How to Write for the World of Work

SIXTH EDITION

How to Write for the World of Work

SIXTH EDITION

Thomas E. Pearsall, *emeritus*
University of Minnesota

Donald H. Cunningham
Auburn University

Elizabeth O. Smith
Auburn University

HEINLE & HEINLE
™
THOMSON LEARNING

Australia Canada Mexico Singapore Spain United Kingdom United States

How to Write for the World of Work/Sixth Edition

Pearsall • Cunningham • Smith

Publisher: *Earl McPeek*
Acquisitions Editor: *Julie McBurney*
Market Strategist: *John Meyers*
Project Editor: *Kathryn M. Stewart*
Art Director: *Van Mua*
Production Manager: *Cindy Young*

Printed in the United States of America
3 4 5 6 7 8 9 10   06 05 04 03 02

For more information contact Heinle & Heinle, 25 Thomson Place, Boston,
MA 02210 USA, or you can visit our Internet site at http://www.heinle.com

ISBN: 0-15-507903-4

Library of Congress Catalog Card Number:
        99-068445

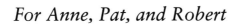

For Anne, Pat, and Robert

PREFACE

Because workplace practices and your needs as a student preparing to enter the workplace have undergone vast and rapid changes since 1994, the year our previous edition was published, this sixth edition in many ways is a new book. We have added four new chapters, extensively revised four other chapters, and have made numerous changes and additions to update all remaining chapters. Our aim in revising the book, as it has been in all previous editions, is to incorporate up-to-date research and communication practices and other current developments in the workplace. Most of the revision this time reflects the increased diversification and professionalism of the workforce, the globalization of the workplace, and the expansion of computers and electronic media into a web of overlapping practices that have influenced all aspects of communication and have led to new perspectives on research, document design, visuals, writing, reading, speaking, and the storage, retrieval, and transmittal of information.

MAJOR CHANGES IN THE SIXTH EDITION

In addition to updating the writing samples, we have made significant revisions for this sixth edition.

• We have expanded Chapter 1, The Process of Workplace Writing, to include more information about setting objectives in writing by discussing writing to solve problems and writing to achieve professional and career goals. In doing so, we hope to help you develop a more sophisticated view of communication as a goal-directed activity and to encourage you to become more motivated about your own writing, reading, and speaking.

• Chapter 2, Computers and Workplace Writing, is a new chapter that deals with computers in the workplace and establishes a framework for the computer-mediated research, writing, and presentations in the rest of the book. This new chapter builds on the writing process presented in Chapter 1 and developed further in Chapter 3, Persuasion and Scientific Argument.

• We have added two new sections to Chapter 4, Style and Tone, one that leads you to consider seriously the cultural differences among writers and readers and speakers and listeners, the other that gives suggestions on how to use language that will not exclude or offend others.

• Chapter 5, Text and Document Design, Chapter 6, Visuals and Document Design I, and Chapter 7, Visuals and Document Design II, update and expand the two chapters on layout and design and on visuals in the previous edition of the textbook. These new chapters examine the current technology for the layout and design and creating visuals and provide guidelines for (1) using page formats and typeface options and headings and displayed lists to forecast the organization and contents of documents and (2) creating specific types of visuals by using currently available word processing and graphics software and by using visuals found on the World Wide Web.

• Chapter 8, Principles of Workplace Correspondence, and Chapter 9, Workplace Correspondence, contain information on using email and sending correspondence and attached documents electronically.

• We have updated Chapter 10, Resumes, Employment Letters, and Application Forms to account for the electronic creation and transmission of employment materials (including electronically scannable resumes and employment information and services found on the World Wide Web).

• Chapter 11, Portfolios and Interviews, is a new chapter that in addition to providing traditional advice about interviewing for jobs also explains how to create a professional portfolio, a notable new form for you to show your qualifications for employment that includes samples of your best research, writing, and oral presentations.

• In Chapter 12, Oral Presentations, we have added information about using presentation software such as Corel's Presentations and Microsoft's PowerPoint.

• The basic coverage of Unit III Reports (Chapter 13, Principles of Workplace Reports; Chapter 14, Recommendation Reports; Chapter 15, Proposals; Chapter 16, Mechanism Description; Chapter 17, Process Description; and Chapter 18, Instructions) remains essentially the same as in previous editions. However, we have updated most of the writing samples.

• We expanded our treatment of research by adding an entirely new unit on research strategies (Unit IV Research—Chapter 19, Research Strategies; Chapter 20, Research Sites and Sources—Library and Internet Research; Chapter 21, Research Sites and Sources—Field Research; and Chapter 22, Documenting Sources). Technology and the electronic environment have changed the way resources are located. Consequently, we discuss extensively the electronic and global environment in research, especially the use of online library catalogs and electronic databases (Chapter 19) and the World Wide Web (Chapter 21). Workplace research also requires professionals to move beyond the library to conduct field research, so we have gone far beyond library research and covered information acquisition through interviews, surveys, and direct observations (Chapter 20). We also explain how to cite sources using the APA (American Psychological Association) style or the MLA (Modern Language Association) style (Chapter 22).

For those familiar with earlier editions of this book, perhaps the most obvious addition is our third author, Elizabeth Overman Smith. She teaches undergraduate and graduate courses in technical and professional communication and serves as coordinator of instructional technology in the Department of English at Auburn University. Professor Smith brings her considerable knowledge of rhetoric and her expertise in computer technology to this sixth edition, especially in those chapters that cover the use of electronic media.

THE CORE OF THE BOOK

Although no chapter in this sixth edition remains unchanged, we have maintained the core of the book to which students and teachers have responded enthusiastically through several editions: We focus on the research, writing, reading, and speaking that goes on in the workplace and on the basic triad of workplace communication—information, audience, and purpose.

• We break these workplace activities into their day-to-day tasks, such as basic correspondence (including email, oral and multimedia presentations, electronically scannable resumes, and professional portfolios), reports (including proposals, recommendation reports, and instructions), and research (including library, field, and internet searches).

• We explain as carefully and precisely as we can how to accomplish each of these activities. We use real examples, most reproduced as they originally appeared in some work situation. Several examples are produced by students. And while we designed the book for the classroom, we want it to have the feel of the world when one day the classroom tasks will become the real thing.

• We continue to regard our audience as the student who is being educated for a specific vocation or profession. We visualize you as practical and industrious, willing to work when shown what needs to be done, and one who wants to continue to develop verbal, visual, and computer literacy. Our purpose, as in previous editions, is to lead you from the simpler forms of correspondence to the challenging complexities of reports and other kinds of documents, including oral presentations.

• We continue to believe that carefully integrated visuals should be a part of nearly every assignment. We regard visuals not as merely aids in writing and speaking but as equal to written and spoken language in documents and presentations. The choice of the appropriate medium should be made on the basis of subject, purpose, audience, and cost.

• We provide planning checklists to guide you through the discovery and organizing stages of the writing process. The revision checklists provide you with an organized approach to revision for both when you write as an individual and when you collaborate with others. The checklists also provide useful evaluation criteria for peer evaluators and the teacher.

The unifying theme of this book continues to be that workplace writing and speaking presents specific information to a specific audience for a specific purpose. To put it another way, an occasion for a piece of workplace writing or for a workplace presentation always exists.

Workplace writing and speaking is usually generated by a specific piece of information that must be presented: *In answer to your query about the pricing of the Delta 5540.... We are on time with the computer conversion.... This is how you build the 86204 Heat Exchanger.* In the workplace, you write or make an oral presentation when you have something to say.

When you present your information, you must think of your audience. You must always be concerned with questions about how the occasion and the audience's expectations and needs shape your report or presentation: *Who will read my report? Who will hear my presentation? Why will they read or listen? What will they want from the report or presentation? What do they already know about the subject? What is left to tell them?*

Purpose is usually closely meshed with the audience's expectations and needs. You write and speak a certain way for bankers so that the bankers can get the information they need. But you go to bankers in the first place because your purpose is to get a loan. Often you will have multiple purposes for writing or speaking. Suppose, for example, you were writing to policyholders of an insurance company to tell them their rates for automobile insurance are to be increased. If your purpose were only to announce the new rates, you could send out a printed table showing the increase. But you would have an additional purpose: keeping the policy holders with the company. Therefore you would justify the increase, showing how circumstances beyond the company's control forced the increase. For good measure, you would remind the policyholders of the good service they have received from the company in the past.

Information ... audience ... purpose ... the basic triad of workplace writing and speaking. We will remind you of it often in these pages, because the bringing together of all these elements is really what this book is all about.

ACKNOWLEDGMENTS

As in previous editions, we thank Professor Frederick H. MacIntosh of the University of North Carolina and John A. Walter of the University of Texas. We thank Professor MacIntosh for his phrase "writing for the world's work," which in modified form has become part of our title. Professor Walter we thank again for his statement that "Scientists and engineers are concerned, when they write, with presenting information to a specific body of readers for a specific purpose." We think all professionals in the workplace have these basic concerns, and we believe they should permeate every portion of writing and speaking—from word to sentence to paragraph to the entire document or presentation. Our version of Professor Walter's statement—*workplace writing presents information to a specific audience for a specific purpose*—is stated and illustrated frequently throughout this book.

We thank those individuals and companies that have given us permission to use materials.

We also thank the following reviewers for their candid and useful advice: Professor Joan Buckley, Concordia College; Professor Hal Guilstad, Grays Harbor College; and Professor Betsy Goebel Jones, Texas Tech University Health Sciences Center.

We owe a great deal of thanks to teachers across the country and in other countries who have used earlier editions of this book in their classes. Many have been kind enough to pass on comments from their students or encouraged their students to write us about how helpful they found the book. We view this book as a collaborative effort of ourselves and the many teachers and students who have written to us.

Further thanks go to the following Harcourt employees who were involved in the publication of this edition: Julie McBurney and Claire Brantley, Acquisitions Editors; Kim Allison, Developmental Editor; Kathryn Stewart, Project Editor; Cindy Young, Production Manager; and Van Mua, Art Director.

Finally, we thank Anne Pearsall, Pat Cunningham, and Robert Smith for their love, understanding, and encouragement.

Thomas E. Pearsall
Donald H. Cunningham
Elizabeth Overman Smith

CONTENTS IN BRIEF

CONTENTS

UNIT I

BASIC PRINCIPLES

CHAPTER 1

THE PROCESS OF WORKPLACE WRITING

Your previous writing courses may have dealt with personal or literary writing. You'll find workplace writing considerably different. Read a few lines of John Donne's "The Bait":

Come live with me, and be my love,
And we will some new pleasures prove,
Of golden sands, and crystal brooks,
With silken lines, and silver hooks.

Donne is making a personal artistic statement with a skill and beauty quite beyond most of us.

Look now at a piece of workplace writing:

Between 1972 and 1990, the proportion of lawyers who were women rose dramatically, from only 4 percent to 21 percent. In 1990, 19 percent of physicians were women, nearly double their 1972 proportion.

Substantial gains in women's share of employment also occurred in other occupations where they had long been under represented. For instance, 56 percent of bartenders were women in 1990, double the proportion in 1972. Over the same period, their proportion of bus drivers increased from 34 to 52 percent.

While women rapidly entered many occupations previously dominated by men, men did not enter the so-called "women's" occupations in significant numbers. Thus, job categories, such as nursing or secretarial work, remained overwhelmingly female.[1]

The writer who wrote this paragraph was making an impersonal statement to convey a specific piece of information. The style is not particularly artistic, but it is competent. The paragraph is easily understandable to its intended audience. To make sure it would be understood, the writer also included a graphic, which we have reproduced in Figure 1.1. The paragraph represents a style and a method of writing within the grasp of most of us.

Workplace writing is a craft, not an art form. As a craft, it is a rational process that can be learned. The process grows out of the underlying theme of this book that workplace writing presents specific information to a specific audience for a specific purpose. We will take you through the steps of the process. As you add the skills of workplace writing to your existing writing skills, you may find some tasks easier and some harder. The process is a bit like learning how to find your way in new territory, as the following metaphor suggests.

You probably know the neighborhood you live in quite well. Whether you walk or drive to school or work, the journey may take you several blocks or a few miles down several streets with several turnings. For these frequently traveled trips you need no maps other than the ones in your

---

[1]The quoted passage and Figure 1.1 are from Bureau of Labor Statistics, *Working Women: A Chartbook* (Washington: US Department of Labor, 1991) 17–18.

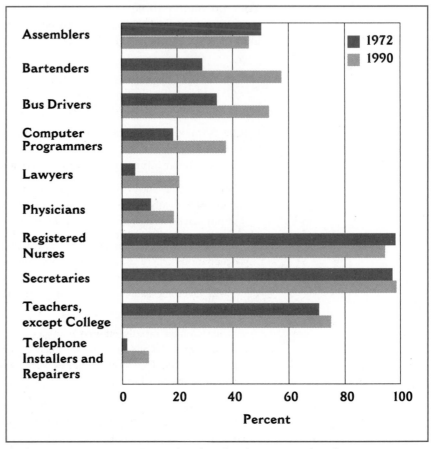

Figure 1.1 Women as a proportion of total employed persons in selected occupations, 1970 and 1990 annual averages.

head. You know the way. As you stray further afield, to confirm the route, you may glance at a map before you start. For a totally strange trip, you obtain a map and prepare an itinerary from it. You keep the itinerary and map close at hand as you travel.

But suppose you are traveling into strange territory for which you have no map. All of us have done that on occasion, perhaps in a city new to us or in rough back country. Here we may make many false starts and turns. We may start in one direction and walk or drive on bravely until we realize that we are not moving any closer to our goal. We back up and start over again. Along the way we may meet someone who gives us better directions for at least part of the way. So we proceed by trial and error and by gathering additional information until we reach our goal.

We hope the map metaphor is clear. Sometimes writing is easy. Writing about familiar subjects and in familiar ways—perhaps writing a letter to a friend or filling in a frequently used laboratory report—resembles our walks and drives to familiar places.

Sometimes writing may be more difficult, but we use "maps"— patterns for organization and format. For example, in creating a resume, you already have the information about your education and work experience, and you can find an acceptable pattern for the resume in Chapter 10 of this book. Throughout the book we present many such patterns to help you find your way.

But sometimes, in writing as in traveling, you enter unexplored territory without a map. This situation presents the highest level of difficulty. A competent writer will attempt to learn as much as possible about the situation, make some conjectures about what the communication must accomplish, and then write. The last step is to double-check everything to be sure no important points or considerations have been overlooked.

In the rest of this chapter we summarize a writing process that you can use at every level of difficulty. The process involves analyzing your audience, setting objectives, discovering and gathering information, planning organization, planning visuals, writing and revising, writing collaboratively (sometimes), and writing ethically. The process can be complex and is not easily reduced to a formula. You can write using paper and pencil or using word-processing software on computers. You may make notes before composing on the computer, or you may compose directly on the computer. Everyone develops his or her own productive process. However, if you are not yet writing on a computer, we encourage you to begin. Computer technology has removed most of the laborious work from drafting, revising, and making corrections. In Chapter 2 and throughout the rest of this book, we discuss the use of computers in workplace writing and we provide suggestions for using them as you communicate in the workplace.

Depending on the level of difficulty, you may need to follow all of the steps only some of the time, but you will need to follow some of the steps all of the time. To give you even more specific guidance, at the end of every chapter that deals with a written product, such as correspondence and reports, we provide a planning and revising checklist. Use of these checklists will help you to consider those key items important to the success of your work. They also help to keep a collaborating group on track.

ANALYZING YOUR AUDIENCE

Because workplace writing deals with audience, purpose, and information, you should start with one of the three. We suggest that you start with your audience for two reasons:

1. Shared communication relies on a shared view of the world, and a writer usually has to look for ways to adjust his or her writing to accommodate readers (in the workplace, the writer or speaker is expected to make meaning clear).

2. Having a reader in mind helps to keep a writer grounded in reality, focused on how the reader will use the document (in the workplace, the reader is not always sitting in a comfortable chair in a well-lighted office).

In workplace writing, you can usually define your reader or readers rather narrowly: an executive with a college degree, a group of technicians with good knowledge of the field, a homeowner installing a lock, a farmer with an associate degree in animal technology, a health-care specialist who needs to know how to perform a specific task on a new piece of software, your boss. They are all intelligent and well educated, but they are uninformed about some aspect of their work or they need certain information to do their jobs. You can define your audiences by experience, occupation, education, and relationship to you. You know to some degree their general knowledge and the special knowledge they already possess about your subject. For the most part, you can assume intelligent readers (otherwise, how could you communicate with them?) who are uninformed about some aspects of the issues or subjects about which you are writing (otherwise, why would you communicate with them?). If they already know the specifics of what you have to say, you need not write, unless it is a means to get on record your shared understandings or for other archival purposes. You may also know their attitude about your subject: friendly, neutral, hostile, or apathetic. Are they predisposed to accept your ideas? Are some of your readers likely to accept some of your ideas but resist others? Jot down everything you can think of about your audience—what you think they know, what you think they want or need to know, what kinds of evidence they are likely to accept, and their reasons for reading the document or what you can do to motivate them to read it.

Audience analysis continues throughout the entire writing process. Keep your real or imagined reader in the forefront of your mind. You need to be on the lookout for the many instances when you suspect that readers won't understand fully your statements or points. As you plan and write, imagine yourself carrying on a dialogue with your reader. What are some of the questions your reader might ask you? We suggest a few here and some of the ways you might respond to them.

Reader's Questions

So what?	A key question. Always be sure your reader knows the significance and implications of the information you present. After you have researched, analyzed, synthesized, and clarified your own thinking about some matter, you may have a tendency to assume that everybody else also understands matters as well as you do. Such an assumption is one of the most frequent traps into which writers fall.

Why is this important to me?	Show where the reader's self-interest is involved. Most readers will not read a document attentively unless they believe it contains information that is relevant to them.
How do you know what you are saying is true?	Provide the needed evidence. Do you have either experience or research to back up what you are saying? What kinds of evidence and what kinds of sources will your readers accept as credible or authoritative?
How does it work exactly?	A relevant and simple example or a comparison can help the reader.
How is the task accomplished?	Provide clear instructions for the work to be done.
Why should I do the task your way and not mine?	If your readers believe they have legitimate reasons for continuing as usual or in some way other than the one you propose, justify your methods and techniques.
How come?	Tell your reader why you're asking that something be done. There is a term in physics, *hysteresis*, which refers to a body's resistance to change or to an extremely slow response to changes that affect it. Many readers will also display symptoms of hysteresis, especially if they think they will have to change their ways of doing or thinking.
What does this word mean?	Provide a definition to ensure that your readers understand your words in the same sense that you do.
How does this idea tie to that one?	If you suspect that some readers will not see how one idea or point relates to another, provide a transition, a bridge of some sort, to link them together.
Now that I understand you what do you want me to do?	Make sure all conclusions and recommendations are firmly stated.

Don't overlook the journalist's always useful questions: Who? What? When? Where? Why? Providing answers to these questions helps clarify and explain more fully your ideas.

SETTING OBJECTIVES

In the beginning of the process, when you have your reader firmly in mind, set your objectives—both yours and your reader's—in terms of achieving professional and career goals and of solving workplace problems.

WRITING TO ACHIEVE PROFESSIONAL AND CAREER GOALS

Whatever your professional work—agronomist, accountant, biotechnician, highway engineer, financial planner, fire control specialist, manufacturing engineering manager, forester, systems analyst, interior designer, nutritionist—you make your living by solving problems. You report your findings, express your opinions, and attempt to persuade your readers that your expertise will contribute to solving the problem. Much of your work comes out in the form of memos, letters, reports, proposals, and manuals. However, writing well comes not merely by doing it, but by working at it intelligently. In fact, writing is not a favorite activity for many professional persons, particularly those who see themselves as already having a full agenda.

However, doing a good job of writing is important. Your ideas will compete with those of others, both inside and outside your organization. You and your group will compete with others for budget, for salary increases and bonuses, facilities, more desirable assignments, higher rank and position, and, of course, for job security. Realizing these potential payoffs should motivate you to create effective workplace documents. Listing the specific professional and career objectives you wish to achieve with a particular piece of writing will motivate you to do the job well.

WRITING TO SOLVE PROBLEMS

What do you hope to accomplish with this piece of writing? What does your reader hope to accomplish by reading it? Usually these questions are two sides of the same coin. You may be trying to sell a certain kind of building material to a contractor. The contractor's purpose is to discover if your product is worth buying. Or you may be explaining to someone how to assemble a device ordered by mail. The reader needs to assemble it. Having a clear sense of your intentions and your readers' expectations is critical to the success of your writing.

Write down your objectives. Nothing clarifies thought as much as forcing yourself to set the thought down on paper or to open a new document on the computer and make notes. The writing process is more than a means of reporting thought. Often it is thought itself. Putting ideas in writing helps you clarify your own thinking. When you compare what you had thought with what you have written down and with what you are now thinking, you gain insight into where your thoughts are leading you. Your objectives as stated should be measurable. That is, they should be stated in a way that allows you to know if they have been accomplished.

An objective such as *the reader will understand how to assemble the device* is not measurable as stated. How do you plan to test the understanding? The objective stated as *the reader will be able to assemble the device in a half hour* is measurable. You could give the reader the unassembled device and the instructions. If the reader, using your instructions, assembles the device in a half hour, your instrumental objective is met. Much workplace writing lends itself to such measurable goals. For example, the objective for the resume and letter of application used in a job campaign could be that at least 10 percent of the people receiving them grant you an interview.

Of course, some pieces of writing have understanding rather than action as their objective. However, even when understanding is your objective, you can still set actions that the reader should be able to take after reading your work. Think of yourself as a teacher who wants to check students' comprehension and understanding. The teacher would devise a test of some sort. You can do the same. If you could go with your document, what questions would you ask the reader about it? In essence, you are continuing the dialogue described earlier, only now you are asking the questions. For example, a writer whose objective is for readers to understand how prejudice develops and operates in society could ask the reader to

- Define prejudice from a behavioral perspective (by describing how prejudiced people behave).

- Cite examples of how our culture often teaches prejudice toward old people, children, women, men, and minorities.

- Illustrate behavior that acts to include people in groups or to exclude them.

Obviously, the writer as teacher must write the paper in such a way that the reader as student could answer the questions.

Writing down, first, your analysis of your audience, and, second, your objectives, fixes them in your mind. You have started the process that, partly through cold rational thought and partly through intuitive insights, will lead you to a complete piece of writing—one that will help achieve common understandings between you and your readers.

DISCOVERING AND GATHERING INFORMATION

The first step in discovering and gathering information is to inventory the information you already have available in your head to satisfy your objectives. If your subject is one with which you are thoroughly familiar, you may already know much or all that you need to know to do the task.

BRAINSTORMING

Write down what you do know about the subject. Use a method known as *brainstorming*. In brainstorming, you set aside thoughts of organization and critical evaluation and write down everything that comes to mind pertinent to the subject. You may use a pad of paper or start a file in your word-processing software. You might name the file *Notes1*. Only by doing so can you truly tell what resources you have available to you. You have probably engaged in some form of brainstorming as part of a group problem-solving effort, such as compiling a list of possible speakers for your club or organization's meetings, with potential ways to raise money, or with possible sites for your company's holiday party. Even though brainstorming was originally developed for small-group activities, you can use brainstorming by yourself to focus on a topic. To guide your brainstorming and, later, to evaluate what it has produced, use the knowledge you generated about the needs and attitudes of your audience. To what person or persons should your writing be directed? Does your reader need any particular information to carry out some process? If you are proposing to perform work or research for your reader, what information is relevant? What information would persuade an employer to hire you?

CONSULTING OTHER PERSONS AND SIMILAR DOCUMENTS

Writers in the workplace consult with their colleagues during this discovery stage of generating information. Just having somebody with whom you can discuss your writing or exchange points of view can be extremely helpful. In addition, writers look at previous documents that they or others in their workplace have produced that are similar to the one they plan to write. Such documents not only may provide useful information but also may guide the discovery process; that is, they may suggest information you need to write your own document.[2] Writers sometimes go online and browse the World Wide Web for information or access a library's online catalog for resources. In the same way, the writer's knowledge of highly evolved and widely used writing-organization patterns is also useful in the discovery process. We discuss many of these throughout this book.

CONDUCTING MORE FORMAL RESEARCH

Obviously, you will rely on your own thoughts based on your own experiences and knowledge. But if your information is thin, the next stage of the discovery process is research. You will often need to use other people's ideas and information from other sources to elaborate on your own thinking. We have a good deal to say about research in Chapters 19, 20, and

---

[2]For an excellent discussion of such techniques, see Jack Selzer, "The Composing Processes of an Engineer," *College Composition and Communication* 34 (1983): 178–187.

21. You may combine library research or investigation of resources on the World Wide Web with empirical research, such as experimentation or polling or surveying, using techniques taught in your own discipline. Or you may interview experts in the field.

PLANNING YOUR ORGANIZATION

As you gather information, your thoughts may leap ahead to organizing your presentation. You may suddenly see in clear outline how your information can best be presented. You may even find yourself writing out drafts of paragraphs that you'll later include in your letter or report. Your mind will be making connections among all the parts of the writing process. Such connections are part of the intuitive creative process of the mind that no one thoroughly understands as yet. But what is clear is that the writing process, like any other creative process, is often *not* an uninterrupted straight path from beginning to end. We leap ahead on the path, and then we double back on our previous tracks. If those unknowledgeable about writing were to see our back-and-forth movements at this stage, they might regard us as sloppy or inept writers. However, knowledgeable and experienced writers know that our process taps, rather than stifles, our skill and creativity.

Use the process; don't fight it. When such connections do occur, write them down; otherwise you will lose them. Many will later prove to be worthless, but one or two of them may be the keys to your report.

At some point in your research, you must turn your attention to the planning chores before you. Now is the time to evaluate your material and to find the coherent organization that will satisfy you and your reader. Sit down with your notes or print out your computer file. Once again review your audience and objective statements. Revise them if necessary.

Although your organizational plan will be more or less tentative as you begin, you must have a deliberate plan or several difficulties could emerge. You might become so overwhelmed by the material you have gathered that you experience writer's block. Or, even if you are able to begin, you might quickly find that your draft is in serious trouble. Developing an organizational plan will help you feel more confident of your grasp of your materials.

STANDARD ORGANIZATIONAL PLANS

In your review of audience and objectives, assess what expectations your readers might have about how particular documents are organized. Check to see if any of the organizational patterns that you know or that are presented in this book would be useful. Just a partial list of such patterns includes such general ones as the time or chronological approach, cause and effect, and scientific argument with its use of induction, deduction, and comparison. In addition, there are more specific patterns, such as application letters, mechanism description, process description, and proposals. Many readers are familiar with these patterns. When you write, take advantage of their familiarity.

If a pattern fits, use it, but recognize that patterns, even at their best, are still rather incomplete maps. In writing all but the most obvious kinds of correspondence and reports, you are usually entering unexplored territory to some extent. And you should relate the map to the audience as well as to the territory. For example, the general outline for most sets of instructions is fairly clear: (1) an introduction that provides an overview of the process to be done, (2) a list of tools and equipment to be used in the process, and (3) a step-by-step account of the process.

Your task is to relate this general outline to what you know about your audience. Will readers need to be persuaded to perform the procedure? If so, you must figure out the reason for resistance and address it. If some readers are ready to accept your instructions, you can dispense with the persuasion. Do the members of your audience already know all about the tools to be used—what they are and how to use them? If so, you need only give your audience a list of the tools. But what if some of the tools are not familiar to your audience? Then you would explain them and instruct your audience in their use. Does your audience know where to obtain the needed equipment? If not, you must supply that information. Does the audience know the significance of all the steps in the process itself? If so, you can run through the steps with little explanation. If not, you'll need to take time for some explanation. In effect, you are carrying on the dialogue with your audience that we recommended earlier (see pages 6–7).

OTHER ORGANIZATIONAL PLANS

Sometimes no ready-made pattern, complete or otherwise, is readily available. At such times, you may organize best by returning to your objectives and breaking them up into subobjectives. As you do so, you should once again keep your audience and its needs in mind. For instance, a psychologist was planning a one-day workshop in which her objective was to teach her audience how to cope with stress and keep it from turning into harmful distress. Her audience was primarily individuals with high school educations. They would probably know what stress and distress are, but possess little real knowledge of how to deal with them. Also, they were rural people who, for the most part, would have little contact with psychologists unless a problem became serious. They would be, the psychologist reasoned, most interested in practical self-help advice and not much interested in theory. Building on that analysis, the psychologist organized her workshop around a series of subobjectives as follows:

- Identify stress in daily life.

- Identify symptoms of distress and causes of distress.

- Recognize a stressful situation and know at what point to take action to prevent stress from becoming distress.

- Learn and apply tension-releasing techniques.

- Learn problem-solving techniques for decision making.

- Identify sources of expert help if needed.

Frequently, as they did in this case, the subobjectives become the topics that make up the organizational plan.

Just how complete you make your organizational plan depends to some extent on how well you know the territory. If you know the territory well, a sketchy plan of the major headings of the report may be all you need to begin. Sometimes, you may want to go a step further and break the topics down into subtopics. For example, for her rural audience, the psychologist divided her first topic, "identify stress in daily life," into two subtopics: (1) problems and pressures of farming and ranching and (2) problems and pressures of basic human needs. To organize the considerable amount of information to be presented on the fourth topic, which explains how to develop a few stress-reducing skills, the psychologist further divided the topic into specific techniques:

- Adopting old-fashioned remedies such as drinking certain kinds of vegetable juices or teas and bathing in botanical oils such as lavender and jasmine.

- Practicing body/mind exercises such as meditation or yoga, which reduce respiratory and pulse rates and lessen the amount of stress hormones that the adrenal gland must secrete.

- Exercising regularly and getting sufficient rest and sleep.

- Avoiding caffeine and other substances that overexcite the body's metabolism.

- Eating fresh fruits and unprocessed foods that contain magnesium and potassium.

When the territory is really unfamiliar, you may want even more of a map. One useful technique is to write summaries of all the major parts of the report. Another is to construct a rough outline.

Whether you begin by deliberately constructing an organizational plan or by intuiting a workable sequence of ideas, you should at some point pause and evaluate your plan critically. This is the time to catch flaws in your plan. It's easy to throw away an outline and start over again. On the other hand, it is painful to discover a fatal organizational flaw when you are well into the writing stage and are forced to scrap hours of work.

At times, the occasion may call for a formal outline. For information on how to construct one, see "Outlines" in Unit V, Writer's Guide. You may also find the outline feature of your word-processing software helpful.

PLANNING VISUALS

While you are still in the planning stage, consider what visuals—photographs, drawings, tables, and graphs, and such—may be available to you or that you can construct yourself. In the workplace, writers rely on visuals of all sorts to help them deliver their message. They see no particular virtue in saying something in words if an illustration or graph will make the concept clear. Also, tables displaying needed statistical information will usually save the writer words and the reader time.

Figure 1.2 Your authors. (That's Cunningham with the beard.)

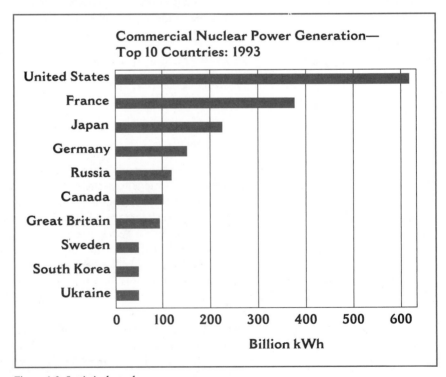

Figure 1.3 Statistical graph.
Source: Statistical Abstract of the United States 1995, 115th ed. (Washington: GPO, 1995) 586.

The bar graph reproduced in Figure 1.1 clearly illustrates the gains women have made in many occupations. And even the proverbial thousand words would not describe your authors as well as the photograph in Figure 1.2 does.

The chart in Figure 1.3 shows the generation of commercial nuclear power in the ten top countries in 1993 in a way that would be difficult to communicate in prose. The table in Figure 1.4 makes the information it displays far more accessible than would a prose passage giving the same information. Putting your information in a table frees you to interpret the material important to your purpose. For example, in Figure 1.4 you might

No. 150. National Health Expenditures: 1960 to 1993
(Includes Puerto Rico and outlying areas)

YEAR	TOTAL[1]			HEALTH SERVICES AND SUPPLIES						
				Private				Public		
					Out-of-pocket payments				Medical payments	
	Total (bil. dol.)	Per capita (dol.)	Percent of GDP[2]	Total[3] (bil. dol.)	Total (bil. dol.)	Percent of total private	Insurance premiums[4] (bil. dol.)	Total (bil. dol.)	Medicare (bil. dol.)	Public assistance (bil. dol.)
1960	27.1	143	5.3	19.8	13.4	67.5	5.9	5.7	—	0.5
1965	41.6	204	5.9	29.9	19.0	63.6	10.0	8.3	—	1.7
1970	74.3	346	7.4	44.0	25.4	57.7	16.9	25.0	7.7	6.3
1971	82.2	379	7.5	48.1	26.9	55.9	19.2	28.2	8.5	7.7
1972	92.3	421	7.7	53.9	29.6	55.0	22.0	31.8	9.4	8.9
1973	102.4	464	7.6	59.7	32.6	54.5	24.8	35.9	10.8	10.2
1974	115.9	521	7.9	65.9	35.8	54.3	27.5	42.8	13.5	11.9
1975	132.6	591	8.4	74.1	39.1	52.8	32.0	50.2	16.4	14.5
1976	151.9	671	8.6	85.7	43.2	50.4	38.5	56.9	19.8	16.4
1977	172.6	755	8.7	98.6	47.5	48.2	46.7	64.7	23.0	18.8
1978	193.2	838	8.7	109.7	51.0	46.5	53.6	73.6	26.8	20.9
1979	218.3	937	8.8	124.0	55.9	45.1	62.2	84.0	31.0	23.9
1980	251.1	1,068	9.3	141.3	61.3	43.4	72.1	98.1	37.5	28.0
1981	291.4	1,227	9.6	164.3	69.6	42.4	85.1	113.9	44.9	32.6
1982	328.2	1,369	10.4	186.5	76.5	41.0	99.1	126.9	52.5	34.6
1983	360.8	1,490	10.6	205.3	83.0	40.4	110.6	139.5	59.8	38.0
1984	396.0	1,620	10.5	228.0	90.4	39.6	125.1	151.6	66.5	41.1
1985	434.5	1,761	10.8	252.9	98.8	39.1	139.8	165.2	72.2	44.5
1986	466.0	1,871	10.9	268.7	105.0	39.1	147.8	180.4	76.9	49.0
1987	506.2	2,013	11.1	291.3	111.6	38.3	162.3	196.6	82.3	54.0
1988	562.3	2,214	11.5	327.5	123.0	37.6	184.8	213.7	89.4	58.8
1989	623.9	2,433	11.9	361.7	127.8	35.3	211.7	240.1	102.6	66.4
1990	696.6	2,686	12.6	399.8	138.3	34.6	236.9	272.5	112.1	80.5
1991	755.6	2,882	13.2	422.8	143.3	33.9	252.8	308.0	123.3	99.1
1992	820.3	3,094	13.6	451.7	150.6	33.3	272.7	341.2	138.3	113.5
1993	884.2	3,299	13.9	484.3	157.5	32.5	296.1	370.9	154.2	122.9

—Represents zero. [1]Includes medical research and medical facilities construction. [2]GDP = Gross domestic product; see table 701. [3]Includes other sources of funds not shown separately. [4]See footnote 2, table 151.
Source: U.S. Health Care Financing Administration, *Health Care Financing Review,* winter 1994.

Figure 1.4 Statistical table.
Source: Statistical Abstract of the United States 1995, 115th ed. (Washington: GPO, 1995) 109.

point out that in the years 1973 to 1993 the portion of the gross national product expended for health care increased by almost 83 percent.

Remember, though, that just as you choose words and write paragraphs in a context, you choose and use visuals in a context. We discuss visuals in Chapters 6 and 7. In our chapters on various kinds of reports we frequently draw your attention to where you can profitably employ visuals. We urge you to always be alert to the possibility of using a visual to carry part of your message. With word processing and computer graphics, you can now easily incorporate visuals into all your documents from memorandums and letters to proposals and instructions.

WRITING AND REVISING

For some experienced writers the organizational stage merges almost without their realizing it into the writing stage. For less experienced writers, the two stages may be quite separate. In either case, you must write. If possible, find a quiet place where you won't be disturbed. Use a large desk or table where you can lay your notes, graphics, and plans around you. Plant your feet firmly under the table and begin. (Sometimes *chain your feet* might be the more appropriate metaphor.) Write as rapidly as you can. Use whatever technology you are comfortable with, whether it's a pencil and a yellow pad or a computer.

Don't worry about writing well yet, and pay no particular attention to such considerations as style and spelling. Just get something on paper or words on the screen. Follow your organizational plan, but don't be a slave to it. If in writing and thinking about your writing, a clearer, less obstructed path to your objectives opens before you, follow it. Also, if one segment of your letter or report seems easier to you than another, begin with it. You can always put elements in proper order later. The copy, cut, and paste features in your word-processing software make rearranging easy. If you are using research material, note in your draft the source so you can cite it correctly later. Most word-processing software enables you to insert footnotes or endnotes relatively easily.

Write for about two hours at a time. In two hours you can produce about a thousand words. After resting and getting your mind off your writing, write for another two hours if need be. Four hours of writing in a day is a lot of writing, usually enough for most people. If your writing is going to carry over to another time, quit when you are in full rush and know exactly what you are going to say next. It makes beginning again much easier. When you have finished, leave your work for at least a day. Letting your work "cool off" for a day or so will help you achieve a little necessary detachment. When you come back to it, the revision process begins.

SUBSTANTIVE REVISION

Begin by revising for clarity and meaning. At this point, don't spend time checking spelling and punctuation or even making fine distinctions of word choice. You might find yourself changing a lot of relatively minor elements that will be deleted or changed substantially later. Attend to big considerations—the *substantive* matters—first. Check your document both in terms of clarity and meaning. Have you achieved your purpose? If you are writing to solve a problem (and you usually will be), readers must be able to grasp what you want to say the first time they read it—the problem, no matter how complex, must be defined well and the solution or solutions must be clear. Look at how clearly you state your intention and purpose in the title, the introduction, the conclusion, and, if there is one, the abstract or executive summary. Are they clearly stated either explicitly or implicitly early in the text of your document? If your document requires a full-scale introduction, have you clearly defined and limited your subject? Perhaps you are answering a letter of complaint. Is your opening sufficiently friendly? Will it calm a tense situation or make more trouble? Perhaps you are explaining how to perform a crucial step that must be carried out precisely as you direct. Will some readers understand your intention and meaning in a way different from the one you intend? Perhaps you are defining a problem and offering a solution. Will readers understand your recommendations and how you arrived at them?

Now examine the body of your document. Have you followed through on your purpose? Does everything in your document speak to your purpose? Are there any gaps or digressions in your writing where you lose sight of your subject as you have defined and limited it? Is the purpose and subject of each paragraph clear? Are you sure of all your facts? Are your sentences well structured? Is your diction appropriate to the occasion? For most workplace writing diction should be straightforward and unembellished—well mannered, neither heavy nor slangy. Good writing has a good sound to it. Read your work aloud. Does it sound right? For help with some of these revisions, see the entries on "Diction," "Paragraphs," and "Sentences" in Unit V, Writer's Guide. Could you replace or supplement some of your writing with photographs, drawings, graphs, or tables?

Put yourself in the reader's place and carry on a dialogue with the writing before you. Some readers will understand quite clearly the points you intend to make. Others won't. Ask the questions we suggest on pages 6 and 7. Are all the *so-whats* answered? Is your work believable? Have you provided evidence where it is needed? Are conclusions and recommendations furnished? Be hard on yourself. Everything is for the reader's convenience, not yours. Where you find fault, reorganize and rewrite. If you are working with a word processor, you can quickly move and rearrange words, sentences, and paragraphs and insert headings or new items of information. A faulty sentence can be deleted and a better one substituted with a few keystrokes. Although revision is never thoughtless work, with the word processor it has become increasingly less painful.

You should save different versions of your revisions. You can easily go back to a previous version if you decide it is better. If you are working with a document you have typed or written with pen or pencil, cut it up.

Literally, cut it up. Take a scissors to it, rearrange it for better organization, and tape it all back together on a new sheet of paper.

It is fair for you to show your work to others to make sure that what you say makes sense to new readers as well as to yourself. Of course, it helps if those who comment on your writing are able to play the role of your intended reader or readers. And, of course, this kind of critique can be painful if you can't take criticism of your work. But it is better to catch the problems early—before your supervisor sees a mistake. You must be prepared for criticism.

MECHANICAL REVISION

When you have the major issues controlled to your satisfaction, look at some of the smaller ones. Begin by reading your document for continuity. Insert better transitions or more cohesive sentences. Get your dictionary off the shelf and check out all the spellings you are doubtful about, even if you have used the spell checker or thesaurus on your computer. If your document is a typical piece of workplace writing, it probably contains numbers, abbreviations, and quotations. Have you handled them correctly and consistently? Do you have a consistent system for capitalization? Keep a look out for grammatical problems you know you have—faulty comma placement or dangling modifiers, for instance. Again, see Unit V, Writer's Guide, for help in such matters.

When you are completely satisfied with your document, make sure it is in the necessary format required by the situation. In Chapters 5, 6, and 7, we discuss layout and design principles. In Chapter 8 we describe letter and memorandum formats. In Chapter 13, we describe the formal elements of workplace reports, such as title pages and tables of contents. Consult these chapters as needed.

Before sending your letter or report on its way, look at it one more time. Proofread it for those little errors that may have slipped through despite all your care. Make whatever corrections are necessary. Then, and only then, send your work to your readers. And good luck.

WRITING COLLABORATIVELY

Because working in a group enables members to pool their labor and take on larger projects, collaborative writing is common in the world of work. It takes three basic forms: **interactive writing, cooperative writing,** and **coauthoring.**[3]

---

[3]For a useful anthology on collaborative writing see *Collaborative Writing in Industry: Investigations in Theory and Practice,* eds. Mary M. Lay and William M. Karis (Amityville, NY: Baywood, 1991). Some of the terminology we use comes from this anthology, in particular from Barbara Couture and Jone Rymer, "Discourse Interaction between Writer and Supervisor: A Primary Collaboration in Workplace Writing," 87–108; and William Van Pelt and Alice Gillam, "Peer Collaboration and the Computer-Assisted Classroom: Bridging the Gap between Academia and the Workplace," 170–206.

Interactive writing is by far the most common. In interactive writing, the writer discusses the work with someone else at some or all of the major steps of writing from analyzing audience through revising. Interactive writing may be something as simple as "Hey, Mary, look this draft over for me, would you?" It can also be a fairly rigid review process in which a supervisor or review panel, right or wrong, has the last word. Beyond knowing how to give and take criticism gracefully, you need no special skills for interactive writing.

Cooperative writing is the next most common method. The cooperative writing process follows essentially the same steps as the individual writing process described earlier in this chapter. The major difference is that, except for the writing step, the group carries out the steps together. The work is divided into major segments to be written by individual writers. These individual writers will likely have to repeat at least some of the steps to plan and write their individual segments. When the writing is done, the group reconvenes to integrate the pieces and prepare a final version. This is the method your authors have used to write this book. To help you with this process, we later provide some principles to follow in cooperative writing. Following that, we point out some problems you may encounter and suggest solutions for them.

Coauthoring is the least common method in the workplace. In coauthoring, as defined here, two or more people sit down together to draft a piece of writing. Although working at a personal computer, where everyone can see what is going on, eases the process, writing in this way normally consumes more time than one person writing alone. Because it is so time consuming, this method is typically reserved for short, important pieces of writing. Although you may think of its three authors as "coauthors," only a few paragraphs in this book have been coauthored in the sense of this definition. Because this method is so seldom used, we do not discuss it further.

PRINCIPLES FOR COOPERATIVE WRITING

You must learn how to work on a team or in a group. There will be times when you work with a mix of men and women, some of whom are more experienced than others in collaborating. Some will be from more technical areas than others. Some will be more enthusiastic about the project. Most will have different reasons for being on the team. Some will be more mature. Sometimes you will be on a group project that has clear instructions; sometimes not. Regardless of the situation, your group must create instant commitment to the project and to the group, maintain that commitment, agree on the division of work and a work schedule, and reach consensus on priorities.

To help you work as a member of a group with common goals, interests, and direction, and to help you develop strategies to manage nonproductive or destructive conflict and to encourage productive conflict, we offer the following principles to guide your behavior.

• Leave your ego at the door of the conference room. Be prepared to listen to criticism of your work and to respond to it cheerfully. Defend your position when necessary, but when it becomes clear that change is needed, agree to the change gracefully and move on. Criticize other people's work constructively. Be as positive as you can be in praising what is good and in pointing out changes that you think are needed. **Always criticize the work, never the person who did the work.**

• Confrontation over major points, such as audience analysis and content, are appropriate, even necessary, to come to problem solutions. But don't waste group time and energy agonizing over less important matters. For example, if a word chosen by one of the writers is objectively wrong, perhaps *infer* for *imply*, reference to a dictionary can quickly straighten out the matter. If the chosen word is not one you would have chosen but is still appropriate, perhaps *upon* for *on,* don't insist on your choice, particularly if the rest of the group doesn't support you.

• Make sure every member of the group understands (1) the common purposes and objectives, (2) the relationship of their work and writing to the purpose and completion of the project, and (3) how the report relates to the overall project and to other related projects, if any. Don't leave the planning steps of the process, such as analyzing audience and setting objectives, until everyone has reached a common vision of the work. Steps poorly conceived early in the process will come back to haunt you later.

• Coordinate format matters before anyone starts to write. Agreeing early on such matters as the level and style of headings, documentation style, margins, spacing, typeface, and layout of the text and visuals will greatly ease final revision. Also, agreeing on which computer environment and software package your group will use will help.

• Establish a firm timetable for completing steps in the process, such as rough draft completion, visuals in final form, and meeting for final revision. Everything will take longer than you think it will, so leave plenty of time for all the steps leading up to report completion and submittal.

• Put the plan in writing and make sure that every member of the group gets a copy. It is important that all members of the group have the same understanding.

• Keep everybody informed about matters, especially if something changes or if new persons join the group either as additional personnel or as replacements.

• If in writing your draft segment you think work you have done will substantially affect another writer's draft, notify the other writer at once. Don't put people through unnecessary work.

• When the drafts are brought together for integration and revision, the group must be alert for redundancies and for gaps in the content. Everything should blend together smoothly in the final draft.

• Revise thoughtfully and seriously, but not excessively. All writing can be revised almost without limit, but the workplace will not allow you time for such a luxury. When the group is in general agreement that enough is enough, it usually is.

• As in interactive writing, either as a group or an individual within a group, share your work with people outside the group. This can be done at any step it seems appropriate.

• Use the planning and revision checklists available in this book. Supplement them if you can from your own experience. Such checklists help tremendously in bringing everyone in the group together.

PROBLEMS AND SOLUTIONS IN COOPERATIVE WRITING

The following are some common problems in cooperative writing and suggestions for solving them.

• People sometimes take critiquing badly. They may grow hostile. If time allows, divert attention for a while to some other subject to allow them time to cool off. When you return to your criticism, relate it to some criterion, for example, to some of the points made about style in this book. It may be that the writer has simply refused to subordinate his or her tone to the tone agreed upon by the group. Perhaps a review of why that tone was chosen may bring the writer around.

When everything else fails, consider how serious the differences are between the writer and the rest of the group. If the differences do no vital harm to the group's intention, perhaps you should move on. If the differences are serious, the group must make the necessary changes. Remember, it is a group project and not an individual one.

Another possible solution may exist if the group includes a writer clearly superior to others in the group. In such a case, the group can designate this person as the lead writer. The group grants the lead writer the right to make final decisions that the group fails to make for itself. Such a method often works well in the world of work, though it may create problems in classroom work. If you do appoint a lead writer, don't second-guess him or her when you disagree.

• Some people seem never to finish their work on time, or forever have questions about format and documentation and such. Such people are hard to deal with in a group. One solution is for the group to appoint a coordinator. The coordinator's job is to see that work is completed according to schedule. The coordinator also serves as a central point to collect finished work and to answer questions about what the group has already decided.

• Some people simply don't know how to give constructive criticism. They react negatively to anything not their own idea and attack people personally, often causing great friction in the group. It's usually better not to correct such people during a group session. It is sometimes effective to take them aside privately and attempt to make them see the dissension they are causing. If this does not work, the group may have to ignore such individuals as best they can.

Sometimes, if such an individual seems able to work better with one person than with the rest of the group, it may be effective to split the group, at least temporarily, to take advantage of this. In a classroom situation, when everything else fails, the group may have to bring the problem to the instructor and ask for relief.

• Some people—either from inexperience or personal inclination—do not understand or value the nature of collaborative work or see the benefits of group efforts as opposed to individual efforts. But the success of collaborative projects depends upon every member making a commitment and maintaining that commitment to the project. Use the questions and procedure outlined in Figure 1.5 to get everybody into a unified group with a shared perspective.

At the beginning of a collaborative project, plan a meeting in which your group works through the following steps. Steps 1, 4, and 8 are to be completed by each group member. Steps 2, 3, 5, 6, 7, and 9 are to be completed by the group. Distribute a copy of the statements produced in steps 3, 6, and 7 to each member of the group. This activity should take a little over an hour.

1. *For each individual:* Define in your own words and in writing what you think a successful collaborative effort is. (5 minutes)

2. *For the group:* Share your definition with others in your group. Take turns reading your definitions with each other. (5 minutes)

3. *For the group:* Arrive at a consensus of what a successful collaboration is. Select a group member to put the statement in writing. (10 minutes)

4. *For each individual:* Describe in your own words and in writing four attitudes or situations that you believe prevent successful collaboration. (5 minutes)

5. *For the group:* Share your list of these four attitudes or situations with others in your group. (10 minutes)

6. *For the group:* Arrive at a consensus of which four attitudes are the ones that most adversely affect collaboration. Select a group member to put the list in writing. (10 minutes)

7. *For the group:* Select one of the difficulties and identify ways to prevent or solve it. Select a group member to put the statement in writing. (10 minutes)

8. *For each individual:* State in your own words and in writing what you believe are the strongest abilities that you bring to a collaboration. (5 minutes)

9. *For the group:* Share individual statements with the group. (5 minutes)

Figure 1.5 Suggested procedure for beginning a new group project.

WRITING ETHICALLY

Communication skills are powerful tools. They can be used for good or ill, ethically or unethically. In your everyday workplace activities, you will encounter situations in which you make ethical decisions: whether to forward to somebody else an e-mail message that deals confidentially with a sensitive issue, whether to include but suppress or downplay data that does not support your position, or whether to use your employer's system to send a strictly social and personal e-mail message to a friend. In many of these situations, the correct thing to do is clear. But other situations offer no clear-cut category of right or wrong acts, only gray areas. Therefore, as a workplace professional, you need to have a practical working knowledge of ethics. Many ethical systems exist, but most are either **utility-based, rule-based, rights-based,** or some combination of the three. We describe each of these systems and present two cases in which we draw everything together.[4]

UTILITY-BASED

In a utility-based ethics system, you judge whether your act is ethical by weighing its consequences. An ethical act should have utility, that is, it should work for the general good of whatever group it concerns. One common expression of this system is that an ethical act will do the greatest good for the greatest number of people. Conversely, an unethical act will harm more people than it helps.

For example, suppose you were asked to write cigarette advertisements. Successfully marketing cigarettes is a positive good for certain members of the community, for example, tobacco farmers, cigarette manufacturers, stockholders in cigarette companies, and so forth. However, evidence clearly shows that far more people are harmed than are helped by the successful marketing of cigarettes. Smokers suffer cigarette-related illnesses and die prematurely. The high health costs associated with cigarette-related illnesses burden health insurance companies and government Medicare programs. Thus most people have higher insurance premiums and taxes whether they smoke or not. Using a utility-based ethical test, it's clear that writing ads to market cigarettes is an unethical act.

---

[4]In writing this seciton on ethics we drew on the following works: William K. Franken, *Ethics* (Englewood Cliffs, NJ: Prentice-Hall, 1963); H. Lee Shimberg, "Ethics and Rhetoric in Technical Writing," *Technical Communication* 25.4 (1978): 16–18; Arthur E. Walzer, "The Ethics of False *Implicature* in Technical and Professional Writing," *Journal of Technical Writing and Communication* 19 (1989): 149–60; and Mark R. Wicclair and David K. Farkas, "Ethical Reasoning in Technical Communication," *Technical Communication* 31.2 (1984): 15–19. A more recent book by Lori Allen and Dan Voss, *Ethics in Technical Communication* (New York: Wiley, 1997), discusses many ethical dilemmas and challenges and presents several case studies that will help you apply the abstract concept of ethics to specific situations.

RULE-BASED

In a rule-based ethical system, the ethical test judges the acts themselves rather than the consequences of the acts; that is, acts are measured against rules. The rules themselves may come from religion, for example, the Ten Commandments. They may simply come from commonly accepted principles. Most people, for example, generally accept the principles that it is unethical to lie, cheat, or steal. In a strict rule-based system, lying is unethical, even if the consequences of the lie are beneficial. In a more flexible rule-based system, lies such as "white lies" might be acceptable but most other lies would be considered unethical.

Lies, incidentally, need not be outright lies. You can lie by promoting false inference even when technically telling the truth. For example, you could write, "Our engineers designed the 100X drive shaft to operate safely between 4,000 and 10,000 rpm." If, indeed, the drive shaft was so designed, technically, you have not lied. However, if, despite the design, the shaft only operates safely between 4,000 and 9,000 rpm, you have lied because you have falsely led your reader to infer that the shaft operates safely at the designed speeds.

To use marketing cigarettes again as an example: In the United States and certain other countries today, cigarette ads must carry a warning that cigarette smoking may be hazardous to health in various specific ways. In that sense, a cigarette ad may be technically telling the truth. However, if the ad shows healthy, attractive models smoking, to lead readers to infer that smoking is a healthy activity, they may be lying by false inference. Depending on the rules in the rules-based system and the statements made or implied in the ad, the cigarette ad may or may not be unethical.

Other legal and ethical considerations concern using ideas, writing, drawings, and research generated by someone else—either persons with whom you work or persons whose publications you read. Many of these are intellectual properties protected by legal and ethical rules. Legal requirements related to copyright and patents require you not only to acknowledge and credit others for their work but also to get their permission to use their work. Even if the work is not protected by law there also exist unwritten cultural and professional conventions to which you must adhere. You must acknowledge your sources.

RIGHTS-BASED

A rights-based system of ethics assumes that everyone has certain rights that, except under certain strictly defined circumstances, cannot be taken away. For example, as stated in the Declaration of Independence, all Americans have the rights of "life, liberty, and the pursuit of happiness." To protect society at large, convicted criminals may lose all three of these rights, but, in general, the rights are assumed to be, as the Declaration states, "unalienable." That is, our rights cannot be taken away.

By the extension of such basic rights as "life, liberty, and the pursuit of happiness" we can devise such rights as the right to expect the tools we use, the cars we drive, and the airplanes we fly in to be safe and not subject our life to unsought dangers.

Another way of looking at rights-based ethics is to say that we must treat our fellow human beings with dignity and not use them solely for our own self-interest or the interest of our organization. We all use people, obviously. We use tailors to alter our clothes, police to protect us, pilots to fly us, customers to provide us profits, and so forth. But a rights-based ethical system implies a fair exchange, such as appropriate payment or a safe and worthwhile product.

Cigarette ads clearly fail the rights test. Cigarettes may rob the smoker of life and the pursuit of happiness. By raising health-care costs, they curtail the rights of nonsmokers. They manipulate people to buy a harmful product solely to benefit those involved in cigarette production.

Acknowledging persons who have contributed to your work can be a sensitive subject. Certainly those who hold patents or copyrights on ideas you make use of have a legal right to be credited. Others who contribute in substantive ways are ethically entitled to acknowledgment as well.

A Case Analysis

Mary Saylor works in a cancer research laboratory that operates totally on grants from federal agencies and large funding organizations. Her job is to write and edit proposals to such agencies and organizations to obtain money for research that the laboratory wants to do. Often, such proposals are for new lines of research suggested by previous research. The more successful the previous research has been, the more likely that the laboratory will be granted the money to proceed with the new research.

Saylor is a writer and not a cancer researcher. However, she has a good background in biology and statistics, and she has worked for the laboratory for five years. Therefore, she has acquired a good knowledge of the way cancer research is conducted and reported. Her current assignment is to edit and polish a draft proposal prepared by Dr. Sam Gregory. Gregory wants to pursue a new line of research based upon his earlier work. He has supplied Saylor with his laboratory notes as well as the rough draft.

In working with the draft proposal, Saylor notices that some of the graphs are unusually smooth and regular. Checking the data in the lab notes, she finds that Gregory has manipulated his data to make his findings appear more precise and accurate than they really are. Looking further, Saylor finds that Gregory has highlighted those data that support his research and buried those data that do not. Furthermore, she finds one successful experiment reported that has no lab notes to support it. When she calls Gregory to tell him this, he says he has misplaced his notes but to proceed anyway.

How does Gregory's work stand up when scrutinized with the three ethical systems?

Utility-Based

If Gregory's proposal is accepted for funding, what will be the consequences? It seems clear that Gregory is fudging his data. Therefore, his past research is not as good as it should be, indicating that future research, too, may be less good than it should be. Money may go to Gregory's potentially inadequate research that could have gone for more successful research in some other laboratory.

Because Gregory's research is likely to waste limited research funds, cancer research will suffer and potential progress in cancer cures will be stymied. Clearly, Gregory's proposal runs a high risk of doing harm to cancer research and cancer patients. Only Gregory, himself, benefits. By the utility test, the writing and submission of Gregory's proposal is an unethical act.

Rule-Based

Gregory's proposal clearly fails the rules test. His smoothing of his graphs and burying his unfavorable data are both forms of lying, either outright or by false inference. Given both these actions, a high probability exists that the reported successful experiment for which no lab notes can be found is an outright lie. In general, rule-based systems prohibit lying. Gregory's proposal is essentially a lie and, therefore, unethical.

Rights-Based

Taxpayers have a right to expect their tax dollars spent on cancer research will go for worthwhile research. Funding organizations have a right to expect their money to be well used. By manipulating his data, Gregory is, in fact, attempting to manipulate the people who control cancer research funding. Therefore, he is using them without offering them the fair exchange of adequate research. Once again, Gregory's research appears unethical.

ACTING ETHICALLY

Once you have decided an act is unethical, the hard part begins. What to do about it? In this case, Mary Saylor, once she has determined that to submit Gregory's proposal would be unethical, has to decide what to do next. Obviously, she can decide to be a party to an unethical act and edit and submit the proposal. If she decides this is impossible for her to do, she has several other options.

She can go to Gregory, tell him what she has determined, and ask him either to rewrite his proposal in an ethical way or withdraw it. If this fails, she can go to the laboratory directors, lay the facts of the matter before them, and let them decide what to do. If they decide in Gregory's favor, she's in a bind with limited options. She can protect herself and say, "I wash my hands of this," and go about her work. She can look for work elsewhere in a more ethical environment. She can "blow the whistle" on Gregory with the funding agencies.

Clearly, these options, perhaps even the first, have the potential of causing Mary Saylor grave problems, perhaps even injuring her own career. It is really not enough to have the ability to determine whether something is unethical. One has to also have the moral sense to know what to do about it. Sometimes, it takes enormous courage to be ethical.

A CASE FOR ANALYSIS

Read the following case. Decide if Bob Davis is being asked to act unethically. If so, what action do you think he should take?

Bob Davis works in the human resources division (HR) of a small corporation. Bob, who has a degree in organizational psychology, has been in HR for five years and is well thought of by his fellow employees, particularly for his writing abilities. He has a new boss, Margaret Tucker, who came on board three months ago as head of HR. Learning about Davis' writing abilities, she asks him to edit for final publication a draft report she has written for the corporate chief executive officer (CEO) and the chief financial officer (CFO) recommending that the corporation expand HR office space and add new employees. The initial cost of the expansion would be $250,000. The ongoing cost of future operations would increase by $350,000 a year, mostly for salary and employee benefits.

The rationale for the expansion is that the increasing complexity of dealing with government regulations, employee health care insurance, and employee pensions has increased HR's work load. The department needs additional employees and space for them.

Davis takes the report and goes to work on it at once. He notices that Tucker does not refer to available HR employee work surveys, but rather uses vague and imprecise language such as, "Large new demands upon employee time brought about by an ever-increasing work load in the areas of government regulations, health care, and pensions lead me to conclude that additional employees and space for them is justified." Thinking to improve her precision, Davis checks out the hourly work-load figures reported in the surveys. To his surprise, they justify less than half of what Tucker is requesting in her recommendation report. Davis takes his misgivings about the figures to Tucker.

Tucker considers his comments and says, "Bob, in a recommendation report, we're dealing with probable truths, not hard facts. My projection may be as good as yours."

"No," Davis says. "My projection is based on the facts in the surveys, and they seem solid and accurate to me. In any case, we should report the data so the CFO and CEO can judge the figures for themselves."

"No," says Tucker. "We won't do that. Anyway, we need to build for future expansion, and this increase will give us a head start. We'll get in ahead of other departments who would do the same to us if they could." Tucker looks at Davis thoughtfully. She says, "Do it my way, Bob, or I'll get someone else who will." Davis leaves her office, wondering what to do.

SUGGESTIONS FOR APPLYING YOUR KNOWLEDGE

Any textbook can supply only a limited number of examples to illustrate its subject matter. Yet, for most of us, an ounce of example is worth a pound of theory. Therefore, we urge you to begin gathering examples of workplace writing that will help you grasp the concepts in this book. Examples bring the use of patterns and visuals to life. Examine them to see how they have been written to meet a specific purpose for a specific audience. Not all the examples you find will be equally good, so they'll provide you with ample material for discussion as well as instruction. There are many potential sources of examples.

GOVERNMENT PUBLICATIONS

Thousands of publications pour out from the federal government every year on a vast number of subjects. The government publishes a wide array of material ranging from scholarly articles to self-help books, such as *Find and Fix the Leaks*, which shows how to reduce air leaks in a home without reducing air quality. Your local or school library probably has a collection of government publications you can use.

If your school is a U.S. government depository, its library receives publications issued by the U.S. Superintendent of Documents, the Department of Energy, the National Aeronautics and Space Administration (NASA), the U.S. Geological Survey, the Defense Mapping Agency, and the National Oceanic and Atmospheric Agency. These government agencies are excellent sources for samples of workplace documents.

Your state land-grant university almost certainly has an extension service. This service prints fact sheets, pamphlets, and booklets on a wide variety of subjects, such as choosing insecticides, detecting oak wilt, choosing a television set, and planning a meeting. Other state agencies, such as the department of transportation, also publish informational pamphlets of many kinds.

MAGAZINES AND PROFESSIONAL JOURNALS

Your library should have a good collection of magazines and professional journals. These publications represent an enormous reservoir of examples. The advertisements in professional and trade journals, for instance, are often fine examples of high-level persuasion and also process and mechanism description. A magazine such as *Consumer Reports* contains numerous examples of analytical essays written to compare various kinds of consumer goods.

COMPANY SOURCES

Companies of any significant size must publish a good deal of material. They can often provide you with examples of handbooks, sales literature, proposals, and so forth. Business and government agencies depend for their very existence on the kinds of correspondence we describe in this book. If you have legitimate access to such correspondence, it will provide you with both good and, unfortunately, bad examples for evaluation and discussion.

INTERNET AND INTRANET RESOURCES

The Internet offers ready access to information on any topic. Companies, governments, organizations, educational institutions, and individuals establish Web sites to provide information about their activities. For example, many companies have developed huge knowledge databases to provide information on the company, its products, and its services. Frequently they include an e-mail address if you want to contact them. You may have access to company documents, such as business plans, mission statements, employee handbooks, and procedures of all kinds. Many organizations also have internal electronic sources (an intranet) for document sharing and employee resources. You will find an abundance of good (and bad) information and examples of documents from electronic sources.

A NOTE ABOUT THE SUGGESTIONS

We have not supplied the traditional exercises at the ends of chapters. We believe that only the classroom instructor, perhaps in collaboration with the students, can design the exact exercises needed to fit the needs of any particular class. This belief stems directly from our basic principle that successful communication presents specific information to a specific audience for a specific purpose. Therefore, we have provided not exercises but "Suggestions for Applying Your Knowledge," addressed to both student and instructor. In these sections we suggest a wide range of possible methods and sources that can be used to construct the out-of-class and in-class exercises needed.

CHAPTER 2

COMPUTERS AND WORKPLACE WRITING

Employers want you to come with the ability to communicate. Read the want ads. One of the most common qualifications you will see is "strong communication skills." They look for workers who write well and have strong oral communication skills. Our purpose is to help you develop successful communication that presents specific information to a specific audience for a specific purpose. In this chapter, we discuss computer-mediated communication—the ways the computer helps you communicate.

The computer environment opens up opportunities to

- Communicate with members of your organization or colleagues at other locations on collaborative projects.

- Maintain files of documents easily accessible and easily revised or printed.

- Share documents instantly and without generating a hard copy.

- Access library databases from your office or home so that you are more efficient in locating information in the library when you get there.

- Locate information on the World Wide Web.

The computer environment gives numerous opportunities to develop effective, well-researched documents, but you control the environment and the activities. You must write solid, well thought out texts. Your reader must have confidence that you provide accurate, complete information.

In this text we supply guidelines for incorporating computer technology into your writing routine. You must adapt the guidelines to your writing habits and to the software available. The examples we give are from current software, platforms (Macintosh, IBM, Gateway, Dell, and so on), and computer environments (Windows or Unix, for example), but no matter whether you are using a personal computer or are a part of a network of computers, you must adjust to rapid development of new technologies.

Employers no longer ask if you can use a computer—they assume you can. In most jobs, you will need a good working knowledge of a word-processing software such as Corel WordPerfect or Microsoft Word. You may also need to know other software that may be used in your profession. For example, accountants must know how to use spreadsheet programs such as Lotus 1-2-3 or Excel. Many companies have software designed specifically for them (proprietary software). Employers will train you or give you a few days to learn the software. However, you need a basic understanding of computers and the capabilities of the software, and you must show confidence in your knowledge of computers. You will then be ready for the ever-changing environment.

In fact, *change* is the word to remember as you read this chapter. As the computer technology changes, and along with it changes in the writing and reading environment, you must change. You must be flexible and adapt to the changes technology brings to your workplace setting.

The computer has changed the writing and reading environment. You will find yourself composing e-mail messages online that you will write quickly and send. You will read messages you receive quickly. You will follow links on the World Wide Web for information and sometimes not remember where you started or how you arrived at the information. You have to read material efficiently so that you can locate the information. You depend upon the cues the writer gives you (such as headings or bulleted lists) and the document design features on the Web (links shown as underlined terms or icons).

The computer is a tool that aids in the writing and reading process. You must know how to use it and control it—just like any other tool. Keep in mind what Jay Bolter, a scholar studying electronic writing, says about computers: "Computers are intelligent only in collaboration with human readers and writers."[1] You may be amazed occasionally—particularly as you surf the World Wide Web. You probably will not use all of the capabilities of the computer, and you may even resist some of the changes that come with each iteration of hardware and software. But, you use the tool, and you control the tool, and as with any tool, the more you use it the more proficient you will become.

We will focus on the capabilities of word-processing software. For example, you may use Microsoft Word, Corel WordPerfect, or Lotus WordPro to produce documents that are predominantly made up of words. These and other word-processing software are frequently integrated with other features that allow you to include graphics, database and spreadsheet information or to create presentations, hypertext documents, or convert a document to the format needed for publication on the World Wide Web (a document using hypertext markup language—html). In the workplace you will also share documents and comment on and edit documents of team members (for example, Lotus SmartSuite identifies itself as the "team approach" software with features such as TeamReview that allows coworkers to review and edit each other's work or TeamConsolidate that lets team members combine files easily). If you have the opportunity, examine several word-processing packages. You will see that their menus are similar, the commands or keystrokes for performing tasks are identical for the common actions (such as copy, cut, and paste), and they have similar capabilities. You must know their capabilities and explore the software to discover how to activate the feature. Word-processing software coordinates directly with other software in a suite of software.

---

[1]Jay Bolter, *Writing Space: The Computer, Hypertext, and the History of Writing* (Hillsdale, NJ: Erlbaum, 1991) 193.

Word-processing software

- Lets you type information once. You can revise documents easily without having to retype information.

- Makes it easier to move text around. You can cut and paste within a document or across documents to build a new document.

- Searches for errors that are repeated and lets you replace the text with correct information.

- Opens up lots of possibilities for document design. You can format a document on your own or use existing company templates.

- Offers many features that enhance the presentation of your document. For example, you can easily add a bulleted list, bold important information, or insert a box to highlight a warning in a set of instructions.

- Automates repetitive tasks so that you have more time for writing the document. For example, if you must complete forms repeatedly, you can construct the form once and then use the form as a template as often as you need it.

- Includes tools such as a spelling checker, grammar checker, and thesaurus so that you can check your work easily. You still must carefully read and edit your text; the software takes care of only the errors that require no decisions, such as *recieve/receive*. It does not catch errors such as *there/their*.

- Allows you to save a document so that you can send it electronically to someone in your office or at another location. It also saves a document so that you can publish it on the Web.

Good word-processing software contains features that allow you to increase your writing productivity. That is, you can spend more time actually writing and less time retyping the text.

In addition to word-processing software, we will discuss ways to incorporate visuals into your documents using the graphics feature of commonly available software (Chapters 6 and 7). In Chapter 12, we discuss how you may use presentation software for effective oral presentations. Again, learning the software is the easy part. Creating effective visuals and presentations means providing text and visuals to support your document or oral presentation. The computer cannot write the text or describe the topic—only you can.

Your employer will train you in the specifics of communications within your organization. You bring to the training curiosity and flexibility to adapt your communication skills to the current software and computer environment. In this chapter we describe the computer environments in which you may find yourself and suggest ways to help you write in those environments. First, we discuss your responsibilities as a writer to your reader but also your reader's responsibilities in using a document. We then overlay the writing process discussed in Chapter 1 with suggestions for incorporating computers into the process. Finally, we look at several online writing and reading environments that require writing and reading strategies somewhat different from working with hard-copy documents.

WRITERS' AND READERS' RESPONSIBILITIES

As a writer, you are responsible for providing your readers with accurate information so that they can use the information for their purposes to solve a problem, perform a task, or gather information. You have the responsibilities, discussed in Chapter 1, of presenting ethical and legally sound documents for decision makers. Medical lab technicians depend on accurate instructions to operate the electron microscope or to handle blood samples safely; personnel directors rely on clearly worded benefit policies to present to employees.

Chapters 4 (Style and Tone), 5 (Text and Document Design), and 6 and 7 (Visuals and Document Design, I and II) provide basic principles for effective writing. The principles apply whether you write a document in longhand or type it using a computer. You must present specific information to a specific audience for a specific purpose. The information must be organized and easy to access. The reader must be able to navigate through the document easily and locate the information needed. In this section, we look at writing and reading online material. Online material is written directly on the computer and is read from the computer. A hard copy of the document may or may not be generated. In fact, frequently the information is gathered from the online document, incorporated into another document electronically, and published electronically.

For example, you may receive an e-mail from your supervisor requesting you to recommend the best computer for the office. You first go to the Web pages for several of the computer manufacturers to get the latest specifications and prices. You copy the information, including a picture of the latest system, into a word-processing document. However, because you want to check with others in your field regarding state-of-the-art equipment, you send e-mail messages to several colleagues at other companies. Your colleagues respond with suggestions that you also incorporate into your report. You may even access your local library in search of a recent article in a computer magazine that compares the latest equipment. You now have a collection of information that you have saved in a word-processing file. You spend a few days organizing the material and drafting the report. You send an electronic copy to a co-worker to double check your report and make suggestions before you revise and print a copy of the report. You proofread the report carefully, make corrections, and print a final version for your supervisor. Or, in some offices, you may send the final report in its electronic form.

WRITING ONLINE

We encourage you to begin your writing on the computer. You will write e-mail online, so you might as well get in the habit of starting all of your documents on the computer. Frequently you will not have time to draft a document in longhand and then type it into a computer before revising and sending the document out. Why not type the document on the computer and revise it from the screen? You will save time transcribing from handwritten notes to computer-generated documents. You can generate a hard copy (or better yet, exchange copies across the office network) for others to comment on before you send the final version of the document. Because you will most likely gather, write, and share information using a computer and you will be working under deadlines, you will need to be efficient. Any tool, in this case the computer, should help the process, not get in the way.

Collaboration is easier if you have your document ready on a disk or in a file to send across the network to give to the project coordinator. Following file-naming conventions and document format established by your office will make the process easier. You will want to establish file-naming conventions that allow you and others to find and work on the document and create a series of versions of the document (for example, *report1* for the first version, *report2* for the second version, . . . *finalreport* for the final version). The *Save As* feature of your software lets you change the name of the file. By saving different versions of a document, you may find that you like all or portions of the earlier version rather than the revised document. Also, you will not have to recreate an entire document if it is lost. Of course, you should always save your document in at least two places (on the hard drive, at a network location, and on a disk).

You also may find that your company has certain templates or boilerplate material available on the office network for you to use in your documents. For example, you can open the template for the office memo and fill in the Date, To, From, and Subject as prompted before writing the body of your memo. You will then know your memo meets the guidelines set by the company. Or, you may need to use a block of information that states the company's affirmative-action policy. Commonly used statements, known as *boilerplate material,* can easily be inserted into your document from the file on the office network or from a company-made disk.

Figure 2.1 illustrates how a document might develop electronically. While you may do most of the writing, you may also coordinate with others as you gather information and produce the document. For some of the information you gather, you may have to acknowledge your source (see Chapter 22); other information that belongs to your company does not have to be acknowledged.

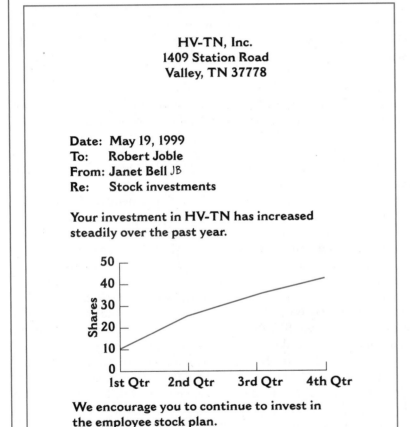

HV-TN, Inc.
1409 Station Road
Valley, TN 37778

Company letterhead

Date: May 19, 1999
To: Robert Joble
From: Janet Bell JB
Re: Stock investments

Memo template

Your investment in HV-TN has increased steadily over the past year.

Graph developed from information in a spreadsheet software. The accounting department supplied the information.

We encourage you to continue to invest in the employee stock plan.

An equal opportunity employer.

Figure 2.1 How a document might develop electronically.

Readers will read documents that are inviting to read, easy to follow, and easy to use (Chapter 5). Word-processing software helps you develop and write such documents. However, you must provide solid information or lose credibility with the reader. Here are a few suggestions that will help.

• **Provide correct and accurate information.** Review the purpose of the document to make sure you have provided what the reader requires. For example, you recommend which computer to purchase or you give the time, date, and location of the meeting. Readers depend upon you to accurately describe the situation and give the needed information.

You have ethical and legal responsibilities (Chapter 1) to provide complete, truthful information. If you use information from sources outside of your company, you will need to acknowledge your sources (Chapter 22). Word-processing software makes it easy to insert *footnotes* (notes that appear at the bottom of the page, like those we use in this book) and *endnotes* (notes that appear at the end of the document). You can establish links between information in a spreadsheet and in a word-processing document so that the changes made on the spreadsheet will also change in the word-processing document. Computers make correcting and updating information easy.

• **Place the most important information where the reader will see it immediately.** Do not force the reader to search for the answer to a problem. Few will come to a meeting if they must search for its time and location. Online text needs even closer attention because readers will spend even less time looking for information. (Readers generally spend 7 seconds or less looking for information on a Web page.) A screen full of text provides little visual orientation for the reader. Keep in mind that readers of online material can move back and forth (following links) or mark pages they visit frequently using the bookmark feature of the Web browser, but they do not always know where they are in the entire work, as in a book.

• **Use visuals to display the information in another form.** (See Chapters 6 and 7.) Large blocks of text may intimidate your reader. If you have information that can be shown in a visual, you should seriously consider doing so. You can create graphs of data or drawings of products and import files with the *.gif* or *.jpg* extensions and other graphic files from the Web or other sources. If you create a line graph and decide a bar graph would better display the data, you can change the selection with a click of the mouse. You have no excuse for avoiding inserting visuals in your documents—it's easy to do!

• **Use the appropriate document format—for example, memo, letter, report, instructions—to help the reader.** (See Chapter 5.) Word-processing software makes formatting your document easy. You will want to establish the format at the beginning of the document. If necessary, consult with group members and company guidelines. When you begin a document, set the margins and tabs, select the font and point size, and insert features such as page numbers, headers and footers, and other features. You can always adjust the format. If you routinely create the same document but change the data (for example, your monthly expense report or periodic memos on safety) consider establishing a style sheet or template that creates the format and keeps it the same for each monthly report. Check your word-processing package; many include commonly used templates and style sheets for documents such as memos, calendars, or sales reports that may save you time. Another way to save time is to put frequently used addresses, signature blocks, and blocks of information (boilerplate material) into macros, separate files, or the address book tool so that you can easily retrieve the information into the document you are working on. Such time savers can help you spend more time on the content.

• **Establish and display the material's organization.** Headers and footers supply information at the top (head) or bottom (foot) of every page. Most headers include the document or section title and page number, and sometimes the date (and file name, if appropriate). The latter two are often placed in the footer. For example:

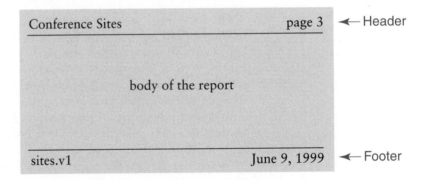

Conference Sites	page 3	← Header
body of the report		
sites.v1	June 9, 1999	← Footer

• **Check spelling and grammar.** You lose credibility with each spelling or grammar error, especially if the errors are easily caught and corrected by a spelling checker or grammar checker.

READING ONLINE

Readers have responsibilities, too, but they might need to be enticed into looking at your document. As you write a document, think about how you read and what makes a document easier to follow. If you think about your experiences as a reader, you can incorporate some of the successful sentence structures, document features, and information into your documents. As you read online material, traveling from link to link, you also become an author. Bolter notes that "electronic writing emphasizes the impermanence and changeability of text, and it tends to reduce the distance between author

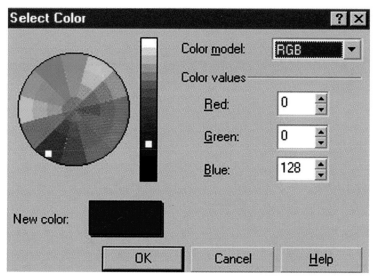

Figure 5.9 An example of a color wheel found in most software programs, often in the area where you make font selections. See pages 116–119 for discussion of using color effectively.
Source: Corel WordPerfect 8.0. Corel and WordPerfect are registered trademarks of Corel Corporation or Corel Corporation Limited.

Figure 7.1 A color photograph best shows the effect of disease on this hedge. The photograph was taken with a digital camera and inserted electronically into the textbook. See page 161 for discussion of using photographs.

(a)

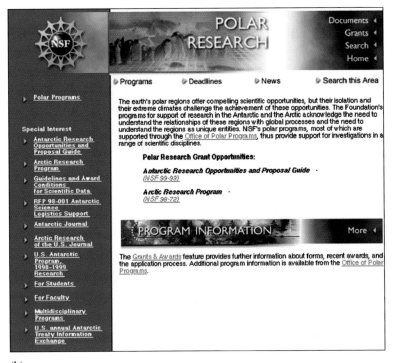

(b)

Figure 2.2 Example of an online reading path for the National Science Foundation Web site, www.nsf.gov. See pages 38–39 for discussion of reading online information.

| News | Publications | Proposal Info | Search | Comments | Contact Info |

ANTARCTIC JOURNAL
OF THE UNITED STATES

Editor :

Winifred Reuning
wreuning@nsf.gov

▶ Article Submissions

▶ Links to individual issues

Antarctic Journal of the United States , established in 1966, reports on U.S. activities in Antarctica, related activities elsewhere, and trends in the U.S. Antarctic Program. Each year, the Office of Polar Programs (National Science Foundation, Room 755, 4201 Wilson Boulevard, Arlington, Virginia 22230; telephone 703-306-1031) publishes and distributes online two review issues, which include papers by members of the antarctic science and logistics community. OPP distributes printed copies of these issues to members of the U.S. and international antarctic science communities, representatives of U.S. private organizations and other Federal agencies with an interest in antarctic research, policy and logistics, and managers of other national antarctic programs.

The *Antarctic Journal of the United States* is also sold by the copy through the U.S. Government Printing Office. To request prices or order individual issues, contact Superintendent of Documents, **U.S. Government Printing Office, P.O. Box 371954, Pittsburgh, Pennsylvania 15250-7954. To place an order by telephone, call 202-512-1800.**

The Director of the National Science Foundation has determined that the publication of this periodical is necessary in the transaction of the public business required by law of this agency.

(c)

(d)

Figure 2.2 (*continued*)

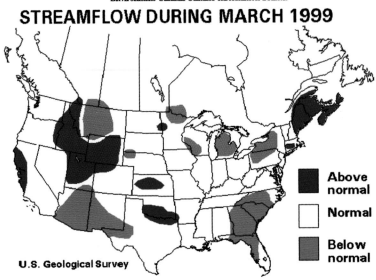

U.S. Geological Survey
Environment Canada Climate Information Branch

STREAMFLOW DURING MARCH 1999

Above normal

Normal

Below normal

U.S. Geological Survey

Figure 7.15 At a glance, the reader can see the water conditions across the continental United States. Maps help readers associate information with an area. See pages 174–175 for discussion of using maps as visuals.
Source: U.S. Geological Survey. National Water Conditions. 12 May 1999 <http://water.usgs.gov/nwc>.

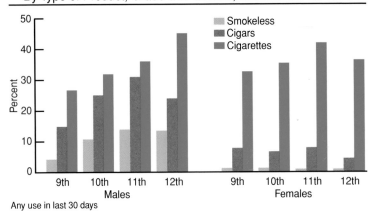

Prevalence of Current Tobacco Use
By Type of Product, Grade and Gender, Massachusetts 1996

Smokeless
Cigars
Cigarettes

Any use in last 30 days

Figure 7.25 The consistent use of color, scale, and categories makes the comparison between male and female high school students easy. See pages 181–185 for discussion of using bar graphs.
Source: National Cancer Institute. Graphs and Charts. 10 April 1998. 24 August 1999 <http://rex.nci.nih.gov/massmedia/pressreleases/cigargifs/cigargraphs.htm>.

and reader by turning the reader into an author."[2] Readers construct the document they read as they follow links to information they need.

Readers share the following common characteristics:

- **They come to the document to gather information.** The writer wants a reader to find the information.

- **They actively seek information.** Writer's cues reveal the organization and point the reader to pertinent information. Readers must know how the author uses arguments and persuasion to present information. They also need the source of the information.

- **They use the document to help complete a task.** Writer's cues, such as headings, bolded text, and summary statements, point the reader to the information.

- **They follow paths through the document to reach needed information.** Readers do not always read workplace documents from front to back as they would a novel. Instead, readers go to the point in a manual that shows how to fix a problem coded as a printer error, or they might look for the anticipated cost for materials and equipment in a proposal for updating a cooling system for a storage facility. Readers may use the table of contents or index to locate requirements for getting a day-care center licensed.

Reading online material requires the reader to follow paths or links to gather information. For example, Figure 2.2 (see the color insert after page 38) illustrates a reading path that begins with the National Science Foundation home page (Figure 2.2a). If readers want to learn more about Polar Research, they click on that link. The Polar Research page (Figure 2.2b) offers a description of the program and more links shown at the top of the page (Programs, Deadlines, News, Search this Area) and along the left margin (for example, Polar Programs, Antarctic Journal [Figure 2.2c], Arctic Research of the U. S. Journal, and so on). Some of the links lead to more information than the reader wants; other links may take the reader to material not of interest. Keeping track of the paths and the information is a challenge for most readers. Reading hypertext material such as that on the Web challenges the reader. Bookmarks, Back key, Return to Home Page links, site maps (Figure 2.2d), and other features help but do not completely solve the problem of orienting the reader.

The writer's and reader's responsibilities depend upon each other. As you write, imagine being the reader and how you would gather information from the document. When you actually are a reader, observe techniques the writer uses to lead you to information. Consider using some of the same techniques in documents you write.

---

[2]Bolter 3.

THE WRITING PROCESS ONLINE

Now that you know your responsibilities as a writer and you know the expectations of readers, you must produce the document. Following our outlined writing process will help you control the process and improve your writing, even if you do not use the computer. However, we urge you to use the computer—it simplifies setting up the document features and gives you more time to work on the content.

The writing process described in Chapter 1 adapts easily to the computer. You can generate ideas into a new file, you can develop the ideas, you can revise and edit the document, and you can send or print the document. Additionally, you can easily share the document with others within the office or at locations around the world.

In this section we review the writing process discussed in Chapter 1 and suggest ways the computer helps you in the writing process. Focus on the portion of the process that seems to give you the most trouble. Maybe the computer can help. For example, if you have trouble getting organized, you might try using the outline tool. Open a new document and select Outline (in MS Word or Corel WordPerfect it's under Tools). Outline automatically numbers each item in your list. If you press Tab, you can add subsections to the outline. You can rearrange your outline until you are comfortable with it. Or, if you need a visual to show what you are trying to say, open a new document and create a chart or graph. You can easily move back and forth between the visual and the text so that you describe the point you are making. Remember—you are not locked into one outline or a particular visual. You might try creating different versions to see what meets the purpose of your document and best presents the information to your audience. The Writer's Guide (Unit V) gives an example under the heading "Outlines."

DISCOVERING AND GATHERING INFORMATION

Open a new word-processing document on a computer. Do not worry about format or sentence-level issues such as spelling and grammar. Instead, type in your ideas. One way to get started is to use a technique called *steamrolling*, introduced by Thomas Barker.[3] Here's what you do:

1. List 5 to 10 words down the left side of the screen that are related to the topic of your document.

2. Place the cursor before the beginning of one of the words.

3. Look at the word and type a sentence that uses the word or that describes the word. The word will *steamroll* across the page, moving as you type.

---

[3]Thomas T. Barker. "Reinforcing the Scheme of Things: Using Word Processors in Writing Across the Curriculum," *Designing Writing Assignments for Vocational-Technical Courses: A Guide for Teachers in the Two-Year College and Technical Institute*, ed. Jimmie Killingsworth, Donald H. Cunningham, and Laurie L. Jones (Lubbock, TX: The West Texas Project in Writing Across the Curriculum, 1988) 39.

4. Erase the word once you have a sentence (or 2 to 3 sentences).

5. Steamroll for the remaining words. You no longer have a blank screen. You now have text to work with.

You might call the file *ideas1*. You are not usually ready at this point to create an outline, but if you want, you can use the outline feature of your word-processing software to organize your ideas. Your main purpose is to gather all of the ideas you have for the document in one place. You are making notes to get you started.

As you work, you will find that you need more data or information. The power of computers moves to the forefront when you begin consulting with others and sharing information. E-mail lets you send a message to someone else within the office or at another location almost instantly. Networked computers let you send a file to another location, or you can transfer the file using a disk. You can exchange ideas and gather information without leaving your desk. Bear in mind, however, that a trip down the hall to ask the computer programmer about a software feature you are writing about may be more effective—especially when you need to ask several questions to clarify the problem. Likewise, a trip to the company library or local library often yields information you might overlook when you gather information only from an electronic database.

If you do exchange information electronically, your technical support department can provide you with the protocol for sending documents. File Transfer Protocol (FTP), attaching a file to an e-mail message, or simply saving a file to the company's network are frequently used means for sharing documents. Formatting problems and multiple platforms may make sending documents troublesome, but once the problems are worked out, you do not have to worry about time zones or playing phone tag.

For example, one of your authors served on a committee that did a feasibility study for an organization looking into holding a conference. The committee members were located at universities in Alabama, Georgia, Iowa, Michigan, North Carolina, Ohio, Pennsylvania, and Wisconsin. The committee formed at a national convention and did not meet as a group again until the next annual convention. All "meetings" were conducted through a listserv on the Internet using e-mail. The document outlining the options for the conference was sent via e-mail. A year later, the committee met in person and reported its findings at the organization's open meeting, where more discussion occurred. The ad hoc committee fulfilled its purpose. It researched the feasibility of holding a conference and reported back to the organization.

PLANNING YOUR ORGANIZATION

After you brainstorm and make notes about the topic, you must organize the material so that the readers can find the information they need. Decide the order in which you want to present the information. We suggest you open your notes file *(ideas1)* and then open another file (maybe *proposal1* for the first draft of a proposal). You can copy notes from *ideas1* and paste them into *proposal1* following the organization you establish for the document. The order probably does not match the order in your notes, but word-processing software gives you the flexibility to move text to an effective location. You may want to use the outline feature of your word processor to structure the outline. Just remember—you probably will deviate from the outline as you write. The structured outline or a set of notes in a file should guide you through the writing. You developed the organization; you can change it as well.

The organization you choose for the document provides the reader with a map of the information. Whether you plan to use comparison and contrast or chronology to set the order of your document, you must make the plan clear to the reader. As you move text in from your notes, consider establishing section headings for placing the information. The headings may be taken directly from your outline, if you developed an outline. Within each section you can then arrange the information following the organizational plan you have established. Figure 2.3 illustrates how the text moved into different sections of a draft for this chapter.

Keep in mind that the organization depends upon the needs of the reader and the purpose of the document. The purpose establishes the format the reader expects—a one-page letter or a report that can be read in 30 minutes. The time and space allotted for a document determines its organization. For example, fitting a set of instructions on the product's side panel will control how much you write and the organization of the information.

PLANNING VISUALS

Including visuals in your document gets easier with each new version of software. If you are using an integrated software package such as MS Office, Lotus SmartSuite, or Corel WordPerfect Suite, you have several options for graphics: constructing tables; drawing visuals; charting data in line, bar, or pie graphs; and importing graphics created in another software package.

One suggestion may make your document more manageable as you write: create the visuals in a separate file and create each visual on a separate page. You can keep the file open and easily go between the text document in one window and the visual document in another window as you work. When you have the text fairly stable, you can move the visual in. The software packages allow you to easily create, label, insert, resize, and format the visuals for your document. Even after you have inserted the visual into your text, you can edit it. Adjusting the size or position of the visual is easy. We describe the features of visuals in Chapters 6 and 7.

WRITING ONLINE

You should now have a computer file full of notes and information that you need to organize. Perhaps as you made notes on the computer, you grouped related information together. Open the notes file and review the

In the *ideas1* file collect your notes and ideas in one file. You can easily copy notes into the draft of the document as you need the information.

For example, the notes shown below moved into sections of this chapter. Your notes
- provide reminders of what to cover in the document.
- record the quotes from other sources that you plan to use.
- identify terms you need to define.

Notes

7 seconds or less looking for information on a Web page

"Computers are intelligent only in collaboration with human readers and writers." (Jay Bolter, *Writing Space,* 193)

include figure illustrating reading path

need source that explains copyright laws for Web material

define FTP, listserv, . . .

Draft of Document

Introduction

. . . Keep in mind what Jay Bolter, a scholar studying electronic writing, says about computers: "Computers. . . ."

Writer's and Reader's Responsibilities

- Place the most important information so that the reader will see it immediately.

. . . Readers will spend 7 seconds or less looking for information on a Web page.

For example, Figure 2.2 illustrates a reading path that begins with the National Science Foundation home page.

Writing Ethically

. . . You must assume that any material you find, whether or not it bears the ©, C, or "Copyright date by source" is copyrighted material. Brad Templeton's Web site, "10 Big Myths about copyright explained" describes implications of using copyrighted material.

Writing Environments

. . . FTP (file transfer protocol) . . . FTPing allows you to send a document electronically.

Figure 2.3 How text moves from notes into the draft of a document.

information or perhaps print out the notes to review them. Now you must begin writing.

Open a second document and establish the format—see the checklist in Figure 2.4. Don't forget to establish a file-naming convention that others working on the document will recognize. You might call this file *proposald1* (for the first draft of the proposal). Also, start a file for the visuals (maybe, *visuals1*). When you create a series of versions of the document, you can always go back to an older version if the changes you make do not work.

Every writer has a way that best suits his or her style of producing a document. You may want to start writing a portion of the document that you are most comfortable with. You need not start with the introduction. In fact, the introduction may be one of the last things you write. Or, you may write the introduction first to give you direction (an outline) of what is to follow. For example, if you cannot clearly state the problem in the introduction, then you probably will have difficulties in the body of the feasibility study presenting relevant findings and supporting your conclusions. You will adjust the introduction as you finish the document.

As this chapter was written, we developed "tricks" to get more writing done. When stuck, we switched to the file with the visuals and created or edited the figures or worked on the references. We worked on what was fun or easy to do before returning refreshed to the document and ready to add more.

You may produce most, if not all, of the document electronically before you print the final version. Or, you may periodically want to print the document to see how it looks and reads in hard-copy form. Of course, if you are producing a document that will remain electronic, you probably will not want to print it at all. We are getting better with editing material that we read online; however, if the document will appear in hard copy, you *must* at some point edit on the hard copy to protect against spacing problems, unreasonable breaks in the text across pages, and so on. You want to see what the reader will see.

Computers give us much more flexibility in where we start and how we move text until we find the best place for the information in the document. With a document developed cooperatively, one member of the group might establish the overall organization and format for the project and then insert the information from electronic documents from other group members. Of course, the final report must be seamless (that is, a reader cannot identify where one writer's contribution ends and another's begins) and the format, including visuals, will be consistent throughout.

The document's purpose and its readers will determine how much time you spend writing. Frequently deadlines determine when a document is finished. Memos generally are written and sent out quickly because they are internal documents that address immediate problems. Letters to clients, however, may need more planning, drafts, and approval from others in the office before they go out.

Checklist for Formatting Your Documents

To create professional documents, you need to know how to control your word-processing software.

Get in the habit of setting up your document first. That is, set the tabs, font, page numbers, and other features, save the document, and then begin writing. You can always adjust the settings.

_____ Select page orientation and paper size.

_____ Insert headers and footers. Headers place information at the top of each page; footers, at the bottom of the page.

_____ Set tabs. To align text, you must use the Tab key instead of the space bar. You may need to move tabs to get the appropriate spacing. Decimal tabs make it easy to align columns of numbers (and other items).

_____ Select font. A serif font works best when you give your reader a lot of text to read. Sans serif fonts work best in headings, in presentation slides, and documents without a lot of text.

_____ Set justification. Only the left justification needs to be set. Readers find it easier to read a ragged-right margin, particularly when there's a lot of text.

_____ Add page numbers. If your document goes beyond one page, you need to add page numbers to help orient the reader.

_____ Select the line space. Will the document be single-spaced, double-spaced, or spaced at 1 1/2 lines?

_____ Save the document. Be sure to Save your document often. Save different versions of each document. You can return to an earlier version if you don't like the changes you have made.

Many of the items can be established as part of your preferences on your computer so that you do not change the items above for each document—but you should check as you begin a document to make sure the format matches the purpose of the document. Consider setting up style sheets if you use the same format for documents.

Figure 2.4 Checklist for formatting a word-processing document.

REVISING ONLINE

The ease with which we can revise computer-generated documents has both advantages and disadvantages. The advantage is that copying, cutting, and pasting within a document, between documents, or across several documents and workstations provides flexibility in providing accurate information. You can change the format to meet the needs of readers and the purpose of the document. You can do this almost endlessly. In the workplace, a deadline frequently limits the revision period. The writer's job is to allow enough time before the deadline to write and revise.

The importance of substantive revision does not change. That is, you must organize the document and work with the information to develop a clear, concise document. The content must satisfy the reader's purpose for coming to the document. If readers can't easily follow instructions for putting a gas grill together, they will return the grill to the store. If the proposal for highway repairs does not clearly state the cost estimates, the company bidding on the job will not receive serious consideration. No matter how good the computer and software make a document look, if the reader does not understand the text or find the information needed, the document has failed. Bad writing is still bad writing no matter how good it "looks"—effective document design invites the reader into the document, but only good, available information will keep the reader there.

Software available on computers, however, does help with some of the mechanical revision—spelling, grammar, and formatting. Spelling checkers and grammar checkers are available as part of the word-processing software you use. We have cautioned earlier, however, to not rely on the spelling and grammar checkers. You still must proofread the document.

Additionally, if you set the format features early in the document, you will have a consistent document design throughout the document. The checklist in Figure 2.4 will help you establish the look of the document and the way the information is presented.

WRITING COLLABORATIVELY

The principles of cooperative writing remain the same whether you are writing online, creating a computer-generated document, or writing longhand. And, the problems and solutions in cooperative writing also remain unchanged on or off the computer. What does change is the environment. We have easier access to each other through e-mail and network connections. More and more companies use local-area networks or wide-area networks to connect computers to each other and share information. The phone, fax, video conferencing, and online discussions through such features as Lotus Notes give us more options for incorporating ideas from others into a project. Although a writer and team have access to information online through the Web and online libraries, they still must cull the important information, interpret it, and present it effectively—not an easy task. Your critical thinking skills are key here. Your ability to work with others is essential.

WRITING ETHICALLY

In Chapter 1 and throughout this textbook, we describe the importance of writing ethically. You accept responsibility for the information you provide your reader when you publish the document in hard copy form, electronically, or orally. You represent yourself and your company or client through the text you produce. In this section we discuss your responsibilities as you gather information from electronic sources—in particular, the World Wide Web.

Evaluating and using information on the Web differs little from evaluating and using information found in print sources such as an environmental impact statement or an insurance contract. Ease of access to a seemingly endless supply of information, speed of copying material, and the appearance of up-to-date information make the Web an attractive source of information. But don't let the ease of access, speed, or recency deceive you. Like information from a report, article, book, or speech, you must evaluate the source of the information, the content for accuracy and completeness, and the timeliness and stability of the Web site.

Source	Who developed the page? What are their credentials? Whom do they represent? How might you verify the information on the page? Can you contact the author(s) by phone or postal address (not electronically) to request more information? Does the author provide an objective viewpoint? Is the information free of advertisements or other indications that the writer is presenting a biased view?
Content	How was the information obtained? Are the sources for information clearly listed so that you can verify them in another source? Is the statistical data easy to understand, are graphs accurate, and is the method explained? Is there a print version of the material on the Web? Is the complete version on the Web? Is the information copyrighted?
Site	Is the information current and kept up-to-date? What are the dates on the page? (When was the page written? When was the page first placed on the Web? When was the page last revised?)
Navigation	Is the site easy to move around in? Is there a site map?

Figure 2.5 gives an example of a Web site and questions for critiquing the Web site.

After you evaluate an information source, you may find you want to include some of the information in, say, your report on improved methods of asphalt repair or in a memo to your boss asking for a new computer workstation. What information do you have to acknowledge?

Source
- Who developed the page?
- What are their credentials?
- Is there a way to verify the information on the page?
- Is the information free of advertisements or other indications that the writer is presenting a biased view?
- Does the author provide an objective viewpoint?

Site
- Is the information current and kept up-to-date?
- What are the dates on the page?

Navigation
- Is the site easy to move around in?
- Is there a site map?

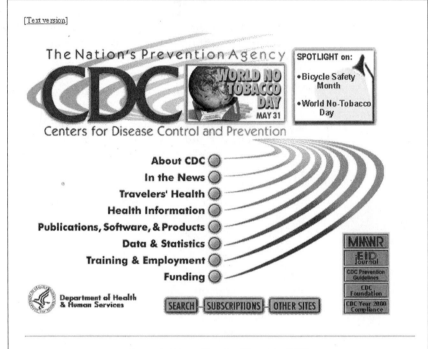

Content
- How was the information obtained?
- Are the sources for the information clearly listed so the reader can verify them in another source?
- Is the statistical data presented in easy to understand and accurate graphs and the method explained?
- Is there a print version of the information? Is the complete version on the Web?

Figure 2.5 Evaluating a Web site, in this example, the Centers for Disease Control and Prevention ⟨http://www.cdc.gov/⟩.

Let's take the computer workstation request first. You visited two local computer stores and Web sites for three manufacturers and you read reviews in *PC Computing* and *PC Magazine*. You also checked with the information technology representative for your company to ensure that what you request will be compatible with the company server. The representative also gave you a range of prices and identified the sources the company has purchase agreements with. How do you present your findings to your supervisor? Your supervisor wants you to identify the computer you want and the total cost of the workstation. How much acknowledgment must you give to the sources you consulted? Very little.

Let us assume, too, that your boss wants assurance that it will help you be more productive—you must justify the cost. You must focus on how each feature (RAM, hard-drive space, monitor size, jazz drive, software, and so on) will improve your output. Depending on your department's budget and how costly your request is, you might offer two or three configurations and the costs for each. Assuming you priced several sources and are confident in your request, you might strengthen your request by adding a sentence or two to review how you arrived at the workstation configurations that you did. Consider the following:

> I tested the computer at our local computer store, ABComputing, and met with Sally Jones (the company's information technology representative). I checked the Web sites for IBM, Dell, and Gateway as well as read reviews in *PC Computing* and *PC Magazine*. The prices for each configuration are guaranteed for 30 days.

Spend most of your time describing the computer and how each feature meets your needs. For example:

> Because the multimedia presentations I create for the department activities frequently exceed 30 MB of disk space, I need the external jazz drive capacity of 100 MB to copy the presentation to Janice Walker's (sales representative) laptop.

You need not provide formal bibliographic citations. Your supervisor trusts you to do the research and report the prices accurately.

However, in certain situations you must document sources in greater detail. For instance, you may be writing a report on the latest research on asphalt repair materials for a panel of civil engineer and highway supervisors. They need to evaluate the options before approving the repairs. The report may also go to the state legislature's subcommittee on highways. Your sources include interviews with civil engineers and asphalt contractors, research published in professional journals such as *Public Works* or *Concrete International*, several government reports on highway maintenance, and Web sites for asphalt suppliers. You might include a sentence such as the following in your report:

> In a study done by the National Center for Asphalt Technology and the Indiana Department of Transportation, Brown et al. found that "fiber stabilizers were found to be more effective in reducing draindown than polymer stabilizers" (16).

You will have a reference section at the end of the report with an entry such as the following:

Brown, E. R., John E. Haddock, Rajib B. Mallick, and Todd A. Lynn. *Development of a Mixture Design Procedure for Stone Matrix Asphalt (SMA)* (NCAT Report No. 97–3). Auburn, AL: National Center for Asphalt Technology. March 1997. 23 July 1999 ⟨http://www.eng.auburn. edu/center/ncat/reports/rep97-3.pdf⟩.

Citing your sources is important when you are using information gathered by another individual or organization. The information is copyrighted. Acknowledging your sources strengthens your report. You show that the information presented has been studied by reliable sources and the findings lend support and credibility to your conclusions.

You must assume that any material you find, whether or not it bears ©, C, or "Copyright (date) by (source)" is copyrighted material. Brad Templeton's Web site, "10 Big Myths about copyright explained,"[4] describes the implications of using copyrighted material.

To sum up, you must acknowledge your sources. You may quote sources and paraphrase information from sources as long as you identify the source. If you borrow more than what is considered "fair use" (less than 20 percent of the source), you must get permission from the author. This applies to linking to Web sites, too. If you create a link to a site, you should get permission first. We discuss the issue of citing print and electronic sources in more detail in Chapter 22.

WRITING ENVIRONMENTS

The writing environment has expanded beyond the boundaries of a quiet corner with a desk and a few select readers. The quiet corner and desk may still be where you initiate a document, but you send your electronically produced documents into environments that can reach anyone—astronauts on a space station or any machine, the land rover on Mars, for example. The global network of satellites and computers links virtually everyone. The *Internet* is a collection of computers networked (connected together) through locations around the world. The global network sends and receives information almost instantaneously. *Intranet* refers to computers networked locally and linked to the Internet. *E-mail* and the *World Wide Web* rely on Internet connections. *Groupware* most frequently relies on intranet connections for collaborative activities. Computers mediate communication. That is, they provide an effective and efficient environment for quick, easy exchange of information.

Banks, for example, rely on internal networks (intranets) for their employees to conduct the daily communication activities of the business. Most banks have branches, sometimes located across several states. Colonial Bank, for example, has offices in several cities in the Southeast that circulate money

[4]Brad Templeton, 1 May 1999 ⟨http://www.clarinet.com/brad/copymyths.html⟩.

electronically, not by sending an armored truck. Likewise, many of us can telephone our bank to access account information and make transactions.

In this section, we describe three widely used writing environments: electronic mail; listservs, groupware, and online chat sessions; and the World Wide Web. These writing environments change constantly, requiring you to develop as a flexible writer who can adapt to the different environments and their changes.

ELECTRONIC MAIL (E-MAIL)

Many companies and individuals now rely on electronic mail (e-mail) as a quick and easy way to get a message to someone. We no longer play phone tag; we send messages. The messages may be sent across the Internet to locations outside your company or they may be messages sent on your company's local network, across a local-area network.

The writing environment for e-mail requires as careful and thoughtful writing as your other writing (see also Chapter 8). Consider e-mail writing as similar to writing an office memo or a letter to a client. You generally will spend little time composing an e-mail message. Consider your reader's needs and expectations: e-mail readers and writers expect prompt replies. Identify the purpose of your message early and provide the information immediately.

However, do not let timeliness get in the way of producing a succinct, error-free message. E-mail readers might overlook one or two typing errors, but they will not overlook repeated errors. For example, the representative of a firm hiring several recent college graduates explained that one applicant contacted her via e-mail as she had requested. However, the applicant misspelled *receive* several places in the message. She was willing to overlook the first error, but when the error was repeated, the representative could not consider the e-mail writer as an applicant. The writer lost credibility as an applicant for the position.

As with any other professional document, you must know the reader, the purpose, and the circumstances behind the e-mail message. Some messages require only a quick one- or two-line response; others may require drafting in your word-processing software before you *FTP* (file transfer protocol) it to others. FTPing allows you to send a document electronically.

You can attach and send documents with an e-mail message. Some companies now ask job applicants to send an electronic version of their resume. Keep in mind that readers associate your writing with the quality of your work. Remember, too, that companies have the right to monitor your e-mail just as they do your other work. You may delete a message from your computer, but the company's server more than likely retains a copy. E-mail appears to be fleeting but in fact is permanent. The host server archives all activity and the activity can be retrieved.

Few people keep a hard copy of e-mail messages. Some use folders within the e-mail system to keep messages that they may want to refer back to or hold until they have time to respond. Know that others may keep a copy of your message or forward it on for others to read.

Here are some suggestions for effective, readable e-mail messages:

• **Keep your messages relatively short and to the point.** Many professionals receive more than 50 messages daily in addition to their other work. They will read their messages quickly.

• **When possible, have your main point appear on the first screen of the message.** That is, write the message so that your main point is seen first. You can follow up with more detail in the message. Between 20 and 30 lines of e-mail text show at one time. The reader should see your main point as early as possible in the first 20 to 30 lines.

• **Include a short description of the e-mail topic in the subject line.** Readers frequently will scan their in-box to see who they have mail from and what the mail is about. Your subject line should signal the content of your e-mail. Be as brief and concise as possible. Tell your readers what they want to know with little interference.

• **Use short paragraphs.** Readers lose their place in long electronic paragraphs.

• **Use upper- and lowercase letters.** The variety in the letters' shape help readers' eyes follow the text.

• **Respond within a reasonable amount of time.** If you can't give an appropriate response quickly, send a short e-mail acknowledging the message and explaining that you will get back to the sender after you have thought about your answer. Keep in mind, however, that, like most workplace correspondence, the writer had a reason for writing and in many cases needs a reasonably quick response.

• **Reread your message before you send it.** Check for grammar and punctuation errors. Use the spelling checker if one is available for your system. Readers of e-mail are generally more forgiving of errors and typos, but you don't want to appear sloppy. Know your reader and your relationship with the reader. You might take more care writing to your boss than to a colleague on a listserv.

• **Understand e-mail addresses to prevent errors and delays in sending and receiving messages.** Internet addresses have two major parts: the username and the address of the host computer: *username@hostcomputer*. Similar to the Web addresses, Internet addresses contain an extension that indicates the type of institution with which the user is associated: .edu (education), .org (nonprofit organization), .com (commercial organization), .mil (military), and .gov (government) are common extensions.

• **Build a signature block for yourself so that you can add it to e-mail messages when needed.** In addition to your name, a signature block frequently identifies your position, company, address, phone, and fax numbers. You don't always have to use it if your reader knows the information, but a signature block makes it easier for someone to recognize you and contact you.

- **Write straightforward messages as you would in a memo, letter, or other workplace document.** Humor and satire rarely are successful electronically because the reader cannot hear your tone or see your face. Some writers use combinations of symbols such as :) for a smile to indicate emotion. Reserve this for informal messages to friends and family. Personal attacks, called *flaming*, also are inappropriate.

- **Keep your in-box organized to avoid overlooking or forgetting to respond to an important message.** Create folders to hold mail you need to keep but remember to periodically clean your folders—as you do electronic and hard-copy versions of other documents.

- **Think twice before forwarding a message written to you.** Writers know that once they send their e-mail message they lose control of it, but you must consider the original writer's purpose before forwarding the message. Forwarding a job announcement to a friend or other members of a list is fine; forwarding a discussion about your company's budget probably is not.

- **Select carefully e-mail that you forward to others.** Sending e-mail such as jokes and other trivia that clutters a reader's in-box is not an acceptable business practice. Sending e-mail messages (particularly promoting your business or service) to multiple addresses, called *spamming*, is also inappropriate.

LISTSERVS, GROUPWARE, AND ONLINE CHAT SESSIONS

The writing environment becomes truly dynamic in listservs, groupware, and online chat sessions. *Listservs* are electronic mail lists that you subscribe to. Many professional organizations have established such electronic forums for their members to discuss issues. Listservs, or discussion groups, have grown in popularity. Organizations and individuals form groups to discuss almost any issue you can think of. One source for a list of discussion groups is http://tile.net/lists. In most cases, you subscribe by sending a one-line message to the address: subscribe *youremailaddress*. Members of a business can discuss a problem, collaborate on projects, and share and write documents using *groupware*, such as Lotus Notes or proprietary software on a company's server. Meetings may be held online with participants in different locations.

IRCs (Internet Relay Chat), *MOOs* (MUD Object Oriented), and *MUDs* (Multi-User Dimension) create environments for online chat sessions. Internet access providers such as America Online (AOL) and others also provide "rooms" for meeting. And, more and more businesses are using Web-based discussion software for online, "live" discussions during meetings within the company and with clients. The discussion sessions frequently are *synchronous* discussions—that is, members are online at the same time much like a face-to-face conversation. Online discussions give everyone equal opportunity to "talk" and read each others comments. (E-mail is *asynchronous*—it cannot be read until it is sent and received.) Such forums provide a writing environment for discussions on any topic imaginable. New forums are created daily—you might even need to create one as part of work on a committee.

Suggestions for effective e-mail messages apply to the messages you send to listservs or through groupware, and they even apply to chat sessions, although chat sessions frequently have their own rules. On any list, or as you participate in group discussions on line, you must know who the readers and writers are. You may want to monitor the conversation on a listserv for a couple of days before you enter the conversation. List members who join but do not enter into the conversation are called *lurkers*. Lurkers read the messages as one way to stay attuned to issues in the field, but they do not respond. You want your comments and questions to be appropriate for the forum. Frequently new members ask questions or raise issues that have already been addressed. Most members are patient with such questions, but if you lurk for a few sessions, you may have a better idea of the discussions of the group.

The writing environments just described are online conversations and, like conversations, they change constantly. The conversations you have online as part of your workplace activities follow the rule of oral workplace conversations: present well-thought out ideas in a professional manner.

WORLD WIDE WEB

The World Wide Web presents an ever-changing writing and reading environment. If you have been on the Web, you know which sites you find easier to read and to locate information on. You know that keeping track of where you are on the Web as you follow links can be confusing. You have followed links and probably forgotten where you were on the site or if you had actually stayed on the site. In this section, we describe some of the ways you may find the Web useful in your work. The Web may help you do your job and provide information to support research you do for school or work, or you may use it to present information about yourself and your work.

The Web can serve as a resource for issues that come up daily at work. If, for example, you are in charge of scheduling deliveries, weather may be a factor and you may consult www.weather.com or www.mapquest.com before you schedule and route the deliveries. If you have a question about your company's benefits, your company's Web site might contain a copy of the policy statement. Say, for example, that your company plans to relocate some personnel to the Pacific Northwest and you have been asked to find cost-of-living information and attractions in the area. When you find the answers on the Web, remember to check the last update of the Web site and evaluate the source to make sure it provides accurate and up-to-date information. Depending on your line of work, the Web might help you locate current pricing and the specifications for an oscilloscope, manufacturers of digital cameras, or background information on copyright laws before you consult a lawyer.

Many of you now have Web sites. You may have developed one for business or just for fun. Perhaps you have developed a Web site to advertise a student organization on campus and link it with a professional organization, for example the Society for Technical Communication (www.stc-va.org). Now may be the time to review your Web site and develop it into a solid example of your writing. If you list your Web address on your resume, companies you are applying to will likely look at the site. Use this to your advantage. The site lets you show your work to others—an electronic portfolio that potential employers can easily access to see your work (discussed in Chapter 11). Because your Web site is so public, you want to represent yourself in text and graphics as you would most like to be seen and in a form appropriate for the work you are doing or plan to do. Showing your interests, your work, class projects, links to sources you find important, and so on gives the reader an idea of who you are. Be sure to represent yourself as you want to be known.

If you have not developed a Web site yet, you will be surprised at how easy it is to do. The newest versions of word-processing software such as MS Word and Corel WordPerfect can convert a document to *html code* (hypertext markup language, the code for Web pages). HTML documents are becoming easier to create. Of course, more complicated features, such as custom graphics, must be written in more flexible code such as JavaScript, but you can create an effective Web site fairly easily using html.

We began the chapter suggesting that you be flexible and open to changes in the writing environment. Our description of the writing process includes suggestions for effectively using the computer and word-processing software, in particular, to be a more productive writer. The writing environments described illustrate some of the situations you will encounter. If you are flexible and adapt easily to the changes, you will continue to succeed as the technology and the writing environment change. Consider the changes opportunities!

SUGGESTIONS FOR APPLYING YOUR KNOWLEDGE

1. Interview a member of the profession you want to join who has a computer on his or her desk. Ask her how much time she spends using the computer and what tasks she uses it to perform. Ask her to describe how she composes a letter or a report to someone outside the company and how she writes an e-mail to a colleague within the company but at another location. Compare the writing processes she describes for each of these activities.

2. Evaluate the Web site of a company you would like to work for. Apply the criteria discussed on pages 47–48 of this chapter.

3. Write and send an e-mail to a company asking a question about one of its products. Before you write the e-mail, review the company's Web site to make sure you cannot find the answer on the site.

CHAPTER 3

PERSUASION AND SCIENTIFIC ARGUMENT

In persuasion, you are trying to sell somebody something—from a piece of merchandise to an idea. In scientific argument, the notion of selling is gone or at least greatly subdued. Rather, you are trying in an emotion-free way to convey to the reader the accuracy of your information and the reasonableness of your interpretation of it. In truth, of course, emotional persuasion and the completely scientific argument are but two ends of a continuum. In the workplace, you will operate most of the time toward the middle of the continuum rather than at the extremes. Figure 3.1 illustrates the continuum and the locations of a few typical pieces of workplace writing on it. When writing for the workplace, you must be aware of this continuum and position your piece of writing on it in accordance with your audience and purpose.

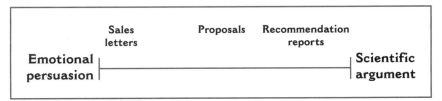

Figure 3.1 The emotional persuasion/scientific argument continuum.

PERSUASION

We make daily use of persuasion, and we are daily exposed to it from others. We engage in persuasion when we try to convince someone to lend us money, to vote for our political candidate, to hire us, or to accept bad news gracefully. We can't pick up a magazine or turn on the television without being exposed to hundreds of persuasive advertisements. One could make a good case that persuasion is our most frequent use of language. Having the right answer or solution to a question or problem is only half our work. To be successful, we also must persuade others to believe that we have the right answer or solution.

Despite its all-pervasive nature, or, perhaps, because of it, persuasion sometimes has a bad name. Perhaps we are merely nervous in the presence of so powerful a force. In truth, persuasion is a tool for good or evil. Winston Churchill's powers of persuasion helped the world survive an evil time in World War II. But, unfortunately, Adolf Hitler's powers of persuasion had helped to bring on that evil time. Somewhat like the parent who teaches a child how to use a hammer and then hopes the child will use the hammer to hit nails and not people, teachers of persuasion hope for a moral use of persuasion from their students. In any event, because we use and are exposed to so much persuasion, it is well that we understand it.

To be persuasive, we must be credible, we may use emotional appeals, and we should use facts and logical analysis.[1]

---

[1] Knowledgeable readers will see in all this our debt to Aristotle, a debt that we cheerfully acknowledge.

CREDIBILITY

You have credibility if your readers perceive you, the writer, as someone reliable in whom they can trust and believe. Many factors can make your credibility rise or fall in the minds of your readers. Cheap stationery, unorganized documents, and poor spelling can bring you down. Conversely, good stationery, organized documents, and correct spelling can bring you up. Evidence of impracticality brings you down—for example, a letter of application for a position that your experience fails to justify. Being seen as open and honest will bring you up, as will having a good grasp of your subject matter. Be careful of extremes. Excessive humility or arrogance brings you down; confidence in your knowledge, ability, or authority brings you up. In some instances, your credibility may be a major component of your persuasive strategy, for example in employment letters and proposals. You may have to spend a good deal of time detailing your education and experience to convince the reader that you are suited for some position or task. In attempting to persuade managers, investors, or customers to approve your new engineering design or business plan, relying on the technical merits of your proposal may not be sufficient. It is not necessarily true that if you invent a better mousetrap, the world will beat a path to your door. You may also have to show that you are credible in dealing with such nontechnical, judgmental matters as budget allocations, long-range marketing plans, possible customer prejudices, or the tendency of an organization to resist certain new ideas or change.

Perhaps most important of all, your readers must see you as a person of goodwill who has their interests at heart. You must have a "you attitude"; that is, you must consider your readers' needs and viewpoints at all times. This is easier said than done. We all view the world through our own eyes, filtered through our own concerns. The writer of the successful letter or report must be sensitive in the extreme. If you know the people you are writing to, try to anticipate their reactions. Think about what pleases them and what annoys them. If you don't know them, you probably won't go too far wrong by asking yourself how you would react in a similar situation. Statements that would make you feel abused or annoyed are likely to do the same to someone else. Also, think about the reader's technical knowledge and whether your information will be self-evident or should be supplemented with analogies and illustrative examples.

Show that your ideas benefit the readers. Remember that we all respond most favorably when we are convinced that our own interests are being served. Every company is in business to turn a profit, yet to stay in business it must provide a service or product that people need or desire. You should emphasize the service, the product, the need or the desire, and not the profit. You needn't say,

Pay your bill because we need the money.

Rather you say,

Prompt payment of bills protects your good credit rating.

Less obviously, we are often misled by our own skill and hard work into making statements of no concern to our readers. Consider this approach:

> We have created at considerable expense in money and time a new fire detector for use in private homes.

All wrong. Readers don't care about your time and money. Also, although the readers may live in "private homes," they won't relate to such a non-specific term. Compare this approach:

> You'll sleep more easily tonight and every night when you and your family are protected from smoke and flame by our new battery-operated fire detector.

In the second example you deal directly with your readers' concerns, not yours. In correspondence, always ask yourself to define your readers' needs and problems. Use that knowledge to give your message from the readers' point of view, not yours.

We have discussed here some of the tactics used to achieve credibility, and, indeed, good tactics will help and bad ones will hurt. And although all people are different and you will have to adjust your persuasive tactics to the person you are persuading, you will also do well to remember the three major characteristics that Aristotle believed underlay true credibility: good sense, good moral character, and goodwill.

EMOTIONAL APPEALS

The use of emotion may be the aspect of persuasion we distrust the most. Partially, this distrust comes from our fear that use of emotional appeals can distort the truth. For this reason, we take emotion out of scientific argument and insist instead upon a logically organized array of facts and well-reasoned opinions. And, in truth, the use of emotion in many situations in which the readers expect logic and factual evidence would probably fail as a persuasive device. Also, our distrust of emotion likely stems from our belief that emotion may persuade us to act against our better judgment. We each can point to times in our lives when we have used our intellect to rationalize a choice that had actually been dictated by our emotions—sometimes to our later sorrow.

Nonetheless, the very power of emotion makes it a force that we are unlikely to avoid using when it can be helpful. You can legitimately appeal to your readers' emotions, especially by showing how your ideas will benefit them, their group, or their organization. Try to fit the appeal to the interests of specific readers. This is easier said than done, but let us examine a few tactics.

An example used earlier shows the use of an emotional appeal, in this case, fear:

> You'll sleep more easily tonight and every night when you and your family are protected from smoke and flame by our new battery-operated fire detector.

It may or may not amuse you to know that advertising copywriters know this kind of appeal as "backing the hearse up to the door."

Notice the use of emotion-laden words in this ad for a man's leather vest:

> Team this vest with a turtleneck sweater or an Eddie Bauer chamois shirt and you have the ultimate in handsome defiance of winter chill.

The word *handsome* appeals to our vanity, *defiance* adds a macho touch, and *winter chill* suggests the discomfort we wish to avoid while being handsome and macho.

Emotional appeals are not restricted to advertising, of course. They also have their place in serious writing. For instance, a passage in an environmental impact study that describes the buildup of debris on a flood plain and wetlands area is likely to include a quantitative table or chart that indicates the type of litter (for example, plastic containers, styrofoam cups, styrofoam pieces, hand plastic items, glass containers, aluminum cans, tires). Such data will likely be effective in communicating with scientists and engineers specializing in environmental work. However, a photograph of the area showing plastic jugs, glass bottles, dead cats and dogs, and old tires is likely to affect citizens and governmental officials in a more directly emotional way, appealing to their anger, disgust, fear, and pride. Such an emotional appeal pulls more sympathetic responses and creates more emotional commitment than tables and charts full of abstract numbers are likely to do. Unless you are engaging in a strict and rigorous scientific argument, you should consider the use of emotional appeals as a persuasive device, but for most readers you must use them with subtlety and discretion. Of course, an argument cannot depend entirely on emotional appeal, but emotional appeal can gain readers' interest and help you lead them to an analysis and interpretation of the data—an appeal to reason and logic.

FACTS AND ANALYSIS

When we are being persuasive, our audience can often be categorized into three groups: those who are already persuaded, those who can be persuaded, and those who will never be persuaded. For the last group, nothing you can do or say will have any effect. For the first group, perhaps establishing your credibility and making an emotional appeal may be enough to keep them persuaded. For the middle group you are likely to need facts and analysis. In a political race, for instance, a candidate may mount a negative attack to persuade the voters that his or her opponent should not be elected. The attack might go something like this:

- My opponent is incompetent (examples of incompetence).

- My opponent would ruin the economy (examples of past economic blunders).

- My opponent would lead us into war (examples of warlike statements and actions).

A positive argument is similarly constructed, only now the statements are positive and in support of the candidate:

- I am competent (examples of competence).

- I have accomplished (identify projects completed).

- (And so forth.)

Few readers will doubt the truth of your information. What will likely be at issue are not facts but such matters as meaning, value, significance, and possible consequences. Much of your analysis will consist of making clear the implications and meanings of your facts. That is, as your readers absorb your facts, they will want to know what our students and we have come to call the *so-whats*. The "so-what" principle is amply illustrated in descriptions of merchandise in catalogs. Read the following description of a bicycle helmet taken from a Recreational Equipment, Inc., catalog:

> Bell Bicycle Helmet High-strength *Lexan*® shell with polystyrene lining for greater shock absorption. Wide air scoops for ventilation, foam pads for comfort. Adjustable sizing by means of *Velcro*® pads assures a perfect fit.

The following two columns list the facts and so-whats of the description:

Facts	So-Whats
High-strength *Lexan*® shell with polystyrene lining	Greater shock absorption
Wide air scoops	Ventilation
Foam pads	Comfort
Adjustable sizing by means of *Velcro*® pads	A perfect fit

Read the description with the so-whats removed:

> High strength *Lexan*® shell with polystyrene lining. Wide air scoops. Foam pads. Adjustable sizing by means of *Velcro*® pads.

People who know about bicycle helmets could no doubt provide their own so-whats. Those less knowledgeable may miss the true meaning of the facts presented. Even those who know may need to be reminded, and the so-whats will help to persuade even them.

The need for so-whats is not restricted to merchandise descriptions, advertising or even persuasion. They are a necessary part of many letters, memorandums, and reports. Providing the so-whats, in fact, is where your professionalism comes into play. Only you may be able to see the implications and conclusions to be drawn from the facts. Suppose, for example, an accountant, after an organizational audit, reports to top company officials that the district office in Auburn, Alabama, is not following Company Accounting Procedure (CAP) 112 to the letter. Higher authority may or may not know the significance of being sloppy about CAP 112. The accountant might add the following:

> Despite the small irregularities in the observance of CAP 112, the records are in good order and no significant problems are evident.

Higher authority relaxes.

But suppose the accountant draws this so-what instead:

> Although the irregularities in the observance of CAP 112 are small, they are significant because they are in an area to which the Internal Revenue Service pays a great deal of attention.

Higher authority is now alerted and, indeed, now probably expects a recommendation to solve the problem, perhaps something like the following:

> I recommend that the district manager at Auburn be brought to the home office for training in CAP 112 and related procedures.

Read over the drafts of every document you write to see if you have clearly stated the necessary implications and conclusions—the so-whats. Without them, you may not have done the job you intended to do. In stating conclusions and recommendations, you have a clear choice in whether you state them before or after your supporting evidence. The placement of your implications and conclusions can be of major importance. When the implications are important enough to be considered warnings, they should be stated early, perhaps as early as the introduction. When the reader is likely to consider the implications good news, you should again state them early. But when the reader is likely to consider the implications bad news, you might be wise to put them later.

In much workplace writing, factual analysis leading to conclusions and recommendations becomes your major mode of presentation. When such is the case, you are moving toward the scientific end of the continuum—toward scientific argument.

SCIENTIFIC ARGUMENT

When is scientific argument your appropriate choice? An example may make the matter clear. Let's imagine for a moment that you are an employee of a small eyewear retail chain that is considering expanding from its present three-office operation in one city to a six-office operation in two cities. Your management gives you the job of gathering and analyzing the information about costs, available credit, markets, profits, and so forth. You analyze the data with no preconceived bias and reach the conclusion that, yes, to expand in the current economy would be profitable, although some risks are involved. When you make your report, you carefully and without emotion present your data and the analysis of that data that underlies your conclusions. You make sure that both the potential and the risks are clearly stated. In other words, you are not trying to sell management on the idea of expanding, but rather you are showing them what is involved in the decision. Because you are not trying to sell, you hide nothing from your audience. Any emotional bias or pressure at such a time might confuse the issue and lead to a bad decision.

In this section we show you how to present such a scientific argument. We talk first about the form of argument itself and then about induction and deduction, comparison, and casual analysis.

THE FORM OF ARGUMENT

In argument we present the facts and the chain of reasoning about the facts that lead us to certain opinions, which we present as conclusions and sometimes as recommendations. (See also Chapter 14, "Recommendation Reports.") In its most basic form, an argument is a thesis supported by opinions that are in turn supported by factual data, something like this:[2]

Thesis: The cost of American health care is out of control.
Opinion:
- Health-care costs as a percentage of the gross national product (GNP) are too high.
   Support: From 1973 to 1993, health-care expenditures as a percentage of GNP rose from 7.6 percent to 13.9 percent.
Opinion:
- Medical expenses are rising too rapidly.
   Support: From 1973 to 1993, health-care expenditures in the United States rose from $102.4 billion to $884.2 billion. From 1973 to 1993, health-care costs had an average inflationary rise of 8.8 percent per year. During the same period, inflationary costs for all items on the Consumer Price Index increased on average only 6.43 percent per year.
Opinion:
- Despite rising costs of health care, we are not getting our money's worth.
   Support: Other industrialized countries have lower infant mortality rates and longer lifespans than the United States. Nearly 40 million people in the United States have no medical coverage whatsoever, private or governmental.

The example also illustrates why it is an argument and not merely a setting down of facts. Even this simple example interprets facts and reaches conclusions. Other interpretations or additional facts may bring about different conclusions. For example, some might argue that the increased costs are largely a result of improved medical technology, which in turn has improved medical care. Others might claim that the real fault lies with an unwarranted increase in malpractice suits, which result in unnecessary medical testing. Still others might argue that we simply are seeing the free enterprise system at work.

[2]Data are from US Bureau of Census, *Statistical Abstract of the United States 1995*, 115th ed. (Washington: GPO, 1995) Tables 150, 151, and 169.

What does this disagreement mean for you other than that human affairs are complex and difficult to interpret? Most importantly, perhaps, it means that you cannot assume that a few supporting facts will make your case. Your facts must be relevant, of course, but you must also attempt to cover as many of the variables as seem to apply. You cannot, for various good reasons, always think of all the variables or find all the information needed. Therefore, you will find that modesty, open-mindedness, and caution are necessary virtues in most scientific arguments.

INDUCTION AND DEDUCTION

In scientific argument, the basic methods of reasoning and presenting that reasoning are induction and deduction. Using *induction,* you analyze your data by generalizing from particular facts to reach your conclusion. Using *deduction,* you analyze your data by applying a known principle to your data to reach your conclusion.

Induction

The following paragraph, written with data from the *Statistical Abstract of the United States 1995,* illustrates induction:[3]

> In 1960, infant deaths among whites in the United States per 1,000 live births were 22.9. In 1975, 14.2 white infant deaths occurred; in 1988, 8.5; in 1992, 6.9. For the same years, infant deaths per 1,000 live births among blacks in the United States were as follows: 1960, 44.3; 1975, 26.2; 1988, 17.6; 1992, 16.8. Therefore, from 1960 to 1992, infant mortality at birth was more than halved for both blacks and whites, but the death rate for black infants has remained more than twice as high as for whites.

Notice two things about this inductive presentation. First, the conclusion, although interpretive, does not exceed the data presented. Nothing in the data tells why the difference exists between white and black infants. Therefore, the conclusion makes no attempt to generalize about causal factors. For causality to be explained, more information on such relevant factors as income, geography, medical assistance available, births at home, births in hospitals, and so forth would have to be gathered and analyzed.

Second, notice that in the presentation the data are presented first, followed by the conclusion. You can reverse the presentation and still present the material inductively:

> From 1960 to 1992 in the United States, infant mortality at birth for both blacks and whites was more than halved, but the death rate for black infants was still more than twice as high as for whites. In 1960, infant deaths among whites in the United States per 1,000 live births were 22.9. . . .

---

[3]*Statistical Abstract of the United States 1995* Table 123.

Both methods are perfectly acceptable, and you should choose the one that presents your material most effectively. Presenting the conclusion first may help the readers' understanding by putting the facts in a better context for them. But by putting your conclusion last, you leave your readers with your main point in mind.

Deduction

When reasoning deductively, you apply a known or generally accepted principle to your data and draw a conclusion based on the application. For example, you may establish a characteristic of some class and then, after determining something is in that class, conclude that the thing has the same characteristic, as in this famous syllogism:

> All men are mortal.
> Socrates is a man.
> Therefore, Socrates is mortal.

Often, in a presentation, you will not give all the terms of a syllogism; for a really well-established principle, you may assume the reader knows the principle without being told. Therefore, you might rewrite the syllogism this way: "Because Socrates is a man, he will die someday."

Whether you are using a fully stated principle or an implied one, be sure not to commit the error of applying the second and third terms in reverse, as in this statement:

> All men are mortal.
> Socrates is mortal.
> Therefore, Socrates is a man.

From this statement of the syllogism, we in fact do not know deductively that Socrates is a man. He could be, for instance, a dog or a goldfish, both of which are also mortal.

Deductive reasoning and presentation are useful as long as you begin with established principles, or at least principles that your readers accept, as in this example:

> Generally speaking, lower-income groups in the United States do not obtain medical care as good as that obtained by groups with higher incomes. According to the *Statistical Abstract of the United States 1995*, in 1993 the median yearly income of black households in the United States was $19,533 as compared to a median income of $32,960 for white households. We would expect, therefore, that blacks in general do not obtain as good medical care as do whites.

For the people who accept your principle about the positive correlation between money and medical care, this deductive argument would be acceptable. If need be, you could strengthen your argument by combining your deductive argument with an inductive one in this manner:

> Possible evidence that blacks in general do not receive medical care as good as that received by whites can be seen in the comparative figures for

the races in infant mortality. From 1960 through 1992, the infant mortality rate for blacks was more than double that of whites. In 1992, among whites, the infant mortality rate per 1,000 live births was 6.9. The comparable figure for blacks was 16.8.

Note that the infant mortality rate is given only as "possible" evidence. As noted before, there may be other variables. Nevertheless, if you use induction and deduction carefully and in combination, you can present your data logically and reasonably.

Some pitfalls lie in wait for the user of induction and deduction. Probably the most common and perhaps the most dangerous is to generalize from insufficient information. We are all guilty of this mistake from time to time. Perhaps we read in the newspapers about the scandalous conduct of a few members of Congress. We shake our heads and imagine Washington, DC, as a hotbed of skulduggery. This would be generalizing from insufficient evidence. As Aristotle long ago pointed out, one swallow does not make a summer. Neither do a scandalous few indicate that all our representatives behave badly.

Walk carefully when you make conclusions and make only those conclusions justified by your evidence. Don't attempt to fool others (or yourself) by building assumptions into the questions you ask about your material. The question Why do men make better business executives than women? assumes a proposition that will produce considerable disagreement.

COMPARISON

As we have seen, induction and deduction are the chief modes of logical thought and of presenting scientific argument. Comparison is a specialized form of induction and deduction. (*Comparison,* as we use the term here, is the examination of things to see both their differences and similarities; therefore, contrast is also implied.) Comparison can form a piece of a longer argument or in some instances the organizational plan for an entire argument. It served as a piece of an argument in the earlier example that compared black infant mortality rates with white rates.

In comparison, we frequently look for *correlation.* For example, suppose we wished further evidence to support the concept that, in general, lower-income groups in the United States do not obtain as good medical care as do upper-income groups. One test of that concept would be to see if a positive correlation exists between per capita income in certain states and the numbers of doctors in the same states. After checking the data in the *Statistical Abstract of the United States 1995,* we could express what we find in this comparison:

Evidence that good medical care correlates positively with income can be found by comparing the numbers of physicians in states with the per capita incomes in the same states. We do not find a perfect positive correlation; for example, Alaska, with a per capita income of $23,070, has fewer physicians per 100,000 population than does Missouri, with a per capita income of $19,557. However, we do find, in general, a positive correlation between numbers of physicians and per capita income as shown in this table, which compares the states ranked top, median, and bottom in per capita income:

States Ranked by Per Capita Income	Average Per Capita Income[a]	Average Number of Physicians Per 100,000 Population[b]
States ranked 1–5 (CT, MA, MD, NJ, NY)	$25,494	322
States ranked 23–27 (KS, NE, MO, OR, WY)	$19,646	185
States ranked 46–50 (AR, MS, NM, UT, WV)	$15,878	170

[a]From *Statistical Abstract of the United States 1995*, Table 713.
[b]From *Statistical Abstract*, Table 177.

In constructing this example, we paid attention to the principle of scrupulous honesty in scientific argument when we pointed out that the positive correlation was not perfect. Also, because we had fairly extensive statistical data to present, we used a table. Tables are great word savers that also often make a comparison more obvious to the reader. (See also pages 178–181.)

In addition to forming part of a larger argument, comparison can make an entire argument. For example, one common workplace analytical report is an evaluation that compares items—anything from machinery to methods—to see which is superior.

In comparing things to each other, you need a set of standards—a way of measuring how one thing stacks up against another. The success or failure of your comparison will depend on how well you choose these standards and on how well you define them. Once the standards are chosen and well defined, you know what you are looking for in your comparison.

When it comes time to report your comparison, you must explain your standards carefully to your audience. In fact, explaining the standards, in some cases, could be the major part of the report. Once that is done, the actual results can often be presented simply, perhaps in a summary table.

To illustrate how this is done, we use excerpts from an article in the March 1998 issue of *Consumer Reports* that compares the merits of ink-jet and laser printers.[4] The purpose of the article is to provide consumers with enough information to make a wise choice of a computer printer that would be suitable for their purposes. The readers are typically intelligent people with some familiarity with computers and printers. However, they are not considered to have full knowledge of all the criteria by which they could judge computer printers.

The introduction to the article comes immediately to the point. It explains the circumstances under which someone might choose a laser or

[4]"Printers: Better, Faster, Picture-Perfect," *Consumer Reports* Mar. 1998: 49–52.

ink-jet printer. Following the introduction, the article sets out the standards, which deal primarily with characteristics that help readers decide which type of printer is better for them. Here is the passage on "Text and graphics":

Text and graphics

A trained panel judged print quality by comparing the output from each printer. To gain a sense of how printing quality has changed over time, we also looked at pages from last year's [1997's] top-rated models. This year's [1998] best printer, the *Hewlett-Packard DeskJet 722C*, performed better overall than the unit we top-rated last year, a clear sign that ink-jet performance continues to improve. Even the lowest-rated models produced text pages that were easy to read.

Text. All the ink-jets produced good to excellent text. Laser printers all produced excellent text, but then, that's their forte.

Graphics and photos. We printed clip art, pie charts, small rectangles with sharp edges, graduated shades, fine lines, and a color reproduced from a negative scanned into a computer at high resolution.

The ink-jets were the clear standouts. The best ink-jets printed deep blacks and colors with smooth gradations; the worst suffered from cruder shading and duller or paler colors.

Most printers produced graphics judged good or better. But none of the laser printers matched the best ink-jets for printing photos.

Resolution. Most printers can deliver 600 to 720 dots per inch (dpi), though some, including two *Epson* ink-jets, can print up to 1440 dpi. But that alone doesn't determine performance. Indeed, most of the time the printer won't even use the maximum dpi setting. For printing in the default mode on plain paper, most printers ranged from 300 to 600 dpi.

Settings and papers. We found little difference in the quality between the manufacturers' default printing settings and the high quality or "best" printing modes when printing on copier paper. In general, the default settings provide the best mix of speed and quality. The high-quality modes may eliminate glitches like "banding" and rough textures in some prints, but they can slow printing considerably.

We compared text and graphics on both regular ink-jet paper and plain copier paper and saw no real quality differences.[5]

Some of the other criteria discussed are costs of ink cartridges, costs of printing text per page, and prices of printers. When the explanation of the criteria is completed, the actual comparison of printers is presented in a table that brings together the standards with the printers being compared. To help the readers interpret the table, a summary of the criteria labeled "The tests behind the Ratings," is provided. We show the table and the summary of criteria in Figure 3.2.

[5]"Printers" 50–51.

Overall Ratings *Within types, listed in order of overall score*

Key no.	Brand and model	Price	Overall score	Text quality	Speed	Print quality B&W GRAPHICS	B&W PHOTOS	COLOR GRAPHICS	COLOR PHOTOS
			0 — 100 P F G VG E						
	INK-JET PRINTERS								
1	**Hewlett-Packard** DeskJet 722C A CR Best Buy	$300		◕	3.2 ppm	●	●	●	◕
2	**Canon** BJC-7000	450		◉	2.2	○	●	○	◕
3	**Lexmark** 7000 Color Jetprinter	350		◉	2.5	○	○	◕	○
4	**Apple** Color StyleWriter 4500	340		◕	1.4	○	◕	◕	○
5	**Epson** Stylus Color 800	350		○	3.5	○	◕	○	◕
6	**Hewlett-Packard** DeskJet 694C	240		○	1.7	○	◕	◕	○
7	**Epson** Stylus Color 600	250		○	1.8	○	◕	○	◕
8	**NEC** Superscript 750C	230		◕	0.7	○	◕	◕	○
9	**Epson** Stylus Color 400	180		○	0.8	○	◕	○	○
10	**Canon** BJC-4304 Photo	240		○	2.8	◕	◕	●	◕
11	**Canon** BJC-620	300		○	0.9	◕	●	◕	◕
12	**Canon** BJC-250	180		○	2.0	◕	●	●	◕
13	**NEC** Superscript 150C	180		○	0.4	○	◕	●	◕
	LASER PRINTERS								
14	**Hewlett-Packard** LaserJet 6Lse	400		◉	3.8	◉	●	—	—
15	**NEC** Superscript 660plus A CR Best Buy	290		◉	4.1	◕	○	—	—
16	**NEC** Superscript 860	370		◉	4.6	◕	●	—	—
17	**Brother** HL-730 Plus	350		◉	4.6	○	○	—	—
18	**Brother** HL-760 Plus	400		◉	3.9	○	◕	—	—
19	**Okidata** Okipage 6e	300		◉	3.8	○	◕	—	—
20	**Lexmark** Optra E+	400		◉	3.8	○	◕	—	—
21	**Okidata** Okipage 4W	200		◉	3.6	○	◕	—	—

The tests behind the Ratings

Overall score is based on print quality and speed, using the printers' "default" mode for everything but photos. **Text quality** shows how crisp and clear each printer reproduced single-spaced text on plain copier paper. **Speed** is for single-spaced pages per minute, based on the time needed from executing an "OK to print" command until the last page was finished. We printed three pages, then calculated an average speed. **Print quality** is based on judgments of identical samples of pie charts, geometric shapes, and photos, both black-and-white and color (the laser printers can't produce color images). Graphics were printed on copier paper, and photos on glossy photo paper. **Price** is the estimated average, based on a national survey.

In the Details on the models: Dimensions are HxWxD, in inches, for the overall space needed to use the printer. **DPI** stands for dots per inch, the maximum number of spots of ink the printer can deposit horizontally and vertically. **CMYK** denotes cyan, magenta, yellow, and black (K) inks. **Printing costs** (per page) include ink or toner and wear on print heads or drum. Text and graphics costs assume paper cost of 0.5¢/sheet; photo costs, 67¢/sheet. Photo printing times are what we measured. All can print envelopes.

Except as noted, all the printers we tested: • Come with and hold one set of color and black ink cartridges (ink-jets) or one toner cartridge (lasers); toner cartridge can usually be changed separately from the drum to cut costs. • All ink-jets (but no lasers) can print banners. • Have an output tray. • All lasers come with 1 megabyte (MB) of memory. • Don't include a printer cable. • Offer technical support by phone, fax, or Web site. • Are compatible with Windows computers. • Can send and receive data through the computer's ECP port. • Have a paper feeder that holds at least 100 sheets. • Have a 1-year warranty.

● Excellent
◕ Very good
○ Good
◒ Fair
◉ Poor

Figure 3.2 Definitions of criteria. Once the rating standards are explained, little needs to be done except to show the comparative results in some easy-to-follow way. Here, as is often the case, a table is used—both for ease of comparison and for cutting down on wordage. Below the table are the definitions of the criteria.

Source: "Printers: Better, Faster, Picture-perfect," *Consumer Reports* Mar. 1998: 51. Copyright 1998 by Consumer's Union of U.S., Inc., Yonkers, NY 10703-1057. Reprinted by permission from CONSUMER REPORTS.

The table provides an easy visual way for readers to make comparisons. We can quickly see, for example, that the top-rated ink-jet printer, the Hewlett-Packard DeskJet 722C, at $300, meets most of the criteria in a very good to excellent way and earns CR Best Buy designation. On the other hand, the NEC Superscript 150C, costing only $180, ranges only from poor to good on specific criteria. It is also nearly three times slower in printing than the top-rated Hewlett-Packard DeskJet 722C.

Given the table, most readers would be able to make a wise choice. Nevertheless, to be on the safe side, the writer presents some recommendations to guide the readers' choices:

Recommendations

An ink-jet is the best type of printer for most households. The top-rated *Hewlett-Packard DeskJet 722C* is the clear standout, at $300. We've judged it A CR Best Buy.

If you opt for a laser printer, look first at the NEC Superscript 660plus, A CR Best Buy at $290. Like all the tested laser printers, the NEC produced excellent text. It was also one of the best for photos and graphics.[6]

The key to writing good comparison reports lies in bringing together the things compared with the standards or other factors by which they are compared. In the computer printer article, the standards are explained and the comparative results are presented in a table. Such a plan, perhaps presented in a report (see Chapter 14) or a memorandum (see Chapter 8), would be quite suitable in a business setting. We look at the comparison organization in more detail in Chapter 14, Recommendation Reports.

CAUSAL ANALYSIS

Causal analysis is yet another specialized form of induction and deduction. In causal analysis, you use inductive and deductive reasoning to establish certain causal relationships. The organizational plans for causal analysis are easy enough to outline, but you must exercise great care when drawing inferences from the evidence presented. The basic plan is that X caused Y. Variations for the basic plan exist, such as

If X continues, Y will result.
Y exists; its probable causes are U, W, X.
In itself, X is not undesirable, but its probable effect, Y, will be.

Here is a fairly straightforward cause-and-effect statement. Notice that it operates on several levels:

Vibration of the table causes the vials to be improperly positioned, which in turn blocks the passageway for insertion bags and jams the machine.

[6]"Printers" 51.

During the past month, we have experienced several failures in the bag injections station at machine 5. These failures are a result of the 45-ml. vials being out of position for the insertion of the bags, thus jamming the machine. These jams are causing an average of 10 minutes of downtime on machine 5 during each 10-hour shift. The resulting loss in production is approximately 66 kits ($802.00 in lost revenue) per shift.

The reasons the vials are not in the proper position at the insertion station are the vibration of the table during operation and the sudden stop at each station. . . .

Here the writer is making a credible case; his causal analysis is really an induction drawn from quite direct evidence of many observations of the machine operating. Because the causal relationships among these occurrences have been discovered through direct observation, we have no trouble accepting the causal analysis.

Other causal analyses prove more troublesome. The troublesome ones are based upon circumstantial evidence rather than direct evidence. Circumstantial evidence is indirect evidence from which we can sometimes, with great care, infer causality. We all know this in a commonsense way. Recently, we read two stories in a newspaper that illustrate the care needed when inferring causality from circumstantial evidence. One story was the report that two children living near a hazardous waste dump had lost all their hair. Two cases would indeed make us suspicious that a causal connection existed between some substance or substances in the dump and the loss of the hair. But without any direct medical evidence of the link, we lack enough substantial evidence to claim any real certainty for the link.

However, in the face of more substantial relevant evidence, we can be more confident of our inferences. The other story reported that teenage licensed drivers are involved in five times as many fatal motor vehicle accidents as are all licensed drivers ages 35 to 64. Even lacking a direct causal link showing that youth was related to dangerous driving, such evidence makes the inference of such a causal link highly probable.

In drawing such inferences, we depend upon the logical methods of sameness and of difference. Each group in this accident study is identified by the sameness of its age—teenage in one group, between 35 and 64 in the other. The groups are different from each other by virtue of their age and fatality records. If one can rule out other possible variables, the inference drawn from the differences between the two groups may be convincing.

Even when the evidence is substantial and relevant, too many variables can lead to doubt about the conclusions drawn. Several studies have been conducted to determine if Vietnam veterans suffer a higher rate of cancer than non-Vietnam veterans because of their having been exposed to the herbicide Agent Orange during their tours of duty in Vietnam. One such study conducted by the Veteran's Administration illustrates the difficulties involved when the variables multiply, as described below:

The study compared the causes of death of 24,235 Vietnam veterans with those of 25,685 non-Vietnam veterans. On the whole, the study found,

Vietnam vets did not die of cancer more often. (Nor, contrary to another popular myth, did they commit suicide more often.) The study did report, however, "statistically significant" excesses of non-Hodgkins lymphomas and lung cancer among marines who served in Vietnam—but not among army Vietnam vets. The authors of the study were unable to explain the contradictions. . . . In the case of the lymphomas, another possibility was an antimalarial drug called Dapsone; most marines, it seems, were stationed in one of the two regions where Dapsone was widely distributed.[7]

Although they exercise great caution, scientists will accept circumstantial evidence if it passes strict tests of substantiality and relevance. For example, most of the evidence connecting cigarette smoking to ill health and early death is circumstantial, a long series of statistical associations. Despite this absence of direct evidence—the "smoking gun," so to speak—the overwhelming nature of the evidence makes virtually all medical experts outside of the tobacco industry willing to accept the causal link. Here is one example of such acceptance, itself a good example of causal analysis.

When experiments on animals turn up carcinogens in our favorite foods and everyday consumer items, some critics invariably dismiss the data as coming only from animals. The tobacco industry has, of necessity, taken the opposite tack; for years it has argued that the evidence incriminating cigarettes shows merely a "statistical association" because it comes from studies of human deaths, not animal experiments. By now, though, the evidence that cigarettes shorten life is overwhelming; the causal connection is as firmly established as any in medicine. "Indeed," writes John Cairns, a molecular biologist and expert on cancer, "in retrospect, it is almost as if Western societies had set out to conduct a vast and fairly well-controlled experiment in carcinogenesis, bringing about several million deaths and using their own people as the experimental animals."

But the cancer connection, which was the most obvious and easiest to establish, is not the major cause of death in smokers. Rather, it is coronary heart disease. Second comes lung cancer. General deterioration of the lung tissue is third. After these three major causes, a variety of other diseases and cancers make a further contribution to the high death rate of smokers. Cancers of the larynx, mouth, esophagus, bladder, kidney, and pancreas are all more common in smokers than nonsmokers. So are ulcers of the stomach and intestine, which are more likely to be fatal in smokers.

Women who smoke during pregnancy run a significant risk that their babies will die before or at birth. The newborns are likely to weigh less, to arrive prematurely, and to be more susceptible to "sudden infant death."

The risk of smoking is, in general, a 70-percent increase in the probability of dying at any age—100 percent for a two-pack smoker. As a rule of thumb, each cigarette knocks about five minutes off the smoker's life.

[7]Gary Taubes, "Unmasking Agent Orange," *Discover* Apr. 1988: 47.

For an average habit, that adds up to six or seven years (more for some, less for others). In the meantime, smokers lose more work days to illness than nonsmokers and spend more time in the hospital.[8]

USES OF PERSUASION AND SCIENTIFIC ARGUMENT

You will find that much of your workplace writing, whether in correspondence or reports, will be devoted to persuasion and scientific argument— trying to get others to think and act as you wish. Correspondence that attempts to sell ideas or merchandise, although it uses facts and analysis, is frequently closer to the persuasion end of the continuum than to scientific argument. In reports, proposals are often somewhere in the middle of the continuum. Recommendation reports generally fall further along the continuum toward scientific argument. Different persuasion strategies and forms of arguments have their advantages and disadvantages. You must use your judgment in deciding which strategies and arguments are best in a specific situation. As in all workplace writing, your purpose and your audience will guide you to the appropriate place on the continuum.

[8]William Bennett, "The Cigarette Century," *Science 80* Sept./Oct. 1980: 42.

SUGGESTIONS FOR APPLYING YOUR KNOWLEDGE

1. Examine several pieces of writing to determine where they belong on the persuasion-scientific argument continuum. See what efforts the writer has made to establish credibility. What emotional appeals, if any, are made? At what level does the writer use factual analysis? You can find your examples in many places: advertisements; direct-mail solicitations; business and college correspondence and reports; Web sites; articles in magazines such as *Newsweek, Consumer Reports, Popular Science, Discover, Scientific American,* and *Business Week;* stories and editorials from newspapers; and technical and scientific articles from journals in your field. Report your findings orally or in writing.

2. Examine closely one of the pieces of writing from Suggestion 1. How well has the writer accomplished his or her purpose? How successful are the persuasive strategies? If you were the intended audience, would you be persuaded or satisfied with the scientific argument presented? How well has the writer handled credibility, emotional appeals, and factual analysis? Look for organizational patterns. Note any errors of logic, such as generalizing from insufficient evidence.

3. Write two advertisements for a technical product such as an automobile, camera, calculator, or computer printer. The first ad will be placed in a daily newspaper, the second in *Scientific American.* Be aware of how you attempt to appeal to credibility, emotion, and facts and analysis and how you suit your persuasive tactics to the responses of the different audiences.

4. In collaboration with several other people, browse through a collection of statistics, such as the *Statistical Abstract of the United States* or the *Canada Yearbook,* for significant trends that interest you. For example, what is happening to the family farm? Are farms growing in size? Does this growth correlate with a drop in farm worker numbers and a rise in crop yields? Do these two trends correlate in some way with increases in the use of machinery and commercial fertilizer on the farm with a consequent rise in energy consumption? Could there be a causal relationship among all these trends?

   For another example, are the numbers of women in the workforce increasing? Are more women marrying later in life? Is the birth rate dropping? Is there a correlation among all these trends? Is there evidence of causality?

   Continuing the collaboration, write an interpretive paper on the subject. Be careful not to press your conclusions beyond the supporting evidence. Also, in all such papers be sure to establish a purpose and an audience before you begin.

CHAPTER 4

STYLE AND TONE

Although most writers and speakers and readers and listeners believe that style and tone really matter, they regard them as abstract concepts and lack a clear understanding of them. Even language specialists and teachers of writing use the terms *style* and *tone* in widely varied ways, further adding to our uncertainty. Nonetheless, it is not too difficult to figure out what creates good style and appropriate tone.

Quite frankly, this chapter is meant to be persuasive as well as instructional. We wish to persuade you that the writing style represented by this example is bad writing:

> Benefits are paid if an insured employee or eligible dependent incurs covered charges because of pregnancy. Reimbursement for hospital and out-of-hospital maternity charges will be made on the same basis as for any non-maternity condition covered under the plan.[1]

We wish to persuade you that the writing style represented by this example is good:

> If you or one of your insured family members becomes pregnant, the Plan will pay for medical care in the same way that it pays for any other medical condition.

The style in the first example is difficult, too formal, and bureaucratic. The style in the second is clear and concise; its tone is positive. If you were trying to figure out your medical coverage, which of the two styles would you prefer? We prefer the second and suspect that you do, too. Most people do.

Effectively communicating with people, persuading people, and managing people are at the heart of most business and professional success. The use of plain language has much to do with that success. Businesses such as Citibank, JCPenney, Aetna Life and Casualty, and Shell Oil have all realized that plain language is good business and have gone to great lengths to use it.[2] Several states have passed plain-language laws—among them are Connecticut, Hawaii, Maine, Minnesota, Montana, New Jersey, New York, and West Virginia. These laws require that consumer contracts be written in an understandable style. In addition, the U.S. Securities and Exchange Commission recently began a program to encourage companies to use more understandable English and early in 1997 issued a publication titled *Plain English Handbook: How to Create Clear SEC Disclosure Documents.* On June 1, 1998, President Clinton wrote a Presidential Memorandum on Plain Language, which is part of his effort to make federal government "more responsive, accessible, and understandable in its com-

---

[1]This example and its rewrite are from "Treating the Whole Document: A Benefits Handbook," *Simply Stated* 21 (1981): 3.
[2]US Dept. of Commerce, *How Plain English Works for Business* (Washington: GPO, 1984) 2.

munications with the public."[3] The recommended practices resemble very much the practices we present in this chapter: the use of

- common, everyday words, except for necessary technical terms;
- "you" and other pronouns;
- the active voice; and
- short sentences.[4]

President Clinton's directive stipulates that by January 1, 1999, all proposed and final rulemakings published in the *Federal Register* are to be written in plain English and that agencies should "consider rewriting existing regulations in plain language" when there are the opportunity and resources to do so.[5] Canadian corporations and government agencies also have developed plain-language guidelines.[6] Clearly, the person who enters the workplace today with the ability to produce plainly written correspondence and reports and with the desire to use a friendly tone has a definite advantage over those who do not.

In this chapter we tell you how you can achieve an effective style by writing with clarity, conciseness, and a proper tone and by considering cultural differences among English-speaking people worldwide. When during your composing should you be most concerned about style and tone? In general, we think you should deal with style and tone while you are revising your work. Too much worry about them during the writing stage can slow you down, even lead to writer's block. To give you a feel for revising faulty style and tone, we have provided "Exercises for Revision" throughout this chapter. Taking time to work with them will help you to understand and apply the principles involved. Beginning on page 99, we have also provided our revisions of the faulty passages that you can check against your own.

ACHIEVING CLARITY AND CONCISENESS

When you write in the workplace, you attempt to accomplish something. To do so, you must convey your message in a way that those to whom you are writing or speaking can read and understand what you intended. Much research has been done in the past fifty years to find out what makes writing more readable. Much of this research has concerned clarity and conciseness. Conclusions from this research boil down to two simple

---

[3]*Plain Language Action Network*. Presidential Memorandum on Plain Language. 21 Apr. 1999. ⟨http://plainlanguage.gov/cites/memo.htm⟩.

[4]*Plain Language Action Network*.

[5]*Plain Language Action Network*.

[6]Ruth-Ann Boyd, "Plain English: Making It Work," *STC Intercom* Nov. 1997: 16–18. You may also visit the SEC's Web site and read the *Plain English Handbook* online or download it. The address is http://www.sec.gov/consumer/plaine.htm.

principles: Don't reach for unfamiliar words, and keep an eye on general sentence length.

In telling you how to make your writing and speaking more understandable, we'll follow these four principles:

- Keep sentences at a reasonable length.

- Use familiar words when possible.

- Eliminate unneeded words.

- Put action in your sentences.

KEEP SENTENCES AT A REASONABLE LENGTH

One measure of whether a sentence is of reasonable length is its efficiency. Does it express the intended thought without a lot of extra words? Using this criterion prevents you from assuming that, for example, a sentence of 11 words is of reasonable length and one of 35 words is too long. Look at this 12-word sentence:

There is a direct line that connects us with the Seattle office.

If we count only the number of words in the sentence, we might call this a short sentence. But if we count the number of words needed to express the thought, we can see that it contains three unnecessary words: *there is*, and *that*. We need only nine words to communicate the idea:

A direct line connects us with the Seattle office.

Compare the following two sentences. Both contain ten words:

The high-quality-type soldering job was done by Glaser.
Because Glaser did good soldering, he was promoted to supervisor.

The first sentence uses 10 words to communicate a 6-word thought: *Glaser did the high-quality soldering.* Maybe even a 3-word idea: *Glaser soldered well.* These two versions would not always be the best possible sentences for the situation, but they are certainly better than the original 10-word sentence. The second sentence about Glaser's promotion contains 10 words, too, but it says twice as much in those 10 words as does the first sentence.

Although efficiency is perhaps the best measure of reasonable sentence length, word count itself is a second criterion. Judging when a sentence has too high a word count is somewhat subjective. The complete answer depends on how well the sentence is constructed and on audience reading ability. In good workplace writing, sentences may range from several words to as many as 30 or 35. We do not give you these numbers as ironclad standards never to be violated, but the numbers do indicate reasonable length in a sentence. You can check the average of your sentences by using word-processing software that provides counts of words, sentences, paragraphs, average word length, and average words per sentence.

EXERCISES FOR REVISION

1. The Dayton Athletic Club, organized in 1908 and in continuous existence since then, today has approximately 3,000 members many of whom have their annual fees paid for by their employers and of whom 70 percent use the athletic facilities of the club and 30 percent use only the dining and hotel facilities.

Use Familiar Words When Possible

Few subjects spark more disagreement among technical experts and businesspersons than the use of specialized language in their communication. Some insist that such language is an absolute necessity, the single most important thing they can do to achieve precision, accuracy, credibility, and legal security. On the other hand, just as many have little use for technical and specialized language when communicating with all except their professional peers. Our position is that unfamiliar language—whether it is technical and specialized or not—makes workplace writing and oral presentations confusing, ponderous, and dull. We think it important to remember the following points when you are writing or speaking about technical and unfamiliar concepts and you are unsure whether your readers and listeners understand them:

- Use technical or specialized language but define it or also use familiar synonyms.

- Avoid using pseudojargon.

Define Unfamiliar Terms and Use Synonyms

Occasionally you must use words unfamiliar to your readers. Every professional and interest group has its own accepted and necessary language. Physicians, for example, need technical language such as *coronary thrombosis* and *coronary sclerosis* to distinguish between these two kinds of heart problems. In the first case a heart artery is blocked by a clot. In the second case a heart artery is blocked by a thickening and hardening of the artery walls.

The paradox of technical language is that although it conveys specialized information economically to those who understand the language, it blocks information to those who don't understand it. The problem lies not in the technical words themselves but with technical people who use such words for a nontechnical audience without definition. In speaking to a lay person, for example, the physician should either use familiar language, such as *heart attack*, or define the needed terms in familiar language as we have done here. When the physician describes the problem to the patient, he or she may say "heart attack caused by a clot or hardening of the artery walls."

The hardest part of all is recognizing what words in our vocabulary are specialized and professional words known only to people who share our profession and interests. Customarily, we use such words so easily and frequently that we forget that most other people lack our knowledge of them. As always in any writing or speaking, audience analysis is a prime factor here. For some audiences, you can write or speak about *Creutzfeldt-Jakob disease*. For others, you can call it *bovine spongiform encephalopathy*. But most audiences will recognize the disease only when it is called *mad cow disease*.

Avoid Pseudojargon

A far worse problem than the use of true technical language is the use of pseudotechnical language. Pseudotechnical language needlessly substitutes unfamiliar multisyllable words for good, everyday, familiar words. A prime example is calling the area of a building where the elevators and stairs are a *vertical access area*. Another bureaucratic example we have seen refers to a person without a car as *transportation disadvantaged*.

Many people become addicted to such language, perhaps in the belief that they thus indicate their high educational attainments. For the most part, when you have a choice between words such as the following in the left column and their simpler synonyms in the right column, choose the simpler words in the right.

Heavy Formal Words	Familiar Words
abate, abatement	drop, decrease, cut down
behest	request
cognizant	aware
delineate	draw, describe
facilitate	ease, help
germane	relevant
hiatus	gap, interval
impair	weaken, damage, hurt
lethal	deadly, fatal
multitudinous	many
nadir	low point

Heavy Formal Words	Familiar Words
obviate	prevent, do away with
palpable	obvious, visible, clear
remuneration	pay
salient	important
terminate	end
utilize	use
wherewithal	means

The list goes on, but you have the idea. Every word, left and right, is an excellent word, but your steady use of words similar to those in the left column would convince readers not of your high intelligence but of your insensitivity—both to your readers and listeners and to the proper use of language.

Users of big words and unfamiliar words seldom stop at single words. Combinations of words to make meaningless phrases seem to have a special place in their hearts. But the impression made by such language is like that of pseudotechnical vocabulary—it's "word static": all noise and little, if any, meaning. Such phrase building is demonstrated ironically by Gerald Cohen's humorous Dial-A-Buzzword, a pseudotechnical vocabulary wheel that makes it easy to string words together until they register on the Richter earthquake scale.

The three dials rotate independently. From Figure 4.1 you might select combinations such as *functional input compatibility, operational systems environment,* or *sequential output approach.* A turn of the dials might result in the alignment shown in Figure 4.2, from which you could choose *overall communications implementation, integrated performance analysis,* or *conceptual interactive criteria.* By adding a few necessary structural words to the selected phrases, we can easily build prefabricated sentences that say nothing:

> The *functional input compatibility* of the *operational systems environment* features a *sequential output approach.*
>
> *Overall communications implementation* follows *integrated performance analysis* of the *conceptual interactive criteria.*

Try a couple of these sentences yourself:

The _____ _____ _____ is a _____
_____ _____ of the _____ _____
_____ .

The _____ _____ _____ , which is the result of a _____ _____ _____ , is a
_____ _____ _____ .

If you didn't know how these sentences were generated, you might think they mean something to somebody.

When unfamiliar language crowds out more familiar language, writing and speech become especially difficult to understand. The

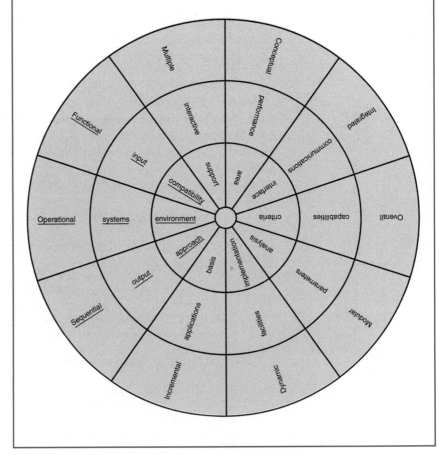

DIAL-A-BUZZWORD offers you a thousand impressive three-word combinations.

Write your next proposal or technical manual in half the time.

Directions:

1. **Turn the dials to line up the words.**
2. **Select the most pleasing 3-word combinations.**
3. **Join the selected combinations into sentences.**

Figure 4.1 Cohen's Dial-a-Buzzword. (Courtesy Gerald Cohen)
Source: Gerald Cohen's Dial-a-Buzzword Wheel. Reprinted by permission from Gerald Cohen.

solution is to avoid technical vocabulary when your readers or listeners don't understand it (unless you define it) and to avoid pseudotechnical vocabulary at all times. Learn to live without it. You'll avoid a lot of foolishness.

DIAL-A-BUZZWORD offers you a thousand impressive three-word combinations.

Write your next proposal or technical manual in half the time.

Directions:

1. **Turn the dials to line up the words.**
2. **Select the most pleasing 3-word combinations.**
3. **Join the selected combinations into sentences.**

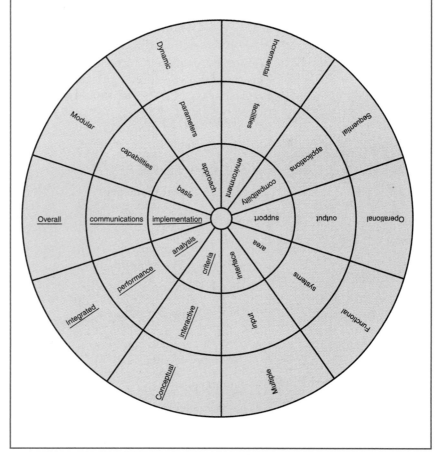

Figure 4.2 Cohen's Dial-a-Buzzword, set for a different combination.
Source: Gerald Cohen's Dial-a-Buzzword Wheel. Reprinted by permission from Gerald Cohen.

EXERCISES FOR REVISION

2. In this strategy-oriented environment, it is vital to trim down complex open-ended problems to key issues, thus forestalling an anticipated ad hoc judgmental scenario at this point in time.[7]

3. The diversity nevertheless represents a burgeoning grass roots sort of pluralism discomforting only to those whose binary temperament eschews any evidence of ambiguity.

ELIMINATE UNNEEDED WORDS

Unneeded words create static in your writing. To help limit your writing to necessary words, follow these three principles:

- Remove unneeded prepositional phrases.

- Remove fillers.

- Cut out unnecessarily repetitious words.

Remove Unneeded Prepositional Phrases

Overuse of prepositional phrases bogs down sentences. The following are typical heavy phrases that should be replaced by lighter ones:

in accordance with	with
in the event of	if
due to the fact that	because
for the purpose of training	for training, to train
pursuant to	under
subsequent to	after
with regard to, in regard to	on, about
in order to	to
in view of the fact that	since, because
with reference to	about
at the present time	now
at this point in time	now
at that point in time	then

[7]This sample and the next are from "Clunker Blight: High Time to Stamp It Out," *M.O.* Oct. 1983: 2.

by means of   by

during the time that   that, while

Remove Fillers

It and *there* often become fillers, words that fill out a sentence until you think of what you are going to say. When a filler is the subject of a sentence, it is followed by a linking verb, such as *appear, seem*, or *be*, and a word that is actually the logical subject of the sentence:

There are three trusses the beam rests on.
There is a suitable airplane available at Newark.
It appears six workers were absent from the night shift.
It is our plan to be in Chicago next Friday.
It seems obvious that we must meet the deadline.

Such constructions as *there are, there is, there were, it is*, and *it seems . . . that* anticipate the logical subject and verb and distract from their natural emphasis. Because fillers take up space and delay the logical subject and verb, removing them returns emphasis to the logical subject and verb and shortens the sentence:

The *beam rests* on three trusses.
A suitable *airplane is* available at Newark.
Six *workers apparently were* absent from the night shift.
We plan to be in Chicago next Friday.
Obviously, *we must meet* the deadline.

In some instances, a *there is, there are* opening is acceptable, such as when the *there is* can only be readily replaced by a verb such as *exist*. An example would be "There is really no sure-fire rule to follow about using the active or passive voice." To get rid of this *there is* construction, we would have to substitute "No sure-fire rule to follow about using the active or passive voice really exists"—not necessarily an improvement.

In any case, go over your sentences carefully to be sure you need each *there is* and *there are* construction.

Cut Out Unnecessarily Repetitious Words

A word or phrase that repeats itself or says the same thing twice is a *redundancy*. A redundant system in engineering is a backup system that provides alternative action if the primary system should fail. Redundant systems in space vehicles are desirable. Certain principles of redundancy in writing and speaking are useful. For example, an overview gives the reader or listener a good mental picture of the content and arrangement of a report, a heading system identifies key topics that are restated and developed in detail in the report text, or a graphic repeats what is described in words. But many redundant expressions are pointless. Examples are *red in color, rectangular in shape, large in size, return back, combine together*, and *25 in number*. Only the first word in each case should be kept. Other redundancies come early in phrases: *The month of* July, *the city of* Woodstock, *the field of* biology, and *a total of* 30. Only the last word should be kept.

Doublets are another source of unnecessarily repetitious words: *any and all, each and every, revered and respected, unless and until, if and when, cease and desist*, and *give and convey*. Many such doublets and even triplets are carryovers from legal language. Lawyers are fond of such redundancies. Legal contracts don't merely sell, they "sell, transfer, and convey," and not merely property but the "right, title, and interest" to property. We don't make a will to merely leave an estate to someone, rather we "will, devise, and bequeath" the estate plus the "rest, residue, and remainder" to our heirs. Lawyers, some of them, anyway, will argue that in law, as in a space vehicle, redundancy is necessary. The point is debatable, but the success of plain-language laws seems to indicate that legal redundancy has been overdone. The problem lies not only with lawyers, however, but with those who imitate legal redundancies unnecessarily. If you write a sentence like "Each and every one of our employees and workers is ready and willing to work and toil long and hard," you should be eager to cut out one of each of the doublets. Such a paring will reduce unnecessary words by 50 percent.

EXERCISES FOR REVISION

4. Upon our receipt of your request, a refund will be sent to you.

5. In connection with your stated view, and in view of the fact that agreement between us is vital, we should put this matter off until some point in time in the future when our views are more likely to coincide.

6. There is a plan we have that might work.

7. The carriers, six in number, who deliver the express mail must deliver the bagged and sacked packages before 11 A.M.

Put Action in Your Verbs

Nouns used for verbs and passive voice create unnecessary sentence length and sluggishness. In using nouns for verbs we substitute the noun form of a word for the verb itself. The process is referred to as *nominalization*. Nominalization often results in unnecessary words and vague sentences. The following sentence uses three nominalizations:

> *Failure* to perform an *adjustment* of the drain valve to the 4,000 liters/minute level will result in a *closure* of the vacuum pump.

The three italicized nouns stand for the verbs *to fail, to adjust*, and *to close*. Not only has nominalization resulted in a longer sentence, as used here it has also resulted in a vague one. For example, who is to adjust the drain valve? What causes the vacuum pump to close? One way to streamline the sentence and make it clearer is to convert the nouns back into verbs and furnish the subjects the verbs need, resulting in this better, clearer sentence:

> If you fail to adjust the drain valve to 4,000 liters/minute, the waste water pressure will decrease, causing the vacuum pump to close.

Certain general verbs create nominalizations by drawing attention away from the true verb. Verbs such as *have, give, take, be, do, get,* and *make* are innocent enough by themselves, but when connected with nouns ending in *-ance, -ence, -ion, -ity,* and *-ment,* they create phrases loaded with static. Here are five such phrases that can be streamlined to single words:

to be in agreement	agree
to give assistance to	assist, help, aid
to have a preference for	prefer
to be desirous of	desire, want
to make application	apply

When you write or speak a sentence like "It is our intention to submit the proposal by the deadline," think about it a bit. Is there a more important verb hiding away in there somewhere? How about *intend* or *plan* for *intention?* With that change we improve the sentence greatly:

> We intend to submit the proposal by the deadline.

Another way to put action into your verbs is to use the active voice. You frequently can choose to make a particular noun either the subject or the object in a sentence, with a resulting difference in verb form.

> ACTIVE VOICE: The company *gave* each employee a bonus.
> PASSIVE VOICE: Each employee *was given* a bonus by the company.

In the active voice the subject acts (*The company gave*). In the passive voice the subject is acted upon (*Each employee was given*). The passive consists of some form of *be* plus the past participle (*is given, was given, has been given, will be given*). Verb tense has nothing to do with whether the verb is active or passive. Nor must the subject in an active-voice sentence be a person:

> ACTIVE: Mr. Brady gave the book to John.
> PASSIVE: John was given the book by Mr. Brady.

> ACTIVE: The pump pushes the fluid into the third receptacle.
> PASSIVE: The fluid is pushed into the third receptacle by the pump.

> ACTIVE: The mirror reflects the light.
> PASSIVE: The light is reflected by the mirror.

An advantage of the active voice is that the actor is always identified because it's the subject:

The *company* gave. . . .

In the passive voice the actor, no longer the subject, may or may not be identified:

Each employee was given a bonus *by the company.*
Each employee was given a bonus.

Most sentences use active voice for a good reason: The logic of the active-voice sentence matches the grammar of the sentence. Whoever or whatever does the action is the subject of the sentence; whoever or whatever receives the action is the object.

At times, however, the passive voice is effective. When the actor is obvious, it may be more efficient to write a passive-voice sentence that refers only to the action and not to the actor. For example, in conducting an experiment, the experimenter may have performed all the procedures. To use the active voice while reporting the experiment, he or she would frequently have to say things like "I tested the solution for titanic acid." In the passive voice, the experimenter can avoid the obvious and repetitive "I" and write "The solution was tested for titanic acid."

Sometimes the receiver of the action is more important than the actor. When this is the case, you can use the passive to emphasize the importance:

The bricks were then moved to the cooling chamber.
The letter has been filed.

And, of course, sometimes you don't know the actor:

The office was burglarized during the night.

There is no sure-fire rule about using the active or passive voice. In general, put what you want emphasized in the subject slot. If the passive buries your main idea the way nominalization and general verbs do, use the active voice.

Often, the biggest obstacle in the way of easy-to-understand writing and oral presentations is a misplaced zeal to appear well educated. Remember, flesh-and-blood readers and listeners are out there; if you want to impress them, do so by writing and speaking clearly and precisely. (For more on sentences, see "Sentences" in Unit V, Writer's Guide.)

EXERCISES FOR REVISION

8. Payment of a refund of your money will be made by us upon your return of the damaged merchandise.

9. To get a solution to the problem of the missing mail, a better labeling process must be found.

10. An examination of the process was made by the supervisor.

CONSIDERING VARIETIES OF ENGLISH AND DIFFERENCES AMONG READERS

Most of us tend to think of the English language as a monolithic language with clear rules and meanings shared by everyone who uses it. However, more than 260 million U.S. residents speak American English (just one variety of English) and in several dialects. Depending on factors such as geographical location, profession or vocation, and social and economic background of the speakers and writers, common words carry different meanings (and sometimes have different pronunciations). For instance, the same object can have different names in different parts of the country. New Englanders tend to use the term *pail*, while Midwesterners and Southerners tend to call it a *bucket*. Depending on the region of the country, *snapbeans*, *string beans*, or *green beans* refer to the same vegetable. In addition, a word can have different meanings in different disciplines. Consider, for instance, the word *culture*. It has different meanings for a microbiologist and an anthropologist. The one thinks of organisms growing in a petrie dish; the other thinks of a group of people who share similar customs and beliefs.

Outside the United States, English has also become the most widely used language in international business. In the mid-1980s, the following was reported:

> Three-quarters of the world's mail, and its telexes and cables, are in English. So are more than half the world's technical and scientific periodicals: it is the language of technology from Silicon Valley to Shanghai. English is the medium for 80 percent of the information stored in the world's computers. Nearly half of all business deals in Europe are conducted in English.[8]

However, with nearly 500 million people worldwide using some variety of English, it cannot be a stable language. While a great common core of English is shared by writers and speakers in the United States, Canada, Great Britain, Australia, New Zealand, and the post-colonial countries in Southeast Asia, Africa, and the Caribbean, idioms and differences in nouns often create difficulties. Idioms in American English, such as *to take a back seat* and *to stay put* are familiar to some non-American English-speaking persons, but they are not to many others.

As close as are American English and British English, confusion can arise over different nouns that refer to the same things. Cover up the left-hand column below and see how many of the British terms you can identify.

American	British
cookie	biscuit
corn	maize

---

[8]Robert McCrum, William Cram, and Robert MacNeil, *The Story of English* (New York: Viking, 1986) 20.

American	British
eraser	rubber
elevator	lift
fried potatoes	chips (vegetables)
gasoline	petrol
ground wire	earth wire
off ramp or exit	slip
passing	overtaking
period (in punctuation)	full stop (in punctuation)
traffic circle	roundabout
truck	lorry
trunk (of an automobile)	boot (of an automobile)

In addition to choosing our words carefully, we must also be aware that other American practices and conventions can also cause confusion for people in other countries. Here are some suggestions for writing to international audiences:

- To be clear about a date, write it out: August 4, 1999, or 4 August 1999. It's customary for Americans to abbreviate a date such as August 4, 1999, as 8/4/99 (eighth month, fourth day). However, in most other countries the date is abbreviated 4/8/99 (fourth day, eighth month).

- To be clear about a time, refer to the month or months instead of the season. In the northern hemisphere a reference to a season can be confusing to persons who live in the southern hemisphere (January is in the middle of the winter in the United States, Canada, and England; it's the middle of the summer in South Africa, Australia, and New Zealand).

- Avoid references to U.S. holidays, such as Thanksgiving, the Fourth of July, Labor Day, or Mother's Day. These holidays do not represent specific dates for users of English in other cultures.

We must be aware of international and transnational developments of the global economy that increase our workplace communication with people of different cultures. International suppliers, manufacturers, distributors, and marketers are becoming our business partners as well as our customers. Whether from the Philippines, Thailand, China, Japan, Germany, England, France, Turkey (the list goes on and on), as users of the English language, we forget how diverse we are—representing many dialects and cultural differences.

There is no single best way to reduce the problems caused by the varieties of English. Sometimes a glossary might actually be needed. But most of the time it is really a matter of remembering to tailor your English to the specific situation and just being a little more conscious of using the variety of English and conventions familiar to most of your readers and listeners. Use the language that others use in your workplace and be aware that a word can have different meanings for different people.

USING LANGUAGE THAT DOES NOT OFFEND

In other sections of this chapter, we discuss the importance of communicating with individuals who are different from you. They may be a different gender, have a different racial or ethnic background, or in other ways belong to a different demographic group from you (for example, readers over the age of 50, teenage readers, or readers primarily concerned with finances). Or, the difference may be less visible, such as a difference in religion, position in a company or a disability. The terms you select will reflect your awareness of individuals and a concern for referring to and representing the individual fairly. In this brief section, we provide guidelines for addressing this workplace diversity.

Gender-biased terms single out men or women when no distinction should be made. For example, not everyone who reads a letter is male, so *Dear Sir* is not appropriate as a catchall phrase. If you do not know who will read the letter, omit the greeting line. (We discuss letter writing in Chapters 8 and 9.) Another example that may be less obvious is the italicized phrase within the sentence:

We must *man the sales booth* during the hardware convention.

Not everyone in the sales force is male so *man* is not appropriate. Instead you might use the phrase *staff the sales booth*.

Racial and ethnic bias affects your working relationship with the individual you are communicating with. Respect requires you to be alert to how you refer to others. For example,

The Japanese computer technician quickly brought the network back on line.

Instead of singling out the technician as Japanese, you should refer to him or her by name (if necessary) or just remove the racial reference.

Differences that cannot be seen or are unknown undermine good workplace communication. For example, in writing a procedures manual you might include a list of points of contact. It is not appropriate to give the first and last name of the technical staff on the list but give only the first name of the secretaries or housekeeping staff. You are not treating the groups equally. Be consistent. For example:

We surveyed people walking in the mall about their use of the local hospital. They were asked to circle one of the following age groups: under 18; 18–20; 21–22; 23–24; 25–30; over 30.

The age groups listed obviously show bias toward 18–30 years old. Will the age breakdown provide an accurate and useful description of the age of those using the local hospital?

We have given you only a few examples. You must be alert to the possibility of offensive terms. You must avoid language that will offend members of a group or single out individuals unfairly.

EXERCISES FOR REVISION

11. The chairman sent out a notice of the meeting for the day-care staff.

12. Ann White, the French woman, manages the largest client's account.

13. The following staff members should attend the meeting: Jim, Nate, Courtney Fen, and Angela Series.

14. All vice-presidents in the company should bring their wives to the dinner.

15. Each volunteer should pick up his packet of material in room 110 of Building C.

16. Mario is handicapped. He cannot hear the fire alarm.

17. The older man found the answer on the Web.

ACHIEVING PROPER TONE

Understanding tone is perhaps best approached first through analogy. We all know, for example, that the way we dress sets a certain tone. If we wake up on a Saturday morning and put on jeans and a sweatshirt, we are saying this is a casual kind of day. If we put on a dark suit with formal accessories, we are saying this is a serious day. We have important things to do.

We also know that certain clothes have the proper tone for certain occasions and not for others. A well-cut business suit is appropriate in most offices but would look pretty silly at a picnic. A party dress suitable for an evening social event would look out of place in church or at a football game.

To move to an analogy closer to writing and speaking, we all know that the words we use in conversation and the sound of our voice as we speak them set the tone for the conversation as serious, friendly, funny, angry, or otherwise. We might use one tone at a football game, another on a fishing trip, and yet another when talking to an authority figure such as a bank's lending officer.

So it is in writing and speaking. You set the tone by the way you write and speak—the words, the sentence structures, and the format of the document you choose. For most workplace writing and speaking, you want to set a tone that's efficient and yet friendly, crisp but not rude, serious but not too formal. Tone is clearly related to style. For the most part, if you follow our advice about achieving clarity and conciseness you will be on your way to a good, businesslike tone.

Our experience in consulting with people at work indicates that faulty tone, particularly in correspondence, results from one of two errors by the writer: trying to be too formal or being so abrupt as to appear rude.

The too formal we have already looked at extensively while talking about clarity and conciseness. The pseudotechnical language we discuss on pages 80–83 usually shows up in the writing and speech of people who believe that to sound educated and professional they have to talk and write as though they have swallowed a dictionary plus a thesaurus. As a result they sound pretentious and pompous and usually irritate their readers and listeners. Here is the body of an actual letter that, although not extreme, illustrates how the writer fell into the pitfall of the too formal.

> I noted with interest your speech on computer-assisted instruction given recently in Los Angeles.
> It is requested that you send a copy to me at the above address.

Take a moment to read aloud the first sentence above. Actually *listen* to what you read. What is the tone of "I noted with interest"? Would you *speak* such a phrase? The tone is faintly patronizing, and we doubt that many people speak that way.

Try speaking the second sentence: "It is requested that you send a copy to me at the above address." Does it sound pompous and impersonal to you? Would you speak such a sentence? How would you react to someone who came up to you at work or school and said, "It is requested that you send a copy to me at the above address"?

The answer is clear. We speak a great many things we shouldn't write. But when we write we should not get too far from the tone of common, courteous, educated speech. Put the "It is requested" sentence into plain speech. It will come out something like, "Please send me a copy of your talk" or perhaps, "I'd appreciate your sending me a copy of your talk."

Notice that in speaking you rather naturally use active voice and personal pronouns such as *I, we, you*, and *me*. Don't be afraid to use personal pronouns in workplace writing such as correspondence and instructions. It gives *your* writing a personal, friendly tone—which is why *we* have used a *we-you* approach in this book.

Notice how cold and impersonal the following is:

> The top portion of this statement will be used to process the payment to the user's account and its enclosure in the envelope supplied with the bill will aid in the accurate crediting of the user's account.[9]

The passage contains no personal pronouns. It is also in passive voice and uses two nominalizations: *enclosure* and *crediting*. For a better tone you would need to make the following changes:

- Change the passive voice to active.

---

[9] This example and its rewrite are from "Three Document Design Principles," *Simply Stated* 29 (1982): 4.

- Drop the impersonal *user* for the more personal *you*.

- Transform the nominalizations into verbal forms.

Here is the result:

> We will use the top portion of your statement to process your payment to your account. If you enclose it in the envelope that we supplied with the bill, we will be better able to credit your account accurately.

The difference in tone is obvious. As an added bonus, research shows that people read material written in this personal, narrative style faster and remember it longer than they do material written in a more impersonal, less narrative style.[10]

The second problem common among businesspeople is sounding rude. We are not talking here about being deliberately stern—as a business might be in telling a customer that an overdue debt is about to be turned over to a collection agency. Rather, we refer to an inadvertent rudeness that results from carelessness by the writer.

In conversation we get immediate feedback from our listener. If we say something friendly, the listener smiles. If we say something rude, our listener frowns. We always know where we are. In writing, we lack this immediate feedback. We may write something that we think is crisp, efficient, and businesslike without realizing that we have fallen into a tone that is abrupt to the point of rudeness. The following letter is a case in point:

> Dear Ms. Cortez:
>
> Enclosed find UPS Express Invoice #4-653-98246. Please let it be understood that it is not the policy of ITC Corporation to accept for payment any shipping charges for packages mailed to our attention.
>
> We request that you look into this matter at once.
>
> Sincerely,

Again, read this letter aloud. Imagine it being spoken to you or your speaking it to someone. No matter how you read it aloud, it sounds rude and unfriendly. The writer, we can assure you, had no intention of being either. He simply wanted to be businesslike.

In writing such a letter, imagine you are in conversation with the recipient. In your mind's eye, place her in front of you. Hear what you are saying and imagine her response. Is she angry when you are hoping for a nod of understanding? If so, rewrite your letter. You have been inadvertently rude. The previous letter rewritten for proper tone might read as follows:

> Dear Ms. Cortez:
>
> With this letter we are returning UPS Express Invoice #4-653-98246 to you. It came with your April shipment of packages to us.

---

[10]"Three Document Design Principles" 3.

Our policy is that the sender pays the cost of such shipments. Therefore, we are returning the invoice to you and ask that you pay it.

Thank you for the shipment. If you have any questions regarding shipping costs, please write or call.

Sincerely,

The rewritten letter is clear about who pays the cost, but the tone, although businesslike, is friendly. Notice also that it contains more useful information than does the first letter.

Reports, when compared to letters and memos, are likely to be less personal in tone. Their tone, nonetheless, should still be courteous and should not be too formal or pseudotechnical. As in most writing and speaking, audience analysis helps decide the proper tone. The following excerpt is taken from a publication aimed at a lay audience. The stated purpose of the publication is "to promote public understanding of science and technology"[11] The excerpt discusses ECCOFLOAT, a chemically created foam used in a small submarine that explored the wreck of the *Titanic.*

Besides adding strength, the foam makes the tiny submarine essentially weightless in water, much as a satellite is weightless in space.

"It's difficult to imagine a remote-operated underwater vehicle without foam," said Dana R. Yoerger, assistant scientist in the Deep Submergence Laboratory at Woods Hole. Aviation gasoline is a buoyancy alternative, but it has less lift than foam. Consequently, using gasoline would result in a huge "dinosaur-like" submersible that could only be towed—not flown or shipped—to a destination, Yoerger said.

At the heart of the buoyant foam are glass microspheres filled with nitrogen. . . . The spheres are formed by blowing nitrogen gas through molten glass under carefully controlled conditions. By changing the conditions, the glass bubbles can be made in sizes ranging from a few microns to half-inch in diameter.

The bubbles themselves are fragile, so they are then added to an epoxy resin as it is formed via polymerization. The resin is strong yet light and when combined with the nitrogen-filled glass bubbles provides a material that is buoyant too. In essence, ECCOFLOAT is a high-tech version of the kickboards used in swimming pools.[12]

The tone in the excerpt is relaxed, a bit informal but not sloppy. The writer gives some of the information in a quotation, which gives the excerpt a personal tone. The sentences describing the process by which EC-COFLOAT is made are a good example of the proper use of passive voice.

The next excerpt, concerning readability formulas, is from a report aimed at experts in the field. More formal that the first example, it nevertheless is plainly written. The sentences use active voice. The vocabulary, although professional, is not chosen to impress anyone. The sentence

[11]*What's Happening in Chemistry* (Washington: American Chemical Society, 1987) 1.
[12]*What's Happening in Chemistry* 10.

lengths, somewhat on the long side, are still reasonable given the intended audience. There is no attempt to personalize the material:

> Readability formulas can make gross distinctions between relatively simple or sophisticated text. They may be useful in making finer distinctions among instructional prose for elementary school students, because the formulas were developed on the basis of materials, readers, and reading tasks at that level. They are not fine-tuned enough to indicate reliably and validly the difference between eighth and ninth or ninth and tenth grade material for adult readers. A computer program that gives a new reading score with each editorial change of sentence length or word substitution may be doing the document designer and the reader a great disservice.[13]

EXERCISES FOR REVISION

18.

Dear Mr. White:

We have in hand your complaint about your premium refund for the policy you canceled. Your refund check was in the amount of $25.32, and you claim it should have been $40.32. We beg to advise you that you are in error.

From a premium paid of $72.00, in accordance with the pro rata cancellation table, a table, incidentally, on file with the State Insurance Governing Board, a charge of 44 percent of the premium for 81 days of coverage in the amount of $31.68 was made, leaving a residue and remainder of $40.32. From the $40.32, in accordance with Item 3 of the General Provisions Clause of your policy, a service charge deduction in the amount of $15.00 was made, leaving a remainder of $25.32, which is exactly the amount of the refund sent to you.

Sincerely,

CONCLUSION

In workplace writing and speaking, work for a plain style and a courteous tone. In certain situations, such as correspondence and instructions, you may also use a personal tone. Certain kinds of reports may be less personal in tone but should still be plainly written and avoid the trap of too formal and pseudotechnical language. In any kind of writing or speech avoid the blown-up, bureaucratic style. *Listen* to your writing and speech. It should sound good to your ear and should never be inadvertently rude.

---

[13]Daniel B. Felker et al., *Document Design: A Review of the Relevant Research* (Washington: American Institutes for Research, 1980) 89.

SUGGESTIONS FOR APPLYING YOUR KNOWLEDGE

1. For each of the following words and phrases substitute a more familiar word or phrase that means the same thing.

assuage	germane	palpable
delectable	impecunious	promulgate
demeanor	inchoate	remuneration
domicile	nadir	substantiate
eschew	neophyte	vitiate

   a natural geologic protuberance

   a geriatric female of the Homo sapiens species

   totipalmated feet

   observed in a state of rapid locomotion

   a sampling of fluid hydride of oxygen

   a member of the team precipitately descended

2. Translate the following statements from British English to American English:

   a. The aircraftsman inspected the undercarriage of the plane.

   b. We recommend that you invest in a unit trust fund featuring ordinary shares instead of using a deposit account.

   c. The supply teacher was unfamiliar with the building and was not able to locate the loo.

   d. The shingles will be stored in a casket.

   e. The vegetables included aubergine and capsicum.

   f. Johnston's shooting brake and Smythe's caravan were stored in the mews off the tarmac.

   g. The company is considering a site just north of the new trading estate at the bottom of Amberjack Lane.

   h. There was not half a crowd at the opening.

3. Streamline the following sentences by substituting verbs where appropriate for the nominalizations. Keep the same verb tense.

   a. We are in agreement that new circuit breakers should be installed.

   b. These payments are in excess of those specified by the contract.

   c. Mr. Donleavy was present when we conducted an inventory of unassembled equipment.

   d. Our staff has done a survey of health needs of the five surrounding counties.

e. The night clerk is supposed to make a record of the daily activities.

f. The committee will give consideration to alternatives.

g. Figure 3 is a list of the centrifugal pump replacement parts.

4. Fillers weaken verb power and distract from the logical subjects of the following sentences. Strengthen these sentences by removing the fillers *it* and *there*, rewriting to emphasize the logical subjects and verbs.

   a. There are many mechanics who own their own tools.

   b. It was noticed by the pilot that the air speed indicator was malfunctioning.

   c. There are two screws that fasten the cover to the wall box.

   d. There is a house at 212 Normal Avenue that is being converted into a day-care center.

   e. It is evident that the time needed to repair the hoses is still too long.

   f. There are two grooves that run the length of the handle.

   g. There are several different types of needles that can be used.

5. Eliminate the unnecessary words in these sentences.

   a. This morning at 8:00 A.M. the prisoners were transferred away to the prison facility by means of a bus.

   b. In view of the fact that the two companies are not in agreement with each other about the important essentials, it is the consensus of opinion of the board that advance planning is of great importance.

   c. It is absolutely essential that the scalpels be sharp-edged in order to bisect the specimens in two.

   d. Prior to the conductance of these tests, we made a decision to make use of disposable culture plates in lieu of glass ones because of the cost factor involved.

   e. I am of the opinion that the city and county agencies are at this point in time cooperating together.

   f. A total of ten (10) registered nurses will be needed to staff the proposed new intensive-care unit.

   g. The locking device that suffered breakage is triangular in shape and red in color.

   h. Remove any and all foreign objects from the sensor mechanism.

   i. Either one or the other of the timetables is totally acceptable.

   j. The received message is decoded into two separate and distinct signals for correct and positive identification purposes.

6. Rewrite verbs in these sentences to make them active voice. Be sure to keep the same verb tense.

   a. A review of the case by the appeals board was requested by the representative.

b. For the final test five dyes were used.

c. At our Newark plant semiconductors are manufactured.

d. The causes of wood warping are discussed in Part 4.

e. A 1 percent earnings tax is imposed by the new ordinance.

f. The necessary equipment for constructing a battery eliminator is listed in Part 1 of this manual.

7. Rewrite the following letter using plain, courteous, personalized language. Tell Mr. Sarver, who owns the policy in question, what he must do to get his loan:

Dear Mr. Sarver:

Your request for a policy loan has been rejected. Although the policy has a loan value in excess of the amount requested, the owner may obtain an advance on the policy only if the policy has been assigned as security. It was not specified in the letter requesting the loan that the policy could be used as security.

Sincerely,

SOLUTIONS TO EXERCISES FOR REVISION

It's unlikely that your revisions will match ours exactly, but make sure your revisions demonstrate your understanding of the principles involved.

1. The Dayton Athletic Club was incorporated in 1908 and has been in continuous existence since then. Today, the club has approximately 3,000 members, many of whom have their annual fees paid by their employers. Seventy percent of the members use the Club's athletic facilities, and 30 percent use only the dining and hotel facilities.

2. We must understand the principal issues in our problems so that we don't base judgments on specific but minor issues.

3. The diversity of the answers nevertheless represents a growing pluralism uncomfortable to those who see the world only in black and white.

4. When we receive your request, we'll send you a refund.

5. Because we must agree about this matter, let's postpone discussing it until our views are closer together.

6. We have a plan that might work.

7. The six carriers who deliver the express mail must deliver the sacked packages before 11 A.M.

8. When you return the damaged merchandise, we'll refund your money.

9. To solve the problem of the missent mail, we must find a better labeling process.

10. The supervisor examined the process.

11. The chairperson [or chair] sent out a notice for the day-care staff meeting.

12. Ann White manages the largest client's account.

13. The following staff members should attend the meeting: Jim Cronin, Courtney Fen, Nate Michaels, and Angela Series.

14. All vice-presidents in the company may bring a guest to the dinner.

15. Volunteers should pick up their packet of material [or Each volunteer should pick up his or her packet . . .] in room 110 of Building C.

16. Mario has a disability that prevents him from hearing the fire alarm.

17. The man found the answer on the Web.

18.

Dear Mr. White:

Thank you for your letter about your insurance refund. We computed your $25.32 refund in this way:

1. You paid $72.00 in premiums.

2. Using the pro rata cancellation table in your policy for our calculation, we deducted $31.68 from the $72.00, leaving $40.32.

3. From the $40.32, we further deducted a service charge of $15.00 leaving the $25.32 refunded to you. For an explanation of the service charge, please see Item 3 under the General Provisions Clause of your policy.

I hope I have explained satisfactorily the way we computed your refund. If you do have a question, please call or write.

Sincerely,

CHAPTER 5

TEXT AND DOCUMENT DESIGN

Chapters 5, 6, and 7 work as a unit to cover two components of document design: the text and the visuals. The text and visuals of any document (whether it be a letter to a client, an e-mail message, or a form from the post office) work together to convey the information to the reader. The rhetoric of text and visuals influences the reader's use and understanding of the text. Although we have divided the discussion into three chapters, you must coordinate the text and visual features together when you write.

Writers can now create and arrange text and visuals to design a document within a single software package. Letters and reports follow document designs not only established by companies as part of their corporate image but also as the format readers expect to see. Electronic documents such as Web pages require the writer to understand design issues that influence how the reader moves through the hypertext environment. Even e-mail requires the writer to consider document design issues. As a writer, you want to present the document so that the reader can easily read the information. Readers will not read a document they must struggle with to find information they need.

There was a time when writers were concerned primarily with organizing content and expressing it in an appropriate style. Almost all considerations about the actual design of the finished piece of writing were the responsibilities of editors and graphic designers who would mark the writer's manuscript with strange symbols and abbreviations that would provide specific instructions for margins, typeface, spacing, headings, and so on. Following these instructions, the compositor (the person who set the type) and printer would actually produce the finished work. Today with computers, word-processing and desktop-publishing software, and laser printers readily available, writers insert most of the design features without the assistance of production people. Because writers have more control over the final project, they need to know something about document design.

Although in some organizations graphic and printing specialists still produce the finished work, more and more you will find yourself responsible for making decisions about the design of your own documents simply because you can easily incorporate the components of document design using software on the computer on your desk. Although you can make these decisions before creating text, while creating text, and after creating text, you should make them as early as possible. And, if the document is written in collaboration with others, everybody should be informed of its design. Whether you are writing solo or as part of a group, leave nothing to guesswork—much time can be lost in changing a design to make it consistent throughout the document.

Almost all features of writing can be regarded as some aspect of the document's design. Capital letters and lowercase letters are part of design. Punctuation is also part of design; bulleted lists and paragraph length are part of design. The space between words is part of design. Anything to do with the arrangement and appearance of the page is a function of document design—including the amount of white space and where it is placed. White space is the areas of the page not used by text or visuals. If we did not have design features, our writing would look like an unbroken string of letters of the same size with no space between them and with no punctuation. Without layout and design, our writing might look like this:

WITHOUTFORMATOURWRITINGWOULDLOOKLIKETHISANDITWOULDBEV

GNOLSECNETNESRUOFYLNOSIEGASSAPSIHTDAEROTTLUCIFFIDYRE

THINKHOWDIFFICULTITWOULDBETOREADSEVERALPAGESLIKETHIS

In designing a document you can use the special features of word-processing and desktop-publishing software to full advantage. However, the principles of design, not the technology, are important to remember and use. You may have been to Web sites that are difficult to navigate and read or you may have tried to read paper documents that are difficult to follow. To help you make wise decisions, you need to know what graphics designers, production editors, and printers have known for decades about

- making documents inviting to read

- making the content easy to follow

- making documents easy to use

Knowing how to accomplish these goals will help you present your information and ideas in an attractive and professional manner. In a real sense, design is a partner with development (Chapter 1), organization (Chapter 3), and style in presentation (Chapter 4). The document's design coordinates the text and the visuals. In this chapter we focus on the text and the visual presentation of the document. In Chapters 6 and 7 we discuss visuals and visual features of a document.

MAKING DOCUMENTS INVITING TO READ

Readers usually look at a document as a whole before they read it. If the text looks inviting to read, readers will probably find it easy to read. However, keep in mind—if the document does not provide information the reader needs, even a good design will not make the document useful.

USE GOOD MATERIALS AND EQUIPMENT

Paper
Print the document on good quality paper that has a nonglare surface and is heavy enough to make the print stand out. Most companies have stationery, referred to as *letterhead,* to use for documents going outside the

company. Letterhead usually has the company logo and address printed on good quality (usually bond) paper. Internal documents frequently are printed on paper with no letterhead or on paper with a preprinted memo structure on a less costly paper. Check your company's guidelines for the paper to use and where to place the information on the page (particularly, when you use company letterhead).

The better grades of paper are made of linen and cotton fibers (20-pound bond paper, for example). They are much more expensive than wood pulp paper and should be used only for the most important and formal occasions, such as your resume. White paper or light shades of blue, tan, or gray provide good contrast between the typeface and the paper. You want the reader to see the print clearly. Dark colored paper may distract from the reading. If the document is large or is expected to be used for a long time or to be handled roughly, use a heavier paper and perhaps a different color for the cover and the divider pages that separate the major sections.

Recycled paper and paper that is recyclable are common now. In fact, many readers check to see if the document can be recycled or if the publisher has used recycled paper as one small way to help the environment.

Paper Size
The standard page size for letters and reports in the United States is 8.5 × 11 inches. The page orientation can be either *portrait* (8.5 × 11 inches) or *landscape* (11 × 8.5 inches). Some organizations have letterhead available on half sheets (5.5 × 4.25 inches) for shorter notes. If you work for a company with sites in other countries, you will see paper measured in the metric system. For example, the closest to 8.5-×-11-inch paper measures 8.26 × 11.69 inches or 210 × 297 millimeters (referred to as *A4* paper).

Of course, the environment or circumstances in which a document will be used can have a significant influence on what size paper is most appropriate. For example, you have received a computer disk with instructions printed on the label for using the software on the disk. Or, someone working in a small space or in a constrained situation (such as an electronic technician working 100 feet above the ground on the superstructure of a wind turbine) probably prefers smaller page sizes. Word-processing software allows you to adjust margins and page size easily.

Printing
Laser printers are standard in the workplace. Laser printers produce a sharp, clean print and superior graphics, at up to 30-plus pages per minute. Top-end models print color as well. They provide a sharp, clean print and they print text and visuals together. Do not use a dot matrix printer for anything other than drafts of documents.

Ink-jet printers that can print in color are also widely used. Some ink-jet printers currently can print at up to 8 pages a minute in black and white. Laser and ink-jet printer abilities in printing speed, character quality, and color application are improving constantly. Color printers let you add emphasis to documents, which we discuss later in this chapter.

If you require multiple copies of important documents, photocopying may not suffice. A better copy may be obtained from a laser printer with 600 dots per inch (dpi) or higher capability. If your company cannot handle the work in house, most copy shops now print directly from an electronic version of the document. They print from the original file (just as you do when you send a file to the printer from your computer).

In choosing how to reproduce a document, you must consider how the document will be used. If you need only a copy for your files or copies for internal use, use the copier in your office. However, documents going outside the company, for example a set of manuals for operating an oscilloscope or a proposal to a client, should be printed by a professional copy shop or by a properly equipped in-house department with adequate equipment and materials. Wherever you have the document reproduced, the printer used is important because it produces the final copy and determines what the text will look like.

Binder

You may consider putting longer documents in a binder. When you select the type of binding to use, consider how the reader will use the document before you select the binder. How often will readers refer to the document? How will they use the document?

A three-ring notebook works well for documents that may be added to, for example a company's procedures manual. Notebooks hold up under repeated use, but this feature also makes them the most expensive binder. Spiral binding allows the user to fold the document back on itself so that one page shows at a time, but pages cannot be added to the document. Plastic binding, often the least expensive method of binding, works for documents that will be used only occasionally and when the user has enough room to open the document fully. There are other types of binding available. Check with your company's printing department or a local printing and copy shop for other options. Be sure to increase the left margin to 1.5 or 2 inches to allow room for the binding.

USE AN UNCROWDED DESIGN

Dense or busy-looking pages will put off all except the most committed readers, even though the document contains useful information and interesting ideas. Judicious use of *white space* and an attractive type (font) can encourage readers to read a document. You want to use white space—the space not used by the text and visuals—effectively.

White Space with Printed Documents

As shown in Figure 5.1, no more than 50 percent of the page of most letters, memos, and reports should be the text area (the part of the page

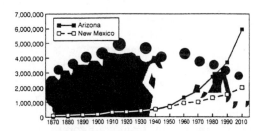

Figure 5.5 Population growth in Arizona and New Mexico 1870-1990 and projected population for the year 2010. (de Gennaro 1990, Vest 1996, Bureau of Business and Economic Research 1994).

Bernalillo County (including Albuquerque) has 650,000 residents.

RECREATION

The transcontinental railroads not only opened the Southwest for resource extraction and settlement, but also opened a market for tourism. In the last quarter of the 19th century, the Santa Fe Railroad expanded its ridership through tourism to the Grand Canyon in Arizona and the Indian pueblos in New Mexico. In its efforts to encourage tourism of the Southwest, the railroad was aided and assisted by the Fred Harvey Company (Howard and Pardue 1996):

> "The Fred Harvey Company and the Santa Fe Railway joined forces at an auspicious historical moment. Borrowing new techniques in marketing and advertising, the companies promoted the American Southwest as an exotic destination. The railroad, the travelers, and the indigenous communities of the region were all integral elements in a partnership that spanned more than three-quarters of a century."

Still, much of the recreation potential of the Southwest remained undiscovered. Only the most spectacular sites that were easily accessible from the railroads attracted significant visitation. Recreation facilities and services in most of the region's arid landscape were sparse and primitive, simply because there was little demand before 1940 (USDA Forest Service 1980):

> "Recreation use of the forest reserves grew slowly at first, then more rapidly as automobiles became

numerous and roads penetrated further into what had previously been remote and inaccessible areas. General prosperity and more leisure time increased the human flow into the national forests, a flow which eventually became a flood."

Beginning in the 1970s, the Southwest was "discovered." The population expansion of the Phoenix and Tucson metropolitan areas was unparalleled anywhere in the United States. At the same time, the mystique of the "Land of Enchantment" and the "Santa Fe" style captured the attention of trend-setters throughout the country, and tourism to New Mexico exploded. Because of the mild weather, the Southwest also became a winter mecca for retired people as well as those with the freedom of long vacations. The Southwest became the nation's number-one target destination for the retired and recreational vehicle (RV) traveler, making it a year-round recreation area.

The Southwest has a diversity of high-quality recreation opportunities ranging from the primitive settings of the Gila Wilderness (first wilderness in the National Forest System) to the urban settings of the Salt River Chain of Lakes outside of Phoenix, Arizona. With the large increase in population and the attraction of the Southwest's climate, culture, and scenery, recreation use has increased tremendously over the past 20 years. Recreation use (as recreation-visitor-days, **RVD**, see glossary for definition) on National Forest System lands since 1965 has increased fourfold:

Year	Recreation–visitor–days
1965	10,147
1976	15,565
1985	21,742
1996	44,342

Developed Site Recreation

There has been an increase in demand for high-quality developments that include toilets, showers, lights, and reservation systems. Modern campers are seeking spaces designed for 40-foot RVs with individual hookups for sewage, water, power, and cable television. They also want trails, mountain bike paths, and interpretive nature walks. Their expectations on safety and security far surpass traditional offerings. The effects on forest health of this localized use include soil compaction, loss of vegetative cover, and soil erosion.

Figure 5.1 A page consists of three basic areas: the white space, the text, and the visuals. On this page, the features combine to create an inviting page to read.
Source: An Assessment of Forest Ecosystem Health in the Southwest, General Technical Report RM-GTR-295, Fort Collins, CO: US Dept. of Agriculture, Forest Service, Rocky Mountain Forest Range Experiment Station, 1997. 36.

```
Date:    Friday, February 8, 2000
From:    Joanne Welsh ⟨welshjh@email.ttu.com⟩
To:      Marie Housen ⟨housenmm@email.ttu.com⟩
Re:      Training Sessions

Here are ideas for my portion of the computer training sessions. I
confirmed this morning the software available in the room with Internet
access. Not only is there Internet access, but there's also access to
presentation software such as PowerPoint—all on PCs, not Macs. The
Internet sessions will focus on sending and receiving e-mail and sending
a file via e-mail as an attachment. The class will meet Wednesday,
February 13, 2-4 p.m. The Web session will cover evaluating Web sites for
accurate, reliable information and how to acknowledge the information in
company reports to clients. The class will meet Wednesday, February 20,
2-4 p.m. The class for developing a computer-generated presentation will
meet Wednesday, February 27, 2-4 p.m. We should send reminders to
everyone the day before the class.

Joanne
```

```
Date:    Friday, February 8, 2000
From:    Joanne Welsh ⟨welshjh@email.ttu.com⟩
To:      Marie Housen ⟨housenmm@email.ttu.com⟩
Re:      Training Sessions

Here are ideas for my portion of the computer training sessions.

I confirmed this morning the software available in the room with Internet
access. Not only is there Internet access, but there's also access to
presentation software such as PowerPoint—all on PCs, not Macs.

INTERNET SESSION
The Internet sessions will focus on sending and receiving e-mail and
sending a file via e-mail as an attachment. The class will meet
Wednesday, February 13, 2-4 p.m.

WEB SESSION
The Web session will cover evaluating Web sites for accurate, reliable
information and how to acknowledge the information in company reports to
clients. The class will meet Wednesday, February 20, 2-4 p.m.

PRESENTATION SESSION
The class for developing a computer-generated presentation will meet
Wednesday, February 27, 2-4 p.m.

We should send reminders to everyone the day before the class.

Joanne
```

Figure 5.2 White space in e-mail helps the reader spot important information.

The Facilities and Information Technology Committee (FITC) met on April 6, 1999, and developed a list of items, which they would like for you to include in your presentation before the division managers. The list is given below.

1. Who and how many employees will be affected by your proposal?

2. How will the proposed renovation or purchase of new equipment save money and/or leverage resources?

3. Explain how your requests will support state-of-the-art research and development as the company moves into the 21st century.

4. Have you addressed the accessibility of the proposed equipment for employees with disabilities, including those who are in wheelchairs, visually impaired, hearing impaired, or disabled in another way?

5. Will the resources be shared with other departments?

6. Be prepared to provide information on specific items in your budget.

7. Indicate how your proposed request works with the strategic initiatives of your division and the company.

Figure 5.3 Spacing problems occur in a document when full justification is used. Fonts such as Courier do not adjust, which means that each letter takes the same amount of space.

where the text and visuals appear). The other 50 percent is white space (comprising the margins around the text area and visuals and the spaces between lines, between words in a line, and between letters and characters). There are, of course, exceptions: letters and memos that are shorter than a full page, and bulletins, brochures, newsletters, and manuals often require more white space.

White Space with Online Documents

White space in e-mail, Web documents, or online help, such as company policy manuals, is as important—maybe even more important—than with documents printed on paper because the reader's eyes must distinguish breaks in the text in order to move through the text on the screen. Readers cannot easily hold their place with their finger or mark the text with a pencil. They must rely on the cursor, the mouse, and the scroll bar to move through the text. The example in Figure 5.2 compares an e-mail message that is one long paragraph and the same message with breaks in the text.

The Facilities and Information Technology Committee (FITC) met on April 6, 1999, and developed a list of items, which they would like for you to include in your presentation before the division managers. The list is given below.

1. Who and how many employees will be affected by your proposal?

2. How will the proposed renovation or purchase of new equipment save money and/or leverage resources?

3. Explain how your requests will support state-of-the-art research and development as the company moves into the 21st century.

4. Have you addressed the accessibility of the proposed equipment for employees with disabilities, including those who are in wheelchairs, visually impaired, hearing impaired, or disabled in another way?

5. Will the resources be shared with other departments?

6. Be prepared to provide information on specific items in your budget.

7. Indicate how your proposed request works with the strategic initiatives of your division and the company.

Figure 5.4 Selecting a proportionally spaced typeface and using a good printer solve most of the problems with spacing. In the example, the font was changed from Courier 12 to Times New Roman 12, right justification was removed, and the tab was moved closer to the number to narrow the gap between the numbered item and the text.

Margins

For 8.5-×-11-inch pages, maintain a minimum of a 1-inch margin (the white space outside the text area) all around. For most documents, do not *justify* the right margin. When the right margin is justified, the text edge along the right side of the page appears in a straight line. Readers may have trouble distinguishing between lines and may lose track of where they are reading. As Karen Schriver points out, "it is much easier to use a ragged-right setting and to limit hyphenation than it is to justify the text with equal word spacing while maintaining a limit on hyphenation."[1] You want to avoid gaps in the text. The gaps interfere with the reader's eyes sweeping the line and do not present a professional looking document. Figures 5.3 and 5.4 show an example of a right-justified document and the same document without justification. Notice the gaps and problems with hyphen on the right-justified document.

[1]Karen Schriver, "Chapter 5: Seeing the Text: The Role of Typography and Space," *Dynamics of Document Design* (New York: Wiley, 1997) 270.

EMERGENCY SUPPLIES

Keep enough supplies in your home to meet your needs for at least three days. Assemble a Disaster Supplies Kit with items you may need in an evacuation. Store these supplies in sturdy, easy-to-carry containers such as backpacks, duffle bags or covered trash containers.

Include:

- A three-day supply of water (one gallon per person per day) and food that won't spoil.
- One change of clothing and footwear per person, and one blanket or sleeping bag per person.
- A first aid kit that includes your family's prescription medications.
- Emergency tools including a battery-powered radio, flashlight and plenty of extra batteries.
- An extra set of car keys and a credit card, cash or traveler's checks.
- Sanitation supplies.
- Special items for infant, elderly or disabled family members.
- An extra pair of glasses.

Keep important family documents in a waterproof container. Keep a smaller kit in the trunk of your car.

UTILITIES

Locate the main electric fuse box, water service main and natural gas main. Learn how and when to turn these utilities off. Teach all responsible family members. Keep necessary tools near gas and water shut-off valves.

Remember, turn off the utilities only if you suspect the lines are damaged or if you are instructed to do so. *If you turn the gas off, you will need a professional to turn it back on.*

4 Steps to Safety

Find Out What Could Happen to You

Contact your local emergency management or civil defense office and American Red Cross chapter — be prepared to take notes:

- Ask what types of disasters are most likely to happen. Request information on how to prepare for each.
- Learn about your community's warning signals: what they sound like and what you should do when you hear them.
- Ask about animal care after disaster. Animals may not be allowed inside emergency shelters due to health regulations.
- Find out how to help elderly or disabled persons, if needed.
- Next, find out about the disaster plans at your workplace, your children's school or daycare center and other places where your family spends time.

Create a Disaster Plan

Meet with your family and discuss why you need to prepare for disaster. Explain the dangers of fire, severe weather and earthquakes to children. Plan to share responsibilities and work together as a team.

- Discuss the types of disasters that are most likely to happen. Explain what to do in each case.
- Pick two places to meet:
  1. Right outside your home in case of a sudden emergency, like a fire.
  2. Outside your neighborhood in case you can't return home. Everyone must know the address and phone number.
- Ask an out-of-state friend to be your "family contact." After a disaster, it's often easier to call long distance. Other family members should call this person and tell them where they are. Everyone must know your contact's phone number.
- Discuss what to do in an evacuation. Plan how to take care of your pets.

Fill out, copy and distribute to all family members

```
Family Disaster Plan

Emergency Meeting Place _____
                                    outside your home
Meeting Place _____ Phone _____
                  outside your neighborhood
Address _____

         _____

Family Contact _____
                                  (name)
Phone ( _____ ) _____ Phone ( _____ ) _____
                    day                              evening
```

Figure 5.5 In this bleed graphic, the organizations want readers to cut the form out and give it to family members. Moving the form into the margin calls attention to its importance and encourages the reader to cut it out.
Source: Your Family Disaster Plan, Federal Emergency Management Agency (FEMA L-101) and American Red Cross (ARC4466), 1991.

All text and visuals should be kept within the margins (see Figure 5.1) except for special effects. There are two exceptions: (1) headers or footers and page numbers, which usually lie two spaces above and below the text area and (2) special texts—usually visuals—or other marks that extend beyond the text area. Such special texts and marks are called a "bleed." Bleed graphics, such as the one shown in Figure 5.5, are designed to look as if they continued beyond the edge of the text. In Figure 5.5, the authors of the brochure want to call attention to the Family Disaster Plan. Bleed marks, such as the one shown in Figure 5.6, serve as tabs to assist readers in locating particular information.

Line Spacing

Letters, memos, brochures, and most newsletters are single-spaced. Single-spaced, space-and-a-half, or double-spaced reports are common. For example, space and a half is frequently used for engineering reports. Proposals are often single-spaced.

You need to check with the corporate style guide or other employees for your company's preferred style. Also, know what your readers expect and the purpose of the document. A one-page, single-spaced document

Figure 5.6 A "bleed" tab is a mark placed at the edge of the page to help readers locate specific sections of a document. It takes the place of a physical tab that protrudes beyond the normal edge of the page.

may be appropriate for a meeting of 100 members of the sales team if you need to get some information to them quickly and inexpensively. The same document may be better presented on two sheets of paper, stapled and double-spaced if you are asking the sales managers to write comments on the document before you give it to the sales team. Remember that the length of the document will determine costs for reproducing and binding.

If the document is single-spaced, provide some eye relief and "breathing room" by double-spacing between paragraphs and above and below headings, indented lists, long quotations, displayed equations and formulas, and visuals. If the document is double-spaced, allow no extra line spaces between paragraphs, but indent the first line of each paragraph. Figure 5.7 illustrates a passage that is crowded, uninviting, and difficult to read. Figure 5.8 shows a redesigned version of the same information that has much better visual appeal because it incorporates more white space that reduces the density of text, allowing for easier reading and providing room for readers to make their own notes. The trade-off of additional length for easier reading is worth it. The result, as you can see, is that the longer versions are much quicker to read and easier to remember because readers can quickly identify the points of discussion and the order in which the points are being made.

USE TYPEFACE EFFECTIVELY

Use a legible, nondistracting typeface (referred to as a *font* in software programs) for body text. Although a wide variety of type styles, sizes, and special features are available in word-processing software, avoid unusual types with fancy lines and flourishes. Design a consistent look for each part of the document. Frequently, writers use a *serif* font such as Times Roman for the body of a document and a *sans serif* font such as Univers for the headings. Random changes in type, or what appear to be random changes, will confuse or annoy readers. This advice applies not only to documents printed on paper but documents published on the Web.

Roman and Italic Type

There are two basic styles of type: roman and italic. Roman (roman) is an upright typeface that is most frequently used for body text because it is the most readable. Italic (*italic*) is a slanted typeface that is not as easy to read as roman and is used for special purposes, such as to designate titles of books, plays, and works of art; names of ships and air- and spacecraft (for example, *Titanic* or *Challenger*); foreign words and other words that are referred to as words (as we used *font* above); and sometimes to emphasize words or phrases of importance.

Serif and San Serif Type

Type can also be classified as serif and sans serif. Serif (serif) contains small features that clearly mark the ends of letters and characters. Sometimes there are also uneven widths of lines that form the character. For instance, the little cross strokes on I, i, C, c, 3 are serifs. Sans serif (**sans serif**) has no such features: I, i, C, c, 3. Frequently, a serif type works best for a document's body text. Readers may have less trouble reading large blocks of text with serif fonts because the cross strokes and uneven lines in serif type make individual letters easier to distinguish and consequently speed up reading. The uncluttered and streamlined shape of sans serif type works well with shorter blocks of text and gives a text a more modern appearance. You will see serif type commonly used in body text and sans serif type used for special purposes, such as for headings or displayed passages where it is desirable to have the type contrast noticeably from the body text. Some recommend that a sans serif typeface be used on Web pages because readers will find it easier to read from the screen.

Occasionally you can justify varying the typeface, but variety should be used sparingly. A sans serif typeface is used effectively in the headings of Figures 5.1, 5.5, 5.8, and 5.12. Type styles other than plain roman and serif stand out from body text. Draw the readers' attention by using *italic,* **boldface** (extra-dark type), underlining, ALL-CAPITAL LETTERS, sans serif type, or different colors. Use highlighting techniques consistently. Do not use boldface one time and underlining another for the same purpose. Most importantly, don't overuse highlighting or the document will look cluttered and confusing. Passages consisting of words formed of all-capital letters should be kept to a minimum. They reduce reading speed and increase the chances that typographic errors and misspellings will be overlooked, partly because capital letters have fewer distinctive features than lowercase letters. It is overkill to combine special effects such as all-capitals, italic, bold, and shadow images. If many items are highlighted, those that really need emphasizing will not stand out.

Use italics and boldface type more frequently than underlining. The underline interferes with the letters that descend (g, j, p, q, y, g, j, p, q, y)—that is, the line crosses through the portion of the letter that descends below the bottom of the letter. Use italics for titles. Boldface works well if you have a good printer and copy machine, but boldface type fades when multiple copies are made on lower-quality copiers.

Use standard type sizes. How large the type should be depends on the distance from which the document will be read. The standard type size for body text 18 to 24 inches away from the reader's eyes is 10 to 12 points as in these examples:

This is 10-point in Times Roman typeface.

This is 12-point in Times Roman typeface.

This is 10-point Univers typeface.

This is 12-point Univers typeface.

Use the same type size and font for all body text. Smaller type, perhaps 8-point, can be used for text that will be read only briefly, such as

Date: January 11, 1999
To: Sales Representatives
From: Ellen Gault *EG*
Re: External Short-Term Customer Contract

Effective February 1, 1999, we will implement the new procedure for approving external short-term customer contracts. Enclosed is the new External Short-Term Customer Contract Request form. We require the form be filled out and signed by the customer. However, we are also asking you to assist customers in filling out the form to ensure that all information needed to fulfill the request is included. We also require you to send a copy of the signature card you have on file for the customer. This is so we may verify the signature on the form. We will also have to have the customer's mailing address so we can send the contract to them. These steps are necessary in order that we may be in compliance with the directives related to our Total Quality Control Plan.

Charges for research are $15.00 an hour. The minimum charge will be $15.00 payable in advance. Charges for document preparation are $25.00 an hour. Additional copies are 20 cents per page. On requests where it appears several hours will be required to complete the work, we need to be contacted in advance so that we can estimate the charge and a 20 percent down payment can be forwarded with the contract request. The actual balance will be due upon completion of the work. The contract request form and the payment need to be sent to my administrative assistant, Warren Thompson.

Please call Warren Thompson at 806-295-6841 or me at 806-295-6842 if you have any questions concerning this matter.

Figure 5.7 The writer uses very little spacing to indicate organization in this memo. Readers will have to read carefully to identify the steps of the new procedure. They may overlook the important classification of contract charges.

Date: January 11, 1999
To: Sales Representatives
From: Ellen Gault   *EG*
Re: External Short-Term Customer Contract

Effective February 1, 1999, we will implement the new procedure for approving external short-term customer contracts.

Enclosed is the new External Short-Term Customer Contract Request form. Below are explanations of the new procedure and contract charges.

New Procedure

The new two-step procedure is designed so that we can ensure the shortest time possible in completing the contract work and be in compliance with our Total Quality Control Plan.

1. Have the customer fill out and sign the form. If necessary, assist customers in filling out the form to ensure that all information needed to fulfill the request is included.

2. Send the completed, signed form to Warren Thompson for approval. Also attach a copy of the signature card you have on file for the customer so that we can verify the signature on the form.

    If appropriate, send the following:

    • The address to send the contract to, if it is different from the customer's address listed on the form.

    • A 20% down payment of the total estimated charges for document preparation that may exceed 50 hours.

Contract Charges

We bill for two kinds of work: 1) research and 2) document preparation. Work is charged by the hour, and any fraction of an hour is charged at the full hourly rate.

Research: $15.00 an hour. The minimum charge will be $15.00 payable in advance.

Document Preparation: $25.00 an hour. Additional copies are 20¢ per page.

On requests where it appears that more than 50 hours of work will be required, contact Warren Thompson in advance so that he can estimate the charge. A 20% down payment is to be paid upon approval of the contract request form. The actual balance will be due upon completion of the work.

Please call Warren Thompson at 806-295-6841 or me at 806-295-6842 if you have any questions concerning this matter.

Figure 5.8 The writer revised the memo shown in Figure 5.7. The use of headings, numbered lists, overview statements, and grouping information into meaningful segments in a consistent manner enhances the layout of the text. The memo is longer, but much easier and faster to read.

labels and captions on visuals, footnotes or endnotes, or legends accompanying visuals.

Unless a document is designed for readers who are visually impaired, do not use type that is larger than 12-point for body text. It wastes space and paper and does not have the professional look required in the workplace. Of course, there are exceptions—the most notable is typeface for overhead projector slides and computer-generated slideshows. The point size for presentations will be between 22–42 depending upon the size of the room, the audience, and the equipment you are using. We discuss creating effective oral presentations in Chapter 12.

USE COLOR EFFECTIVELY

Color, when used effectively, enhances the readability of a document. Readers use color cues to locate information in the text and to distinguish the importance of information. Writers use color to signal important information or to show relationships among items, for example a warning in a set of instructions or the different colors used for bars in a bar chart. Web sites and other electronic documents incorporate color almost without exception. The document appears more accessible to the reader. Elizabeth Keyes refers to color as an "information structure signal."[2] In this section, we describe several ways color may be used to signal the reader about the organization (structure) of the information.

The following guidelines are selected and adapted from Keyes' article:

- Use color to call attention to important information. Because you want to signal important information, use it only on the most important information. Often you will see the word *WARNING* in red to alert the users to read the warning that follows.

- Use color to help a reader navigate through a document. Figure 5.6 shows a color tab along the edge of a page. When several pages are grouped together, the color shows on the edge of the document. The reader knows that the information in the section is related. The reader can move quickly to the section. Links on Web pages are another example. The links on Web pages appear in one color until the link is followed but changes color to indicate when the link has been followed. Readers find this helpful in keeping track of where they have been on a Web site.

- Use color to simplify information that contains many details and multiple relations among the details. You can use it to separate the information but at the same time show that the information is related. In Figures 2.2a–d (color insert), for example, color is used on the National Science Foundation Web site to help the reader navigate the Web site. By now, you have used this textbook for a few weeks. Have

---

[2]Elizabeth Keyes, "Typography, Color, and Information Structure," *Technical Communication* 40 (1993): 638–54.

you used the color of the headings and the typeface to help you understand the hierarchy of information in the textbook?

You have ready access to the color spectrum and more colors than you will ever use. Look for the color feature on the software package you are using (for example, Figure 5.9 in the color insert after page 38). It may be in the same area that you select font or the graphics. If you follow some simple guidelines, you can effectively coordinate the colors. If at all possible, have several colleagues review your document before you send it to clients or to others in your company. Here we provide some guidelines that William Horton[3] and others suggest you follow when integrating color into a document.

- Use colors that your reader expects to see—blue, red, green, and yellow. Leave experimenting with color and color combinations to the marketing and entertainment departments. You have information to deliver to your reader; do not let color detract from the information.

- Use colors commonly associated with the action. For example, in the United States, red signals danger.

- Keep in mind that different cultures associate certain colors with different meanings. For example, black signifies death in the United States; white signifies death in China. Test the document with different audiences, particularly if it will be distributed internationally.

- Coordinate the colors selected with the company logo and colors in documents going to clients to look unified and well thought out.

- Use complementary colors. On the color spectrum, look for colors of the same hue, that is, shades of the same color. Complementary colors are next to each other on the color spectrum. (See Figure 5.9, color insert after page 38.)

- Use low contrast and darker shades of colors across the pages of larger documents. For example, the color used for the headings in this textbook is not the brightest shade of blue.

Remember two things if you use color in a document. First, adding color to a document may increase the cost of reproducing the document. You must decide if the cost increase is justified by the improvement in helping your readers find the information. Second, you can use any color imaginable for text and background for any document (especially Web documents); however, if your reader cannot read the information, you have not succeeded as a writer.

As you develop your documents, always keep your readers' needs in mind. When you write important documents (such as your resume or a report for a client) or any documents to be distributed to more than one

[3]William Horton, "Overcoming Chromophobia: A Guide to the Confident and Appropriate Use of Color," *IEEE Transactions on Professional Communication* 34 (1991): 160–73.

reader, ask others to read and comment on not only the content but the document's design. We have provided an overview of the most common document design features. As a writer, you must remain flexible and adjust to your readers' needs; as a reader, be alert to what text and document design features work for you and incorporate them into the documents you write. Know your audience, the purpose of your document, and the information you are providing.

MAKING THE CONTENTS EASY TO FOLLOW

In spite of the work you may have put into organizing and expressing your information as clearly and logically as you can, your document should be designed so that its organization is obvious to the reader. You want the reader to navigate quickly through a document whatever the length—memos, e-mail messages, 40-page reports, procedures manuals, or Web sites. As a writer, you must provide the navigation cues. In Units 2 and 3 in this book, we discuss a great many organizational plans, including correspondence, process and mechanism descriptions, instructions, recommendation reports, and proposals.

Because we can express only one idea at a time, out of necessity we must organize our letters, memos, and reports in some way. Readers expect related documents (genres such as instructions or letters) to have similar textual, visual, and document design cues.[4] That is, readers look for numbered steps in instructions to find out where to start or the signature box in a letter to know who wrote the letter. Readers come with experience reading other documents. Readers are familiar with moving around hard-copy documents. They know the table of contents is in the front, the index is in the back. They can find each quickly. Readers know how much information is between the front and the back of a book or a report or a letter—they see it and they can flip through the pages. You can build on their experience while presenting your ideas.

Navigation cues perhaps are more important with electronic documents. For example, electronic documents have no fixed boundaries as do hard-copy documents. Although site maps, as shown in Figures 2.2d (color insert) and 5.10, give us an overview of the Web site, we have no way of knowing how much material is a part of each page of the site as in hard copy. We can move around the site, but we can also lose our place there. If we do not understand the categories (topics in the index), we may have trouble. In both hard copy and electronic documents, you must provide your reader with ample appropriate and consistent cues.

But knowing how to organize a document is not enough. You, as a writer, know what you are driving at and have as a map your inner picture of the organization of your document. You have spent so much time

---

[4]Schriver 358.

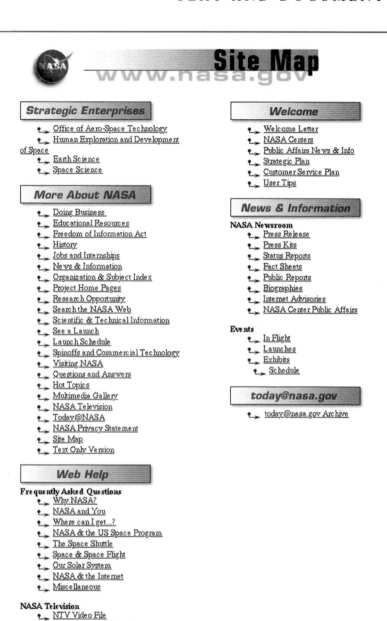

Figure 5.10 The site map for NASA provides an overview of the paths the reader can take to find information about the National Aeronautics and Space Administration.

Source: National Aeronautics and Space Administration. *Site Map*. 5 Aug. 1999 〈http://www.nasa.gov/siteindex.html〉.

thinking about organization that you have internalized it. However, your readers may not share that same picture.

Whether you are writing a document for publication in hard-copy form or electronic form, you need to transfer your organization to your readers. You must provide the reader with navigational cues and tools: cues such as headings or chapter breaks; tools such as Web-site maps or table of contents. Layout and design cues help transfer this picture. Good readers scan a document before they begin reading to understand the organization of the information. They then select where to start reading and how much reading to do. However, not all readers are good readers. Some may lack good reading strategies or may have a first language different from that of the document. You must provide navigation cues for all readers.

Many workplace documents are not read from beginning to end. Readers go to the document to find specific information. Headings, displayed lists, paragraphs to show organization, and Web site links will help them quickly understand the organization of large blocks of information. We use many such design features in this book. Notice in particular the size and color of the various levels of headings and how we distinguish lists from normal text.

The value of headings, numbered or bulleted lists, and organizational paragraphs should be self-evident. Posters, brochures, illustrated magazines and books, and television and movies have responded to and, in turn, shaped an audience that would rather look than read. Readers want their information highlighted. If your documents are to succeed, they must have the willing participation of these visual-minded readers. It is not so much a question of whether readers will *understand* what you have to say as of whether they will be willing to *read* what you have to say. When readers are put off by pages of information unbroken by headings or lists, they probably will not read the report, or at best will read it grudgingly. If they become discouraged and stop trying to wade through pages of solid text, all the interest and firmness of purpose you had in creating your document will do you no good, for it is the reader, not you, who measures how successfully you have communicated your ideas.

USE HEADINGS

Headings help fulfill the readers' assumptions that your information is shaped into an organized and meaningful whole. Without headings to display your plan of organization, the reading becomes tedious and the main ideas remain lost from view, buried in the mass of words and sentences that make up the document. The reader should be able to pick out the major ideas of your document well enough to set them down in writing. Note, for example, that the passage in Figure 5.7 makes the reader's work difficult for the very reasons we have just outlined.

To grasp the major ideas in Figure 5.11, you probably would have to read it and note the major ideas, separating them from subordinate ideas and details by bolding them or by reconstructing the outline of the material in brief notes or marks in the margin. Understanding the document would require considerable work.

Now look at another version of this memo in Figure 5.12. Notice how the headings make it easier to read and understand what the writer has written. In a single brief exposure, the reader sees immediately the writer's inner picture of organization. The more visible the content and arrangement, the greater the impact on the reader. Headings stand out best when slightly larger than the body text or printed in bold or italics.

The version in Figure 5.8 is longer than the version in Figure 5.7 because headings take up space. However, in spite of this, it is quicker to read and easier to understand and remember because the reader can quickly identify the points of discussion, the order in which they are made, and how much discussion is devoted to each.

Remember to make distinctions between the different levels of headings you use so that your reader will see the relation among the different sections of the text. Just as headings in your textbooks signal different sections and the relation of sections to each other, so do headings within documents you write. When you write, the purpose of the document, the information presented in the document, and the reader's expectations determine how many levels of headings you will need.

Find an example of a document without headings and consider how you might add them. For example, you might include headings in a one-page memo (Figure 5.12) or in an e-mail message (Figure 5.2). You will probably need just one level of heading; you might use a sans serif font such as Univers and bold the typeface. If your e-mail software does not let you bold or use a different font, then use all capitals. Frequently, with proposals and other requests for information the headings are given to you. That is, the request for proposal (commonly called the RFP) identifies each area that must be addressed or a request from another division in your company outlines what information is needed. The information needed determines the headings. In Figure 5.13 the boxed words can become the headings for each section of the proposal.

Each document will be different. Some general guidelines include using a sans serif font such as Arial and using **bold** instead of <u>underline</u> to set off the heading. Use *italics* sparingly and then only for sections within major sections. You may use all capital letters, but for short blocks of text only. Readers have a harder time distinguishing the letters when the block of text is uniform (no ascenders or descenders). Look at the headings in Figures 5.1, 5.8, and 5.12. Figure 5.14 illustrates possible formats to distinguish levels of headings and to show the hierarchy of information in the document.

For further guidance on the logic and rules of headings, study the comments on the samples provided in "Outlines" in Unit V, Writer's Guide.

Date: May 20, 2000
To: T.Y. Lee, Supervisor, Greentree District #7 *TLee*
From: Allen McClure, Area Chief, Reforestation Project

Subject: Recommendation of Replacement of Fire Suppression Tractor in Area 1

The purchase of a new Caterpillar D4D dozer will give Area 1 the dependable equipment needed for fire suppression, fire protection, and routine management activities. This purchase will result in the continued maximization of fiber yield and minimum loss to wild fire.

The potential loss of Area 1 plantations, due to fire, because of the downtime is critical with the present unit. The area has 58,191 acres of timberland; 22,629 acres are in plantations one to 20 years old. To ensure development of these plantations fire suppression is essential.

The new fire suppression tractor is also essential in developing a road system in these plantations to give better fire protection and aid in suppression.

Our commitment to maximum yield from our timberlands and the future dependency of the DePhalant Mill to this commitment makes dependable equipment a must. The fire suppression tractor is also used in minor road construction projects and tree planting, which are also essential in the commitment to maximum yield.

The present tractor had maintenance costs of $10,101 and $9,600 for the past two years. In contrast, during this same period the 2-year-old tractor in Area 2 had maintenance costs of $1,500 and $3,000. These tractors are for the same purposes and the hours of operation were essentially the same. The cost of operating the present tractor in Area 1 is prohibitive.

The unit to be replaced is a D4D diesel crawler, purchased in May 1980, asset no. M548, which is totally depreciated. This crawler has no book value and will be traded in or sold.

The alternative to purchasing a new tractor would be to lease a tractor or continued use of the present tractor. Experience indicates that this type of equipment is more costly to lease than to own. Continuing to operate our present tractor would be impractical due to extensive downtime, high maintenance costs, and its potential unreliability.

Figure 5.11 A document without headings or displayed list, even in a short passage, does little to make the work of readers easier. To grasp the full meaning of this memo, readers will probably have to read it more than once and separate major ideas from subordinate ones and details by underlining or marking with highlighters, or by constructing an outline of the material with brief notes in the margin.

Date: May 20, 2000
To: T.Y. Lee, Supervisor, Greentree District #7   *TLee*
From: Allen McClure, Area Chief, Reforestation Project

Subject: Recommendation of Replacement of Fire Suppression Tractor in Area 1

I recommend the replacement of the fire suppression tractor in Area 1 for the following reasons:

- loss of production to downtime is critical
- the maintenance cost of the tractor is excessively high
- the tractor is completely depreciated

Loss of Production to Downtime

The potential loss of Area 1 plantations, due to fire, because of the downtime is critical with the present unit. The area has 58,191 acres of timberland; 22,629 acres are in plantations one to 20 years old. To ensure development of these plantations fire suppression is essential.

The new fire suppression tractor is also essential in developing a road system in these plantations to give better fire protection and aid in suppression.

Our commitment to maximum yield from our timberlands and the future dependency of the DePhalant Mill to this commitment makes dependable equipment a must. The fire suppression tractor is also used in minor road construction projects and tree planting, which are also essential in the commitment to maximum yield.

Excessively High Maintenance Cost

The present tractor had maintenance costs of $10,101 and $9,600 for the past two years. In contrast, during this same period the 2-year-old tractor in Area 2 had maintenance costs of $1,500 and $3,000. These tractors are for the same purposes and the hours of operation were essentially the same. The cost of operating the present tractor in Area 1 is prohibitive.

Depreciation

The unit to be replaced is a D4D diesel crawler, purchased in May 1980, asset no. M548, which is totally depreciated. This crawler has no book value and will be traded in or sold.

Purchase of New Tractor

The alternative to purchasing a new tractor would be to lease a tractor or continued use of the present tractor. Experience indicates that this type of equipment is more costly to lease than to own. Continuing to operate our present tractor would be impractical due to extensive downtime, high maintenance costs, and its potential unreliability.

Figure 5.12 Notice how the displayed list and the headings make this memo easy to read and understand. In a single brief pass, readers see immediately the writer's inner picture of organization. The more visible the content and arrangement, the greater the impact on the readers.

REQUEST FOR PROPOSAL

**Nancy and Edward Grover Endowment
for Research in Teaching in the
Computer-Mediated Classroom**

1. Describe the specific objectives of the proposed project for improving computer class-room teaching.

2. How do the project objectives relate to and promote the enhancement of teaching and accomplishment of the general objectives in course(s) taught in the computer classroom? How many students will be reached by the proposed project? Describe the rationale and significance of the proposed project.

3. Outline what you plan to do and how you plan to accomplish and evaluate the results.

4. Outline plans for dissemination of the project results and methods of assessment.

5. Explain any use of graduate student labor planned for this project. These funds may not be used to support a graduate student's thesis or dissertation; however, you may use graduate student labor on the project.

6. Provide a detailed budget for this project. List by major expenditure category: faculty salary and employee benefits (14% of requested salary, when appropriate), wages (provide hourly rate and number of hours requested), expendable supplies (include examples of this category), travel required to conduct project (number of trips planned, where, when, etc.), requested equipment (include estimates for each item).

Figure 5.13 This Request for Proposal identifies the six areas that the proposal writer must address. The writer can develop headings for each area of the proposal from the words marked in boxes. Proposal readers will then be able to quickly locate information.

USE DISPLAYED LISTS

Present important information or other significant data in vertical list form instead of in sentence and paragraph form. Lists help break up long bodies of text and call attention to specific items. Readers find them useful for giving information in a concise, easy-to-read format. Readers of online text find lists helpful because lists provide shorter chunks of information that can be scrolled through and read with less chance of losing the location. Readers of documents written in a language other than their first language find lists helpful for the same reason. The shorter chunks of information do not overwhelm the reader. In Figure 5.12, notice how the bulleted list at the beginning of the memo identifies the organization of the

Title	bold, all caps, centered, sans serif font	**UNDERSTANDING THE ROTH IRA**
1st level heading	left margin, upper/lowercase, bold, sans serif font	**Selecting the Account Holder** You want to select a financial institution that provides quarterly statements of your investments.
2nd level	part of the paragraph, upper/lowercase, italics, sans serif font	*Banks.* Banks provide services in addition to IRAs that you may want to use. For example, you can get cash when you need it from an ATM machine.
Title	bold, upper/lowercase, 14 point font, centered, sans serif font	**Understanding the Roth IRA**
1st level heading	left margin, upper/lowercase, 12 point, bold, line space between heading and paragraph	**Selecting the Account Holder** You want to select a financial institution that provides quarterly statements of your investments.
2nd level	left margin, upper/lowercase, 10 point (same as the text), bold, line space between head paragraph	**Banks** Banks provide services in addition to IRAs that you may want to use. For example, you can get cash when you need it from an ATM machine.

Figure 5.14 Two panels from a bank brochure on the Roth IRA show different formats for the headings. Headings should enable the reader to quickly see the organization of the information.

memo and the headings use terms from the list to signal the reader where the discussion for each point begins.

As you construct your list, consider the following guidelines:

- If the sequence of the items in a list is random or arbitrary, use a bullet (•). If the order is important, as in a set of instructions, use Arabic numerals (1, 2, 3 . . .). Most word-processing software will fill in the pattern (bullets or numerals) when you start the sequence. Be sure to change the tab so that you do not have a large gap between the bullet or the numeral and the text. You want the equivalent of 2–3 spaces between the bullet or number and the text. Use indent to align the lines following the first line of text.

<u>Problem</u>
-     Too much space

<u>Solution</u>
- Change the tab settings to move the text closer.

<u>Problem</u>
1.   Too much space. Large gaps make it more difficult for the reader

and look unprofessional.

<u>Solution</u>
1. Proper spacing simplifies reading, looks more professional. And, readers will see the numbers more clearly if you align ("stack") all lines following the first.

- Use the same spacing for all lists throughout a document. Readers quickly determine the pattern and hierarchy of the information. If you are inconsistent, you will lose your reader. Figures 5.4, 5.5, and 5.8 show acceptable spacing.

- Use parallel sentences or phrases throughout the list. If the grammatical construction shifts, readers may slow down or stop reading. Consider the lists below:

Parallel (Acceptable)	Not Parallel (Unacceptable)
- Use bullets to signal items in a list.	- Bullets signal items in a list.
- Align the text in the list to help the reader to see bullets and distinguish between items in the list.	- Aligning the text in the list helps the reader see bullets and distinguish between items on the list.
- Insert lists to highlight a series of items that might otherwise be lost in a long paragraph.	- If I want to call attention to a series of items that might otherwise be lost in a long paragraph; I use a list.

USE TEXT TO FORECAST

As you write the document, you will provide the reader with cues as to what is coming. The text forecasts for the reader what comes in the section with transition statements and summary paragraphs that point to the next part of the document. For example, the following paragraph introduces Chapter 1: Literacy in the Older Adult Population.

This chapter profiles the prose, document, and quantitative literacy skills of older adults in the United States—those age 60 and older. *In addition* to examining differences in performance within the older adult population, we analyze the literacy proficiencies of older adults in comparison with those of younger adults. *The latter part* of the chapter compares older adults' self-assessed literacy skills with their demonstrated proficiencies. *Finally,* we examine the extent to which adults in various age groups receive assistance with various types of everyday literacy tasks, another indicator of their proficiencies.[5]

We have added italics to the words that signal statements that forecast the content of the chapter.

Paragraphs, frequently short and at the end of a section, signal transition to the next section of a document. Transition paragraphs tell the reader what will follow. Do not hide information in a document because readers frequently skim until they find the information they need. Transition paragraphs and headings that forecast what follows help the reader.

MAKING DOCUMENTS EASY TO USE

All the features of effective design and layout discussed so far in this chapter contribute toward creating documents that are easy to use. Chances are great that documents that look inviting to read and that are designed so that the progression of thought is easy to follow will also be easy to use. That is, readers will read the document with the purpose of locating information they need.

Here we discuss two strategies for making documents easy to use: (1) matching the document design to the readers' purpose and (2) matching the document design to the readers' environment.

MATCH DOCUMENT DESIGN TO READERS' PURPOSE

To make a document easy to use, you must understand clearly the purpose of the document and how readers are likely to use it. That is, you must consider the document from the readers' points of view. Some readers will want to read a document from beginning to end. Others will want to read only the sections that are relevant to their needs. Still others will want to locate a specific piece of information that is crucial to their immediate need.

Figures 5.15, 5.16, and 5.17 show directions for claiming speaking and instructional fees and for claiming reimbursement for professional travel. The directions in Figures 5.15 and 5.16 are ineffective because the information is not presented in a way that helps readers gain access to the specific information they will need. At the least, document design should help readers perform any one of the tasks easily. The best design will help readers undertake several of the tasks, as necessary. The directions in Figures 5.15 and 5.16 force the reader to scan the document from beginning to end because there are few visual cues to what information is where. However, not all readers will want to start and finish at the same places, so the design is poor. Figure 5.16 has information paragraphed according to tasks, but that is still not enough.

[5]Brown, Helen, Robert Prisuta, Bella Jacobs, and Anne Campbell, *Literacy of Older Adults in America: Results from the National Adult Literacy Survey,* NCES 97-576 (Washington: US Dept. of Education, National Center for Education Statistics, 1996) 15.

Central Business Office
Drawer 6000
Empire-Juniper Professional Consultants
Meyer Road and State Route 7
Sandpoint, ID 83864

<u>Procedures for Claiming Expense Reimbursement</u>
<u>and Instructional or Speaker's Fee</u>

Please use this sheet as a guide to assist you in providing us with the proper receipts for your professional travel expense reimbursement and fee payment. Following this guide will ensure payment with a minimum of difficulty and time.

To claim mileage, provide us with a memo requesting that you be reimbursed for personal auto mileage. Cite the purpose of the travel, the function of the meeting, dates, and round-trip mileage for each day at 25¢ per mile. Please include your mailing address. To claim lodging, provide us with the original hotel receipt. If you share a room with another person also participating in the meeting, ask the hotel to print two separate receipts. To claim airfare, provide us with the original receipts. To claim meals, provide us with the original receipts. To claim taxi fare, provide us with a signed receipt from the driver.

To be paid an instructional or speaker's fee, if your fee is to be paid directly to you, submit a bill stating the service you provided, the unit for which you provided the service, and the dates of the work in accordance with the letter or memorandum of agreement. Payments made to individuals will be made in accordance with the letter or memorandum of agreement by PAV (Payment Authorization Voucher) or DAV (Departmental Authorization Voucher). These are initiated upon completion of your service or work. Taxes are deducted from compensation paid to individuals.

Figure 5.15 Readers will find it difficult to locate the steps they must take to claim expenses. See Figures 5.16 and 5.17 for revised instructions.

Central Business Office
Drawer 6000
Empire-Juniper Professional Consultants
Meyer Road and State Route 7
Sandpoint, ID 83864

Procedures for Claiming Expense Reimbursement
and Instructional or Speaker's Fee

Please use this sheet as a guide to assist you in providing us with the proper receipts for your professional travel expense reimbursement and fee payment. Following this guide will ensure payment with a minimum of difficulty and time. Please include your mailing address.

To claim mileage, provide us with a memo requesting that you be reimbursed for personal auto mileage. Cite the purpose of the travel, the function of the meeting, dates, and round-trip mileage for each day at 25¢ per mile.

To claim lodging, provide us with the original hotel receipt. If you share a room with another person also participating in the meeting, ask the hotel to print two separate receipts.

To claim airfare, provide us with the original receipts.

To claim meals, provide us with the original receipts.

To claim taxi fare, provide us with a signed receipt from the driver.

To be paid an instructional or speaker's fee, if your fee is to be paid directly to you, submit a bill stating the service you provided, the unit for which you provided the service, and the dates of the work in accordance with the letter or memorandum of agreement. Payments made to individuals will be made in accordance with the letter or memorandum of agreement by PAV (Payment Authorization Voucher) or DAV (Departmental Authorization Voucher). These are initiated upon completion of your service or work. Taxes are deducted from compensation paid to individuals.

Figure 5.16 The design of this example helps the reader, but see Figure 5.17 for further document design features that make the information easier to locate.

Central Business Office
Drawer 6000
Empire-Juniper Professional Consultants
Meyer Road and State Route 7
Sandpoint, ID 83864

Procedures for Claiming Expense Reimbursement
and Instructional or Speaker's Fee

Please use this sheet as a guide to assist you in providing us with the proper receipts for your professional travel expense reimbursement and fee payment. Following this guide will ensure payment with a minimum of difficulty and time. **NOTE:** Please include your mailing address with requests for reimbursement.

To claim **Mileage**	provide us with a memo requesting that you be reimbursed for personal auto mileage. Cite the purpose of the travel, the function of the meeting, dates, and round-trip mileage for each day at 25¢ per mile.
To claim **Lodging**	provide us with the original hotel receipt. If you share a room with another person also participating in the meeting, ask the hotel to print two separate receipts.
To claim **Airfare**	provide us with the original receipts.
To claim **Meals**	provide us with the original receipts.
To claim **Taxi Fare**	provide us with a signed receipt from the driver.
To be paid an **Instructional** or **Speaker's Fee**	if your fee is to be paid to your place of employment, submit a bill stating the service you provided, the unit for which you provided the service, and the dates of the work in accordance with the letter or memorandum of agreement.
	if your fee is to be paid directly to you, it will be made in accordance with the letter or memorandum of agreement by PAV (Payment Authorization Voucher) or DAV (Departmental Authorization Voucher). These are initiated upon completion of your service or work.
	Taxes are deducted from compensation paid to individuals.

Figure 5.17 The information is easier to locate in this example.

Figure 5.17 contains the same information as in Figures 5.15 and 5.16 but in an extraordinarily different design. It uses self-contained blocks of information, judicious use of white space, and varied type styles to help readers understand the underlying logic of the document and how to find the specific information they need. It is straightforward, helpful, and friendly.

MATCH DOCUMENT DESIGN TO READERS' ENVIRONMENT

When you consider your document's purpose and how the reader will use it, you should also consider the environment in which the reader will use the document. Although you cannot control the environment, you can create a design that will work well in most situations for which the document is intended.

Let's consider several examples. Golfers use a scorecard. Most of the cards have the scoring table for the first nine holes on one side and the second on the other side. A heavier paper, sized to fold and put in a pocket, provides golfers with something fairly substantial to write on and keep safely during play. Frequently, color is used and the layout of each hole is given as well as a review of some of the basic rules of courtesy. The scorecard matches the needs of most golfers.

The instructions on a cake mix fill one side of the box. The reader need not turn the box over to continue making the cake. Pictures show a measuring cup with the amount of water needed and the number of eggs. The text is easy to read, with white space and color to emphasize the easy steps to making a cake.

A company's cleaning crews' carts have a set of laminated cards that give instructions for using cleaning supplies. The cards hang on the crews' cart for easy reference if a spill occurs. The cards have few words but a lot of visuals because the cleaners may not have time to read the warnings or may not be efficient readers.

Figure 5.18 shows a list of documents you are likely to receive with a new computer. Notice the range of formats the documents take, from a poster to a book of more than 100 pages to a CD-ROM and online documents to read.

Electronic documents are no different. You must know how your reader will read the document. For example, what about the service representative who must troubleshoot and repair an oscilloscope at a hazardous-waste-monitoring facility? The online manual you write will provide the instructions, but you must also consider the size of the computer screen, the amount of light, the amount of space to work in, and the power source as you write the instructions. An index or fast-search feature, white space, lines that do not run off the screen, visuals sized to fit the screen, and color that shows clearly on a screen in variable light are just a few of the choices you must consider.

Similar to printed documents, you have control over the text and visuals—to a point—in the electronic environment. The reader's environment

Document	Purpose	Some of the Features
Poster-size 19″ × 20″	Shows how to set up the computer quickly.	• Large typeface • Numbered steps • Visuals showing the parts of the computer dominate • Color used to highlight key parts of the computer and step numbers
7½″ × 9″ 88-page book	Gives step-by-step instructions for setting up and troubleshooting the computer. Similar books come with the monitor, the system board, the CD-ROM, the speakers, and the zip drive. The booklets vary in size and length.	• Chapters with sections clearly signaled by headings with the contents listed at the beginning of each chapter • Color used occasionally to highlight key information; visuals used to show parts of the computer • Text and photographs bleed into the margin to emphasize the information
5¾″ × 8¼″ 126-page book	Provides instructions for installing and troubleshooting the operating system.	• Computer screens shown throughout the instructions • Tips given in the margins • Headers identify the chapter and topic • Software licensing information included • Soft cover, perfect binding
6″ × 6″ envelope	Contains 3½″ disk with controller software for emergency use if system failure.	• Bright pink envelope to call attention to importance • Bolded, large-point font used for DO NOT THROW AWAY! • Instructions printed on the envelope
5¾″ × 6″ envelope	Contains CD-ROM with software to install.	• Envelope is plastic sheath with holes punched for storing in CD binder • Instructions printed on the disk
Online Help	Provides instructions for user.	• Window appears • Index • Gives numbered steps for task selected

Figure 5.18 A partial list of the documents received with the purchase of a new computer. The list of features for each document identifies some of the document design elements, not all.

and the computer environment (hardware and software) the reader uses will affect the presentation of the document. For example, the size of the monitor may affect the amount of text the reader sees without having to move the scroll bar, color may change, or the size of the print on the screen may be reduced depending upon how the user has the monitor set. The Web browser or e-mail software the reader uses also may affect the presentation.

As you review the documents you develop, consider the purpose of the document and information it provides, but also consider how the reader will use the document. Your choices for the design of the document, and the content will follow easily from a careful analysis.

PLANNING AND REVISING CHECKLIST: TEXT AND DOCUMENT DESIGN

Think about the following while planning and revising the design of your documents.

PLANNING

- Are there ways that you can make your document more visually attractive and more inviting to read?

- Do you have access to a computer with a word-processing program, desktop-publishing software, and a good printer? Do you know how to use these software and equipment?

- What are the specifications for the document?

  Size of paper _____

  Page orientation _____

  Size and style of font for the body text _____

  Size and style of font for displayed passages _____

  Size and style of font for headings _____

  Single- or double-spaced text _____

  Right margin justified or unjustified _____

  Width of margins _____

  Position of page numbers _____

  Text of header/footer _____

- If there are no specifications, what do you think would be best?

- How best can you display the organization of the document?

- What devices can you use to highlight the major ideas and important pieces of information?

- How can you help readers recognize the difference between major ideas and subordinate matter?

- Does the document provide for direct access to particular pieces of information?

- If others are also working on the document, do they know the specifications for the design?

REVISING

- Does the document conform to the specifications for size of paper, size and style of font, and so on?

- Is the overall design attractive?

- Are the pages of the document broken up to avoid long stretches of solid text?

- Does the design of the document match the underlying logic and the use of the document? Do headings and subheadings mark main points and major sections of the document? Are major sections of the document visually distinct? Can readers make their way easily through the text? Can readers gain quick access to specific information?

- Is the overall design consistent throughout the document?

SUGGESTIONS FOR APPLYING YOUR KNOWLEDGE

1. At the end of Chapter 1, "The Process of Workplace Writing," we suggest that you start gathering examples of writing found in the workplace. Either as an individual or as a member of a group, examine one that uses a variety of design features. Write a memo or prepare an oral report for your instructor and classmates that explains the following:

   - What type of document it is

   - Its intended audience

   - What features aid or hinder a smooth reading

   - What features provide clues to its organization

   Evaluate what the writer or writers have done well. What additional features could have been used?

2. Revise the following memo using design principles discussed in this chapter to make its meaning as clear as possible to the reader. You will have to do more than rearrange the text. You may decide the information can be sent by e-mail to the reader. If so, be sure to send a copy to your instructor. The memo is part of the correspondence related to the inventory of a direct-mail marketing company specializing in gardening supplies. The warehouse manager identifies problems with returned merchandise and recommends solutions. Write a brief memo to your instructor explaining your reasons for the design features you used.

<u>MEMO</u>

September 15, 1999
To: Ruth J. Wades
Vice President, Operations

From: Jerome Dean
Warehouse Manager

Subject: Returns

The number of returns has doubled over the past six months. There are several reasons for this. We changed primary shippers. The new shipper has had repeated delays in picking up and delivering the merchandise in the time specified in the contract. Repeated phone calls and visits have not resulted in improved service. Customers do not accept delivery on items received after the promised delivery date. I recommend we use On-Time Shipping for all of our regional customers. The addition of crystal vases to our inventory has created problems. The foam packing material seeps through the gift boxes for the vases. We have not found a plastic wrap that will protect the box from the foam. We need to use bubble wrap. Machines for dispensing bubble wrap cost: $55,000 for sheets 36″×45″; $75,000 for 45″×60″; $150,000 for adjustable sheet size. Currently the 36″×45″ sheets cover the crystal boxes, but if we carry larger vases, we will have problems. There's a two-day delay between the time an order is taken and when the warehouse receives the order. Incompatible computer systems in customer service and in the warehouse further delay the processing. Customer service and the warehouse need a direct link via computer.

3. Compare the use of color in a paper document and an electronic document. Locate a set of instructions or a company report for the paper document and use a noncommercial Web site for the electronic document. How does each use color to provide information-structure signals? What colors are used? How many colors are used?

CHAPTER 6

VISUALS AND DOCUMENT DESIGN I

Think for a moment of anything that you have studied recently in one of your courses—the double-helix structure of DNA, the Federal Reserve Board, the hydrological cycle, how to add antibiotics to livestock feed, the relationship between exposure to carbon monoxide and human health, a method of predicting lateral pressure transmitted to nonyielding and rigid basement walls by swelling expansive soils, or what have you.

Some of these concepts and events can be difficult to understand in abstract language, but a visual may clarify them. They probably were illustrated in whatever you studied, whether textbooks, articles, reports, or slides projected on a screen. The visuals helped you to understand the subject and later to recall and think about it. Long after you have forgotten the words, you are probably able to recall the visual.

Text conveys many ideas; however, when text reaches its limits of effectiveness, visuals are more effective. Visuals can make certain kinds of data and relationships more apparent than is possible in text and can emphasize or clarify information that might otherwise go unnoticed or be difficult to understand. Take, for instance, an idea that is primarily pictorial, such as the proper distribution of lawn fertilizer using a drop-type spreader. The reader can understand more easily how to distribute the fertilizer evenly by looking at the drawing in Figure 6.1 than by reading a statement such as "For even distribution, apply one lot of fertilizer lengthwise and the other crosswise over the lawn."

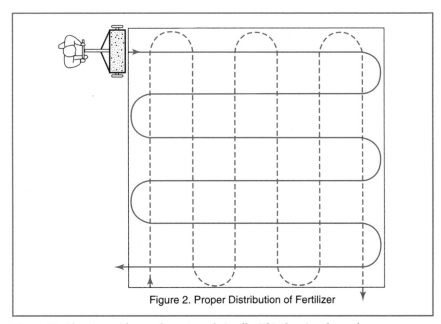

Figure 2. Proper Distribution of Fertilizer

Figure 6.1 Almost any idea can be conveyed visually. This drawing shows the proper distribution of lawn fertilizer using a drop-type spreader.
Source: Texas Agriculture Extension Service, The Texas A&M University System.

Even when the information is not normally regarded as primarily visual, visuals can succinctly present data that would otherwise take many words to explain. For example, Figure 6.2 shows how text and visual combine to give an overview of how Java, a programming language, works. Some readers will find the visual easier to understand; others, the text. The text and the visuals support each other, as in the bar chart in Figure 6.3, which shows almost at a glance the number of tornadoes in Alabama 1950–95.

Visuals have become an essential and conspicuous part of presentations, reports, and even correspondence. The care with which they are

---

of these characteristics made Java appropriate for the Internet. However, it was not until 1995 that the world recognized Java's potential as an Internet language.

During 1994, with the growing popularity of the World Wide Web and the need to display a vast variety of media elements, Sun realized that the Java language would be well suited for creating a graphical Web browser. Sun created *HotJava*, which was programmed in Java and ran Java applets. HotJava was unveiled at SunWorld in May 1995 and became a showcase for Java and its unique features.

Then, in January 1996, Netscape Communications Corporation released Netscape *Navigator 2.0*, a Java-enabled graphical Web browser. Because Netscape *Navigator* was the most widely used Web browser, this was the effective date when Java was born into the world at large.

What Makes Java Unique?

Java is a programming language. What, exactly, makes it different from other programming languages? Java can be characterized as follows:

Optimized

Optimized language code is compiled to an intermediate level, which is then interpreted. The resulting code is called bytecode or, in other programming languages, p-code.

Optimized language code is portable and can be moved from platform to platform without modification.

Platform-independent

A platform-independent language is not dependent on any particular processor. However, it does require a runtime module, and the runtime module is dependent on the platform.

Java code is generic for any operating system or platform. Users must have a Java-enabled Web browser, such as Netscape *Navigator*, to run applets. To run a Java application, you need to have a Java runtime system installed on your computer. In this way, Java code can run on any hardware platform, with any operating system.

Object-oriented

Java is an object-oriented programming language. In object-oriented programming, programs consist of reusable components called objects. The use of objects makes it possible to reduce the amount of code necessary to write a program. Each function—for example, the function to open a dialog box—is written once and can be used by any part of the program at any time.

How Java Works

Java source files are compiled into bytecode, which is stored and distributed by a network or file system.

For Java applets, the bytecode file can be transported over the Internet from the server to the user's Web browser when a user visits the Web page. (The user must be running a Java-enabled browser.) For Java applications, the bytecode file can be distributed on traditional media or over the network.

The Java virtual machine (VM) handles program execution, including file access, security checking, and the runtime system.

When the bytecode file reaches the Java platform, the bytecode loader associated with the VM places it into memory.

Before executing the program, the VM runs the program through the bytecode verifier (the VM's security mechanism) to ensure that it will not generate a stack overflow; that it obeys the private, protected, and public access rules; and that it does not create pointers to modify anything illegal.

Once a program is verified, it moves to the Java interpreter, unless the Java runtime system has a just-in-time (JIT) compiler. A Java interpreter reads Java bytecodes and passes commands through the Java runtime system to

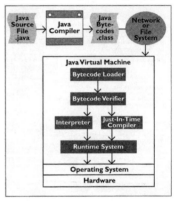

Figure 1. Steps in Creating and Executing Java Programs

the operating system as the program executes.

By turning Java bytecodes into machine code native to the user's platform, a JIT compiler acts as an accelerator, making Java applications and applets run much faster.

The Java runtime system consists of threads, memory, and other resources required to run Java on a given platform. Both the interpreter and JIT compiler run in the context of the runtime system.

The Hype Versus the Facts

There is so much hype surrounding Java that it is easy to get a distorted view of its features and capabilities. To dispel the myths, review the information in Table 1.

When to Use Java

In general, Java is an appropriate tool when your environment includes the following:

• Networked computers
• Multiple platforms
• Security issues
• Limited funding
• Unknown future

Of course, there may be other factors that will influence your decision to use Java.

Figure 6.2 The writer gives the reader the information in the text and in the visual. The reader chooses which to focus on to gain a better understanding of how Java works.
Source: "The Basics of Java" written by Cynthia Currie and reprinted with permission from INTERCOM, the magazine of the Society for Technical Communication. Arlington, VA. U.S.A.

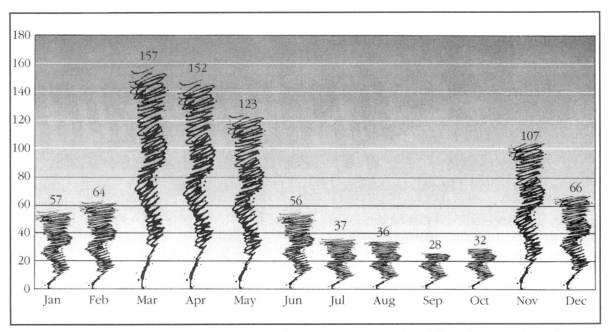

Figure 6.3 **At a glance, the reader can see which months Alabama has the most tornadoes. If the reader wants to know the actual number of tornadoes, he or she can look closer at the graph. Bar graphs such as this one show comparisons.**
Source: Tornado Safety in Alabama, Alabama Cooperative Extension System, Circular ANR-983.

created greatly affects readers' impressions of the value of information contained in correspondence and reports. Therefore, the choice, execution, and placement of visuals should not take a back seat when you plan your writing. You should strive to be as fluent in using visuals as in using words and sentences. There is a "symbiotic relationship between the visual and the verbal [what we are calling the text]."[1] The extra care in coordinating the visuals and the text will pay off by making the document easier to read and by making your work look professional.

One cautionary note: Incorporate visuals in your document only when the reader needs the visuals, when the purpose of the document calls for a visual, and when the information is best conveyed in a visual. You omit unnecessary words to convey information; do the same with visuals—omit any unnecessary clutter from the visual to present a clear, concise representation of the information you want the reader to have.

In this chapter, we use examples from a variety of sources to illustrate factors that influence the reading of visuals. The quality of the visuals you create will affect how clear an understanding of the information readers gather from the visual. Also, you have a responsibility to your readers to present the information accurately and without intentionally misleading the reader. We provide several guidelines for using visuals to present information

[1]Charles Kostelnick and David D. Roberts, *Designing Visual Language: Strategies for Professional Communicators* (Boston: Allyn and Bacon, 1998) xix.

ethically. In Chapter 7, we provide guidelines for creating effective visuals. We assume you will create the visuals for your document using a computer.

FACTORS INFLUENCING COMPREHENSION OF VISUALS

To use visuals, readers must be able to differentiate them from surrounding text, identify the important information in them, and comprehend the information. The following seven factors determine the ease, speed, and accuracy with which visuals are read. The factors apply to hard-copy documents, although much of the advice applies to online documents such as Web sites. For more information on Web-site design see William Horton's *The Web Page Design Cookbook*[2] or sites such as www.w3.org, the site for the World Wide Web Consortium. The Consortium is an international organization that establishes protocols for the Web to ensure relatively

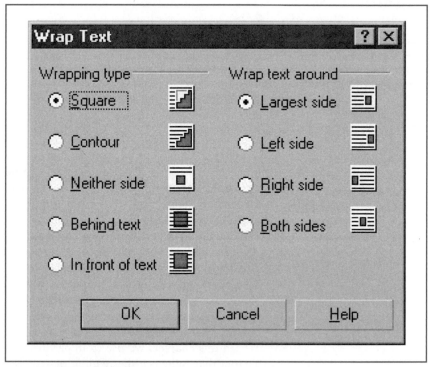

Figure 6.4 Text-wrapping options in Corel WordPerfect 8.0.™ All current word-processing software offers similar options.
Source: Screen shots are Corel® WordPerfect® Suite 8 Copyright © 1996–1997 Corel Corporation Limited, reprinted by permission. Corel and WordPerfect are registered trademarks of Corel Corporation or Corel Corporation Limited.

[2]William Horton, ed., *The Web Page Design Cookbook: All the Ingredients You Need to Create 5-Star Web Pages* (New York: Wiley, 1996).

consistent global Web access. We suggest you review a variety of Web sites before you create your own Web document.

VISUALS SHOULD BE PERCEPTIBLE

To aid readers in immediately recognizing visuals, separate visuals from the text around them with adequate white space. The defaults set by the software will take care of most spacing issues and placement of the labels and text. Only occasionally will you have to adjust the spacing. You will want to select the most effective placement of the visuals within the text. The *text wrapping* feature of the software controls the location; Figure 6.4 shows some possibilities. You may also select a border for the visual that will define the area of the visual. Readers find borders helpful when distinguishing between the visual and the text. Again, the software lets you select a border. For most documents you will want a thin-ruled line (see Figures 6.2 and 6.5 and the visuals in the instructions in Chapter 18).

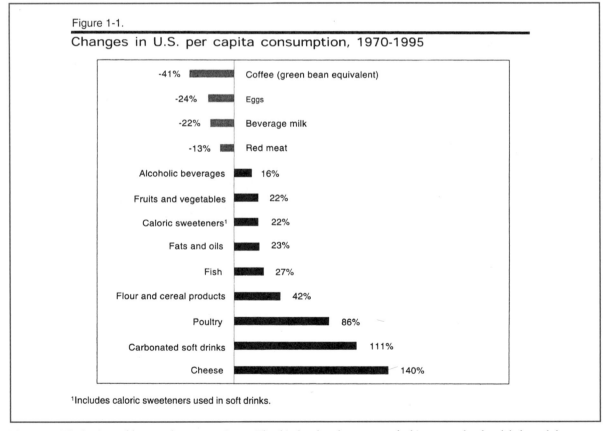

Figure 1-1.

Changes in U.S. per capita consumption, 1970-1995

- -41% Coffee (green bean equivalent)
- -24% Eggs
- -22% Beverage milk
- -13% Red meat
- Alcoholic beverages 16%
- Fruits and vegetables 22%
- Caloric sweeteners[1] 22%
- Fats and oils 23%
- Fish 27%
- Flour and cereal products 42%
- Poultry 86%
- Carbonated soft drinks 111%
- Cheese 140%

[1]Includes caloric sweeteners used in soft drinks.

Figure 6.5 The horizontal bar graph compares items. The thin border, the amount of white space, the clear labels, and the descriptive caption make this an effective graph.
Source: US Dept. of Agriculture. "What Do Americans Eat?" *Agriculture Fact Book 1997.* 5 Aug. 1999 ⟨http://www.usda.gov/news/pubs/fbook97/la.pdf⟩.

Size and place the visuals to meet the purpose of the document and to best display the information. You can easily change the size and placement of visuals through the software. When visuals are too large to fit on a page with text, put them on a page by themselves immediately following or facing the page on which you analyze their contents. Orient the visual on the page so that the reader does not have to turn the document to read the information. If the visual is too large and must be turned, then place it so that the binding of the report is at the top of the visual. (Be sure to increase your top margin for any bound document.)

VISUALS SHOULD BE ACCESSIBLE

Accessibility refers to the ease with which readers can locate individual visuals. Distinguishing visuals from text contributes to making them easy to find. Placement of visuals is equally important. Readers move back and forth between the text and visuals as they gather information. For example, when you are using a Send-N-Return Envelope (Figure 6.6), you probably look at the visual and then the corresponding text before you begin to reassemble the envelope. Place the visual at or near your discussion of it, as near as possible following the first reference to it (for example, the flowchart in Figure 6.2 is right with the text describing the Java programming process).

Think of the pages of your document as a collection of blocks of text and of visuals. Review how your reader will use the document, the reader's expectations for the document, and where the most important in-

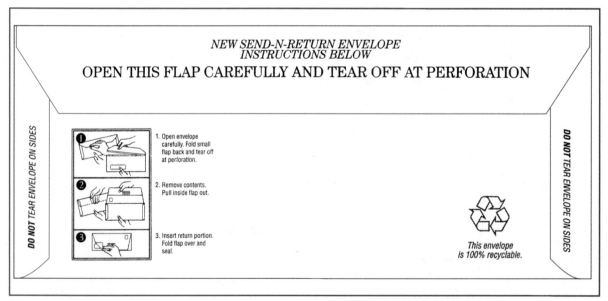

Figure 6.6 Three visuals and the corresponding text fit on the back of the Send-N-Return envelope.
Source: The Send-n-Return envelope is a patented product of the Tension Envelope Corporation, headquartered in Kansas City, Missouri.

formation should be placed to be seen. You also need to know the general design of the document. For example, if you are creating a brochure, you are limited to two sides of an 8.5 × 11-inch sheet of paper. You can make it a bifold or a trifold brochure. The information must fit in that area. If you are writing a report, your outline and the topic should give you an idea of how long to expect the document. It is not at all unusual for a Request for Proposal (RFP) to specify the maximum length for the submitted proposal (see Chapter 15, Proposals). Once you have an overall idea of the plan for the document, you can lay out your text and visual blocks, as illustrated in Figure 6.7. The examples throughout this textbook illustrate some of the options.

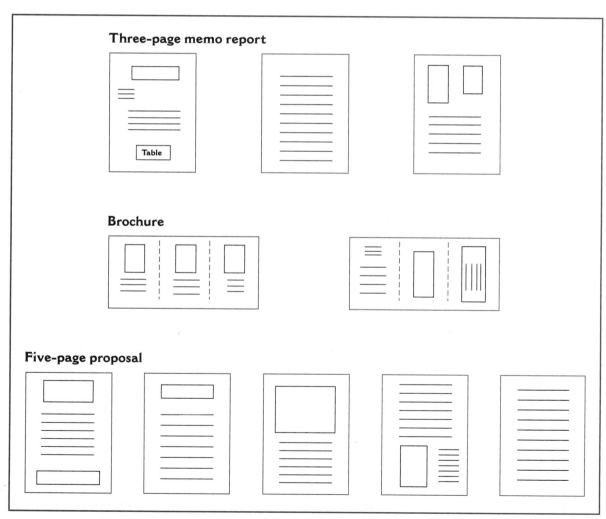

Figure 6.7 Think of the text and visuals as blocks that must fit on a page. The purpose of the document, the information presented, and the amount of space available will determine how to arrange the blocks. The sketches above give three possible arrangements.

Sometimes, however, you may include visuals that have only indirect relevance to your discussion or that are relevant to only a portion of your audience. When this is the case, place them in an appendix so they do not interrupt the flow of your discussion.

A report that contains several visuals (more than five is a good guideline) should include a list of tables and figures in the prefatory elements (see the report in Chapter 13) to aid readers in selectively locating individual visuals.

VISUALS SHOULD BE CLEARLY LABELED

Caption and label everything clearly so readers can scan visuals quickly and know exactly what they are looking at. Standardized labeling practices increase reading speed and comprehension. If possible, arrange all lettering to be read from left to right. If it is necessary to place labels on vertical scales, run the lettering so it can be read from bottom to top. Select the appropriate position using the features of the software program.

- Caption formal figures by arabic numerals and descriptive titles below the visual, as in

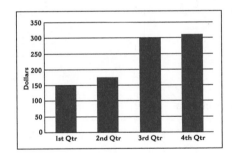

Figure 1 Growth of Investment

All visuals are labeled as figures except information displayed in columns and rows. These visuals are referred to as *tables*.

- Caption formal tables by arabic numerals and descriptive titles above the table, as in the following table:

Table 1   Overview of Walsh Inc. Finances

	Income	Expenses
1999	$29,500	$25,375
2000	$35,000	$24,000

- Number figures and tables consecutively in the order of their reference in the text and refer to them as Figure 1, Table 1, and so on. Use your software's caption feature to identify the visuals. The software will also automatically number the visuals.

  The suggested numbering system and placement of the caption has shifted over the past several years. Roman numerals no longer are required for captioning tables. And, frequently, all of the captions may be located above or all below the visual. Our advice: be consistent throughout the document. That is, if you label the first table with arabic numbers, you must use arabic numbers for all of the table captions. If you begin by putting the caption above tables and below the figures, do so throughout the document. Number tables and figures consecutively—but separately. If you have 5 tables and 10 figures in the same document, you would have Table 1, Table 2, Table 3, . . . Table 5 and you would have Figure 1, Figure 2, Figure 3, . . . Figure 10.

- Label by name or symbol the parts of objects and components of diagrams that you want readers to pay attention to. As you examine the sample visuals in this chapter and elsewhere in the book, notice how labels are used.

- Arrange labels neatly and straight in the background area of the visual.

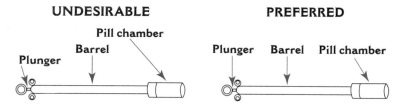

- Use right-hand justification of labels when the arrow comes from the right side of the label.

- Use left-hand justification for labels when the arrow comes from the left side of the label.

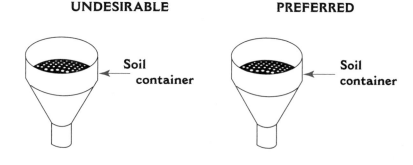

- Where there is adequate space, label the parts directly.

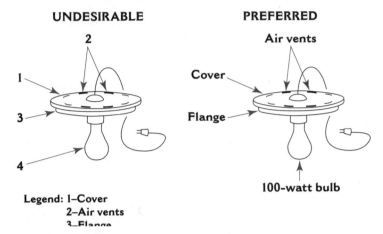

UNDESIRABLE   **PREFERRED**

Legend: 1–Cover
        2–Air vents
        3–Flange

- If direct labeling results in a cluttered and crowded visual, use a key to identify the items.

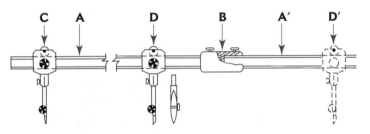

Legend: A–Beam
        B–Coupling attachment
        C–Center pin
        D–Writing head
        A′–Extension
        D′–Writing head at end
            of extension beam

- If possible, center an arrow that comes from the top or bottom of the label.

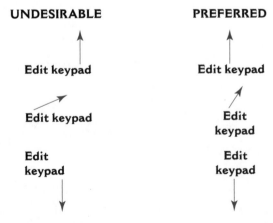

UNDESIRABLE   **PREFERRED**

Edit keypad   Edit keypad

Edit keypad   Edit
                         keypad

Edit   Edit
keypad   keypad

- Draw an arrow so that it does not touch the label.

UNDESIRABLE	PREFERRED

- If possible, draw arrows so that they barely touch the items.

UNDESIRABLE **PREFERRED**

- In charts, graphs, and tables, label every column, row, axis, bar, and line. Use consistent terminology and symbols. Terms and symbols in a visual should be identical to those in the text.

- If you borrow or adapt data or a visual from another source, give credit to the source below the visual. Review how we have identified the source for visuals used in this and other chapters in this textbook, for example Figures 6.1 or 6.2 or the Web site in Figure 2.2 (color insert).

  Graphics software allows you to control the label. Spend a few minutes learning how to use the feature.

VISUALS SHOULD BE INTEGRATED INTO THE DOCUMENT

As we have seen in Figure 6.2, text wrapping integrates text and visuals. Other ways to integrate the information in visuals with the surrounding text are to (1) refer readers to the visuals, (2) use consistent nomenclature and symbols in visuals and text, (3) make the visual reflect the levels of organization in the related text, and (4) fully extract information from the visuals.

Refer Readers to the Visuals

If possible, introduce visuals before readers reach them. Such an introduction or reference to a visual written into the text of the report is known as a *call-out*. Place the call-out where you want readers to stop reading the text and to look at the visual, as we have done throughout this textbook. Among the options you have for pointing to a visual are

Figure 1 shows. . . .
. . . as shown in Figure 1.
. . . (see Figure 1). . . .

Table 1 shows . . .
. . . as shown in Table 1.
. . . (see Table 1). . . .

If the visual is not near the call-out, include its location in the call-out, for example:

Recommended storage tanks (see Figure 12 on page 61) can be either buried or above ground.

An actual survey form sent to customers is found in Appendix B.

Make sure that everything about the visuals match:

- They are numbered or lettered consecutively.

- They appear in the proper order.

- They are referred to by call-outs.

- The visual referred to is the correct one.

- All this is reflected correctly in the list of visuals in the prefatory pages.

- Type fonts and sizes and border lines have been used consistently.

Maintain Consistency Between Text and Visuals

Don't call an antenna an *antenna* in the text and label it an *air terminal* on the visual. Such inconsistent terminology can easily confuse readers. Abbreviations in visuals should also follow the same style used in the text. Use the same standard symbols in text and in visuals.

Make the Visual Reflect the Organization of the Text

When a visual illustrates a hierarchically arranged concept in the text, make the levels distinctive in the visual through the labeling, as in Figure 6.8.

Discuss the Significance or Meaning of the Data in the Visual

Do not assume that a visual is clearly understandable in and of itself; therefore, do not include one unless you discuss it in the text. Point out the significance of the data or direct the reader's attention to particular relationships among the data presented in the visual. For instance, the discussion accompanying the bar graph in Figure 6.9 targets the time of day tornadoes frequently hit Alabama:

Tornadoes occur with greater frequency during the late-afternoon to late-evening hours, according to National Weather Service records. In Alabama, five o'clock in the afternoon is the time of the maximum tornado incidence.

Providing both a bar graph and a description helps merge the information in the minds of readers and helps state your interpretation of the

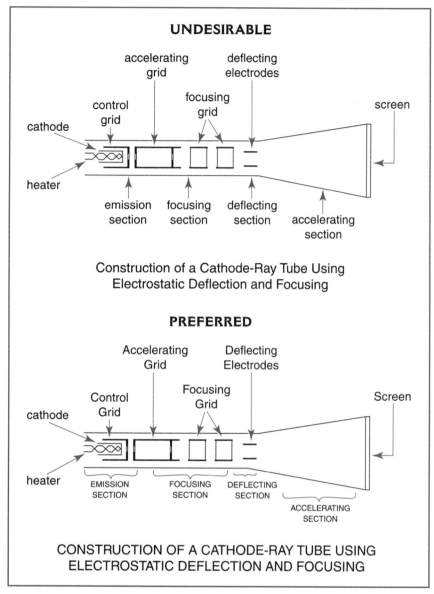

Figure 6.8 The labels on the preferred graphic cue the reader to the hierarchical arrangement of information. The highest level is the title of the graphic in oversized uppercase letters. The next highest level is the names of the main parts (EMISSION SECTION, FOCUSING SECTION, DEFLECTING SECTION, and ACCELERATING SECTION) in normal uppercase letters. The third level is the names of the subparts of the main sections in mixed uppercase and lowercase letters (Control Grid, Accelerating Grid, Focusing Grid, Deflecting Electrodes, and Screen). The lowest level is the names of the elements of the subparts in lowercase letters (the cathode and heaters are elements of the Control Grid). Type size and capitalization are only two methods of using labels to indicate hierarchy. Word-processing programs offer a wide range of type sizes and colors and type styles such as bold and italic.

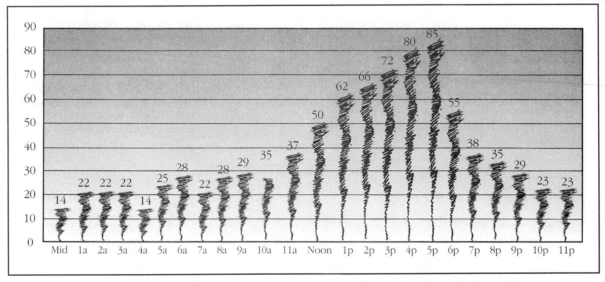

Figure 6.9 The writer makes sure the reader understands that tornadoes hit Alabama most frequently about 5:00 p.m.
Source: Tornado Safety in Alabama, Alabama Cooperative Extension System, Circular ANR-983.

data explicitly. (Figure 6.9 and Figure 6.3 are found in the same brochure, *Tornado Safety in Alabama.* Notice the consistent format between bar graphs that help the reader see the patterns.)

When you edit your manuscript, be sure you have not placed visuals amidst unrelated text, you have left no apparent contradictions between visuals and the text, and the data in the visuals are easily understood or interpreted.

VISUALS SHOULD BE EASY TO UNDERSTAND

Visuals present abstract concepts visually and concisely. They distill into a relatively small space information that would otherwise require a great deal of text. However, because they are so succinct they can be difficult to understand if they are not easy to read. Careful attention to captions and labels and to explaining the significance of the information helps make visuals almost self-explanatory. Here are four more tips for making visuals easy to read.

1. **Use digital images whenever possible.** Scanners that convert images electronically into digital form allow you to copy existing artwork, including photographs, and incorporate them into your document. (Figure 7.1, color insert, was taken with a digital camera.) You can easily copy an image off a Web site or from another electronic source. In fact, all the figures in this textbook that show Web sites were inserted into the textbook in digital form.

Just make sure you acknowledge your source. If you must use an original hard copy of an image, make sure it is a sharp, clean image that will reproduce well. Images that are too dark, too light, or are blurred will reproduce poorly and will be virtually useless. As long as the printer is working well, visuals that you create on a computer will probably produce well. If you reduce the size of a visual, make sure that labeling and any text or important features on the visual remain legible.

2. **Use specialized visuals and language only if readers can understand them.** A circuit diagram or other schematic drawing or a scatter diagram or logarithmic chart is not much good to readers who cannot read it. In such a case, choose another form of representation such as a block diagram, a photograph or drawing, or a bar chart or line graph that readers can interpret.

3. **When appropriate, accompany visuals with legends.** A legend adds to the information presented and makes the visual more understandable. Legends identify the color, shading, or line style used with the topic represented. For example, the legend identifies what each pattern represents in the pie chart below:

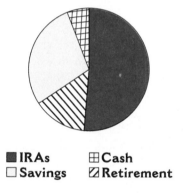

■ IRAs   ⊞ Cash
□ Savings   ▨ Retirement

4. As a final check, ask another person if he or she can understand the visual. It almost always helps to have another person look over the visuals, especially if that person's experience matches your reader's.

VISUALS SHOULD BE RELATIVELY EASY AND INEXPENSIVE TO PREPARE

Not only do visuals provide information and illustrate relationships, they also improve the appearance of a page. Readers are quicker to review a document that does not overwhelm them with text. But readers also don't want visuals to detract from the text by appearing to clutter the page. Excessively varied type fonts and sizes, different kinds and widths of borders, distracting colors, and dizzy patterns to fill in the background or foreground make your visuals look inconsistent and unprofessional. Use visuals when they meet the identified purpose and provide the information needed.

Use Color Carefully

Review the guidelines in Chapter 5 on color combinations. Be aware that color affects how the reader interprets the information. Shading and patterns that fill in bars and other shapes you draw increase the attractiveness and readability of charts over those drawn in outline form. Using shading from black to various tones of gray or using different patterns of diagonal lines, cross-hatching, stippling, and other simple designs may be as effective as color.

VISUALS SHOULD BE APPROPRIATE FOR THE MATERIAL AND PURPOSE

Determine what information you want to convey visually, so you can choose the type of visual that best shows what you want to convey. Before you begin a visual, ask yourself such questions as

What is the purpose of this visual?

What am I trying to show in this visual?

What do I want the reader to see in this visual?

What should the reader understand after reading this visual?

Choose the visuals that best display the facts for the intended audience and place them where they are most accessible, within the time and budget allowed.

ETHICS OF VISUALS

Creating visuals requires more than following the suggested guidelines. You want to portray the information accurately and fairly to readers. Readers expect to read a visual quickly and interpret the information easily. Think about how you read visuals found in *USA Today* or in *Newsweek*. If you are like most readers, you look at the relationship but don't read the scale or exact points on the graph unless you need exact numbers. Instead you are looking for trends or getting an impression of the information the writer wants to convey. You probably trust the writer to present the information accurately.

Consider the following scenarios adapted from a survey of professional communicators by Sam Dragga.[3] We leave these descriptions for you to discuss in class; we encourage you to read the results of Dragga's survey.

- You want to show that your company encourages the disabled to apply for positions and provides an environment that accommodates the needs of the disabled. You want to show this on the company Web site; however, you do not have any employees using a wheelchair. You

---

[3]Sam Dragga, "'Is This Ethical?' A Survey of Opinion on Principles and Practices of Document Design," *Technical Communication* 43 (1996): 255–65.

ask one of the employees to sit in a wheelchair so you can get a photograph. Is this ethical? What might you do instead of photographing an employee who is not disabled to visually illustrate the company's accommodative environment?

- You have been asked to write a letter of recommendation for a colleague applying for promotion. To call attention to his good qualities, you list them in a bulleted list. You write a paragraph describing his weaker qualities. Is this ethical? If you list both either in a bulleted list or in paragraphs, will this take care of any ethical issues?

- In the annual report for the nonprofit organization you work for, you want to call attention to the activities of the organization. You use red to call attention to the money spent on activities, even though it is less than that spent on administrative costs (which you color in green because cool colors make things look smaller). Is this ethical? Do you think the readers will notice? What other color combinations might work better?

As you see from these scenarios and the class discussion, you have decisions to make as a writer and reader. As a writer, you decide the best way to present the information so that it is a fair representation. As a reader, you must evaluate the visual carefully. The suggestions we give in the next two sections build upon the discussion earlier in this chapter that visuals should be:

Perceptible

Accessible

Clearly labeled

Integrated into the document

Easy to understand

Relatively easy and inexpensive to prepare

Appropriate for the material and purpose

WRITER'S RESPONSIBILITIES

The writers Dragga surveyed believe that adjusting the design of the document to get more information on a page creates a problem only if the reader cannot read the information. However, these same writers think that distorting graphs and using inappropriate photographs and other pictorial representations is not acceptable workplace communication.[4] We have six suggestions to help you create visuals that present your information ethically:

- Do not use a scale that distorts the data.

- Do not distort the size using three-dimensions or different thicknesses of pie segments or bars.

[4]Dragga 262.

- Do not use different colors, shades of black and white, or fill patterns to distort the data. (Figure 6.10).

- Do not go against commonly accepted practice to intentionally mislead the reader. For example, keep the years along the x-axis in chronological order (Figure 6.11) or use a drawing if a photograph cannot be taken of the actual situation.

- Do not clutter the visual with unnecessary information that will interfere with interpretation of the information.

- Do not combine types of visuals that interfere with interpretation of the information.

Stephen M. Kosslyn has a more comprehensive list of 25 recommendations for avoiding distortion of visuals.[5] Consult his list if you will be presenting a lot of data in visual format to colleagues and clients.

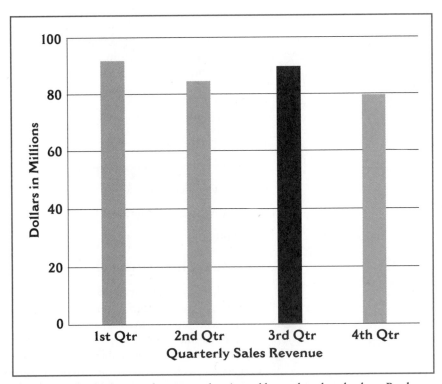

Figure 6.10 The third-quarter bar appears heavier and larger than the other bars. Readers might mistakenly see the third-quarter as the most successful quarter, when the first quarter actually yielded more revenue.

[5]Stephen M. Kosslyn, "Chapter 8: How People Lie with Graphs," *Elements of Graph Design* (New York: Freeman, 1994) 206–35.

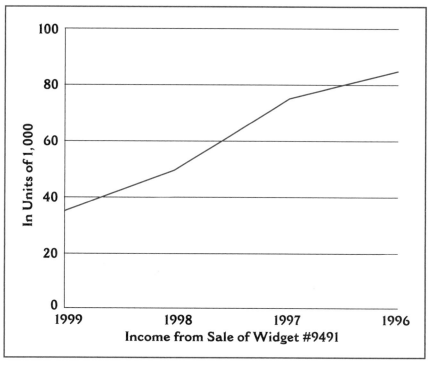

Figure 6.11 The line graph climbs from left to right when the sale of widgets is shown in reverse chronological order. Will the reader see that sales actually have declined over the four-year period?

READER'S RESPONSIBILITIES

How closely readers evaluate a visual depends upon their purpose. If the reader intends to include the visual's information in a report to a client or to a colleague, he or she must confirm that the information is presented accurately. In revising your visuals, put yourself in the place of readers.

- Look at the scale to verify that the data is represented accurately.

- Evaluate three-dimensional pie segments or bars graphs carefully. If possible and appropriate, convert the visual to two dimensions.

- Confirm that the colors, shades of black and white, or patterns of fill do not interfere with evaluation of the data.

- Use commonly accepted formats. For example, keep the years along the x-axis in chronological order or use a drawing if a photograph cannot be taken of an actual situation.

- Make sure there is no unnecessary information that will interfere with interpretation of the information.

- Confirm and evaluate the source of the visual.

In Chapter 7, we provide guidelines and examples of effective, accurate, and ethically sound visuals. Use the Planning and Revising Checklist for visuals at the end of Chapter 7 to guide you through developing visuals for the documents you write.

SUGGESTIONS FOR APPLYING YOUR KNOWLEDGE

1. Select a visual from a newspaper such as *USA Today* or a weekly magazine such as *Time* and bring both the visual and the accompanying article, if there is one, to class with enough copies for everyone to review it. First, have everyone look briefly at the visual and write two to three sentences stating the conclusion they can make about the topic of the visual. Share your conclusions. Next, evaluate the effectiveness of the visual—particularly if classmates disagreed about the information the visual was showing. Ask the following questions: Is the information perceptible? Accessible? Clearly labeled? Integrated into the article or self-contained? Easy to understand? Relatively easy and inexpensive to prepare? Appropriate for the material and purpose?

2. Locate a visual that you think misleads the reader. If you review a newspaper or a weekly magazine for a couple of weeks, you will probably find a visual you can discuss. Show the visual to others in your class but do not comment on what you consider questionable tactics by the developer of the visual. After the class has discussed the visual for a while, call attention to the problem you see if no one else has noticed it. Should this be considered a problem if most of the class does or does not notice the biased presentation?

3. In a short memo, import a visual from the Web and write a two- to three-paragraph analysis of the visual. Be sure to cite the source of the visual. (Copying a visual from the Web is easy. Simply put the cursor on top of the visual and use the right mouse button on a PC or hold the mouse down on a Mac. Follow the menu prompts to save the visual. You can then open a word-processing document and insert the file with the visual.)

CHAPTER 7

VISUALS AND DOCUMENT DESIGN II

In Chapter 6, we discussed the general factors that contribute to the quality of visuals. In this chapter, we tell you how to use specific types of visuals to explain objects and processes and to report totals, trends, and relationships. Throughout, we also discuss some of the ways that graphics software and high-quality printers have enhanced the production of visuals. You can accomplish the techniques we discuss in this chapter with any of the currently available office *suites* (integrated software packages that provide word-processing, spreadsheet, presentation, and database capabilities). Although you may need more specialized software for your workplace communication activities, the basic guidelines that follow will provide solid support for your communication activities.

It is worth repeating our caution from Chapter 6: Incorporate visuals in your document only when the reader needs the visuals, when the purpose of the document calls for a visual, and when the information is best conveyed in a visual. Just as you select your words carefully to convey the information you want your reader to gather from the text, you also must select the appropriate visual to convey the information. For example, will a photograph or will a drawing best show the front panel on an oscilloscope? Or, is the increase in golfers using public courses best represented as a line graph or a bar graph? Or, are the instructions for holding a tennis racquet best shown only as drawings with little or no text? You must decide which visual representation will best represent the information you want the reader to have. Review Chapters 5 and 6 as you combine text and visuals in your documents.

In this chapter we describe the ease with which you can incorporate visuals into your document using computer-generated visuals. We then describe different types of visuals you can use and suggest when you might select a particular visual. We have grouped the visuals as those that best explain objects, processes, and trends.

COMPUTER-GENERATED VISUALS

You no longer have an excuse for not including visuals in your document when one is needed. Graphics software and hardware range from fairly simple and inexpensive drawing programs, color inkjet printers, and laser printers to sophisticated and expensive computer-aided design (CAD) systems and large visual plotters. These enable you to automate drawing and graphing tasks that until recently were done manually. Most importantly, once a visual is created, you can make changes in a fraction of the time required with pencil, paper, and drafting tools. Visuals can be created, stored, retrieved, and edited on computers just as text is. Thus, you no longer must spend a lot of time bent over a drawing board and a T-square to create line drawings, nor must you redo an entire drawing to correct a mistake or make a minor revision.

Using a graphics program is fairly simple and easy to learn. You create a visual on the computer screen and save it in a file (frequently with a file extension such as .jpg, .gif, or .bmp). You then insert the visual electronically into your text file. Or, you create the visual within the program you are using (for example, WordPerfect, Word, Lotus, or Excel). The visual appears at the point where your cursor is in the document. Not only can you create graphs or line drawings, you can easily copy a visual from a Web site and paste it into your document. You can scan visuals or use a digital camera for photographs. The scanner or camera creates a digital image captured in a file that may easily be inserted into your document. Audio and video clips may also be incorporated into your document.

Graphics programs and good quality printers provide an impressive array of visuals and special effects that can make documents look like they are professionally typeset.

Drawing and paint programs enable you to use lines of various widths and styles and fill with color to create images. These programs also make it easy to create precise geometric shapes and manipulate them to make them larger, smaller, or skewed.

Chart and graph programs allow you to make a wide variety of charts and graphs, including bar, line, pie, and organizational. To create charts and graphs on most of these programs, you enter data on a spreadsheet and convert the spreadsheet to the desired chart or graph form. Programs have split-screen features that let you see the chart or graph and enter data at the same time. You can change the type of graph, for example a line graph to a bar graph, with a few keystrokes; you need not reenter the data.

Most **graphics programs** allow you to create visuals to import into a document or print or record on several types of output devices (black-and-white printers, color printers, and film recorders). Presentation software such as Microsoft PowerPoint or Lotus Freelance simplify creating slides for projection through an LCD projector. In Chapter 12, we provide guidelines for giving professional oral presentations using a computer-generated slideshow.

Clip-art programs allow you to reproduce ready-made electronic images. These programs contain from dozens to hundreds of clip-art files. Many of these programs are organized into thematic categories, such as business, leisure (such as sailing, basketball, or hiking), government, and education, which makes it easy for you to select images related to specific topics or themes. One word of caution here: Use clip-art images only when they are needed—don't sprinkle your document with unnecessary clip-art.

Visuals from Web sites can be quickly and easily copied off the Web and incorporated into a document. However, before you use a visual from the Web, you should ask permission from the site manager. You *must* ask permission if you plan to use the visual in a document intended for publication. In any case, you must acknowledge your source. Note how we acknowledge the sources for figures used throughout this textbook.

Optical scanning programs and hardware "copy" line artwork and photographs, including video images, and format them for use in your own computer files. The copied artwork is actually a bit-map image (a series of black-and-white or color squares or dots) that can be displayed on a computer screen or printed. Many scanning software packages and desktop publishing systems allow the scanned images to be modified fairly easily, although the editing can be tedious.

Although word-processing software lets you combine text and visuals, **desktop-publishing software** (Adobe PageMaker, for example) and **multimedia software** give you more flexibility and are easier to use with larger documents. You can transfer word-processing and visuals files into formatted pages, merging text and images similar to those of newspapers and magazines. Most of the visuals used in this textbook, including examples from other sources, were created with software commonly found in office-related software suites.

Web-page design software (such as Microsoft FrontPage) prepares files in *html* (hypertext markup language) for loading on to the Web. Effective Web sites blend text and visuals to present information to the readers.

These programs allow you to achieve the technical precision of manual drawing, to enlarge or reduce the size of the visual, to add special touches such as variations of shades and shadows and reverse type (white images on a black background), to fill in shapes with selected patterns or color, and even to tilt and rotate images. They also allow you to reproduce visuals or touch them up. The programs have similar features and follow many of the same keystroke conventions. If you learn one program, you can quickly learn another. Explore the options in the programs—just save different versions of your work so you can return to an earlier version if you don't like the changes you make. You may want to create the text and visuals in separate files to make each file easier to manage. You can move them together after the text and visuals are close to final form. You will find it easier to edit text and visuals separately (particularly if you have imported the visuals into the document).

USING VISUALS TO EXPLAIN OBJECTS

If you have ever tried to visualize something that you have never seen before or something that you cannot easily recall, you know the value of photographs and drawings. When you want readers to understand an object, pictorials (photographs and drawings) are the most exact method of communication. Although compressed in size and usually one-dimensional, pictorials closely resemble the objects they refer to and thus illustrate physical appearance and spatial relationships better than do words.

The following information on photographs and drawings should help you choose and prepare the appropriate pictorials for showing objects.

PHOTOGRAPHS

Photographs present the exact appearance of actual objects. Realism is their greatest asset. They are often essential in showing the appearance of newly created objects, objects readers have never seen before, objects at the end of a particular stage of development, and worn or damaged objects. Photographs are also useful in comparing sizes of objects by scaling them against more familiar objects, such as a hand or coin, or an actual scale such as a ruler.

Photographs, such as the one in Figure 7.1 (color insert after page 38), are indispensable in showing the exact appearance, in validating the existence or the condition of an object, and in presenting its actual appearance when it or a model is not available for direct observation. Drawings would not be suitable in these instances because they would not provide realistic appearances and would be time-consuming to prepare.

Whether you or somebody else takes the photographs, you need to be able to distinguish effective from ineffective photographs. The most common problems with ineffective photographs are

- irrelevant material in the background

- overexposure of light objects and underexposure of dark objects

- lack of contrast between main subjects and the background

- unintentional out-of-focus areas or subjects

- poor camera angles

You will use a digital camera or a scanner to import a copy of a photograph into your document. If necessary, you can *crop* (trim to eliminate unnecessary peripheral details), size, and enhance a photograph quickly and easily in most software with graphics capability.

DRAWINGS

Like photographs, drawings show what objects look like. And though they are less realistic than photographs, they can better convey certain kinds of information. For example, they can depict objects that exist only as concepts (such as the proposed International Space Station, as in Figure 7.2) or provide specific dimensions (such as showing the floor space needed for a wheelchair, Figure 7.3).

Because drawings are further removed from reality than are photographs, they allow much greater flexibility than do photographs and can be used to illustrate specific aspects of an object. You will see as you examine Figures 7.4 through 7.8 that this selectivity enables you to concentrate the reader's attention on particular features. Computer-aided design programs such as AutoCAD create professional-level drawings. The graphics components of office software such WordPerfect and Word have enough features to create basic drawings.

The most commonly used views are external, cutaway, sectional, exploded, and phantom.

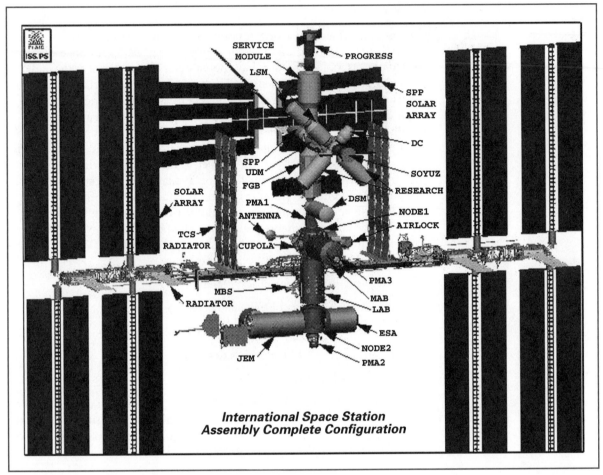

Figure 7.2 The drawing of the International Space Station provides the model for a station that has not been built yet. If you click on a label, you will see a drawing of that part of the station, for example, the cupola.
Source: National Aeronautics and Space Administration. International Space Station. 21 July 1999. 5 Aug. 1999
⟨http://spaceflight. nasa.gov/gallery/vrml/station/index.html⟩.

External Views

External views, like photographs, show the outside of an object to give readers an idea of its appearance. The outline drawing is a special kind of external view that shows, as the name suggests, an object in outline form. The clear, uncluttered appearance of outline drawings avoids the realistic clutter of photographs and makes them useful for selecting and emphasizing significant features. The outline drawing in Figure 7.4 shows different ways that helicopters can lift heavy loads by various combinations of tether cables, spreader bars, and bridle cables. The drawing eliminates irrelevant material that would have been included in

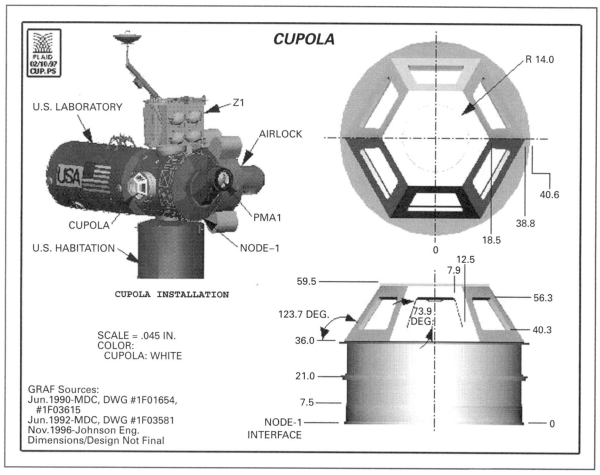

Figure 7.2 (continued)

a photograph and also allows the three different lifting methods to be depicted in the same illustration for easy comparison, which would be difficult to achieve in a photograph.

Photographs and external views do not show the inside parts of objects, how parts fit together, or the transportation of material through an object or device. However, hidden lines, which may be used with any kind of view, show features that ordinarily can't be seen. The unseen features are represented by short dashes, as in Figure 7.5. Interior parts that cannot be photographed or shown well by hidden lines can be illustrated by cutaway, sectional, and exploded views. These views are useful when objects contain so much housing that readers see only the exterior.

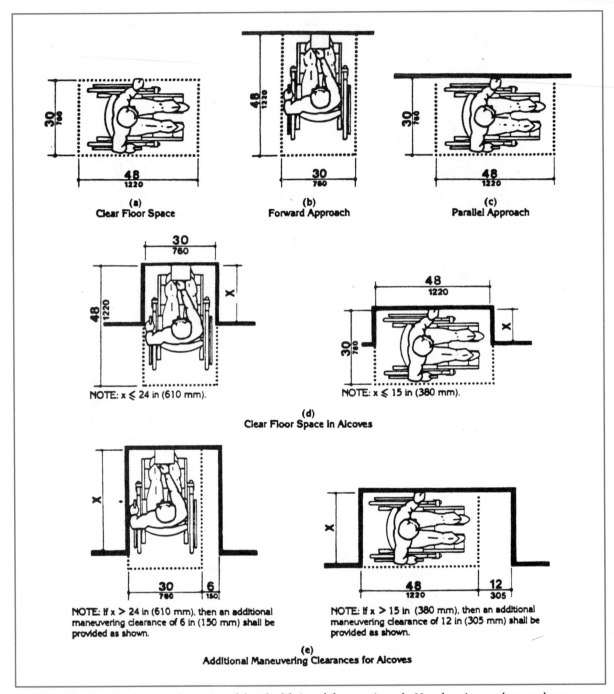

Figure 7.3 The drawing gives a topdown view of the wheelchair and the room it needs. No other view or photograph can so clearly show the wheelchair and the space needed.
Source: Americans for Disabilities Act Handbook EEOC-BK-19. Washington: US Equal Employment Opportunity Commission and the US Dept. of Justice, 1992. App. C, 16.

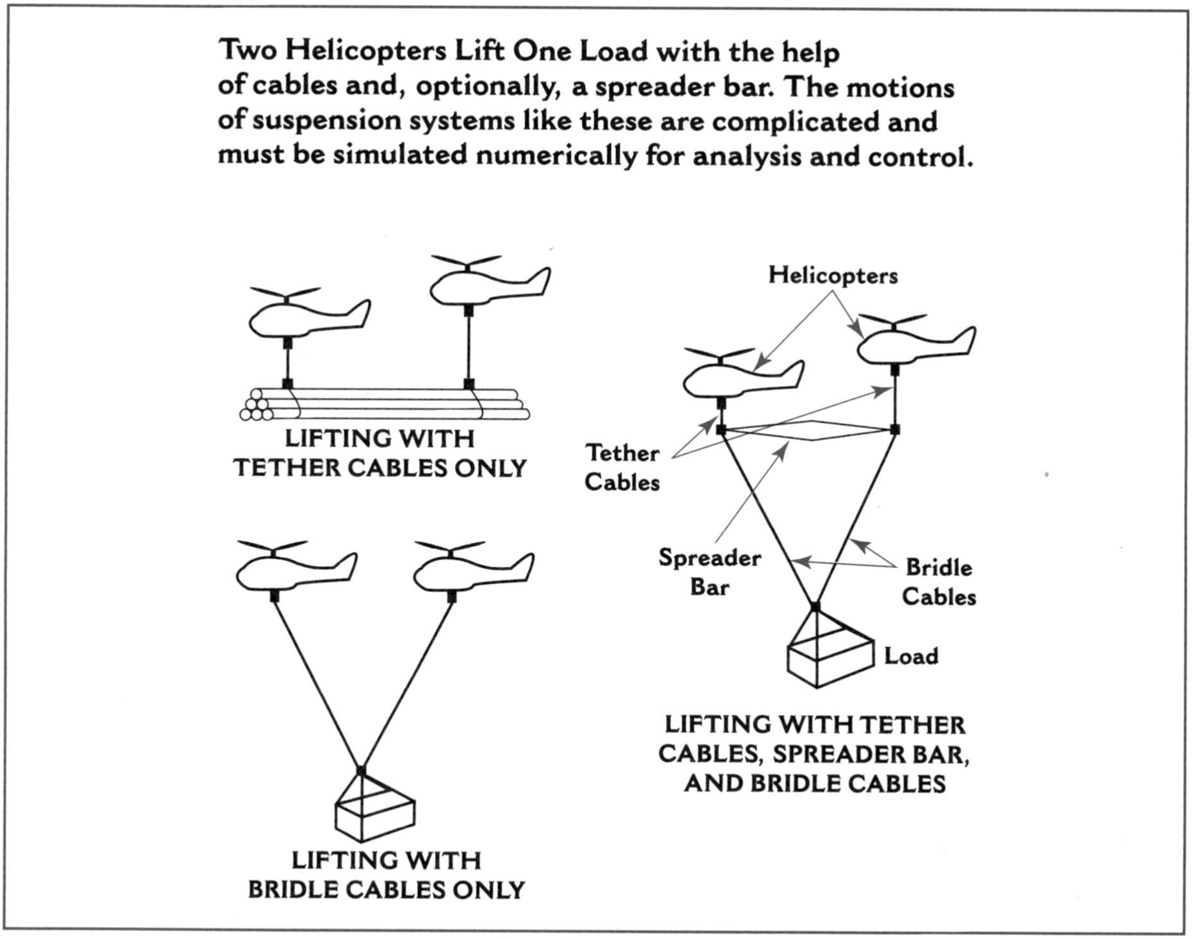

Two Helicopters Lift One Load with the help of cables and, optionally, a spreader bar. The motions of suspension systems like these are complicated and must be simulated numerically for analysis and control.

LIFTING WITH
TETHER CABLES ONLY

LIFTING WITH
BRIDLE CABLES ONLY

Helicopters

Tether
Cables

Spreader
Bar

Bridle
Cables

Load

LIFTING WITH TETHER
CABLES, SPREADER BAR,
AND BRIDLE CABLES

Figure 7.4 Line drawings present views that are difficult, if not impossible, to show in photographs. Notice the legend at the top of the drawing that provides additional information.
Source: "Calculating Dynamics of Helicopters and Slung Loads." *NASA Tech Briefs* (PB91–924912). Dec. 1991: 970.

Cutaway Views

Cutaway views, as the name implies, show an object as if some part of its exterior nearest the viewer had been cut away. They are used to show both internal and external constructions in the same drawing. Figure 7.5 illustrates the use of hidden lines and a cutaway view to show unseen rear parts and interior parts of the ammunition magazine of an M-14 A-1 military rifle that would not be visible in an external view. Notice also the exploded view to show the bottom plate.

Sectional Views

Sectional views, as the name indicates, show an object as if some section of the object nearest the viewer had been removed. Similar to cutaway

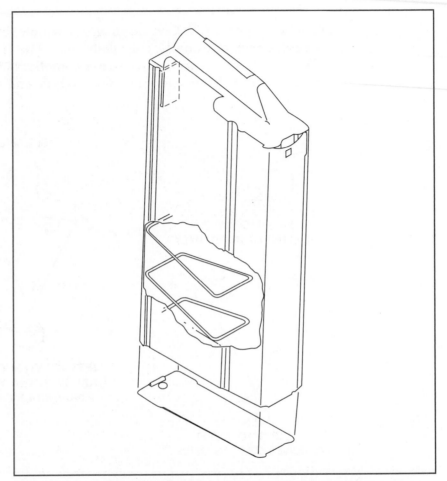

Figure 7.5 In cutaway views, a portion of the exterior of the object is removed to reveal internal parts. In this drawing, the cutaway shows the loading spring of the ammunition magazine for the M-14 A-1 military rifle. Note also the use of hidden lines and exploded view to reveal the base plate.
Source: Courtesy Betty L. Bradford.

views, sectional views allow readers to "see" through the exterior cover almost as if they have x-ray vision. Sectional views may be partial or full; that is, the sectional cut may be through just a portion of the object or may run completely through it. In Figure 7.6 the door and the covering for the wave guide channel of a microwave oven have been removed. A cross-sectional view, which runs completely through the object, shows an object as if it had been split down the middle and the half nearest the viewer removed. In Figure 7.7, diagonal lines indicate the cut lines where the exterior cover has been removed to display the interior parts, including the specially designed electrode holder.

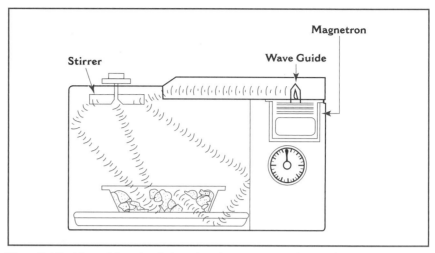

Figure 7.6 In this partial sectional view, the microwave oven's door to the oven cavity and housing for the wave guide channel are removed to illustrate the movement of microwaves. *Source:* Agricultural Extension Service, University of Minnesota, St. Paul.

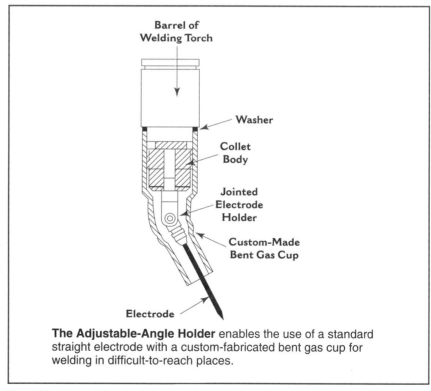

Figure 7.7 Diagonal lines in this sectional view represent where the external cover has been removed to reveal interior parts. Note the legend beneath the drawing that provides additional information.
Source: "Jointed Holder for Welding Electrode." *NASA Tech Brief* (PB92-925903). Mar. 1992: 195.

Exploded Views

Exploded views separate parts so readers can become familiar with the parts of an object or system or can see how the parts relate or fit together. They often are necessary in instructions to show readers how to assemble or disassemble complicated parts. The axis lines in Figure 7.5 (between the base plate and the main housing) and Figure 7.8 show how the parts are aligned.

Phantom Views

Phantom views suggest the way objects would look in alternative positions. The drawing of the adjustable beam compass (page 146) illustrates many of the drawing techniques we've been discussing. Hidden lines indicate the existence of the beam inside the center pin and writing head. Break lines cut the beam in two to shorten the view. A partial sectional view shows the inside of the coupling device, indicating that the base beam and the extension beam are separated by a partition. A phantom view indicates where the writing head would be on the extension beam. In Figure 7.9, the light, broken lines show the changing positions of the ratchet handle in tightening and releasing the cargo tie-down strap.

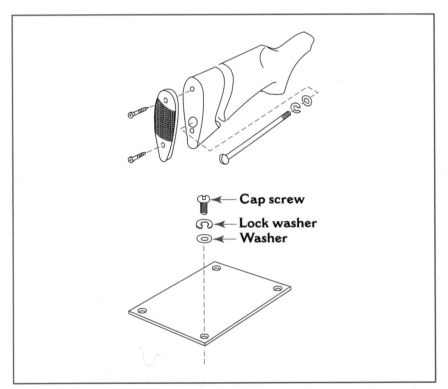

Figure 7.8 Exploded views show parts of objects in a disassembled, but aligned, state. If necessary, axis lines illustrate how the components fit together.

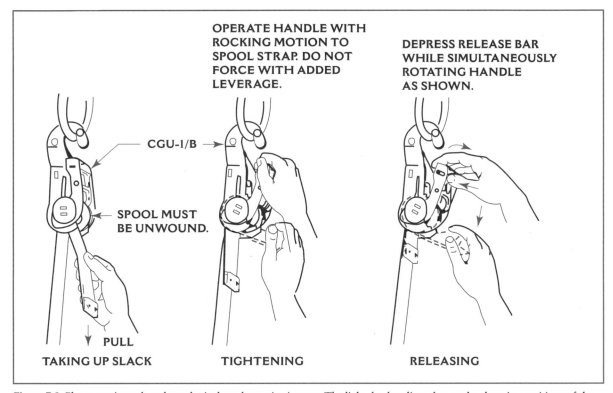

OPERATE HANDLE WITH ROCKING MOTION TO SPOOL STRAP. DO NOT FORCE WITH ADDED LEVERAGE.

DEPRESS RELEASE BAR WHILE SIMULTANEOUSLY ROTATING HANDLE AS SHOWN.

CGU-1/B

SPOOL MUST BE UNWOUND.

PULL

TAKING UP SLACK   TIGHTENING   RELEASING

Figure 7.9 Phantom views show hypothetical or alternative images. The light, broken lines denote the changing positions of the ratchet handle.
Source: "Preparation of Freight for Airlift Transportation." *Dept. of the Army Technical Manual* TM 38-236. Washington: Dept. of the Army, 22 Dec. 1991. 2–16.

USING VISUALS TO EXPLAIN PROCESSES AND SHOW RELATIONSHIPS

You may find after you have explained a relationship verbally that you would like to show your reader the relationship visually. The relation may take the form of one of the flowcharts described below, or it may be a less formal drawing. The graphics features of your software give you unlimited options. The only caution we offer is to focus on getting the text in place before you start creating the visual. Often the visual will take more time to create than you have allotted for the project. On the other hand, occasions may arise in which, if you "see" the relationship, you can explain it better. We've emphasized throughout this book that your writing must be easy to understand. The same holds true for flowcharts: Draw them clearly, for they have a story to tell.

Figure 6.2 shows an example of text and a flowchart that work together to provide the reader with two representations of the same information. The title of the article, "The Basics of Java," leads the reader to expect an overview of how Java works. Skimming the three-page article,

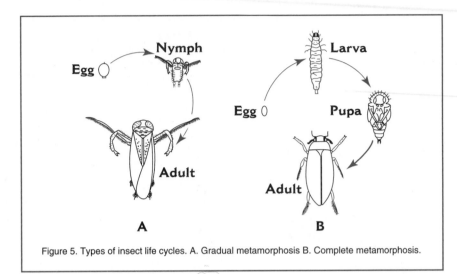

Figure 5. Types of insect life cycles. A. Gradual metamorphosis B. Complete metamorphosis.

Figure 7.10 Circular pictorial flowcharts are appropriate to illustrate cyclical processes. *Source:* Slack, Keith V. "Stream Biology." *Biota and Biological Principles of the Aquatic Environment.* Ed. Phillip E. Greeson. Alexandria, VA: US Geological Survey, 1982. A13.

the reader may first review the flowchart and then look for the text that provides an explanation, or the reader may review and understand the flowchart to get all the information he or she needs for now.

When you must describe a process, flowcharts can help readers visualize steps and activities that might otherwise take paragraphs of prose to explain and still be difficult to comprehend. Flowcharts may be prepared in different ways, ranging from simple block diagrams to pictorial flowcharts to specialized schematic diagrams. They may be single-level or multilevel. Software is available especially for drawing flowcharts, or you can use the draw feature of any of the software office suites to create a simple flowchart.

Most flowcharts are designed to be read from left to right, and, if more space is needed, from first row to second row to third. A flowchart that illustrates a cyclical process might be best arranged as a circle, designed to be read clockwise. The circular flowchart in Figure 7.10 compares the gradual and complete metamorphic life cycles of insects.

BLOCK DIAGRAMS

The block diagram is the simplest of flowcharts. Simple block diagrams and their modifications are easy to draw, easy to read, and easy to understand. As shown in Figure 7.11, a block diagram represents the main stages of a process by means of labeled blocks connected by arrows. The arrows indicate the direction of the activity flow. Almost any simple geometric shape can be used as long as the shape is consistent.

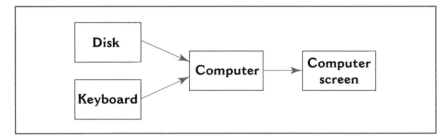

Figure 7.11 Block diagrams, the simplest of flowcharts, indicate the major steps of processes. The arrows represent the direction of activity in the process.

DECISION TREES

A decision tree is sometimes called a yes-no chart or an algorithmic chart. Figure 7.12 shows a decision tree that uses the block and arrow-line features of block diagrams to assist readers in making decisions at specific points during a procedure.

Specialized shapes are used in certain kinds of flowcharts to indicate specific kinds of actions, such as the standard computer template symbols

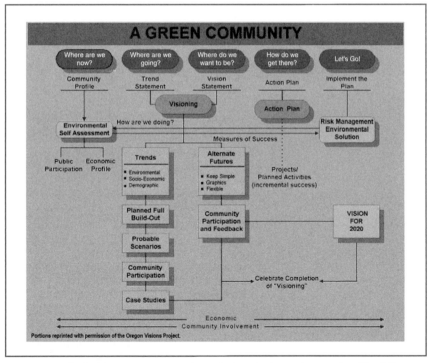

Figure 7.12 The decision tree maps out the activities of a Green Community. The different shapes and lines and the use of color on the Web site provide an overview of the activities and the relation of each to the other.
Source: US Environmental Protection Agency. Green Communities. 26 May 1998. 5 Aug. 1999 ⟨http://www.epa.gov/region3/greenkit/flow_chart.htm⟩.

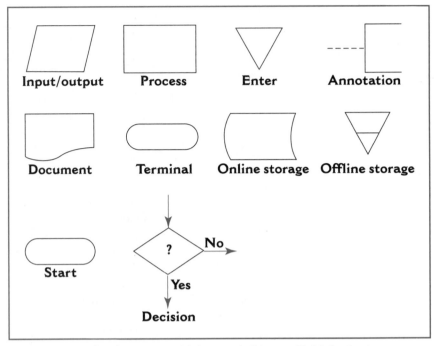

Figure 7.13 Some flowcharts use special shapes to indicate specific kinds of action. Illustrated here are several symbols used in computer documentation.

for computer documentation in Figure 7.13. Remember, though, the same symbol must be used consistently from one diagram to another. If *start* and *end* of a procedure are represented by ovals in one diagram, they should be ovals in the next. The shapes are part of the template found in software for creating flowcharts.

Constructing a Block Diagram or Decision Tree

You should know how to make block diagrams and decision trees because they are relatively easy to make and to read. Here is the way to make them using the graphics feature of a software package:

1. Draw geometric figures to represent stages in the process. Make each one large enough to contain the name of the stage it represents or other relevant information.

2. Label each geometric figure with the name of the stage it represents. The labels may be centered in the geometric figure (as in Figures 7.11 and 7.12) or aligned flush left.

3. Connect the geometric figures by using the line feature provided in the software. Add arrows as needed on the ends to indicate the direction of the activity flow.

4. If desired, put a border around the flowchart and use a caption.

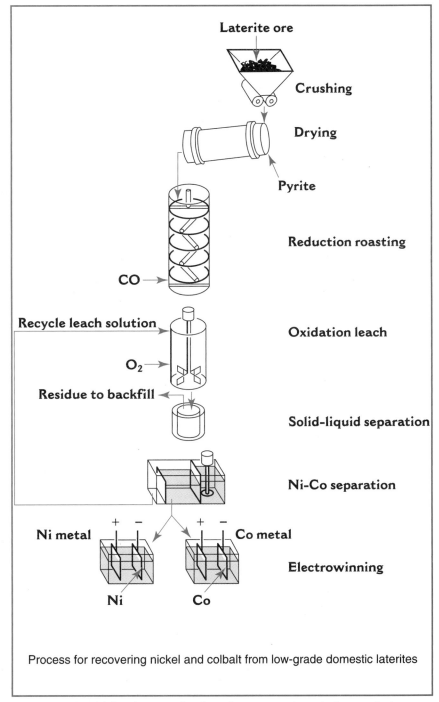

Laterite ore

Crushing

Drying

Pyrite

Reduction roasting

CO →

Recycle leach solution

Oxidation leach

O₂ →

Residue to backfill ←

Solid-liquid separation

Ni-Co separation

Ni metal   + −   + −   Co metal

Electrowinning

Ni   Co

Process for recovering nickel and colbalt from low-grade domestic laterites

Figure 7.14 Pictorial flowcharts use drawings of components instead of geometric shapes or schematic symbols.
Source: Daellenback, C. B. "Nickel-Laterite Pilot Plant Testing." *Bureau of Mines Research, 1981* Washington: US Dept. of the Interior, 1981. 14.

PICTORIAL FLOWCHARTS

Some flowcharts use pictorials or schematic symbols to indicate activity at specific points in the process. Instead of labeled blocks, you may use drawings of components. Pictorial flowcharts, such as that illustrated in Figure 7.14, are interesting ways to provide concrete images as well as a broad visual overview of a process. Imagine how many words and sentences it would take to describe these processes without using visuals such as these.

MAPS

Maps provide helpful visuals for readers concerned with associating data with particular locations or regions. For example, the map of the United States in Figure 7.15 (color insert after page 38) clearly identifies the water conditions for regions of the country and the map in Figure 7.16 shows

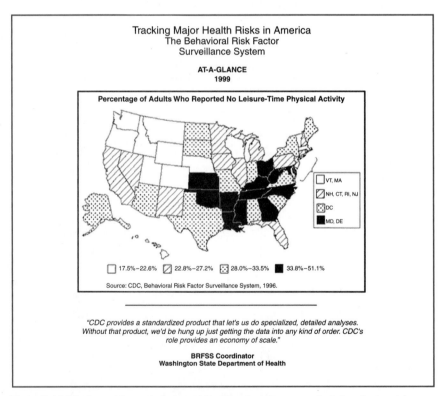

Figure 7.16 The legend beneath the map identifies the percentage of adults who participate in a physical activity for leisure. The reader not only sees which states have the highest percentage of adults not participating, but the reader can make observations about the location. For example: What region(s) of the country have the least active adults? What factors might influence this inactivity?
Source: Centers for Disease Control and Prevention. Behavioral Risk Factor Surveillance System. 1996. 11 May 1999 ⟨http://www.cdc.gov/nccdphp/brfss/⟩.

the percentage of adults across the United States who do not participate in physical activity for leisure. Maps such as these can be downloaded from the Web and incorporated into a document.

USING VISUALS TO EXPLAIN TRENDS AND RELATIONSHIPS

We frequently rely on numerical data and statistical information in our problem solving and decision making. Consequently, tables, charts, and graphs showing such data and information are primary means of analyzing, interpreting, and presenting data. Each of the following sections begins with a model for the visual type. Keep in mind that models provide guidelines, but you must adjust the visual to meet the needs of the reader and the purpose of the document.

Graphics software allows you to change the features of the graphic easily. You can view the data as a bar graph, a line graph, a pie chart, or versions of these before deciding which to use in your document. If you follow these general guidelines and work through the options available on the software you are using, you should create an effective visual.

1. Enter the data carefully, including the data labels, in the order you want the information to appear. That is, if you want to show changes over several years, you must enter the years consecutively with the corresponding data. Once you have the data entered, you can view and modify the graph without having to adjust the data.

2. View the data in several forms (for example, as a bar graph and a line graph) and in horizontal and vertical orientation to see which is the best representation for the data. Three-dimensional graphs are unsuitable for most information. The extra lines required to give the appearance of three dimensions interfere with the data.

   Most software defaults to three-dimensional graphs, and many graphics packages create three-dimensional charts; change the default. Figure 7.17 shows an example of a three-dimensional graph changed to two-dimensions. Which do you think is easier to read?

3. The software adjusts the scale automatically. In most cases, you will not have to change the scale, but you can, if necessary. Simply find the menu item for the adjustment.

4. Shade the bars or use color to better display the data. If you have access to a color printer, if the information you are presenting will work best in color, and if color visuals will fit with the overall design of the document, use color. Chapter 5 provides some guidelines for coordinating colors. We have selected several examples that use color effectively to display the information (see Figures 7.1, 7.15, and 7.25 [color insert after page 38]). If you are using black-and-white imagery, select shades and patterns that will effectively set off the data.

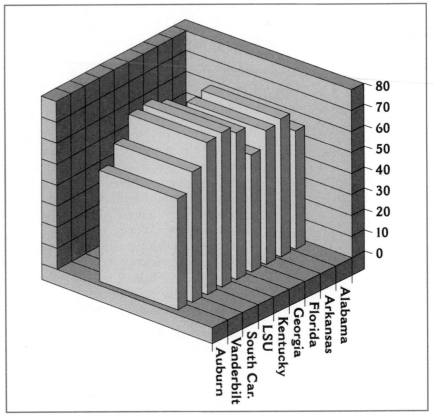

Figure 7.17 Compare the data shown in the bar graphs. Most people find it easier to read the two-dimensional graph rather than the three-dimensional graph.

5. Label each bar, line, or segment of the pie (what it represents) and each scale (quantities and units of measure). Again, if you entered the data correctly, the software will automatically place the information on the graph if you select the option to display the labels. Include a legend if necessary (for example, Figures 7.15, 7.16, and 7.26).

6. Select a border that will help set off the visual from the text. Graphics software provides several options, including color. Our advice is to consider your audience and the purpose of the document but be conservative. You don't want to detract from the information or interfere with the reading.

7. Use a caption to identify the information in the visual.

TABLES

Tables are word savers. They present simply and clearly large blocks of information without all the connecting devices needed in prose. They pro-

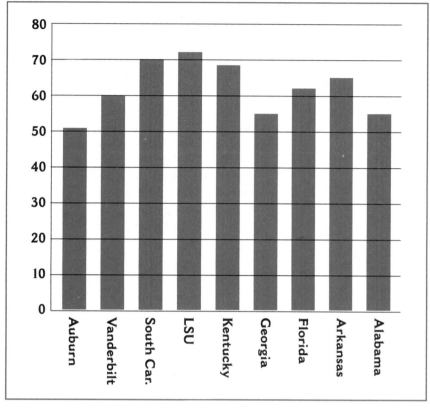

Figure 7.17 (continued)

vide a lot of visibility to the main points presented, such as in Figure 7.18, which reports data on five crops. The column headings at the top of the table (Crop, District 1, District 2) project down the table. Only the captions in the first column project across the table.

Tables are sometimes informal listings incorporated into the regular flow of the text, especially when the tabulation is simple and consists of only one or two columns. As such, they are part of the information within a paragraph—and generally part of the sentence structure—and are not set apart or identified by a number, a title, or a lined boundary. An informal table, for instance, might be presented as shown in Figure 5.1 (in the right column, the four years are parallel with Recreation-visitor-days in the left column). More complicated tables are often set apart from the text, either through the use of a lined border or by being placed on a separate page. When separated from the normal flow of the text, tables are usually given titles. If more than three or four tables are used in a report, they are usually numbered in the order of their appearance. Tables handled in this manner are regarded as formal tables.

Tables have two primary uses:

1. Report totals for comparative purposes (as in Figures 7.18, 7.19, and 7.20)

2. Serve as a ready reference, such as a timetable or schedule, or as instructions (as in Figure 7.21), and so on

The table feature of your word-processing software makes creating tables easy. (The table feature is so easy that you can use the table structure to control the blocks of text and visuals on a page without showing the table lines. Tables also are used to contain and control information on a Web page.) Figure 7.22 illustrates how a table may be used to organize textual information—in this case, comparing the features of three revenue crop insurance plans.

The following general rules will help you set up tables properly:

• Whenever possible, orient the table so that it appears on the page in normal fashion, not turned sideways forcing the reader to rotate the page to read it. Center it between the left and right margins. White space around the table will help set off the table for easier reading.

• Adjust each column or row as needed. The width of the row or column should be the same for like information. For example, in Figures 7.19 and 7.20 most of the data columns have the same width, but the first column is wider.

• Label each column and row to identify the data. If a column shows amounts, state the units in which the amounts are given, using standard symbols and abbreviations to save space. Center a column heading above the column.

• If columns are long, double-space after every fifth entry (Figure 7.19) or, as in Figure 7.20, highlight every other row.

TABLE 1. DISTRICT CROP IRRIGATION REQUIREMENTS 10-YEAR AVERAGE		
Crop	District 1	District 2
Corn, grain	69	57
Corn, silage	13	12
Grain Sorghum	11	18
Alfalfa	5	7
Winter Wheat	2	6
Total	100	100

Figure 7.18 Tables display information arranged in columns and rows.

Table 1.6

Percentages of adults, by amount of help received with different literacy activities and by age

Activity/ age	n	WGT N (/1,000)	Row percentages			
			A lot	Some	A little	None
Filling out forms						
16 to 24	4,571	34,873	16 (0.9)	27 (1.0)	26 (1.1)	32 (1.1)
25 to 59	17,768	116,817	9 (0.3)	16 (0.4)	21 (0.5)	54 (0.6)
60 to 69	2,265	20,164	15 (0.9)	16 (1.0)	17 (0.9)	52 (1.6)
70 to 79	1,001	13,789	17 (1.2)	16 (1.4)	18 (1.3)	49 (1.6)
80 and older	440	5,413	32 (2.9)	12 (2.1)	18 (2.1)	37 (2.7)
Reading newspapers						
16 to 24	4,569	34,867	6 (0.5)	15 (0.9)	24 (0.8)	54 (1.1)
25 to 59	17,764	116,758	5 (0.2)	9 (0.3)	16 (0.4)	70 (0.5)
60 to 69	2,266	20,167	5 (0.6)	10 (0.9)	16 (1.0)	69 (1.4)
70 to 79	1,002	13,807	7 (0.9)	11 (1.3)	14 (1.0)	68 (1.5)
80 and older	440	5,413	14 (2.1)	11 (1.9)	12 (1.5)	62 (2.9)
Reading printed information						
16 to 24	4,561	34,780	11 (0.7)	22 (1.0)	28 (0.8)	39 (1.1)
25 to 59	17,745	116,681	7 (0.3)	14 (0.4)	23 (0.4)	56 (0.5)
60 to 69	2,262	20,155	9 (0.8)	15 (1.0)	21 (1.2)	55 (1.5)
70 to 79	1,000	13,785	13 (1.2)	13 (1.3)	19 (1.7)	55 (2.0)
80 and older	440	5,413	25 (2.3)	15 (2.3)	16 (2.1)	45 (3.0)
Writing letters						
16 to 24	4,560	34,821	4 (0.4)	8 (0.6)	14 (0.7)	73 (0.9)
25 to 59	17,744	116,683	4 (0.2)	7 (0.2)	11 (0.4)	77 (0.4)
60 to 69	2,262	20,132	6 (0.5)	6 (0.7)	9 (0.8)	79 (1.2)
70 to 79	999	13,756	7 (0.8)	7 (1.1)	7 (1.0)	79 (1.7)
80 and older	438	5,384	18 (2.1)	8 (1.9)	4 (0.9)	70 (2.8)
Using arithmetic						
16 to 24	4,570	34,856	5 (0.4)	9 (0.6)	14 (0.7)	73 (1.0)
25 to 59	17,765	116,796	4 (0.2)	6 (0.2)	8 (0.3)	83 (0.3)
60 to 69	2,266	20,167	5 (0.6)	6 (0.6)	7 (0.7)	82 (1.0)
70 to 79	1,002	13,807	8 (0.8)	7 (1.1)	6 (0.7)	78 (1.5)
80 and older	439	5,388	17 (2.1)	8 (1.3)	7 (1.1)	68 (1.9)

n = sample size; WGT N = population size estimate / 1,000. The sample sizes for subpopulations may not add up to the total sample sizes, due to missing data. Numbers in parentheses are standard errors. The true population values can be said to be within 2 standard errors of the sample estimates with 95% certainty.

Source: U.S. Department of Education, National Center for Education Statistics, National Adult Literacy Survey, 1992.

Figure 7.19 The reader can compare the literacy activities within each age group or across age groups using the information in this table. The tabular format, the white space between columns, the headings, and the explanation below the table contribute to the effectiveness of this table.

Source: Brown, Helen, Robert Prisuta, Bella Jacobs, and Anne Campbell. *Literacy of Older Adults in America: Results from the National Adult Literacy Survey* NCES97-576. Washington: US Dept. of Education. National Center for Education Statistics, 1996. 27.

NEISS Data Highlights — Calendar Year 1996 cont.

Product Groupings	Estimated Number of Cases*	CV*	Number of Cases*	Estimated Number of Product-Related Injuries* per 100,000 Population in the United States and Territories that were treated in Hospital Emergency Departments									
				Age						Sex		Disposition	
				All Ages	00-04	05-14	15-24	25-64	65+	Male	Female	Treated & Rel.	Hosp. & DOA
Heating, Cooling, Ventilation Equipment													
Air Conditioners	12,459	.11	301	4.7	2.6	5.3	3.9	5.4	3.2	7.0	2.5	4.6	0.1
Chimneys, Fireplaces	20,288	.15	504	7.6	72.2	6.1	2.0	1.5	3.5	9.9	5.5	7.6	0.1
Fans (excl. Stove Exhaust Fans)	16,543	.10	371	6.2	12.7	6.1	6.8	5.2	6.3	7.4	5.2	6.0	0.2
Furnaces	13,042	.25	257	4.9	9.1	8.9	2.6	4.2	3.5	4.4	5.4	4.6	0.3
Heating & Plumbing Pipes	38,312	.08	902	14.4	21.5	25.2	12.0	12.9	7.0	20.2	8.9	14.1	0.3
Heating Stoves, Space Heaters	29,492	.12	626	11.1	54.2	14.4	7.1	5.6	9.6	11.4	10.9	10.5	0.6
Radiators	14,106	.16	506	5.3	36.0	9.2	1.5	1.6	2.6	6.5	4.2	5.1	0.2
Home Furnishings & Fixtures													
Bathroom Structures & Fixtures	226,145	.07	5,490	85.2	204.7	57.5	50.9	61.9	179.9	79.1	91.1	79.1	6.0
Beds, Mattresses, Pillows	416,985	.07	10,675	157.2	667.6	198.8	79.5	48.6	343.1	153.1	161.1	144.4	12.6
Carpets, Rugs	123,775	.10	3,351	46.7	117.0	31.5	21.5	26.1	134.1	32.9	59.9	41.9	4.6
Chairs, Sofas, Sofa Beds	395,409	.07	9,754	149.1	634.0	150.5	72.2	73.0	262.3	132.7	164.7	139.4	9.4
Desks, Cabinets, Shelves, Racks	220,947	.07	5,510	83.3	302.6	115.1	55.9	50.7	84.0	83.1	83.4	81.7	1.5
Electric Fixtures, Lamps, Equipment	52,051	.07	1,302	19.6	44.5	26.8	20.3	14.8	16.3	23.0	16.4	18.9	0.7
Ladders, Stools	165,868	.07	3,773	62.5	30.3	20.3	27.5	79.4	97.6	92.2	34.0	56.9	5.5
Mirrors, Mirror Glass	22,135	.09	593	8.3	16.6	10.8	18.7	5.4	1.6	8.5	8.1	8.2	0.1
Misc. Household Covers, Fabrics	17,514	.09	417	6.6	6.0	3.0	5.8	5.7	15.5	3.9	9.2	6.1	0.5
Other Misc. Furniture & Accessories	60,578	.10	1,467	22.8	30.5	9.8	26.4	25.5	18.7	23.0	22.7	22.5	0.3
Tables, not elsewhere classified	308,793	.07	7,882	116.4	753.8	129.9	59.6	42.6	98.4	129.6	103.7	113.4	2.8
Home Structures & Construction Materials													
Cabinet/Door Hardware	19,763	.09	490	7.4	27.0	11.7	6.7	3.8	7.0	8.4	6.5	7.2	0.2
Fences	114,055	.06	2,778	43.0	45.9	106.2	59.1	27.1	16.8	65.0	21.9	41.8	1.1
Glass Doors, Windows, Panels	180,754	.07	4,412	68.1	99.1	97.0	131.4	48.4	30.0	83.8	53.1	65.8	2.3
Handrails, Railings, Banisters	39,299	.10	1,079	14.8	34.7	27.1	13.4	8.5	16.5	17.0	12.7	14.4	0.4
Non-glass Doors, Panels	334,522	.07	8,895	126.1	392.9	198.6	135.3	72.6	98.7	125.1	127.0	123.7	2.3
Outside Attached Structures & Materials	23,353	.10	488	8.8	5.6	7.0	8.6	10.3	6.8	14.8	3.1	8.2	0.6
Stairs, Ramps, Landings, Floors	1,972,553	.09	48,259	743.6	1,425.8	556.4	586.9	504.0	1,707.2	563.5	916.0	669.6	73.3
Window, Door Sills, Frames	53,101	.08	1,201	20.0	65.4	25.3	15.3	12.4	24.2	20.1	19.9	19.5	0.5
Miscellaneous Products													
Dollies, Carts	43,636	.08	1,100	16.4	114.7	14.1	5.6	7.4	11.4	17.9	15.1	16.0	0.4
Elevators, Other Lifts	15,261	.11	491	5.8	8.6	3.9	3.8	4.1	14.9	4.4	7.0	5.4	0.3
Gasoline, Diesel Fuels	15,634	.12	301	5.9	14.7	6.6	8.9	4.5	2.6	10.3	1.7	5.2	0.7

Source: National Electronic Injury Surveillance System (NEISS), U.S. Consumer Product Safety Commission

* **Estimated Number of Cases:** Since NEISS is a probability sample, each injury case has a statistical weight. National estimates of product-related injury incidents are derived by summing the statistical weights for the appropriate injury cases.

* **CV (Coefficient of Variation):** The CV, the standard error of the estimate divided by the estimate, is a measure of sampling variability (errors that occur by chance because observations are made only on a population sample).

* **Number of Cases:** This is the actual number of injury cases collected from the hospitals sampled. Since injury cases have different statistical weights, these "raw" numbers should not be used for comparative purposes.

* **Product-Related Injuries:** These are national estimates of the number of persons treated in U.S. hospital emergency departments with consumer product-related injuries during the given time period. The data system allows for reporting of up to two products for each person's injury. Therefore, a person's injury may be counted in two product groups.

Figure 7.20 Tables organize and display numerical data in less space than a written explanation. Readers must read the explanation for each column to fully understand the data.
Source: US Consumer Product Safety Commission. "NEISS Data Highlights-Calendar Year 1996." *Consumer Product Safety Review,* Fall 1997. 12 May 1999. ⟨http://www.cpsc.gov/cpscpub/pubs/cpsr_mnws6.pdf⟩.

Oven Temperature	350°	350°	325°
Baking Time	25 min.	30 min.	40 min.
Pan to Use	round	13″ × 9″	glass

Figure 7.21 The table structure gives the cook an easy-to-read reference.

- Align the data using expressed or implied decimal points as a guide. If the table is word- or phrase-based, align entries on an imaginary left margin in each column.

- If a particular column or row lacks data, use three periods or dashes in each space lacking data.

- Use lines sparingly. Your software may use a default of lines around each cell—change this. A thicker line at the top and bottom of the table set the information off from the text. Lines separating the column and row headings may be the only other lines you need. You can easily change this. If they improve legibility, use vertical lines to separate columns. See Figures 7.19 and 7.20, for example. Compare the use of lines in the tables in Figure 7.23. Which do you find easier to use?

GRAPHS AND CHARTS

Like tables, graphs and charts show relationships, save words, have strong visual impact, and help break up what would otherwise be pages of solid text. There are several different types of graphs and charts; each is appropriate for a particular task.

Bar Graphs

Bar graphs report totals and show trends in ways that simplify comparisons.

- They report amounts that exist at any one time. Figure 7.24 shows three simple bar graphs reporting the percentages of literacy level. Because the bars report comparable information, the literacy levels and proficiencies and the scales for each bar graph are the same, the reader can also make comparisons among the bar graphs. Figure 7.25 (see color insert after page 38) compares the use of cigarettes, cigars, and smokeless tobacco in Massachusetts high school students.

- They report changes over a period of time, with the horizontal axis representing time and the vertical axis representing the amount. Figure 7.26 shows two bar graphs found on the same page of a report describing the U.S. fishing industry. Both bar graphs show changes over a 9-year span.

1998 Side by Side Coverage Comparison Chart

Feature	Crop Revenue Coverage (CRC)	Income Protection (IP)	Revenue Assurance (RA)
Unit organization	Basic and Optional Enterprise for corn and soybeans	Enterprise unit (all acreage of the insured crop in the county in which the insured has an interest).	Basic, optional, enterprise, and whole farm. Whole farm coverage includes all corn and soybean acreage in the county in which the insured has an interest.
Basis for insurance guarantee	Higher of: 1) APH yield x Base price x coverage level or 2) APH yield x Harvest price x coverage level. Insurance guarantee can increase if the Harvest Price exceeds the Base Price.	APH yield x Projected price x coverage level.	APH yield x Projected County price x coverage level.
Maximum protection unit price increase	corn $1.50 cotton $.70 soybeans $3.00 grain sorghum $1.50 wheat $2.00	Not applicable.	Not applicable.
Reference commodity price	95 or 100 percent of selected commodity contract traded on a commodity futures exchange for coarse grains and cotton. A set price for wheat.	100 percent of selected commodity contract traded on a commodity futures exchange. Grain Sorghum is 90% of the corn futures.	100 percent of the USDA posted county price (calculated by averaging the daily USDA posted county prices for the month of November for corn and October for soybeans).
Eligibility for insureds with special rating: High Risk Land and Nonstandard Classification System	High-risk land is eligible for coverage if elected by insured. NCS Eligible for coverage	High-risk land is not eligible for coverage. NCS Not eligible for coverage	High-risk land is eligible for coverage if elected by insured. NCS Not eligible for coverage
Coverage levels	50 - 75 percent in 5 percent increments.	50 - 75 percent. 30 percent CAT.	65 - 75 percent.
Hail and fire exclusion	Not available.	Not available.	Not available.
1998 Pilot scope-crops	Corn, cotton, grain sorghum, soybeans and wheats.	Corn, cotton, grain sorghum, soybeans and wheat.	Corn and soybeans in the 99 counties of Iowa.
Rating	APH base rate plus low price factor plus high price factor plus CRC factor.	New rating model incorporating yield and price variability.	New rating model incorporating yield and price variability and yield and price correlation.

Figure 7.22 Tables do not have to be columns and rows of numbers. More and more you will see tables used to condense and organize information. In this example, three types of revenue crop insurance are compared.
Source: 1998 Revenue Crop Insurance Plans: Crop Revenue Coverage, Income Protection, Revenue Assurance. Washington: US Dept. of Agriculture, Risk Management Agency, 1998. 8.

Example 1: Table with Interior Lines

	W	L	Pct	GB	L10	Str	Home	Away	Intr
New York	20	6	.769	—	z-9-1	W-5	9-1	11-5	0-0
Boston	20	9	.690	1½	1-7-3	W-1	13-4	7-5	0-0
Baltimore	16	14	.533	6	4-6	W-1	9-8	7-6	0-0
Tampa Bay	12	17	.414	9½	1-9	L-3	5-8	7-9	0-0
Toronto	12	17	.414	9½	4-6	W-2	5-8	6-10	0-0
Cleveland	17	12	.586	—	z-5-5	W-3	9-7	8-5	0-0
Kansas City	12	18	.400	5½	3-7	L-3	4-11	8-7	0-0
Minnesota	12	18	.400	5½	4-6	L-1	4-10	8-8	0-0
Chicago	10	17	.370	6	z-4-6	L-3	5-6	5-11	0-0
Detroit	7	20	.269	9	3-7	L-2	4-7	3-13	0-0

Example 2: Table without Interior Lines

	W	L	Pct	GB	L10	Str	Home	Away	Intr
New York	20	6	.769	—	z-9-1	W-5	9-1	11-5	0-0
Boston	20	9	.690	1½	1-7-3	W-1	13-4	7-5	0-0
Baltimore	16	14	.533	6	4-6	W-1	9-8	7-6	0-0
Tampa Bay	12	17	.414	9½	1-9	L-3	5-8	7-9	0-0
Toronto	12	17	.414	9½	4-6	W-2	5-8	6-10	0-0
Cleveland	17	12	.586	—	z-5-5	W-3	9-7	8-5	0-0
Kansas City	12	18	.400	5½	3-7	L-3	4-11	8-7	0-0
Minnesota	12	18	.400	5½	4-6	L-1	4-10	8-8	0-0
Chicago	10	17	.370	6	z-4-6	L-3	5-6	5-11	0-0
Detroit	7	20	.269	9	3-7	L-2	4-7	3-13	0-0

Figure 7.23 The baseball box scores are easier to read when there are fewer lines and the column widths are adjusted to fit the information. Too many lines give the table a dense, cluttered look. White space gained with the removal of lines makes the table easier to read. Because every table is different, you will have to decide which lines are needed and which are not. Begin with three lines—a top and bottom line to frame the table and a line to separate column labels from the data. Consider carefully each line you add after those.

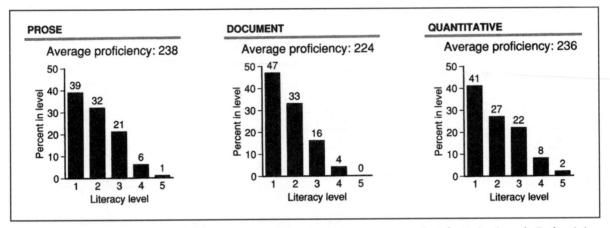

Figure 7.24 The three bar graphs have identical format so that the reader can compare the information in each. Each axis is labeled; the scale is proportional; the title and subtitle clearly identify the data.
Source: Brown, Helen, Robert Prisuta, Bella Jacobs, and Anne Campbell. *Literacy of Older Adults in America: Results from the National Adult Literacy Survey* NCES97-576. Washington: US Dept. of Education. National Center for Education Statistics, 1996. 17.

- They can report more extensive information by subdividing each bar into increments. The segmented bars in the bottom graph in Figure 7.26 represent the number of fish-processing plants. Each bar is divided to indicate the number of plants entering, exiting, or remaining in the industry. The legend at the top of the chart identifies each pattern.

Many readers find bar graphs easier to understand than line graphs. Each bar represents a quantity; the height or length of the bar indicates the amount of the quantity. It makes little difference whether the bars run horizontally or vertically, but horizontal bar graphs are often used to report quantities of time, length, and distance; vertical bar graphs report heights, depths, and so on.

Divided- or Segmented-Bar Graph

Consisting of a bar divided into segments, a divided- or segmented-bar graph (Figure 7.27) effectively shows and compares percentages. The entire field of the bar represents 100 percent; each segment represents a portion of the 100 percent. The order of the segments should be the same in all bars. If a legend or key is used, its segments should be arranged like those in the bar. The bar can be presented vertically or horizontally.

The attributes of a bar graph and a divided- or segmented-bar graph can be combined, as shown in Figure 7.26. With complete bars representing the total data, the subdivision within each bar shows the distribution of the amounts represented by the whole bar (Figure 7.27).

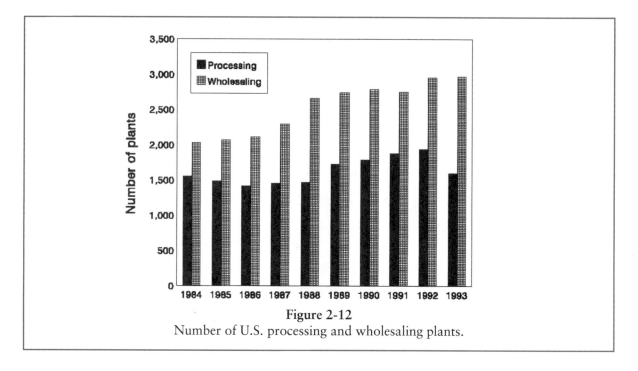

Figure 2-12
Number of U.S. processing and wholesaling plants.

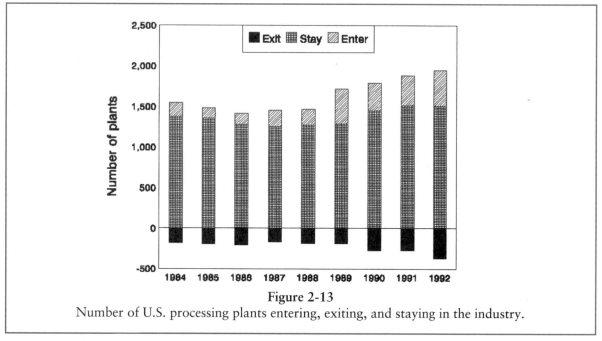

Figure 2-13
Number of U.S. processing plants entering, exiting, and staying in the industry.

Figure 7.26 Readers can see trends and make comparisons easily with well-constructed bar graphs. Each axis is labeled, a legend is given, a border surrounds the graph, and a descriptive caption identifies the topic of each bar graph.
Source: Our Living Oceans: The Economic Status of U.S. Fisheries, 1996. NOAA Fisheries. 1996. 12 May 1999 ⟨http://www.st.nmfs.gov/st1/econ/oleo/chap2.pdf⟩.

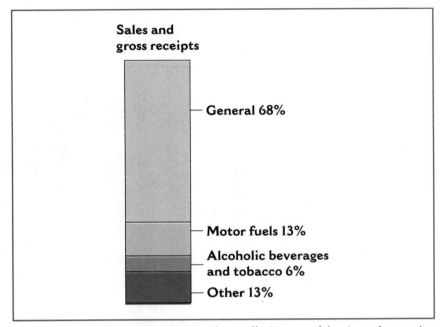

Figure 7.27 Divided- or segmented-bar graphs are effective ways of showing and comparing percentages. The field of the bar represents 100 percent; each segment represents a portion of the whole.
Source: US Bureau of Census. *Statistical Abstract of the United States: 1991.* 111th ed. Washington: GPO, 1991. 270.

Line Graphs

Like bar graphs, line graphs show comparisons between two or more quantities and trends. The curved line or lines help readers quickly grasp the results of comparative data because the fluctuation of the line or lines shows the variation in the data. Use a line graph when the emphasis is on a relationship between variables, as in Figure 7.28 or on a trend, as in Figure 7.29, rather than on an actual amount.

Keep line graphs simple, particularly if your audience is unskilled in reading them.

Pie Charts

Like a divided- or segmented-bar graph, the pie chart (Figure 7.30) compares percentages of a whole. Each segment expresses a part of 100 percent.

The practice of beginning at the 12 o'clock position and moving clockwise from the largest to the smallest slice has changed with the widespread use of graphics software. While it is possible to orient the segments to begin at 12, it is not easy in many of the packages to make the adjustments. If possible, organize the data in decreasing order so that the segments of the pie chart move from largest to smallest. However, some software packages

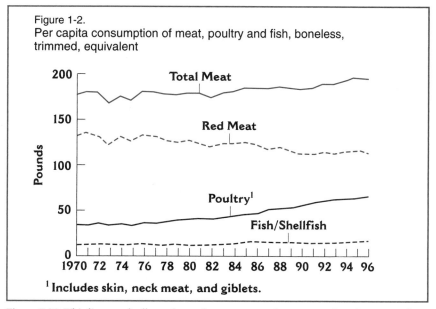

Figure 1-2.
Per capita consumption of meat, poultry and fish, boneless, trimmed, equivalent

¹ Includes skin, neck meat, and giblets.

Figure 7.28 This line graph allows the reader to compare the consumption of meat, poultry, and fish from 1910–1996. What are some conclusions the reader might make about what Americans eat based on this line graph?
Source: US Department of Agriculture. Office of Communications. *Agriculture Fact Book 1997.* 12 May 1999 〈http://www.usda.gov/news/pubs/fbook97/contents.htm〉.

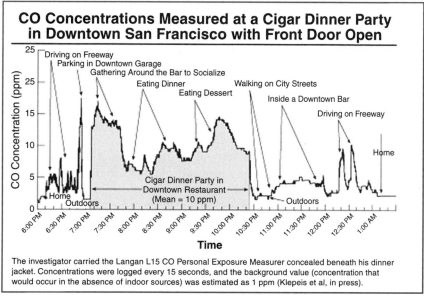

CO Concentrations Measured at a Cigar Dinner Party in Downtown San Francisco with Front Door Open

The investigator carried the Langan L15 CO Personal Exposure Measurer concealed beneath his dinner jacket. Concentrations were logged every 15 seconds, and the background value (concentration that would occur in the absence of indoor sources) was estimated as 1 ppm (Klepeis et al, in press).

Figure 7.29 This line graph plots the level of CO. The high and low levels are obvious. Note the use of shading (color on the Web site) to call attention to one part of the evening's exposure to CO.
Source: National Cancer Institute. Graphs and Charts. 10 April 1998. 12 May 1999 〈rex.nci.nih.gov/massmedia/pressreleases/cigargifs/cigargraphs.htm〉.

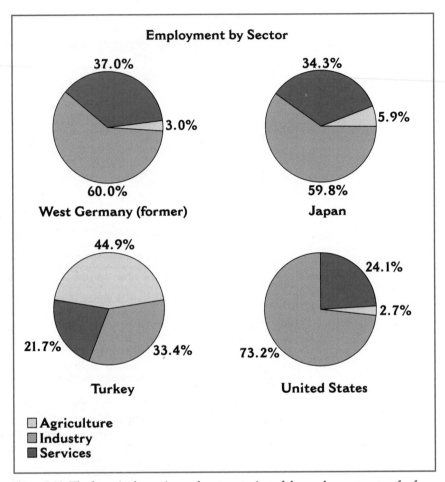

Figure 7.30 The four pie charts give readers an overview of the employment sectors for four countries.
Source: National Center for Education Statistics. *International Education Indications: A Time Series Perspective* NCES97-069. 12 May 1999 ⟨http://ncesed.gov/pubs/97059.pdf⟩.

do not follow this order. If you are comparing in side-by-side pie charts, the segments in all charts should be in the same order. Group extremely small percentages (less than 2 percent) into one segment. The grouped segment may be labeled *miscellaneous* or *other,* with the individual groups and percentages given in parentheses or in a footnote.

Study the side-by-side pie charts in Figure 7.31 and evaluate the presentation of the information. Check the order of the segments, the fill associated with each species, the use of three dimensions, and the use of the "other" category.

VISUAL COMBINATIONS

With more sophisticated software, we can create visuals that combine features described in this chapter. Robert Harris defines a *combination graph*

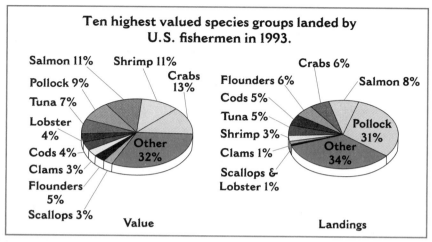

Figure 7.31 Readers can compare data in side-by-side pie charts easily if the presentation of the information is consistent. Evaluate these pie charts reporting on what U.S. fishermen caught.
Source: Our Living Oceans: The Economic Status of U.S. Fisheries, 1996. NOAA Fisheries. 1996. 12 May 1999 〈http://www.st.nmfs.gov/st1/econ/oleo/chap2.pdf〉.

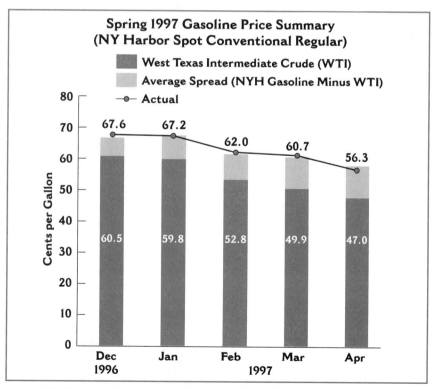

Figure 7.32 The stacked bar graph and the line graph combine to give the reader an overview of gasoline prices.
Source: US Dept. of Energy. Energy Information Administration. Office of Oil and Gas. *Petroleum 1996: Issues and Trends.* Washington: GPO, 1997. 47.

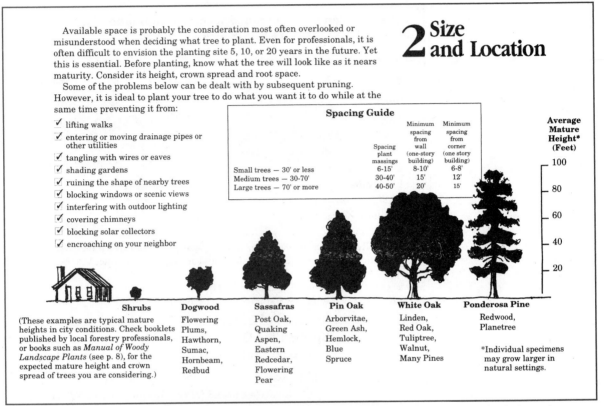

Available space is probably the consideration most often overlooked or misunderstood when deciding what tree to plant. Even for professionals, it is often difficult to envision the planting site 5, 10, or 20 years in the future. Yet this is essential. Before planting, know what the tree will look like as it nears maturity. Consider its height, crown spread and root space.

Some of the problems below can be dealt with by subsequent pruning. However, it is ideal to plant your tree to do what you want it to do while at the same time preventing it from:

✓ lifting walks
✓ entering or moving drainage pipes or other utilities
✓ tangling with wires or eaves
✓ shading gardens
✓ ruining the shape of nearby trees
✓ blocking windows or scenic views
✓ interfering with outdoor lighting
✓ covering chimneys
✓ blocking solar collectors
✓ encroaching on your neighbor

2 Size and Location

Spacing Guide

	Spacing plant massings	Minimum spacing from wall (one-story building)	Minimum spacing from corner (one story building)
Small trees — 30' or less	6-15'	8-10'	6-8'
Medium trees — 30-70'	30-40'	15'	12'
Large trees — 70' or more	40-50'	20'	15'

Average Mature Height* (Feet)

— 100
— 80
— 60
— 40
— 20

Shrubs	**Dogwood**	**Sassafras**	**Pin Oak**	**White Oak**	**Ponderosa Pine**
(These examples are typical mature heights in city conditions. Check booklets published by local forestry professionals, or books such as *Manual of Woody Landscape Plants* (see p. 8), for the expected mature height and crown spread of trees you are considering.)	Flowering Plums, Hawthorn, Sumac, Hornbeam, Redbud	Post Oak, Quaking Aspen, Eastern Redcedar, Flowering Pear	Arborvitae, Green Ash, Hemlock, Blue Spruce	Linden, Red Oak, Tuliptree, Walnut, Many Pines	Redwood, Planetree *Individual specimens may grow larger in natural settings.

Figure 7.33 Combining visuals allows the writer to show a number of relationships in one visual. In this visual, the reader gets a comparison of tree height next to a house. In addition, the table identifies the space trees will need around a house.
Source: Visual from *Tree City USA Bulletin, no. 4,* reprinted by permission of The National Arbor Day Foundation.

as a graph that "displays multiple data series using two or more different types of data graphics . . . to improve clarity and highlight relationships between the various data series" (97).[1] This definition encompasses visuals such as the combination of a bar graph and line graph in Figure 7.32 or the combination in Figure 7.33.

We expand this definition to include drawings and other visual designs, not just data graphics such as bar or line graphs. Figure 7.33 provides examples of just such combinations. The visual supports the second point, Size and Location, of three points in the article "Tree Factors to Consider." Note how the house and trees are placed across the x-axis in increasing size, similar to a bar graph. Each is labeled with examples of trees included in the height category. A scale on the right (the y-axis) gives the height the tree reaches when mature. The Spacing Guide is a 4-column table that provides suggested distances for planting the trees. The checklist at the left

[1]Robert L. Harris, *Information Graphics: A Comprehensive Illustrated Reference* (Atlanta: Management Graphics, 1996) 97.

identifies other factors to consider when planting trees. Review other features of this visual and its relation to the text surrounding it. Consider the white space, the amount of text, the placement of the visual and the text.

One final note about Figure 7.33. The visual in Figure 7.33 is found in a bulletin printed on recycled and recyclable paper using soy ink. The paper color is a light shade of grey, and the ink colors are black and green. The green is used for many of the headings, the fill in the trees, and to shade one box of text. The selection of paper and ink reinforce the interests of the type of organization, The National Arbor Day Foundation, and the topic of the document, selecting the right tree to plant.

Visuals that combine different graphic features have become more prevalent because of the ease of creating them. Create them with your reader and your purpose in mind. They can easily become overloaded with details that hide the information. Edward Tufte calls this *chartjunk*, the unnecessary, unrelated data that interfere with the purpose of the visual.[2] Review your purpose, your reader, and the information you want the reader to gather from the visual.

PLANNING AND REVISING CHECKLIST: VISUALS

PLANNING

- Can any concepts or data in your document be clarified by visuals?

- How familiar is your audience with certain kinds of visuals? Can they understand specialized schematic drawings, charts, and formulas?

- Have you planned your layout so that your visuals will be located in the best places? Will visuals that relate directly to information in the text be placed within the document? Will visuals that contain supplemental information be placed in an appendix?

- How much explanation will you provide for visuals? Will any of the visuals need legends and interpretation?

- Do you need to explain objects? Would photographs or drawings, or both, be most helpful? What kinds of photographs and drawings (for example, exploded or cutaway) best serve your and your audience's purposes?

- Do you need to explain processes and procedures? What photographs or drawings would be appropriate? Would block diagrams, pictorial flowcharts or decision trees serve your and your audience's purposes?

- Do you need to explain trends or relationships? What tables, charts, and graphs would be appropriate?

[2]Edward Tufte, *The Visual Display of Quantitative Information* (Cheshire, CT: Graphics Press, 1983).

REVISING

- Are your visuals suited to your and your audience's purposes?

- Are your visuals well placed and easy to find?

- Are your visuals legible?

- Are all variables and values specified clearly? Are all labels and captions horizontal?

- Do your visuals and written text complement each other? Have you introduced and discussed each visual? When necessary, have you helped your audience interpret your visuals with legends or commentaries?

- Have you identified the sources of your visuals?

SUGGESTIONS FOR APPLYING YOUR KNOWLEDGE

1. Visuals are used to depict concepts, objects, processes, trends, and relationships. Either as an individual or as a member of a group, find examples of each use in reports, newspapers, magazines and professional journals, textbooks, and on the World Wide Web. Examine the strategies used in each visual and determine how well the visuals serve the writer's and readers' purposes. If your instructor makes such an assignment, photocopy the examples—making enough copies for the other students in your group or in the class—and be prepared to discuss the way each visual works in its document. If appropriate, explain how you would revise a visual for more effective format and placement and increased clarity.

2. Prepare both a line graph and a bar graph to show the closing volume of shares traded on the New York Stock Exchange from September 26 through September 30 (in millions of shares):

September 26	110
September 27	110
September 28	112
September 29	165
September 30	170

3. A. Prepare a table and a bar graph to depict the following data about cigarette smokers who are at least 20 years old:
   In 1990, 34 percent had less than a high-school education; 38 percent were at least high-school graduates; 36 percent had some college education; and 28 percent were college graduates.

In 1995, 36 percent had less than a high-school education; 37 percent were at least high-school graduates; 32 percent had some college education; and 24 percent were college graduates.

In 1999, 34 percent had less than a high-school education; 33 percent were at least high-school graduates; 26 percent had some college education; and 16 percent were college graduates.

B. Write a paragraph interpreting the data presented about cigarette smokers who are at least 20 years old and their educational attainments. Incorporate the bar graph into your paragraph.

4. Either as an individual or with another student or with a group designated by your instructor, analyze the following information about applications for immigration amnesty in the United States from May 5, 1998 to April 28, 1999. The information is provided by the Immigration and Naturalization Service. Discuss the kinds of visuals that would be appropriate for displaying the information. Create the visuals.

A. The number of regular and farm applications for amnesty:

Area	Regular	Farm
Eastern (VA, WV, PA, NY, MD, DE, NJ, RI, MA, NH, VT, ME, CT, PR)	126,608	25,452

Area	Regular	Farm
Northern (WA, OR, ID, MT, ND, SD, MN, WI, CO, UT, IN, OH, AK, MI, WY, NE, IA, IL, MO, KS)	126,426	45,576
Southern (NM, TX, OK, LA, MS, AR, GA, TN, KY, FL, NC, SC, AL)	307,846	121,941
Western (CA, NV, AZ, HI)	750,204	256,379

B. Percentage of applications for amnesty by country of citizenship:

Mexico	73.3%
All other countries	13.3
El Salvador	6.5
Haiti	2.7
Guatemala	2.2
Philippines	1.0
Colombia	1.0

5. Prepare a pie chart that depicts the following data about new entrants to the U.S. labor force in 1999.

Native white males	47%
Native white females	36%
Native nonwhite males	5%
Native nonwhite females	5%
Immigrant males	4%
Immigrant females	3%

6. Locate or write a letter or a report that contains a large amount of statistical data. Construct a table that will summarize the data. Alternatively, locate or write a letter or report that explains a process or procedure. Construct a flowchart or decision tree that will aid your audience in understanding your message.

7. Visit the Web site http://spaceprojects.arc.nasa.gov/Space_Projects/pioneer/ PN10&11.html#plaque. Study the drawing placed on the Pioneer Plaque. What is the purpose of the plaque? Who is the audience? Can you decipher the message in the visual?

UNIT II

CORRESPONDENCE AND PRESENTATIONS

CHAPTER 8

PRINCIPLES OF WORKPLACE CORRESPONDENCE

Letters and memorandums (memos) travel by various routes ranging from the post office or interoffice mail to fax machines or electronic mail (e-mail). But no matter the route, surveys reveal that letters and memos are by far the most common form of written communication in the workplace. Professionals—from human resources specialists to maintenance coordinators—know that they spend much of their work day writing letters, memos, and e-mail like the ones illustrated in Figures 8.1, 8.2, and 8.3. They use these types of correspondence in many ways: to convey information, to describe procedures, to argue for change, to make and cancel appointments, to share drafts of documents, to report the results of work and research. Virtually every communication purpose is served at one time or another by letter or memo, whether hard-copy (printed on paper) messages or e-mail.

You may wonder why in an age of rapid telephone and telecommunication networks letters and memos are still so much in use. The answer is, at least, threefold:

- Organizations need records that oral communication often does not provide. For example, two people may reach an agreement orally and in a week each may have a different memory of the agreement. A letter on file prevents such misunderstandings.

- You can reach a wide audience quickly with a letter or memo. You may, for instance, wish to send a set of instructions to 20 workers, each in a different location. One memo containing the instructions copied 20 times and sent to the workers is far more efficient than 20 telephone calls. In addition, the memo serves each worker as a constant reference for the instructions.

  Also, it is a common practice in the workplace to send copies of correspondence to other people concerned with the subject matter addressed. As a writer at work, you may send copies of your correspondence to supervisors and people in other departments of your organization. For example, the research and development department of an organization may send copies of some of their correspondence to the sales and legal departments of the organization.

- Finally, sometimes, a situation is too sensitive to be handled in a phone conversation. You may be trying to satisfy an angry customer or tell someone he or she cannot have a desired job. Often such situations can be handled with less pain to all concerned in correspondence rather than a phone call.

Because you will likely have a computer connected to your workplace network and to the Internet, you will also send and receive letters and memos as e-mail (see Figure 8.3). You can send and receive e-mail to and from co-workers, consultants, suppliers, and clients around the world as easily as you can to and from co-workers just down the hall from your office.

MOUNTAIN PIONEER TECHNICAL SERVICES, INC.

605803 Twentieth Avenue South
Kellyville, CA 96022

11 July 2000

Ms. Linette Barton
242 Katie Lane
St. Louis, MO 63130

Dear Ms. Barton:

We are delighted that you have accepted our offer of employment. This letter confirms the offer
to you for the position of Program Analyst at a starting salary of $30,600.

Upon coming to work for Mountain Pioneer, you become eligible for our comprehensive benefits
package. Our total package includes life, disability, dental, and medical insurance, plus a
retirement income program that includes both a pension and savings investment program.

Your first day with us will be Monday, 24 July. Please come by to Human Resources, Room
222, at 8:30 a.m. Ask the receptionist for me. We look forward to seeing you and are confident
that you will find a great deal of challenge and opportunity with our organization.

Sincerely,

John Meldahl
Human Resources Officer

JM:evc

Figure 8.1 Sample letter.

ELITE INSURANCE

Date: 15 November 2000

To: Frank Werner-Kramer
             Claims Analyst
             Mail Stop 362

From: Nancy Ingram   *n. d.*
             Retirement Specialist
             Mail Stop 465

Subject: Loan Information Requested

You are eligible to take out a loan from your company retirement account. We offer both general loans and residential loans. A general loan does not require explanation of purpose and must be repaid within five years. A residential loan does require explanation of purpose and must be repaid within ten years. I've enclosed an application in case you wish to request a loan.

All loans are subject to the following conditions:

Loan Amounts

- Minimum loan amount is $500.
- Maximum loan amount is the lesser of $50,000 or 50% of the balance in your retirement account.

Interest Rate

- The interest rate will be set at prime rate at the time of the loan plus 1%.

Repayment of Loans

- Minimum loan payment is $25.00 per month, made through payroll deductions.
- Loans may be repaid in full without penalty at any time.

Enclosure: Loan application blank

Figure 8.2 Sample memorandum.

```
Date:      Fri, 28 March 2000 14:14.15
From:      Lee Callaway ⟨lcalla@sunstor.com⟩
To:        Building G Personnel ⟨abettel@sunstor.com⟩
           ⟨bbettle@sunstor.com⟩
           ⟨kwang@sunstor.com⟩
           ⟨lsoders@sunstor.com⟩
           ⟨ntimmon@sunstor.com⟩
Cc:        ⟨dmatthew@sunstor.com⟩
Subject:   Possible Defect in Storage Units, Units 115-119

There is a possible defect in the panels of the storage units in
which the files and sales displays for Building G are located.
The defect might allow water damage during or after hard rains.

Would you please stop by my office Monday through Friday 9:00
a.m. to 5:00 p.m., at your earliest convenience so that we can
arrange to inspect the panels of your storage unit(s).

If it is not convenient for you to come by, please use company
mail service to send us a copy of your key and we will return it
as soon as the inspection and repair (if needed) is made.

If you should have any questions, please do not hesitate to
contact me.

Thank you,

Neil Bustamantes
Maintenance Coordinator
114 Administration Building
255-3300
```

Figure 8.3 Sample e-mail.

In planning and writing hard-copy memos and letters and e-mail, you should follow basically the same process we described in Chapter 1, The Process of Workplace Writing:

- Analyze your audience.

- Set objectives.

- Discover and gather information.

- Plan your organization.

- Plan your visuals.

- Write and revise.

As discussed in Chapter 1, you will want to be ethical in your correspondence, and occasionally, if the situation seems to call for it, you may collaborate with others in some manner. Because correspondence is usually shorter and sometimes allowably more informal than reports, you may abbreviate all the steps to some degree, but you shouldn't overlook any of them.

When people in the workplace are asked to rank the writing skills needed on the job, clarity ranks number one, followed in order by conciseness, organization, and good grammar. In this chapter we discuss ways to achieve these top-ranked skills in letters and memos, discuss the importance of courtesy in workplace correspondence, and give you some basic format principles. In Chapter 9 we present some situations that generate basic workplace correspondence, show you the resulting correspondence, and analyze it for you. In Chapter 10 we deal with employment letters and resumes, subjects close to the hearts of most college students. Chapter 11 includes a section on portfolios. In portfolios, you collect the best examples of your work (including workplace writing samples) to show to future employers or to your current employer at your job performance review.

CLARITY AND CONCISENESS

In part, you achieve clarity and conciseness by attention to style. As we discussed in Chapter 4, Style and Tone, you can make your writing more readable by following four basic principles:

- Keep sentences a reasonable length.

- Use familiar words when possible.

- Eliminate unneeded words.

- Put action in your sentences.

Putting action in your sentences sometimes calls for you to use *I* or *we* in your sentences. Generally speaking, you should use *we* when you are speaking for your organization and *I* when you are speaking for yourself as a representative of the organization. For example, "Because company policy does not allow payment for transfers, we cannot refund your costs in this matter." But, "I have looked over your proposal carefully, and my reaction to it is favorable."

Beyond applying these stylistic principles, you can achieve clarity and conciseness by careful selection of content. In general, a letter or memo should have only one guiding purpose. You should choose your content to satisfy that purpose, whether it is to obtain a job interview, sell a product, recommend a change in a procedure, or ask for a raise. Content that doesn't help you meet that purpose should generally be left out. (An exception to this principle is the kind of social content that workplace friends may allow into their correspondence to one another.) Furthermore, don't reiterate your point endlessly. If you tell someone you can't keep an appointment because you'll be in Atlanta, don't also explain that you can't keep the appointment because you have a "conflicting appointment." Choose one of the two.

The more you know about your audience, the clearer you are likely to be. Many letters and memos are unclear because the writers assume that information known to them is also known to their readers. Think carefully, of course, about your readers' knowledge of the language and concepts you are using. When need be, define and explain professional terminology. But think also about what has gone on before in relation to the issue being discussed. For instance, if there have been earlier meetings and correspondence about the issue, does your reader have enough knowledge about them? If not, you will probably have to provide a context for your letter or memo by bringing your reader up to date. How much information you provide is a judgment call. Provide enough so that your reader can understand the letter or memo you are writing, but don't lovingly rehash irrelevant history.

Keep in mind that you may have more than one reader. You may be writing to a colleague and sending a copy of the memo to your supervisor. It may be that your supervisor doesn't know the past history of the project as well as you and your colleague do. When such is the case, you'll be wise to supply the information that your boss needs.

Finally, although you may regard e-mail letters and memos as informal notes, you should minimize the use of such abbreviations as IMHO (in my humble opinion), IOW (in other words), and TIA (thanks in advance) and of *emoticons*, such as smileys :-) and frowns (:-(. These abbreviations and emoticons are acceptable in rapid responses to personal messages and to lighten the tone of personal messages, but they can be stylistic blunders when discussing substantive workplace matters that are more public and professional than private. Remember to use style appropriate to the occasion.

ORGANIZATION

Throughout this book we suggest many organizational patterns for such elements of correspondence as argument, process descriptions, and instructions. Mastering these patterns and applying them when appropriate will enhance your correspondence greatly. Often, as we demonstrate in Chapter 9, a careful analysis of purpose, audience, and situation will suggest a suitable organization. Beyond such particular patterns and the value of analysis, several general principles of organization for letters and memos should prove helpful to you.

Introduce Your Letters, Memos, and E-mail   Begin by making your purpose clear and by providing any information your reader needs to understand what comes later. Sometimes making purpose and context clear may call for a full introduction, something like this one:

> In this memo I provide the credit analysis of the H. C. Hunt Company that you requested on 6 May. The analysis covers three areas: customer evaluation, financial situation, and credit structure and pricing.

With such an introduction the reader is reminded of the occasion for the memo and is given the outline that the memo will follow. Both reader and writer are off to a good start.

In other situations—for example, an e-mail note written following a phone conversation—the writer can plunge more swiftly into the body of the letter, something like this:

> Thanks for the good chat about the problems with the visuals. Below is a list of the faulty visuals that need replacing.

The appropriate beginning is a matter of judgment. The major principle you should follow is that the reader (and any secondary readers) should be left in no doubt about the purpose of the correspondence and the context from which the correspondence comes.

Organize Your Letters, Memos, and E-mail for Your Readers

Think about your reader's interests and organize to satisfy those interests. For example, suppose you are arguing in a letter for a new procedure to be adopted. You could argue pro and con, perhaps, explaining the advantages and disadvantages to the procedure. That's a better organization than none at all, but it is probably not the best plan. Perhaps a few moments of audience analysis might tell you that your reader is primarily interested in the cost, convenience, and timely introduction of the new procedure. If such is the case, organize your material into three sections that deal with those interests.

Display Your Organization for the Reader

In part, you can reveal your communication's organization in your introduction. You could, for instance, in your letter introducing the new procedure, forecast your organization for your reader by saying that the three reasons for adopting the new procedure are "low cost, greater convenience, and a short transition time."

In a letter, memo, or e-mail, you can also display your organization by using headings. In the example we're using, your headings could be Cost, Convenience, and Transition Time.

GRAMMAR

Grammar, as business people use the term, is a catchall for several different aspects of writing, including correct spelling, accurate punctuation, and clear sentence structure. Business people want good grammar for at least two reasons. First, faulty grammar may produce writing so unclear that the purpose and content of the correspondence remain indecipherable. At the very least, faulty grammar can delay the readers' understanding, thus annoying the readers by making them work harder than they should have to.

Second, even when clarity is not the issue, professionalism is. A difference exists between school and the workplace in this regard; school is more forgiving to those learning skills. An instructor may pass a letter that is good except for some sloppy punctuation. In business, the letter may be considered totally unsatisfactory. It may lose you the job you seek or the order you want, or it may convince someone that you are irresponsible. For example, more than one-third of the executives surveyed in America's largest companies said they would "'categorically' reject a job applicant whose resume contained a typographical error."[1] Letters, memos, and e-mail that fail to accomplish your goals are unsuccessful, no matter how close they come.

To be an effective workplace correspondent you must be proficient in grammar. Use Chapter 4, Style and Tone, and Unit V, Writer's Guide, to help you. If they are not enough, ask your instructor to recommend a more complete handbook of grammar to you. Ask your instructor to explain concepts you don't understand. If you master grammar to the point where you can write without embarrassing errors, you will avoid the risk of seriously limiting your potential in any job you take that requires you to write letters and memos.

COURTESY

Simple courtesy goes a long way in the workplace. Courtesy helps to keep people working together toward a common goal. If you follow the advice we give you about tone in Chapter 4, Style and Tone, you will be well on your way to a courteous tone in your correspondence. Be sensitive to people's feelings. Memos to peers that sound like commands rather than recommendations will be resented. Brusquely stated requests will often fail to achieve the desired results. Refusing a request without adequate explanation is a discourteous act. Be positive in your statements, not negative. Do not say, "Your plan for reorganization will never work." Rather, say, "Here is an alternative organizational plan that seems promising for our purpose." Courtesy should work in all directions—peer to peer, supervisor to subordinate and vice versa, and organization to client and the reverse.

As important as courtesy is, sometimes it has limits. Usually, the implications, the *so-whats*, of your data can be stated courteously. However, when the stakes are high, do not allow courtesy to prevent you from stating the *so-whats* clearly and openly, sometimes even bluntly. As one student of the *Challenger* space shuttle disaster put it, "Politeness can be fatal when it is used for the wrong purposes."[2]

In the *Challenger* accident, a faulty rocket seal rendered inoperative by cold weather caused the fatal explosion. Months before the catastrophe, an engineer working for the rocket's manufacturer, Morton Thiokol, Inc. (MTI), wrote to NASA providing data about the seal's faulty performance in cold weather. He concluded as follows: "The conclusion is that

---

[1]Annetta Miller, "Spelling Bees for Business," *Newsweek*, 4 July 1988: 29.
[2]Patrick Moore, "When Politeness Is Fatal," *Journal of Business and Technical Communication* 6 (1992): 288.

the secondary sealing capability in the SRM field joint cannot be guaranteed."[3] He had expressed a *so-what*, but he had expressed it politely and somewhat vaguely. The engineers at NASA who received the letter later testified that they did not understand the significance of the stated conclusion. They may have understood it better if the MTI engineer had stated it more bluntly, something like this: "Because the rubber o-rings lose their resiliency in cool weather, the secondary sealing of the SRM joint is likely to fail in cold weather. Data from our tests and the history of o-ring damage in previous cool-weather launches clearly support this conclusion. Such a failure would likely cause a catastrophic explosion with the resultant destruction of the space shuttle." Perhaps, just perhaps, such a direct statement would have changed the decision to launch the next morning, when the ambient temperature was 30 degrees Fahrenheit, and might have prevented the tragic explosion that killed seven people and nearly destroyed a multibillion-dollar program.

As we tell you often, express *so-whats* clearly. Although courtesy and politeness are important in day-to-day correspondence, when the situation is urgent, the need to be absolutely clear may take precedence.

Another matter of courtesy relates to the handling of both hard-copy letters and memos and e-mail. Frequently, messages that announce meetings and programs, changes in policy, and requests for information are considered public and are forwarded to interested readers. In certain instances, however, you must decide whether or not correspondence you receive is personal and private and should not be shared with others, either by making photocopies and giving them to others or by forwarding an e-mail message electronically to others.

LETTER FORMATS

Workplace letters must be neat and follow consistent formats. They must be typed or printed. Sloppiness and inconsistency indicates carelessness and lack of professionalism on your part. In Figures 8.4 to 8.7, we have demonstrated acceptable formats and indicated the conventional spacing and punctuation. Choose a format you like and follow it. We comment in the text about a few major points concerning the letter and its parts.

STATIONERY

Go to the campus bookstore or an office supplies store and choose a good-quality white bond paper of about 20-lb weight—a paper that looks good and feels good in your hand. Don't buy cheap, lightweight paper. It's a false economy. The organization or company you work for will provide letterhead stationery. Use it when you are writing about company business.

---

[3]Dorothy A. Winsor, "The Construction of Knowledge in Organizations: Asking the Right Questions About the *Challenger*," *Journal of Business and Technical Communication* 4 (1990): 14.

1260 Hazel Avenue
Gallatin, IL 60404
April 7,2000

(2 line spaces)
Ms. Mary Bolt
Customer Service
Sunset Van Lines
2224 Wake Boulevard
Contra Costa, CA 90233
(2 line spaces)
Re: Your letter of March 29, 2000
(2 line spaces)
Dear Ms. Bolt:
(2 line spaces)

_____
_____
_____

(2 line spaces)
_____
_____
_____
_____

(2 line spaces)
_____

(2 line spaces)

Sincerely,

(4 line spaces)   *Mary H. Palmer*

Mary H. Palmer

(2 line spaces)
MHP:els
(2 line spaces)
Enclosure: Furniture inventory
(2 line spaces)
copy: United Services Automobile Association

Figure 8.4 Block-format letter.

1492 Columbus Avenue
Biloxi, MS 39530
October 4, 2000

(2 line spaces)
Mr. Richard Ferguson, Head
Public Documents
Distribution Center
Pueblo, CO 81009
(2 line spaces)
Dear Mr. Ferguson:
(2 line spaces)
Subject: Shipment of *Index of National Park System*
(2 line spaces)

_____
_____
_____

(2 line spaces)

_____
_____
_____
_____

(2 line spaces)

_____
_____

(2 line spaces)

                                    Sincerely,

(4 line spaces)   *Maria G. Cortez*

                                    (Mrs.) Maria G. Cortez

(2 line spaces)
Enclosures
(2 line spaces)
copy: Superintendent of Documents

Figure 8.5 Modified block-format letter.

E-Z Workouts

5200 Gatlin Road
Fayetteville, VA 22212

(2 line spaces)
21 February 2000
(2 line spaces)
Mr. James W. Whittaker
General Manager
Recreational Equipment, Inc.
1225-11th Avenue
Seattle, WA 98122
(2 line spaces)
Dear Mr. Whittaker:
(2 line spaces)

(2 line spaces)

(2 line spaces)

(2 line spaces)
Sincerely,

Gerard B. Hewlett   (4 line spaces)

Gerard B. Hewlett
(2 line spaces)
copy: Anne K. Chimato

Figure 8.6 Full block-format letter.

2098 Colfax Avenue
Denver, CO 80279
12 January 2000
(2 line spaces)
The Harvard Medical School
79 Garden Street
Cambridge, MA 02138
(3 line spaces)

SUBSCRIPTION RATES
(3 line spaces)

_____
_____
_____

(2 line spaces)
_____
_____

(2 line spaces)
_____
_____

(5 line spaces)

Bladon Penny, M.D.

BLADON PENNY, M.D.
(2 line spaces)
Enclosures (2)

Figure 8.7 Simplified letter.

FONTS AND PRINTERS

Choose a standard font such as Times Roman or Bookman. For workplace correspondence, don't choose a font style such as italic except for purposes of emphasis. Using an unusual font is considered unprofessional.

In addition, be sure, for important work, to use a laser or ink-jet printer that prints darkly. If your printing is unevenly shaded or unacceptably light, replace the toner or ink cartridge in the printer.

MARGINS

Letters should never look crowded or off balance on the page. Leave generous margins, at least one inch on either side and one and one-half inches on top and bottom. For a short letter, come down farther on the page so that your letter doesn't hang at the top like a balloon on a string. The center of the body of a one-page letter should be just above the center of the page.

HEADING

The heading includes your complete address but not your name. Do not abbreviate words such as *street* or *avenue*. You may abbreviate the state, using the postal service's two-letter abbreviations. (See the list of abbreviations in Figure 8.8.) The date is part of the heading. It may be written *January 18, 20xx* or *18 January 20xx*. Do not write date numbers as ordinals *(9th* or *3rd)*. Use the number by itself.

Alabama	AL	Montana	MT
Alaska	AK	Nebraska	NE
Arizona	AZ	Nevada	NV
Arkansas	AR	New Hampshire	NH
California	CA	New Jersey	NJ
Colorado	CO	New Mexico	NM
Connecticut	CT	New York	NY
Delaware	DE	North Carolina	NC
District of Columbia	DC	North Dakota	ND
Florida	FL	Ohio	OH
Georgia	GA	Oklahoma	OK
Guam	GU	Oregon	OR
Hawaii	HI	Pennsylvania	PA
Idaho	ID	Puerto Rico	PR
Illinois	IL	Rhode Island	RI
Indiana	IN	South Carolina	SC
Iowa	IA	South Dakota	SD
Kansas	KS	Tennessee	TN
Kentucky	KY	Texas	TX
Louisiana	LA	Utah	UT
Maine	ME	Vermont	VT
Maryland	MD	Virginia	VA
Massachusetts	MA	Virgin Islands	VI
Michigan	MI	Washington	WA
Minnesota	MN	West Virginia	WV
Mississippi	MS	Wisconsin	WI
Missouri	MO	Wyoming	WY

Figure 8.8 State and territory abbreviations.

INSIDE ADDRESS

Set up the inside address as you do your own address in the heading. Do, however, include your correspondent's name and any titles. The titles *Mr., Mrs.,* and *Dr.* are abbreviated. *Ms.* is the preferred form for most women in business. Most other titles are written out in full, such as *Professor* and *Sergeant.* Do not use a title after a name that has the same meaning as the title before the name. Write *Dr. Isadora Paludan* or *Isadora Paludan, M.D.,* but not *Dr. Isadora Paludan, M.D.*

REFERENCE AND SUBJECT LINES

A reference line is frequently used in workplace correspondence. Placed above or below the salutation, it is preceded by the term *Re* followed by a colon. (See Figure 8.4.) The reference line may refer to the correspondence that generated your correspondence or to a file number, for example "Claim #G4562." A reference line allows your correspondents or their secretaries or assistants to locate previous correspondence on the same subject. It also saves your readers from trite, trivial openers like, "With reference to your letter of July 7, 20xx."

A subject line identifies the subject of the letter or memo. It is preceded by the word *Subject* followed by a colon. (See Figure 8.5.) You may use both a subject line and a reference line in the same letter or memo.

SALUTATION

Most of us are still slaves to convention in the salutation and use *Dear* _____ when we are writing to someone whose name we know. Most people accept the *Dear* as a convention and don't take it seriously. Yet they would probably notice and even resent its absence. Therefore, you should probably continue to use salutations such as *Dear Dr. Coney, Dear Ms. White*, and *Dear Professor Souther.* Use a first name if you and the letter's recipient are on a first-name basis. Use a colon after the salutation.

The issue of what form of salutation to use when you don't know the name of the individual you address has been complicated by the fact that exclusively male salutations such as *Dear Sir* and *Gentlemen* are in general no longer considered appropriate. No universally accepted substitute has been found as yet. Some people have begun to address a department directly, as in *Dear Credit Department* or *Dear Consumer Complaints.* Others prefer the conversational approach of beginning with *Hello* or *Good day.* Perhaps the best approach is to use the simplified letter shown in Figure 8.7, in which no salutation is required. In routine correspondence it may matter little which of these alternatives you use, but in important correspondence do everything you reasonably can to get a name to address. Usually, a quick call to the business or department in question will get you the name.

BODY

In the letter body, single-space the paragraphs and double-space between them. In short letters of several lines, you may use double-space or space-and-a-half for everything. In the modified block format (as shown in Figure 8.5), indent the paragraphs five spaces; in the other formats, do not. Keep sentences and paragraphs short. Average 14 to 17 words a sentence and don't let paragraphs run more than six or seven lines. Generous use of white space in a letter invites readers in. Cramped, crowded spacing shuts them out.

COMPLIMENTARY CLOSE

Use a conventional close such as *Sincerely* or *Sincerely yours* for people you don't particularly know. For people with whom you have some friendship, you may close with *Warm regards, With best wishes*, and so forth. Capitalize only the first word in the close. Follow the close with a comma.

SIGNATURE BLOCK

Type your name four spaces below the complimentary close. A woman without an honorific title, such as *Colonel* or *Professor*, who prefers the title of *Miss* or *Mrs.* to *Ms.* should indicate the title preferred in parentheses to the left of her typed name. Otherwise *Ms.* will be the understood preference as *Mr.* is understood for men. A married woman should use her own first name, not her husband's. Below the typed name, put your business title if you have one. Sign your name legibly above your typed name.

SPECIAL NOTATIONS

Three special notations—identification, enclosure, and copy—are frequently made below the signature block. Their order and spacing are indicated in Figures 8.4 to 8.7.

Identification
When a typist rather than the writer prepares a letter, an identification line is used. Usually the writer's initials are uppercase letters, and the typist's are lowercase, as in

AJB: whm

AJB is the person who writes and signs the letter; *whm* identifies the person who prepared the letter for the writer's signature.

Enclosure
The enclosure line tells the reader that something is enclosed with the letter. The format of the line and the amount of information given varies.

Typical lines might be

Enclosure

Enclosures (3)

Encl.: Medical examination form

Copy Line

In most circumstances, you will use a copy line to inform your primary reader of others who have been sent copies of the letter. The notification requires a simple notation such as the following:

copy: Ms. Janet Kimberly

CONTINUATION PAGE

The format for one or more continuation pages is shown in Figure 8.9. Use plain bond paper for page two and beyond; do not use letterhead stationery. Plan your spacing so that at least two or three lines of the body are carried over to the continuation page.

ENVELOPE

The envelope format is shown in Figure 8.10. Notice that the format is in all capital letters and has no punctuation. This is the form now preferred by the postal service.

Letters sent to business people will sometimes quite legitimately be opened by their co-workers, for instance, when the person addressed is ill or on vacation. The assumption is that the letter concerns company business, and business goes on regardless of who is present to conduct it. Therefore, if you are writing a personal or confidential letter to a person at a workplace address, mark it with the words *PERSONAL* or *CONFIDENTIAL,* directly under the address on the envelope.

MEMORANDUM FORMATS

Most organizations have preprinted memo forms that differ from the forms used for letters. Generally, these forms contain the organization's name or logo, but not address, and guide words for *Date, To, From*, and *Subject*. See Figure 8.11 for an example of a typical memo layout.

Because of the preprinted formats, memos require no salutation or complimentary close. Frequently, though, people do provide job titles with their names and sign or initial next to their names on the *From* line (see Figures 8.2 and 8.11).

The body of a typed or printed memo is spaced in the same way as the body of a letter, with similar margins. As in a letter, use headings when they are appropriate. As shown in Figures 8.2 and 8.11, memos may have notations for identification, enclosures, and copies, just as letters do. A

Page 2
Ms. Janet C. Huer
5 April 2000

—————————————————————————
———————————————————————————
——————————————————————
—————————————————————————
————————————————————————
————————————————————

Sincerely,

John R. Gilmore

John R. Gilmore
DOT Technician

JRG: hrw

Figure 8.9 Continuation page.

SUNSET VAN LINES
2224 WAKE BOULEVARD
CONTRA COSTA CA 90233

MARY H. PALMER
1260 HAZEL AVENUE
GALLATIN IL 60304

Figure 8.10 Envelope.

continuation page for a memo will look exactly like a continuation page for a letter (see Figure 8.9) except, of course, it will have no signature block. Instead of signing the memo, you will write your initials next to your name (see Figure 8.2).

E-MAIL FORMATS

Local computer networking, Internet connections, and e-mail are linking people together much the way the development of the telephone enabled people all over the world to talk with each other. Physical distance is now less important than electronic connection, and e-mail has become one of the most used media of communication now that people want to share and discuss ideas as well as to create and retrieve documents. Once your work-station is on-line, you are able to send and receive messages electronically to and from persons hundreds or thousands of miles away more economically than by telephone or postal mail and almost as quickly as a telephone call. In general, e-mail software programs are easy to use and have clear menus and on-line help. Your e-mail program will enable you to send messages, read and reply to messages, forward messages, and save, print or delete messages just like any other kind of writing.

As e-mail grows in importance in the workplace, it is becoming regarded as more than just a way to send brief notes that can be written quickly, with little planning, sloppy organization, and little attention to revision or proofreading. As with regular letters and memos, you should

Office Memorandum

Property Consultants Inc.

Date: 10 December 1999

To: Elizabeth R. Arnold-Maricharel
         Liquidation Assistant

From: Xiaoping Zhang X.Z.
         Liquidation Assistant

Subject: LP-28 Asset No. 4377, In Receivership
         Principal Balance $142,460.10
         Samuel J. Oliverson

On December 8, 1999, Frank Malone and I visited with Jason Flynn at the Second Peoples Bank, Woolum Heights, Kentucky, concerning Samuel J. Oliverson.

In our conversation, Mr. Flynn offered the following information:

1. Samuel J. Oliverson actively farmed in 1998. His operation consisted of a section of land he owned, plus approximately a section to a section and a half of rented land.

2. In 1999 Samuel J. Oliverson was not actively farming. Mr. Oliverson sold the last one-half of Section 15, Block F-108, to Mr. Ambrose Weatherly. The other one-half section Mr. Oliverson owned was farmed by his nephew, Alpha Oliverson.

After leaving the Second Peoples Bank, Frank and I went to Section 15 to identify any equipment on the farm, as well as to inspect the crop. It appeared that there were approximately 600 pounds of tobacco in the barn. There were three items of equipment in the field:

1. One (1) 9500 Series, 2-row IHIC, self-propelled tobacco harvester.

2. One (1) 4020 J. Deere LPG tractor.

3. One (1) 32-foot Bush Hog module builder.

XZ:jjs

copy: James Flynn, Second Peoples Bank

Figure 8.11 Another sample memorandum.

present your ideas in readily understandable and useful ways when using e-mail.

E-mail messages consist of three major parts: the heading, the text body, and the signature block (see Figure 8.12).

HEADING

The heading includes the *Date* and the *From* lines, which the e-mail software program automatically completes, and the *To*, *Subject*, and *Cc* lines, which the writer must complete. E-mail addresses, entered in the *To* line, must be carefully keyed in, for if they contain an error the e-mail will not be deliverable. For your convenience, your e-mail program contains an address book in which you can enter abbreviations for long addresses (for instance, *abe* can be typed in and the entire e-mail address, *Abe_Lincoln@republic.UI.edu*, will be entered). The *Subject* line allows you to specify the recipient of your e-mail, if the address is a general one, or to summarize the message topic. The *cc* prompt allows you to send other persons a copy of the e-mail message. (You need not copy yourself, because you will automatically receive a copy of what you send.)

BODY

The body of an e-mail message is typed the same way as that of a hard-copy letter or memo, using paragraph indentations, lists, headings, and double-spacing between paragraphs. Most e-mail programs handle messages up to 20 to 25 pages easily, although you will seldom write such lengthy e-mail.

SIGNATURE BLOCK

The signature block or closing consists of a block of text that provides additional information about the author—name, title or position, telephone and fax numbers, and postal address. Although the procedure varies in different e-mail programs, you can select to have the signature block automatically attached to your outgoing e-mail. Look for the feature in the e-mail program you are using.

ATTACHMENTS

More and more frequently we now send whole documents in electronic files along with an e-mail message. The file (a proposal, a resume, or a list of parts, for example) is attached to the e-mail message. Once sent, the receiver can open the attachment and use it as if it had been created on his or her machine.

To create an e-mail message, you need only to respond to the *To*, *Cc*, and *Subject* prompts in the heading and type the message. You can also create a special file to which you can save all e-mail related to a specific project.

```
Date:        Friday, 20 October 2000 14:20.09
From:        Safenhe@dubcorp.com
To:          Department Heads and Project Directors
             〈fcabson@dubcorp.com〉
             〈msellars@dubcorp.com〉
             〈tbeards@dubcorp.com〉
             〈vmorro@dubcorp.com〉
             〈ysimmo@dubcorp.com〉
Cc:          Cynthia Jackson 〈cynjac@dubcorp.com〉

Subject:  Halogen Lamps

As a result of several fires and deaths nationwide related to
the use of halogen lamps, the Corporate Safety and Environmental
Health Committee is issuing a ban on their use in DubCorp
facilities.

If your area has any halogen lamps, they are to be removed and
are to be replaced with non-halogen bulbs.

The Corporate Office of Safety and Environmental Health is
currently conducting building inspections to ensure compliance
with the ban. We ask your assistance in ensuring that these
potentially dangerous lamps are quickly removed and disposed of
properly (see Safety Code Handbook, page 6).


Anne Barnett, Corporate Safety Officer
for the Corporate Safety and Environmental Health Committee
```

Figure 8.12 Another sample e-mail.

PLANNING AND REVISING CHECKLIST: CORRESPONDENCE

Think about the following while planning and revising letters, memos, and e-mail.

PLANNING

In planning letters, memos, and e-mail think about your purpose, content, and organization and your reader.

Purpose, Content, and Organization

- What do you hope to accomplish?

- Is your guiding purpose informational, persuasive, or argumentative?

- What do you want your reader to know or do?

- What information will fulfill your purpose?

- What are the *so-whats* of your information?

- How best can your information be organized?

- Does any particular existing organizational pattern fit your purpose and content?

Reader Analysis

- What are your reader's interests and needs? How can you best organize to meet those interests and needs?

- How strong is your reader's vocabulary in the subject area?

- Are there concepts you will need to explain to your reader?

- How much explanation of context will your readers need?

- Do you have secondary readers whom you must consider?

- What will be your reader's attitude?

- If your reader will be hostile or indifferent, how can you overcome such a barrier?

REVISION

In revision, pay attention to content and organization, style and tone, and format and grammar.

Content and Organization

- Is your purpose clear?

- Do your first few sentences provide the organizational and contextual information your reader needs?

- Is your organization clear and coherent?

- Have you displayed your organization with appropriate headings?

- Does your content and organization satisfy your purpose?

- Does your content and organization satisfy your reader's needs and interests?

- Have you stated clearly the *so-whats* of your information?

- Have you eliminated unneeded content?

- Is any action you want the reader to take clearly stated?

Style and Tone

- Have you kept your sentences to a reasonable length?

- Are your word choices familiar to your readers?

- Have you eliminated unneeded words?

- Are your sentences active?

- Is your tone suitable to your purpose and the occasion?

- Have you used personal pronouns such as *I*, *we*, and *you* appropriately?

- Have you avoided brusqueness and rudeness?

Format and Grammar

- Have you followed a format suitable for the occasion and your purpose?

- Are your paragraphs a reasonable length, allowing for sufficient white space?

- Have you used good-quality white paper?

- Is the letter or memo well typed or printed?

- Have you proofread carefully, eliminating all grammatical errors and typographical errors?

- Does your letter or memo present an overall good appearance?

SUGGESTIONS FOR APPLYING YOUR KNOWLEDGE

We suggest that you prepare for your study of correspondence by gathering as many examples of real workplace letters, memos, and e-mail as you can. They will be invaluable in your study of correspondence. Most members of the class have probably received various kinds of sales letters. Many students generate correspondence with department stores, book clubs, and similar institutions. Some students already work and have legitimate access to both hard-copy and e-mail workplace correspondence.

The staff members of your school send and receive an enormous amount of correspondence. People such as the dean, bursar, placement officer, maintenance superintendent, and admissions officer do much of their business by mail, so much so that they often use form letters. Most may use e-mail more than postal mail. Some members of the class can go to these school officials and ask permission to reproduce some samples of their correspondence for classroom use. The names of people involved should be removed, of course, when letters are reproduced.

When you have the letters, memos, and e-mail in class, use them as the basis for discussion. What is your honest opinion of them? Do they work? Are they clear, concise, and well organized? Is their information complete? Is their tone appropriate to their purpose? Have their writers sufficiently considered audience and purpose as well as the information they intended to convey? How successful are their persuasive strategies? How have the writers handled credibility, emotional appeals, and facts and analysis? Do any of the formats differ markedly from the norm? If so, do the differences help or distract? Have the writers avoided grammatical and typographical errors?

CHAPTER 9

WORKPLACE CORRESPONDENCE

Workplace correspondence can range from the simple to the complex, from informal to formal. In the workplace, there really is no rigid categorization of informal and formal. Rather, there is a continuum ranging from the very informal to the very formal. Where you place yourself on that continuum depends on audience and situation. For example, an e-mail message between two colleagues who know and trust each other might be as informal as this:

To: Bill

From: Cynthia

OK on 9 a.m. Tuesday meeting in your office. You make the coffee; I'll bring the doughnuts.

The formal might range from e-mail and letters and memos that look like those in Figures 9.1, 9.2, and 9.5 on up to memos and letters that are really short reports.

Using the principles discussed in Chapters 1 through 8, you can generate almost any kind of correspondence you need. Those principles are summarized in the planning and revising checklist following Chapter 8 (pages 219–220). To illustrate the process you would follow, we (1) describe several situations, (2) show the correspondence generated in those situations, and (3) show how attending to checklist items produced the results achieved. A few types of correspondence are specialized enough that you might not produce them using the general checklist. When such is the case, we provide the additional necessary information.

A ROUTINE REQUEST

People in the workplace commonly request information from one another. For example, business thrives on potential buyers of a product requesting information about that product.

SITUATION

George Santiago owns a garage that specializes in working with car hobbyists. In the magazine *Road and Track*, he has read about a new fuel pump that he may want. But the article he read does not provide all the information he needs. He decides to write to the manufacturer, whose e-mail address is included in the article, and request the information. Figure 9.1 shows his e-mail query.

ANALYSIS

George Santiago needs specific information. He knows that if his questions are vague, he will receive vague answers or no answers at all. He need not be particularly persuasive—his address and title are in the signature block of his e-mail, and his specific questions identify him as

```
Date:     3 Nov 2000 08:27.12 (CST)
From:     sasinc@mindup.com
To:       EngDyn@rockhill.com
Subject:  Request for Information on Fuel Pump, Type AK306J

Please send me the following information about your new
adjustable-pressure electric fuel pump, type AK306J:

1.  Can it be mounted anywhere and in any position?
2.  Does it come with a mounting bracket?
3.  Does it operate independently of the engine?
4.  How many pounds of pressure does it adjust to?
5.  Is the flow adequate for a Continental 0-470 engine?

If you have literature available that answers these questions, I
would be pleased to receive it.

George Santiago
Owner/Manager
Santiago Auto Service, Inc.
2089 Fair Oaks Boulevard
Bellflower, CA 90706
```

Figure 9.1 An e-mail routine request.

a potential customer who merits a serious answer. He knows that his e-mail request will be read and answered by someone who is familiar with engine terminology.

Because he lacks the name of a company employee to address, he chooses not to use a salutation. His opening sentence provides all the context and purpose statement needed for such a routine request. He lists and numbers his questions for two reasons: He wants to make each question stand out so that it will be answered. His enumeration makes it easy for the receiver to answer each question.

Santiago's style is clear. He wastes neither words nor his reader's time, but his tone is courteous, not brusque. His grammar is correct, helping to demonstrate that he is someone the company should take seriously.

A SPECIAL REQUEST

You can be reasonably sure that people will answer a routine request either because it is easy to answer or because answering may benefit the answerer in some way. You won't have the same assurance with a special request. You will be making work for the person who responds to the request, and it may well be that the answerer perceives no immediate benefit.

SITUATION

Jill Kehoe is a student at Southern Polytechnic Institute, majoring in industrial technology. For a paper she is to write, she is researching how medium-sized companies screen recent college graduates. Using the *College Placement Annual*, she has obtained the names of the personnel directors of six such firms in her area. She will send similar letters to all six. Figure 9.2 shows one of her letters.

ANALYSIS

Jill Kehoe must be persuasive in her letter. She has little to offer Robert Bradley in return for his answer, so she must depend largely on his goodwill. To encourage that goodwill, she identifies herself as a student and, without being obsequious, is particularly polite in her request. The purpose and context of her letter are clearly stated in the first two paragraphs. She offers Bradley what she can: She will share her paper with others, thus drawing Ace South Transport to the attention of students who may someday be potential customers or employees. Further, she offers Bradley a copy of her report.

As in George Santiago's routine request, Kehoe makes her questions quite specific and enumerates them for ease in answering. Because Bradley is an experienced personnel director, she can be sure that he will know the answers to her questions without the need for any research on his part.

Bradley is not likely to be hostile in any way, but he could well be somewhat apathetic and inclined to put off answering her letter. To help prevent that, Kehoe politely states the time by which she must have an answer. She then builds goodwill with a courteous close. (But notice she avoids the trite expression "Thanking you in advance.")

Her good grammar, clarity of style, and courteous tone identify Kehoe as someone who should be taken seriously. Because her coherent organization and businesslike format smooth the way for an answer, they build goodwill for her with Bradley.

INFORMATIONAL CORRESPONDENCE

Many letters pass along information. Often an informational letter or memo is a response to either a routine or special request. At other times the information is something the writer thinks the reader or readers should know. Let us look at two such situations.

SITUATION: A RESPONSE LETTER

Robert Bradley has received Jill Kehoe's request for information (see Figure 9.2). He is impressed by her coherence and businesslike approach. When he finds some time to spare from his busy schedule, he writes her a letter answering her questions (see Figure 9. 3).

86 Needham Hall
Southern Polytechnic Institute
Bailey Springs, MS 39320-1502
March 14, 2000

Mr. Robert Bradley
Vice President of Human Resources
Ace South Transport, Inc.
1000 By-Pass I-440
Memphis, TN 31111

Dear Mr. Bradley:

I am an industrial technology student at Southern Polytechnic Institute. I'm writing a report for my Transportation Management 3160 class on how firms such as yours screen for employment recent graduates of college programs.

I have done considerable library and Internet research on the subject, but I want to augment them with information collected from some of the larger industrial firms in the tri-state area. The results of my study will be shared with my classmates. I would also be happy to send a copy of my final report to you, should you want one.

Would you spend a few minutes answering the following questions about the way your firm screens employees?

    1. What priorities do you place on applicants' academic performance, experience, and on-campus or in-plant interviews?

    2. What do you expect of applicants' behavior and dress when they report for an interview?

    3. How much importance do you place on recommendations from faculty, school officials, and previous employers?

    4. Do you give any standard or in-house tests to applicants? If so, how much weight do you give to the scores?

My paper is due April 10. I appreciate your taking the time to read my letter and hope to receive a reply from you in early April.

Sincerely,

Jill Kehoe

Jill Kehoe

Figure 9.2 A special-request letter.

Ace South Transport, Inc.
1000 By-Pass • Memphis TN 31111

24 March 2000

Ms. Jill Kehoe
86 Needham Hall
Southern Polytechnic Institute
Bailey Springs, MS 39320-1502

Dear Ms. Kehoe:

I am happy to answer your questions about how we screen recent college graduates. I'll take your questions in the order you ask them.

1. Our first priority is generally to consider whether the applicant's major field of study fits him or her for the job sought. For instance, we like to hire drivers who have been through an extensive training program, such as those now provided in many two-year colleges. In descending order, we consider academic performance, work experience, and interviews. The only exception to this priority order might be when someone's extensive work experience makes up for a lack of academic preparation.

2. We expect that applicants come prepared to ask good questions of us and to listen to us as we will listen to them. They should be clean and neat in appearance.

3. Recommendations from people who have worked with an applicant, either on the job or in school, serve primarily as a check on what we find out from an applicant's resume and records and from the interview process.

4. We give in-house tests to prospective drivers and clerical workers. As with recommendations, we use tests primarily as a check on education and experience. A good score on a test would not guarantee an applicant a job, but a bad score would put his or her employment by us in doubt.

A useful source you may not have run across in your library search is *The Fleet Owner*, which frequently publishes information about the hiring and training of employees in our industry. I would be pleased to receive a copy of your report.

Sincerely,

Robert Bradley
Robert Bradley
Vice President of Human Resources

Figure 9.3 A response letter.

ANALYSIS: A RESPONSE LETTER

Bradley's purpose is to answer the questions posed by Jill Kehoe. Because she has wisely enumerated her questions, he chooses to follow her order in answering her questions. A reference to her letter will provide sufficient introduction and context for his reply. Because she has done her homework before writing him, he knows he can forego lengthy explanations. By mentioning *The Fleet Owner*, he provides another reference for her, always a good idea when possible. His letter is clear, courteous, and complete. The friendliness apparent in the tone will help to create goodwill for his company with both Kehoe and her classmates.

SITUATION: INSTRUCTION

Ruth Phillips is the personnel director for a small but growing corporation. To help with the process of hiring, training, and evaluating new employees, the company has asked department heads to write descriptions for all the positions within their departments. The program has been in effect for three months, and Ruth Phillips is responsible for seeing that it goes well. In reviewing recent position descriptions, she realizes that the department heads are having difficulty describing the duties of a position. Although Phillips' message will be a bit longer than most e-mail she sends or receives, she decides that an e-mail message to each of them may help correct the situation quickly. For her e-mail, see Figure 9.4.

ANALYSIS: INSTRUCTION

Good position descriptions are not easy to write. Therefore, Phillips realizes that some department heads may resist her e-mail message. Too much resistance will prevent her from effecting the change she wants. The key to the success of this e-mail is getting off to a good start and having the department heads see it as useful information and not as criticism. To that end, she begins her message with a compliment.

The first sentence in the second paragraph is the only criticism in the entire memo. In that sentence, Phillips states the problem and the *so-whats* of the problem clearly. She does so without a hint of sarcasm or hostility toward the department heads. The second and third sentences of the paragraph describe the material that is in an FTP file attached to the e-mail. An FTP (file transfer protocol) is a program for transferring a file from one computer to another. Check the feature on your e-mail program. You may simply have to check the Attachment box to send a file or you may have to FTP the file before you attach it to your e-mail message. By asking for comments in the final sentence of the paragraph, Phillips makes it clear that she is open minded about other ways of solving the problem.

In organizing, Phillips organizes her information by separating it into the three problem areas she sees in the position descriptions. She makes her plan of organization clear in her third paragraph and with her three headings. She uses a neutral tone in her instruction. She describes what needs to be done without dwelling on the mistakes of the past. She does not talk down in any way to her readers. Because most people learn well from examples, she provides them in her e-mail message and provides three additional sample duties sections as well.

GOOD-NEWS LETTERS AND MEMOS

Most letters, memos, and e-mail, we're happy to say carry good news. Any correspondence that moves business forward is good news, even a routine notice that a shipment is on the way. In a good-news letter or memo, announce the good news first:

- We're pleased to tell you we want you to come to work for us.

- Your bicycle is repaired and ready for pickup.

- Congratulations on your promotion to head of merchandising.

Following the good news, supply any needed details, explanations, and analyses. Third, in some cases, you will *resell* the reader. You may not be familiar with the notion of reselling. Let us illustrate. Recently, we bought a fax machine. As we were completing the purchase, the salesperson said, "You will be happy with this machine. It speeds up the transmission of letters and other documents in a way you'll really come to appreciate." Although he had already made the sale, he was reselling us—he wanted us to go away happy, convinced that we hadn't thrown our money away on an expensive gadget. You will frequently end good-news correspondence in the same way.

The three steps of good-news communication, as illustrated in the following situation, are

- Report the good news.

- Supply the necessary information.

- Resell the reader.

SITUATION

Mark Johnson, Director of Human Resources (DHR) for Columbia Electronics, has been trying for some time to convince the executive council of the company that a company child-care center would pay for itself by reducing absenteeism, improving worker morale, and preventing rapid turnover among women employees. He has finally succeeded, and Ann Manchester, the company's chief financial officer (CFO), has the pleasant task of writing a memo to Johnson to confirm the good news. See Figure 9.5 for the memo.

```
Date:      7 June 2000 13:20.6 (EDT)
From:      phillipr@faircog.com
To:        All Department Heads <cranmerj@faircog.com>
           <jamisow@faircog.com>
           <millerrb@faircog.com>
           <oliphanjr@faircog.com>
           <tsuimilrr@faircog.com>
Cc:        <andertob@faircog.com>
Subject:   THE DUTIES SECTION OF POSITION DESCRIPTIONS
Parts/Attachments
1 Shown 35 lines text
2 38 KB Application
```

Our new position description program is going well. You have all
done an excellent job in working with your department staffs in
gathering the information needed for useful descriptions.

The Duties sections of some position descriptions, however, have
not covered the duties well enough to aid in training and
evaluating new employees. Please look over the following
material written to help with organizing and writing the Duties
section. I have also attached three sample Duties sections.
Please send me any comments that you think will help us achieve
the goals we have set for our position descriptions.

Our purpose in the Duties section is to describe what someone in
that position does to fulfill the function of that position. A
good Duties section will have a useful introduction, a coherent
organization, and plain, clear language.

Introduction:

Introduce a Duties section with a general description of what an
employee in this position does. For example, you could write,
"Serves as executive secretary to the department head."

Organization:

Because duties vary from position to position, there is no set
way to organize a Duties section. The following three
organizational plans work well, however:

 • Write a narrative describing in sequence what the employee
does, hour by hour, day by day, or week by week, whichever fits
the duties best.

 • List the duties in order of their importance.

Figure 9.4 A set of special instructions sent via e-mail.

- In cases where employees perform several different functions, you can categorize the description into those functions. For example, in some of the smaller departments, executive secretaries have clerical, accounting, and managerial functions. Within the categories you could organize by sequence or order of importance.

Plain, Clear Language:

Use plain, clear language to describe duties. File clerks file, illustrators illustrate, janitors sweep, mop, and wax floors. Be specific, and don't gild the lily with statements such as "Provides organizational support for cleanliness activities within the facility."

Because you are describing activities, use active verbs, such as these:

- Maintains computerized department budget and provides department head with weekly budget status reports.

- Takes dictation and uses word-processing equipment to type memos and letters free of spelling and grammatical errors.

Thanks,

Ruth Phillips, Director
Human Resources Department

[Part 2, Application/MAGNET-STREAM (Name: "Duties" 38 KB]
[Cannot display this part. Press "V" then "S" to save in a file]

Figure 9.4 (continued)

Columbia Electronics, Inc.

Date: 17 April 2000

To: Mark Johnson
            DHR

From: Ann Manchester A. M.
            CFO

Subject: Executive Council approval of company child-care center

Mark, I'm delighted to tell you that the Executive Council has approved your recommendation concerning a company child-care center. The case you made for it was quite convincing. The Council was particularly impressed by your figures on the number of mothers working in the company with preschool children.

You may be interested in how closely your figures match national figures. I ran across this graph in a government publication (Bureau of Labor Statistics, *Working Women: A Chartbook* [Washington D.C.: U.S. Department of Labor, 1991] 36.):

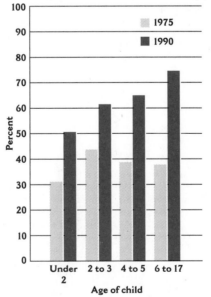

Chart 18
Labor force participation rates of mothers
by age of youngest child, March 1975 and March 1990

Figure 9.5 A good-news memo.

Page 2
Mark Johnson
17 April 2000

As you have requested, Human Resources will be in charge of the project. The Council hopes you can have the center in place by August. I will be your coordinator with the Council for space and funding. Please schedule an hour's appointment with me at your earliest convenience.

Once again, congratulations. You have already put much time and enthusiasm into this project. The Council knows you will continue your good efforts in carrying your plans through to completion.

Figure 9.5 (continued)

ANALYSIS

Ann Manchester has three major purposes in this memo. First, she wishes to convey the good news to Mark Johnson. This she does, as she should, in her opening sentence.

Second, she wants Johnson to know how pleased the council is with his work on this project. She does this in two ways—one directly, one indirectly. Directly, she tells him his case was "quite convincing" and that the council was "impressed by his figures." She is indirectly expressing her approval by taking the time to share the chart of national statistics with him. In doing so, she also shows him that her interest in the project extends to discovering helpful statistics. (As we point out in Chapter 6, Visuals and Document Design I, and Chapter 7, Visuals and Document Design II, computer graphics software now makes it possible to integrate graphics into memos and letters.)

Third, she wants to set a deadline for the project and get Johnson started on it. Her next-to-last paragraph accomplishes that goal.

Finally, she resells Johnson on the project by once again complimenting him. Johnson will be greatly pleased and ready to work on the project with great enthusiasm.

Manchester's memo is a good example of the importance of considering human values in correspondence. Johnson would have been satisfied with hearing that his project was approved and underway. However, Manchester's additional effort in the memo improves his self-esteem and increases the efforts he will make in the matter of the daycare center and in other matters as well.

BAD-NEWS LETTERS AND MEMOS

In the workplace, a small number of letters, memos, and e-mail carry bad news. Examples would be memos telling someone an expected raise is not coming or that a proposed project will not be funded. Bad-news correspondence is tricky to write. Normally, you will want to be courteous and tactful, but at the same time you must be honest and explicit. The following situation is fairly typical.

SITUATION

The motor of John Rhodes' clothes dryer has overheated and been damaged beyond repair. John Rhodes has called the appliance store where he purchased the dryer and demanded a new motor under the provisions of his replacement guarantee. A service representative sent to examine the motor finds that it was improper operation on Rhodes' part and not a defect that caused the overheating. Willoughby Osgood, the store's service manager, has the task of telling Rhodes the bad news. See Figure 9.6 for his letter.

AMBROSE APPLIANCES
2215 West Barnes Avenue
Denver, CO 80204

February 7, 2000

Mr. John Rhodes
3295 West Avondale Drive
Denver, CO 80204

Dear Mr. Rhodes:

Thank you for your call about your dryer. As you know, following your call, our service representative, Sophia Montana, examined your dryer.

She found that the dryer's motor had been overheated so much that it is damaged beyond repair. She also noted that the lint filter was so clogged with lint that it was not functioning properly. As a result, the lint packed into the motor, causing the overheating. She also reported that on a previous service call to your house, she had found the lint filter clogged. At that time, she showed you the warning in your operating manual that points out that failure to clean the lint filter after every use of the dryer may result in overheating and damage to the motor.

Your replacement guarantee covers only defects by the manufacturer and improper installation by us. Since neither was a factor in the motor's overheating, we cannot replace your motor free of charge as you have requested.

However, we are anxious to help you get your dryer working again. If you want our service representative to install a new motor, please call us. We can bill the installation as a continuing service call at $30 rather than the normal installation fee of $60, saving you $30. The cost of the motor itself is $150, so your total cost would be $180.

We value you as a customer, and we hope that our solution for replacing your motor will be acceptable to you.

Sincerely,

Willoughby Osgood

Willoughby Osgood
Service Manager

Figure 9.6 A bad-news letter.

ANALYSIS

Willoughby Osgood has two goals in this letter. He wants to let John Rhodes know that his service guarantee does not apply in this situation and at the same time keep as much of his goodwill as possible. He has to be clear about the way in which Rhodes caused the problem and yet not insult or humiliate Rhodes in any way. He expects that Rhodes will be hostile. Because of Rhodes' expected hostility, Osgood chooses to write to him rather than telephone. In a letter, Osgood can control the tone better than he might on the phone with an angry Rhodes. Also, the letter provides a record that could be useful in case of litigation at a later time.

Osgood maintains a neutral tone in the letter. He starts with a "thank you" and sets the context for the letter. In the second paragraph, he objectively points out the facts of the situation. In the third paragraph, he clearly states the *so-what*, the bad news that Rhodes will not get a free motor. In the fourth paragraph, he offers an alternative solution that he hopes may be acceptable to Rhodes. Finally, he closes in a friendly way.

Most bad-news letters, like this one, are ultimately persuasive; that is, the writer hopes to persuade the reader that his or her request is denied. If you, the writer, have an alternative to offer, you hope to persuade the reader to accept that. To be persuasive, you must delay the bad news until you have provided a rationale for it. A letter to Rhodes beginning with a blunt statement that because of his faulty use of the dryer, no free motor was forthcoming would make the problem worse, not better.

In writing his letter, Osgood followed a standard bad-news organization that has served many businesspeople well:

- Begin with a friendly buffer opener.

- Carefully and objectively explain and analyze the problem.

- Clearly state the *so-what*, the bad news.

- Offer the best alternative possible.

- Close in a friendly way.

PERSUASIVE CORRESPONDENCE

Many letters, memos and e-mail, even those we think of as informational, are at least partly persuasive. For example, Ruth Phillips in her informational e-mail to the department heads (Figure 9.4) wishes to persuade the department heads to write position descriptions her way. But some correspondence has no goal other than persuasion. Most such correspondence in the workplace is somewhere in the middle of the emotional persuasion-scientific argument continuum (see Figure 3.1, page 57). Below we describe two situations where persuasion is the goal.

SITUATION: FUND-RAISING LETTER

Dorothy Forbes is the president of a small, newly established, nonprofit village library. She and everyone else who works for the library is an unpaid volunteer. The library receives free space from the village but has to pay its own utilities and buy its own books. The library has no support other than yearly dues, rental fees, and donations from library patrons. In several years, when the library is finished and all the shelves are in, it should be self-sustaining, but for now it still needs help. Forbes decides to raise money with a fund-raising letter to people in the village. For her letter, see Figure 9.7.

ANALYSIS: FUND-RAISING LETTER

Dorothy Forbes has one major goal—raising money for the library. Because she is sending her letter to every householder in the village, many of them will be unfamiliar with the library. Therefore, she has to tell them something about the library. Furthermore, she has to tell them about the library in a way that will capture their attention and awaken their desire to use and, she hopes, support the library.

Forbes' readers are unlikely to be hostile, but they may find it all too easy to lay down and subsequently forget the request for money. Therefore, she knows that she must ask for immediate action and make such action easy for the reader. Her letter meets all these requirements.

She begins with a boxed, attention-getting line above her salutation. For her attention-getter, Forbes aims a question directly at the readers. She hopes their wish to see an answer to the question will encourage them to read on. Her question also appeals to her readers' self-interest, another reason to continue. Alternatively, she might have chosen an attention-getter such as proclaiming the newness of something, for example, "New from NRI! A 25-inch color TV with split-screen capability."

The first part of Forbes' letter answers her question. She lists some of the books available in the library. She sets off the books she lists to draw attention to them and further draw the reader into the letter. She is careful to list a variety of books that will appeal to a variety of tastes. She mentions the tapes that are available and suggests a specific use for them.

After she awakens interest and desire in her readers, she begins her fund-raising effort. She tells specifically why the funds are needed. She reassures her readers that they will not be continually pressured for donations. She appeals again to her readers' self-interest, telling them that dedicated volunteers are working hard to meet their needs.

Finally, she asks for immediate action. With her attached form and enclosed envelope, she makes such action as easy as possible.

The Village Library
16 Front Street
Fairfield, FL 33063

> The Village Library—What's in it for you?

Dear Neighbor:

Well, to begin with, the Village Library has more than three thousand hardback books for you to borrow. The Village Library buys copies of the latest books, including those on the *New York Times* bestseller list, almost as soon as they're off the press. Right now on our shelves you can find the books you want to read, such as,

Kissinger, by Walter Isaacson
Diana: Her True Story, by Andrew Morton
Head to Head, by Lester Thurow
Rum Punch, by Elmore Leonard
Walking on Water, by Randall Kenan

You'll find a fine stock of mysteries and a table full of paperbacks from which you can borrow without even checking them out. Simply bring back the paperback when you can, or swap your paperbacks for ours. Some titles currently on the table:

Danger, by Dick Francis
Ernest Hemingway, by Carlos Baker
A Taste for Death, by P. D. James
Nemesis, by Isaac Asimov

Are you going on a long trip on the Interstate? Before you leave, drop into the library and, for a small fee, check out a few tapes and wile away the boring hours listening to a novel or a biography.

If you have been by the Village Library's new location at 16 Front Street, you know that our shelves are full, but we have room for many more shelves to be stacked with books for your reading pleasure.

In the next year, we will spend approximately $8,000 for shelving and $4,000 for books. When the Village Library reaches its full growth, it will be nearly self-sustaining, but, for the moment, we need your help. When you contribute, dedicated volunteers will see to it that your money is spent in your best interest—to bring you the books and tapes you want.

Figure 9.7 A persuasive letter.

Please use the attached form and enclosed addressed envelope to send your contribution to the Village Library today.

Yours for good reading,

Dorothy Forbes

Dorothy Forbes, President
Village Library

Enclosure

- -

The Village Library

Yes! Count on my support. Enclosed is my check, fully tax deductible (made to The Village Library).

Donor $20 ( )   Patron $100 ( )
Sponsor $50 ( )   Angel $100 + ( )

Name _____

Address _____

Mail in the enclosed envelope or drop it off at the Village Library.

Donations entitle you to a complimentary family membership card and our great thanks.

Figure 9.7 (continued)

In her letter, Dorothy Forbes has used the classic sales-letter organization, know as **AIDA**:

- Get the reader's **Attention**.

- Awaken the reader's **Interest** and **Desire** in what you are selling.

- Call for the reader's immediate **Action** and make that action as easy as possible.

SITUATION: SEEKING APPROVAL FOR A CHANGE IN COMPANY POLICY

Dorothy Forbes' fund-raising sales letter, positioned to the left of center on the emotional persuasion-scientific argument continuum, would not be appropriate in every persuasive situation. At times, you must be more discreet and closer to the right side of the continuum. The following situation illustrates this point.

Donna Jackson is vice president for information services for Southeastern Department Stores (SDS), a twelve-store chain located in small- and medium-sized cities in the southeastern United States. SDS is struggling to stay solvent. Because it collects and uses sales information so poorly, it prices items badly and is forced to maintain excessive and costly inventories. Jackson realizes that certain technological solutions would resolve many of SDS's problems, and if they are not adopted soon, SDS may go under. She decides that an e-mail message to SDS president Thomas Hovey pointing out some of the technological advantages competitors have over SDS may initiate some of the changes needed. She chooses e-mail because it will reach Hovey much faster than a memo. Even though speed is an important advantage here, Jackson also knows that Hovey expects recommendations to be carefully thought out and that he doesn't tolerate grammatical errors or misspelling. Jackson also is aware that Hovey prefers to receive e-mail because he can forward messages electronically—with his comments—to others whose advice he seeks. For her e-mail, see Figure 9.8[1] on pages 242–243.

ANALYSIS: SEEKING APPROVAL FOR A CHANGE IN COMPANY POLICY

Donna Jackson has a clear purpose in this e-mail message. She wants to persuade her president, Thomas Hovey, of the potential for SDS of technological developments in transmitting and processing information. She needs to grab his attention quickly in a way that a long memo or report might not do. Therefore, she opts to describe one major technological innovation that could significantly improve the way SDS operates. Thomas

[1]Figure 9.8 is based upon Alice LaPlante, "Shared Destinies: CEOs and CIOs," *Forbes ASAP* 7 (Dec. 1992): 32–42.

Hovey understands department stores, but he doesn't speak computerese. Therefore, computerese is notably absent from Jackson's memo. There's no mention of local area networks or Unisys U6000/65 Unix servers to boggle his mind.

Instead, in plain language, Jackson describes one major technological innovation and gives three important *so-whats*, the significance of which Hovey will immediately grasp. She uses a format to make the *so-whats*, labeled "Advantages," stand out.

Jackson knows that Hovey will not immediately make expensive investments in technology without the input of major segments of the SDS management. Therefore, rather than suggesting immediate action, she suggests the formation of a research and development (R&D) committee to investigate information technologies useful to SDS. However, to prevent needed changes from bogging down in committee, she bluntly states her belief that SDS is headed for further failure if it fails to take advantage of information technology.

Jackson hopes her memo will bring about a discussion with Hovey in which she can open his eyes to other innovations that will help SDS. Once on the R&D committee, which as vice president for information services she is sure to be, she hopes to persuade others of the advantages of integrating information technology into every level of SDS.

PLANNING AND REVISING CHECKLIST: CORRESPONDENCE

Please refer to the Planning and Revising Checklist: Correspondence following Chapter 8 (pages 219–220).

```
Date:      29 Mar 2000 10:20.15 MST
From:      Jaxdon@sds.com
To:        Hoveyth@sds.com
Subject:   A SOLUTION FOR SDS PRICING AND INVENTORY PROBLEMS
```

As discussed at the recent SDS Executive Council meeting, SDS is losing money because of poor pricing decisions and the need to carry excessive inventory. One suggestion at the meeting was to decentralize control over pricing and inventory and place more responsibility for both at the store level. I agree that our present centralized control system is inefficient. However, I believe the answer is not to decentralize, but to develop a new computerized central control system that works.

Many of our competitors are introducing technological innovations that are helping them in the very areas where we have problems. I'll describe one such major innovation (there are many others) and close with a recommendation of how SDS might proceed.

INNOVATION:

- Through computer and space satellite systems already available, it's possible to collect complete sales data from every store every evening and transmit it to SDS headquarters for analysis.

ADVANTAGES:

- SDS can make immediate price corrections when needed to move an item and still maintain a profit margin.

- SDS will know when inventory of an item has reached the point where it needs to be replenished, removing the need to stock excessive inventory. Our competitors have cut their inventories by 30 percent using this technology.

- SDS will have precise knowledge of what items and what types and colors of items sell best in different stores. For example, if blue sweatshirts sell best in Charlotte and gray sells best in Ashville, we can stock accordingly. At the present time we stock all stores with equal amounts of blue and gray. As a result, we have an excess of gray sweatshirts in Charlotte and a shortage of blue, and the reverse in Ashville.

With the right technology, SDS can get the right merchandise to the right stores at the right price and at the right time. To

Figure 9.8 E-mail using scientific argument.

begin using such technology successfully, SDS has to make decisions at the highest levels of the company that affect all divisions of the company. To that end, I recommend that you form a Research and Development Committee composed of senior people from all the major divisions of SDS. Your charge to that committee should be to study information technologies useful to SDS and report back concerning their use to the Executive Council.

Failure to make use of technological resources available to us will lead inevitably to the failure of SDS to keep pace with its competitors.

I would like the opportunity to meet and discuss these issues with you at your earliest convenience.

Donna Jackson
Vice President for Information Services
SDS, Inc.

Figure 9.8 (continued)

SUGGESTIONS FOR APPLYING YOUR KNOWLEDGE

1. Analyze and discuss in class the following inquiry letter. Is it a routine or special request? Will the reader be motivated to answer it? Why or why not? Does the reader receive enough information to provide the desired suggestions? If so, why do you think the information is sufficient? If not, what information do you think should be added? How do you think the letter should be answered?

WESTLAKE COMPUTER SYSTEMS
UNION STATION PLAZA B
PORTLAND, OR 97201-9999

January 19, 2000

Mr. Pete Markham
Technical Representative
Hughes Lighting Company
4420 Bear Creek Road
Raymond, MS 37703

Dear Mr. Markham:

Your firm was recommended to me as a possible supplier of lighting fixtures.

We are renovating our Mountain View plant and would like to install more powerful and intensive illumination to support the meticulous nature of the work that our production personnel must perform in the production area.

Our production area is approximately 45,000 square feet and has no outside windows. The lighting system must be suspended from eighteen-foot ceilings.

We have looked through your latest catalog (Fall 1999), and we find nothing that seems to fit our basic lighting needs. We look forward to receiving your suggestions.

Sincerely,

WESTLAKE COMPUTING SYSTEMS
Ann Abernathy Norwood
Assistant Plant Manager

---

2. If you believe that Norwood's letter needs to be revised, write the revised letter. Write a memo or e-mail to your instructor or classmates or both that identifies the nature of the revision and gives the rationale for the changes you made.

3. Assume that you are Pete Markham and write a response to Norwood's letter. Give a copy of your letter to a classmate or your instructor or both for their comments.

4. The following are just a few opportunities that call for writing inquiry, request, and order letters, memos, or e-mail and writing responses to such correspondence. You may be able to think of others:

A. Select an advertisement that invites you to send away for a free catalog, brochure, or sample. Write a letter requesting the material. Include with your letter a photocopy of the advertisement so your instructor or fellow students can better evaluate your letter.

B. Select an advertisement in a nationally circulated publication or a Web site and write a letter or e-mail asking for more information about the product or service advertised. Include a copy of the advertisement or Web site so your instructor or fellow students can better evaluate your letter or e-mail request.

C. If you are writing a research report for one of your courses, supplement material you have found locally by writing or e-mailing several companies or organizations for additional information. Ask for your instructor's or some of your classmates' opinions of your correspondence before you mail them.

5. Occasionally an unhappy customer or client vents anger by being sarcastic and making idle threats, as in the following letter by Daniella LaCosta. Analyze and discuss LaCosta's letter in class. What effect do you think the letter would have on the reader? If you were to receive the letter, how would you respond? Would you take it seriously? Assuming that you would take the letter seriously, does it contain enough information for you to decide whether to allow an adjustment or not? If not, what additional information would you need? If you were to answer the letter, would you ignore the sarcasm and handle the complaint as if it were a routine one? Explain your opinions in a memo or e-mail to your instructor or classmates or both.

DANIELLA'S SALON
Old Merchants Building
1100 Main Street
Merced City, CA 96340

March 17, 2000

Customer Services Office
Mollenbrockt Skin Care Services
Attn. Ms. Sigrid Bramberg
800 West Covina Avenue
Los Angeles, CA 90016

Dear Sigrid:

This afternoon I'm returning three boxes, collect, so you can see what a fine job your shipping department certainly made of that order of perfume, cologne, and face powder. I smelled it before the driver unloaded it off his truck. What didn't leak out of the boxes got into the face powder cartons, and you'll see what a nice batter it makes.

My order was long enough in coming anyway, and now some ignoramus shipping clerk of yours has sent me pancake batter. What do you think I run here, anyway, a restaurant?

If you can get someone who knows how to pack goods, and get my order here by March 30, I'll take it. Otherwise, I'll order from a local distributor. I must have the goods for my new spring promotional. Do you get that?

Yours in anger,

Daniella LaCosta
Manager and Owner

6. Assume that LaCosta has realized that she has relieved some of her anger by writing the above letter, and that she has asked you to help her revise it for mailing. Do you have sufficient information to rewrite the letter? If not, what information would you need? Revise the letter, providing additional information if needed, for LaCosta's signature and mailing.

7. Discuss how you would handle the following situation. You are the owner of Farmington Lighting Systems, 4120 East Third Street, Jenkins, MO 65883. On March 17, you ordered three ceiling fans and light fixtures from The Better Fan & Light Company, 5215 Big Bend Boulevard, St. Louis, MO 64508. This is the first time you have ordered merchandise from this company. The merchandise, which cost $500 and was paid for in advance by your check #908 in order to get a 10 percent discount on the wholesale price, was delivered by River City Transport on March 28. The order, however, was incomplete. One of the light fixtures was not sent, and the fans were the wrong size. You have no e-mail address for the company. Your calls to the company, which is 50 miles away, have not been returned.

It is now April 5 and too late for you to include the merchandise in your store's special promotional sale. You prefer to return the items and receive a refund. However, you would be willing to accept the complete shipment if the company sent the correct sizes and would adjust the price accordingly or provide some other adjustment that would satisfy you.

What should you do next? Would you consider trying again to contact the company by telephone, write a letter explaining the problem and your desired solution, contact the Better Business Bureau, or drive to St. Louis and explain the problem in person? Discuss which seems the best course of action and why.

Assume that you have decided that writing a letter is the best solution. Write the letter.

8. Discuss how you would handle the situation in the previous exercise if you were a customer relations representative for The Better Fan & Lighting Company. You have received a letter requesting a refund for the merchandise that will be returned or an adjustment on the complete shipment. Your records show that the six packages were sent on March 27, and you are checking with River City Transport to trace the missing light fixture. You have checked the order, and you realize that the wrong size fans were shipped, but you have no idea why. You are interested in supplying the ordered merchandise at an additional discount or with some other adjustment, because the store that ordered them is an area where you have no established retailers.

How would you respond to the letter? What seems a reasonable adjustment to make? Would you contact the store by telephone or by letter? Regardless of how you contact the store, you will need to write a letter so that you have an official record of the adjustment. Write the letter.

9. Analyze and discuss the following letter. The letter obviously carries bad news and does it in a way that is sure to alienate the reader. Assuming that Chambers is fully justified in granting no credit, how would you rewrite the letter? Assuming that Chambers may be able to grant partial credit, how would you rewrite the letter?

Rewrite the letter explaining that you cannot grant credit. Rewrite the letter explaining that you can grant partial credit.

```
                    THE COMPUTER CONNECTION
                      419 OWINGTON AVENUE
                      BROOKLYN, NY 11206

November 10, 2000

Ms. Sonya Troy
Computer Sales and Support Center
Suite G, 5307 East Blake Street
Englewood Heights, NJ 07635

Dear Ms. Troy:

I have just been informed by our shipping and receiving
department that on November 7 you returned for credit
cartons containing four ZHAP-1100 color monitors and two
Sigma KB-52 printers.

Because you have been in business for many years it
would seem to me that you would be aware that once
merchandise has been removed from its original carton
(as these have obviously been) and put on display (as
these apparently have been), they can hardly be returned
for credit. Furthermore, our return policy is that
unsatisfactory merchandise must be returned within ten
days of receipt. This condition is printed on all our
```

invoices. This policy has obviously been violated as we have shipped none of these items since July 11 of this year. I am assuming that you are well aware of our policy and believe that you intended to request full payment for their return regardless of the ethical question involved.

I would also like to point out that one of the monitors is slightly damaged. So for these reasons you can see why we must refuse your request, although we are delighted to cooperate in any way possible with good customers such as your firm.

Sincerely,

F. Martin Chambers
Customer Support Staff

10. Write a thank-you letter, memo, or e-mail to someone who has done something helpful for you. Be sure to be specific about the nature of the assistance and express your awareness of how you have benefited from the reader's help. Ask your instructor or classmates to critique the message before you send it.

11. Interview the director of the local Better Business Bureau or an official of a business who is responsible for handling customer complaints and inquiries to identify consumers' rights and the company's policy concerning adjustments. Write a memo or e-mail to your classmates that summarizes your findings.

12. Write a sales letter for some activity such as going to the cafeteria, student center, library, or learning resources center. Remember, you must research an activity and its potential users before you can sell it successfully. Ask your instructor or classmates to critique the letter before you send it.

13. Write a letter, memo, or e-mail persuading someone to take on a challenging job or to make a contribution. Use AIDA (see page 240). Ask your instructor or classmates to critique it before you send it.

14. Plan, write, and revise a letter on one of the following topics in collaboration with at least one but not more than four other classmates.
    Every school has problems of some sort. For example, many schools have registration practices that seem cumbersome and slow to students and faculty alike. Or perhaps there are problems such as inadequate access to computers or dimly lit parking lots, unsafe for men and women alike. Choose such a problem. Find out who would be responsible for correcting the problem. Find out as much as you can about the person or group and write them a letter. Make clear in your letter what the problem is and what you think the solution should be. Use methods of persuasion and argument that best suit the situation and your reader. If your instructor thinks it appropriate, send the letter.

15. You work for the National Aeronautics and Space Administration (NASA). Your job is to answer inquiries about NASA operations. The following letter has come in from Mr. Marion Smith's third-grade class at J. S. Harris Elementary School, 112 Mitchell Street, Estrin, OH 44530.

```
Dear NASA,

We have a color photo of Saturn that NASA took in space.
It is on our classroom wall. How do you get such
wonderful color? Our senator, Mr. John Glenn, flew with
you once. When we asked him, he said we should ask you.

Sincerely,

Members of Mr. Smith's third-grade class
```

Answer the letter using language and concepts third-graders could understand. To aid you in writing your answer, we provide you with source material published by NASA.[2] You need not document your source in your letter. Your letterhead reads as follows:

National Aeronautics and Space Administration
Washington DC 20402

Your title is "Educational Specialist."

SOURCE MATERIAL FOR EXERCISE 15

Color images can be made by taking three black-and-white frames in succession and blending ("registering") them on one another in the three color-planes of a television screen. In order for that to work, however, each of the three frames has to be taken by the camera on board the spacecraft through different filters. On *Voyager,* one frame is taken through a blue filter, one through a green filter, and one through an orange filter.

Filters have varying effects on the amount of light being measured. For example, light that passes through a blue filter will favor the blue values in the image, making them appear brighter or transparent, whereas red or orange values will appear much darker than normal. On Earth the three images are given the appropriate colors of the filters through which they were measured and then blended together to give a color image.

An important feat the interplanetary spacecraft must accomplish is focusing on its target while traveling at extremely high speeds. *Voyager* sped past Uranus at more than forty thousand miles an hour. To get an unblurred image, the cameras on board had to steadily track their target while the camera shutters were open. The technique to do this, called image-motion compensation, involves rotating the entire spacecraft under the control of

---

[2]Robert Haynes, *How We Get Pictures from Space* (Washington: GPO, n.d.) 9.

the stabilizing gyroscopes. The strategy was used successfully both at Saturn's satellite Rhea and Uranus. Both times, cameras tracked their targets without interruption.

Once the image is reconstructed by computers on Earth, it sometimes happens that objects appear nondescript or that subtle shades in planetary details such as cloudtops cannot be discerned by visual examination alone. This can be overcome, however, by adding a final "contrast enhancement" to the production. The process of contrast enhancement is like adjusting the contrast and brightness controls on a television set. Because the shades of the image are broken down into picture elements, the computer can increase or decrease brightness values of individual pixels, thereby exaggerating their differences and sharpening even the tiniest details.

For example, suppose a portion of an image returned from space reveals an area of subtle gray tones. Data from the computer indicate the range in brightness values is between 98 and 120, and all are fairly evenly distributed. To the unaided eye, the portion appears as a blurred gray patch because the shades are too nearly similar to be discerned. To eliminate this visual handicap, the brightness values can be assigned new numbers. The shades can be spread farther apart, say, five shades apart rather than the one currently being looked at. Because the data are already stored on computers, it is a fairly easy task to isolate the twenty-three values and assign them new ones: 98 could be assigned 20, 99 assigned 25, and so on. The resulting image is "enhanced" to the unaided eye, while the information is the same accurate data transmitted from the vicinity of the object in space.

The past twenty-five years of space travel and exploration have generated an unprecedented quantity of data from planetary systems. Images taken in space and telemetered back to Earth have greatly aided scientists in formulating better and more accurate theories about the nature and origin of our solar system. Data gathered at close range, and from above the distorting effects of Earth's atmosphere, produce images far more detailed than pictures taken by even the largest Earth-bound telescopes.

In our search to understand the world, as well as the universe, in which we live, we have in one generation reached farther than in any other generation before us. We have overcome the limitations of looking from the surface of our planet and have traveled to others. Whatever yearning drew those first stargazers from the security of their caves to look up at the night sky and wonder still draws men and women to the stars.

CHAPTER 10

RESUMES, EMPLOYMENT LETTERS, AND APPLICATION FORMS

Every step of seeking employment is highly competitive in matters both large and small and whether the unemployment rate is low or high. A letter from a former student to one of the authors illustrated this point rather painfully. He told us that in one instance he and his staff were choosing between two recent graduates who seemed equal in every professional way. The decision was finally made by taking the person who had prepared the neatest application. As you read Chapters 10 and 11, take note of the different communication activities you will engage in and the number of people you will encounter as you look for a job. Whether the deciding factor is a neat application or if you answered your home telephone in a professional manner or if you showed respect for the receptionist taking your application, you must have solid oral and written communication skills to present your credentials to an employer.

Seeking employment will thrust you into many competitive communication situations, both written and oral. Your first contact with a potential employer may be by means of a letter of application and a resume showing your education and experience. Or, a friend may tell you about an opening at the company she works for and suggest you send her supervisor an e-mail message. Or, the guest speaker at the student professional organization you belong to (for example, the Society of American Foresters or the Association of Nursing Students) may suggest that you send him your resume. If you present yourself effectively in the initial contact—frequently a spoken one—you will most likely be asked to send your resume. If your letter and resume succeed, you will probably be interviewed. If you obtain an interview, consider your resume and letter successful whether you receive a job offer or not. Remember those interviewing you are looking for someone who will contribute to their team's activities and work well with other members of the team.

The job search requires that you do more than write a resume to obtain an interview. You may also need to write requests for letters of recommendation and several follow-up letters, such as thank-you notes to those who interviewed you and those who wrote you letters of recommendation. You will also write letters of acceptance and refusal. You will likely complete an application form. To help you successfully reach your goal of a job, we discuss all these communication situations in this chapter. Read what we have to say about letters, resumes, and application forms, but also review library and Web resources and talk with your school's career placement advisers, a recent graduate, friends, and someone doing what you want to do. Some of the advice you gather may contradict other advice. You must decide what advice best fits your personal and career goals.

This chapter and Chapter 11 provide information on the job hunting process. At the end of this chapter, we provide a self-inventory that will help you evaluate your interests and abilities. We describe the features of letters of application, resumes, and application forms and show you several examples. You must adapt the information to your needs. Keep in mind our definition of workplace writing: writing for a specific purpose, to a specific audience, to convey the information the audience needs. Your purpose is to find a job. You will need to evaluate what each employer wants and present your credentials (information about yourself) in such a way that employers (your audience) will see how you meet their hiring requirements.

Obtaining an interview and a job offer are your goals. In Chapter 11, we describe portfolios and interviews and suggest some techniques for having successful interviews. In an interview, employers want to see evidence of your expertise in your field (whether it is building houses, designing Web sites or writing instructions or press releases). A portfolio contains samples of your communications and area-of-specialization activities to show potential employers during an interview.

TIMING

You should begin the job-search process early and allow enough time to research and apply for positions that best fit your personal and career goals. You also must add in the time it takes for companies and organizations to work through the hiring process. Looking for a position that is part of your career plans is not the same as looking for a part-time position to earn income while going to school. The more specialized the training needed for a position, the more time you may need to find a position.

Figure 10.1 provides a time line to help you plan your job search. You will fill in the dates that fit your plans. You cannot expect to graduate, look for a job for a week or two, and then start to work. If you want to start work shortly after you graduate, you need to begin looking three to six months ahead of time, depending on the current demand for workers in your field. Employment counselors, teachers, and friends working in the field have a pretty good idea of what the job market is like.

Few companies can fill an opening immediately. They must advertise the position, review the applications, interview a select few of the applicants, and meet state and federal employment guidelines providing equal opportunities for employment before they can make a job offer. Companies invest a lot of time and money when they hire you (more than just the amount you receive in your paycheck). Training you, providing health insurance and other benefits, and equipping your workstation are just a few of the additional costs. They want to make sure their investment is worthwhile. The process may take two weeks; it may take three months. Most likely the time will be four to six weeks from the time the company first approaches you for an interview.

PREPARATION

Before the letter writing begins, you must prepare yourself in at least two ways. First, inventory your own interests, education, experience, and abilities. Second, explore the job market to find out what is available for you.

Suggested Time Line for Job Search

	Month to Begin Job Search Activity *Fill in the months. For example:*							Graduate
	Nov	Dec	Jan	Feb	Mar	Apr	May	June
Preparation								
Self-Inventory	█	█	█	█	█			
Job Exploration								
Professional Organizations			█	█	█	█	█	█
Career Placement Office	*check your school's schedule for interviews* →							
Teachers			█	█	█			
Web Sites			█	█	█			
Resume								
Content	*revise as needed for each application* →							
Send Format								
Traditional Hard Copy	█	█						
Scannable				█	█	█	█	█
Electronic				█	█	█	█	█
Web				█	█	█	█	█
Letters								
Application				█	█	█	█	
Other						█	█	█
Application Form					█	█	█	█
Portfolio	*add to as you develop writing projects* →							
Interview					█	█	█	█

Figure 10.1 Construct a time line to help plan your job search. When you start your search will depend upon the job market, your school schedule, your career goals, and your personal goals. The self-inventory, traditional resume, and portfolio should be your first activities.

Self-Inventory

Begin by reviewing relevant significant events in your life. What did you accomplish in high school and college? What do you remember of your course work? Which courses did you enjoy? Which courses could you barely tolerate? Where did you earn your highest and lowest grades? Focus your attention on the most relevant part of your schooling. Rarely will you refer back to your high school activities if you have an associate or bachelor's degree, military experience, or other specialized training such as in heating and air conditioning installation or maintenance of a UNIX mainframe environment.

What were your extracurricular activities? Have you any long-standing hobbies such as photography, needlepoint, rebuilding engines, or gardening? Have you been active in political, social, religious, or civic groups? Do you enjoy sports, music, or surfing the Web? Be sure to include appropriate activities that might set you apart from other applicants. For example, if you have a private pilot's license, include that information. Having the license says something about you—your personality, your level of ability, and so on. The employer sees a pilot as someone who invested considerable time in an activity that carries great responsibility for the safety of others. Child-care responsibilities have similar connotations for employers. If you took care of three children under the age of six, you were entrusted with a responsibility that not everyone can handle.

What has been your work experience? What was your first job? Your most recent? What have been your duties and responsibilities? What sort of work have you enjoyed? Have you been in the military? What training and jobs did you have there? Did you work while going to school?

In the planning and revising checklist at the end of this chapter we provide a self-inventory—a series of questions you should ask yourself as a way of discovering the information you need. Open a file on your computer and type in the answers to the questions. This written self-inventory is a useful document for at least two reasons.

1. **A self-inventory helps you get in touch with your own identity.** Consider those activities you have succeeded in and enjoyed. Which did you enjoy more, computer programming or English? Do you prefer math to psychology or the other way around? Do you relate best to people or to working with equipment such as computers? Which would you rather do, read a book, go to a large, noisy party, or play charades with a few close friends? Never mind which you think you *should* like. Which do you *really* like? Have you ever sold merchandise in a store? Did you enjoy it? Is money extremely important to you or not? Do you stick to jobs? Do you see new ways to get an old job done? Are you willing to take a chance on people or on jobs? Do you find the most satisfaction in stability or change? Do you work well independently or would you rather have your tasks spelled out for you?

   Be honest in your answers and analysis. It's your life. You would not want to spend it doing something you don't enjoy. And you're more likely to succeed at work you truly enjoy and have the capabilities for. A good sales representative might make a terrible horticulturist and vice versa.

2. **The self-inventory highlights the education and experience that will make you attractive to a potential employer.** While you're analyzing yourself, be alert for evidence of those qualities employers value: loyalty, willingness to shoulder responsibility, ability to stick to a task until it is done, initiative, enough flexibility and a positive attitude to realize that things don't always go perfectly but that most problems can be solved. You must be a good communicator and work well with others no matter what job you have.

You'll be able to draw upon the self-inventory information in all the communication activities of the job search, such as writing your resume and letters of application and filling in employers' application forms. Such information is particularly useful during an employment interview when you are expected to describe your qualities and abilities.

JOB EXPLORATION

As you begin the search for a job, first let everyone know that you are looking for a job and what type of job you would like. Some of the people we identify below you may want to provide with a short summary of your career goals and experiences, or you may want to give them a copy of your resume. Others you may want to make an appointment to visit or take them to lunch so that you can describe your career plans to them without interruptions. Your self-inventory will provide you with the information to share.

Networking—letting as many people as possible know that you are actively looking for work—is important. Employers like to know a little bit about you before they contact you. They depend upon formal and informal recommendations from others as they evaluate you. Your networking should include the following:

• Student chapters of professional organizations offer opportunities for students to meet members of the profession. Become active in such an organization. You may be surprised at how many doors this will open. More and more organizations also have Web sites with job listings.

• Career counselors at your school can be invaluable. Register with your school's career center. Employers routinely contact career centers and make campus visits to interview students. Career counselors have resources available to help you with your search and will help you target your search.

• College faculty and training instructors can be helpful networkers. Employers frequently call schools and ask about graduating students. Frequently the employers have hired a graduate of the school who has done outstanding work, and they hope to find other graduates with similar abilities. Let your teachers know how to reach you. You also may want to ask them if you may list them as a reference.

• Friends and relatives can spread the word that may reach someone who is looking for a dependable worker. They work in places where you might want to work and can tell you a good deal about working conditions, opportunities for advancement, company policies, needed skills, and so forth. They are valuable sources of information.

Once you get the word out, gather as much information as possible about potential jobs and potential employers. The Planning and Revising Checklist at the end of this chapter provides a series of questions in the Employer Inventory (page 290) to help you gather the information you need. Where can you obtain such information?

• Use the World Wide Web to gather information from three sources. One is the company Web site for the company you want to work for. Such sites describe the activities of the company and frequently list job opportunities. For example, Hewlett Packard's homepage (www.hp.com) links to *Jobs at HP*. From there, you can follow numerous paths to find out about working at Hewlett Packard and how to apply. You may choose to follow links that use terms such as *college recruiting* or *recent graduates* and avoid wasting time reading about positions that require several years of experience.

A second Web source you should review is the site for the professional organization that represents your field: for example, American Public Health Association (www.apha.org), the Institute of Electrical and Electronics Engineers (www.ieee.org), and the National Agri-Marketing Association (www.nama.org).

Companies that specialize in career information are a third source (Figure 10.2). These companies have Web sites for posting your resume and accessing job banks. You may find the amount of information overwhelming. Use the questions at the end of the chapter to help guide you with the information gathering. Figure 10.2 lists a few of the many career service and job bank sites on the Web.

• Register with your school's career placement office. We noted under networking that you should contact your school's career placement office. Contact the office at least one semester or quarter before you plan to graduate—earlier is better. Many schools now have you enter items from your self-inventory into a database either on disk or across the Web. When they receive a call for an education major with experience in teaching kindergarten, piano, and computers, they will search the database using keywords such as *early childhood education, kindergarten, music, piano, word processing, ClarisWorks,* and so on. Few students' resumes will match all of the keywords entered—that's expected. You will be notified if you meet a significant number of the requirements.

• Read the newspaper, including the want ads. Not only will you keep up on the activities of your community, but you will also read about where the new bank will be located or when the local manufacturer is hiring. The want ads list specific openings.

Web Resource	Web Address (http://)
America's Employers	www.americasemployers.com
America's Job Bank	www.ajb.dni.us
CareerMart	www.careermart.com
CareerMosaic	www.careermosaic.com
CareerPath.com	www.careerpath.com
Career Resource Center	www.careers.org
College Grad Job Hunter	www.collegegrad.com
Cool Works	www.coolworks.com
HeadHunter.net	www.HeadHunter.Net
JobTrak	www.jobtrak.com
JobWeb	www.jobweb.com
U.S. Office of Personnel Management	www.usajobs.opm.gov

Figure 10.2 Companies and the U.S. government provide career services across the World Wide Web. We have listed only a few of the many commercial sites. The Web site for your school library or career placement office probably links to some of these and to others.

- Check with your state employment office or human resource department about state employment. The federal government also lists jobs. If you have access to the Web, you might begin with America's Job Bank (www.ajb.dni.us), a site developed by the U.S. Department of Labor and states' employment services, or www.usajobs.opm.gov, the site maintained by the U.S. Office of Personnel Management.

- Your librarian and school placement officer can direct you to many other sources, including many that relate to specific industries, organizations, and geographic areas. We have listed some of these resources in Figure 10.3. Much of this information is on the World Wide Web and may be linked through your library's home page.

One source you should be sure to check is the *Occupational Outlook Handbook* available in most libraries and on the Web (http://stats.bls.gov/ocohome.htm). Figure 10.4 illustrates information you can gather from the *Handbook*—information that may help you target your career search.

Finding information about jobs and employers should be part of your preparation for the job hunt. You will ask better questions in an interview if you know about the company. You will show the employer that you have a real interest in the position and want to work for the company.

Check your school's library or career placement office for the following resources:

College Placement Annual
Dun's Census of American Business
Global Company Handbook
International Directory of Company Histories
Million Dollar Directory
Moody's International Manual
Occupational Outlook Handbook
    (http://stats.bls.gov/ocohome.htm)
Standard and Poor's Register of Corporations, Directors,
    and Executives
Thomas Register of American Manufacturers
    (www.thomasregister.com)
Ward's Business Directory

Figure 10.3 Most libraries subscribe to at least two of the resources. The resources provide information such as products and services, lists of directors, contact names, company size, company location, and telephone and fax numbers.

The ten occupations with the fastest employment growth, 1996–2006.
(Numbers in thousands of jobs)

Occupation	Employment 1996	Employment 2006	Change, 1996–2006 Number	Change, 1996–2006 Percent
Database administrators, computer support specialists, and all other computer scientists	212	461	249	118
Computer engineers	216	451	235	109
Systems analysts	506	1025	520	103
Personal- and home-care aides	202	374	171	85
Physical, corrective therapy assistants, aides	84	151	66	79
Home health aides	495	873	378	76
Medical assistants	225	391	166	74
Desktop-publishing specialists	30	53	22	74
Physical therapists	115	196	81	71
Occupational therapy assistants, aides	16	26	11	69

Adapted from the *Occupational Outlook Handbook*.

Figure 10.4 The Occupational Outlook Handbook provides an enormous amount of information you might find useful as you make career choices. This table identifies 10 fields that are predicted to grow and need more employees.
Source: Bureau of Labor Statistics. Employment Projections. 8 Sept. 1998. 12 May 1999 ⟨http://stats.bls.gov/news.release/ecopro.table6.htm⟩.

RESUMES

If you will remember in Chapter 2, we discussed *change*. *Change* may be the key word to remember as we describe *resumes* (pronounced *rez-uh-may* and sometimes given its original French accent marks *résumé*). In the past three years, changes in technology have affected the way we produce and distribute resumes. The content of resumes has changed little, but the format and method of delivering the resume to the employer have changed. In this section, we first describe the content of a resume—that is, what information you include in a resume. We then describe current (but changing) ways to send a resume.

Spend your time on the content. Once you have the content in place, you can easily adapt the format to send the resume. You must create your resume electronically and use a laser printer or a high-quality ink-jet printer for hard-copy versions. Don't even consider submitting a typed or handwritten resume.

CONCENTRATING ON THE CONTENT

You will gather the content for your resume from your self-inventory. Select information depending upon the type of resume you plan to produce and the job you are applying for. Remember that the job description establishes your purpose, and your reader is the person(s) who reviews the resume and interviews you. We include several examples of resumes in this chapter. Use the examples for ideas but modify the content (the information) you include and the order of the content depending upon the job description.

Figures 10.5, 10.6, 10.7, 10.8, and 10.9 illustrate variations on two common resume types: chronological and functional. With either resume, you must identify your purpose and audience and adapt the content and format for the specific job. Chronological (Figures 10.6, 10.7, and 10.8) resumes are the most common and familiar. They are perhaps best used when most of your education and work experience seem to point toward a specific career goal.

If you have gaps in your work or educational experience or if you decide to change careers, the functional resume (Figure 10.9) may be your best choice. It allows you to list your experiences under functional categories that will best demonstrate those of your capabilities that relate to the jobs you are seeking. In the example, the student has chosen categories such as technical writing, technical editing, Web design, presentations, and creative writing. Headings on your resume might be *technical support, computer programming, sales, organization, management, research, teaching, construction*, and so forth.

Word-processing software lets you vary your resume from employer to employer. Review the job description and pull information from your self-inventory that will support the job description. Figure 10.10 shows a job description with keywords highlighted. Keywords are words that you

Kelly J. Bennett

School Address: 8th Street, Apt. 10A Boise, ID 83700 208-111-9999 kjbennett@mail.com	Home Address: 1611 Wafer Lane Marytown, ID 82200 208-456-7899

Education	Chemical Engineering, Idaho University, Bachelor of Science, 2001
Military Training	Infantry, Ft. Benning, 1995 Airborne, Ft. Benning, 1996 Advanced International Morse Code, Ft. Bragg, 1996 Special Forces Qualification Course, Ft. Bragg, 1997
Experience	Firefighter, Boise Fire Department, Boise, ID, January 1999–present Responsibilities: firefighter, apparatus operator Special Forces Communications Sergeant (SSG), National Guard, Boise, ID, January 1999–present Responsibilities: Operate and repair $500,000 communications equipment Computer service technician, ComputExperts, Boise, ID, June 1993– May 1995. Responsibilities: Repaired hardware problems on personal computers.
Skills	Spanish, Ft. Bragg, June 1996–November 1996 EMT/Firefighter I, Boise, ID, January 1999–May 1999 Firefighter II, Boise, ID, June 1999 Apparatus Operator, Boise, ID, June 1999
Activities	Boise Softball League Champions 1999
Expertise	Speak, write, read Spanish fluently Use computer programs C++, AutoCAD

Figure 10.5 The first draft of your chronological resume may look like this. If you open a word-processing file and create a two-column table, you can copy and paste in information from your self-inventory. Figure 10.6 shows a revised version of the resume.

Kelly J. Bennett

School Address:
2011-8th Street, Apt. 10A
Boise, ID 83700
208-111-9999
kjbennett@mail.com

Home Address:
1611 Wafer Lane
Marytown, ID 82200
208-456-7899

Education	**Idaho University,** Boise, ID Bachelor of Chemical Engineering Expected graduation, June 2001
Military Training 6/95–12/98	Special Forces Qualification Course, Ft. Bragg, 1997 Advanced International Morse Code, Ft. Bragg, 1996 Airborne, Ft. Benning, 1996 Infantry, Ft. Benning, 1995
Experience 1/99–present	**Boise Fire Department,** Boise, ID *Firefighter II* • Apparatus Operator • Unit Supervisor
1/99–present	**Idaho National Guard,** Boise, ID *Special Forces Communications Sergeant* • Operate and repair $500,000 communications equipment • Deployed to Bosnia • Spanish School, Ft. Bragg • Special Forces Qualification Course, Ft. Bragg
6/93–5/95	**ComputExperts,** Boise, ID *Computer service technician* • Repaired hardware for all makes of personal computers • Managed listserv for three clients
Expertise	Speak, write, read Spanish fluently Program in C++ Use AutoCAD for design projects
Activities	Pitcher, Boise Softball League Champions 1999

Figure 10.6 A revised version of a chronological resume shown in Figure 10.5. Helpful changes include the use of white space, headings, and a san serif typeface for the headings. The table structure holds the information in place even though the lines are removed.

Mark G. Patterson
956 Roberts Street
Rochester, NY 14622
716-554-6231

Education   Forest Park College, Rochester, NY
Candidate for Associate in Applied Science, June 1999

Concentration in Electronic Technology with emphasis on
reading schematic drawings and sketches, building and testing
prototype circuits, and modifying electronic apparatus.

Have FCC license: second-class radiotelephone.

Member of Drama Club
Treasurer of Student Government Association

College expenses 100% self-financed.

Use clauses
and phrases,
not complete
sentences.

Work Experience

1997–present   Radio Shack, Rochester, NY

Work 20 hours a week as salesperson. Sell all types of radio and
electronic equipment, which involves explaining the equipment,
showing people how to operate it, and demonstrating tuning and
minor report procedures. Top salesperson of month for five
months in 1998.

Note reverse
chronological
order for
education and
experience.

1989–1993   Newspaper delivery, record announcer at roller skating rink,
request line operator at radio station.

Military Service

1993–1997   United States Navy
Highest Rank Aviation Electronics Technician 2/c
Assigned to U.S.S. *Kitty Hawk*.
Repaired, tested, calibrated, and maintained electronic devices
including airborne radio and radar equipment.

Personal Background

Grew up in Rochester, New York. Have traveled in Spain, Italy,
and Greece. Interests include singing, amateur dramatics, ham
radio operation, and cross-country skiing.

Figure 10.7 The order of the information may change. The examples given put education first. If you are a student working toward an associate or bachelor's degree, your education is the qualification you want to stress. However, if Mark Patterson wants to apply for a position with an electronics firm with military contracts, and the position does not require a college degree, he might place his education information below his military experience.

ANNA MOOSAD

1509 Oxford Road	Charlottesville, VA 22901	804-205-3333

EDUCATION **VIRGINIA COLLEGE,** Charlottesville, VA
Bachelor of Science, Biology, December 2000

100% financially responsible for all college expenses.

RELEVANT Environmental Biology   Plant Ecology
COURSES Organic Chemistry   Herpetology
Biological Statistics   Silviculture

HONORS AND 4-Year Scholarship, Biology Council
ACTIVITIES Member, Wildlife Society

WORK **COUNTRY'S BBQ** Charlottesville, VA
EXPERIENCE *Head Server*
9/98–present Establish workstation rotation and shift schedules. Ensure customer satisfaction.

Trainer
Explain restaurant policies and procedures to new employees. Conduct health and safety training sessions.

Cashier
Processed customer receipts. Closed register at the end of the shift and deposited weekend receipts averaging $3700.

11/99–present **VAC RADIO** Charlottesville, VA
Production Manager
Coordinated air time schedules, planned programs, set up remote sites for broadcasting sporting events. Filed FCC quarterly reports.

Summer 1998 **U.S. NATIONAL PARK SERVICE** Luray, VA
Trail Maintenance Crew
Cleared trails in the Shenandoah National Park.

REFERENCES Enclosed.

Figure 10.8 A resume created using a resume service database follows similar formats. You can modify some of the headings and the format, but you cannot make a lot of changes. The database searches for keywords within the major fields (education, work experience, and so on).

Angela Maria Chang
922 Burke Place
Lubbock, TX 79401
806-967-9071
changam@tx.mail.edu
www.tx.edu/~changam

Objective	To research, design, and write descriptions for displays at museums, zoos, and entertainment parks.
Education	West Texas University, Lubbock, TX Bachelor of Arts in English, June 1999 GPA: Major 3.64; Overall 3.21

Writing Experience

Technical Writing	• Developed documentation for file management features in Windows 98 • Interviewed prospective users, compiled a user analysis, and oversaw user testing • Designed page layouts in WordPerfect • Collaborated with team members
Technical Editing	• Performed a substantive edit on grant proposal for Plains Museum of West Texas • Determined style guidelines including font, justification, and spacing • Completed numerous copyediting tasks using standard copyediting symbols
Web Design	• Created a personal Web site with online resume and portfolio • Self-taught basic- and intermediate-level HTML codes • Researched Web page layout and design
Research	• Researched guidelines for entertainment park information for customers • Investigated the use of symbols, such as $, %, and &, in technical documents • Interviewed the chief editor of *Phi Kappa Phi*, a national scholarly magazine
Presentations	• Developed a 20-minute/16-slide presentation on Plains Museum of West Texas information signs for visitors using Corel Presentations • Created a 15-minute/12-slide presentation on online editing using Microsoft PowerPoint
Creative writing	• Published a poem, "Sweet and Sour Reverie," in the university's literary magazine • Drafted, revised, and prepared for submission eight short stories and many poems
Computer Knowledge	Windows 98; WordPerfect 8; Microsoft Word 97; Corel Presentations; Microsoft PowerPoint; Intermediate HTML; Basic Microsoft Excel; Basic Microsoft Access
Honors	*Alpha Lambda Delta,* national honor society *Phi Eta Sigma,* freshman honor society *Dean's List,* Fall 1993, Spring 1995, Winter 1997

Volunteer

Summers 1998–99	**Plains Museum of West Texas University** Children's Group Leader

Work Experience

8/98–6/99	Papa John's Pizza, Lubbock, TX; Driver
Summer 98	Ruby Tuesday, Lubbock, TX; Server
Summer 97	Denaro's Restaurant, Lubbock, TX; Server
Summer 96	Main Dining Room, Big Sky Resort, Big Sky, Montana; Busser
Summer 95	Camp Greylock, Becket, Massachusetts; Senior Counselor/Soccer Instructor

Figure 10.9 The functional resume may be used to highlight skills that most likely are not revealed in your work experience. The student in this example had work experience that was good, but unrelated to her career objective.

MAJOR DUTIES:

— Coordinates and conducts a **radio telemetry** study on young **sandhill cranes,** involving **locating nests and young, ageing eggs and chicks, attaching radios to chicks, following chicks** daily in difficult terrain, **recording locations,** and **determining causes of deaths** by examination of carcasses and other evidence at the death scene. Uses a **rocket-net** to capture and band cranes.

— Conducts **North American Breeding Bird Surveys** involving identification of western passerine birds by sight and call.

— Assists in operation of a migrant passerine bird monitoring station on the refuge, involving **mist-netting,** species identification by sight and call, **banding, and ageing and sexing passerines** in the hand through knowledge of specific techniques such as **skulling and plumage** features.

— Coordinates and conducts **wildlife and habitat inventory projects** requiring **ground, water and aerial observations,** which provide scientific data for monitoring and evaluation of wildlife management on the refuge. Monitors effects of **land management practices** on wildlife and wildlife habitat and provides recommendations for improved wildlife management.

— Coordinates and conducts **duck banding operations,** including ageing and sexing ducks in the hand and keeping accurate records. **Reads color markers** on geese, cranes, and trumpeter swans and keeps accurate records of observations.

— Prepares **biological reports,** and assists in **writing of environmental assessments, management plans, and scientific papers** for publication.

— Assists in **tabulating and applying statistical analyses** to wildlife data. **Maintains computer wildlife databases.**

— Operates and provides **routine maintenance for refuge biological equipment** (canoes, motorboats, airboats, ATV-type motorcycles, and refuge vehicles including 4-wheel drive).

QUALIFICATION REQUIREMENTS:
Selective factors: The applicant for this position must possess skill in identification of western passerine birds by sight and sound and in aerial census of waterfowl.

Candidates must meet the basic requirements specified under either A or B below:
A.   A bachelor's or higher degree from an accredited college or university with major in a biological science which included:
—At least 9 semester hours in such **wildlife subjects** as mammalogy, ornithology, animal ecology, wildlife management, or research courses in the field of wildlife biology; and
—At least 12 semester hours in **zoology** in such subjects as general zoology, invertebrate zoology, vertebrate zoology, comparative anatomy, physiology, genetics, ecology, cellular biology, parasitology, entomology, or research courses in such subjects; and
—At least 9 semester hours in **botany** or the related plant sciences.
(Note: Excess courses in wildlife biology may be used to meet the zoology requirements where appropriate.)

B. Combination of education and experience ...

Figure 10.10 As you write your letter of application and resume, review the job description. Incorporate some of the words used in the description into your letter and resume. Include only those that apply to your experience. We have bolded some words an applicant for the above job might include. In Figure 10.15, we illustrate the application letter for a student responding to this job description.
Source: US Office of Personnel Management. USA Jobs. 12 June 1998. ⟨http://www.usajobs.opm.gov/wfjic/jobs/BD3771.HTM⟩.

should include on your resume if at all possible. No one will be able to include all of the keywords, but you should include some. Always give an accurate, honest picture of your qualifications, and always present them in language that is familiar to your readers.

In Figure 10.5 and 10.6, we show the first draft and final version. The student, Kelly Bennett, had significant work experience including military experience before returning to school. The student copied and pasted information from her self-inventory into the table structure of a word-processing document. The final version shows how the student rearranged information and worked on the document design. The information is still in a table but with the lines removed. More white space and headings help the reader see the information.

You will select information from the self-inventory and adapt headings to best describe the information you include. In the following paragraphs we talk briefly about the types of information you probably want to include (name/addresses, education, experience, activities, and so on) and mention others you may want to consider (objective, religious or political activities). You select the information and format based on the information the reader wants.

Name and Address

In the section with your name and address(es), you might also include your e-mail address and Web address. Only include the e-mail and Web address if you check your e-mail regularly and if you want the readers to see your Web site. They *will likely* visit your Web site before they contact you because it is one more way to evaluate your work before interviewing you.

Career Objective

Many recommend you state your career objective and list those capabilities and achievements that fit you for such an objective. Remember that although a stated career objective may open some doors, it may shut others. If you omit the career objective from your resume, you can always include it in your letter of application. On the other hand, the resume may be scanned in to a database and a letter probably won't be, so you may want to include an objective on your resume.

Education and Experience

Whether you choose to emphasize the chronological or functional for your resume, keep it brief but with good coverage of your education and experience. Use phrases and dependent clauses rather than complete sentences. Don't give a mere list of your courses and job titles. Rather, describe what you have actually learned, done, and accomplished in school and on the job. The order on the page and where you boldface information affects what the reader will see. Create several versions of your resume and ask others to critique them.

Activities

You must set yourself apart from others with similar training. Your activities and other interests do this. Employers want to see this side of you. As you select information from the self-inventory, think about how others will interpret the information. Your religious and political activities may or may not be appropriate information. For example, if you are applying for a position with a service organization such as United Way, you might include your volunteer activities with the Girl Scouts and Sunday school class. If you are applying for a position as a computer programmer at an international company, you might omit the church-related activities.

Your computer skills may be important to include if they go beyond the basic office software. (College graduates are expected to understand basic word processing and file management.) Use the space to identify expertise in software and programs that members of your profession use, such as AutoCAD, Java, or C++.

Document design options for your resume are unlimited. Just keep your reader in mind. We have several recommendations to start you off:

- Don't crowd elements on the page.

- Leave plenty of white space.

- Keep bold and italic text, typeface changes, and border lines to a minimum. (Faxed and scanned resumes should have no lines and no unusual spacing or characters. The machines have trouble "translating" the characters.)

- If you must, don't be afraid to go to a second page. However, most employers will be more attracted to a well-organized, brief summary than to a long, detailed discussion of everything you have ever done. They are busy people. A one-page resume works for most situations; if you go to two pages, be sure to fill the second page. You want the reader to think you have more to say.

Most word-processing software has a resume template. That is, you can open a resume-formatted file that establishes the document's design. All you must do is fill in an area as you are prompted. Resume templates are fine but they restrict your ability to adjust the content. You must follow the established format, and your experience may not fit neatly into the assigned categories. Resume database forms also are structured such that you may have trouble matching your qualification with the established categories.

SENDING THE RESUME

You have several options for delivering your resume to a potential employer. You can fax the resume or send a hard copy through the mail. Or, you can send your resume electronically as an attachment, across the Web, or entered into a database. You cannot go wrong sending a traditional, hard-copy resume. In fact, we recommend that no matter how else you send the resume you should also send a copy laser printed on good quality paper. On the Disney Web site, you find the following advice:

> For certain positions, you may want to have two versions of your resume:
>
> 1. For the computer to read—with a scannable format and detailed information. Submit this one.
> 2. For the recruiter to read—possibly with a creative layout, enhanced typography, and summarized information. Carry this one to the interview.[1]

Not only does the Disney description distinguish between how you submit the versions, it also notes the extent of the information to submit. The length of the scannable resume doesn't matter. What matters is that you give "detailed information" with keywords (nouns) that the search engine of the database will pick up. The resume for the recruiter "summarizes" information about you. You should still use descriptive nouns but keep your description to one to two pages.

Traditional Hard-Copy Resumes

You must have a hard copy of your resume. When you go to the interview, have several copies with you (in your portfolio, see Chapter 11) even though you know the person interviewing you has one. You may meet others who do not have a copy.

You must send

- A perfect resume—no spelling errors or incorrect information. It must *look good.*

- A *clean* copy. Your resume will be copied and passed around the company. (We have seen several examples of resumes printed on paper that, when copied, shows streaks of cotton or other marks. These marks will distract the reader.)

- The resume in a large enough envelope that you do not have to fold it. The folds may fall in the wrong place and make some lines harder to read. If the resume is faxed or scanned, the fold lines may create problems for the fax machine or the scanner.

- A resume that will fax and scan cleanly. Large companies scan resumes. The recommendations for designing scannable resumes changes with each improvement in scanning technology. Many of the formats you use for the traditional resume will work *if* you (1) remove any lines, (2) use a 12 point sans serif font, and (3) remove unusual graphics and typefaces other than bold. If you send the traditional resume and a resume formatted for scanning in your letter of application, be

[1]*Disney,* Resume Tips, 12 Aug. 1999 ⟨www.disney.com/disneycareers/resumetips.html⟩.

sure to note that you have enclosed two resumes. (Most human re-source managers will recognize what you are doing.)

Figure 10.11 shows the guidelines for sending in a resume found on the Tennessee Valley Authority's (TVA) Web site. You are given several options for sending the resume, and you are also given specific instructions on what to do (for example, including your social security number). The TVA guidelines resemble recommendations given by other companies and organizations.

Figure 10.12 is an example of a resume prepared for scanning. Note the 12 point sans serif font, no unusual spacing or characters, and no lines. Use bold and all-capital letters for emphasis but keep these to a min-imum. Make sure your name is the first item on the page and list phone numbers on separate lines.

The scanned resume is designed to be searched by a database search engine, not be printed out and evaluated for how it looks. However, sometimes the scanned resume is printed out and circulated so that your qualifications can be reviewed. Figure 10.13 illustrates the problems that may occur when a resume is scanned. One of our students reported that the person interviewing him had a copy of his scanned resume but all of his work experience had been omitted. Always have copies of your tradi-tional resume with you. You will then have a complete version of your re-sume with good document design if you need it.

Electronic Resumes

You can distribute your resume electronically in several ways without gen-erating a hard copy. You can (1) send your resume via e-mail as an ASCII file or as an attachment, (2) post your resume on your Web site, (3) submit your resume through a database, or (4) follow other instructions given by the employer. Rapid technology changes demand that you adapt your sub-mission to the requested format of the employer (Figure 10.11). When submitting your resume electronically, you should verify that it was re-ceived. We recommend following an electronic submission with a tradi-tional hard-copy version of your resume if you cannot confirm that your resume was received or if you want to make sure the interviewer sees a complete and well-formatted version of your resume.

When e-mailing your resume, it will help if you know how the re-ceiver will handle it. If the receiver will print the e-mail message directly, most likely you should convert and adjust your resume to an ASCII file (a document with little formatting) that is inserted into the e-mail message. With current e-mail software, you can use the attachment feature to attach the electronic file in which you created your resume to an e-mail message. The receiver opens the attachment and has a clean copy of your resume with all of the formatting in place. If the receiver prints the attachment, he or she will have a hard copy of your resume just as if you sent a copy through the mail. Be aware that this does not always produce a perfect transfer—keep in touch with the person receiving your resume.

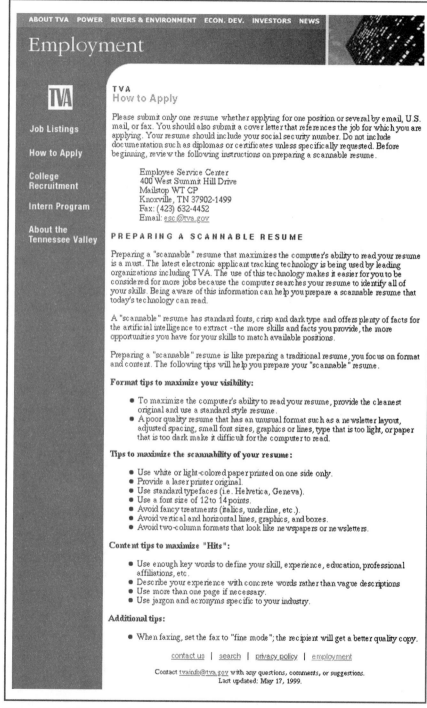

Figure 10.11 TVA suggestions for producing a scannable resume.
Source: TVA. How to Apply. 17 May 1999. 12 Aug. 1999
⟨http://www.tva.gov/people/employment/apply.htm⟩.

Mark G. Patterson
956 Roberts Street
Rochester, NY 14622
716-554-6231

Education

Forest Park College, Rochester, NY
Candidate for Associate in Applied Science, June 1999

Concentration in Electronic Technology with emphasis on reading schematic drawings and sketches, building and testing prototype circuits, and modifying electronic apparatus.

Have FCC license: second-class radiotelephone.

Member of Drama Club.
Treasurer of senior class.

College expenses 100% self-financed.

Work Experience

Radio Shack, Rochester, NY

Work 20 hours a week as salesperson. Sell all types of radio and electronic equipment, which involves explaining the equipment, showing people how to operate it, and demonstrating tuning and minor report procedures. Top salesperson of month for five months in 1998. (1997–present)

Newspaper delivery, record announcer at roller skating rink, request line operator at radio station. (1989–1993)

Military Service

United States Navy 1993–1997
Highest Rank Aviation Electronics Technician 2/c
Assigned to U.S.S. *Kitty Hawk*.
Repaired, tested, calibrated, and maintained electronic devices including airborne radio and radar equipment.

Personal Background

Grew up in Rochester, New York. Have traveled in Spain, Italy, and Greece. Interests include singing, amateur dramatics, ham radio operation, and cross-country skiing.

Figure 10.12 Compare this resume prepared for scanning with the traditional resume in Figure 10.7. Note the sans serif font, use of bold, and placement of text along the left margin. Figure 10.13 show the results of scanning this resume.

Mark G. Patterson   *7 7 7 7 7 7 7*
956 Roberts Street
Rochester, NY 14622
716-554-6231

Education
Forest Park College, Rochester, NY
Candidate for Associate in Applied Science, June 1999

Concentration in Electronic Technology with emphasis on reading schematic drawings and sketches, building and testing prototype circuits, and modifying electronic apparatus.

Have FCC license: second-class radiotelephone.

Member of Drama Club.
Treasurer of senior class.

College expenses 100% self-financed.
Work Experience
Radio Shack, Rochester, NY

Work 20 hours a week as salesperson. Sell all types of radio and electronic equipment, which involves explaining the equipment, showing people how to operate it, and demonstrating tuning and minor report procedures. Top salesperson of month for five months in 1998. (1997–present)

Newspaper delivery, record announcer at roller skating rink, request line operator at radio station. (1989–1993)
Military Service

United States Navy (1993–1997)

Highest Rank Aviation Electronics Technician 2/c Assigned to U.S.S. *Kitty Hawk*. Repaired, tested, calibrated, and maintained electronic devices including airborne radio and radar equipment.
Personal Background
Grew up in Rochester, New York. Have traveled in Spain, Italy, and Greece.
Interests include singing, amateur dramatics, ham radio operation, and cross skiing.

Figure 10.13 Compare the results of scanning the resume in Figure 10.12. Some of the spacing collapsed and some of the boldfacing disappeared. The information is intact, however, and a search using keywords such as *electronics, FCC license,* and *associate* degree will bring up this resume. (When we tested this resume, we found that using a san serif font such as Univers or Geneva is important because the scanning program we used did not recognize several words where the comma and the last letter were too close together. We cannot explain why our test also put sevens at the top of the resume.)

Sending a resume as an attachment is becoming a popular way to send the resume. Recent developments allow the database you use to create a resume for your school's career placement service to send your resume as an attachment that pulls directly from the data. The receiver simply double-clicks on an attachment icon to open the resume information directly into word-processing software. The receiver has a good-quality resume without you printing a copy and mailing it. If your school's career placement service has this capability, be sure to send a couple of practice attachments with your resume to friends to make sure you know how and to make sure the resume arrives in good shape.

You may put your resume on your Web site. Most likely you cannot simply convert your word-processing file to an html file and place it on the Web. You will need to adjust the spacing and other features. You will probably want to take advantage of the color and graphic options available to you on the Web. You can link to pages from your resume that show projects you have done, to organizations you are active in, or to companies and organizations you have worked for. (You should obtain permission from the organizations or companies that you link to.) We suggest that you review other resumes on the Web before posting yours. Remember, once your resume is posted, your information is public and accessible to everyone. For security reasons, you may choose not to list your address and telephone number; you may just give an e-mail address.

Submitting your credentials through a database such as one established by your school's career placement office is common. Many Web-based career services (such as the ones listed in Figure 10.2) provide an electronic form. You may have some trouble "fitting" your credentials into the categories. Do the best you can. Use descriptive nouns—words that an employer will likely use as keywords to search the database.

The recommendation now is to use more nouns in your resume than action verbs. Employers tend to enter nouns as keywords. For example, instead of computer *programming*, use *programmer* and list the programs you work with, COBOL, AutoCAD, and Java. A teacher's aide might use nouns such as *phonics in reading groups, student evaluation,* and *parent contact.*

LETTERS

In this section, we describe several types of letters you may write and we give some examples. You must adapt the letters to your situation. And, you may find that some of the letters will actually be e-mail messages. More and more we hear from our students that employers are contacting them at some point in the interview process by e-mail. The e-mail message may simply be confirmation of the interview time or it may include a list of questions that the applicant needs to be prepared to answer. Whether you send a letter by mail, fax, or e-mail, you must take special care in writing and sending the letter. The letters and e-mail messages you write and the phone conversations you have are as much a part of the evaluation process as the resume and interview.

LETTER OF APPLICATION

The letter of application is a way of introducing yourself to an employer. When accompanied by your resume, it should present a picture that is complete enough so that prospective employers can decide whether or not they want to find out more about you. Your desire, of course, is for the letter to result in an interview. The letter of application, therefore, is a selling letter.

Letters of application should be neat, correct, and well written. They should be created on a computer and printed on good bond paper of about 20-lb. weight. You may be short of cash when you're job hunting, but letters and resumes are not the places to be cheap. They represent you, and they should represent you well. Your letters of application and resumes should be perfect. Have a friend read them before you send them out.

The letters in Figures 10.14 and 10.15 are examples of letters of application. Notice that the salutation uses a name. If necessary, you can acquire such names through telephone calls and letters of inquiry. The introduction of each letter tells the employer how the writer learned about the job. It names the job and makes it clear that the writer seeks the job. Avoid tricky openers. One of us recently received a letter that began, "If you don't want to hire a well-educated, fine, industrious instructor, stop right here." Unfortunately for the writer, his reader took him at his word and stopped. Courtesy, tact, and solid information will take you further.

In the middle of the letter in Figure 10.14, the writer does several things. First, he makes it clear that he knows something about the company, thus letting the reader know that he has been doing his homework. In the late-middle part of the illustrated letter, the writer digs into his self-inventory and produces facts that should interest the employer. Normally, these will concern past work and educational experience, but don't overlook the value of referring to extracurricular activities that relate to the job you seek. This portion of the letter may repeat information in the resume, but try to include additional information as well.

Knowing something about the employer helps you choose appropriate facts. Stick to the facts. Don't express opinions about yourself. Let employers form their own opinions. If you have the right facts and choose them well, the opinions will be favorable. Have the job description (Figure 10.10) next to you as you write the letter. Use keywords from the description in your letter and resume when possible, Figures 10.8 and 10.15. Match your credentials with what the employer is looking for but don't stretch the truth. Be honest. Rarely does anyone meet all of the qualifications.

In the closing part of the letter, the writer refers the reader to his resume for additional information. Finally, he attempts to set up an interview—almost always the object of a letter of application. Make scheduling the interview as easy and convenient for the employer as possible.

956 Roberts Street
Rochester, NY 14622
24 March 1999

Ms. Joan B. Mills
Employment Manager
Warren Radio Company
252 Foss Avenue
Bedford, MA 01730

Dear Ms. Mills:

The placement director at Forest Park College has drawn my attention to your need for an FCC licensed Communication Technician. I have a second-class radiotelephone license and will be available for work in June of this year.

Identify position sought and the way you heard of it.

I have had considerable theoretical training and practical experience in your company's field of designing, manufacturing, and selling electronic instruments and testing and measuring systems. As a Navy Aviation Electronics Technician 2/c, I had more than three years of practical experience doing first- and second-echelon maintenance of radio and radar equipment. My experience includes working with most of the sophisticated electronic testing equipment that the Navy furnishes its electronic maintenance units.

Show knowledge of employer and give details of education and experience.

At Forest Park, I have majored in Electronic Technology, with courses in electronic circuit theory, tests and measurement, and microwaves.

Please see my enclosed resume, which gives the details of my education and experience.

Refer to resume.

May I drive over to Bedford to talk with you? I can arrange my schedule to be available for an interview on any weekday afternoon.

Request interview.

Sincerely,

Mark G. Patterson

Mark G. Patterson

Enclosure: Resume

Figure 10.14 Letter of application.

1509 Oxford Road
Charlottesville, VA 22901
804-205-3333

October 19, 2000

U.S. Fish & Wildlife Service
Malheur National Wildlife Refuge
HC 72 Box 245
Princeton, OR 97721

Announcement Number: 98-116708

I am applying for the position of Wildlife Biologist on the Malheur National Wildlife Refuge. I learned about this position on the Web site usajobs.opm.gov. I have enclosed a copy of my resume.

I will graduate from Virginia College in December with a Bachelor of Science in Biology. I have 12 semester hours in zoology, 12 semester hours in wildlife management, and 9 semester hours in botany. I have a portfolio with samples of class projects for Environmental Biology and Biological Statistics, and sets of instructions and FCC reports I have done as part of my work experience.

One of the projects for the campus Wildlife Society is the annual Thanksgiving field trip to Assateague Island, Virginia, to inventory species of birds as they migrate. We band ducks and geese as they migrate south. For the past two years, I have been responsible for entering the sightings from each member into the database. We use Microsoft Access. I helped write the environmental assessment report that was sent to the National Audubon Society.

Last summer I worked on the trail crew in the Shenandoah National Park. We worked in teams to clear the main trails and re-route less used trails in the more isolated parts of the park. Frequently we had to backpack in with equipment and supplies for 3- to 5-day work projects.

I will be in Oregon in December. I will call for an appointment to discuss my application.

Sincerely,

Anna Moosad

Anna Moosad

Figure 10.15 Letter of application. The student wrote this letter in response to the job description shown in Figure 10.10. Her resume is shown in Figure 10.8.

Never send out duplicated letters of application. You may have one standard letter that you modify only slightly from employer to employer, but each letter must be an original and printed on good-quality paper using a high quality laser or inkjet printer.

OTHER LETTERS

Several other letters are either necessary or desirable during the job hunt: requests for recommendation, interview follow-up letters, acknowledgments of job offers, job refusals, and job acceptances. Always be as courteous as possible in workplace correspondence and especially in employment letters. The sample letters in Figures 10.16 to 10.22 illustrate how to proceed in each of these matters. As you examine them, consider the following additional points.

Thank-you letters following an interview will set you apart from other applicants. The letter will be appreciated, and your name will become that much more familiar to the employer. You simply thank the interviewers for their time and courtesy (see Figure 10.16 for an example). The thank-you letter is the one letter you can hand-write on nice notepaper. (Most campus bookstores stock notecards with the school emblem.)

As you begin the job search, you may need to write letters to former teachers or employers requesting a letter of reference. Figure 10.17 shows one example of a *request for a recommendation*. The letter is not a long one. In it you should give a specific date when the recommendation is needed and give any special instructions. Enclose a stamped and addressed envelope and your resume so the person is reminded of your activities. Afterward send the person a thank-you note and keep him or her posted on your job search (see Figure 10.22).

APPLICATION FORMS

Look briefly at Figure 10.23, a company application form. Most employers will ask you to complete such a form before they hire you. Notice that it covers many of the same areas we have urged you to cover in your self-inventory. Most often you must complete the application at the employer's office. Be sure to have all the needed information with you—from your social security number to specific details of education and experience. Your self-inventory is a good source for this information. Use a pen with black ink and print your answers neatly. (Black ink is preferred because it duplicates better than blue ink or pencil. Your application will be copied and distributed to those interviewing you.)

More and more companies and organizations ask applicants to complete the application form online in the office. You will also find application forms on the Web, for example, http://apps.usajobs.opm.gov. Fill out the forms just as you would a paper copy—providing accurate and complete information.

The job-search process takes time and is stressful. The reward comes when you find a satisfying job.

2011-8th Street, Apt. 10A
Boise, ID 83700

May 20, 2001

Mr. Jack B. Smith
Human Resource Manager
Rockford Products
2930 Creek Road
Rockford, TN 36888

Dear Mr. Smith:

Thank you for the opportunity to interview with Rockford Products.
I particularly enjoyed the chance to tour the Bedford plant and to
talk with Jim Brunson about the production line for the fire
protection products.

Thank for the interview.

I would like to follow up on Jim Brunson's suggestion that I
consider the position of regional technical representative. I did not
realize the importance of my Boise Fire Department experience and
my fluency in Spanish.

Give or request additional information.

After thinking over whether or not I would like to travel to
Rockford's customer sites in Latin and South America, I have
decided I would like such an opportunity.

Will you forward my application materials to the International
Division? I will call you early next week to see what I need to do.

Thank you,

Kelly J. Bennett

Kelly J. Bennett

Figure 10.16 Interview follow-up.

922 Burke Place
Lubbock, TX 79401
April 15, 1999

Dr. Susan DuBois
Plains Museum of West Texas University
4th Street Northwest
Lubbock, TX 79401

Dear Dr. DuBois:

May I give your name as a reference?   **Ask the question.**

I volunteered last summer in the Welcome Children to the Museum   **Recall the association.**
program. I helped develop activities for the 4-5-6th-grade classes.

I will graduate from West Texas University with a B.A. in English in   **Give some background.**
June. I hope to find a position in a museum where I can design and
write descriptions for the displays.

I have enclosed a copy of my resume to bring you up to date on my   **Establish to confirm**
activities. I will call you next week to confirm that I may use you   **that you use the**
as a reference, or if you want to send me an e-mail message before   **reference.**
then I can be reached at changam@tx.mail.edu.

Thank you,

Angela Chang

Angela Chang

Enclosure: Resume

Figure 10.17 Request for a recommendation.

1509 Oxford Road
Charlottesville, VA 22901

January 14, 2000

Dr. Amanda Groves
Biological Research Center
1600 Main Street
Columbus, GA 31901

Dear Dr. Gross:

Thank you for offering me the position of Wildlife Biologist I for the Biological Research Center.

Acknowledge offer.

I am considering several other employment opportunities as well. I will, however, decide by January 15 and give you a definite answer at that time.

Give reason for delay and request or give a deadline.

Again, thank you for the offer.

Sincerely,

Anna Moosad

Anna Moosad

Figure 10.18 Acknowledgment of job offer.

1509 Oxford Road
Charlottesville, VA 22901

January 14, 2000

U.S. Fish & Wildlife Service
Malheur National Wildlife Refuge
HC 72 Box 245
Princeton, OR 97721

Dear Mr. Clayton:

I enjoyed meeting you and Tamara Jones on December 10. At the
time you indicated that I would have some word about my
employment with you by the end of December.

Recall the meeting.

I have been offered another position, and the company expects an
answer from me by January 25.

State reason for letter.

I am still interested in the position as Wildlife Biologist at the
Malheur National Wildlife Refuge. Would it be possible for you to
give me a definite answer about my employment before January 20?

Request information.

Sincerely,

Anna Moosad

Anna Moosad

Figure 10.19 Status inquiry.

1509 Oxford Road
Charlottesville, VA 22901

January 14, 2000

Dr. Amanda Groves
Biological Research Center
1600 Main Street
Columbus, GA 39101

Dear Dr. Gross:

Thank you for the offer of a position with Biological Research   **Acknowledge and**
Center. However, I have decided to accept another offer. My career   **decline offer.**
goals and family responsibilities influenced my decision.

The choice was a hard one to make. I appreciate the time you and   **State your**
Allan Jordan spent with me.   **appreciation.**

Sincerely,

Anna Moosad

Anna Moosad

Figure 10.20 Job refusal.

922 Burke Place
Lubbock, TX 79401
March 20, 2000

Ms. Joanne Hoff
Vice President, International Division
Total Services Corporation
1919 Circle Texas Drive
Austin, TX 78751

Dear Ms. Hoff:

I accept the offer to work as a Technical Communication Specialist for **Accept the offer.**
Total Services.

I understand that my salary will begin at $35,000 annually and I will **Confirm the salary**
receive $1,000 in relocation expenses. **and other benefits.**

I will report to Thomas Martinez on April 15 for orientation and training. **Confirm the start**
date.

Thank you. I look forward to beginning my career with Total Services.

Sincerely,

Angela M. Chang

Angela Marie Chang

Figure 10.21 Job acceptance.

922 Burke Place
Lubbock, TX 79401
April 15, 1999

Dr. Susan DuBois
Plains Museum of West Texas University
4th Street Northwest
Lubbock, TX 79401

Dear Dr. DuBois:

Thank you for responding to my request for letters of recommendation.

I have accepted the Assistant Curator position with the Grove Zoo.
Not only am I working outdoors and with animals, but I also help
design and write the information boards beside the display areas
and brochures mailed to members. I began work two weeks ago
and already I am busy planning a display for elementary school students.

Again, thank you for the recommendation.

Sincerely,

Angela M. Chang

Angela Marie Chang

Thank for the recommendation.

Describe the position accepted.

Figure 10.22 Thank-you note for a recommendation.

Chick-fil-A®

APPLICATION FOR EMPLOYMENT

PLEASE TELL US ABOUT YOURSELF

Name (print): Last ______ Middle I. ______ First ______ Date ______
Present Address: ______ City ______ State ______ Zip ______
Home Phone: ______ Work Phone ______
In case of an emergency, please notify: Name ______ Phone (H) ______ (W) ______
Address: ______ City ______ State ______ Zip ______
Do you have a reliable means of transportation to work? ◯ Yes ◯ No What wage are you expecting? ______
If you are younger than 18 years old, how old are you? ______ Social Security # ___ ___ ___ / ___ ___ / ___ ___ ___ ___
Are you eligible to work in the U.S.? ◯Yes ◯No (PROOF OF ELIGIBILITY IS REQUIRED UPON EMPLOYMENT)
Have you ever been convicted of a felony? ◯ Yes ◯ No

AVAILABILITY

	MON	TUE	WED	THU	FRI	SAT
FROM						
TO						

Summer ______ School Year ______ All Year ______
Minimum number of hours needed to work: ______
Maximum number of hours able to work: ______

PREVIOUS EMPLOYMENT HISTORY

PLEASE LIST YOUR THREE MOST RECENT JOBS (including babysitting, lawn care or volunteer work):

Have you ever worked for Chick-fil-A? ◯ Yes ◯ No If YES, which Unit? ______

Employed From	To	Name & Address of Employer	Phone #	Supervisor	Earnings	Reason for Leaving

Job skills acquired: ______

EDUCATION

High School (Last attended) Location Did You Graduate? ◯ Yes ◯ No
______
College & Vocational Schools Location Did You Graduate? ◯ Yes ◯ No If yes, Degree & Major Grade Pt. Average
______
______

PERSONAL BACKGROUND

What are your interests and activities? ______
______
Please list awards and/or leadership positions held (work or school): ______
______

Figure 10.23 Sample application form. Most application forms require the same information and ask similar questions. Be prepared when you go for an interview to complete an application form. You may want to take your self-inventory so that you have information about the jobs you have had: dates of employment, salary, employer's address and telephone number. Give accurate information about how to contact references. You need not say much in the Reason for Leaving section. Phrases such as "returned to school," "moved," or "took better job" are sufficient.
Source: Chick-fil-A Employment Application, reprinted by permission of Chick-fil-A, Inc., 5200 Buffington Rd., Atlanta, GA 30349.

MILITARY SERVICE

◯ Yes ◯ No   Branch: _____   Rank: _____   Start Date: _____   End Date: _____

Please describe your duties: _____
_____
_____

PERSONAL REFERENCES

PLEASE PROVIDE FOUR REFERENCES TO WHOM YOU HAVE BEEN ACCOUNTABLE. PLEASE INCLUDE NO MORE THAN TWO FAMILY MEMBERS.

Name	Address	Phone	Relation	Years Known

PLEASE READ THE FOLLOWING STATEMENTS CAREFULLY AND SIGN

I understand that completion of this application does not indicate that there are any positions currently open and does not obligate the Chick-fil-A Operator to hire me. I certify that all of the answers given in this application are true and complete to the best of my knowledge and are subject to confirmation by Chick-fil-A.

Chick-fil-A may make such investigations and inquiries of my personal, employment, financial, academic history and other related matters as may be necessary in determining whether I can perform the essential functions of the position which I seek. I hereby release past employers, schools, and all persons contacted from all liability in responding to inquiries in connection with my application.

If I am employed, I understand that false or misleading information given in my application or interview(s) may result in termination. I understand that I am required to abide by all employer rules and regulations.

_____   _____
Date   Applicant Signature

THIS SECTION TO BE SIGNED BY EMPLOYEE ONLY AT THE TIME OF HIRE

I understand that it is the objective of Chick-fil-A, Inc. and the Chick-fil-A Operator to provide the highest quality of food at competitive prices with the highest caliber of employees possible. I also understand that one of the hardest things to prevent is the mishandling of cash and store property from within. Therefore, I acknowledge the reasonableness of and consent to the following:

1. Chick-fil-A and the Chick-fil-A Operator reserve the right to use any lawful method of investigation which either one of them may deem necessary in determining whether any person has engaged in conduct which either Chick-fil-A or the Chick-fil-A Operator feel interferes with or adversely affects the business of either one of them.

2. Persons entering and leaving any Chick-fil-A premises are subject to questioning and searches. All packages, bags, purses, coats, containers, accessories, or possessions of any sort brought onto or taken from any Chick-fil-A premises are subject to thorough inspection.

3. Chick-fil-A or the Chick-fil-A Operator may engage in a variety of security procedures, as deemed necessary by either one of them. These may include, but are not limited to, surveillance of employees or premises. I understand that these security procedures may be conducted in secrecy, unannounced to me or other persons.

I understand each of these provisions and consent to each and every provision. I also understand that cooperation with any action encompassed by these provisions is expected of all employees, and failure to cooperate may result in termination of employment.

_____   _____
Date   Employee's Signature

Chick-fil-A, Inc. is an equal opportunity employer and considers all applicants equally without regard to race, sex, age, religion, national origin, color, disability, citizenship, or veteran status.

©1998 Chick-fil-A, Inc., CT002, Rev 7-98

Figure 10.23 (continued)

PLANNING AND REVISING CHECKLIST: THE JOB HUNT

Think about the following at the beginning of your job hunt. Review the time table in Figure 10.1.

THE SELF-INVENTORY

The first step in preparing for the job hunt is to inventory your education, experience, interests, and abilities. Why not create a file in your word-processing program called *self1?* Using the headings below, list everything you can think of that might be relevant to your job search. If the file grows to several pages, that's fine. You are brainstorming—an early part of the writing process.

As you write a resume, letter, e-mail inquiry, or other document, select information from the self-inventory that describes you to a specific employer (the reader) for a specific job (your purpose). Have at least two files open: the *self1* and the *resume1*, for example. Copy and paste between the two. As you update each file, change the name to show the update: *resume1, resume2, . . . self1, self2. . . .* You can always go back to an earlier version if you do not like the change, and you always have a backup if something happens to the current version. ALWAYS save your files in at least two locations (on a disk and on a hard drive). Update the files as you gain work experience or add to your educational credentials.

EDUCATION

For each school and program you have attended or are attending since high school, provide the following information:

- Name, location, and dates of attendance

- Kind of degree or certificate (for example, B.S or A.A.)

- Major or emphasis

- Courses most relevant to job you seek. Grades for these courses

- Internships or co-op programs

- Grade point average

- Courses in your education that you enjoyed the most and the least

- Courses in which you earned the highest and lowest grades

ORGANIZATIONS

List any organizations you have belonged to, both in and out of school. For example, have you been a part of student government, student clubs, athletic teams, or civic groups? Identify political and religious activities as well. (We discuss how to represent these activities in the resume section of this chapter.) State the purpose of the organization. For each organization list any positions you may have held, such as secretary, and define your responsibilities in the organization. Be sure to include committee work you may have done.

WORK AND MILITARY EXPERIENCE

List all the jobs, full time and part time, you have held, including any military experience. You may go as far back as you like, but for jobs held during and before high school, you need provide only summary information. For each job held since high school, provide the following information:

- Name, location, and Web address of company or organization

- Business of company or organization (for example, restaurant, trucking, computer, or medical laboratory)

- Name, address, telephone, and e-mail address of supervisor

- Dates of employment

- Job title

- Description of your activities and responsibilities

- Description of any special training received

- Important accomplishments

- What you enjoyed most and least about the job

HOBBIES

List the hobbies that you do for relaxation and enjoyment.

SKILLS

Look back over your experience in education, organizations, jobs, and hobbies. What skills have you gained through these experiences? Think not only of specialized professional and technical skills, but also of supporting skills in areas such as teamwork, leadership, communication, and problem solving. List and describe any such skills and tell how you achieved them. Pay particular attention to those skills relevant to the jobs you seek.

HONORS AND RECOGNITION

List and describe any honors or recognition you have received from school, work, or organizations.

REFERENCES

List those people you may want to attest to your abilities, skills, and character. Think about employers, teachers, and family friends who know you well enough to provide a reference for you. For some positions, you will be asked to provide work-related references (people who can describe your work habits and skills) and personal references (people who can comment on your character). Choose several who not only think well of you but who have enough skill in speech and writing to convey their thoughts about you to a potential employer. List their job titles, addresses, telephone numbers, and e-mail addresses.

EMPLOYER INVENTORY

On pages 256–258, we describe ways of gathering information about potential employers. Here are some of the things you should find out about them:

- Telephone number, e-mail address, Web address for the location where you want to work

- Size (by number of people employed, financial strength, annual sales, and so forth)

- Products or services

- Position of organization within its field (by reputation, sales, financial strength, and so forth)

- Kinds and numbers of positions open

- Training and educational possibilities

- Technology important to company

- Growth potential

- Names of officers

- Management philosophy

- Names and addresses of human resource managers and people for whom you might work

PLANNING AND REVISING CHECKLIST: JOB-HUNT COMMUNICATION

Think about the following when planning and revising the communications for your job hunt.

PLANNING THE RESUME

- What type of resume best fits your needs? Chronological? Functional?

- Do you want to state your job objective firmly?

- Do you have all the information you need about your education and experience, including dates, names, locations, courses, grades, job descriptions, and so forth?

- If you want to use a functional resume, which categories will best display your skills and experience?

- What capabilities and achievements in your background fit you for your job objectives?

REVISING THE RESUME

- If you have included a job objective, is it stated specifically and succinctly?

- If you have produced a chronological resume, have you listed your education and experience in reverse chronological order?

- Is all the information in your resume accurate?

- Have you included experiences, achievements, honors, and skills relevant to the job sought?

- If you were an employer, would the resume interest you? Would you want to interview the person who wrote it?

- Have you used phrases and dependent clauses rather than complete sentences?

- Is the information on the page uncrowded?

- Do the headings reveal the organization?

- Is your resume absolutely free of errors of any kind, whether of content, spelling, or grammar?

PLANNING THE LETTER OF APPLICATION

- Remember the goal of your letter: to obtain an interview.

- How did you learn about the job?

- How well does the job meet your job objectives?

- How well do your skills and attributes match the job?

- What can you do for the employer?

- How can you make it easy for the employer to schedule an interview with you?

REVISING THE LETTER OF APPLICATION

- Is your letter addressed to someone by name?

- Have you clearly stated the job you want and how you heard about it?

- Have you briefly discussed the skills and attributes that fit you for the job?

- Have you shown that you know something about the organization and the job?

- Have you made it easy for the employer to reach you to schedule an interview?

- Is the letter professional in all aspects? Tone? Style? Appearance? Format? Grammar?

PLANNING OTHER WRITTEN CORRESPONDENCE

You also will write letters or e-mail messages that request recommendations, follow up on interviews, thank people for help, and accept or reject a job. In planning them, take care with the following:

- Obtain accurate names and addresses. Spell names correctly.

- Be accurate about any dates you refer to, whether in the past or in the future.

- Answer any questions that need answering.

- Furnish any requested information.

REVISING THE OTHER WRITTEN CORRESPONDENCE

- Have you included all the information needed for your purpose?

- Is your tone courteous and professional?

- Is your letter or e-mail message correctly formatted and error free?

SUGGESTIONS FOR APPLYING YOUR KNOWLEDGE

The employment situation, with its correspondence and interviews, is one place where your practice can approach or even be the real thing. The facts you must work with are the real facts of your own life along with information you can gather about real employers you might want to work for.

Begin with a self-inventory. Keep it as reference material for the other assignments you may write, such as letters of application and resumes.

With the help of your school placement officer or advisor, make a list of potential employers for people with your skills and interests. Using the resources available in your library, on the Web, and in your school's placement office, look up companies and organizations you might want to work for. Check Web sites for information on the companies. Check with friends and relatives. In other words, you can obtain a good deal of information about employers from many sources. Gather as much as you can.

All job-hunting communications are potential assignments: self-inventory, letters of application, resumes, interview follow-up letters, and so forth. All should be completed on a computer using word-processing software, printed using a high-quality printer, and have a thoroughly professional look—good document design and no errors.

CHAPTER 11

PORTFOLIOS AND INTERVIEWS

If your resume and letter have been successful, you now must prepare for your interview with potential employers. Employers want to interview you to make sure you will fit their team. They want to confirm that you have the knowledge and special abilities they are looking for and that you can work with others. In this chapter we describe portfolios for showcasing your special abilities and your communication activities. We also provide guidelines for interviewing with an employer.

PORTFOLIOS

Whatever your training, you will need to show your work to future employers. One way to do this is with a portfolio. A portfolio collects samples of your work in a notebook, on a Web site, on a CD-ROM, or in a form your field expects. We describe a portfolio in which you carry hard-copy documents. Electronic portfolios are becoming more and more prevalent—particularly Web folios. We suggest you review several Web sites before designing your own site. Whatever format you use, the purpose is the same: to show your best work to a reader who is gathering information about the quality of your work.

Portfolios give you an effective means of gathering samples of your work and showing your communication activities to employers and clients. You put your best work in your portfolio to show your range of communication experience and the extent of your talent. Future employers and clients can see how your abilities match their needs. Both in your letters of application and on your resume, you should mention that you have a portfolio. In the letter, you might add the following sentence: "I will bring a portfolio containing samples of my work to the interview." On your resume, you might replace the overused phrase "References upon request" with the phrase "Portfolio available."

You collect samples of your work in a portfolio to

- Demonstrate your special skills, abilities, and subject matter knowledge.

- Show your communication activities—particularly written communication.

- Show your experience working with several types of documents and media.

- Illustrate your organization and presentation skills.

- Distinguish yourself from others applying for the same position.

Take your portfolio with you to interviews. When the interviewer asks about your class and work projects and other communication activities, you will have examples to show.

CONTENTS

The documents included in the portfolio should represent a cross section of your work. Be sure to present your best work. If you are a student majoring in graphic art or architecture, you would show several of your major design projects; a technical communicator would include documents written and edited in different media for different readers; an education major would include lesson plans and course materials; an engineer would include his or her senior project and, for example, a proposal written to solicit funding for a solar car project; a medical technician would include lab reports and work done on a practicum; an accountant would select writing from English classes and accounting classes, such as an analysis of a financial statement.

Most job descriptions include the phrase "must have good communication skills." With your portfolio you can proudly (and selectively) display your writing. Don't overlook your extracurricular activities such as president of a student organization or volunteer for Big Brothers/Big Sisters. Flyers you have created and distributed, letters you've written to guest speakers, the Web page you developed, all show your communication activities.

Electronic documents such as computer-generated slide presentations or Web pages create special problems for presenting in hard-copy format. You may want to print the presentation as a handout, and you might print a portion of your Web site. If you have access to a color printer, you can display the presentation or Web page more effectively. If you give your Web address, be assured reviewers will look at your Web site.

You may want to revise assignments and documents so that the best possible document is included in the portfolio. Have someone with a critical but friendly eye review your portfolio.

A copy of your resume will also help the reader. If the resume is first in the portfolio, you give the reader an overview of your education and work history. The reader then moves on to the documents that show what you have developed. If the resume is placed at the end of the portfolio, you assume the reader has already reviewed your resume. Putting the resume in the back ensures that you have a copy available if one is needed.

DESIGN

The reader should readily understand the organization of your portfolio. Some readers will work through the portfolio carefully, but most will flip through the portfolio stopping at documents that catch their attention. A *title page* with your name provides the reader with a clean, crisp opening to the portfolio (Figure 11.1, for example). A *list of the contents* provides a guide for the reader and an overview of the organization of the portfolio. The list should show how you have grouped the documents. Section dividers distinguish the different sets of documents. Placing your best work at the beginning of the portfolio may help call attention to your strongest work. Don't overlook the entire "picture" of the portfolio. The portfolio

Portfolio

Kelly J. Bennett

Figure 11.1 Sample title page. Your title page establishes the design for the rest of your portfolio. Instead of a vertical line, you can use a horizontal line, a different color, or another graphic feature to introduce your portfolio. Do not clutter the title page with unnecessary information or visual effects. Your name is the most important information. You may want to put a date on the page, or information about how to contact you.

represents you—the type and color of notebook and dividers you select and the organization and display of your work say something about you.

A *description of each document* or section of the portfolio will help the reader. The description may be a cover sheet for each document or section. Figure 11.2 shows the description for a set of instructions on a feature of WordPerfect and the first page of the instructions. Figure 11.3 describes an oral presentation presented as part of a student contest before a

The Instruction Assignment

Assignment

This collaborative assignment, which was done in English 2116 in Spring 1999, required us to prepare a set of instructions on a process. We learned a new process and then provided instructions for this process.

Parameters

This set of instructions includes the following to ensure effectiveness:
- an introduction that provides a brief overview of the process and our reason for describing it
- a list of tools, equipment, and software necessary for the completion of these instructions
- visuals to help orient the user with difficult stages of the instructions
- clear and succinct directions for this process

The set of instructions is for students using 486 computers with WordPerfect 7 in the English department's computer classroom.

Construction

This assignment followed a recipe-like construction of an overview, a list of ingredients, and instructions for how to assemble the graphics. We divided the process into three sections to promote manageability. We imported graphics from the Internet for our visuals and employed them as landmarks for the user. This assignment was constructed in WordPerfect; the visuals were chosen via Netscape and configured with L View.

I was the most computer literate of the group members, and I had a computer at home. I constructed most of the document with another group member working beside me helping to write the instructions. A third group member worked through the instructions and checked the final document.

Comments

Our largest problem with this assignment was its collaborative nature. This collaboration manifested itself in many drafts of the project that corrected the same errors repeatedly. Beyond that, we were uncertain how technically specific we needed to be for our audience.

Figure 11.2 Sample description for a set of instructions. The description identifies the purpose and audience for the instructions and describes some of the issues the group faced as they developed the instructions. We have included the first page of the instructions in this example.
Source: Unpublished student project, printed with permission of Julie Bouchard, the author.

Importing AU Graphics
from the WWW

Putting together the EGO newsletter for new graduate students can be time consuming, especially if you're not used to producing desktop-publishing documents. After completing the text, you will want to add graphics to the newsletter to make it more appealing. In the past, we have used generic graphics in regular clip-art software, but with these instructions, you can now incorporate AUNet's official Auburn graphics to give the newsletter a real "War Eagle" feel. The following instructions assist you in importing those graphics from the WWW. These directions are to be used in Haley Center 3116.

Tools: computer in HC3116
      3.5" disk (containing the newsletter file)
      software—Web browser, L View in AUNet, WordPerfect

Selecting the Graphic

1. From the opening screen of Windows 95, double click on **Netscape Navigator.** (Figure 1)

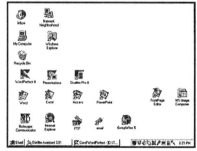

2. When the **Auburn Home Page** (http:www.auburn.edu) appears on your screen, decide from which area of the home page your graphics will be chosen. For example, the News and Events area has Auburn logos for use.

3. Click on your choice of areas and wait for the new page to appear.

Figure 1

4. Once you are in your desired area, find the graphic you wish to copy. You can only choose one graphic at a time.

5. Move the point arrow onto the graphic. Hold down the **right** mouse button and choose **Save Image As ...** from the menu.

6. The graphic's name will already be in the filename box of the **Save Image As ...** screen, which should look like Figure 2.

You must make certain that you have chosen to save this image to your floppy disk (drive a:).

IMPORTANT: You must also note the *complete* name and the three-letter extension (found after the "." in the filename or in the **Save File as Type** box.) For example, *au.gif* is a complete filename.

Figure 2

Figure 11.2 (continued)

Oral Presentation

This oral presentation began as a component of my senior marketing project. For my marketing project, I developed a marketing plan for an agricultural product assigned by Professor Jonathan Fenwick. I was encouraged by my professor to enter my marketing plan in a contest for student professionals sponsored by the National Agri-Marketing Association. I presented my plan and this presentation at the national conference in San Francisco in April 1999.

Purpose Present a marketing plan for the agricultural product *FastGrow,* a fertilizer developed for increasing soybean growth.

Audience Judges for National Agri-Marketing Association. The judges were marketing directors from three international corporations.

Information Described how I conducted a market analysis for introducing *FastGrow* as a new product. Presented the proposed marketing plan for *FastGrow.*

Specifications 20-minute computer-generated slide show

Software Used Microsoft PowerPoint 97

Special Features Incorporated three visuals captured from the Web and two graphs created in Microsoft Excel

Results Earned an Honorable Mention among the 49 students competing.

I had never created a computer slide show before this. At first I struggled with the software and had some trouble getting access to a computer, but once I learned how to add and delete slides, I created the slides in about 45 minutes. A friend showed me how to insert pictures from the Web and the graphs.

After seeing the presentations of the winner, I now know that I probably should have used fewer slides. I included so many that I had to rush through the slides to finish in 20 minutes. My visuals seemed to impress the judges.

Figure 11.3 Sample description for an oral presentation. The description identifies the purpose and audience for the oral presentation. A copy of the presentation is included in the portfolio immediately after this description. The presentation is printed as a handout with six slides on the page.

national organization. The descriptions reflect the different writers' experiences and document design preferences. Describe the context for the document. Questions to answer:

Why was the project developed?

Who is the intended audience for the project?

How was the project developed? What software and hardware were used?

When was the project developed? What was the time frame for development?

Who created the project? Was it an individual- or a team-developed project?

What was your contribution to the project?

What are the special features of the project?

PRESENTATION OF THE PORTFOLIO

You can display your work in a three-ring notebook or in a leather-bound, zippered case specially designed for portfolios. The case must securely hold the material but also allow the material to be easily reviewed. Clear plastic sheet covers, dividers, disk holders, and envelopes are aids that may also display the material effectively. You may want to use color on the title page, the description pages, and the color dividers. How you display your work is as much a part of the evaluation of the portfolio as what you put in the portfolio.

You may want to have with you a sample of your work that you can leave. A three- to six-page sample, called a *leave-behind* by graphic artists, should illustrate your best work and the type of work you want to do. If you want to move into another area, the leave-behind should include a description of how the material shows you can handle a new assignment. Don't leave your complete portfolio unless you are sure you will get it back.

One last point: Show confidence and enthusiasm for your work during the interview. You will be presenting the portfolio to potential employers, clients, or supervisors as part of your annual review. Know the material in the portfolio and be prepared to discuss each document.

INTERVIEWS

If your letters of application succeed, the next stage of the job hunt is the interview. If the company is large enough to have a human resource department, you may first be interviewed by someone there before you meet with someone in the department where you will work. If the company is small, you will likely meet with the people with whom you will work. Alternatively, you may be interviewed in an interactive video conference where you sit in front of a computer with a camera and microphone and meet with one or more interviewers at another location who are also sitting before a computer. Just as technology has affected how we send resumes so has it opened up the possibilities for interviews.

When you are asked for an interview, you probably will be told what to expect—if not, ask whom you will be seeing and how long you should expect the interview to last. Also ask if you will be tested (for example, on how to use a special piece of equipment such as an oscilloscope) or if you will need to make a presentation (common for training and sales positions). Interviews frighten a great many job hunters, probably more than they should. The more you know about the interview process planned for you, and the more you know about the company, the more comfortable and confident you will be during the interview. Use the guidelines we gave in Chapter 10 for finding out information about potential employers before the interview.

You have certain responsibilities for the interview as well. You should prepare for the interview beforehand. Here again, your self-inventory is good preparation (see Chapter 10). Look through it and select those items from your background that demonstrate those characteristics employers value, such as loyalty and initiative. Also, look for jobs, education, and extracurricular activities that relate to the job sought. If you did your job exploration thoroughly, you'll already know something about the employer. If you haven't, find out what you can before the interview.

Interviewers from the human resource department, recruiters who visit college campuses, and others who may meet with you aren't out to trap you. Their job is to evaluate you, to find someone that their employers need, and also to help you find out for what position you are best suited. Experienced interviewers know how to assess your qualifications. They ask questions to determine if you are a responsible person. They want to see if you are friendly and good humored, someone who will work well with other people. They examine your vocational and professional skills. You will find most professionally trained interviewers helpful and friendly.

How should you dress for the interview? Like it or not, first impressions are important. Studies show interviewers are more favorably inclined toward suitably dressed people. For men this means shined shoes, sport coat, slacks, shirt, and tie. For some positions, particularly office work, a suit is probably even better. It doesn't matter that you may wear informal clothes on the job sought; dress well for the interview. For women, a dress or suit appropriate for business use is the best attire. However, if a tour of the plant is part of the interview process, you might be told to wear casual slacks and shoes with low heels. Follow the guidelines. Avoid extremes of all sorts: For men, hair too long and beards too bushy are extremes, as are sloppy, ill-fitting, or unclean clothes. Excessive makeup or perfume, many jangling bracelets, or flashy, dressy clothes are extremes for women. Naturally, you should be well groomed. Dirty knuckles and fingernails have lost as many jobs for people as low grades. Don't chew gum during the interview. Don't smoke even if invited to—in fact, avoid smoking before the interview so that you will not smell of smoke.

Arrive at the place of the interview at least 10 minutes early. When you meet the interviewer, get his or her name straight and shake hands firmly but comfortably—avoid bone crunchers or limp-as-a-fish shakes. You offer a copy of your resume if the interviewer doesn't already have one. If you have a portfolio, mention it. More than likely other candidates for the position will not have a portfolio, so you begin the interview with one advantage. You sit down erectly but comfortably.

Interviews with individuals within a company usually last about 30 minutes, but you may meet with more than one person separately or at the same time. After introductions are over, interviewers usually spend a few minutes setting you at ease. They do not want you to be tense. The best interviews are relaxed and friendly, even a bit casual. Neither party should dominate. After some casual talk, perhaps about sports or current events, the interviewer may shift into telling you something about the company or organization. If so, listen closely and be prepared to come in at natural pauses with intelligent questions, but don't interrupt the interviewer while he or she is talking. Ask questions that demonstrate you have done your research on the company.

Sometimes this talk about the employer comes later in the interview. In any event, questions and answers about you are the heart of the interview. Frequently, testing may be part of the interview. The questions may be deliberately vague to see if you can develop ideas on your own, or they may be quite specific and penetrating. Here are some samples:

- Why do you want to work for us?

- Tell me something about yourself.

- What sort of summer or part-time work have you had?

- What were your responsibilities?

- Why did you leave your last job?

- Do you enjoy _____ (sales), (office), (experimental), (manual), (troubleshooting) work? Why?

- Can you take criticism?

- Why have you chosen your vocation?

- What subjects did you enjoy most in school? Why?

- How have you paid for your education?

- What are your strong (weak) points?

- What do you want to be doing five years (ten years) from now?

- If you were rich enough not to have to work, how would you spend your life?

Be aware that various state and federal laws prohibit interviewers from asking you for information that is not job related or that could be discriminatory—for example, "Are you married?" or "Do you have children?" In general, all questions about race, color, creed, national origin, religion, sex, age, ethnic background, marital status, family relationships, and political beliefs are off limits to interviewers. You should not provide such information on resumes or in letters of application.

What do you do if interviewers ask improper questions? (Most will not.) You can refuse to answer, of course, but that would likely guarantee you will not get the job. One expert suggests that a wiser choice is to deflect the question by getting at the real concern of the interviewer[1]:

QUESTION: Are you married?
ANSWER: Yes, but my spouse also works in this city and plans to remain here.
QUESTION: Do you have children?
ANSWER: Yes, a two-year-old boy, and we have found an excellent day-care center for him.

If in doubt about how to answer such questions, ask a question of your own, such as "How does that relate to working for your corporation?" The interviewer's answer may lead you to a response that allays the interviewer's concern without violating your privacy and legal rights. Whatever you do, don't lie as a way of evading an answer.

Like athletic events, no two interviews are exactly alike. But certain situations and questions do repeat. Good answers prepared for the questions listed here would go a long way to get you ready for any interview. And you can practice. Get together with friends and interview each other. Practice talking about yourself and your accomplishments and articulating your desires. Learn how to be assertive about your qualifications.

At some point in the interview, the interviewer will discuss with you the job or jobs the employer has to offer. Here you should be able to display your professional knowledge about jobs for which you are suited. You should be fairly firm about your goals but flexible enough to discuss a related job if it looks good. Avoid the appearance of being willing to take any job at all. Ask job-related questions, such as these:

- What qualities (or skills) does this job require?

- What is the experience of the person I may work for?

- How many people are in the office?

- Is there training for the job? Is the training formal or on the job?

- Does the job offer opportunities for professional growth?

- How will I be evaluated on the job?

When the interviewer discusses salary and job benefits, such as hospitalization insurance, pensions, and vacations, you are free to ask questions about these items. But don't ask about them until the interviewer brings them up.

---

[1]James M. Jenks, "Tactful Answers to Illegal Interview Questions," *National Business Employment Weekly, Managing Your Career* (College ed.) (Spring 1988): 37.

You will rarely be offered a job at a first interview. Sometimes this may occur at a second interview. Normally, however, the job offer will come at some later time. Don't try to extend interviews. When the interviewer closes up your folder and indicates that the interview is over, for better or for worse it is. Stand up, shake hands once again, thank the interviewer, and leave.

What characteristics should you display to have a successful interview? According to many interviewers, the following rank high on the list:

- Be neat and well groomed.

- Be natural, friendly, and relaxed, but not sloppy or overly casual.

- Be more interested in the work involved on the job and in its potential than in salary and benefits.

- This may be most important: Have definite goals. Know your abilities and what you want to do. Be ready to articulate these goals.

PLANNING AND REVISING CHECKLIST: THE INTERVIEW

PLANNING FOR THE INTERVIEW

- Have you done your homework? Do you know yourself and the organization with which you will interview?

- Do you have your career goals well defined? Can you speak easily about them?

- Have you thought about where you would like to live and work? How flexible are you about this matter?

- Are you realistic about your goals?

- Do you know what people really do in the job you seek?

- Are you truly interested in and enthusiastic about the job you seek? If not, should you rethink your career goals?

- Have you thought about yourself from the employer's point of view? Can you show how your interests and skills will benefit the employer?

- Can you speak easily about your strengths and weaknesses?

- Have you thought out answers to the sample questions on page 303?

- Have you examined your wardrobe and obtained the right kind of clothes?

- Are you neat and well groomed?

- Do you have extra copies of your resume to give to the interviewer?

- Does your portfolio contain your best work?

REVISING THE INTERVIEW

It may seem strange to speak of revising an interview, but it's entirely possible. First, you should practice interviews with your friends. Sit down with them and role play interviewee and interviewer in turn. If you have access to video equipment, tape at least three or four practice interviews. View each taping analytically, looking for successful responses and poor responses. Watch for the improvement that will come with practice. Second, you will certainly have a number of interviews during your job hunt. Following each one, take time to analyze objectively how well you did. Jot down interview questions for which you were unprepared and be prepared if they come up again. In analyzing both practice and real interviews, think of these questions:

- Was the interview relaxed and friendly? Did you appear good humored?

- Did you make your career goals clear?

- Were you able to consider alternatives to your goals and yet maintain the impression that your goals are well thought out?

- Did you exhibit enough knowledge about the kind of work you feel best suited for?

- Did you know enough about the organization you were interviewing with?

- Did you have enough evidence of your abilities to be convincing?

- Did you come across as being either too passive or too aggressive?

- Did you look at the interviewer during the conversation?

- Were your expressed expectations realistic?

- Did you sit comfortably during the interview?

- How did your manner of dressing compare to the interviewer's?

- Did you seem more interested in money than the job?

- Did you ask questions of your own about the organization and the job? Did you get satisfactory answers?

- Do you think you and the organization are a good match?

- Do you really want to work for the organization as represented by the interviewer?

- What do you do next? What points can you raise or answer in a follow-up letter to the interviewer?

SUGGESTIONS FOR APPLYING YOUR KNOWLEDGE

To practice interviewing, pair up with a classmate. Interview each other, developing important information about the interviewee, as mentioned in this chapter—favorite courses, job experience, hobbies, and so forth. You and your partner should show your portfolios and answer questions about the work in the portfolio. This interview relaxes students unfamiliar with the process and gets them talking freely about themselves. Some people have difficulty drawing attention to their own strong points but can do it easily for others. A good follow-up to this interview is to have the interviewer write a letter of application for the interviewee.

Conduct mock interviews before the entire class. You can even role-play in these interviews. One student can play an ill-prepared, unsuccessful interviewee, another a well-prepared, successful one. If your school has the proper equipment, videotape interviews for later study.

Students who have participated in real interviews should tell the class about their experiences. Outside of class, you can practice interviews with friends until you are familiar with the process and totally at ease with it.

CHAPTER 12

ORAL PRESENTATIONS

No matter what kind of job you have, you are likely to be called upon to give oral presentations. Four brief scenarios identify the range of possible occasions for oral presentations:

- A creative director and chief graphic designer make an oral presentation on their firm's capabilities and attempt to win a prospective client's next project.

- A product development specialist presents orally her innovative control system for machine tools to her company's production managers and assistant production managers and answers their questions about its implementation.

- A forester researching the types of pollution caused by local industries explains her preliminary findings to a meeting of environmental and safety engineers from local industry, government officials, and a committee of local citizens.

- As part of a health promotion campaign, an occupational nurse speaks at an employee meeting to inform production workers in his company's factories how to prevent repetitive-motion injuries.

In these and similar situations, the person must speak so that he or she can be heard and understood. Its personal, live nature makes spoken communication something rather special. We see an immediate response to our presentation. An oral presentation is a highly effective way of communicating, necessary in almost every professional occupation. It's worth doing well.

Our purpose in this chapter is to guide you from the moment you know you must give an oral presentation or speech to the moment you sit down after completing your successful presentation. We talk about how to prepare an oral presentation, how to integrate visuals, and how to deliver the presentation.

PREPARING FOR ORAL PRESENTATIONS

One of the keys to a successful oral presentation is the conviction that you are well prepared. Preparation is much more than gathering material for an oral presentation and even more than organizing that material. Successful preparation involves, first, considering to whom you're talking and where. What is the occasion for your presentation? After you know the audience and the occasion, you can consider your purpose. When you know occasion, audience, and purpose, you can select the right material to satisfy all three and organize that material. These important matters we will discuss in this section.

ANALYZING CONTEXT

Conversations differ depending upon where you are, what you're doing, and whom you're with. A conversation with a potential employer is not the same as a conversation with a close friend. You don't use the same tones or language at a noisy party that you do in church or in a library. As the context changes, so do the content of your conversation and the manner of its delivery.

So, too, do oral presentations differ with context. Specifically, we refer to occasion and audience.

Occasion

When you are invited to speak, find out as much as you can about the occasion for your presentation. What is the purpose of the occasion? Is it social, business, or some mix of the two? Are you the only speaker? If there is a program of speakers, where do you fit in? Why were you specifically invited to talk? What is expected of you? Knowing the answers to these questions may help you avoid embarrassing pitfalls. An oral presentation entirely suitable for one occasion may be utterly unsuitable for another.

Case in Point   Let us suppose students from colleges and universities around the state have gathered at your school for a two-day conference. The first meeting of the group occurs at an evening social hour and a dinner. The group eats a heavy meal, after which a faculty adviser from your school is introduced to deliver a welcoming talk. He proceeds for 40 minutes to deliver an excellent, informative talk about programs at your school, complete with statistics, success-failure ratios, and so on.

How successful was the speaker on this occasion? He was a complete flop. He was at a social occasion, but he treated it like a business meeting. He put half his audience to sleep and annoyed the half that stayed awake. He delivered a presentation that would have been successful and appropriate on another occasion—say, the annual report to your group's advisory committee. The dinner, however, called for a short, light talk of perhaps 5 to 10 minutes duration in which he welcomed the group, reiterated the purpose and focus of the conference, and perhaps told a humorous anecdote or two.

Location and Facilities

It is also important to know the physical location of where you are going to talk. What size is the room? Does the room fit the number of people in the expected audience? It can be more depressing than you may think to talk to 40 people in a room meant to hold 200. Conversely, it's often exciting and successful to talk to an overflow crowd of 40 in a room meant for 30 people. What kind of equipment is available? Is there an overhead projector, a flipchart, or a whiteboard if you need it? Will you have a lectern and a light?

Case in Point   A prominent tax specialist is invited to give a presentation to a group of accountants and tax consultants. It's expected that the talk will be fairly serious. The speaker is respected, and the accountants and consultants want information and her opinions about recent changes in federal tax laws. The speaker comes with her speech written out, although she also has several slides she plans to use to illustrate certain key points in the new tax tables. The meeting room is dimly lit. There is neither lectern nor light at the speaker's place. There is a projector, but its bulb is burned out. While she gives her presentation, she holds her manuscript about ten inches from her face in order to see it. She eventually gives up trying to read in the dim light and tries to give the presentation extemporaneously. Because there is no replacement projector bulb, she has to give up on the slides she had planned to use. However, she has quotes she has to read, and when she tries to find them in the manuscript, she loses her place. Finally in frustration she sits down to light, polite applause.

What should have been an excellent presentation was ruined by a lack of equipment and a poor physical setting. Two preparatory actions could have prevented the disaster. The tax specialist could have let the meeting's organizers know that she required a light and a lectern, and the host should have checked to make sure that the projector worked. If light and lectern were not available, the speaker should have been warned in ample time to prepare an extemporaneous speech. Speaking from a brief outline, as one does in extemporaneous speech, she could have survived in the dim light. Her quotes could have been typed in large type on separate, numbered cards and placed in the order she needed them. She could have relied on the slides to illustrate her major points.

The moral in these two tales is clear. Know beforehand what you are getting into and plan accordingly. Be familiar with the site of your presentation as well as the purpose of the meeting. If you have any control over the situation, ask for needed changes: the right-sized room or the necessary equipment, for example. Although occasions will arise when you will have little or no control over the physical arrangements for your presentation, you may be able to improve the setting anyway. But you must check out the setting beforehand. If possible, do these things:

- *Know how to use the equipment.* An overhead projector is easy to use, but you must check its position to project your whole slide on the screen and in focus. Systems projecting computer-driven presentations all work about the same; however, you cannot set one up at the last minute. Arrive early and check your presentation.

- *Check all materials and equipment.* Having a felt-tip pen that won't write, a burned-out projector light bulb, and a screen that won't lower is frustrating and is likely to hinder an effective presentation.

- *Remove any distractions.* You don't want to be competing with a previous speaker's material, exhibits, or drawings on a whiteboard or flipchart.

- *Rearrange the seating if necessary.* If possible, arrange the seating so that everyone is facing you and can see you and your visuals or exhibits.

- *Position yourself away from the entrance.* If possible, speak from a place where latecomers or persons who must leave early won't distract you and others by walking in front of you to find a seat or to leave the room.

- *Set a comfortable temperature in the room.* Check the room temperature and whether sunlight is streaming in through unshaded windows. If possible, keep the room comfortable, but cool. A hot, stuffy room makes people drowsy, especially when your presentation is scheduled right after lunch or late in the day and the lights have been dimmed or turned off for viewing slides.

If you can't arrange the environment to your satisfaction, at least you will be forewarned. You can probably adjust your plans to achieve the proper results.

The occasion will also influence the mode of presentation you choose—impromptu, memorized, written, or extemporaneous.

• *Impromptu:* As the name implies, impromptu oral presentations can't be prepared. Or rather, you can't plan the specific presentation. Your best preparation is knowledge of the subject matter. At a social occasion you may be asked to give a little impromptu speech to introduce yourself. Or at a business meeting you may be called upon to stand up and discuss an arrangement, a contract, or the operation of your shop or office. At a meeting you may stand up to question or support an action. Some of our later discussions of content and organization will offer you some guidance, but to deliver a good impromptu, you had better know your subject thoroughly.

• *Memorized:* Memorized presentations have extremely limited uses. They probably serve best when you must repeat a speech many times. For instance, the guides at Disneyland and such places memorize their talks: "Good afternoon, ladies and gentlemen, we're about to enter darkest Jungleland. If you are fainthearted. . . ." Experienced lecturers, actors, and politicians go about the country giving the same speech over and over. But for most of us, memorizing a speech is too much effort and can get us into trouble. When you learn something word-for-word and forget a word, the whole speech can depart from your mind— instant blank.

• *Written:* Written speeches are quite suitable for some occasions. People running for political office often use written speeches to avoid making misstatements of fact or overheated spur-of-the-moment statements that may plague them later. But reading a speech usually bores workplace audiences. A light, ad-lib effect is destroyed by a written speech. And often, as in the case of the tax specialist in the dimly lit room, conditions are not right for reading. In addition, reading from a manuscript creates two additional problems. For one thing, as you read from your written text, you will not be able to maintain good eye contact with your audience and you may miss some of their reactions. For another, if you stand before your audience with a hefty sheaf of papers in your hand or on the lectern, there will always be some listeners distracted from what you are saying by eyeing the stack of pages trying to estimate how much longer you will be talking.

• *Extemporaneous:* The most suitable oral presentation for the widest variety of occasions is the extemporaneous presentation. This mode calls for a good deal of preparation. You organize, outline, and rehearse it, but you do not write it or memorize it. You know what ideas and facts you're going to work with and have them well in hand. The major points of your presentation are literally at hand, either in the form of notecards or, better yet, in your visual aids. But you form the actual wording of the presentation with each delivery. It's a good presentation mode—sound, safe, flexible. It's the primary mode that we consider.

Audience

Find out as much about your audience beforehand as you can. First, to how many people will you speak? For 20 people you might plan an informal presentation that is mainly discussion—a short talk followed by an extensive question-and-answer period. For a large group meeting in an auditorium, discussion might be unwieldy, so you would plan for a longer, well-organized presentation. But most of your decisions based on audience, regardless of its size, will be based on the context and the audience's knowledge and expectations.

• *How closely do you relate to your audience?* For instance, is it composed mainly of friends and co-workers? Is it an audience with which you have many shared interests? Are you a student talking to students? A nurse to nurses? A computer programmer to computer programmers? If so, in some ways your job is easier. Your language can be a bit casual, your speech patterns relaxed. You can leave some things unsaid because everybody knows them anyway. On the other hand, speaking to this group can be tough. They are likely to question your expertise. You may need more evidence to prove your points with this audience than with another that doesn't know you as well.

Groups that don't share your experiences present different kinds of problems. They may expect more structure and more formal language from you. They may not take you seriously because you are too young or too old. When you move out of your normal workplace context, expect difficulties. Your presentation must be well prepared to overcome them. For instance, if you were an inspector for an environmental agency speaking to chemists or chemical engineers employed by pulp mills, you would undoubtedly discuss some safety measures and environmental regulations to which some of the listeners will be sympathetic. But you could expect several who would not agree with some of your viewpoints. You should be aware of likely resistances and know what to do to overcome them.

• *What adaptations should you make for multicultural audiences?* In addition to the considerations mentioned above, you may need to make adjustments for audiences whose English is limited or whose culture may prefer a different approach from your normal one. Although you may not always be able to determine the particular needs and interests of culturally diverse audiences, you can take certain steps to respond to ethnic diversity. Repeat key points and have the key points on visuals. Use visuals that contain captions and labels in both English and the other language or languages to ensure that the audience understands them. Define or explain phrases or words that may be misunderstood. You may even want to distribute translated handouts of crucial passages. In addition to considering verbal language, you should also be aware of cultural differences in body language. In maintaining eye contact, for instance, be careful not to appear too aggressive for audiences that might regard a strong gaze as disrespectful.

Humor can be a mine field of difficulties with a multicultural audience—some members of the audience may not understand the humor (which is always based on mutual understanding) and others may fail to find the humor funny. Sometimes more substantive problems arise. Some persons of other cultures do not share what we might hold as American values. By the same token, as Americans, we might fail to appreciate fully the values of another culture.

• *What does the audience know about your subject?* If they already know all the basics, you can start at a more advanced level. If not, you may have to give background information. We all learn a specialized vocabulary with the jobs we are educated to do. Sometimes we forget that others don't share that vocabulary. A highway engineer speaking about horizontal and vertical curves may forget that nonengineers would call the first simply *curves* and the second *hills.* When you can, use simple expressions for a nonexpert audience. If you can't, define the needed terms. But judge your audience carefully. An audience that doesn't need background, simple language, or definitions will feel talked down to if you speak at that level.

• *What does the audience expect of you?* Most workplace audiences can be classified as management, technical, or nontechnical. By technical we mean those people who work closely with whatever it is you're talking about.

Suppose you develop a new process in an auto shop for taking off old tires, putting new ones on, and balancing the wheels. If you were talking to the management about this new process, they would expect cost data. Will this new process cost more or less than the old? Will it require fewer or more technicians? Are safety problems involved? The technicians would also want to know some of these same things, but they would also want more details about the process itself. How do you do it? What are the major steps in the process? Does it require new equipment? The nontechnicians primarily expect to be told how the process relates to them. In the case of new tire-changing techniques, the nontechnical customers would want to know two things: Will the new process be cheaper, and will it get cars in and out of the garage faster?

To do your best, you must know your audience, for you can't get through to an audience unless it lets you through. In that sense, the audience is in control, not you. But don't despair if you can't always analyze an audience perfectly. Most audiences will listen carefully if they sense that what you have to say is important to them and that you have their interests in mind.

DEFINING PURPOSE AND DEVELOPING CONTENT

Purpose and content are closely related, and both relate closely to occasion and audience. Most speech involves speaking socially, to inform, or to persuade, or some mixture of the three. For a specific presentation to a specific audience you would narrow a broad purpose down to a specific one:

- I propose to welcome and amuse for a few minutes a group of 20 visiting salespeople.

- I propose to inform 20 visiting salespeople how the new billing system works.

- I propose to persuade 20 visiting salespeople that the new billing system is better than the old.

- I propose to inform 20 visiting salespeople about the new billing system and to persuade them that it is better than the old.

When you have your specific purpose clearly in mind, you have completed the criteria you need to choose your content. You should ask four questions about anything you intend to include in your presentation:

- Will it meet the needs and expectations of my audience?

- Will it move my purpose forward?

- Does the occasion call for it?

- Does accurate presentation of the topic call for it?

Leave out any item that fails to meet at least one of these criteria. Your best items will meet all four. The more criteria each item meets, the more economical you will be of both your and the audience's time.

Time is always a problem. Accuracy may say to include an item. Time may say to leave it out. It's a conflict that goes on in all speaking and writing. Also, you must set priorities among your criteria because they will often be in conflict. For instance, an item that your audience really doesn't expect may be needed for accuracy. Which of these two criteria is your highest priority? Go for accuracy.

What sort of material makes up the content of oral presentations? Let's analyze a few excerpts from actual ones to see.

In our first excerpt, a United States senator offers a series of examples to support his contention that New Hampshire has been hard hit by recession:

> Much of the country is hit by an ongoing recession, possibly no state harder than New Hampshire. Signs of the recession in my state include an increase in the state's unemployment rate from 3.5 to nearly 8 percent in the last 3 years, a 53 percent reduction in construction employment, the collapse of the real estate market, a tripling in the number of bankruptcy filings, and a doubling in the number of AFDC recipients.[1]

In this next example, an American business leader uses an anecdote to illustrate a point about the role of creativity in achieving success:

> What makes people creative? Sometimes, it's having your life shaken up. George Valassis is a pal of mine. For 19 years he worked as an advertising salesman for his father's brother. One day his uncle decided to retire and his cousin took over the business. The cousin fired him. Without warning, George lost a modest though comfortable job, and he realized then and there that job security could vanish like a puff of smoke. So, he put his 19 years of experience to use in order to come up with an innovative idea. He knew that advertisers like Procter and Gamble and General Foods were having a really tough time delivering coupons to customers quickly, so he came up with the idea of inserting books filled with coupons in newspapers. To this day, when you open the Sunday edition of your newspaper and see a book of coupons inside, you're looking at what the ad industry calls a "Valassis Insert." George sold the company he built for big bucks. If he hadn't gotten fired, would he have come up with this great idea? George doesn't think so. He says he just played the hand he was dealt. Pretty creative though, wasn't it?[2]

Speakers may appeal to authority to support their points, as in this example where a commencement speaker quotes the essayist Henry David Thoreau:

> If [Thoreau] were here today, advising those of you who plan to enter business he would say fine, good choice, there is nothing wrong with that. It was not that he was against commerce, but rather that he was for responsible commerce. In his essay, "Civil Disobedience," he wrote: "It is truly enough said that a corporation has no conscience; but a corporation of conscientious men is a corporation with a conscience."
>
> He would have you work for corporations whose directors are conscientious men and women who place right action above profit, who are morally responsible, who will not engage in commerce of the kind that

[1]Warren Rudman, "The Federal Budget Deficit," *Vital Speeches* 58 (1992): 386.
[2]Dave Thomas, "What Makes for Success? Achieving Excellence," *Vital Speeches* 62 (1996): 721.

takes unfair advantage of workers, risks the public's health, or contributes to the wanton destruction of the environment.[3]

Speakers may use statistics to support generalizations, as in this excerpt that emphasizes the need for banks to provide more capital to women business owners:

The paradox is that there is equally compelling data that woman-owned businesses are a large and growing force in our economy. And, more to the point from a banker's perspective—no worse than businesses in general at repaying their loans and staying in business.

In fact, woman businesses do even better on a number of those counts:

- Today there are 7.7 million businesses owned by women in the U.S.;

- They employ 15.5 million workers—35 percent more than the Fortune 500 companies do worldwide;

- They generate $1.4 trillion in sales;

- Woman-owned businesses increased at a rate of 57.6 percent between 1982 and 1987 and at a rate of 87.8 percent between 1987 and 1992.

And female business owners are just as likely as their male counterparts to pay their bills on time and to stay in business.

- More and more research is being done on this subject. According to Dun & Bradstreet, the financial and business research firm, woman-owned businesses pay their bills on time just as often as do businesses in general;

- Fewer than 10 percent of female-headed firms are at the highest risk level;

- 72 percent of woman-owned businesses active in 1991 are still in business—compared to 67 percent of all businesses nationwide.[4]

The pattern is clear, we hope. General statements, such as "Much of the country is hit by an ongoing recession, possibly no state harder than New Hampshire," are preceded or followed by support. The support can be almost anything and everything—facts, numbers and statistics, authoritative opinions, comparisons, examples, anecdotes, and so forth. All are suitable as long as they pass through the screen of your four criteria—audience, purpose, occasion, and accuracy.

---

[3]John A. Synodinos, "Some Advice for the Graduates from Henry David Thoreau," *Vital Speeches* 58 (1992): 55.

[4]Sandra Maltby, "Banks and the Woman Business Owner: Dissolving the Paradox," *Vital Speeches* 62 (1996): 186.

Recognize that general statements need support unless they're widely accepted. But there is a limit to the amount of support you can supply or be reasonably expected to supply. When you reach the point where your material is adequate to satisfy a reasonable person, stop.

ORGANIZING MATERIAL

After you have considered context, purpose, and content, the next step is organization. In looking at the content of speeches, we saw that most moved back and forth between generalizations and support for the generalizations. Indeed, this general-to-particular or particular-to-general development is a good overall organizational plan. (See Chapter 3.) Also we discuss a great many other organizational plans in this book. We talk, for instance, about mechanism and process descriptions (in Chapters 16 and 17), good- and bad-news approaches (Chapter 9), and problem solving (Chapter 14). Most of the organizational schemes good for writing are also good for speaking, so don't overlook any of them. Choose the plan or combination of plans that best fits the same criteria we have discussed for content: audience, purpose, occasion, accuracy.

One of your organizational chores is to prepare your presentation. If you were to write your presentation, you would first outline it (See Outline in Unit V, Writer's Guide.) and then write it, much as you would any other piece of writing. Knowing it was meant to be read aloud, you would be particularly careful about either using shorter sentences than usual or building your longer sentences on a series of parallel phrases. You would avoid putting complicated phrases or clauses between subject and verb. You would use contractions except when you wanted emphasis.

When you are to speak extemporaneously, stop at the outline stage. We recommend making two outlines, actually. The first one would look like the outline for written work, complete with subdivisions and sub-subdivisions. You'll need this complete outline to bring all your material into order. But such an outline is too complex to speak from. You'll depend on it too much and be forever peering at it and losing your place, thus throwing away the whole graceful effect of extemporaneous speech.

Cut the first outline down to fit onto several 4-by-6 cards or several screens. Make one card for each major division of your speech. Put just enough on each card to keep you on track, following the main points in the order you have planned. Print your outline in rather large letters (but not all capitals; they're hard to read) on the card. You might also choose not to use notecards at all, but use information on your visuals as prompts for talking. Figure 12.1 shows an outline that could be used on a notecard or as a slide or screen that both speakers and audiences can follow. In preparing a presentation on Microsoft PowerPoint or a similar presentation software, you can create a note page that reproduces a miniature version of the slide you show the audience and contains notes for yourself (Figure 12.2). The advantage of the note page is that your notes and the slide are always together. With such simple notes and

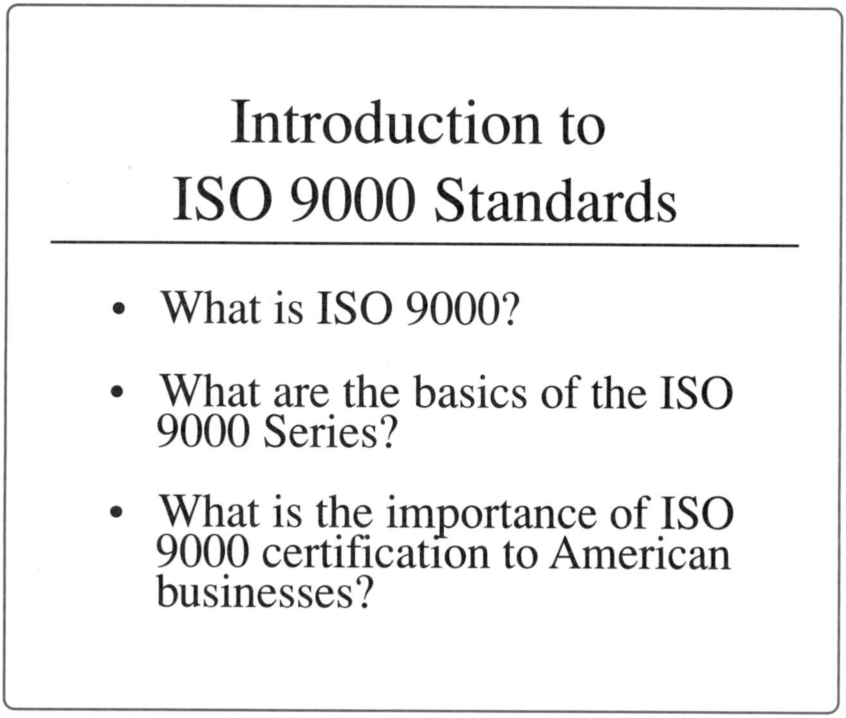

Figure 12.1 Slide that presents an outline for both the speaker and the audience.

prompts, you must rehearse your presentation beforehand. But such notes and visual prompts enable you to see at a glance where you're going. Thus, most of the time you can keep your eyes where they belong—on your audience. Figure 12.3 shows the set of screens used in a Microsoft PowerPoint presentation.

INTRODUCING AND CONCLUDING ORAL PRESENTATIONS

Both the introduction and conclusion are critical to your presentation; they should be well prepared.

INTRODUCTIONS

Actually, most successful introductions come in two parts. The first part is often called the *icebreaker*. You want to slip gracefully from the introduction to the introduction of your presentation. Various devices can be used. You can open with a quotation or an anecdote that illustrates your major point.

Introduction to
ISO 9000 Standards

- What is ISO 9000?
- What are the basics of the ISO 9000 Series?
- What is the importance of ISO 9000 certification to American businesses?

← Reduced image of the slide or screen.

Notes that remind speaker of important points to elaborate.

Notes:

What is ISO 9000?

• Clarify that ISO 9000 applies not to products and services but to the processes that create them.

• Give brief history of ISO as offspring of the International Organization for Standardization, founded in 1947 in Geneva, Switzerland.

• Point out that current ISO 9000 core series was first published in 1987 and has been adopted by more than one hundred nations. (U.S. represented in ISO by the American National Standards Institute.)

What are the basics of the ISO 9000 series?

• Explain that ISO 9000 is a guidance standard. It is ISO 9001, 9002, and 9003 for which companies must be certified.

What is the importance of ISO 9000 certification to American businesses?

• Empahsize the importance of achieving ISO 9000 for businesses that plan to compete seriously in a global economy.

• Point out that the European Community already mandates ISO certification for makers of certain types of products (telecommunications terminal equipment, industrial safety equipment, gas appliances, commercial scales, etc.).

Figure 12.2 Note page created in computer-generated presentation software.

**Proposed Redesign
of Parking Lot C**

Proposed by
Lee Fu-Chang, Traffic and Parking Office
Anne Norwood, Traffic and Parking Office
James Ostrander, Traffic and Parking Office

October 10, 2000

Topics to be Considered

- Factors contributing to parking problems
- Recommended changes
- Steps to implement changes
- Estimated costs to implement changes

**Factors Contributing
to Parking Problems**

- 90-degree parking spaces require wide lanes
- Number of employees has increased by 25 percent
- Compact-sized vehicles take as much space as larger vehicles

Recommended Changes

- Redesign parking lot to accommodate an additional 20 parking spaces (an additional 10 percent).
- Fund changes by additional money from employee contingency fund and by increasing parking permits $10 a year.

Steps to Implement Changes

- Remove parking islands
- Seal coat parking lot
- Paint new 45-degree parking spaces and directional arrows
- Install new curbing
- Install compact-car signage

**Estimated Costs
to Implement Changes**

- Remove existing parking islands $10,000
- Seal coat parking lot   61,500
- Stripe 45-degree parking spaces   3,300
- Add curbing   2,000
- Paint directional arrows and signs   2,000
                          total $78,800

Figure 12.3 Set of screens or slides for computer-generated presentation.

You can get audience participation in some manner. Ask for a show of hands: "How many people visited the company's exhibit at last week's trade show?" You can compliment the occasion or the audience. You have many options. We have only two warnings. Your quotations and stories should apply to your topic. Don't let them seem dragged in. Second, although some people use a joke to put people at ease, be careful of humor. If you can't handle it, don't touch it. And if the occasion for the presentation is a serious one, humor would likely be seen as inappropriate. Your introduction should match the occasion.

After your icebreaker or brief opening remarks, get to your main points quickly. State your purpose and plan plainly and clearly:

> In the next 20 minutes, I'll explain to you why the speed limit on our state's highways should be rolled back to 60 miles per hour. It saves gasoline, highway maintenance, and lives.

In this statement the audience is told the main purpose and the major subdivisions of the presentation. All purpose statements, with one exception, should be this complete. The exception: If your purpose involves bad news, use the bad-news approach (see pages 234–236). That is, build through a factual analysis to the bad news. Keep it out of the introduction.

An introduction can accomplish two other tasks, as well. If your presentation is to include several key terms or theories unknown to your audience, explain them at the beginning of your talk. Don't make people suffer from a lack of knowledge. Also, in a persuasive presentation the introduction is often a good place to seek common ground with your audience:

> I'm sure we all agree on the need to conserve energy, money, and lives. Where we perhaps don't agree is on how to go about it. Let's consider. . . .

CONCLUSIONS

Conclusions also come in two parts, sometimes three—all short. Once you move into a conclusion, move through it quickly. It should take no more than a minute, even for a long presentation.

Summarize your major points in a sentence or two:

> Driving at 60 instead of 70 miles per hour cuts gasoline use by 10 percent and cuts down highway maintenance statewide by as much as $14 million a year. Most important of all, reducing the speed limit to 60 miles per hour will, according to projections provided by the Department of Transportation's Office of Highway Safety, save more than 200 lives a year in our state.

Note the repetition of the key points of the introduction, but with the addition of some important support data.

If your presentation has been persuasive, you may wish to add a "call to action" to the summary:

> If I have persuaded you of the need for a 60-miles-per-hour speed limit on our state highways, write your state representative or senator today.

You can be sure that the truck lobbies are bringing pressure to bear to keep the limit at 70 miles per hour.

You may also want to close your presentation with a memorable quotation or story—something like an icebreaker. If you do close with a story, keep it brief.

USING VISUALS

As in writing, visuals are often indispensable in speaking. Think of the words saved in describing how to tie a square knot by a simple illustration like the one here.

Even when visual aids are not absolutely necessary, they add variety and interest to your presentations. They support, clarify, and expand your points. They can snap a wandering audience to attention. They help the audience understand and retain your information.

What exactly is a visual? As in writing, it can be a graph, drawing, table, photograph; it can be a computer-generated presentation. In speaking, however, the possibilities broaden. Visuals can be models. Your pictures can be animated. And you can use objects—even people and animals. In this section we give some criteria for selecting effective visuals and a rundown on some of the most used visual tools.

CRITERIA

Good visuals enhance oral presentations; bad ones detract. Any visuals you use should be easy to read, clear and simple, and easy to use—visibility, simplicity, clarity, and control.

Visibility

The notion of visibility in visuals seems obvious enough, but it is all too often overlooked. If your audience can't read or see the features of your visual, it's worthless. A 9-by-12-inch photograph held in your hand and waved about does nothing for your audience. Because of the ease with which transparencies can now be made, speakers are tempted to reproduce printed pages and to show them on overhead projectors. Unfortunately, the print is usually so small that it's unreadable beyond the first few rows. If you use too small a point size, a difficult font or too much information on a computer-generated slide, your audience is not going to be happy.

For printed material, we can give you two simple rules:

1. First, to be read, letters and other characters should be at least 1-inch high for each 25 feet between the visual and the audience. If you

project a transparency on a screen, the letters on the screen should follow the same 1-inch-to-25-feet ratio. This means that you must prepare the originals for your transparencies by using oversized type or use a larger print size than you normally would. Point sizes between 30 and 40 points are a good starting point. You may have to adjust the point size after you do a practice run.

2. Second, use headings and bulleted lists, restricting texts to no more than 6 or 7 lines and no more than about 40 words. Any more will make screens too dense. Figures 12.4 and 12.5 use an appropriate amount of blank space and text.

For other visuals, such as drawings, photos, graphs, objects, and even clips from videotapes, the rules of visibility are less easily laid down. You may scan them in to your computer presentation and enlarge them. If that isn't possible, you may have to experiment a bit. You should know beforehand how far the last row of your audience will be from your visuals. Stand that far yourself and see if you can understand the material presented. If you can't, it's too small. Don't use it. It is frustrating to an audience to have a speaker point knowingly to a visual that they can't see well enough to comprehend. Remember, you will probably be within a few feet of your visuals, but most of your audience will be much farther away.

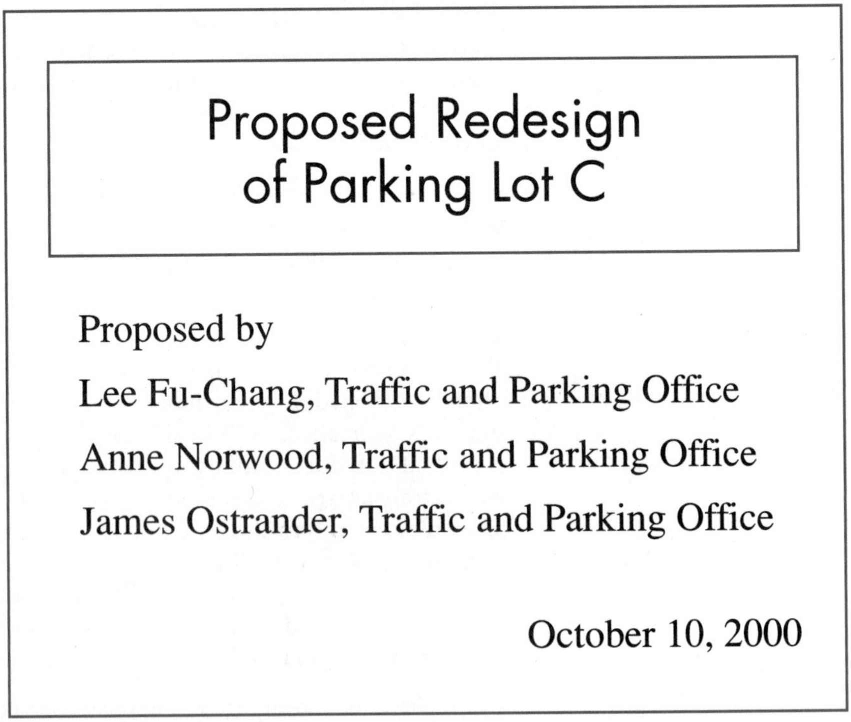

Figure 12.4 Title screen or slide for computer-generated presentation.

Topics to be Considered

- Factors contributing to parking problems
- Recommended changes
- Steps to implement changes
- Estimated costs to implement changes

Figure 12.5 Overview screen or slide for computer-generated presentation.

Simplicity and Clarity

Visuals that are suitable in printed work may be too complicated for use in speaking. The reader, after all, can stop and study a visual. But in oral presentations the listener has only a limited time to take in the visual before the speaker sweeps it away and goes on to the next point. Therefore, the rule for presentation visuals is to simplify and then to simplify again. Cut down to only absolutely vital information. The audience should be able to take in a visual's meaning at a glance. Use graphs to show the shapes of trends without worrying too much about the actual numbers. Break up tables and extract only needed information. Eliminate all unneeded features from maps. Use block diagrams rather than schematics.

The graph in Figure 12.6 is too complicated for use in a speech. Viewers must refer back and forth between the key and the surfaces to orient themselves. A surface graph is difficult for many readers to interpret, let alone for a viewer who may only have a short glimpse of it. The graph in Figure 12.7 is more suitable. Here, viewers can easily grasp the percentages. Labeling the graph directly instead of using a key makes reading the graph a simple matter.

Figure 12.8 shows the layout of the interstate highway system in Minnesota. This illustration would make a good transparency or poster. The lines are bold and the print large. The interstate roads, major cities, and state boundaries are clearly located. All other detail has been eliminated.

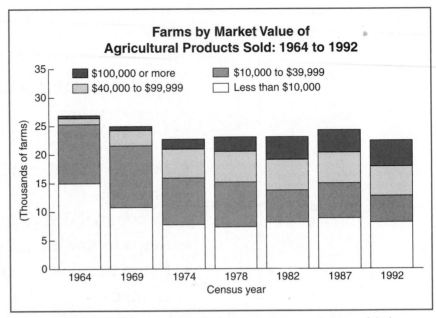

Figure 12.6 Complicated graph. The use of a legend and the many divisions of the bars make this graph too complicated for use in an oral presentation.
Source: US Dept. of Commerce. *Geographical Area Series—Montana* (AC92-A-96). Vol. 1 of *1992 Census of Agriculture.* Washington: GPO, Aug. 1994. 5.

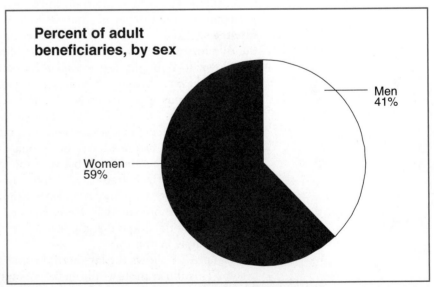

Figure 12.7 Simple graph. Simple pie and bar graphs work well for oral presentations.
Source: Social Security Administration.

Figure 12.8 Minnesota interstate system.
Source: Minnesota Department of Transportation, St. Paul.

The table in Figure 12.9 is far too complex to be of any use in a speech. The simplified, large-print table in Figure 12.10 would work well if made into a transparency. If you must use a detailed visual, consider building it across several screens or slides.

Remember that few visuals found in books are satisfactory for use in speaking. They will likely be too small and contain too much information for speech audiences. Resist the temptation merely to reproduce them without first redesigning them. Eliminate unneeded material and provide bold lines and large lettering. However, even when you redo visuals taken from other sources, remember to acknowledge the source.

Ease of Control

When you make an oral presentation, you should control your audience as much as you can. Properly made and used, visuals can increase an audience's concentration and keep attention focused on your subject matter. Visuals draw attention when you want them to and are invisible when you

Table 3b. Gross Book Value of Depreciable Assets, Capital Expenditures, Retirements, Depreciation, and Rental Payments: 1992

[Million dollars. For meaning of abbreviations and symbols, see introductory text. For explanation of terms, see appendixes]

Item	Tires and inner tubes (SIC 3011)	Rubber and plastics footwear (SIC 3021)	Rubber and plastics hose and belting (SIC 3052)	Gaskets, packing, and sealing devices (SIC 3053)	Mechanical rubber goods (SIC 3061)	Fabricated rubber products, n.e.c (SIC 3069)
Gross book value of depreciable assets:						
Total:						
Beginning of year	6,823.8	234.9	1,019.4	1,216.4	1,808.9	2,564.7
New capital expenditures[1]	506.1	12.9	74.1	90.3	154.0	204.2
Used capital expenditures	30.5	2.2	6.9	17.3	12.3	19.3
Retirements	103.6	5.1	12.2	44.2	61.1	52.9
End of year	7,256.8	244.8	1,088.1	1,279.9	1,914.1	2,735.3
Buildings and other structures:						
Beginning of year	1,268.3	58.6	227.8	255.3	388.3	618.4
New capital expenditures	52.2	2.3	8.4	15.1	22.6	29.3
Used capital expenditures	.1	.1	(D)	1.3	(D)	3.6
Retirements	6.3	.1	(D)	3.3	(D)	3.1
End of year	1,314.3	60.8	236.6	288.4	409.9	648.2
Machinery and equipment:						
Beginning of year	5,555.4	176.3	791.5	961.1	1,420.6	1,946.3
New capital expenditures[1]	453.9	10.6	65.5	75.2	131.4	175.0
Used capital expenditures	30.4	2.2	(D)	16.1	(D)	15.7
Retirements	97.2	5.0	(D)	40.9	(D)	49.8
End of year	5,942.5	184.00	851.6	1,011.5	1,504.2	2,087.1
Depreciation charges during 1992:						
Total	409.9	21.2	64.9	92.6	134.9	184.0
Buildings and other structures	45.7	3.4	9.7	14.1	20.7	27.8
Machinery and equipment	364.2	17.8	55.1	78.6	114.1	156.1
Rental payments:						
Total	45.3	7.3	15.2	32.7	36.23	59.6
Buildings and other structures	8.9	5.2	7.4	19.1	21.0	30.8
Machinery and equipment	36.4	2.1	7.8	13.5	15.2	28.7

[1]Data on new machinery and equipment expenditures by type are provided in table 3c.

Figure 12.9 Complicated table. Members of the audience simply can't pick up information from this table in the time it will be on view.

Source: US Dept. of Commerce. *1992 Census of Manufacturing.* Industry Series, MC 92-1-31A. Washington: GPO, Apr. 1995. 23.

TABLE IV   COMPREHENSIVE COST COMPARISON, PRESENT HEATER AND PROPOSED HEATER

Construction Costs	Present Heater	Proposed Heater
Materials and Labor	$3500.00 per heater	$1047.00 per heater
Monthly Costs	**Present Heater**	**Proposed Heater**
Operating	42.12	35.10
Maintenance	125.00	76.00
Total Monthly Costs	167.12	111.10

Figure 12.10 Simple table appropriate for oral presentations.

are through with them. Poorly made visuals distract audience attention toward irrelevancies.

For instance, large models or mockups of equipment are often excellent visuals. But they have the disadvantage of sitting there on the rostrum like a lump after you are done with them. The audience may stare at them, running over their operation, instead of listening to you. If possible, arrange to have them removed or at least covered when they are not in use.

Small exhibits passed through the audience are deadly for proper concentration. Members of the audience get involved in the mechanics of passing them about. They examine them when they receive them, ignoring the speaker. Passed-around objects are perfect examples of visuals you can't control.

For proper control, then, you should be able to show and remove a visual at will. You'll be even farther ahead if you can easily change it by adding or deleting material. Computer presentations give you some flexibility here. You can advance or go back to a slide with a couple of keystrokes. You can use the mouse or a laser pointer to point to one of your statements.

Visual Tools

You have a wide range of visual tools to choose from—videotapes, movies, 35mm slides, models, chalkboards or whiteboards, flannel boards, computer screens, and many others. We deal here with four such tools, all recommended for their effectiveness and ease of use: chalkboards or whiteboards, posters, flipcharts, and overhead projectors and liquid crystal displays (LCDs).

Whiteboards or Chalkboards

Whiteboards or chalkboards have the major advantage of being easy to use. They rarely require extensive preparation beforehand. They also provide eye-appealing action as you move about, writing and drawing on them as you make impromptu sketches and notes. Their major disadvantage is slowness. It takes time to produce your drawings, lists, or whatever on the board. If you plan to create complicated drawings, do them ahead of time. If you do, cover them until you use them and erase them as soon as you are done with them.

Write or print legibly and in large letters. Drawings can be rudimentary but must be understandable. It takes experience to draw and talk at the same time. Avoid talking to the board exclusively. Remember that you have an audience out there. Don't turn your back on them for too long. And make sure you have plenty of chalk or felt-tip markers and an eraser.

In an age of technology the old-fashioned whiteboard's or chalkboard's effectiveness is often underrated, but it meets the important criterion of control excellently. You need not draw your visuals until the moment you need them, you have all eyes on you as you are drawing them, and you can erase them whenever you like.

Posters

Words, drawings, and graphics can be displayed on posters prepared ahead of time. Display the poster on an easel. Keep the poster a convenient size: 2-feet wide by 3-feet high is a common dimension. Be sure that all lettering is at least 1-inch high for every 25 feet from your audience. Do not use all capital letters. A normal mixture of capital and lowercase letters is easier to read. Confirm that all drawings and graphs are easily visible from the back row.

Posters are controllable and quite effective if you keep their contents visible and simple. Put them on the easel only when you need them.

Flipcharts

The flipchart in its simplest form is a large tablet (about 2-feet wide by 3-feet high) securely fastened to an easel. When you are through with one page, you flip the page over and reveal the next. When no chalkboard or whiteboard is available, you can substitute the blank pages of a flipchart. Or, if you want to prepare ahead, you can construct each page as you would a poster.

A combination of the two approaches is to draw your visuals lightly on the flipchart before your talk. (If you do it lightly enough, your audience won't see your sketches, but it won't matter particularly if they do.) Then, during your presentation, you cover the light lines with bold strokes of a felt-tipped pen. This method effectively combines action with accuracy.

You have good control with a flipchart. Be sure to leave the top page blank, so that you can cover visuals when not using them. Here are a few additional points to keep in mind when using a flipchart:

- *Make sure the flipchart is of appropriate size.* It should be large enough to be seen from the back of a large room. It can be smaller if you are talking to a handful of people seated around a conference table.

- *Make sure the flipchart is in a well-lighted area.* It does little good to use a flipchart that is hard to read.

- *Check all equipment and materials before you begin.* Make sure you have enough sheets on the pad for your complete presentation. Make sure your markers are fresh and will write. Test to see that the easel is sturdy and won't tip over when you write on the chart.

Overhead Projectors and LCD (Liquid Crystal Display) Projectors

At the risk of sounding like salespersons for overhead projectors and LCD projectors, we must say that they are probably the most effective visual tools ever devised for speakers. These relatively simple machines allow you to project transparencies or computer screens on a screen or wall. Never assume, however, that you can walk up to a computer, insert your presentation disk, and begin running it. Make sure the software has full compatibility with your presentation file.

Ease of Preparation   Most of the copy machines readily found in offices and libraries make transparent copies as well as opaque ones, if you insert the correct blank transparency into the paper tray to make the copy. These transparencies are your visuals. It's so easy to reproduce almost anything for a transparency that you must guard against reproducing inappropriate material, such as pages of small print or complex graphs. You can also use computerized presentation software such as Microsoft Power-Point and Corel Presentations to create colorful and sophisticated visuals. Computer-generated visuals can be prepared easily and can be revised with just a few keystrokes.

Ease of Operation   With your projector in the front of the room, you can remain in front of your audience and easily control your own visuals. You lay transparencies directly on the machine in a position that allows you to read them. Turn on the machine, focus the image, and you're in business. There are no trays of slides to jam. Room lights can remain on. You can project on either a light-colored wall or a screen. About the only thing that can go wrong with an overhead projector is a burnt-out light bulb. Keep an extra bulb handy and know how to change it. Computer-generated images are even easier to use because you do not handle transparencies or slides.

We cannot overemphasize the importance of running through your computer presentation ahead of time—if at all possible on the computer and projector you will be using. The LCD projects the visual on the screen. If you are using presentation software, it's best, if possible, to use your own laptop computer and LCD projector because you will be familiar with their operation. Make sure that the computer you use has the type and version of software that will run your presentation file. At a recent meeting, four presenters had delays of 10 to 15 minutes while they connected and adjusted their laptops to the projector. One presenter never did get his to work. He admitted that he had arrived only an hour before the presentation and he was using a friend's laptop.

Ease of Control   Overhead and LCD projectors offer more control over your visuals than any other tool. You can prepare transparencies ahead of time, or you can put a blank transparency on the projector and use it like a chalkboard. You can prepare a transparency partly and finish it with a felt-tipped pen or a crayon while you talk. By sliding a piece of paper around on your transparency, you can reveal as much or as little of your visual as you like. You can prepare other transparencies to superimpose over a first transparency to add material as you go along. With computer-generated presentations, you can build in special transition effects that enable you to move one slide off the screen and bring the next one on in several interesting ways with just a keystroke. You can also create a special effect on a slide by using an automatic-build feature that enables you to reveal points one at time and to dim or gray out earlier points when a new point is added. You can shut off the entire visual with a flip of the switch.

In preparing your transparencies or computer screens, keep our criteria in mind: Keep visuals visible, simple, and clear. Your projected image must be of sufficient size to be seen in the back row. For printed material this generally means your letters must be about twice the size of ordinary print. The default point size for presentation software is between 25 and 40 points. If you must use small print, move the projector farther back from the screen wall and thus enlarge the letters.

An overhead projector or a computer (especially a laptop) is small enough not to block anyone's view. Place it in front of your audience and stand slightly to the side. Face your audience while you talk and work with your visuals. You may point to material on the transparency with a pencil, use the mouse to point to an area on the slide, or use a laser pointer and point to locations on the screen. The pencil's shadow will point to the image on the wall. Always turn the projector off immediately when you are not using it. This helps prevent heat build up that can blow the bulb and eliminates the distracting noise of the cooling fan and the large, illuminated but empty square on the screen or wall. However, remember that if the projector has been on for several minutes, you may have to allow the cooling fan to run to prevent the bulb from blowing.

Because of their effectiveness, overhead projectors and computers and LCD projectors are used in many schools and businesses. You almost certainly have seen them in action. Observe carefully how they are used. Learn what to do from the people who use them well, and what not to do from those who use them poorly.

DELIVERING ORAL PRESENTATIONS

Your first job was to prepare well for your oral presentation. Now your task is to make a presentation that will achieve your goals.

Let's assume you have made all the preparations we have suggested. You've organized your presentation and have your outline and notes ready. You've planned your visuals and integrated them into your presentation. You now have only one task left—delivering the oral presentation.

An oral presentation is a performance. Whether you choose a low-key conversational style or a more formal rhetorical style, you're giving a performance. In this section we talk about the preparation period, the delivery of your presentation, and the question-and-answer period that often follows a presentation.

PREPERFORMANCE PERIOD

No matter whether you plan to give your oral presentation from a manuscript or extemporaneously from cards or overhead screens, you must rehearse it. If you can find a sympathetic but critical audience of one or two persons, fine, but rehearse, if only in front of a mirror and, if possible, to a tape recorder. Play back the tape and listen critically to your pace and delivery. Listen for effective use of the techniques we'll discuss shortly. Timing is critical. Tailor your presentation to fit precisely into whatever time is allotted you. Running seriously under or over your allotted time can greatly inconvenience a good many people and gain you nothing but bad marks from your audience. Pay attention to the pronunciation of words. Rehearsal is the time to discover the words that you can't pronounce or that you feel shaky about. Look them up; practice them until you have mastered them. Rehearse several times—your confidence will increase as you become more familiar with what you will cover and how it feels to move through your presentation, working with your notes (if any) and visuals. You will know your rehearsals are adequate when you can run through a speech comfortably—on time, with no major hesitations, and with all the words properly pronounced. You should feel comfortable in your movements and know how you're going to work with your visuals.

On the day of your presentation pay some attention to your appearance. Dress for the occasion, whatever it is. Some occasions are shirt-sleeves affairs; others are more formal. In general, you should be neat and well groomed for your presentation. The simple truth is that people feel better about themselves when they feel attractive, and proper dress enhances whatever nature gave us to work with.

DELIVERY

The moment has arrived. You have done all you can to get ready. You are introduced, and it's time to make your way to the front of the audience. For many people, this is an absolutely terrifying moment. For others, it's a stimulating, enjoyable experience. In either case, however, the right delivery techniques will enable you to do a better job. Let us consider here the beginning of an oral presentation, some general techniques, and the ending.

The Beginning

Rule number one: Don't hurry your beginning. Walk slowly to the lectern or to where you will begin your presentation. You'll be in a brief transition period. This movement will help relax your muscles and give you a few seconds to adjust from sitting to being on the verge of speaking. If you speak from notecards, place them in front of you and arrange them as you want them. Incidentally, don't try to hide the fact that you're speaking from notes or a manuscript. Use them openly. Pause; survey your audience pleasantly. If water is available, pour some and take a sip. All this business may take only twenty seconds, but if you're an inexperienced speaker, it may seem like an hour. This unhurried approach is essential. It gives you time to prepare yourself, and it relaxes your audience. It tells them they are about to listen to a calm, composed individual, and they will be happy for that.

Begin by greeting your audience in whatever manner is appropriate for the occasion. Perhaps a simple "Good afternoon" will do. If appropriate, express your appreciation for the opportunity to make your presentation. On more formal occasions you may need to acknowledge the person who introduced you and greet important people in the room: "Thank you, Ms. Robinson, for that kind introduction. Mr. Weaver, Ms. Goodding, coworkers. . . ."

Now begin firmly and authoritatively with your icebreaker. At this moment your adrenaline will be pouring into your bloodstream. You will be experiencing what physiologists call the fight-or-flight response. You can't fly, so let the response carry you not into fight but into vitality and enthusiasm.

At the beginning of a presentation never apologize for conditions or set up a rationale for failure: "If I had a little more time, I could have prepared better charts" or "At the last minute, I was unable to get my printer to. . . ." Instead, have your icebreaker and the rest of your introduction well in hand and get on with your business.

Techniques

When you have good feelings about someone, you feel comfortable and rate the person highly. With bad feelings the reverse is true. Researchers in communication are well aware of good and bad feelings between listeners and speakers. Such feelings are produced by subtle interactions between people. It isn't too difficult to figure out what it takes to create good rapport with your listeners.

• *Show enthusiasm for the occasion and conviction for your ideas.* There is no substitute for being eager and excited about your presentation. An audience will give their attention to a speaker who appears genuinely interested in his or her topic. But an audience that detects a speaker who is weary of or bored by the subject will quickly lose interest. Don't be reluctant to display enthusiasm, to deliver your presentation with self-confidence, and to feel the conviction of believing what you say. Having an organized presentation, showing attention to details, and using only the best tools (no amateurishly produced visuals or outdated or other inappropriate data) can improve your ability to hold people's attention. Once you become enthusiastic and committed, the presentation will be a lot less stressful for you and more enjoyable for your audience.

• *Stand erect but not stiff.* Body motions, or body language, and the way peoples' voices sound may produce greater rapport with an audience than what is actually being said. For instance, a man may be addressing you as a friend, but the whole tenseness of his body, the stiffness of his neck, may be shouting his hostility toward you. You will instinctively trust what his body says rather than believe his words. A great many politicians over the years have ultimately failed because, say what they would, they were never able to project sincerity through their bodies and voices. So proper body actions and voice sounds are important for success in speaking.

A stiff, motionless speaker comes across as a frightened speaker. A slouchy, too-laid-back speaker comes across as an uncaring, lazy speaker. Don't stand stiffly with your hands clasped behind your back, permanently rooted in one place. Don't lean nonchalantly on the lectern or drape yourself casually over a table. Motion is important in convincing people—and even yourself, for that matter—that you are relaxed and assured. Use all the normal body motions while you are speaking. Shake your head yes and no. Indicate size with your hands and arms. Clench a fist for determination or righteous anger. Point for emphasis. Almost every gesture you would use in normal conversation, perhaps broadened a bit, is appropriate in speaking. Have a mobile face. Smile or frown as you feel like it. Move about if you can, especially when you move from one main point to another or from one part of your presentation to another. But don't fall into a pattern of pacing back and forth across the front of the room. The use of visuals is important here; they encourage natural movement as you draw or write or move a poster or transparency.

• *Maintain eye contact.* Eye contact is an important part of body language for two reasons. First, people aren't really persuaded that you're speaking to them unless they feel your eyes on them. They will think you're insincere if you fail to meet their eyes. Second, if you look at people, you get feedback. Read their body language: People sitting alertly with faces pleasantly composed are giving you positive feedback. You can continue as you are. People slumping, yawning, or looking away from you are giving you negative feedback. If that happens, don't panic, but recognize a need for change, perhaps a different speech rate, more motion, or more explanation. Or you might try addressing one statement to a person on the first row, another point to someone to your left, another point to someone to your right and farther back, and so on until you have looked at most of the audience. If you work with a chalkboard, whiteboard, or flipchart, make sure you don't turn your back on the audience. Stand slightly to the side and write or draw. Move away from the overhead projector to be sure that your audience can see the information on the screen. If there is a problem you can correct immediately, do it. If curing the problem is beyond you for the moment, file it away as a lesson for next time. After the presentation, analyze what you did wrong and try not to do it again.

• *Speak vigorously but normally.* The very sound of your voice carries part of your message. Obvious as it may seem, pay attention to whether or not you're being heard. If possible, arrange to have someone farthest from you to signal if you need to speak louder. If you can't arrange for someone to signal you, early in your presentation look carefully at the seats farthest from you. If people there are frowning, stop and ask them if they can hear you. If not, crank up the volume. Besides volume, you can also control pitch and rate. High pitch and high rate both suggest excitement and enthusiasm. But too high in either one suggests hysteria. Low pitch and rate suggest confidence and stability. Too low, however, and boredom sets in. Practice varying volume, pitch, and rate to get the effects you want.

Be careful to say your words clearly. Again, practice your presentation and make sure you can pronounce each word clearly and correctly and that you know the meaning of the words.

In short, stand up straight, move freely, speak loudly and clearly, and look directly at the faces of the people in front of you. If you appear enthusiastic and seem both vital and composed, people will take their cues from you.

The Ending

It's important that you stop speaking before your audience quits listening. If you are one of several speakers at a meeting, don't take up more than your allotted time. If you have planned to give a 15-minute presentation, stick to it. Before you begin to speak, take your watch off and have it on the podium or table where you can see it. As we have said elsewhere, once you suggest you are going to end, end quickly. Have your final summary or quote or whatever firmly in mind or handy on a card so that you won't miss a beat when it's time to conclude. Close firmly, but don't hurry from the rostrum. As you did at the beginning, pause. Hold eye contact with your audience for five seconds. In certain situations applause can be expected and will come. Wait for it and take it standing on the rostrum, not back in your seat. In situations such as a classroom session or a company briefing, applause is unlikely. But hold eye contact for five seconds anyway and then look away as you gather up your notes and move from the lectern.

QUESTION-AND-ANSWER PERIOD

Many presentations conclude with a question-and-answer period. In some business situations the entire talk, after a brief introduction, could be questions and answers. Sometimes a chairperson or moderator will take the questions; in other situations you will. In any case, pay attention to your audience. Be sure everyone in the audience understands the question before you begin your answer. We can sum up your goals during the question-and-answer period with five C's. You should be *courteous, correct, complete, concise,* and *careful.*

Courteous

Give everyone in the audience a fair chance to hear the questions and to ask questions. We're sure that you have experienced the frustration of being unable to hear a question asked by somebody in the first row of seats or hear the speaker's response. A questioner and an answerer who are close to each other sometimes speak too quietly and exclude the rest of the audience. When you have a large audience, always repeat the question so that everybody can hear it. In addition, you may have to rephrase a long, involved question. Before answering, ask the questioner if you have rephrased the question fairly.

Look around and answer questions from different parts of the room. Don't zero in on one area or let one person monopolize you. Sometimes questions may indicate hostility to you or your ideas. Don't rise to the bait. Be polite and objective in your answer, but don't take abuse either. If someone is obviously more interested in harassment than information, say something like "Under the present circumstances, I cannot answer that question objectively," and move on to the next question. Whatever you do, don't play for laughs at the expense of someone who may have innocently asked a foolish question. You embarrass the person needlessly, probably make a lifelong enemy, and lose the rest of the audience.

Correct

Be sure your answers are accurate. Quite frankly, in the excitement of playing expert, speakers sometimes get carried away. They make up facts or give dubious answers rather than appear ignorant. Answer a question only if you can do so accurately. If you can't, don't be afraid of saying, "I don't know." Or get the questioner's name and address and promise to send the information. If you do, keep your promise.

Complete and Concise

Complete and *concise* are obviously somewhat in opposition. Answer as fully as time allows and the question deserves. Questions often indicate that major points in your talk have not been understood or, worse, have been misunderstood. Elaborate as needed until you reach a correct understanding. In many situations you would be wise to bring additional material with you for the question-and-answer period—reports, tables, charts, and so forth. Take enough time if you have such material with you to look up the answers needed. Be complete, but keep your eye on the clock. Don't get carried away into a whole new talk. When you really have answered the question, stop.

Careful

Keep your head when answering questions. If you're not careful, you can be trapped into many unhappy situations. Be careful not to be angry or sarcastic. Be careful not to let playing the expert lead you into inaccurate answers or into giving authoritative answers to questions outside your field. Be ready to say, "My opinion on that matter would be no better than anyone else's." Be careful not to make elaborate promises to people. In other words, be careful to be courteous, correct, complete, and concise.

PLANNING AND REVISING CHECKLIST: ORAL PRESENTATIONS

Think about the following while planning and revising oral presentations.

PLANNING

- What is the occasion for your oral presentation: social, business, formal, informal?

- Where are you talking? What kind of facilities and aids will you have?

- Will an extemporaneous or written presentation serve the occasion best?

- Who are your audience? What is their level of knowledge?

- What is your audience's attitude toward your purpose, subject matter, and you? Why are they there?

- Are there special adjustments you must make for a multicultural audience?

- What is your purpose: social, informative, persuasive?

- How much time do you have?

- How can you support your generalizations? Examples? Anecdotes? Appeal to authority? Research?

- What is the best way to organize your presentation? General to particular? Particular to general? Argumentative? Other?

- Do you have an interesting fact or anecdote to begin your presentation?

- What visuals are available for your presentation? Are they simple enough for the speech context?

- What visual tools will you use? Chalkboard or whiteboard? Poster? Flipchart? Overhead projector? Computer and LCD projector? Other? If you plan to use a computer presentation package, are compatible hardware and software available at the site of the presentation?

REVISING

For true revision you must practice your oral presentation, preferably before an audience, before you deliver it. You can also "revise" in the sense that you can analyze speeches and oral presentations after they are given to aid you in preparing a better one on the next occasion. Consider the following:

- Are you within your allotted time?

- Is your purpose clearly stated?

- Does your introduction preview your presentation?

- Does your content meet these four criteria: meets needs and expectations of audience; moves your purpose forward; satisfies the occasion; provides needed, accurate information?

- Do your visuals meet the criteria of visibility, clarity, simplicity, and control?

- Are you unhurried at the beginning and end of your presentation?

- Do you have good body movement? Eye contact?

- Are your gestures suitable to your subject and audience?

- Is your speech clear and distinct?

- Do you have information to handle questions that may come?

SUGGESTIONS FOR APPLYING YOUR KNOWLEDGE

If you have time, speaking and oral presentations can be tied into many of the course writing assignments. A sales letter can easily be made into a persuasive talk. Descriptions of processes and mechanisms can be given orally as well as in writing. Proposals are often accompanied by briefings that cover their major points. The possibilities are wide.

Often the major report of the term is given orally as well as in writing. Because the major report is usually based on the information of a specific discipline, it furnishes a good opportunity for cooperation with other departments of your school. Instructors who are experts in the subject matter can be brought into the class to help evaluate the oral presentation. Their presence in the classroom ensures a combined audience of experts and nonexperts, a situation common in real life.

Create a context for the talk, such as a sales meeting, a proposal briefing, a demonstration of a new process or mechanism to its users. Role-play as an executive, technician, member of a community group, and so forth.

Create a real-life situation in other ways. Have a lectern for the speaker. Put out a pitcher of water and some glasses. Invite guests. Schedule time for a question-and-answer period.

Speeches and oral presentations should not be considered complete without visuals. You can create transparencies if an overhead projector is available. Flipcharts and posters are easily assembled. A chalkboard is almost always available. Presentation software and LCD projectors, too, are often available for use.

UNIT III

REPORTS

CHAPTER 13

PRINCIPLES OF WORKPLACE REPORTS

Successful business and industrial organizations and government agencies get their jobs done by gathering information and moving it to those who need it or to those whom they want to have it—employees, suppliers, customers, sponsors, government regulators, and so on. They transfer all kinds of information in all forms of print and electronic correspondence and reports. They store these documents in easily accessible forms because correspondence and reports are usually the most permanent record of their valuable work. Unsuccessful organizations fail to keep records or transfer information efficiently. Productivity decreases. Ignorance and guesswork replace knowledge and information. The idea is simple: The effectiveness of an organization is tied to its reporting—it will thrive on its successful reporting of information.

Because good reporting is so important to an organization's functioning, all organizations are in the business of communication. Whether your job is in accounting, engineering, production, sales, research, or service, as a professional in the workplace you can expect report writing to be an important part of your work. No one works in a vacuum: Every form of employment requires us to work with and through other people and to communicate with them. Our ability to inform and persuade is critical to our success.

The basic principles that apply to all your writing and speaking were discussed in Unit I of this text. The major types of correspondence that you might be expected to write were covered in Unit II. In Unit III we cover the more complex task of writing reports and discuss choices you must make while planning and preparing reports.

But before we take up those tasks and choices as they relate to different types of reports in Chapters 14, 15, 16, 17, and 18, we present helpful ways for you to look at specific types of reports and at your obligation to make information in your reports easy to access, read, understand, and use.

TYPES OF REPORTS

Reports carry information to those who want it or need it. The information is usually expected or requested by those receiving the report.

When you prepare a report—regardless of its length, content, and form and whether it is primarily written or oral—you will be presenting specific information to a specific audience for a specific purpose. The information you include and the relationship you establish with your audience will depend largely on your reason for reporting. Exactly what information does your audience need or expect? Of what use will the information be? In what order should the information be presented to provide the most help? The answers to these questions will give you a good idea of you and your audience's purposes.

Purpose, in the most general sense, refers to the intentions that both you and your audience bring to the report. Most reports either inform; inform and analyze; or inform, analyze, and persuade. The informational report informs the audience what you have found out, and it usually includes a minimal amount of commentary and interpretation. The analytical report presents the facts together with an analysis of them. The persuasive report seeks to influence the audience's belief or action. However, keep in mind that seldom are there "pure" examples of such reports. Most reports have a combination of purposes.

Purpose is only one way to classify reports, but it is a good way to begin thinking about what suits you and serves your audience. Learn to think about the purpose or function of the information in your report, and you will know what to put in your report. You will be better able to decide what information to include, what information to emphasize, and how to organize your report.

How beneficial your report is to your audience depends on how well you meet their interests, purposes, and needs and how accurately you estimate their ability to understand what you are trying to tell them. So get to know your audiences and their needs and keep them in mind while you plan and prepare your report. If you know your audience well, you have a leg up on the job. If you do not, you will fail to prepare a good report—no matter how much you hack away at it.

Two important points to remember when considering your audiences: they are real persons like yourself and they likely will be eager to gain the information you offer.

An eager audience, however, is not necessarily a captive audience. Do not let your knowledge of the subject and your personal convenience totally govern how you prepare the report. In the heat of on-the-job reporting always remember the courtesy that you naturally owe your audiences. You must get the report to them in plenty of time—when *they* need it or want it. By all means, if you have doubts about any aspect of the report and if you have access to your audience, ask them if they have any special requests concerning the report. They may give you information that will help you cut down on their reading or listening time and increase their comprehension. At times your audience may make the conditions for the report and establish specific requirements concerning the content, organization, format, and publication procedure or delivery. At other times, your organization or agency may have its own established specifications.

In such situations, your anticipation of the audience's desires or your adherence to prescribed specifications is relatively easy. Sometimes, though, in the case of written reports, you may be unable to consult your readers or your organization or agency may have no specifications. In the absence of such clear identification of the readers' needs or specifications, there still exist several principles you can follow to make your reports easy to read and to make your information easy to find and understand. In Chapter 1, we discuss ways to develop a profile of your readers. In Chapter 5, we provide guidelines for creating effective layout and design. In Chapters 6 and 7, we discuss using visuals to present certain types of information. In Chapter 22, we explain how to document a report to indicate the sources of information gathered from various sources. Here, we discuss the formal elements of a written report, such as a title page, a letter of transmittal or preface, an abstract or executive summary, a table of contents, a list of visuals, the introduction, and so on, and provide you with strong and simple principles that help guide you as you design a report for readers who need information to perform their work.

FORMAL ELEMENTS

Reports can take many forms: four or five sentences scribbled on a notepad, the preliminary results of a laboratory experiment, a dozen paragraphs on how to identify phytoplankton, or perhaps a twenty-two-volume feasibility study on the development of a supersonic transport. No clear-cut distinction exists between informal and formal reports: Simple problems and situations require only simple reports, perhaps most closely resembling letters, memos, and e-mail messages. Complex and lengthy reports, those with audiences that are distanced from the reported project, and reports that have value as long-term references, have a greater need for formalized presentation to save readers time and effort and to prevent confusion. Well-designed reports form a series of modules—related but also independent at the same time—where closely related information is usually in one place and does not necessarily require reading other parts of the report. The formal elements help readers (1) keep in view the big picture of the main ideas of the report and (2) recognize the various units of a report, consequently speeding up the retrieval process by highlighting important information and leading readers to the specific information they want. The number and type of formal elements of a report vary with its size and purpose. Short reports designed to be read from beginning to end may have a brief introduction and use some headings. Other reports may add a title page and table of contents. Others designed to provide selective access to information may have these elements and a letter or memo of transmittal, an abstract, and an index. In short, formalizing certain elements of a report fights against the loss of meaning, however slight, that inevitably takes place when a message is transmitted.

Some companies and organizations use a rigid, standardized plan for long reports; others are more flexible. Our advice is that you learn whatever plan you are expected to follow. If your organization or agency has an established plan, you should follow it. It probably has been developed and evolved into standard practice because it serves writers and readers well. Still, no one plan is best for all purposes. Our discussion of the formal elements of long reports is purposely general and flexible, so that you can design each report to fit its own subject matter, purpose, and audience.

You may need to arrange for your work to be produced on a word processor or do it yourself. Typing a report is not hard, but it does take time and patience. Whether you type 80 words a minute or "hunt and peck" 8 words a minute matters little once you have the report printed. What matters is how it looks—if it is neat and easy to read and if it follows the principles of good document design discussed in Chapters 5, 6, and 7. Most companies and organizations agree that attention to these principles is important. Editors and readers can be quite picky about elements such as margins and documentation form. They tend to frown on design, organization, and layout that break the rules, and they smile on reports that look good and are well organized. Why? Because well-designed reports help reduce the work of reading. Instead, the reader focuses on using the information contained in the report.

Here is a list of formal elements. Long reports may have any or all of them. Although companies and organizations do not design their formal elements exactly alike, the differences are usually minor.

Prefatory Elements

- Cover (Figures 13.1, 13.2, 13.3, and 13.4)

- Title page

- Letter or memo of transmittal or preface (Figures 13.5 and 13.6)

- Table of contents (needed for all except short reports) (Figure 13.7)

- Lists of figures and tables (usually needed when the report contains three or more formal visuals) (Figure 13.8)

- Abstract or executive summary (Figures 13.9 and 13.10)

Main Elements

- Introduction (Figure 13.11)

- Body (with headings and subheadings) (Figure 13.12)

- Ending (which may include a summary, conclusions, and recommendations)

Supplemental Elements

- May include endnotes, lists of references (Figure 13.13), a glossary (Figure 13.14), appendixes (Figure 13.15), and so forth.

PREFATORY ELEMENTS

The prefatory elements present the contextual information of the report—its author, audience, date, subject, coverage, and organization—to readers before they begin to read or scan the report. This context helps a diverse group of readers begin to activate their prior knowledge about the topic and occasion of the report and to begin integrating what they already know with what they will read.

Prefatory pages are usually numbered in small roman numerals—iii, iv, v, and so on.

COVER

The cover (see Figures 13.1, 13.2, 13.3, and 13.4) is of heavy paper or plastic to protect the typed pages from wear. It gives identifying information about the report: the title, the name (and if appropriate, the position) of the person or group for whom the report is prepared, the name (and if appropriate, the positions or job titles) of the person or group who prepared the report, and the date of the report. It may also include a distribution list (if anybody other than the primary reader receives a copy). Occasionally, as shown in Figure 13.4, the cover (as well as the title page) includes a brief table of contents. This information is important because it introduces the subject, identifies the primary audience and author, establishes the currency of the information, helps in filing and retrieving the report, and makes the report easy to refer to. Here are some suggestions on providing the necessary information for the cover.

Title

Think of the title as a one-phrase summary of the report. It should indicate the subject as briefly and specifically as possible. Avoid unhelpful expressions like *A Report on . . .* , *A Study of . . .* , *An Investigation . . . .* Four to eight words are usually enough. One or two words often are vague; more than ten words work against easy comprehension. Here are some acceptable titles that describe succinctly the purpose and subject of reports:

Proposed Changes in the Traffic Patterns at Lockwood Mall

Recommendations for Preventing Workplace Violence in Late-Night Retail Establishments

Comparative Merits of Copy Machines on the Market

Tooth Transplantation in Pediatric Dentistry

Battery Eliminators Save Money in the Shop

Recommendation for Providing Accounting Support to SBDC Clients

Such key terms as *Proposed Changes, Traffic Patterns, Lockwood Mall, Recommendations, Preventing Workplace Violence, Late-Night Retail Establishments, Copy Machines, Tooth Transplantation, Pediatric Dentistry, Battery Eliminators, Recommendation, Accounting Support,* and *SBDC Clients* identify and emphasize the topic, purpose, and scope of the report. Equally important, they facilitate indexing and cross-referencing reports in files and databases.

Name and Position of Primary Reader

Identify the reader or group of readers of the report and, if appropriate, add their positions and organizations. If the report is distributed to a large group, identify the group or groups (for example, *Current HBK Investors* or *Prospective Environmental Sciences Majors*).

ACCESS TO MULTIMEDIA TECHNOLOGY BY PEOPLE WITH SENSORY DISABILITIES

National Council on Disability
March 13, 1998

Figure 13.1 Cover for a formal report. The cover of a formal report contains much the same information that is included on a title page, but it is usually made of heavier paper or plastic to protect the report from wear. The material typically is balanced with all information aligned center.
Source: National Council on Disability. *Access to Multimedia Technology by People with Sensory Disabilities.* Washington: GPO, March 13, 1998.

ACCESS TO MULTIMEDIA TECHNOLOGY BY PEOPLE WITH SENSORY DISABILITIES

National Council on Disability

March 13, 1998

Figure 13.2 Unbalanced cover. This cover is unbalanced by having the information aligned flush left. Although placed at the top and bottom of the page, the elements are tied together by the vertical left alignment of the first letter in the lines of the title and the first letter of the organization and the date of publication.

ACCESS TO MULTIMEDIA TECHNOLOGY BY PEOPLE WITH SENSORY DISABILITIES

National Council on Disability

March 13, 1998

Figure 13.3 Unbalanced cover. This cover is unbalanced by having the title aligned center and the name of the organization and the date of publication aligned flush right. Although the alignment is unbalanced, the elements are tied together by the vertical right alignment of the last letter in the third line of the title and the last letter of the organization and the number in the date of publication. This placement is no accident.

Recommendations for Preventing Workplace Violence in Late-Night Retail Establishments

Phillip Clemons, 04, Criminal Justice

Sharon Flippen, 03, Social Work

Jackson Olivieto, 04, Business Administration

4 December 2000

Figure 13.4 Report cover with table of contents. This cover contains a brief table of contents that adds balance to the page and provides a quick reference for readers. Notice the left alignment of the horizontal lines above and below the title with the first letter of the names of the authors of the report. Also notice the right alignment of the page numbers in the brief table of contents with the right edge of the date of the report. These alignments are done on purpose to connect different parts of the cover and to add some balance to the page.

Distribution List

Identify by name and, if appropriate, by title and organization, others who receive the report. It is courteous to indicate to the primary reader who else will be receiving the report.

Name and Position of Author

Identify yourself by name and organization. If appropriate, give your position or job title, too. If the report has been written by a team, the authors' names should be in alphabetical order or in some other customary order, such as listing the principal investigator, team leader, or senior author first.

Date of the Report

Date the report according to when it is submitted to the reader. Never abbreviate the date; give the month, day, and year: *March 17, 1999* or *17 March 1999.*

The cover text may be of a typeface larger and different from that of the text of the report. The finished cover can look balanced, as in Figure 13.1, or it can be unbalanced, as in Figures 13.2, 13.3, and 13.4. The balanced look (Figure 13.1) is standard, but it is regarded by most graphic designers as overly formal and a trifle dull looking. The flush left alignment of Figure 13.2 or the centered top and flush right alignment of the bottom in Figures 13.3 and 13.4 are appealing in that the two elements are still aligned (notice in Figure 13.3 the alignment of the last letter in the title and the last letter in the name of the organization and in the date). The title of the report should be in a prominent font at the top of the page. Single- or double-space and divide the title into two lines if it looks too long for one line. Place the dateline about two inches from the page bottom. The cover is not included in the numbering of pages in the prefatory section of the report.

TITLE PAGE

The title page usually contains the same information as the cover. It may differ from the cover in these ways:

- It may provide additional information regarding date of publication and approving authority.

- It is the same weight paper as all the other pages of the report (the cover is usually of heavier stock).

- It is usually of the same font as that of the text of the report (the cover may have a different and larger font).

The title page is understood to be page i of the prefatory elements, although it is not numbered.

LETTER OF TRANSMITTAL

The letter of transmittal (Figure 13.5) or the preface (Figure 13.6) officially transmits or presents the report to the readers. The "letter" of transmittal may be in memo or letter form. Addressed to the readers, it provides sufficient background by

- explaining the authorization or occasion of the report (readers in the workplace are subject to many distractions and pressures, and they need to know whether the report is important enough to commit the time to read it);

- restating the title of the report (in case the letter is mailed separately from the report);

- stating the purpose of the report (readers in the workplace want to focus immediately on the task at hand);

- pointing out features of the report that may be of special interest (all readers look for this information, but this information is especially important for when certain parts of a report are of significance to different segments of a diverse audience);

- acknowledging special assistance in performing the study or preparing the report, especially from those who funded the project or provided materials, equipment, or information and advice.

This background information establishes a base from which all readers—regardless of their interests or needs—can start reading the report. Close the letter or memo politely by stating your willingness to provide similar services in the future or to provide further information if the readers desire it, whichever is appropriate.

Like any good workplace correspondence, the letter or memo of transmittal should be in a format that makes it easy to read (see Chapter 8 for letter and memo formats). If the letter or memo is bound with the report, it is understood to be a page of the prefatory elements, though it usually is not numbered. If it is placed in front of the title page, it is not regarded as part of the report and is not counted as a page of the prefatory elements.

PREFACE

The preface (Figure 13.6) contains introductory material similar to that in the letter or memo of transmittal. It usually contains statements about the background, purpose, scope, and content of the report and acknowledgment of assistance received. If you include a letter or memo of transmittal, a preface usually is unnecessary (although it is common to see both in formal reports). The preface may be placed before the table of contents (especially if the preface takes the place of the letter or memo of transmittal) or after the table of contents. If it follows the table of contents, it is included

NATIONAL COUNCIL ON DISABILITY

An independent federal agency working with the President and Congress to increase the inclusion, independence, and empowerment of all Americans with disabilities.

LETTER OF TRANSMITTAL

March 13, 1998

The President
The White House
Washington, DC 20500

Dear Mr. President:

On behalf of the National Council on Disability (NCD), I am pleased to submit a report entitled *Access to Multimedia Technology by People with Sensory Disabilities.* The report was developed with the advice of NCD's Tech Watch Task Force, a group of experts in technology and disability from around the country.

The rapid advances in technical capability and affordability are exciting. For America's 54 million people with disabilities, however, such technological developments are a double-edged sword that can release abundant opportunities or sever essential connections.

On the one hand, they can be revolutionary in their ability to empower people with seeing, hearing, manual, or cognitive impairments through alternative means of input and output to typical screens and keyboards. This is true because digital information generally is not inherently visual, auditory, or tactile. Rather, it can be expressed in any of those forms with appropriate programming. This allows previously inaccessible tasks to become possible and practical for individuals with disabilities, for example, a blind person using a CD-ROM-based encyclopedia on a computer equipped with synthetic speech output.

On the other hand, technological developments can present serious and sometimes insurmountable obstacles when principles of universal design are not practiced in their deployment. A distance learning course broadcast over the Internet, for example, is inaccessible to a deaf person if a text transcript is not also available.

This NCD report provides an overview of multimedia access barriers and solutions, including public policy interventions that we recommend as part of an overall strategy to make the electronic bridge to the 21st century available to all Americans. Thank you for the opportunity to play the independent role that our mission requires and to offer an assessment of progress and prospects in this area. NCD stands ready to work with you and stakeholders outside the government to see that the agenda set out in the attached report is implemented.

Sincerely,

Marca Bristo

Marca Bristo
Chairperson

(The same letter of transmittal was sent to the President Pro Tempore of the U.S. Senate and the Speaker of the U.S. House of Representatives.)

1331 F Street, NW ■ Suite 1050 ■ Washington, DC 20004-1107
(202) 272-2004 Voice ■ (202) 272-2074 TTY ■ (202) 272-2022 Fax

Figure 13.5 Letter of transmittal. The letter of transmittal introduces readers to the report. Typically, it identifies the occasion, authorization (if any), or other pertinent information concerning the report and its topic and major findings. It often explains how the report is organized and points out any major ideas to which the author or authors wish the reader to pay close attention. The letter of transmittal typically closes by acknowledging whatever assistance the authors received and by stating the author's or authors' readiness to provide further information if desired.
Source: National Council on Disability. *Access to Multimedia Technology by People with Sensory Disabilities.* Washington: GPO, March 13, 1998.

PREFACE

In August 1994, members of the National Council on Disability (NCD) began meeting with representatives of the computer industry to discuss the accessibility of graphically based software for people with disabilities, particularly people with severe visual impairments. To obtain ongoing information and advice about technology-related issues, NCD then established Tech Watch, a community-based, cross-disability task force. The 12-member task force advises NCD on issues concerning access to emerging technologies and helps monitor compliance with relevant laws.

This report was commissioned by NCD on the advice of Tech Watch. It is an overview of computerized multimedia technology, barriers for access for people with disabilities, and progress to date on addressing these issues. The report concludes with recommendations to policy makers and industry officials to solve problems raised in the report.

xi

Figure 13.6 Preface. The preface contains similar information to that of a letter of transmittal or abstract. It is not necessarily an abridgement of the report, but it does provide readers with the background and occasion of the report and sometimes includes a brief summary of the coverage of the report.
Source: National Council on Disability. *Access to Multimedia Technology by People with Sensory Disabilities.* Washington: GPO, March 13, 1998. xi.

in the table of contents. Whether you use the letter or memo of transmittal or the preface depends on the audience:

- Use the letter or memo of transmittal when the audience is one person or a well-defined group.

- Use the preface when the audience is more general and you don't know specifically who will be reading the report.

The tone of the preface is often less personal than that of the letter or memo of transmittal.

Center and make prominent the word *Preface* at the top of the page. When the preface takes the place of the letter or memo of transmittal, number it as a page of the prefatory elements. Center the lowercase roman numeral at the bottom of the page.

TABLE OF CONTENTS

The table of contents (Figure 13.7) lists (1) the prefatory elements that follow it and (2) the major headings and subheadings in the report, including appendixes. These provide a handy overview of the report that helps readers understand the organization of the report as a whole and also locate any major section or sections quickly. More than any other elements of formal reports, the table of contents provides a map of the contents that enables readers to make choices of what to read. Preparing the table of contents involves two major steps: (1) making a rough copy, gathering headings and subheadings from the finished report, and (2) putting it in correct form on the page.

- *Making a rough copy:* First, make a rough draft of the table of contents by listing every part of the report that comes after the table of contents. Follow each entry with the page number on which it appears.

  Second, make the wording, capitalization, and order of entries in the table of contents exactly as they are in the headings in the report.

  Third, indent the subheadings under each main heading to show their subordination, and indent progressively subordinate subheadings under their headings. If you numbered the chapters or major sections of the report, those numbers should be placed before the main headings in the table of contents.

- *Putting it in correct form on the page:* Occasionally, as illustrated in Figure 13.4, the table of contents is incorporated into the cover or the title page or both. More frequently, though, it is on a page or series of pages of its own (Figure 13.7). If it is on a page of its own, center and make prominent the words *Contents* or *Table of Contents* at the top of the page. Arrange the information into three columns. The left column contains capital roman numerals as major divisions or chapter numbers. The center column contains the main headings and subheadings of the report. Remember to indent to show subordination of subheadings. The

CONTENTS

Figure 13.7 Table of contents. The table of contents provides quick access to various parts of the report. Although there is no unanimous practice in this matter, the major sections of the report proper are in all capital letters; subsections are in capital and lowercase letters. The periods (single- or double-spaced) lead the reader from the main headings and subheadings to the page numbers in the right margin. The words *Contents* or *Table of Contents* are usually centered at the top of the page, and the page number is usually centered at the bottom.
Source: National Council on Disability. *Access to Multimedia Technology by People with Sensory Disabilities.* Washington: GPO, March 13, 1998. vii–ix.

viii

Figure 13.7 (continued)

Figure 13.7 (continued)

right column contains the page numbers on which the headings appear. The right side of the numbers should be even. Use single- or double-spaced dots, called *leaders,* to connect the headings with the page numbers.

Double-space between entries and single-space any heading that is too long for one line.

Number the table of contents page as a prefatory page.

LIST OF FIGURES AND TABLES

The page that lists figures and tables (Figure 13.8) shows readers the location of visuals and tables. You should include it only if the report makes significant use of visuals—say, more than three figures or tables. If your report includes many figures and tables, you may group them into separate categories: *List of Figures, List of Tables,* and so on.

The list of figures and tables is set up just like the table of contents. Center at the top of the page and make prominent the words *Figures and Tables* or whatever is appropriate.

Arrange the information in three columns, similar to the table of contents: The left column contains the figure or table number (normally tables are given capital roman numerals and figures are given arabic numbers, but the practices are not universal); the center column contains the title of the figure or table; the right column contains the number of the page it is on or is facing. Use dot leaders to connect titles of figures and tables with the page numbers.

ABSTRACT OR EXECUTIVE SUMMARY

The abstract (Figure 13.9) is a brief, condensed statement of the most important ideas of the report. It provides the readers with a compressed overview of the report by mirroring both its content and organization.

The length of the abstract depends primarily on the length of the report. The typical abstract is a paragraph of 150 to 200 words. But longer reports, say 20 or more pages, probably would require additional paragraphs. A good working estimate for the length of an abstract of a longer report is that it should not be more than 5 percent of the whole report. Thus, a 40-page report would have an abstract of approximately two pages at most. The abstract for a longer report might consist of a series of brief paragraphs, each paragraph summarizing a major section of the report.

Although the abstract is a compressed version of the report, you should not write it in a telegraphic style. Its words and sentences must be in good prose style.

Center and make prominent the word *Abstract* at the top of the page, double-space, and begin the abstract.

An executive summary (Figure 13.10) is similar to an abstract, although it tends to be longer.

List of Illustrations

iv

Figure 13.8 List of illustrations. Formatted similar to the table of contents, the list of illustrations identifies the visuals that illustrate specific information in the report.

Abstract

Chlorofluorocarbons (CFCs) are key contributors to the problems of ozone layer depletion and global warming. CFCs exist in common products such as refrigerants, aerosols, and foams. Depletion of the ozone layer and global warming are threats to all forms of plant and animal life. Therefore, there is a need to control the production of these harmful chemicals. The 1987 Montreal Protocol was the most important international regulation placed on the production of CFCs. The original Protocol called for a 50 percent reduction worldwide in the use of CFCs by 1998. In June 1990, the original protocol was amended to require the complete elimination of CFC production by 2000. In April 1992, President Bush announced a new policy that required the United States to stop producing CFCs by 1995. These regulations have had great impact on the refrigeration industry because most refrigerants contain the CFCs that are being banned. As a result, two important solutions are being researched. First, used refrigerants that contain CFCs are either being recycled, reclaimed, or incinerated. Second, alternative refrigerants are being tested. Currently, the alternative refrigerants are hydrochlorofluorocarbons and a hydrofluorocarbon. However, each potential solution is a trade-off of such aspects as ozone-depleting potential, global-warming potential, and toxicity. The search continues for an environmentally safe refrigerant to use in the future CFC-free era.

Figure 13.9 Sample abstract. The abstract is essentially a summary of the information presented in the report. The word *Abstract* **is usually centered at the top of the page, and the page number is usually centered at the bottom of the page.** *Source: Chlorofluorocarbons (CFCs): Problems and Solutions,* an unpublished student report by Kelly Carman, Kelly Bradberry, and Charles Smith. Used with permission of the authors.

EXECUTIVE SUMMARY

This report by the National Council on Disability (NCD), an independent federal agency, focuses on the barriers to use of computerized multimedia technology by a significant segment of the disability community—people who have visual or hearing impairments—and recommends actions that would reduce or eliminate those barriers.

Advances in computer and telecommunications technology have made it possible to combine high-quality computerized video, audio, text, and images into attractive and compelling interactive multimedia presentations. As this new information technology increasingly renders the sounds, images, and textures of the real world in a virtual environment, people with visual or hearing disabilities face a troubling, uncertain future in which opportunities for employment, education, and recreation may be greatly enhanced or diminished as a direct result of new technology.

Publishers, schools at all levels, employers, and a host of cultural and civic-oriented institutions are grappling with multimedia technology. If a commitment to accessibility for all individuals is not ensured now, individuals with disabilities, particularly those with sensory disabilities, will suffer the loss of educational opportunities and employment options. On the other hand, a commitment by the information technology industry to develop and support multimedia products that are accessible to and usable by people with disabilities, and a commitment by government to purchase only accessible products, will give persons with disabilities heretofore-unrivaled opportunities to learn and contribute to society.

In an attempt to educate policy makers, manufacturers, and consumers about these issues, NCD, through its Tech Watch task force, commissioned a study on multimedia access for people with visual and hearing impairments. The research was conducted by the American Foundation for the Blind (AFB) and the National Association of the Deaf (NAD).

1

Figure 13.10 First page of an executive summary. Sometimes an executive summary is used in the place of an abstract or preface or letter of transmittal. Sometimes it is used with the other elements. Its purpose is to prevent an overview of the report for busy readers who must make decisions or act on information contained in the report.
Source: National Council on Disability. *Access to Multimedia Technology by People with Sensory Disabilities.* Washington: GPO, March 13, 1998. 1.

MAIN ELEMENTS

The main elements of the report follow the prefatory elements and consist of three parts—the introduction, the body, and the ending. These elements are often referred to as "the report proper."

THE INTRODUCTION

The introduction (Figure 13.11) attracts attention, sets the context, and presents a general idea of the topic of the report. The quality of the introduction can make or break your report's success.

When busy readers turn to your report, they will start looking for answers to several questions as they try to settle into the report. They will want to know or be reminded why you are writing to them now, what you have to say, how you are going to say it, and how difficult or time-consuming it will be to read what you have written. They will also want to know the importance of the report to them and their work. And they will want the answers to these questions right away.

To hold the readers' attention and prevent mental wandering, you must pave a road that is easy to follow, build an entrance that is unavoidable, and close the gates to the sides. These are the jobs of the introduction, the first main portion of the report.

The introduction may consist of a few paragraphs or perhaps several pages. When it is lengthy, you should consider using subheadings to indicate its subparts. Whether the introduction is short or long, it should perform the following functions:

• *Explain the subject or research problem.* Readers need to know what they are going to read about. The title, letter or memo of transmittal or preface, and abstract give them some information, but they might not provide adequate orientation. Often it is necessary to define the subject, state the research problem, explain some of the key terms used in the discussion, or give historical and other background information about the subject or research problem—including a review of the literature. Finally, you should comment on the significance of the information—the *so-whats*. Work a bit on arousing the readers' interest. Why is the subject important? Why should they want to know about it? The more the readers want or need the report, the less you must do to arouse interest.

• *Explain the purpose.* Although the purpose of the report should be self-evident to you, make sure it is equally evident to readers. Your purpose might be to report on a study requested by the readers. If so, review the facts of the request or authorization: When did they make the request? How did they make it? Did somebody else make it? Such a review is especially important if you include no letter or memo of transmittal. If the report is unsolicited, explain thoroughly the situation that led to your writing the report.

CHLOROFLUOROCARBONS (CFCs):
PROBLEMS AND SOLUTIONS

Introduction

Throughout recorded history are accounts of how humans have tried to improve their quality of life through increased technology. However, as our technology has increased, so have the complexities of our problems. In the past, numerous environmental problems have occurred, but nothing on the scale of today's problems. In the twentieth century, technology development has become particularly threatening as is evidenced by environmental changes such as depletion of the ozone layer and global warming. Key contributors to these changes appear to be chlorofluorocarbons (CFCs).

CFCs, which have come to prominence since their first use in the 1920s, are synthetic gases that are used as refrigerants in refrigeration and air-conditioning units, as propellants in spray cans, as agents in producing plastic insulation foams, and as solvents for cleaning electronic components. When the energy crisis of the early 1970s began, CFCs were in high demand as foaming agents in the production of polyurethane and polystyrene foam used to improve home insulation. Polymar foams are also used in furniture and car seats and in the manufacture of fast food containers and disposable coffee cups. Leaking refrigeration and air-conditioning systems (especially from discarded air conditioners and refrigerators and abandoned automobiles at junk yards and disposal sites) and spraying from aerosol cans release CFCs into the atmosphere. CFCs can also escape into the atmosphere during the manufacture of polymer foams and are gradually released as the foams age (Kemp).

Evidence shows that CFCs have a direct affect on depletion of the ozone layer and on global warming. Therefore, CFCs are an environmental threat, and their production must be controlled. The 1987 Montreal Protocol and the 1990 Amendment to the Montreal Protocol were legislative actions taken to reduce and eventually eliminate the amount of CFCs being produced. Since CFCs are common components of refrigerants, the refrigerator industry will be greatly impacted by the phaseout. As a result, scientists are actively researching alternative replacements. In addition, the handling and disposal of existing refrigerants that contain CFCs can be accomplished by either recycling, reclamation, or incineration. Although CFCs are harmful substances that adversely affect

1

Figure 13.11 First page of a report introduction. This introduction begins by orienting readers to the problems of CFC pollution and giving a brief history of the problems. It continues onto another page by describing the attempts at solving the problems.
Source: Chlorofluorocarbons (CFCs): Problems and Solutions, p. 1, an unpublished student report by Kelly Carman, Kelly Bradberry, and Charles Smith. Used with permission of the authors.

The value of the report and the objectives and purposes of your reporting should be clear to the readers. Be sure that you are clear on the purpose of the report and on the problem to which it relates. For instance, say you are working on a project to redesign a piece of machinery to reduce the vibration when it is operating and to prevent material jams caused by misalignment of the machine parts. The purpose of your report might be to persuade your readers that your redesign will solve the problem and will be within the budget of the project.

- *Explain the scope.* Let the readers know the extent of the presentation or the limits of the study. In other words, explain just how much ground the report is covering. The statement of scope tells readers what you see yourself responsible for reporting.

- *Explain the plan and order of presentation.* Always preview the report for readers. Tell them the order of topics. This statement usually is the last function of the introduction and serves as a transition to the body of the report.

Almost every important or long report will need a formal introduction that fulfills these four functions. For special circumstances you may need to do any of the following:

a. Discuss in detail the problem or problems the project and report are designed to solve.

b. State a hypothesis and explain how it was or will be tested.

c. Review the literature relevant to the problem or hypothesis.

d. Explain the nature of the investigation—the sources and methods of collecting data.

e. Define important terms used in the report that you feel readers will be unfamiliar with.

f. Summarize your significant findings or recommendations and point out the limits of the validity of your conclusions, if the purpose of the report is to communicate your position on a set of issues.

In short, the introduction should include whatever is needed to prepare readers for the information they are about to receive. Don't be hasty in an introduction, but neither should you be long-winded. Get on with the main event as soon as possible.

THE BODY

The body, the longest section of the report, presents the detailed message (Figure 13.12). It has no set organization, but its contents should be arranged in some logical, unified order. Regardless of the content and arrangement of the report, you must help readers to skim the report, to read it thoroughly, or to refer to specific parts of it by using headings and subheadings, which separate the text into major divisions

ATTEMPTS AT SOLVING THE CFC PROBLEM

Although much focus has been placed on the search for alterative refrigerants, the issue of existing refrigerants that contain CFCs still remains. The main concern from the service sector is how to dispose of these used refrigerants in an environmentally responsible manner.

Handling and Disposal of Used Refrigerants

At the end of 1992, the Environmental Protection Agency released regulations regarding the management of CFC-based materials (Roth 35). Three options appear to be available to the refrigeration industry. One option (recycling) is performed on-site. The other two options (reclamation and incineration) are performed off-site (Grant 43).

Recycling. The on-site option consists of a two-step recycling process. First, a recycling machine removes refrigerant from a system and processes it by oil separation and circulation through filters and driers. This process can be used periodically to remove contaminants from the refrigerant. After this processing, the refrigerant is returned to the same piece of equipment from which it was removed (Grant 43). Although recycling removes common contaminants such as air, moisture, oils, and acids, the process cannot guarantee to return the refrigerant to original specifications. This unknown purity is a major disadvantage to the recycling process. Refrigerant contamination could damage equipment or result in poor operating conditions (McCain 32-33). Another disadvantage is the high cost of recycling equipment. On the other hand, the primary advantage of recycling is the cost savings of not having to purchase new refrigerant. By using recycled refrigerant, companies do not have to buy new refrigerant (Grant 44).

Reclamation. The second option is off-site reclamation, a process consisting of two stages. First, the refrigerant is collected in a special container and transported to an off-site facility. Second, the recovered refrigerant is analyzed to determine if it can be reprocessed (Grant 44). If it can be reprocessed, then a complex distillation procedure is used to remove contaminants. The new refrigerant must meet ARI Standard 700-88, a standard for refrigerant purity defined by the Air-conditioning and Refrigeration Institute. If the refrigerant cannot be reclaimed because of its serious contamination, then it is destroyed by incineration (McCain 32, 35).

14

Figure 13.12 Headings provide cues to readers about the organization, topics, and contents of a document. In the body of this report, as with many reports, each major section begins on a new page, and headings and subheadings display the organization of each section and its subsections. The use of headings and subheadings does not lessen the need for conventional overview statements and transitions.

Source: Chlorofluorocarbons (CFCs): Problems and Solutions, p. 14, an unpublished student report by Kelly Carman, Kelly Bradberry, and Charles Smith. Used with permission of the authors.

(similar to chapters in books) and divide each major division into sections. The outline of the report is a good source for headings and subheadings.

Probably no other scanning aid will help readers more than the liberal use of headings. To test this claim find any report, article, or manual more than two or three pages long, remove the headings, and see how suddenly the text appears to be tediously uninterrupted and how the major topics disappear into the text. (See also pp. 120–125 in Chapter 5.)

For those who read the entire report, the headings will be a comforting reminder of the readers' progress. However, most readers read selectively, and headings provide them with easy reference to the parts they seek by indicating key topics. The headings and subheadings should agree with the entries in the table of contents; in fact, the headings are an "exploded" table of contents inserted at appropriate places throughout the text. Each heading and subheading should be worded to convey the topic of the section it heads. For example, in a section about medical needs of elderly prison inmates, the heading *Section II* or *Analysis of Medical Facilities* is too general and uninformative. A heading such as *Medical Needs of Elderly Prison Inmates* is far more informative.

Although slight variations exist in the use of headings, their format is usually handled as shown in Figure 13.12. In addition to making sure that their positions clearly indicate the levels of importance of the headings, you should make sure of the following:

- Headings are worded so that they point to the text that follows and relate to each other grammatically.

- Headings are not followed immediately by a pronoun that refers to a word or phrase in them.

- Headings have written text between them, even if it is only an explanation of subdivisions to come.

- Headings have at least two lines of text between the last heading and the bottom of the page.

Remember that headings serve as excellent clues to the content and arrangement of material. Think three times before you submit a report that does not have them.

As readers begin to read a major section of a report, they need similar kinds of introduction to that section that they needed at the beginning of the report—they need an introduction to the section that gives them at least a brief overview of the contents of the section and its purpose, scope, and organization. They have the same desire to grasp the overall picture, to find the information they need quickly, and to understand the information immediately as they did when they began reading the report. Major sections that do not adequately introduce readers to content and organization can be difficult and frustrating to work through.

THE ENDING

The last major part of the main elements of the report is the ending. Like the introduction, the ending should emphasize the most important ideas in the report, so make it as strong as the introduction. Some typical functions of formal end sections are (1) to summarize the major points of the report, (2) to state conclusions, and (3) to state recommendations. Depending on the type of report and the needs of the readers, the ending may contain any one or a combination of these functions. You may at times want to provide up-front visibility for the conclusions and recommendations—for instance, when readers are primarily interested in results, conclusions, and recommendations and regard the body of the report secondarily. In such instances, you should move them to the front of the report. Long sections of reports usually have their own formal ending as well as an introduction.

• *Summarizing major points:* Reports that are primarily informative usually end with a summary that helps readers make sense of the mass of details presented in the body by recalling the essential ideas covered. Just as the introduction offers readers a preview of the body, a summary at the end offers readers a postview.

• *Stating conclusions:* Reports that are primarily analytical end with a conclusion, which lists the logical implications of the findings—the *so-whats*. Sometimes the formal end section combines a statement of the major points and the conclusions reached. When it is appropriate to present several precise conclusions, they should be numbered.

• *Stating recommendations:* Reports that are primarily analytical and persuasive usually end with recommendations, which fulfill the advisory function of the report. That is, the recommendations tell the reader what to do or not to do. The recommendations should be laid out in a series of parallel statements, each separately paragraphed.

SUPPLEMENTAL ELEMENTS

After the main elements of the report come the supplemental elements, which contain information related to the report that may be of interest to readers but is not essential enough to interrupt the main line of discussion. You must decide what information can be placed in the supplemental elements to help reduce the length and complexity of the main body of the report.

• *The list of references* (see Figure 13.13) provides complete publication information for each citation in the report. Although there is universal agreement that credit must be given to sources of borrowed information, there is no universal agreement on how to do it. See Chapter 22 for information on documentation.

• *A glossary* (see Figure 13.14) is included if the report contains many technical terms or words that many of the readers may not know.

REFERENCES

Allan, James, Ph.D., teacher of the visually impaired, Texas School for the Blind and Visually Impaired. Personal communication. May 16, 1997.

American Foundation for the Blind. Comments of the American Foundation for the Blind, October 28, 1996, before the FCC WT Docket #96–198, in the Matter of Implementation of Section 255 of the Telecommunications Act of 1996, Access to Telecommunications Service, Telecommunications Equipment, and Customer Premises Equipment by Persons with Disabilities.

American Society for Training and Development (ASTD) (1996). (http://www.astd.org/industry/trends/trend1.htm)

Annenberg Washington Program in Communications Policy Studies of Northwestern University (1994). *Communications Technology for Everyone: Implications for the Classroom and Beyond.* Washington, DC: Annenberg Washington Program, p. 15.

Apple Computer (1995). (http://hed.info.apple.com/aie-multimedia.html)

Bassi, L., Gallagher, A. L., and Schroer, E. (1996). *The ASTD Training Data Book.* Alexandria, VA: American Society for Training and Development.

Berke, S. J. (1997). Closed Captioning Web Site. (http://www.erols.com/berke/)

Bolnick, David, accessibility program manager, Microsoft Corporation. Personal communication, May 16, 1997.

75

Figure 13.13 Report references. References are listed in alphabetical order by author's last name. The format conforms to the *US Government Printing Office Style Manual.*
Source: National Council on Disabiltiy. *Access to Multimedia Technology by People with Sensory Disabilities.* Washington: GPO, March 13, 1998. 75.

GLOSSARY

Analog captioning: Subtitles in video materials, configured for analog transmissions.

Closed captioning: Subtitles embedded in video materials and visible only to those who have a caption decoder, which is usually built into television sets.

Digital captioning: Subtitles embedded in video materials, configured for digital transmissions.

Digital video disc (DVD):   A new media storage format intended to replace audio CDS, CD-ROMs, videotapes, and laser discs. DVD players will fall into two categories: (1) stand-alone devices attached to televisions and (2) DVD-ROM drives in computers (similar to today's CD-ROM, but with eight times the storage capacity). Originally scheduled for release in June 1996, DVD players were delayed because of copyright negotiations between the entertainment and computer industries.

Open captioning: Subtitles that are visible to anyone viewing the video material (broadcast, cable, videocassette, and otherwise).

Remote captioning: Captioning services provided through remote means, usually through telephone lines. May require use of on-site interpreters to supply audio.

Screen reader: Device that enables blind and visually impaired people to use a computer as a sighted person would, either by magnifying the text on the screen or by converting the text to speech or braille.

Telecommunications relay service (TRS):   Provides a link between voice and text telecommunications users.

85

Figure 13.14 Sample glossary. This is the first page of the glossary from *Access to Multimedia Technology by People with Sensory Disabilities*.
Source: National Council on Disabiltiy. *Access to Multimedia Technology by People with Sensory Disabilities.* Washington: GPO, March 13, 1998. 85.

APPENDIX A

FRAMEWORK OF MULTIMEDIA CATEGORIES

In an attempt to circumscribe our working definition of multimedia and our parameters for this project, we sought a useful way to categorize multimedia-related terminology. Gregg Vanderheiden, director of the Trace Center, divides information technology into a three-part typology consisting of source material, transmission mechanisms, and viewer/controller equipment. We tentatively suggest the following organizing framework[1] as a useful way to approach multimedia issues.[2]

Interactive Multimedia[3]

I. Delivery[4]

    A. Transmission

        1. Fixed transportable media (e.g., CD-ROMs, digital video disks, floppy disks)

        2. Phone lines and other wired communications (e.g., cable)

        3. Short- and long-range wireless (e.g., infrared, satellite)

---

[1] The list of examples below is not meant to be exhaustive, but to be representative of those technologies that currently exist while being flexible enough to incorporate new technologies that are currently being developed or are not yet in existence.

[2] This typology differs from Vanderheiden's in that it elaborates on the different types of visual and aural outputs that exist. In addition, it categorizes viewer/control devices and transmission under the larger heading of "delivery" and adds under this major heading the separate category of "underlying control software."

[3] We do not include videotape materials in this list as they are not interactive.

[4] The Internet, including the World Wide Web, is not specifically mentioned on this list as it is a "meta-construct"—it uses varying combinations of transmission, control devices, and control software and does not fit neatly into any one of the delivery categories.

47

Figure 13.15 **Sample appendix. This is the first page of an appendix from** *Access to Multimedia Technology by People with Sensory Disabilities.*
Source: National Council on Disabiltiy. *Access to Multimedia Technology by People with Sensory Disabilities.* Washington: GPO, March 13, 1998. 47.

Arrange the words or phrases alphabetically, beginning each entry on a separate line.

• *Appendixes* (Figure 13.15) contain information or documents that, although useful, might hamper easy reading of the text. Although it is not always easy to decide what material to put in appendixes, we suggest material that has direct—but secondary rather than primary—importance to the reader. Appendixes often include glossaries, copies of questionnaires, related correspondence, reports, the text of speeches or interviews, samples, exhibits, and all kinds of supplemental tables, figures, and case histories. A glossary or list of symbols that may be too lengthy to place in the introduction of the report could be placed in an appendix.

PLANNING AND REVISING CHECKLIST: FORMAL ELEMENTS OF WORKPLACE REPORTS

Think about the following while planning and revising formal elements of reports.

PLANNING

• What is the purpose of the report? If it is to be used as a reference work, does it have a detailed table of contents and plenty of headings and subheadings?

• What formal elements are appropriate for the report?

• Is a cover required?

• Does the report require a letter or memo of transmittal or a preface?

• Is an abstract required or preferred?

• What is the format for headings and subheadings?

• What, if any, material will be placed in an appendix?

REVISION

• Are the required elements present?

• Is the overall design attractive, effective, and consistent?

• Do the entries in the table of contents agree with the headings?

• Do the lists of figure and table captions agree with the captions and page numbers of the visuals?

• Does the report provide direct access to information through a table of contents, headings and subheadings, and other cues?

• Are the elements mechanically correct, consistent, and accurately typed?

SUGGESTIONS FOR APPLYING YOUR KNOWLEDGE

1. At the end of Chapter 1, The Process of Workplace Writing, we suggest that you start gathering examples of workplace writing. Examine one of the more formal, but relatively brief, examples you have collected and write a report for your instructor and classmates that explains the following:

   • What type of report it is

   • Its intended audience

   • What features aid or hinder legibilityZ

   • What features provide clues to its organization

   • What formal elements it contains

   • Correctness of spelling, grammar, and punctuation

   Evaluate what the writer has done well. What additional strategies and techniques were available that the writer could have used?

2. On pages 466–468 is a report titled *Controlling the Fire in Bevo #3 Mine* and our analysis of the report. Assume that you have written the report. Provide the following prefatory elements:

   • Title page

   • Letter of transmittal to Shawn Payne, Director of Mining Safety and Security, Nickeltown Coal Corporation, Warsaw, Pennsylvania 19455

   • Table of contents

   • List of figures and tables

   • Abstract

     Information that you will need from the original report but that is not included in the version in Figure 17.1 follows:

     Figure 1. Vicinity Map of Sherman Township Showing Location of Fire Areas, facing page 1

     Figure 2. Cross-section through Fire Area, facing page 1

     Figure 3. Photograph of Isolation Trench to Newcome Bed, Showing Evidence of Hot Area over Courtney Bed, facing page 1

     Figure 4. Surface Map of Fire Area, Showing Various Phases of Fire Control Work, facing page 2

     Figure 5. Photograph of Wet-sand Seal on Exposed Newcome and Courtney Beds, facing page 2

Figure 6. Aerial Photographic Showing Fire Project Area after Completion of Fire Control Work, facing page 3

Appendix A: Invoices, Contracts, and Work Orders Related to Stage 1, pp. A-1 through A-6

Appendix B: Invoices, Contracts, and Work Orders Related to Stage 2, pp. B-1 through B-9

Appendix C: Sales Receipt for Coal Shipments, pp. C-1 through C-3

CHAPTER 14

RECOMMENDATION REPORTS

A frequent task for people in the workplace is reporting and explaining recommendations and decisions. Such recommendations and decisions, usually growing out of a problem-solving situation, must be explained and justified. The resulting reports—for simplicity's sake, we'll label them all *recommendation reports*—present the results of exercises in practical logic. Before we get to the reports themselves, let's pause for a moment and talk about what we mean by practical logic.

PRACTICAL LOGIC

You may or may not have taken a course in formal logic, but you have been practicing practical logic and coming to decisions since you were a child. When you stood before a candy showcase weighing the merits of buying four licorice sticks for 20¢ against buying five jawbreakers, also for 20¢, you were analyzing a problem. You were comparing and contrasting alternatives. You were doing a cost analysis—four for 20¢ versus five for 20¢. You remembered the flavor of the two candies and realized that the licorice in your estimation was superior. You weighed quantity versus quality. You reached a series of conclusions:

- The jawbreakers were cheaper.

- Each piece of candy lasted 10 minutes.

- The jawbreakers would give you 50 minutes of pleasure.

- The licorice would give you 40 minutes of pleasure.

- However, the flavor of the licorice was superior.

- For you, 40 minutes of superior pleasure were better than 50 minutes of inferior pleasure.

- Therefore, for you, the licorice sticks were a better buy.

If you proceeded to plunk down your dimes for the licorice, you were backing your conclusions with a decision.

As you grew older, your analyses became bigger and more complicated. Perhaps you wanted to buy a bicycle. You considered cost, naturally. You also considered the comparative weights of bicycles. You compared 10-speed bikes against 12-speed bikes. You made these comparisons not in an abstract way but by considering them against your own needs. If you were a serious biker who planned long trips through hilly country, a lighter, expensive 12-speed might be the answer. On the other hand, if you were an occasional bike rider who simply wanted to combine some exercise with transportation around the flat streets of town, you probably would have chosen a heavier, less expensive, 10-speed bike.

In such analyses you were following the processes of induction and deduction that we describe for you on pages 64–66. You were drawing upon information that you already possessed or that was easily obtainable.

Analyses you will conduct in the workplace are different in degree but not in kind. That is, the process will be more complex and involve more information but will still draw on essentially the same practical logic you have frequently used. We'll look at the process in more detail. With some variations practical logic is likely to follow a course similar to this:

- Defining the problem
- Creating solutions
- Testing solutions
- Choosing a solution

DEFINING THE PROBLEM

A problem can be either a question or a situation. In the candy and bike examples, the problem is a question: Should I buy licorice sticks or jawbreakers? What sort of bike should I buy?

A problem situation is always a situation that deviates from the norm. For example, you're cruising smoothly down an interstate highway. Your car is performing in its normal manner. Suddenly, you hear a loud whooshing sound and see clouds of steam pouring out through the hood. You have a problem.

In defining the problem, the approach is approximately the same whether you are dealing with a question or a situation. In defining a problem, you must both relate the problem to its environment and break the problem down into its components. You must be clear-eyed about your objectives in solving the problem. Finally, you must recognize any limitations set upon you in solving the problem. We'll illustrate these points by using a problem that a student, Scott Pahl, dealt with.[1]

Scott looked at a problem in the state department of transportation. In the past few years, the department's grass-mowing budget has been getting out of hand. In a recent year, mowing costs totaled almost $4 million. What was to be done?

Relating to the Surrounding Environment

Where does grass mowing fit into the total picture of the department's responsibilities? As big a chore as mowing the grass on the state's highways is, it's only one of many department responsibilities. It's a small part of a budget that exceeds $600 million. Considerably more important to the state are the maintenance of existing highways and the construction of new

---

[1]All excerpts from "The Feasibility of Using *SlowGrowth* Plant Growth Regulator Instead of Mowing to Maintain Grassy Areas Along Minnesota's Highways," an unpublished student report, printed with the permission of Scott Pahl, the author. We have modified the report slightly to update the information and to emphasize the points we want to make about recommendation reports.

ones. Although the citizens of the state expect the grassy areas near their roads to be neatly kept, they do not want money taken away from road building and maintenance to achieve this neatness. Solving the grass-mowing problem is important, but it is not a problem of crisis proportions.

In this manner, Scott looked at the grass mowing problem in relation to the surrounding environment of the department's other tasks and problems. Any problem must be seen in proper perspective before you begin seeking its solution. Consider again the loud whooshing sound coming from your automobile. If that occurred at 3:00 A.M. on a lonely country road, it would be a totally different problem from if it occurred at 3:00 P.M. at a spot 100 feet from a full-service gas station.

Breaking Down the Problem

In defining your problem be specific about its elements. What are its components? If you don't analyze your problem carefully at the beginning, you'll find yourself out of your depth when trying to find a solution. In analyzing your problem, you must look beneath the surface problem—high costs in Scott's problem—and search for its causes. The solution almost certainly will attack these subproblems and not the surface problem as such. In breaking down your problem, you will often find valuable the journalist's questions of *who, what, when, where,* and *how.* Using these questions, Scott came up with such facts as these:

- *Mowing season:* 15 May to 1 October.

- *Total miles mowed:* 9,910 miles, broken down into metro areas, the interstate system, and the nonmetro state highways.

- *Number of mowings per season:* 10 in metro areas, 6 on interstates, 3 on state highways.

- *Cost:* $3,855,000 in 1999. Costs include wages, equipment operating and maintenance, equipment replacement, storage, worker's compensation, and insurance.

- *Associated problems:* The work is tedious and dangerous. Mowers tip over on steep slopes; motorists throw things at the mower operators. Every year workers are seriously injured, and over the years several have been killed.

Scott found much more, but you get the idea. Look at all the possible causal factors in your problem. Make a list of related problems: for example, the danger to the mower operators. As you examine these factors, use the software on your computer to record your findings and help you to analyze the information. For example, you might use a spreadsheet program to develop the cost analysis or find a map on the World Wide Web that shows the area affected by the mowing. The more you document early, the better off you'll be later.

Setting Objectives

Knowing your objectives is an important key to solving the problem. The solution to our bicycle-choosing problem above rests on the objectives. The objective of cross-country travel calls for a different solution from the objective of riding a few miles to work each day. You must be absolutely clear-eyed about what you want as the outcome of the solution. You should have one major objective. You may have other objectives of lesser importance. State them all clearly, preferably in writing. Know the priority you set on each.

Scott's major objective was clear: Lower the cost of grass management on the state's highways. He had lesser objectives as well, including lowering the operators' accident rate and freeing the operators for other kinds of maintenance work.

Knowing the Limitations

Almost always there are limitations you must observe in solving a problem. They might include available funds and technology, people's attitudes, environmental problems, time, and so forth. One test for any solution is that it can be accomplished within the limitations.

The limitations in the grass-maintenance problem were these:

- Citizens expected grass bordering the highways to be maintained neatly.

- Any solution had to be ecologically safe.

CREATING SOLUTIONS

Creating solutions and the next step, testing solutions, are understandably closely related. Given the speed with which the human mind makes connections, it's likely that most of us, at least some of the time, test a solution almost as quickly as we form it in our minds. However, we separate the steps here for two reasons. First, we want to suggest that if you make snap decisions about solutions, you may overlook the solution that would ultimately be best. Second, if you are seeking solutions in a group, you may do better if the group creates solutions without the pressure of immediately testing them. By doing so, group members can present solutions, even silly sounding ones, without fear of someone immediately jumping on their ideas. It's not at all unusual for a solution that at first glimpse seems ridiculous to prove to be the best one.

Obviously, creating solutions calls for the problem solver to possess knowledge relevant to the problem. Someone with no knowledge in the appropriate subject matter will have difficulty in forming solutions. For example, a problem solver who didn't know about the various kinds of bikes available would be in no position to frame an answer to the question, "What bike should I buy?" If you lack the needed knowledge from your education and experience, you must seek it as part of the problem-solving process. If you want to buy a bike, you might first go to the manufacturer's Web sites to read about the bikes, or you might check with friends to see what bikes they have and ask to ride them, after which you would go to the bike shop with questions to ask. As you'll see, Scott's knowledge as an agronomy student enabled him to come up with the solution that he ultimately chose.

Wherever your knowledge comes from, begin creating solutions. Write down all your ideas, even the outlandish ones. Scott's possible solutions were these:

- Leave the situation as he found it.

- Stop mowing the grass.

- Mow the grass at less-frequent intervals.

- Pave over some or all of the grassed areas.

- Stop the grass from growing.

When he was satisfied he had thought of all the possible solutions, Scott was ready to test them.

Rarely in the workplace will you work alone on a problem. You may come up with a list of possible solutions, but you will meet with others and probably modify some of the solutions and more than likely add to the list. If you find yourself working alone on a problem, seek out the advice of others. Scott interviewed members of the department of transportation and the sales representative from AgriHighway. Almost everyone likes to talk about his or her work. One of your authors recently had the responsibility of building a computer classroom. After identifying 10 to 12 specific questions about the computers to buy and how to set up the environment, she met with seven other faculty members on campus responsible for computer classrooms. She came back with suggestions that made setting up the new classroom easier. She learned about the best way to give every workstation access to sound without having a room full of computers with speakers, how to add locks to each computer, and how to ensure a stable desktop environment with an image-creating software program.

TESTING SOLUTIONS

Solutions may be tested logically and empirically. To test a solution logically, you'll work with the objectives and limitations you have already stated. These objectives and limitations lead you to the criteria—the standards of judgment—you'll use to measure the effectiveness of the proposed solutions. In the bike example, let's consider the major objective as buying a bike suitable for cross-country travel. Let's also assume a cost limitation of $1000. Such an objective and limitation might lead to these criteria:

The bike should

- be lightweight

- have gearing suitable for long hills

- have an effective braking system

- be sturdy and easily maintained

- not cost more than $1000

Think your criteria through carefully. Without proper standards of comparison, you'll be unable to test your solutions. You should also set priorities for your criteria. Which of the preceding criteria is the most important? It may well be the $1000 limitation. If that is the case, no matter how lightweight a bike is and how effective its gearing system, if it costs more than $1000 it will not be considered.

Once the criteria are set, testing the solution becomes fairly simple. You gather information on the relevant attributes of bikes in the below-$1000 dollar range. You compare their weights, gearing systems, and so forth, much in the manner that *Consumer Reports* compared the attributes of ink-jet and laser printers in the example in Chapter 3 on page 69. The bike that best meets the criteria will emerge as the choice.

In Scott's grass-management problem, his objectives and limitations led him to several criteria. A proposed solution had to

- lower the cost of grass management

- be aesthetically pleasing

- be ecologically safe

- lower the exposure of workers to danger and free them for other jobs

His first priority was lowering the cost. However, the solution had to meet the other criteria to be seriously considered. Scott was then ready to examine his solutions against his criteria.

- Leaving the situation as it was, although it met all the lesser criteria, obviously did not lower the cost.

- Stopping the grass mowing lowered the cost but would not be aesthetically pleasing.

- Mowing the grass at less-frequent intervals lowered the cost but also failed the aesthetic test.

- Paving all the grass areas was too expensive to consider and would not be aesthetically pleasing.

- Stopping the grass from growing was possible. Scott was an agronomy student and knew of a product manufactured by the AgriHighway Company, *SlowGrowth,* that would retard grass growth. He examined this solution thoroughly and found that it passed all his criteria. It lowered costs. It left the grass in good enough condition to be aesthetically pleasing. It was ecologically safe. The necessary spraying took much less time than the mowing; therefore, workers would be less exposed to danger and would be free for other work.

Logically, Scott had his solution. He also considered empirical testing. By empirical testing, we mean testing a solution's effectiveness through either physical means or social scientific means such as polls or questionnaires. For example, the directions that come with a carpet-cleaning fluid tell you to test the fluid in some inconspicuous place. If the cleaner removes all the color from your carpet under the couch, you'll know not to use it on the rest of the carpet. That is the empirical physical test. If your solution might affect people, perhaps the workers in some section of a plant, a questionnaire polling their attitudes toward the change might be advisable. This would be an empirical social scientific test. You systematically ask a group of people the same questions and analyze their answers.

CHOOSING A SOLUTION

Scott knew that *SlowGrowth* had been empirically tested by AgriHighway and had proven effective. That fact had entered into his logical testing. However, he was not prepared to recommend on the strength of Agri-Highway's testing that the state spray the grass along 9,910 miles of highway. Obviously, further large-scale testing was called for. Scott decided that his recommendation would be that the department conduct a major test of *SlowGrowth* on several hundred miles of state highway. Furthermore the testing should be in several spots in the state. Parts of the state are warmer and dryer than others, and cities have microclimates of their own, different from the nearby suburbs and rural areas. If the testing proved successful, the state could consider a grass-management program that included the use of *SlowGrowth*.

Scott had arrived at his recommendation. It was time for him to report it.

REPORTING THE SOLUTION

If you have followed a reasoning process similar to the one just described, most of your work is done when it is time for you to write your report. You have defined your problem. You know what solutions you have seriously considered and the criteria you have used to compare them. You know your conclusions and the recommendations they lead to. Your task now is to plan the organization and format of your report and write it so that it is understandable and acceptable to your readers. Before beginning, however, you would be wise to think about your objective and your audience.

In Scott's case his objective was clear: to persuade his audience that his proposed solution was the appropriate one. His primary audience was well defined. It consisted of several department of transportation managers, a neutral if somewhat skeptical audience. They were engineers by education and experience. They were an educated audience who, at the most, might need a few agronomic concepts explained. Secondary readers might be members of citizen groups, particularly those concerned about ecological effects.

As you'll see, Scott kept his objective and readers in mind as he planned and wrote his report. For example, he knew that his report would have to provide specific information to support his recommendation. He would provide AgriHighway's test results; he would include a spreadsheet that showed the comparison of costs. The order in which he presents the information and how he presents the information (in bulleted lists or in paragraphs, for example) will influence what information the readers gather from his report.

Review Chapters 3 and 4 for help with setting up your recommendations (arguing for the point you want to make) and persuading your audience. Chapters 5, 6, and 7 suggest ways to design and present the text and visuals so that the reader can easily review the information. Like other workplace documents, recommendation reports have similar features. A complete recommendation report may consist of all of the following:

Prefatory Elements	Letter of Transmittal
	Title Page
	Table of Contents
	List of Illustrations
Main Elements	Introduction
	Body
	Summary and Conclusions
	Recommendations
Supplemental Elements	List of References
	Appendix

In this chapter we discuss only the introduction, body, summary and conclusions, and recommendations. For the other parts we refer you to Chapter 13, Principles of Workplace Reports, where they are thoroughly discussed. Keep in mind that you will follow the conventions established by the company or organization you work for. Your report may be a 3- to 5-page memo without a list of references or an appendix, or it may be a 300-page report, presented in a 3-ring binder with a computer-generated slideshow summarizing the key points. You must adapt your presentation to meet the purpose of the report, to meet the needs of the audience, and to provide the information needed.

INTRODUCTION

In describing a typical introduction on pages 364–366, we tell you to explain your subject, purpose, scope, and plan to your readers. The introduction to a recommendation report follows this basic format. In a recommendation report, your subject is the problem you are working with. Your purpose is to present your solution and show how you have arrived at it. Your scope includes the definition of the problem, the solution or solutions you are considering, the evaluation of the solutions, your conclusions, and your recommendations. Your plan is how you intend to present your material. Scott's introduction demonstrates all the basic parts of a successful introduction.

Introduction

Last year, the Department of Transportation spent almost $4 million, out of a total budget of slightly over $600 million, on mowing the grass areas along the state's highways. This grass mowing is a major summer-time chore for state highway crews. In the struggle to keep the many miles of highway medians, ditches, and embankments mowed, other important projects are delayed and limited budgets are depleted.

Under contract to the Department, I studied the problem. I considered four possible solutions:

- Leaving the situation as is

- Lowering the frequency of mowing or stopping it all together

- Paving over the grass

- Retarding the growth of the grass

The major criteria used to evaluate the solutions were that the acceptable solution had to lower the cost of grass management, be aesthetically pleasing, and be ecologically safe. Lesser criteria were lowering the exposure of the workers to danger and freeing them for other jobs.

Only the solution of retarding the growth of the grass met all the criteria. Therefore, it is the only one considered in this report.

Immediately following this introduction, I present a summary of my data and major conclusions followed by my recommendations. Following my recommendations are three sections in which I describe the problem fully, present a solution to it, and evaluate the solution.

We draw your attention to several things in this introduction. First of all, in it, Scott disposes of all his solutions but one. This is advisable only when one solution clearly stands out as the best. When the solutions are more balanced, you may have to carry over a consideration of the alternative solutions to the body. We'll discuss that further in a moment. Second, Scott's plan reveals that he has chosen what is frequently called an *executive format* for his report. That is, he presents his summary, conclusions, and recommendations *before* he presents the body of his report. We discuss the rationale for doing so when we discuss the summary and conclusions.

BODY

The body of your recommendation report should display your reasoning in complete enough detail to allow your readers to judge for themselves if your analysis has been adequate. You should in your report, as in your reasoning, describe the problem, present your solution or solutions, and evaluate them. With only one solution, your organization might look like this:

- Definition of problem

- Presentation of solution

- Evaluation of solution by criteria

If the problem can be simply defined, that task may sometimes be done in the introduction. In that case, the body would consist of only the last two items on the list: presenting and evaluating solutions.

When you have two or more solutions to evaluate, your organization will be slightly more complicated:

1. Definition of problem

2. Presentation of solutions

3. Evaluation of solutions
   a) Criterion A
      i) Explanation of criterion A
      ii) Evaluation of solutions 1 and 2
   b) Criterion B
      i) Explanation of criterion B
      ii) Evaluation of solutions 1 and 2

(And so forth.)

You can also organize the evaluation of solutions by solution rather than by criteria, in this manner:

1. Definition of Problem

2. Explanation of Criteria

3. Solution 1
   a) Presentation of solution 1
   b) Evaluation by criteria

4. Solution 2
   a) Presentation of solution 2
   b) Evaluation by criteria

We find that most people can demonstrate the differences among their solutions more sharply when they organize by criteria. No matter which plan you choose, be sure both criteria and solutions are carefully explained before you begin your evaluation. Scott's table of contents, reproduced in Figure 14.1, illustrates how he used the general plans we have shown you for his purposes.

In **defining his problem**, Scott discusses the existing mowing program, its costs, and its associated problems. Here is Scott's description of the mowing program:

The Mowing Program

The state normally starts its mowing season May 15, about one month after the grass begins to green up, and ends it on October 1. The state's mowing responsibilities can be divided into three major groups of roads: the metro area roads, the nonmetro interstate highways, and the nonmetro highways. The crews attempt to mow the metro highways every two weeks. Some metro areas will be mowed ten times during a season. The areas along the nonmetro interstates are mowed, on the average, six times per season. The nonmetro highways receive three mowings per season.

Table of Contents

Figure 14.1 Table of Contents. The headings in the table of contents match the headings in the report in wording and in typeface. You want to show the reader the hierarchy of information in your report and help the reader easily locate the information.

In **presenting his solution**, Scott begins with a clearly stated overview of his solution to the grass management problem:

SlowGrowth **Grass-Management Program**

SlowGrowth, a plant-growth regulator, developed and released by the AgriHighway Company, shows a good deal of promise in the area of chemically assisted turf grass management. *SlowGrowth* works by suppressing cool-season grasses' vegetative and reproductive development. The plants remain a healthy, normal green color. With proper application, grass growth can be suppressed for up to eight weeks, eliminating the need to mow.

The overview allows the readers to grasp the solution in its entirety before they are hit with the details. It's a good technique. Scott follows the overview with technical descriptions of *SlowGrowth*'s chemistry and mode of action. He concludes by describing how *SlowGrowth* would be applied.

You must be careful in describing your solution not to provide too much detail. Executives, the usual readers of recommendation reports, are unlikely to want the same detail that someone implementing the solution would need. In other words, executives would not need a full set of instructions, but they would need enough detail to understand how the solution will work. As you construct your report, be careful to use language that your readers can understand. Define any technical terms you must use and that your readers are unlikely to know. Here is how Scott explained the application of *SlowGrowth*:

Proper Application

The product should be applied after the grass greens up and is actively growing but before the seedheads start to emerge. This normally occurs in late April. Applied in this manner, *SlowGrowth* will give vegetative and reproductive growth suppression for up to eight weeks.

In situations where full-season grass suppression is needed, *SlowGrowth* may be applied more than once per season. To avoid plant injury, there should be a six-week wait between applications.

As you will see when we discuss the summary and conclusions section, Scott included material useful in supporting his conclusions.

In **evaluating his solution**, Scott applies his criteria of cost, aesthetics, ecological safety, and solution of associated problems. Here is a piece of his evaluation of the ecological safety of *SlowGrowth*:

Ecological Safety

SlowGrowth is a safe compound. It is nonirritating to either whole or abraded skin and only slightly irritating to eyes. Its toxicity to fish and birds is quite low. However, it should not be sprayed on lakes or streams, and animals should not be allowed to graze on treated areas. As with any chemical, care should be taken to avoid prolonged or unnecessary contact with *SlowGrowth*.

Mefluidide, the chief component of *SlowGrowth,* is unstable in the soil, with a half-life of only two days. It is rapidly broken down by soil microbes. Therefore, it will not build up in the soil or cause serious problems for birds or other wildlife.

In evaluating your solution, you are using practical logic to make your argument (see pages 377–383). You need not show your reasoning in every detail, but you must show enough so that readers can judge the validity of your argument. Also, if your solution involves any risks, you should draw them to your readers' attention. They will need to weigh them in their decisions. Scott, for example, pointed out that, despite *SlowGrowth*'s safety, animals should not graze on grass treated with it. Also be careful to point out *so-whats* to your readers as Scott has done in his statement, "Therefore, it will not build up in the soil or cause serious problems for birds or other wildlife."

SUMMARY AND CONCLUSIONS

The summary and conclusions section often may be the only part of the report many readers read. Therefore, it must be well done. Also, most of the time, executive readers will find the summary and conclusions and read them before they read anything else in the report. When read in this sequence, the summary and conclusions become the overview of the report that helps readers understand the report. Furthermore, this section helps the readers to select those parts of the report they may wish to read more thoroughly.

For example, an executive reader might be satisfied with Scott's summary statements concerning ecological safety. Consequently, she might not bother to read the body section, where greater detail about ecological safety can be found. On the other hand, she might doubt Scott's cost figures and choose to read the section on cost with great care. Many reports place summaries, conclusions, and recommendations immediately following the introduction on the principle that if executives are likely to read them early, these parts will serve best up front where they are easily found. As you see in Scott's table of contents, reproduced in Figure 14.1, that is the format he chose.

To write a good summary, you must read through your report body, selecting those key facts that have led you to your conclusions. Generally, such key facts will be surrounded by supporting details. To summarize, you leave out the details and report only the key facts. Do not merely pile up facts in a random way. Rather, place facts together in a context that allows you, through induction and deduction, to demonstrate how you reached your conclusions. Figure 14.2 illustrates the sequence that leads you from facts through conclusions to recommendations. We can illustrate these principles by comparing the material in several sections of Scott's reports with his use of the same material in his summary and conclusions.

> SUMMARY
> Key facts drawn together in a related context
> ↓
> CONCLUSIONS
> The implications of the facts—the *so-whats*
> ↓
> RECOMMENDATIONS
> The actions that follow as a result of the conclusions

Figure 14.2 Logic sequence.

In his evaluation, Scott showed some of his cost calculations:

The per-gallon cost of *SlowGrowth* is $79.00. At the recommended application rate of 1.5 pints per acre, the chemical costs per acre would be $14.80. To this must be added the average application cost of $5.00 per acre, for a total cost per acre of $19.80. By comparison, mowing costs, on average, are $13.00 per acre for each mowing. One mowing costs less than one application, but two mowings at a total cost of $26.00 exceed the cost of the application by $6.20.

While describing the state's grass-mowing program, Scott described the different number of mowings used in the state, depending on the type and location of the highway (see page 386). In his section on the solution, Scott, in discussing the application of *SlowGrowth*, said that one application would retard grass growth for up to eight weeks (see page 388). Now, read through Scott's summary and conclusions and see how these key facts and others are condensed and properly related to one another, allowing Scott to reach his conclusions and state them in a convincing way.

Summary and Conclusion

The state's current highway grass-management program is costly at $3,855,000 a year. It is also dangerous. Every year workers mowing grass are injured, and fatalities have occurred. A possible solution to this problem of high costs and injuries is the use of *SlowGrowth,* a plant-growth regulator manufactured by the AgriHighway Company. A single application of *SlowGrowth* retards the growth of grass for up to eight weeks. Although its growth is retarded, the grass retains its natural healthy green color. *SlowGrowth* is ecologically safe. It is noncorrosive to machinery and, if used properly, nontoxic to human beings and wildlife. However, the manufacturer does recommend that animals not be allowed to graze on grass sprayed with *SlowGrowth*.

SlowGrowth breaks down quickly in the soil, having a half-life of only two days. Because *SlowGrowth* is rapidly broken down by soil microbes, it will not build up in the soil and cause serious problems for wildlife.

A comparison of the costs involved in mowing and in applying *SlowGrowth* shows that a grass-management program using *Slow-Growth* can be worked out that will lower costs. Currently, the mowing season runs from May 15 to October 1. During that time, the metro roadways are mowed, on average, 10 times, nonmetro interstates 6 times, and nonmetro highways 3 times. Each mowing costs, on average, $13.00 per acre. The comparable cost for each *SlowGrowth* application is $19.80 per acre. The break-even point in cost for using *SlowGrowth* thus comes between the first and second mowing. Given the 8-week period of retardation following each *SlowGrowth* application, two applications—one before the spring grass-growing season and one before the late summer grass-growing season—would be cost effective on the metro and interstate areas. For the highway areas, a single *SlowGrowth* application in early spring coupled with a fall mowing would be the most cost effective. Because the combined number of mowings and applications under the *SlowGrowth* program would be considerably lower than under the current all-mowing program, the workers' exposure to danger would be greatly reduced, and they would be free for other maintenance work.

AgriHighway Company's testing of *SlowGrowth* has been thorough, but it would seem prudent for the Department to run a series of tests of its own before launching a statewide program. Climatic conditions vary throughout the state. Also, metro areas have microclimates different from surrounding areas. Therefore, any testing should include both metro and nonmetro areas and enough locations in the state to test *SlowGrowth*'s performance under the state's various climatic conditions.

Notice that Scott's final conclusions form a bridge to the recommendations that follow. In fact, your conclusions should always be written so that the recommendations can be anticipated by the reader. The recommendation section of a report is no place for surprises.

RECOMMENDATIONS

Recommendations are action steps. The recommendation section is the place in your report where you tell the readers what they *ought* to do. (If you're writing a decision report rather than a recommendation report, this is the place where you tell your readers what *is* going to be done.) The recommendation section should be short. Your reasoning has been displayed elsewhere in the body and in the summary and conclusions. You need not repeat any of it in the recommendations. Confine yourself to action statements.

The first recommendation should always answer the key question of the problem. What is the solution to the problem, the answer to the chief question asked? Later recommendations, if any, will supplement the first recommendation and show how it should be implemented. In our bicycle example, the first and only recommendation might be simply, "Buy Brand-X bicycle." In Scott's report, the recommendation section is necessarily more complex, but it demonstrates the principles stated here.

Recommendations

1. The Department of Transportation should begin a statewide test on the state's highways of the effectiveness of AgriHighway's *SlowGrowth* in grass management.

2. The testing should be conducted in both metro and nonmetro areas. Enough testing areas should be chosen to reflect the varied climatic conditions in the state.

3. The test grass-management program should be as follows:
   a. Apply *SlowGrowth* twice per season, spring and late summer, on interstate and metro right-of-ways.
   b. Apply *SlowGrowth* once in the spring on nonmetro highway right-of-ways, and follow with a late-summer mowing.

When the recommendations are stated, your report is done. You have studied your problem, found a solution for it, and reported both your reasoning and your solution.

RECOMMENDATION REPORTS AS CORRESPONDENCE

Recommendation reports that do not exceed four or five pages are frequently given a letter or memo format. In Figure 14.3, a report by Donna Smith illustrates a recommendation report written as a memo. Donna organized her report using the comparison mode of argument. Her introduction establishes the purpose, occasion, and plan of the report. She establishes her criteria and puts them in priority order. She takes time to define a term, *high-intensity bulb,* that her reader will need.

After describing the committee's investigation, she gives the key findings in a table. Drawing upon the table, she presents her conclusions and recommendation. Although the memo format does not call for a table of contents, she provides enough headings to guide the reader through the report. All in all, the report is an excellent example of a short recommendation report.

Date: 20 March 1999

To: Mary A. Young
               Director
               Tribble Residence Hall

From: Donna Smith DS
               Committee Chair
               Tribble Hall Improvements Committee

Subject: Recommendation for the Purchase of 200 Study Lamps for
               Tribble Residence Hall

At your request the Tribble Hall Improvements Committee investigated the purchase of two study lamps each for the 100 student rooms in the Tribble Residence Hall. The available ceiling lighting in the rooms is insufficient for studying, and no lamps are provided. In this report, I explain the criteria used by the Committee in this investigation, describe our method of gathering information about the lamps, and present our findings followed by our comparison of the lamps and our recommendations.

Features Compared

You set a price limitation on the lamps of $25 each. Another major criterion was that the lamps could be used at night by one roommate without disturbing the other roommate. We did not consider halogen lamps. The university has banned halogen lamps from the campus because of the fire hazard. For this reason, only lamps using high-intensity bulbs were considered.

A high-intensity bulb is an incandescent bulb that gives a highly concentrated light over a small area, thus lessening the effect on anyone outside the circle of its light. High-intensity bulbs have an additional advantage of long life and, therefore, require fewer replacement bulbs than regular incandescent bulbs.

The Committee found several high-intensity lamps within the $25 limit and compared them by the following criteria, arranged in order of priority:

1. *Size*—to fit available space, lamps must be 12 inches or less in height, and lamps with folding arms must have a reach of 20 inches or less.

2. *Price*—low price (under $25) is an important consideration.

Figure 14.3   Recommendation reports may be presented in a memo format. You are recording the information for others to read once and make a decision.

Page 2
Mary A. Young
20 March 1999

> 3. *Availability of special features*—features such as a high/low switch and a swivel shade are desirable.

Stores Visited

The Committee visited two major office supply stores (The Carson Company and Warner's Office Center), two major discount stores (K-Mart and Walmart), two bookstores (Varsity Bookstore and Anderson's Books), and two merchandise warehouses (Best Products and Service Merchandise).

The office supply stores, bookstores, and discount stores did not have high-intensity lamps within the price limitation. Best Products and Service Merchandise had the best selection within the price limitation. Committee members talked to sales representatives about special features, reviewed catalogs, and examined the lamps. We also asked about a special price for the purchase of 200 lamps.

Comparison of the Lamps

Store	Model	Unit Price[a]	Total Price[a]	Special Features
Best Products	Ledu	$14.97	$2994	• all metal
	Mobilite	9.99[b]	1998	• all metal • folding arm • high/low switch • swivel shade
Service Merchandise	Mighty Mite	9.92	1984	• all metal • folding arm • high/low switch
	Tensor Asteroid	19.97	3994	• all metal (brass) • cool inner reflector • folding arm

[a]price does not include sales tax.
[b]Mobilite's regular unit price is $14.93. However, Best Products will offer a special unit price of $9.99 for the purchase of 200 lamps.

Because all lamps compared met the size criterion, the Committee compared special features available against price. As shown in the table, all the possible lamps have several special features. The cool inner reflector (the inner wall of the shade) absorbs heat and keeps the shade from getting hot. Folding arms and swivel shades give versatility to setting the angle of the lamp and its distance from the desk top. The

Figure 14.3 (continued)

Page 3
Mary A. Young
20 March 1999

advantage of a high/low switch is that the high setting can be used for studying and the low setting for lighting the room just enough to move around without bothering a sleeping roommate.

The Mobilite has the greatest number of special features for the price.   While it does not have the brass finish and cool inner reflector of the Tensor Asteroid, the advantage of its low price and high/low switch outweigh the disadvantages of not having these features.

Recommendation

The committee recommends the purchase of the Mobilite from Best Products.

Figure 14.3 (continued)

PLANNING AND REVISING CHECKLIST: RECOMMENDATION REPORTS

Think about the following as you plan and revise a recommendation report.

PLANNING

Recommendation reports report the solutions to problems. You must therefore begin by defining the problem, creating solutions for it, testing the solutions, and choosing a solution. In doing so, you will create a good deal of information. After you have reached your conclusions and recommendations, you must report them and, as well, report as much of your reasoning as is necessary to be credible to your readers.

Defining the Problem

- Describe the problem.

- Describe the components of the problem.

- Relate the problem to the surrounding environment.

- State your objectives in solving the problem.

- List any limitations you have in solving the problem.

Creating Solutions

- State as many solutions to the problem as you can. Brainstorm; put down every solution that occurs to you.

- Inventory your information. Do you have enough to solve the problem? If not, where can you get the needed information?

Testing Solutions

- Using what you know about your objectives and limitations, form criteria to use in testing your solutions.

- If appropriate, set priorities for your criteria.

- Test your solutions against your criteria.

- Conduct any available and appropriate empirical tests on your solutions.

Choosing a Solution

- Step back from the testing and review the results.

- On the basis of your reasoning and testing, choose the best solution.

Planning the Report

- Who are the readers of your report?

- What is their purpose in reading it?

- Will they have problems with any of the technical vocabulary or concepts involved?

- Are they likely to want a fully detailed report or a summary?

- Do you have several readers, perhaps some with different needs?

- What will be your reader's reaction to your recommendations? Enthusiastic? Indifferent? Hostile?

- What organization and format will present your report the best?

- Will an executive format, placing the conclusions and recommendations before the body of the report, be an appropriate choice?

- Can you dispose of some or all of the unacceptable solutions quickly, perhaps in the introduction, or must you treat some of them fully?

- Would it be best to organize by solution or by criteria?

- Are there visuals such as tables or charts that would be useful?

- Are there *so-whats* of your information that need special emphasis?

- Should you answer some of the special questions that executives frequently have? How big is the problem? How important is solving it? Who should carry out the solution? When should the solution be implemented?

REVISION

In revision, pay attention to organization, content, style, format, and grammar.

Organization and Content

- Does your introduction make the problem clear?

- Does your introduction make clear the solutions you considered?

- If appropriate, does your introduction state your criteria clearly and succinctly?

- Does your introduction give the plan of your report?

- Does the body of your report display your reasoning well enough to allow your readers to judge your work?

- Are your criteria and solution(s) adequately explained?

- Does your organization sharply illuminate how your proposed solution(s) is measured by your criteria?

- Could some of your data be better displayed in a visual?

- Have you displayed your organization with appropriate headings?

- Can your summary, conclusions, and recommendations stand alone?

- Do your conclusions prepare the way for your recommendations?

- Is your chief recommendation clearly stated?

- Have you stated needed supplementary recommendations?

- Do you provide any needed details about implementing your recommendations?

Style

- Are your sentences active?

- Is your vocabulary appropriate for your audience?

- Have you achieved clarity and conciseness?

Format and Grammar

- Have you chosen an appropriate format? Report, letter, or memo?

- Does your report follow good document design conventions and present the information so the reader can find what he or she needs?

- Have you proofread carefully, eliminating all grammatical and typographical errors?

- Will your work present a good appearance to your reader?

SUGGESTIONS FOR APPLYING YOUR KNOWLEDGE

Community and school problems can provide excellent practice in writing recommendation reports. A glance at a local paper will reveal community problems ranging from potholes in the streets to curbside pick up of recyclables. Most schools perennially have problems such as inefficient use of energy, poor food service, and delays in phone registration. You may already be at work and be aware of job-related problems. Perhaps your office is trying to decide what brand of computer to buy. Choose such a problem. Be sure to choose a problem that suits your interests and knowledge. Narrow the problem to a manageable study for the time frame you are working in. For example, you cannot solve the recycling problems for the entire campus, but you can certainly study paper recycling in a computer classroom. After a preliminary study of the problem, submit a proposal to your instructor that you do a recommendation report presenting a solution. (See Chapter 15, Proposals, for advice on how to make such a proposal.)

When you and your instructor agree on the project, analyze your problem by using the logical method described in this chapter. When your analysis is complete, present the results in a recommendation report. Depending on the length of the report, use either a report or a correspondence format.

Problem-solving and recommendation reports lend themselves particularly well to collaborative efforts. If you choose to work collaboratively, review the section on collaboration in Chapter 1, The Process of Workplace Writing.

CHAPTER 15

PROPOSALS

Proposals are made for many purposes and come in many lengths and formats. An insulation contractor, for example, called in to examine an old house, may submit a proposal to the house's owner. He may outline the quantity and type of insulation needed and describe how the job will be done. He'll estimate how soon the job can be done and set a price for it. If he's a good salesperson, he may provide the names and phone numbers of satisfied customers. He may provide an incentive for quick action: "For the rest of August, we offer a summer discount of 10 percent. In September our prices go back up." The whole proposal, or bid, as it may be called in this instance, may be on one page. At the other end of the scale, an aircraft manufacturer, proposing to build a new aircraft for a large airline, may submit a proposal that fills several books. The aircraft proposal will contain information on plans, facilities, schedules, costs, key engineering and management personnel, and much more.

A proposal contains specific information: the work you or your organization want to do for someone, including details about the need for the work, how the work will be done, schedule, price, and personnel. In other words, you answer the questions: who?, what?, when?, where?, how?, and why? Figure 15.1 illustrates the questions you should ask, and answer, as you write a proposal. The answers appear in the appropriate section of the proposal identified in the request for proposal (RFP) or headings similar to the ones identified in Figure 15.1. The specific audience is the people you are trying to convince to have the work done. Your purpose is to get your audience to select and pay you to do the proposed work.

The proposal is a persuasive document. Achieving credibility will help you as much in a proposal as it does in a sales letter. Adopt the you-attitude. Focus on how your proposal will benefit the company or organization paying you for the work. Clearly state your *so-whats* in a proposal. Usually, the major *so-what* is the relevance of your work in solving some problem of concern to the organization to which you are making the proposal.

Proposals fall into two general categories—solicited and unsolicited. A *solicited proposal* is in answer to a request for a proposal—commonly referred to as an RFP. The RFP is usually developed and published by some branch of government, a company, or an organization. Individuals or other companies or organizations respond to the RFP with a proposal for how they will complete the work. For example, the National Science Foundation publishes the *Grants Proposal Guide* (which includes instructions and proposal forms) at www.nsf.gov/bfa/cpo/gpg; funding opportunities—the RFPs—are found at www.nsf.gov/home/grants.htm. If you or your organization wants to work with the National Aeronautical Space Administration (NASA) or the Environmental Protection Agency (EPA), for example, go to the Web site and you will find the link to information for research grants or calls for proposals for work that these agencies need done. Many organizations now publish their RFPs on the Web.

Commercial Web sites also publish RFPs. Figure 15.2 is an example from the *Commerce Business Daily* published by the Loren Data

Questions		Possible Section Headings
Who?	Who will do the work? Who will solve the problem? Identify their qualifications and the special skills and qualifications they bring to the task that others cannot provide.	**Personnel** **Consultants** **Technical Support**
What?	What is the problem? What work will be done? Identify the problem (or restate it to make it clear you understand the problem) and describe the work that will be done to solve the problem. Answer the *so-whats*.	**Introduction** **Problem** **Solutions**
When?	When must the work be completed? Establish a time line of events for completing the work. Depending upon the size of the project, you may identify completion dates for individual tasks leading to the final completion date.	**Schedule** **Time Line** **Calendar of Events**
Where?	Where will the work be done? Describe the location and work environment for the project or where the final product will be delivered.	**Facilities** **Location** **Work Sites**
How?	How will the work be completed? How much will the project cost? Identify and describe equipment and supplies needed. Provide a detailed budget.	**Work and Management Plan** **Budget** **Equipment and Supplies**
Why?	Why will you or your organization be the best choice for completing the work.	**Overview** **Executive Summary** **Services Provided**

Figure 15.1 Questions to ask as you respond to a request for proposal (RFP). Your answers will be placed in the proposal sections that call for the information. We identify section headings that might be used, but the order will depend upon the RFP requirements. An RFP is issued when the organization cannot complete the work themselves. You are explaining how you can do the work in a reasonable amount of time at a reasonable cost to them. Open a file on your computer, put in the headings, and begin writing (making notes).

Corporation (www.ld.com). The *Commerce Business Daily* describes work the government and other organizations need completed and identifies whom to contact for more information on submitting a proposal or requesting a form for submitting a quote or bid on a job. The example in Figure 15.2 identifies the problem: a smoking shelter for Building #31 at the VA Medical and Regional Office Center in Vermont. Proposers (bidders) can get an idea of the size of the project from the budget range given: $25,000 and $100,000. And, they can bid only if they are a small business. The time schedule and a source for more information on the project are identified. This is just one example of how companies find work to bid on.

COMMERCE BUSINESS DAILY ISSUE OF SEPTEMBER 8,1999 PSA#2427

SA-ALC/Contracting Directorate/LDKSF; 485 Quentin Roosevelt Road Suite 12; Kelly AFB, TX 78241-6419

41 -- TURBINE SOL F41608-00-Q-74007 DUE 091899 POC The Point of Contact is DAVID W. ANDRETTI, LDKSF, Phone: 210-925-6603, FAX: 210-925-1073, E-MAIL: david.andretti@kelly.af.mil E-MAIL: Send your E-Mail request to the POC, david.andretti@kelly.af.mil. REPAIR OF 30 EACH TURBINES TECH. ORDER # 35E9-90-51,52 OR BEST COMMERCIAL PRACTICES NSN: 4130-01-306-6309 P/N: 571745-2-1 FUNCTION: THE TURBINE DRAWS AIR FROM THE -60 GENERATOR, COMPRESSES IT AND OUTPUTS CONDITIONED AIR. PART OF THE "EVALUATION" WILL BE PAST PERFORMANCE. DUE TO THE EMERGENCY STATUS OF THIS REQUISITION, OFFERORS WHO HAVE NOT REPAIRED THIS ITEM FOR THE GOVERNMENT IN THE PAST WILL BE CONSIDERED FOR "FUTURE" REQUISITIONS ONLY. SOLE SOURCE CONTRACTOR: ALLIED SIGNAL (CAGE 02LU7) WARNER ROAD TEMPE, AZ 85285 All potential offerors should contact the buyer/PCO identified in this notice for additional information and/or to communicate concerns, if any, concerning this acquisition. If your concerns are not satisfied by the contracting officer, an Ombudsman has been appointed to hear concerns from offerors or potential offerors during the proposal development phase of an acquisition. The Ombudsman does not diminish the authority of the program director or Contracting Officer, but communicates Contractor concerns, issues, disagreements, and recommendations to the appropriate Government personnel. When requested, the Ombudsman shall maintain strict confidentially as to the source of the concern. The Ombudsman does not participate in the evaluation of proposals or in the source selection process. Interested parties are invited to call the SA-ALC Acquisition Ombudsman at AC 210-925-5133 or send E-Mail to: ombudsman@www.kelly-afb.org. See Note(s) 26 Posted 09/03/99 (D-SN376325). (0246)

Loren Data Corp. http://www.ld.com (SYN# 0206 19990908\41-0001.SOL)

41 - Refrigeration, Air Condition and Air Circulating Equipment Index Page

Figure 15.2 Example of an RFP from *Commerce Business Daily* found on the Web site of Loren Data Corporation.
Source: Loren Data Corporation. Commerce Business Daily. 17 June 1997. 24 July 1998 ⟨http://www.ld.com/cbd/today/41wo1001.htm⟩.

An *unsolicited proposal* is made on the initiative of the proposer. The proposer sees an opportunity or a need to solve a problem and proposes a solution that will fulfill the need or solve the problem.

In this chapter we look at both types of proposal and also at a useful classroom project, the proposal for a paper.

SOLICITED PROPOSALS

A request for a solicited proposal will state carefully what goods or services are wanted. The RFP will specify how the proposal should be organized and what information to include.

You can learn a good deal about how to organize and write a proposal by looking at such requests. To that end, we reproduce in part, and slightly modified, a National Science Foundation (NSF) solicitation that requests proposals for student-originated studies. Most of the information found in proposals of any size at all is requested in this NSF solicitation—

information on cost, people, facilities, and schedule. NSF wants to know precisely what will be done and why, and it is particularly interested in the value and significance (the *so-whats*) of what is to be done.

STUDENT-ORIGINATED STUDIES (SOS)

GUIDE FOR PREPARATION OF PROPOSALS

1. **Introduction** In conducting a competitive program for the support of student-originated studies, the National Science Foundation is pursuing three closely related goals:

   (1) to provide talented students with science learning opportunities above and beyond those normally available in most science education programs in the Nation's universities and colleges.

   (2) to increase the variety of instructional modes and of institutional patterns of instruction by demonstrating to both students and faculties the capacity of students to be motivated by independence and thus to accept greater responsibility for planning and carrying out their own learning activities, and

   (3) to encourage college students to express in productive ways their concern for the well-being of our Nation by applying their scientific and technological expertise to the study of significant societal problems.

To request Foundation support through Student-Originated Studies (SOS), student groups will submit proposals that describe the scientific or technological studies they wish to carry out and that give details as to the funds required for that purpose. In almost every academic institution there are faculty members who are familiar with this "proposal process" who can provide information to interested students. There are also officials in the institution's business office who are experienced in estimating the cost of projects. Although the competition requires that proposals be developed by students, the Foundation recognizes their need for faculty and business office advice, and has no objection to applicants' obtaining this sort of assistance.

Guidelines for the Student-Originated Studies Program are being kept as brief and straightforward as possible to encourage diversity and flexibility in the supported projects—within the general framework outlined below:

- Each project proposed is to be problem-oriented to deal with a local problem (or set of associated problems) that has immediate relevance to society, and that poses yet-unanswered questions of a scientific or technological nature on which the student group can collect meaningful data. Ideally, a prospective user's needs become a relevant consideration in the design and conduct of the project.

- The approach to understanding the problem(s) and the search for a solution are to be *interdisciplinary* or *multidisciplinary* in nature, hence,

- Each proposed study or set of studies is to be conducted by a group of students (a minimum of 5 students, but usually not more than 12)—primarily made up of undergraduates, although some graduate students may be included within each group.

- Projects proposed are to be *student*-originated, *student*-planned, and *student*-directed, and are to be carried out under the leadership of one of the students in the group (hereinafter referred to as the *Student Project Director*). In discharging his or her duties, the Student Project Director may be assisted by a Steering Committee chosen from and by the group of participants. The extent to which each group seeks consultation with one or more college faculty members or members of the community at large is a matter for decision by the students, but it is required that there be associated with each grant a specifically-named *Project Advisor* who is a member of the science faculty of the host institution.

- Projects are to be planned to occupy fully the time of the student investigators (predominantly undergraduates) for an uninterrupted period of 10 to 12 weeks. This means that most projects will be conducted during the summer, although projects may be conducted at other times in institutions with schedules that provide 10 to 12 uninterrupted weeks for individual work or independent study during the academic year.

When you answer a solicited proposal, pay careful attention to the guidelines. For instance, in this case a proposal for study by a single student would be unacceptable. The request specifies a study to be made by a group of about 5 to 12 students. The group must designate a faculty member as project adviser. And in proposing a schedule, you would not want to ignore the advice that the project is to last for an uninterrupted period of 10 to 12 weeks.

The NSF solicitation also lays out with care the content of the proposal and how it should be organized:

CONTENT OF PROPOSAL

COMMENTARY
The NSF guidelines for content and organization are fairly standard. See Figure 15.3.

A proposal consists of the following items arranged in the order given: (A) Cover Sheet, (B) Summary Budget Page, (C) Budget Explanations, (D) Abstract, (E) Narrative, (F) Appendices.

(A) *Summary Cover Sheet*—prepared in strict accordance with the sample on page 15.

See Figure 15.4. Budget information is high in importance. What will the proposal cost, and what will the money be spent for?

(B) *Summary Budget Page*—see format, page 16.

(C) *Budget Explanations*—This section must provide a brief but convincing justification for all direct costs listed on the Budget Summary Page (except participant stipends). Items should appear in the same order as entries in the Budget Summary, with corresponding numbering. In drawing up the budget, only essential costs should be included.

COVER SHEET

1. Program: STUDENT-ORIGINATED STUDIES

2. Descriptive Title of Study: _____
   (Maximum: 12 words)

   _____

3. Host Institution: _____

   Address: City _____   State _____   Zip Code _____

   Grant to: _____
   (Full official name of institution to which grant should be made)

4. A. _____   _____   _____
   Student Project Director's Name   Social Security No.   Department

   Telephone: _____   _____
                  Summer Office Number   Number where you may be reached during current academic year

   B. _____   _____   _____
   Faculty Advisor's Name   Social Security Number   Department

   Telephone: _____ _____ _____   _____   _____
              Area Code   Office Number   Department Number   Home Number

5. A. Major Disciplinary Code: IN

   B. Field of Science and Engineering: 9900000, OTHER NEC

   C. Field(s) of Interest and Application : _____

   D. Type of Project: NEW

6. Period of Full-time Participation: _____ 199___to _____ 199___
                                        Starting Date   Ending Date

7. Does the host institution intend to grant academic credit in appropriate amounts and levels for work on this project?
   (   ) Yes   (   ) No

8. Participants and Cost of Proposed Project:

   FULL TIME

   No. of Weeks   No. of Participants   Amt. Requested

   _____   _____ $ _____
                                      (Budget Item 32)

9. Signatures:

   _____   _____
   Signature of proposed Student Project Director   Signature of authorizing official

   _____   _____
   Signature of proposed Project Advisor   Typed name and title of official authorized to sign
                                                            for institution

10. Date of Submission: _____

_____
*List 1 to 3 codes with their abbreviations, in descending order of importance. See pages 13, 14.

15

Figure 15.3 Summary cover sheet.

SUMMARY BUDGET PAGE

Institution: _____

_____

Project Director: _____

_____

NUMBER OF PARTICIPANTS	
Full Time	Acad. Year

19____

19____

19____

A.   PARTICIPANT SUPPORT

_____ Participants for _____ weeks @ $ _____ /wk.
(Minimum 10 weeks; Maximum 12 weeks); (Maximum $90/wk.)

10.   Total Participant Support . . . .

B.   OPERATING COST
Salaries and Wages
12.   Staff* *(Faculty Advice)* . . . .
13.   Assistants and Technical Personnel* (No._____) . . . .
15.   Secretarial and Clerical* . . . .
16.   TOTAL SALARIES AND WAGES (12, 13 & 15) . . . . . .
17.   Staff Benefits *(When charged as direct costs)* . . . .
18.   TOTAL SALARIES, WAGES AND STAFF
             BENEFITS (16 & 17) . . . .
20.   Staff *(Faculty Advisor's)* Travel* . . . .
21.   Field Expenses* . . . .
22.   Laboratory and Field Materials* *(Consumables)* . . . .
23.   Office Supplies, Communications, Publicity* . . . .
24.   Fees† . . . .
25.   Insurance, Health Services & Activities Fees* . . . .
26.   Permanent Equipment* *(Note Restrictions)* . . . .
27.   Publication Costs and/or Miscellaneous Expenses* . . . .
28.   TOTAL DIRECT OPERATING COSTS
             (18 thru 27) . . . .
29.   INDIRECT COSTS_____% . . . .

30.   TOTAL OPERATING COSTS (28 & 29) . . . .

C.   TOTALS
31.   Total Budget *(Participant Support (10) + Total Operating
Costs (30))* . . . .
32.   TOTAL REQUESTED FROM NSF
             (Round to nearest $50) . . . .

_____

* *Itemize in "Budget Explanations", with adequate justifications.*
† *Justify in "Budget Explanations". Other operating costs (lines 12–29) must be reduced to fully offset this item.*

Figure 15.4 Summary budget page.

Abstracts are needed in all but the shortest proposals. Proposals are oftern read by busy executives who want to get the big picture early.

In describing the work to be done in the narrative, the proposal writer has to strike a nice balance that provides enough detail without being wordy.

Notice the call for any visuals that may be needed.

The sales skill required in writing good proposals is pointed out by NSF's call for "evidence that the project's findings hold promise for utilization by civic, governmental, or industrial entities responsible for planning and/or decision making in matters related to the project," NSF's so-what. In writing a proposal, keep your eye on what your work will do for the people paying the bills. Try to find and show something unique about the goals or service you can provide— something that your competiton can't duplicate.

In many proposals you are really selling the services of people. Therefore, it's important to provide details about previous education and relevant experience. (The term curriculum vitae used here refers to such significant biographical data.) Buyers of services are often willing to pay more for people they feel sure they can trust to do a job properly and on time.

(D) *Abstract*—a not more than one-page summary of the problem(s) to be investigated and the proposed experimental approach(es) or study plan(s).

(E) *Narrative*—the following points should be addressed in the order indicated: (Although there is no limit on number of pages, proposers should remember that a concisely written document will present a stronger case for support than one distinguished primarily by its wordiness.)

(1) A one-paragraph description of the host institution and its science program, including local experience in project-type studies, if any.

(2) A brief description of the institution's surroundings (natural and social), if these are relevant to the proposed problem(s).

(3) A description of the problem or group of problems, and of the methodologies to be employed in the study. The several coordinated disciplinary approaches that are to be applied must be outlined in all proposals. Provide any maps or other aids needed by reviewers seeking to understand the project plan. This analysis of the problem and the detailed discussion of the students' plan for attacking it form the core of the proposal. It is here that a merely "good idea" is fleshed out into a competent strategy. *Sufficient detail must be provided* to enable reviewers to reach an affirmative finding as to the adequacy and scientific merit of the proposed study.

(4) Evidence that the project's findings hold promise for utilization by civic, governmental, or industrial entities responsible for planning, and/or decision making in matters related to the project. This evidence should be as specific as possible, naming persons and organizations contacted, quoting or attaching to the Appendix (see F below) their expressions of interest and the like.

(5) A description of the student group that organized the group submitting the proposal and how this was accomplished. (Was it, for example, a science club, an individual, an informal group of concerned students, or who?); how the topic or topics were selected:

- the number of participants for whom support is being requested (with any special justification required);
- who has already been selected to participate in the project (a brief curriculum vitae for each principal participant should be included in the Appendix, emphasizing any previous experience in research or project-oriented studies);
- the disciplinary distribution and balancing of skills to be sought in filling remaining vacancies on the SOS team, by what criteria the remaining participants will be chosen, methods for recruiting participants from other institutions if this is to be done (or if not, the factors that decided the group

against it); the function of the student Steering Committee or reason for not having such a committee;

- any other details that will assist reviewers to understand the personnel aspects of the project. (Curricula vitae should appear in the Appendix.)

(6) Presummer preparation of individuals and coordination of their efforts prior to formal initiation of the study.

Time and work schedules are important. They show that you know where you're going and how you intend to get there.

(7) A time schedule for the project in outline form, sufficient to convince reviewers that realistic consideration has been given to the amount of work contemplated relative to available time and personnel.

More personnel information.

(8) The Project Advisor—name; description of the process by which the advisor was nominated by the students; statement of institution's confirmation of the nomination; curriculum vitae showing highlights of his or her academic training, scholarly productivity, and other qualifications for advising the group.

Facilities are important. If you can't prove that you have the facilities and equipment to do the project, your proposal is not likely to be accepted.

(9) A description of the institutional facilities (including the library) and equipment, specifically identifying what is to be available for use in the SOS project, and its adequacy for the project's needs.

(F) *Appendix—*

See Figure 15.5. Detailed information about personnel, facilities, and other aspects of the proposal is often presented in an appendix.

(1) Curricula vitae of Student Project Director and other principal participants already selected, following the format set forth on page 17.

Note, too, the possibility of including testimonials, again a good selling technique. In many instances a bibliography can be a good way of showing that you have done your homework. (See Chapter 22, Documenting Sources.)

(2) Supportive statements or materials that bear on the expected quality of the proposed project. This evidence should be as specific as possible. Testimonials are useful only if written by local authorities who possess detailed factual information concerning the problem and current efforts to deal with it. Broad, general statements of support from officials remote from the problem or policy issue under investigation are of little value.

(3) Bibliography of sources consulted in background research during preparation of the proposal. The inclusion of key references here will assure reviewers as to the thoroughness of the group's preliminary study.

Remember that the proposal is a persuasive document. Emphasize the value and quality of your own products and services. Point out the unique advantages offered by the experience and education of the members of your organization. If possible, provide testimonials covering your previous work or the work of the organization you work for. Use a persuasive argument and problem-solving techniques in the proposal. Provide information that shows you understand the problem and what is expected from you and your organization to solve the problem. Adapt the questions identified in Figure 15.1 to help you develop the proposal. Present your facts and the implications of those facts in a thorough and attractive manner.

CURRICULUM VITAE FORMAT FOR
STUDENT PROJECT DIRECTORS AND PARTICIPANTS

Name: _____
             (Last)   (First)   (Middle)

Present Institution: _____

Other Institutions Attended: _____

Major Field(s): _____ Minor(s): _____

Class: _____

Courses already completed which are relevant to proposed project (Faculty advisor will please submit in confidence grades for students in those institutions where policy prohibits their being shown to students.):

Course Title	Grade	Course Title	Grade

Additional relevant courses to be completed before project begins:

Previous experience in research or project-oriented studies:

Skills, hobbies, interests pertinent to the proposed study:

Please note briefly why you wish to participate in the projected studies:

Figure 15.5 Curriculum vitae form.

When preparing a solicited proposal, take care to follow precisely the required organization—even if you don't like it. Use headings (with corresponding numerals, if given) that correspond to information asked for in the RFP. (Figure 5.13 illustrates how you can pull the headings out of the description if they are not given.) The requesters will be looking for information in the places where they have specified they want it. Make special note of the date the proposal is due. To be fair to everyone submitting a proposal, a set day and time (usually the normal close of business hours for the organization that issued the RFP) are announced. Rarely will your proposal be accepted if it is late—even a couple of minutes late.

UNSOLICITED PROPOSALS

Unsolicited proposals are much like solicited ones. Essentially, they each require the same information, with one major difference. In a solicited proposal the solicitors recognize a need. Therefore, you don't have to sell them on the need, only on your ability to understand and interpret the need and to meet it. In an unsolicited proposal you must first convince the audience the need exists. If you can't, they will have no particular interest in your goods or services.

For example, a roofing contractor called in by a homeowner to bid on reshingling a roof does not have to establish the need for the job. But an enterprising contractor who sees a roof in need of repair may have to convince the owner that reshingling is necessary. Often, establishing a need calls for a problem-solving organization. The problem establishes the need. Your goods or services supply the solution.

When preparing an unsolicited proposal, you can devise your own organization. A small, simple, unsolicited proposal might fall into six parts:

1. *Summary*—provides a concise statement of the proposal

2. *Introduction*—establishes need

3. *Overview section*—defines the process to be followed or describes the goods to be furnished, or both

4. *Work and management plan*—outlines the tasks to be done and schedules their accomplishment

5. *Detailed budget*—gives precise information on costs

6. *Personnel section*—briefly gives the relevant qualifications of the people involved

Often, short proposals are drafted in the form of a letter or memorandum. Even so, headings and applicable visuals should be used—particularly easy-to-read informal lists and tables.

The proposal in Figure 15.6, modeled after an actual successful proposal, follows the six steps just outlined. Take the time to read it now.

Battle Creek College

Kellogg, Michigan 48108   **Department of Criminal Justice Studies**

DATE: December 10, 1999

TO: Janice H. Grumbacher, Director
        Center for Educational Development
        317 Clark Library

FROM: Martin A. Doyle M.D.
        Student, Criminal Justice Studies

RE: Request for Funding a Peer Advising Program for Criminal Justice Studies Students

Project Summary (A)

A survey shows that students and faculty in Criminal Justice Studies (CJS) favor the concept of peer advising. Peer advising is being successfully used in other colleges in the United States. This proposal requests $3,926 to set up an operational experiment in peer advising in CJS. The experiment would run for 13 months from May 2000 through May 2001. The experiment will be monitored by senior CJS faculty. Evaluative reports will be written and disseminated at the end of the experiment.

Introduction (B)

A new development in many two- and four-year colleges is the successful use of students for advising their fellow students regarding course registration, program development, and job opportunities. Called peer advising, this new development supplements but does not replace normal faculty advising.

In the Fall of this year, I surveyed the faculty and students of the Department of Criminal Justice Studies regarding their opinions about peer advising. A complete copy of the survey results, "Response to Peer Advising in the Department of Criminal Justice Studies," is available from me upon request. The results can be summarized briefly:

- Rightly or wrongly, many students believe they are imposing upon their advisers' time by seeking assistance. Some students view their advisers as having more important matters to contend with.

- Students believe that peer advisers will be better able to relate to the problems of their fellow students.

- Students stated frequently that they would feel freer and more comfortable in bringing their problems to peer advisers.

- Faculty acceptance of peer advising was high. Most believed it would be a welcome addition for both faculty and students.

Figure 15.6 Example of an unsolicited proposal. The letters next to the headings correspond to comments about the sections, pages 417–418.

Page 2
Janice H. Grumbacher
December 10, 1999

The study showed such strong support for peer advising among faculty and students that such a program seems to have a good potential for success. If successful, peer advising will remove a significant burden from the CJS faculty, freeing them for additional time to pursue their teaching and professional development. The experiment may lead to similar innovative advising techniques in other departments of the college.

In the remainder of this proposal, I describe the program and how it will be established (the methodology), a work and management plan, a detailed budget, and the qualifications of the key personnel involved.

Description of the Program (C)

If instituted, peer advising will be conducted for 13 months as an operational experiment. A peer advising unit of two students will be set up in Spring 2000. William Morrell, Chief Adviser for CJS, has agreed to train the two peer advisers and to supervise the program through the year. Beginning in Fall 2000, regular office hours will be maintained with one or both peer advisers present at all times.

The advising unit will deal with

- registration and scheduling difficulties
- guidance on classes and instructors
- sequence of classes and prerequisites
- recommended classes
- questions on the CJS program
- information for potential majors
- information on jobs and placement
- information on University services and agencies

The peer advising unit will work closely with

- current faculty advisers
- the director of CJS
- Admissions and Records

The peer advising unit will collect statistics and information on

- number of students
- types of problems dealt with
- where and who solved the problems
- feedback from CJS students and faculty

In the Spring of 2000 the peer advisers will prepare a full evaluation consolidating all the data collected and presenting conclusions concerning the potential of peer advising in CJS. William Morrell will prepare a separate evaluation of the program. Both evaluations will be submitted to Dr. Carlos Montoya, Director of CJS; Dr. Mary Baker, Dean of the College of Arts and Sciences; and your office.

Figure 15.6 (continued)

Page 3
Janice H. Grumbacher
December 10, 1999

Dr. Montoya and Dean Baker will decide whether to continue the peer advising in CJS or not. Dean Baker will also consider the possibility of peer advising in other departments of the College.

Work and Management Plan

This section provides details on the facilities, the task breakdown, and management of the peer advising program.

Facilities (D).   Dr. Montoya has agreed to provide an office for the peer advising unit. The office will be located in an area easily accessible to CJS students. CJS will furnish the office with a desk, telephone, filing cabinet, bookshelves, a swivel desk chair, three straight chairs, a computer, and a computer table. The peer advisers will have the use of CJS office supplies, including stamps and stationery.

Task Breakdown (E).   There will be three major tasks: training, holding office hours, and evaluating the program. The accompanying graph shows the task timetable.

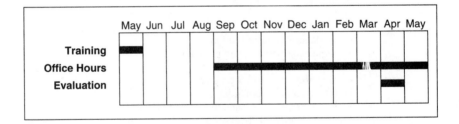

Training.   In May 2000, William Morrell will give the two peer advisers 10 hours of training in advising procedures to include filling out registration forms and procedures for adding and dropping courses. He will provide information concerning other college programs, particularly those that provide aid in needed study skills such as note taking,

reading, listening, and library research. He will aid the peer advisers in learning the interpersonal communication skills needed for effective advising.

Office Hours.   September 3, 2000–May 28, 2001. Office hours will be scheduled from 11 a.m. to 2 p.m., Monday through Friday, holidays and school breaks excluded. During each of the heavy advising months of September and January, an additional 20 hours of advising time will be scheduled and two advisers will be present during peak hours.

Evaluation.   April 1–30, 2001. During April 2001, the two peer advisers will consolidate the information they have gathered throughout the year and write their evaluation report. A total of 16 hours is scheduled for this task.

Figure 15.6 (continued)

Page 4
Janice H. Grumbacher
December 10, 1999

Management (F).   William Morrell will supervise the entire peer advising experiment as part of his duties as Coordinator of Advisers for the CJS program. He will be readily accessible to the peer advisers. He will monitor their procedures and provide advice and counsel when needed. Throughout the year he will provide informal reports to Dr. Montoya. At the end of the experiment he will provide an evaluation of the peer advising program.

Budget (G)

Because CJS is furnishing office space, office supplies, and clerical help, the entire budget needed is for salary for the two peer advisers. The normal student hourly wage of $6.50 per hour is requested. The budget breaks down in the following manner:

Training Time	Salary for 2 peer advisers	20 hours	$130.00
Office Hours	Salary for 3 hours of advising a day for 176 days	528 hours	3,432.00
	Salary for additional advising time in September and January	40 hours	260.00
Evaluation Time	Salary	16 hours	104.00
	TOTAL	604 hours	$3,926.00

The budgeted $3,926 will be divided equally between the two peer advisers. If this grant request is approved, your office is requested to transfer $130 to the CJS budget in April 2000 and the remaining $3,796 in September 2000. Normal college accounting procedures will be used by CJS to account for expenditures.

Personnel (H)

I request that I be one of the peer advisers. In March 2000, the other peer adviser will be chosen from among applicants for the job by a secret ballot of the CJS students.

My qualifications are as follows. After graduation from high school in 1992, I served four years in the U.S. Air Force as a police officer. I left the service with the rank of sergeant. From November 1997 to the present I have been a sheriff's deputy in Battle Creek County. I am currently working half-time while I complete my CJS studies. I have a special interest in counseling. To develop myself in this area, I have taken Social Science 1104, Dynamics of Small Groups, and I am currently taking Social Science 2111, Interpersonal Communication. My current grade point average is 3.2.

William Morrell, who will supervise the program, is Coordinator of Advisers for CJS. Before taking his degree in Criminal Justice Studies at the University of Washington, he was a police officer with the Seattle, Washington, Police Department for eight years. He also has a Master's degree in Educational Administration from the University of North Dakota. With Battle Creek College for the past six years, Morrell has been Coordinator of Advisers since 1995.

Figure 15.6 (continued)

Page 5
Janice H. Grumbacher
December 10, 1999

Conclusion (I)

Evidence gathered at other schools indicates that peer advising is successful—a positive benefit to students, faculty, and the school. I have reports concerning established programs at two major universities that I will send to you at your request. Preliminary studies here indicate that both faculty and students favor peer advising in CJS.

I will be happy to discuss this proposal with you at your convenience. I will be open to any modifications in the plan you might suggest.

copy: William Morrell
     Dr. Carlos Montoya
     Dean Mary Baker

Figure 15.6 (continued)

The letters next to the headings in the model proposal correspond to the following comments.

A. *Project Summary.* The proposal is set up in a memorandum format commonly used for short proposals. It includes, as do most proposals, a summary of the proposal. Executives like to have a concise statement of a proposal before they study it in detail. You will impress them favorably if you compress the major points of your proposal into a short summary.

B. *Introduction.* The beginning of the introduction defines the subject, peer advising, and points out its successful use elsewhere. The survey presented shows that early and careful planning has taken place. The results of the survey do not show that an outright problem of student dissatisfaction exists. The results do show that students might feel more comfortable with another approach. The survey results also set to rest the thought that the faculty might object. The statement about more faculty time and possible innovative advising techniques presents significant *so-whats*.

C. *Description of the Program.* A description of the program, the methodology, outlines the strategy and some of the timing of the operational experiment. Again it shows that a good deal of thought has gone into the proposal. The final paragraph again suggests that the money spent for the proposal may result in a new and more desirable advising procedure than currently exists. Such a development is likely to please the Center for Educational Development, an organization charged with developing innovative methods to improve the college's educational process.

D. *Facilities.* Facilities must be explained somewhere. In a simple report like this one, the work and management plan is a good location. If facilities were extensive, they would rate a section of their own.

E. *Task Breakdown.* The tasks to be accomplished are presented in a chronological sequence. A simple visual shows the time relationship of the tasks.

F. *Management.* Proper management is always a concern. People want to know that the spending of their money will be overseen by experienced, responsible managers.

G. *Detailed Budget.* The budget is presented in a simple table form. Don't overlook any possible expenses. Figure 15.4 provides a good checklist. If appropriate, specify the time and method of payment. Tell how the money will be accounted for.

H. *Personnel.* In a simple proposal, a short narrative biography that gives relevant education and experience is usually enough. Use your sales skills here. The facts chosen for the student's biography emphasize his maturity and experience. The two courses listed establish an interest in counseling that is a strong selling point for the project. The information on William Morrell establishes his credibility as a supervisor and points out that the project will have high-level direction.

I. *Conclusion.* The conclusion resells the proposal. It emphasizes previous successes for peer advising and offers to provide evidence for this claim. Indicating flexibility and the willingness to negotiate is also important. Often proposals can't be carried out exactly as proposed.

Proposals are unique documents. They combine the skills needed for information giving, analysis, and persuasion. Remember, too, they are legal documents. Whatever you say you will do, you must do. You can be held legally accountable. More than likely you have signed a contract confirming the cost of the project and the work to be done. The satisfaction of writing a successful proposal is considerable. When someone gives you money on the strength of a proposal you have written, you have direct evidence of your writing and persuasive skills.

PROPOSAL FOR A PAPER

Frequently instructors ask students to propose what they intend to do for their major term report. Many of the principles used in writing business proposals can be applied equally well in such proposals for papers. Such a proposal will assure you and your instructor that you know where you are heading and will not waste time and energy following dead-end paths. Also, it is an excellent rehearsal for the larger proposals discussed in this chapter.

Figure 15.7 is an example of such a proposal. Look at Figure 15.7 before reading the rest of this chapter.

SUBJECT, PURPOSE, AND AUDIENCE OF THE PROPOSED PAPER

A proposal for a paper should clearly state the subject, purpose, and audience for the paper. To introduce her subject and purpose, Ann Osborn briefly defines the problem she proposes to address. For a different kind of paper, a set of instructions, for example, the writer might describe the paper to be written and explain its purpose. Ann next specifies her audience, in this case the Director of the Technical Communication Computer Center. For a class project, the audience may be fictional or, as in Ann's case, a real person with use for the proposal. If at all possible, a real audience is best because you can identify the specific information your reader needs. Rarely, the audience will be the instructor to whom the proposal is addressed.

METHODOLOGY AND RESOURCES FOR RESEARCHING AND PRODUCING THE PAPER

Your reader will want to know how you plan to carry out your work and what your resources are. In her methodology and resources section, Ann describes the results of her preliminary research into the problem and proposes the solutions she intends to examine. She does not suggest that one

Date: February 2, 2000

To: Professor Richard Cohen
           302 Haecker Hall

From: Ann Osborn   *A.O.*
           Campus Box 342

Subject: Proposal for a report on the feasibility of protecting the Technical Communication Computer
           Center from new computer viruses

I propose to conduct and report on a study on how to best protect the Technical Communication
Computer Center (TCCC) from destructive computer viruses.

The viruses enter the lab across the campus network and through student and faculty disks that have
been contaminated. While the campus network administrators, students, and faculty may take
precautions, we can do more in the TCCC to protect the computers.

The audience for my report will be Carole K. Yang, the Director of TCCC. Yang has an M.S. in
Management of Information Systems and five years experience working in computer labs.

Plan and Resources

My preliminary research indicates that to be feasible any protection plan will involve at least four stages:

1) Gather information on the new viruses: how they operate, how they can be detected, and what
   virus-detection programs protect most effectively against them.

2) Train the TCCC technical support staff on installation and management of the virus protection
   programs and develop instructions for users of the computers in TCCC.

3) Develop an action plan that will go into effect the instant a virus is detected in the TCCC.

4) Submit a plan for routine monitoring and upgrades to the virus protection system.

For this study and report, I will gather information needed in the first stage. I will then use the
information to prepare ways of accomplishing the second, third, and fourth stages.

In my initial search, I have found good sources in the library as well as people with knowledge that will
be helpful. My sources include:

- Steven Levy, *Hackers.* New York: Dell, 1985.

- Ann Mendocino, Director, University Computing Services.

- Paul Mungo and Bryan Clough, "The Bulgarian Connection," *Discover* February 1993: 54–61.

- Andrew Rosenberg, Associate Professor, Management of Information Systems.

- Clifford Stoll, *The Cuckoo's Egg: Inside the World of Computer Espionage.* New York:
  Doubleday, 1989.

Figure 15.7 **Student's proposal for a paper—in this example, a recommendation report.**

2

Schedule

Week of Semester	Task
5th week	Complete research and planning
6th week	Submit organizational plan for report
7th–9th weeks	Draft report
10th–11th weeks	Revise report
12th week	Submit final report

Credentials

I am a Management of Information Systems major. My course work has made me familiar with computer programming and the problems of computer viruses. I have worked part time for both Computer Information Services and the TCCC. I have experience in detecting and destroying computer viruses.

copy: Carole K. Yang

Figure 15.7 (continued)

solution might be superior to another. If in preparing the proposal for your paper you have done enough research to suggest a favored solution, you may do so. However, be careful not to eliminate options that further research may prove better than the one chosen.

The writer's resources are a list of articles and people that her preliminary research show to be valuable. Some instructors like an annotated bibliography that describes what information each source provides. In any case, the resource section must be complete enough to convince the instructor that you have made a good start on your study and that you know where to find relevant information.

SCHEDULE OF WORK

In most proposals for a paper, the schedule of work need not be elaborate. As Ann has done, indicate the major milestones in your work and propose a completion date for each. If there are some complications to the schedule, you might consider showing it in a table or other visual, such as a flow chart (see Chapters 5, 6, and 7).

CREDENTIALS FOR DOING THE PAPER

Finally, you should state why you are qualified to carry out the work proposed. Ann states both the academic and work credentials that provide evidence that she can do what she proposes to do. Credentials should not be overblown, but they should be complete enough to convince the instructor that you will not get bogged down for lack of knowledge, skill, or experience.

PLANNING AND REVISING CHECKLIST: PROPOSALS

Think about the following as you plan and revise a proposal.

PLANNING

Proposals, like recommendation reports, often deal with problems and their solutions. Therefore, you must frequently begin your planning by defining the problem and creating several solutions for it, much as we describe the process in the recommendation report checklist on pages 396–398. If your proposal is a solicited proposal, be sure to read and follow the RFP directions carefully. Plan answers for all the questions asked and note carefully the format required.

- What problem(s) does your proposal aim to solve?

- What solution or solutions are you proposing? What are the *so-whats* of your solutions? In what ways do they benefit your readers?

- Who are the readers of your proposal? What is their purpose in reading it? Do you have several readers, perhaps some with differing needs?

- Will the readers have problems with any of the technical vocabulary in the proposal?

- What will be the readers' reaction to the proposal? Enthusiastic? Indifferent? Skeptical? What can you do to counteract negative reactions and reinforce positive ones?

- What will be your methods in carrying out the work proposed? How will you do the work?

- What facilities and equipment will you need? Who will furnish them? Are needed equipment and facilities readily available?

- What is your schedule of work? Can you show your schedule in a visual?

- How will the project be managed? Who will be the manager?

- What is the cost of what you are proposing? Who pays what? What are the details of the budget?

- Who will do the work proposed? Why are they fitted to do the work?

REVISING

In revision, pay attention to organization, content, style, format, and grammar.

Organization and Content

- Have you provided a summary that can stand by itself for a busy reader?

- Does your introduction make clear the problem you propose to solve?

- If appropriate, does your introduction describe your proposed solutions?

- Does your introduction define any terms or concepts your readers may find difficult?

- Does your introduction state a few significant *so-whats* to interest your readers in reading further?

- Does your methodology section make clear the strategy and timing of the methods you will use? Can any significant *so-whats* be mentioned here?

- Is your work schedule clear? Would a visual help?

- Is your budget complete? Are all expenses accounted for and justified?

- Will the facts presented convince your readers that the people proposed to carry out the work will do a competent job?

Style

- Have you achieved clarity and conciseness?

- Is your vocabulary appropriate to your subject and audience?

Format and Grammar

- Have you chosen the most appropriate format? Report, letter, or memo?

- Is your proposal neat and free from errors?

- Have you used an effective document design to obtain a good layout with some typographical interest?

- Have you provided sufficient headings to guide the reader through the proposal?

- If you have used a report format, do your table of contents and headings match?

SUGGESTIONS FOR APPLYING YOUR KNOWLEDGE

Proposals provide a rich field for both long and short writing assignments and for class discussion.

- You could submit a proposal for a paper such as the one illustrated in Figure 15.7.

- Short proposals can be bids. You can bid to furnish products or services in construction, research, interior design, food service, health services, and so forth. You could bid to build a porch, install track lighting, furnish carpets or drapes, or cater a party. The possibilities are enormous. The proposals can come from school work or off-campus work or some combination of the two. Include only information absolutely relevant to the bid, such as what is to be furnished, by whom, and at what cost. You might also include a few sales touches such as experience and testimonials.

- Long proposals could be a term project. Like short proposals, they could relate to major fields of study or to off-campus work. They could relate to community problems. They could involve extensive research in the area involved, perhaps even including surveys and interviews, as in the model proposal about peer advising. In long proposals you would have more sections, such as facilities, equipment, schedules, and personnel. You would establish the need for the product or service offered. You would promote your ability to fulfill the terms of the proposal. You would devise an organization and a format that present your proposal in the best way possible.

- Long proposals can also be team or even class projects. There are certainly enough sections to go around. You could even try a proposal that is real and not just an exercise. Most colleges have an office that deals in grants. You could go to the grants office in your college and see if they have any student-oriented requests. The NSF solicitation used as an example in this chapter was just such a request. Or search the World Wide Web for requests for proposals. If you find such an RFP, it might be a stimulating group project that could end in real accomplishment.

- Long proposals frequently have to be sold with an oral presentation as well as a written document. They provide good applications of persuasive speaking skills.

- A good deal of material can be gathered for class discussion. The grants office at your college or university will likely have on hand out-of-date requests for proposals they would be happy to let you have. These requests can furnish material for good class discussions as you analyze the types of information, organization, and format they call for. They provide fine examples of our constant theme: workplace writing provides specific information to a specific audience for a specific purpose. Compare and contrast the organizational plans and formats called for. You can learn from all of them, but decide which ones are best, and why. If you cannot obtain actual proposals submitted by various units of your college or by companies in your area, go to Web sites for government agencies, companies, and organizations to find current requests for proposals. Discussion of how they were researched, organized, and written will help you learn how to do your own proposals. The originator of the proposal might be willing to enter into the discussion.

CHAPTER 16

MECHANISM DESCRIPTION

Mechanism description explains the purpose, appearance, physical structure, and sometimes the operation or behavior of a mechanism. The word *mechanism,* as used here, refers to any object that takes up space and behaves in a predictable manner or performs work. In this sense, a driver's license is as much a mechanism as is a clutch or an automobile. A mechanism or object can be small or large, simple or complex, artificial or natural. It can be so large that we cannot see it in its entirety with our naked eye. It also can be so small, so fleeting, so far away, so deeply hidden that we cannot see it without the assistance of special cameras and recording devices used with computers, electron microscopes, and powerful telescopes. Hand tools (scissors, pen, nail punch), devices (oil pump, artesian well, electric dust extractor, geodetic satellite, tesla coil, laser printer), natural objects (egg, knee joint, flower, kidney, meteor, volcano, paramecium), and synthetic objects (the molecular arrangement of fluorocarbons, olean, the plastic in milk cartons) suggest the wide range of mechanisms. In addition, the layout of a wastewater treatment plant or the floor plan of an office complex or an abstract entity such as the Federal Reserve System might also be regarded as mechanisms.

The world we live in is highly artificial and engineered—from crossbreeding and cloning of animals and plants to improved roadways and measuring systems. Mechanisms may even be otherwise unseeable until they are described. Scientists often work with entities that cannot be seen by optical means, especially in the world of astronomy, physics, and molecular biology. The shape and size of atoms, the double helix structure of DNA, the synaptic ends of nerves, black holes, and many concepts of modern physics and molecular biology cannot be seen directly, but they can be objectified and visualized from data that convince us that they are present. Mechanism description is an important means of conveying evidence of their presence and of making visible to the mind what may not be visible to the eye.

At work, at home, at leisure, we are surrounded by mechanisms and objects. To evaluate them or use them, we need to know all their functions, features, and how their parts work together or relate to one another. Mechanism description helps meet our need to know.

Regardless of the mechanism or object to be described, the main problems confronting you when you describe it are (1) how much information to provide, (2) how best to create an image of the mechanism or object in your readers' minds, and (3) how to arrange the details of the description.

DECIDING HOW MUCH INFORMATION TO PROVIDE

One of the universal problems of mechanism description is the decision of how much information to provide. You can potentially include so much in the description that it becomes unacceptably long and provides information that readers cannot use. You must select what information to include and what to leave out. Four familiar considerations face you immediately when you prepare to describe a mechanism or object:

1. What is the purpose of your description?

2. Who is your audience?

3. How familiar is your audience with the mechanism or object?

4. What is the audience's purpose in reading the description?

Mechanism description is always selective. You probably will never describe a mechanism or object just to describe it. The information about it you include depends on whether you are describing it to readers who will approve its manufacture, make it, buy it, ship it, store it, operate it, evaluate it, repair it, or in some instances, identify it well enough to locate it. You must focus on what is important.

A special use of mechanism description is the detailed description required in patent applications, conventionally referred to as the "description of the preferred embodiment."[1] A major part of a patent application is a description of an invention in "full, clear, concise, and exact terms" that "distinguish the invention from other inventions and from what is old" and describes "completely the process, machine, manufacture, composition of matter, or improvement invented."[2]

Mechanisms have specially designed features built into them that are important to readers, and describing these features is one of your most important tasks. You do not want to burden readers with unnecessary information, but you also don't want to omit meaningful information. Sometimes it is difficult to determine when simply to state a feature and when to explain its significance. You must estimate how familiar your readers are with the concepts you are describing. For instance, if it is important to point out that a certain element is made of tungsten, is it also necessary to explain the *so-what*—that tungsten is used because of its hardness and its capability to withstand corrosives and high temperatures? Or, in another example, if there must be a clearance of 18 inches above a device, is it important to explain that that much clearance is needed to open the top cover of the device? In a way, you walk the tightrope between the legal maxim that "the fact speaks for itself" and the often-proclaimed scientific principle that "a fact in itself is nothing."

Because you know so well the features of the mechanism you describe, it may be difficult for you to remember that such knowledge might appear isolated and unimportant to your readers unless you explain the importance of the feature. How many readers do you think would have

[1] *A Guide to Filing a Utility Patent Application* (Washington: US Dept. of Commerce, Patent and Trademark Office, Mar. 1998) 5.
[2] *A Guide to Filing* 5.

the technical background to understand the significance of the following information?

> The protective shroud is made of 3003 aluminum and is flared to the outer edges as shown in Figure 7.

Providing a couple of additional sentences explains the *so-whats,* the significance, of the features (the composition of the material and the tapered design):

> The 3003 aluminum is used because it is malleable, resists corrosion, and is lightweight. Flaring the outer edge of the shroud extends the heating surface to the outer edge of the shroud.

Of course, you might need to elaborate further and explain why the material should be malleable and lightweight and resist corrosion, and why the heating surface should extend to the outer edge of the shroud.*

Let us look at an example of how you can be sure you know enough about the features to explain them to readers. Assume that you are describing an electric paper shredder that reduces paper to unreadable ¼-inch strips and that you want to point out several important features. In preparing your notes, you might find the following two-column format handy. The left column identifies the feature, and the right column identifies the significance of the feature: the *so-what.*

Feature	Significance
1. Built-in shredder continuously feeds through the shredder	Works automatically, without supervision.
2. 3/4 hp motor	Has 70 percent more shredding power than most other models, shreds 14 sheets of 20-lb. bond paper at one time.
3. 12″ throat	Accepts computer printout pages.
4. Hardened cutter blades	Cannot be damaged by conventional staples and paper clips.
5. 10″ high × 21″ wide × 22″ deep	Compact and small enough to use on table or desk top.
6. Soft rubber feet	Won't mar furniture.
7. Brown, gray, or beige finish	Fits most office decors and color schemes.

When you mention the features in your presentation, immediately explain the significance of the feature so that it has meaning to your readers. The two-column format will do, or you can combine the information like this:

The Shredmaster 180 has seven major features:

- Built-in shredder continuously feeds forms through the shredder. Works automatically and without supervision.

- ¾ hp motor has 70 percent more shredding power than most other models. Shreds 14 sheets of 20-lb. bond paper at one time.

---

*You should know this level of detailed information in case it is important to provide it for readers. So as you plan your description, ask yourself if you know the significance, importance, or implications of such features. If you don't then you need to research those matters.

- 12″ throat accepts computer printout pages.

- Hardened cutter blades cannot be damaged by conventional staples or paper clips.

- Size—10″ high × 21″ wide × 22″ deep—small enough to use on a table or desk top.

- Soft rubber feet won't mar furniture.

- Brown, gray, or beige finish matches most office decors and color schemes.

When you review and revise your description, keep asking yourself if your intended reader is likely to need certain features translated into more meaningful terms. By doing so, you will ensure that your readers will take in the full meaning of what you say about the mechanism. Concern about insulting the intelligence of your readers by providing information that they already know is often overemphasized. Even readers who understand the significance or importance of a feature will likely appreciate the reminder and proceed to skip over the material they know. However, readers who don't know the significance or importance of a feature will need the information if they are to understand fully the concept you are describing.

DESCRIBING A FAMILIAR MECHANISM

If your purpose is to remind readers of the major features and parts of a mechanism with which they are somewhat familiar, you can rely on visuals to describe its appearance and on a few words to describe its materials, connections, and functions. Figure 16.1 is a description of a device provided by the manufacturer to acquaint customers with their purchase. The description, appearing at the front of the customer's manual for the blender, is brief, yet sufficient for its purpose, and well organized. The mechanism is described in terms of its major parts and their functions.

DESCRIBING AN UNFAMILIAR MECHANISM

Often your purpose will be to acquaint readers with mechanisms or objects with which they are unfamiliar. In such cases you will need to explain more thoroughly the purpose, physical structure, and use or operation of the mechanism. Let us assume, for instance, that you are introducing a group of students or field assistants to a device they must know forward and backward—the Berlese funnel, a common collection device used by entomologists to collect and test samples for insect habitation (Figure 16.2).[3]

The description of the Berlese funnel provides more detail than does the description for the Oster liquefier-blender in Figure 16.1. The extent to which a mechanism or object is to be described (and consequently, the length of the mechanism description) depends on what readers need to

[3]From an unpublished student report, used with permission of the author, Jim Johnson.

Know Your *Osterizer*
LIQUEFIER-BLENDER

cover

The cover for your Osterizer blender consists of two parts, the plastic feeder cap (1) and the vinyl cover (2). The cover is self-sealing and is made of vinyl and resistant to absorption of odors and stains. The feeder cap is removable for use as a measuring cap and provides an opening for the addition of other ingredients.

container

The 5-cup container (3) for the Osterizer blender is graduated for easy measurement and is molded of heat and cold resistant material. The convenient handle and pouring lip permit easy removal of liquid mixtures, while thicker mixtures are more easily removed through the bottom opening.

agitator or processing assembly

Consists of three parts: (4) a sealing ring of neoprene used as a cushion between the container and the agitator; (5) agitator of high-grade stainless steel; (6) a threaded container bottom.

motor and motor base

The powerful multi-speed motor is the heart of the appliance and designed just for this unit. It is completely enclosed within the housing (7).

The Osterizer blender motor uses a "free-floating" feature to reduce noise and wear. This feature allows the square post which protrudes from the motor base to move slightly from side to side.

Your Osterizer blender contains a powerful food processing motor, but it can be overloaded. To avoid this possibility, closely follow the instructions and the quantities specified in the recipes in this book.

The illustration and photography of Osterizer blenders found in this book do not necessarily depict the particular model Osterizer blender that you have purchased. These photographs are merely a guide to illustrate the versatility of your Osterizer blender.

care and cleaning of your Osterizer blender

Never store foods in your Osterizer blender container. Always remove the agitator assembly and wash and dry container and agitator assembly thoroughly after you have finished blending. Re-assemble container after cleaning so it will be ready for future use. Never place processing assembly on motor base without the container. See page 2 for proper assembly and tightening instructions.

Osterizer blender parts are corrosion resistant, sanitary, and easily cleaned. Wash in warm, soapy water and dry thoroughly. DO NOT WASH ANY PARTS IN AN AUTOMATIC DISHWASHER.

NEVER IMMERSE THE MOTOR BASE IN WATER. It does not require oiling. Its outside can be cleaned with a damp cloth (unplug cordset first).

©Oster Corporation, 1975, Milwaukee, Wisconsin 53217. *Oster, Osterizer, Pulse-Matic, T.M. Mini-Blend, Cyclomatic, Spin Cooker.

203287-Rev.-N   [1]

Figure 16.1 The first page of manufacturer's booklet describing a product (Courtesy Oster Corporation). The description is brief, yet sufficient for its purpose and is well organized. The two-column format, placing an exploded view of the blender to the right of the written description, enables readers to move back and forth from the writing to the pictures with ease. The headings and numbered parts help readers identify parts.
Source: Know Your Osterizer Liquefier-Blender, 203287-Rev-N, page 1. Reprinted with permission of Sunbeam Oster Corporation.

The Berlese Funnel

You have several methods for sampling soil, leaves, or trash for insect habitation. You can simply pick out insects from a sample by hand, use a sieve to separate insects from a sample, or "bake" insects from a sample by using the Berlese funnel. The first two methods are not always satisfactory, because some insects will probably be overlooked. When an absolute count of the insects is required, use the Berlese funnel, named after the Italian entomologist who invented it in 1912. The Berlese funnel uses heat from an incandescent bulb to dry the sample and force the insects to burrow away from the heat source and ultimately drop through a funnel into a collection jar. Although Berlese funnels vary in size, depending on how large a sample needs testing, they all have the same parts and appearance and work the same way. As shown in Figure 1, the three main parts of a workbench-sized Berlese funnel capable of holding up to a half gallon sample are (1) the cover, (2) the container, and (3) the stand. Its overall height is 15 inches.

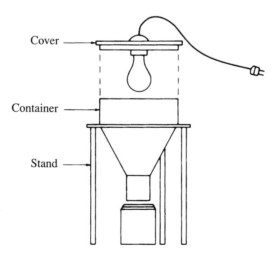

Figure 1. The main parts of the Berlese funnel
and the collection jar

Figure 16.2 Description of a mechanism involves both written and visual description. For such description, you will have to select the details to include and what to omit, based primarily on what you believe readers will need or want to know. Notice the placement of visuals and the references and labeling of the parts.
Source: An unpublished student report, used with permission of the author, Jim Johnson.

The Cover

The metal cover (Figure 2) resembles a miniature trash can lid. It covers the container and serves as a mount for the 100-watt bulb. Air vents in the cover allow excess heat to escape and enable you to observe the sample without removing the cover. A 1/2-inch flange holds the cover in place.

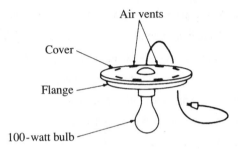

Figure 2. The cover

The Container

The container (Figure 3), which fits into the steel retaining ring of the stand, is divided into an upper and a lower section. The upper section is the 4-1/2-inch deep plastic reservoir that holds the sample, and the lower section is the plastic funnel through which the insects drop into the collection jar. A galvanized screen with a 1/4-inch mesh, upon which the sample is placed, separates the two sections. The container has an overall height of eleven inches and a diameter of 8-1/2 inches before narrowing to a diameter of 1 inch at the bottom of the funnel.

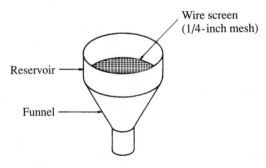

Figure 3. The container

Figure 16.2 (continued)

The Stand

The stand (Figure 4) supports the container and allows room for the collection jar to be placed beneath the funnel. It is composed of a 1/2-inch steel retaining ring with a 9-inch diameter into which the sample container is placed and of three legs made of 1/2-inch steel cylinders 11 inches long. The legs are attached to the retaining ring by screws, allowing the stand to be disassembled for storage or transportation.

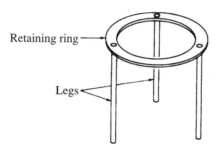

Figure 4. The stand

Using the Berlese Funnel

The Berlese funnel works like an oven. The heat from the 100-watt bulb "bakes" the sample, forcing the insects to seek a moister area. As the top of the sample dries, the insects burrow down toward the remaining moist sample. When the entire sample is dry, the insects have passed through the wire screen and dropped through the funnel into the collection jar. Depending on the size and dampness of the sample, it takes approximately 24 to 36 hours for the sample to dry thoroughly.

Figure 16.2 (continued)

know about the mechanism. If your purpose were to provide specifications so that someone could make the mechanism, you would need to include detailed information that would provide a pattern to be copied. Not even the most minor dimensions or features could be omitted. Once you have established in your mind the purpose of your description and what your readers need to know of the mechanism or object, you will know what and how much to include in your description.

HELPING READERS VISUALIZE THE MECHANISM

One of the major aims of mechanism description is to create for readers a clear mental picture of the mechanism or object you are describing. Thus, it is natural for you to want to show readers what it looks like. The four common ways of doing this are to use pictorials, adjectives and other modifiers, analogies, and geometric shapes.

USING PICTORIALS

When visual understanding is involved, pictorials (photographs and drawings) are the most exact method of communication. Verbal language, written or spoken, simply does not measure up to visual language in showing physical appearance and spatial relationship.

The old saying that "one picture is worth a thousand words" is true only if the picture is a good one and if it communicates better than words. Unless you are skilled in photography and drawing, you will need help in making pictorials. Digital cameras and graphics programs give you the tools to create pictorials; however, consider your level of proficiency and your time as well as your audience's expectations and the purpose of the document. If you have any doubts, have a professional graphic artist create the pictorials. If you work for an organization that has a presentations department that will do your artwork for you—count your blessings. If you do not, you must hire someone to do them. You may find an appropriate visual on the World Wide Web. Remember, though, to acknowledge your source if it is for a school paper. If you include borrowed visuals in a document that you plan to publish, you must get permission to use the visual, including those from sources on the World Wide Web. However, even when others prepare pictorials for you or you borrow a pictorial, you should know what defines a good one. You may be required to supply preliminary sketches to be made into finished pictorials. And, of course, as author of the document, you are also responsible for the quality of the pictorials.

The choice, execution, and placement of pictorials should be at least equal in importance to text when you plan your description. Determine what aspects of the object you want to convey, so that you can decide which type of pictorial best illustrates that information. Use as many visuals as necessary to show the mechanism or object: exploded views, sectional views, partial views, and separate views to show alternative positions of mechanisms or objects. For information about using visuals, see Chapters 6 and 7.

USING ADJECTIVES

As useful as visuals are, words (especially adjectives and other modifiers) are also essential in description. Adjectives describe visual appearance: *narrow, short, curved, round.* They also describe texture and other tactile features: *dry, sticky, bumpy, smooth, rough, sharp.* They describe sounds: *squeaky, screeching, hissing, high-pitched, humming,* and so forth. They also describe taste and odor: *acrid, sweet, sour, smoky.* When using adjectives, keep two goals in mind. First, be as specific as necessary to reduce ambiguity. For instance, *curved, crooked, undulating, wavy,* and *bent* are adjectives that describe lines or planes that are not straight. Because they are not synonyms, you should select the adjective that most accurately depicts the configuration you mean. Second, use adjectives that are familiar to your readers. For instance, *saw-toothed, serrated, crenelated, dentate,* and *dentiform* refer to tooth-shaped features or objects. *Oval, ovoid, elliptical,* and *ellipsoidal* refer to egg-shaped features or objects. Use adjectives that most readers are likely to recognize. *Coin-shaped* is a lot more familiar to most readers than are *nummiform* and *nummular.*

USING ANALOGIES

Suppose we want to describe something that we have seen for the first time or that our readers have never seen. How do we describe the unknown? Usually the best way is by comparing it to the known.

Can you remember the tremendous feeling of excitement when you first looked at objects under a microscope? Those magnified images revealed a world previously hidden from you. In 1665, Robert Hooke, a seventeenth-century English scientist, constructed a microscope that allowed him to examine many objects never before seen by the human eye. Below is part of his description of what he saw when he looked at a piece of outer bark of the cork oak with the microscope as he recorded it in *Micrographia* (1665). We have modernized the spelling.

> I took a good clear piece of cork, and with a pen knife sharpened as keen as a razor, I cut a piece of it off, and thereby left the surface of it exceedingly smooth, then examining it very diligently with a microscope, I thought I would perceive it to appear a little porous; but I could not so plainly distinguish them, as to be sure that they were porous, much less what figure they were of. But judging from the lightness and yielding quality of the cork, that certainly the texture could not be so curious, but that possible, if I could use some further diligence, I might find it discernible with a microscope, I with the same sharp pen knife, cut off from the former an exceedingly thin piece of it, and placing it on a black object

plate, because it was itself a white body, and casting the light on it with a deep plano-convex glass, I could exceedingly plainly perceive it to be all perforated and porous, much like a honeycomb, but that the pores of it were not regular; yet it was not unlike a honeycomb in these particulars.

First, in that it had a very little solid substance, in comparison of the empty cavity that was contained between, as does more manifestly appear by the Figure A and B of the XI scheme, for the *interstitia*, or walls (as I may so call them) or partitions of those pores were nearly as thin in proportion to their pores, as those thin films of wax in a honeycomb (which enclose and constitute the sexangular cells) are to theirs.

Next, in that these pores, or cells, were not very deep, but consisted of a great many little boxes, separated out of one continued long pore; by certain diaphragms, as is visible by the Figure B, which represents a sight of those pores split the long-ways.

Although Hooke's style may seem strange to modern readers (especially his long sentences), he used two conventional methods to convey impressions of what he saw. As his references to "Figure A and B" indicate, he used drawings. His comparison of cells to "honeycomb" and "little boxes" shows that he relied on analogies to describe what the cells looked like.

Take a lesson from Hooke. When an object resembles something else your readers are more familiar with, analogies can be helpful in explaining its shape, size, and structure. A common way to do this is to use metaphors of shape based on the letters of the alphabet: A-frame, C-clamp, I-beam, O-ring, S-hook, T-square, Y-joint, and so on. Another way is to name parts of objects after parts of anatomy: head, eyes, ears, mouth, teeth, lip, throat, tongue, neck, shoulder, elbow, arm, leg, foot, and heel. Gears and saws have teeth; pliers and vises have jaws; needles have eyes; and so on. A third way is to use resemblances to other well-known objects: a mushroom-shaped anchor; a barrel-shaped container; a canister the size of a tube of lipstick.

Analogies also can be used to suggest structure and size.

Each stair tread on an escalator is like a small four-wheel truck.

Some bearing sleeves are porous and under a microscope look like very fine sponges, but are rigid.

The simplest portable hair dryer looks a little like an oversized handgun in which a small fan blows hot air out of a screened nozzle.

The tape-recording head is a small C-shaped electromagnet the size of a dime.

The barometer case looks like a small metal shoe box with a glass lid.

The islands hang like a loose necklace from the entrance of the bay.

The combustion chamber is shaped like a fat figure eight.

Our galaxy may be surrounded by an ultraviolet halo emitted by neutrinos.

If you cannot make the comparison by using a well-known and easily visualized analogy, you can often compare a new mechanism with an older one or a more complex one with a simpler one.

> Disposable syringes are just like rubber ones except they are made of plastic and can be discarded after use.

> A compact disc is a secondary storage medium for computer data and programs. It is identical in shape and size to the compact discs used for recording music.

> An automobile battery is a much larger and chemically different version of the battery that powers a flashlight.

How good an analogy is depends on how well the comparison clarifies the object being described. It would not do to describe something as resembling a pair of dividers or a lemur unless your readers could be expected to know what a pair of dividers or a lemur looks like. You would be using one unknown to describe another unknown. Furthermore, an analogy can mislead rather than clarify if it does not suggest the right features. For instance, comparing an object to a circle is ineffective if the object looks more like a wheel or a donut. Likewise, comparing an object to a funnel is misleading if it is only cone-shaped. Everyone knows what a tree is, but to refer to an object as "tree-shaped" does not take into account the differences between oaks, pines, palms, and weeping willows. Be sure your analogy is familiar, is appropriate, and reveals as many specific characteristics as possible.

Using Geometric Shapes

When an object has an easily identifiable geometric shape, you can refer to that shape—assuming that you and your readers know geometrical terminology. However, if your readers cannot be expected to know what a rhombus or a parallelepiped is, do not refer to them. And if the object you are describing is three dimensional, do not refer to a two-dimensional shape. For instance, if your readers look at a two-dimensional drawing of a three-dimensional object, they might mistake a cone for a triangle. You must either provide a three-dimensional view or explain that the object is conical. Following is a brief review of terms from your geometry class that can be greatly useful in mechanism description.

Two-Dimensional Shapes
Two-dimensional shapes include angles, polygons, and circles.

Angles   Angles are shapes formed by two straight lines that meet. When two straight lines meet at a 90° angle, the angle is said to be a *right angle*. Angles less than a right angle are called *acute* angles. Angles greater than a right angle are called *obtuse* angles.

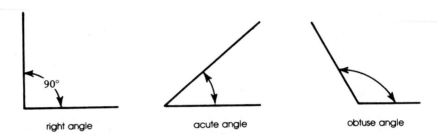

Polygons   Polygons are two-dimensional shapes bounded by straight sides. The most usual kinds of polygons are illustrated in Figure 16.3. Most of these shapes exist around us. The face of an Egyptian pyramid is a triangle. A musical percussion instrument, the triangle, is an example of an equilateral triangle. If you fold a square sheet of paper diagonally so that its opposite corners meet, you have made a right triangle. The court-house squares in traditional county seats are laid out on a square parcel of land. The face of a length of board is a rectangle if the length exceeds the width. Home plate on a baseball diamond and the five-sided building in Arlington, Virginia, that is the headquarters for the U.S. armed services are pentagons. The cells in a honeycomb are hexagons.

NUMBER OF SIDES	NAME OF SHAPE	SHAPES		
3	triangle	equilateral	isosceles	right
4	quadrilateral	square	rectangle	
		parallelogram	rhombus	
5	pentagon			
6	hexagon			

Figure 16.3 References to geometric shapes are important in describing mechanisms.

Circles   A circle is a shape bounded by a curved line that is at all points at an equal distance from its center. A hula hoop, the face of a coin, and wedding rings are circular.

A half-circle, or semicircle, is half a circle with a diameter line connecting the end points. Half a circle without a diameter line is a type of arc.

An oval is a shape that looks like a stretched-out circle. The orbit of a satellite and the layout of a race track are examples of ovals.

Three-Dimensional Shapes

Technically speaking, a three-dimensional shape is a solid object. For our purposes in mechanism description, however, the object need not be solid—it is the shape with which we are concerned. For example, a container or housing for a piece of machinery may be referred to as cubical or cylindrical even though the object is not solid. The most common three-dimensional shapes are polyhedrons, cylinders, cones, spheres, and ellipsoids.

Polyhedrons   Polyhedrons are "solid" objects bounded by plane surfaces. The most familiar type of polyhedron is the cube. Children's blocks, dice, and even some kinds of ice "cubes" are cubes.

Cones   Cones are shapes that come to a point at one end with the opposite end a circle. The upper part of a funnel, the nose "cone" on a space capsule, cinder-coned volcanoes, and even some kinds of ice cream "cones" are examples of cones.

Cylinders   Cylinders are shapes that look like jars, drinking glasses, cans, rods, dowels, and tubes.

Spheres   Spheres are "solid" objects bounded by a surface that is at all points the same distance from its center. Tennis balls, globes, and marbles are examples of spheres. A hemisphere is half a sphere. Domes are typically hemispherical.

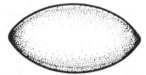

Ellipsoids   Ellipsoids are egg-shaped objects. An egg, a football, and various seeds and pills are shaped like ellipsoids.

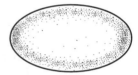

ARRANGING THE DETAILS OF THE DESCRIPTION

Because you have multiple details to tell readers about a mechanism or object, and because a mechanism or object has more than one part, it is impossible to describe it all at once. Thus, you must lead readers through a particular order of presentation. The following three-part arrangement will usually be satisfactory:

- An introductory overall description of the function and appearance of the entire mechanism.

- A description of the function and appearance of each major part of the mechanism.

- An explanation of how the mechanism operates or is used.

What you are doing, in effect, is explaining what the mechanism does and looks like, what each part does and looks like, and how the mechanism as a whole works. Proportions of the description usually work out this way: For a mechanism of five major parts, the presentation will have seven main sections—an introduction, five sections describing the five functional parts, and a concluding section describing the operation of the mechanism. Figure 16.4 is the basic organizational pattern.

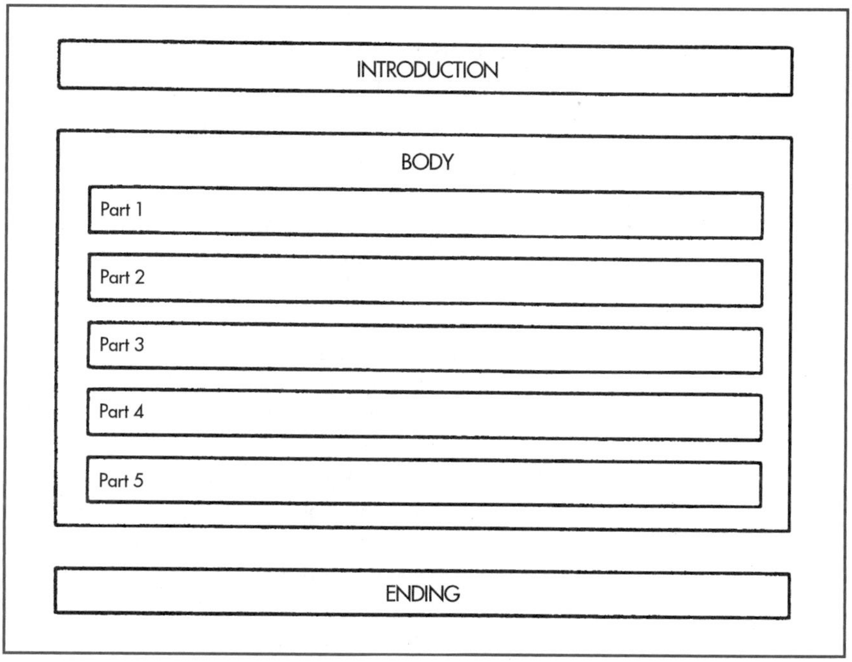

```
┌─────────────────────────────────────────────────┐
│  ┌───────────────────────────────────────────┐  │
│  │              INTRODUCTION                 │  │
│  └───────────────────────────────────────────┘  │
│  ┌───────────────────────────────────────────┐  │
│  │                  BODY                     │  │
│  │  ┌─────────────────────────────────────┐  │  │
│  │  │ Part 1                              │  │  │
│  │  └─────────────────────────────────────┘  │  │
│  │  ┌─────────────────────────────────────┐  │  │
│  │  │ Part 2                              │  │  │
│  │  └─────────────────────────────────────┘  │  │
│  │  ┌─────────────────────────────────────┐  │  │
│  │  │ Part 3                              │  │  │
│  │  └─────────────────────────────────────┘  │  │
│  │  ┌─────────────────────────────────────┐  │  │
│  │  │ Part 4                              │  │  │
│  │  └─────────────────────────────────────┘  │  │
│  │  ┌─────────────────────────────────────┐  │  │
│  │  │ Part 5                              │  │  │
│  │  └─────────────────────────────────────┘  │  │
│  └───────────────────────────────────────────┘  │
│  ┌───────────────────────────────────────────┐  │
│  │                 ENDING                    │  │
│  └───────────────────────────────────────────┘  │
└─────────────────────────────────────────────────┘
```

Figure 16.4 **Basic organization pattern of mechanism description. The introduction provides an overview of the purpose, appearance, and major parts of the mechanism. The body describes each major part of the mechanism. The ending explains how the mechanism works or is used, if this information is not provided in the introduction.**

The title is usually no more than the name of the mechanism being described: Multipurpose Police Vehicle, Field-Effect Transistor, Underground Storage Tanks, and so on.

THE INTRODUCTION

Your readers must have an understanding of the overall mechanism or object and a mental framework in which to fit all the details before they get to the details, or they will be swamped. The introduction provides this kind of frame of reference and overview for the entire mechanism or object. It names the mechanism or object again (in many cases explaining the origin of its name when it is not obvious), explains its function or behavior, describes its overall appearance, and lists its individual parts. Here is an introductory paragraph that does these things:

> A volcano is a cone-shaped mountain with a crater in the top that from time to time erupts, spewing gases, rock, ash, and molten lava. The main features are its crater (the opening in the earth's surface) and the conduit connecting the opening to the interior of the earth, which contains magma (hot, molten lava). The largest active volcano in the world is Mauna Loa in the Hawaiian Islands, which towers more than 13,500 feet above sea level.

See also the introduction to the description of the Berlese funnel (Figure 16.2). Following are some principles to keep in mind when you introduce a mechanism or object.

- **Explaining its name helps readers develop a richer conception of the mechanism or object.** Although much current nomenclature is unnecessarily abstract and jargonistic (for example, the tendency to call a container a "functional storage and transportation module" or a stairwell a "vertical egress and exit area"), several traditional methods exist for naming things, and you should be aware of them and use them. Here are just a few of the more frequently used methods.

One of the most common sources of names is to add the suffix *-er* or *-or* to a verb to indicate its function. Thus, *engraver, opener, propeller, recorder, sprinkler, trimmer, circuit breaker* and *elevator, modulator, oscillator, refrigerator, antenna rotator,* and *sensor* are named for their functions. As long as it is clear what is being accelerated, trimmed, oscillated, and so on, you need not elaborate on the significance of the name. However, when the function is not obvious, you need to clarify. For instance, a *multiplexer* and *demultiplexer* (obviously things that create a "multiplex" or perform multiplexing and "demultiplex" or perform demultiplexing) are components of modern telephone systems. These devices convert voice into digital sounds, a process called *multiplexing.* The conversion allows multiple communications to travel simultaneously on an individual line. Demultiplexing, as you can imagine, is the conversion of the digital signal back into the sound of a human voice.

When Latin or other foreign words are incorporated into a name, some explanation may be necessary: For instance, the word *meter* refers to a measuring device (*measure* = meter) as in *thermometer* (*thermos* = heat, *meter* = measurer). Do you have any idea what a *sphygmomanometer* measures? In some instances, the suffixes *-er* and *-or* are omitted, as in *cruise control* and *brake*—instead of *cruise controller* and *braker.*

A second method of naming items is to shorten and combine words, as in *ammeter* (am[pere]+meter), *altimeter* (alti[tude]+meter), *transistor* (trans[ference]+[re]sist[ence]+or), and *maglev train* (mag[netic]+lev[itation]+train). Acronyms are another form of shortening and combining words, especially using only the initial letter or two of a series of words to form another word. For instance, *radar* comes from *ra*dio *d*etection *a*nd *r*anging; *scuba* from *s*elf-*c*ontained *u*nderwater *b*reathing *a*pparatus.

A third common method of naming, especially in physical, natural, health, and social sciences, is to name items after their inventor, developer, or discoverer, or to honor someone. The *Wangensteen suction* is named after the nineteenth-century American surgeon who invented a suction machine to use in the treatment of gastric and intestinal disorders. The *Mercator* grid is a type of map projection that is named after its inventor, Gerhardus Mercator, a sixteenth-century Danish cartographer. The *Furbish loutwort* is a plant named after Kate Furbish, the botanist who discovered it. The *Maginot Line,* a defensive line built in the late 1920s on France's eastern border, was named after Andre Maginot, the French Minister of War at the time. *Halley's Comet* is named after the astronomer who predicted its return. The rover that sent back so many photographs of the Martian terrain in the summer of 1997 is named *Sojourner,* partly in honor of the abolitionist Sojourner Truth and partly as an allusion to its primary mission of conveying truth about the Martian surface.

And, most relevant to description, many items are named for some aspect of their appearance: alligator clamp, programming comb, mushroom anchor, mouth of a river, bottlenose whales and dolphins, and a c-strap on a motorcycle seat or saddle.

• **The most important statements you make about a mechanism or object early in your description relate to its function, parts, and appearance.** If you are familiar with the mechanism or object, it's easy to assume that your readers share your knowledge. But you must remind yourself that most readers will need information about what the mechanism or object does (if known), what it looks like, and what its major parts are. Here are a few sample explanations of the function and listing of the major parts of mechanisms and objects:

> A hand hacksaw is a metal-cutting saw of three parts: a handle, a C-shaped frame, and a thin, narrow blade fastened to the open side of the frame.

> An amoeba, a one-celled animal found in fresh water, consists of a nucleus, the surrounding protoplasm, and an enclosing outer membrane.

> A cantaloupe is a small melon with a ribbed, netted rind; yellow, delicately flavored flesh; and seeds.

> A microwave oven consists of a housing, power unit, magnetron, wave guide, and oven cavity.

> The steering system on a sailboat consists of the rudder, the rudder post, and the tiller.

> Venetian blinds, horizontally slatted window shades that can be adjusted to control the amount of sunlight that enters a room, from unimpeded sunlight to nearly complete darkness, consist of the following parts:

> 1. control cords to lift and lower the blinds,
>
> 2. control cords to adjust the tilt of the blinds, and
>
> 3. slats resting on crosspieces between pairs of tapes.

> A miter box is a device used to guide a saw in cutting stock to form angle joints. The simplest form consists of a wood or plastic trough with saw cuts through the sides, usually at angles of 45 degrees and 90 degrees.

The heart consists of four chambers (two atria for receiving blood and two ventricles for pumping blood), valves to prevent a back flow of blood, and numerous vessels that help this part of the circulatory system to work.

These examples partition the mechanism or object into main parts. You can provide a more extensive forecast of the parts and subparts by "nesting" the subparts with each main part, as in these examples:

The UJ1000 Printing Calculator has three main parts:

1. the upper panel (composed of the display screen and the printer),

2. the control board (composed of the power, decimal, and printer switches), and

3. the keyboard (composed of the function pad, the number pad, and the memory pad).

The cell, as shown in a magnified cross section in Figure 1, includes three principal parts:

1. the membrane, which holds the cytoplasm together and separates the cell's internal parts from the external environment;

2. the cytoplasm, the substance between the nucleus and the membranes; and

3. the organelles, which are highly specialized components such as the nucleus, mitochondria, endoplasmic reticulum, golgi complex, and lysosomes.

Such extended partitioning provides readers with an outline of the main parts and subparts of the mechanism or object. Occasionally such detailed forecasting can be done, providing that it does not present too much information too fast. In general, you should identify only the main parts in the introduction and introduce the subparts later.

• **Every mechanism is designed or has the form to fulfill a particular function.** The question to answer is: why is the mechanism designed as it is? or why is the object shaped as it is? Sometimes you can explain this in the first sentence of the introduction, as in several of the examples given earlier. Other times, you'll have to devote a sentence or more to explaining the function:

A drafting compass is designed for drawing circles, arcs, and ellipses.

A torque wrench is used to tighten bolts to a specified degree of tightness.

A joystick is a lever that can be tilted any direction (360 degrees) to control the position of the cursor on the display screen. It is used primarily in computer graphics and games.

In explaining the function, be sure to describe all the important functions the mechanism is designed to perform. For instance, an air conditioner has more functions than to cool a space. Most air conditioners also circulate the air, remove moisture from the air, and filter the air. An explanation of the function of an air conditioner should fully reveal the kinds of "conditioning" it is designed to do.

• **When the mechanism or object you are describing is part of a larger mechanism or object, you should explain how the mechanism or object relates to the larger whole.** An ammunition clip or magazine is part of a rifle; a distributor is part of the ignition system of an automobile; a speaker is part of a stereo system. Providing a larger context for the mechanism or object helps readers understand it better.

• **Your readers always need a notion of the size, shape, and general appearance of the mechanism or object.** Size can be explained by giving dimensions (the metal plate is $2'' \times 3'' \times \frac{1}{4}''$) or by comparisons (the film canister is about the size of a tube of lipstick). Shape can be expressed by geometric shapes (the bookend is shaped like an equilateral triangle) or comparison to shapes of the letters of the alphabet and numbers. A drawing that shows the entire mechanism or object is often placed in the introduction to give readers some idea of its general appearance as a whole and to orient them to the physical viewpoint from which they are viewing it.

• **Every mechanism or object has at least two parts.** Partitioning the mechanism or object into its major parts usually presents no problems, unless it is extremely simple or complicated. In either instance you must make some arbitrary decisions. Try to come up with not less than two parts and not more than five or six. Something as simple as a piece of chalk, when thought of as a mechanism, has two ends for marking on a chalkboard and a cylindrical body used for a handle (unless some kind of handle or holder is provided). Just because the mechanism or object is in one piece is no sign that you should not look for at least two parts. Do not confuse a physical piece with a part. Similarly, if a mechanism or object has lots of pieces, you should group several of them under one large part. For example, an adjustable beam compass can be separated into as many as thirty pieces, but it can be regarded as having only three major functional parts: the writing head, the center pin, and the adjustable beam. The thirty or so pieces are grouped as subparts of these major functional parts.

• **The list of parts indicate the order in which the parts will be discussed.** The order may be one of three sequences:

1. *Function:* The parts are described in the order of their activity—Part A moves Part B, which moves Part C, and so forth.

2. *Space:* The parts are described from left to right, top to bottom, outside to inside, front to back, and so on.

3. *Importance:* The parts are described from the most significant to the least significant.

Random order is seldom satisfactory.

THE BODY

The body of a mechanism description explains each major part in the order indicated by the list of major parts in the introduction. The parts description provides much the same information for each part that the introduction does for the mechanism or object as a whole. Simply think of the parts as a miniature mechanism or object. Give at least one section of details for each major part.

The following example describes a bolus gun, which is used by veterinarians and other persons who work with livestock to administer medication in pill or tablet form.[4] In the introduction (which is not included here), the writer explains the function of the bolus gun, compares it to a hypodermic syringe in design and use, indicates the different sizes it comes in, provides an overview of the instrument by listing its three main parts (the plunger, the barrel, and the pill chamber), and provides the following drawing:

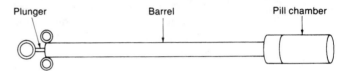

Figure 1. The bolus gun

In the body of the description (see Figure 16.5), the writer devotes a section of details to each main part, explaining the part's function and appearance and identifying its subparts. In the rest of each section, the writer gives the details of material, finishes, weight, connections, and use needed to give readers a visual and functional understanding of the part.

THE ENDING

The ending explains how the mechanism works or is used. Here you divide its function or behavior into meaningful stages and explain what happens in each. For instance, if the writer who described the bolus gun had not provided such information in the introduction, he might have described its use like this:

> The bolus gun, designed like a hypodermic syringe, can be used with one hand. The operator grips the gun with one hand, opens the animal's mouth with the other, and inserts the end of the gun deep enough into the animal's throat to prevent the pill or tablet from being coughed up.

Another way to end your description is to explain briefly the principles involved in its action. (The next chapter discusses process description, of which mechanical processes are a major type.) For instance, a toaster broils thinly sliced materials, such as bread; or an air conditioner cools a space by removing heat from it. If you have included this information in your introduction, you need not write a separate ending.

[4]From an unpublished student report, used with permission of the author, Don Bowles.

THE PLUNGER

The plunger (Figure 2) fits inside the barrel and pushes the bolus out of the pill chamber into the animal's throat. It consists of a ring grip, stem, and knob. Located at the back of the plunger, the ring grip is used to maneuver the plunger. The stem is that part of the plunger between the ring grip and the knob. When the stem is pushed forward in the barrel, it causes the knob to move forward and eject the bolus from the pill chamber into the animal's throat. The knob is attached to the front of the plunger and fits inside the pill chamber. It is the knob, shaped like a disc measuring 3/16 inch thick and 7/8 inch in diameter, that ejects the bolus.

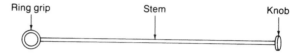

Figure 2. The plunger

THE BARREL

The barrel (Figure 3), which is 10-3/4 inches long and 1/2 inch in diameter, is long enough to insert the pill chamber well into the animal's mouth and is large enough to enclose the plunger. Two ring grips, through which the operator's forefinger and middle finger are inserted, provide the necessary grip on the gun while administering the medicine.

Figure 3. The barrel

THE PILL CHAMBER

The pill chamber holds the bolus before it is ejected into the animal's throat. As shown in Figure 4, it consists of a base, clip, and cover. The base connects the pill chamber to the barrel and supports the clip and the cover. The clip holds the bolus steady while the gun is being positioned in the animal's mouth. It is 2 inches long and 1/4 inch wide to accommodate large pills. The cover is made of pliable plastic to protect the animal's mouth and throat.

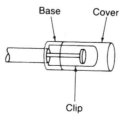

Figure 4. The pill chamber

Figure 16.5 Description of the main parts of a bolus gun, an instrument used to administer medication in pill (bolus) form to large animals.
Source: An unpublished student report, used with permission of the author, Don Bowles.

PLANNING AND REVISING CHECKLIST: MECHANISM DESCRIPTION

Think about the following when planning and revising a mechanism description.

PLANNING

- How familiar are your intended readers with the mechanism? Will some terms need to be defined? Should any *so-whats* be explained?

- What is the purpose of the description? Is it to help your intended readers to understand the function, appearance, and parts of the mechanism or object? Is it to help them manufacture, pack, store, ship, unpack, assemble, or service it? Is it to help them identify it?

- What visuals, adjectives, analogies, and geometric shapes enable your readers to visualize the mechanism or object?

REVISING

- Is the description complete and accurate for your and your readers' purposes?

- Have you provided a clear initial overview of the function, appearance, and parts of the mechanism or object?

- Are the function, appearance, and components of each major part explained clearly?

- Are details, measurements, adjectives, analogies, and references to geometric shapes clear and reasonably specific?

- Are the visuals clear and easy to understand, considering the intended readers?

SUGGESTIONS FOR APPLYING YOUR KNOWLEDGE

1. Explain the visual analogy behind the name of each of the following:

A-frame	chip
alluvial fan	claw hammer
band saw	cradle roof
bottle-nosed dolphin	deadman
caterpillar gate	death's head moth

dining ell	kidney bean
disk brake	leaf spring
dovetail joint	malleus, stapes, incus (the three small bones in the inner ear of humans)
fiddlehead fern	
fiddler crab	monkey wrench
forklift	needle-nose pliers
foxhold	organ pipe cactus
gateleg table	pineapple
hair spring	rocker arm
hammerhead shark	sea cucumber
hip roof	T-hinge
J-stroke	U-bolt
kangaroo rat	wing nut
kettledrum	

2. Explain the visual analogy behind the names of five items from your field of study (excluding any that are listed above).

3. Choose a mechanism or object with which you are familiar and you believe that most of your fellow students are not. Explain its function and overall appearance, partition it into not fewer than two and not more than six major parts, and explain the order of parts that you would use to arrange your description. Explain the visuals that you would use.

4. Write a description of some mechanism or object with which you are familiar and you believe that most of your fellow students are not. Be prepared to explain to other students in the class the intended audience, the purpose and the arrangement of the description, and the methods to help readers visualize the mechanism or object and its parts.

5. Form a panel with two other students in your class to give an oral description of a mechanism or object with which the three of you are familiar. Arrange to have a visual or visuals of the mechanism or object or the thing itself in class. Decide who will make the initial introduction of the mechanism or object, who will describe its major functional parts, and who will describe the way it operates or behaves. Time: 10 to 15 minutes.

6. Analyze the description of the bolus gun or the Berlese funnel for its use of *so-whats*. Divide a sheet of paper into two columns and list the features and their *so-whats*. If you find instances in which additional *so-whats* would be helpful, include them, too.

7. Analyze and discuss in class the description of the field sprayer in Figure 16.6.[5]

[5]William Mayfield. *Field Sprayer Equipment and Calibration* (Auburn, AL: Alabama Cooperative Extension Service, n.d.) 3–15.

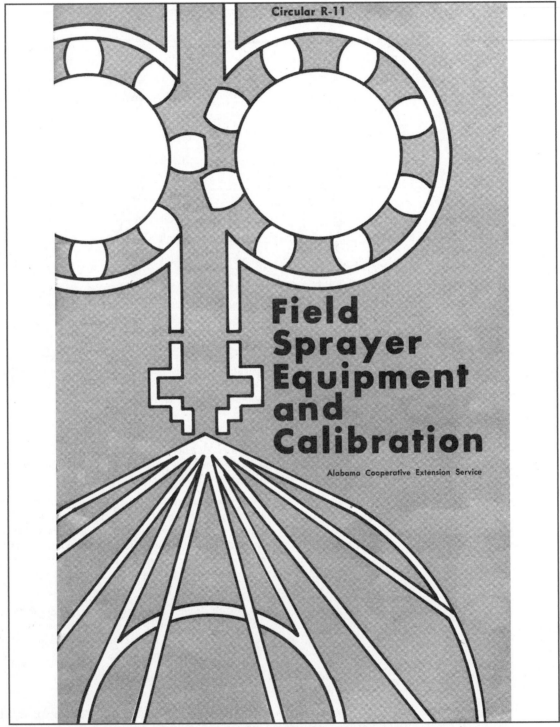

Figure 16.6 Sample description of a mechanism titled *Field Sprayer Equipment and Calibration.*
Source: Alabama Cooperative Extension.

by
W ILLIAM M AYFIELD
Extension Agricultural Engineer

THE MODERN FARMER has many good chemicals to use, but they must be applied properly to be effective. Many of these materials are toxic to crops, animals or humans, and it is absolutely necessary that they be delivered only to the target area.

Study and carefully follow the instructions from equipment and pesticide manufacturers. All spraying equipment should have instruction manuals when you buy it. Keep these manuals in a safe and convenient place.

EQUIPMENT

Conventional sprayers usually consist of a pump, a pressure regulator and gauge, strainers, a tank cut-off valve, nozzles and agitators (Figure 1).

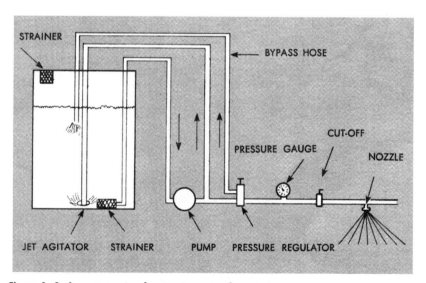

Figure 1. Basic components of a tractor-powered sprayer.

—3—

Figure 16.6 (continued)

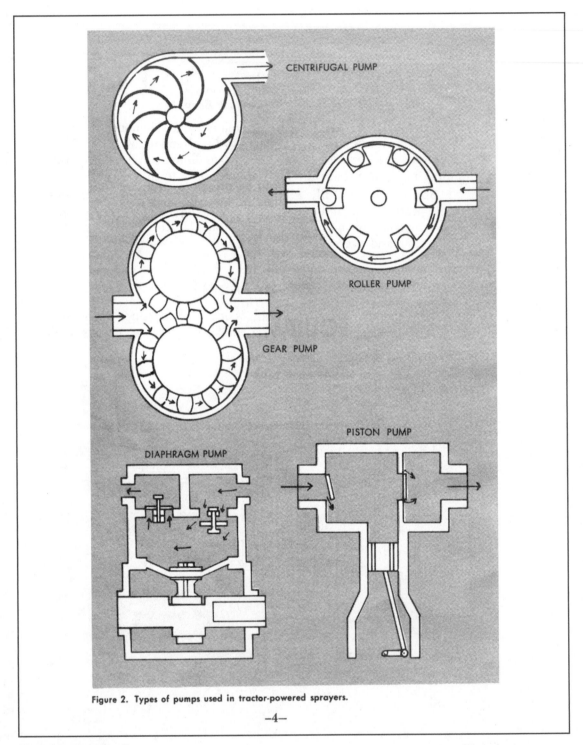

Figure 2. Types of pumps used in tractor-powered sprayers.

—4—

Figure 16.6 (continued)

PUMPS. Types of pumps that are normally used for sprayers are shown in Figure 2, and the advantages and disadvantages of each are listed in Table 1. Gear and roller pumps are satisfactory for emulsions and solutions. Piston and diaphragm pumps are satisfactory for all materials including wettable powders. You can also use roller pumps to apply wettable powders, but wettable powders are abrasive and pump rollers must be replaced often. The pump should be able to supply the required volume of spray (and some bypass volume for agitation) at 100 pounds per square inch when operating at 550 revolutions per minute. This will insure enough capacity under spraying conditions.

Table 1. Advantages and Disadvantages of Pump Types

Pump Type	Operating Pressure	Advantages	Disadvantages
Piston	0-1000	Adaptable to all spray formulas. High pressure. Resistant to wear. Parts easily replaced.	Expensive. Heavier than most.
Gear	0-200	Inexpensive. Medium pressure.	Low volume. Short life. Unsatisfactory for wettable suspensions.
Roller	0-350	Durable when made of noncorrosive steel and plastic. Medium volume and pressure.	Rollers must be replaced frequently when spraying wettable suspensions.
Diaphragm	0-100	Low wear from abrasive materials. Parts are easily replaced. Medium price. Medium pressure.	Low volume. Synthetic rubber diaphragm is nonresistant to some pesticides.
Centrifugal	0-65	Adaptable to all spray formulas. Low wear from abrasive materials.	Expensive. Low pressure. High speed is necessary but not always available on tractor PTO.

—5—

Figure 16.6 (continued)

STRAINERS. There should be a strainer at the tank opening, on the suction hose and at each nozzle. Line and suction strainers should be 50- to 100-mesh screen. Nozzle strainers should be 50- to 200-mesh screen, depending on the size of the nozzle's orifice. The strainers should always have smaller openings than the orifice or nozzle opening with which it is used.

PRESSURE REGULATOR AND GAUGE. The pressure regulator lets enough material return to the tank to keep the desired pressure on the boom (Figure 3). The regulator should be a by-pass type with a screw adjustment. The gauge should be mounted near the pressure regulator and have a capacity of at least 100 pounds per square inch.

NOZZLES. The nozzles determine the spray distribution pattern and affect the volume of spray delivered. Therefore, the nozzles must be the correct size and must deliver the best distribution pattern for the job to be done. The parts of a spray nozzle are illustrated in Figure 4. Nozzles are classified by capacity, type and angle of spray pattern. Some common spray patterns are shown in Figure 5.

Nozzles are commonly available in brass, stainless steel, aluminum, plastic, nylon and ceramic. Usually, brass, aluminum and

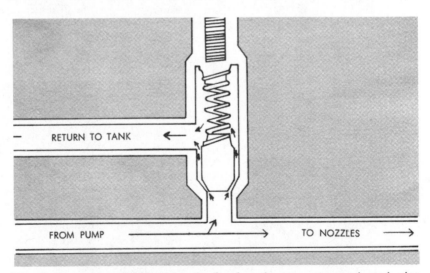

RETURN TO TANK

FROM PUMP

TO NOZZLES

Figure 3. The pressure regulator. It lets the flow from the pump return to the tank when there is enough boom pressure to compress the spring. The load on the spring adjusts the boom pressure.

—6—

Figure 16.6 (continued)

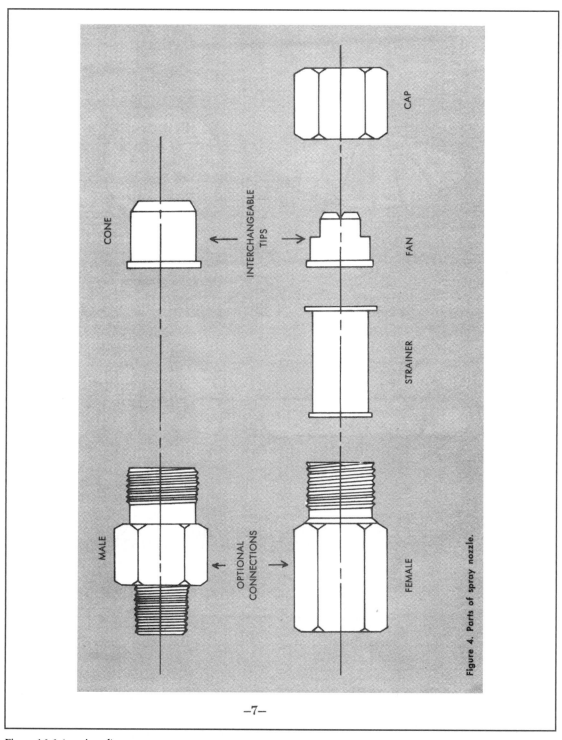

Figure 4. Parts of spray nozzle.

Figure 16.6 (continued)

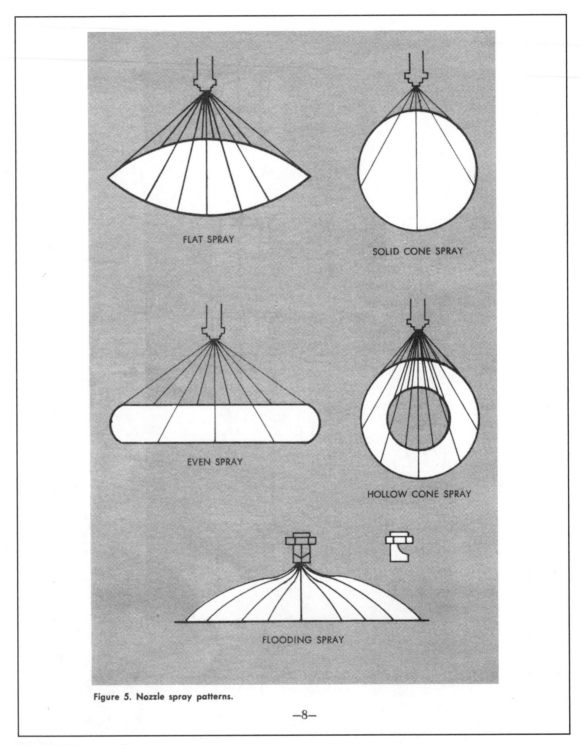

Figure 5. Nozzle spray patterns.

Figure 16.6 (continued)

plastic nozzles have about the same life. Stainless steel should last about 3 times as long as brass; hardened stainless steel about 10 to 15 times, and tungsten carbide about 180 to 200 times as long.

FOR PREEMERGENCE HERBICIDE APPLICATION, fan-type nozzles with 65- to 110-degree angles are used. The 80-degree angle is most used. With the common 20-inch boom spacing, operate 80-degree nozzles 18 inches above the ground (Figure 6). Use a pressure of 20 to 50 pounds per square inch. *Even-flow fan-type nozzles* are best for band application.

FOR POSTEMERGENCE HERBICIDE APPLICATION, use 65- to 95-degree fan-type nozzles at a pressure of 15 to 40 pounds per square inch under most conditions. Directed spray equipment may use a combination of fan-type and cone-type nozzles but must be equipped according to the manufacturer's recommendations.

FOR LAY-BY, flooding-type wide-angle nozzles are usually operated at pressures between 10 and 40 pounds per square inch. Check instructions and charts carefully for speed, pressure and nozzle capacity.

FOR INSECT CONTROL, arrange cone-type nozzles with the required number per row to give complete coverage of plants. One or two nozzles per row may be enough for smaller plants, but for large plants, three nozzles per row may be needed.

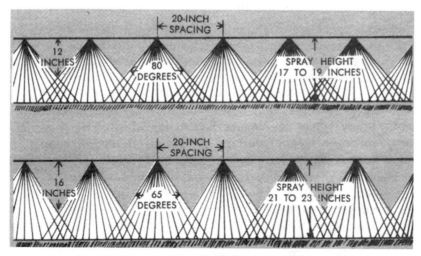

Figure 6. Nozzles with different angles need different boom heights.

—9—

Figure 16.6 (continued)

FOR FUNGICIDE APPLICATION, arrange three *hollow cone noz-zles* per row to give complete foliar coverage. Use pressure of at least 70 pounds per square inch. It is important to use as much water per acre as recommended on the fungicide label.

TANK. Select a tank with a large opening for easy filling, inspection and cleaning. The opening should have a strainer. Be sure the tank can be completely drained. You can get tanks of corrosion-resistant metals, plastic linings and fiber glass. A tank can be mounted in many positions, but the tractor balance and ease in filling should be considered.

AGITATOR. Liquid concentrates, emulsions and soluble powders need very little agitation. The return flow in the bypass usually gives enough agitation for these materials. However, wettable powders need vigorous agitation; jet agitators are needed in addition to the bypass agitation. Connect the jet agitator between the pump and the pressure regulator so that full pump pressure can be used for agitation (Figure 1).

CUT-OFF VALVE. Be sure you have a quick acting, cut-off valve between the pressure regulator and the boom where it can be easily operated from the tractor seat.

HOSES AND FITTINGS. Select hoses that resist sunlight, oil and chemicals, and are flexible and durable.

Nozzle Arrangement on Boom

Nozzle spacing and alignment on the boom are important for uniform coverage. The height of the nozzle tip above the area to be sprayed, nozzle spacing and the angle of spray patterns are all related and should be carefully considered when spraying. Figure 6 shows two types of nozzles and the relationships between spray angles and nozzle heights. Notice that with different spray angles the height has to be adjusted to give uniform coverage. Manufacturers' spray manuals give you the boom heights for various spray angles and nozzle spacings.

Figure 7 shows other boom and nozzle relationships. The top illustration shows that if you let the boom droop, you get uneven coverage and skips. The middle illustration shows what happens when nozzles with different spray angles are used along the boom. The bottom illustration shows skips that occur when nozzles are plugged or when operating pressure is higher or lower

–10–

Figure 16.6 (continued)

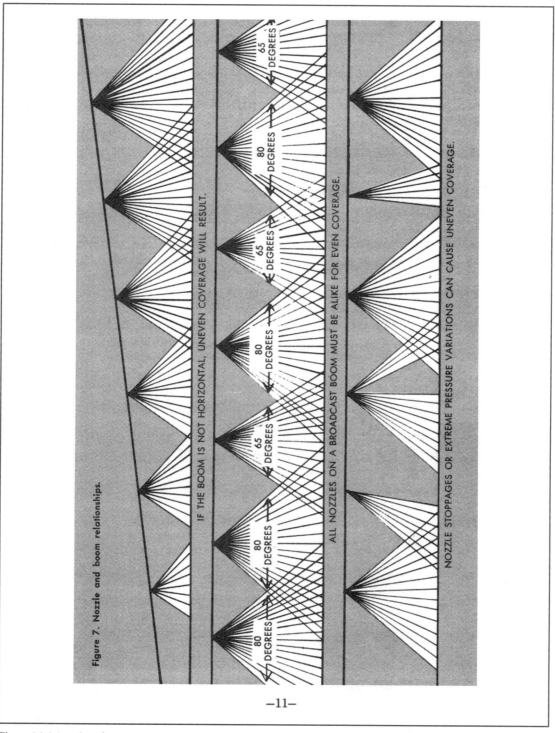

Figure 7. Nozzle and boom relationships.

—11—

Figure 16.6 (continued)

than recommended. Although the required amount of material per acre may be discharged, the coverage is not uniform.

Misalignment of nozzle tips is a common cause of uneven coverage (Figure 8). Be sure fan-type spray patterns are parallel with the boom when installing nozzle tips. Figure 9 shows four arrangements of nozzles on a boom; parts B, C and D are drop-nozzle arrangements.

When you need a band application of herbicides, apply spray with an even-spray nozzle. The nozzle height can be adjusted to give the desired band width.

Boomless or Broadcast Sprayers

A boomless or broadcast sprayer is different from other sprayers because of its nozzle arrangement. A cluster of nozzles or a special nozzle is used to give a wide spray path. This sprayer has fewer nozzles and is better adapted to rough or steep terrain than a boom type. However, it is harder to get uniform coverage and accurate placement with a broadcast sprayer because the spray material simply falls onto the plants while the conventional boom-type sprayer forces the material into the plant foliage. The slightest wind disrupts the spray pattern of the broadcast sprayer, causing drift and uneven distribution.

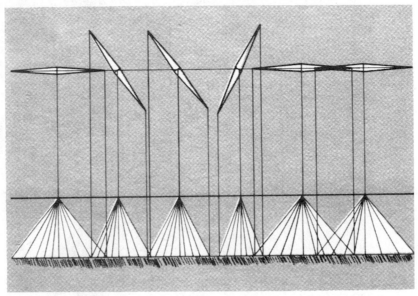

Figure 8. Nozzle alignment. For good coverage, nozzles must be aligned with the boom.

—12—

Figure 16.6 (continued)

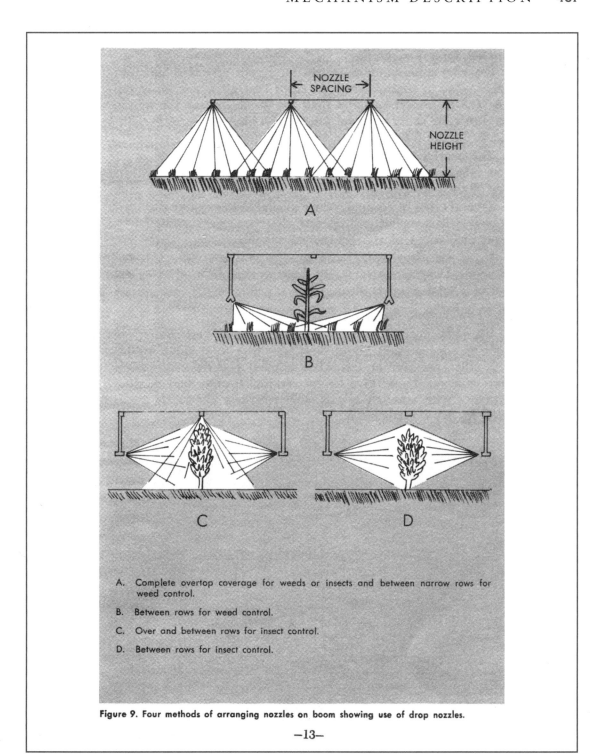

Figure 9. Four methods of arranging nozzles on boom showing use of drop nozzles.

A. Complete overtop coverage for weeds or insects and between narrow rows for weed control.

B. Between rows for weed control.

C. Over and between rows for insect control.

D. Between rows for insect control.

—13—

Figure 16.6 (continued)

Directed Spray Equipment

Directed spray equipment can be a very effective and inexpensive way to control weeds in crops that grow tall fairly rapidly. The crop must be taller than the weeds so that the nozzles can direct the spray material toward the base of the crop plants and strike the foliage of the weeds (Figure 10).

The nozzles must be mounted below and to the side of the crop foliage and must be supported and directed toward the base of the plant.

Several types of equipment are available to support the spray nozzles. Select, mount and operate the nozzles according to the recommendations of the equipment manufacturer.

Using a directed spray with sweeps on a cultivator is a very economical way to control weeds, but this must be used as a single part of a total weed control system.

Ultra-Low Volume Sprayers

Ultra-low volume (ULV) application of a pesticide means applying concentrated liquid pesticides in a total spray volume of ½ gallon per acre or less. ULV-applied pesticides are faster, more convenient, and give longer residual toxicity and wash-off resistance with some chemicals. However, few chemicals are labeled for ULV application.

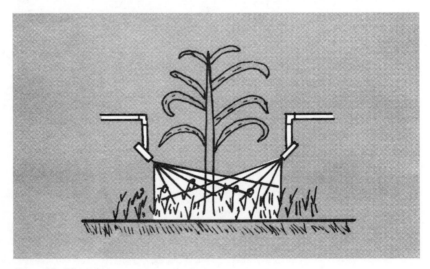

Figure 10. Directed spray.

—14—

Figure 16.6 (continued)

ULV sprayers have many problems, especially with ground equipment. Calibration, distribution, flow rate, drift and safety are some of the more serious.

The physical properties of each pesticide formulation are different and flow rates are not the same; therefore, calibration must be done with the pesticide itself. Flow rates often are so low that the volume of spray caught for measurement in the short calibration time is too small for accurate measurement and calibration. Low flow rates and the small-orifice spray nozzles often result in nozzle stoppage. And, because of the low flow rate, it is difficult to detect a stoppage.

Distribution studies have indicated that it is very difficult to get a uniform distribution pattern across the spray swath. The extremely small particles delivered from a ULV sprayer drift easily. This is true with both the multirow, mist-blower-type sprayer and those with a single spray orifice for each row.

Special safety precautions must be followed when applying concentrated ULV insecticides. The potential dangers to the operator during calibration, nozzle cleaning, filling and spraying are greater because of the greater concentration of toxic material.

–15–

Figure 16.6 (continued)

CHAPTER 17

PROCESS DESCRIPTION

A process is a specific series of actions that brings about a specific result. Process is essentially chronological or sequential—this happens, then this, then that. Because business and industry are concerned with processes, much of the writing and speaking you may do will be explaining processes. You may need to explain to a coworker, an oversight committee, a supervisor, or a customer the way something happened, the merits of a particular process, or the way a mechanism or system works. Or you may need to explain a natural process such as photosynthesis or how parasites change hosts or how peat bogs are formed. Almost any action can be regarded as a process.

Such explanations are useful only if they are clear. Thus, you must plan your explanation carefully. In this chapter, we show you, through explanation and several examples, how to determine the purpose of your description and how to organize and illustrate your description.

DETERMINING THE PURPOSE OF THE DESCRIPTION

You first must decide on the purpose of your explanation. An important distinction is the difference between explaining a process and giving instructions for performing it. If you expect readers to perform the process, you should write a set of instructions. (We take up writing instructions in Chapter 18.) If you do not expect your readers to perform the process but only to understand it, you should write an explanation of it. After reading your explanation, your readers should know the process well enough to understand what happens during a chain of events, to evaluate the reliability or efficiency of the process, to diagnose a possible problem in the process, or to understand the operational sequence of a mechanism or system.

EXPLAINING HOW SOMETHING IS DONE OR MADE

Much process description tells how something is done or made: how ships are mothballed, how coal is mined, how money is coined or printed, how riots are controlled, and how a particular procedure is or was carried out (for instance, how the value and cost of housing is estimated in determining rental subsidies). Organizations use process description to tell the story of their products. Professional persons are often asked by their supervisors how something was accomplished. For example, the report in Figure 17.1 is written by a supervisory mining engineer of a coal company to explain the work and costs in controlling a large fire in an abandoned mine. The intended primary readers are the engineer's superiors in the company: the director of mining safety, other senior administrators, and the board of directors. Significant secondary readers are personnel in the government agencies that regulate and oversee mining operations and environmental safety and members of environmental organizations, such as the Audubon Society. Read the report before you read the discussion that follows.

Controlling the Fire in Bevo #3 Mine
11 July 1998 to 1 May 1999

Background

On 11 July 1998, a mine fire was discovered in the central portion of Bevo #3 Mine. Although situated about two miles east of the Sherman Township residential area, the site was only 300 yards north of the Armistead Industrial Park (Figure 1). Containment of the fire protected that important area.

The fire is believed to have started in a partly backfilled strip pit that had been used since 1965 as an ash and garbage disposal site. Garbage apparently began burning from an unknown source, and then probably ignited the coal in some of the exposed portions of the pillar remnants in the highwall of the strip pit. The outcrops of both the Newcome and Courtney beds that had been strip-mined at this site are part of the abandoned Bevo #3 Mine.

From 1 October to 1 November 1998, some of the burning material in the strip pit was excavated and ten exploratory boreholes were drilled. From the elevated temperatures in the pit and the boreholes it was concluded that the fire had spread to the Newcome bed and possibly to the underlying Courtney bed (Figure 2).

The Fire Control Plan

Because there was evidence that the fire would spread beyond the limits determined by our exploratory drillings, a two-stage plan to extinguish the fire was developed, as follows:

1. Drilling a sufficient number of boreholes from the surface to the mine voids to determine the extent of the fire in the Newcome bed and its possible existence in the lower Courtney bed; excavating and extinguishing hot material encountered above the floor of the Newcome bed; and restoring the surface, if it proved unnecessary to excavate to the Courtney bed.

2. If fire were present in the Courtney bed, excavating and extinguishing hot material to the floor of the Courtney bed and restoring the surface.

The proposed plan was approved on 6 November 1998 by the Office of Mining Operations in the State Department of Economic Activity and the State Department of Environmental Safety.

Ultimately the second stage of the plan had to be performed.

Exploratory Drilling and Trench Excavation to the Courtney Bed

Drilling boreholes. Drilling boreholes to determine the perimeter of the fire and the location of the proposed isolation trench was started on 12 November 1998. Temperatures obtained from boreholes drilled to the voids in the Newcome bed ranged up to 1000° Fahrenheit. Temperatures from boreholes to the Courtney bed were not high enough to indicate that the fire had spread to those mine workings at that time.

Excavating the isolation trench. The location and the shape of the isolation trench to the floor of the Newcome bed were planned to conform with the limits of the heat zone indicated by the temperatures obtained from the boreholes. During excavation, a hot area was encountered, and this required widening the original trench at that location (Figure 3). Upon completion, the isolated "hot island" was bounded by a trench on two sides, and on its third side by a natural deep gully south of the Courtney bed outcrop in which Nifonger Creek flows.

1

Figure 17.1 One of the most frequent jobs you will have as a professional person is to describe processes. You may describe a process you have developed or one that you would like to develop. You may describe a planned course of action or one that you have completed. This sample process report explains how a large fire in an abandoned coal mine was controlled.

Additional holes were drilled in the isolation trench from the floor of the Newcome bed to the underlying Courtney bed. Elevated temperatures up to 500° Fahrenheit obtained from some of these holes established that a fire was also burning in the Courtney bed in an area northwest of the isolation trench in the Newcome bed.

At this time, it was decided to widen the original Newcome trench at one point to overlie a cold area in the Courtney bed and then deepen the entire trench to encircle the fire in the Courtney bed. The resulting hot area was therefore considerably greater than originally planned (Figure 4).

Work on the first stage was completed 20 December 1998. After this work was completed, the active fire area in the Newcome and Courtney beds had been successfully isolated.

Table I provides detailed data on the extent and cost of work conducted during this stage. Appendix A contains copies of invoices, contracts, and work orders related to work performed during this stage.

Table I. Cost of Exploratory Drilling and Trench Excavation Stage 1, Bevo #3 Mine Fire 1 October 1998 to 20 December 1998			
Item	Quantity	Cost per unit	Total cost
6-inch drilling	893.0 linear ft	$2.00	$1,786.00
3-inch drilling	718.5 " "	1.85	1,329.25
6-inch casing	450.0 " "	2.50	1,125.00
Excavation	70,288.0 cubic yds	.55	38,658.40
Excavation	18,197.0 " "	1.25	22,746.25
Recasting spoil	18,197.0 " "	.25	4,549.25
Bulldozer rental	12.0 hours	30.00	360.00
Total			$70,557.15

Removing Remaining Hot Material and Subsequent Backfilling of Project Area

The work planned under the second stage involved the following three steps: 1) sealing off the hot area, 2) excavating all the material that had been isolated, quenching the hot or burning material, and 3) backfilling and regrading the surface in the project area to its approximate original configuration.

Sealing off the hot area. Work was started 4 January 1999 by placing a seal of wet sand on the exposed Newcome and Courtney beds along the cold side of the entire isolation trench (Figure 5). This seal was intended to prevent any hot material thrown during blasting in the fire zone from igniting carbonaceous material in these beds. The seal at the Courtney bed level also acted as a dam to impound water used in quenching and cooling the fire area. During the course of the work, a pool of water approximately 6 feet deep on the floor of the Courtney bed was created. During January and February 1999 the pool of water froze, indicating that no fire existed in an unmined thin leader bed a few feet below the Courtney bed. Water for quenching

2

Figure 17.1 (continued)

extremely hot or burning material was obtained from nearby Nifonger Creek, across which a temporary impounding dam was built. A gasoline-driven pump powered the two 6-inch water cannons, which sprayed constant streams of water on the excavation and disposal area.

Excavating material in the isolated hot zone. The second step under this stage involved excavating all material in the isolated hot zone that covered the floor of the Courtney bed. The operation consisted of blasting and quenching a total of 45,000 cubic yards of material.

Recasting spoil and restoring the surface. The third step consisted of recasting spoil, which had been excavated from the trench during the first stage, back into the excavated area. Finally, the surface was graded to its form contours (Figure 6).

A final inspection of the completed work was made 1 May 1999. Table II provides detailed data on the amount and cost of work during the second stage. Appendix B contains copies of invoices, contracts, and work orders related to work performed during the second stage.

Table II. Cost of Excavating and Backfilling Stage 2, Bevo #3 Mine Fire 4 January to 1 May 1999			
Item	Quantity	Cost per unit	Total cost
Excavation	45,000.00 cubic yds	$1.00	$45,000.00
6-inch drilling	113.00 linear ft	2.00	226.00
6-inch casing	50.00 linear ft	2.50	125.00
Recasting and grading	150,000.00 cubic yds	lump-sum payment	75,000.00
Total			$120,351.00

Cost Summary

The total of the fire control project is summarized as follows:

Stage 1	$70,557.15
Stage 2	120,351.00
	$190,908.15

During excavating operations, marketable coal from the relatively few pillars that remained in the various beds was recovered. The money received for the coal ($65,000) was used to help defray the cost of controlling the fire. Appendix C contains copies of sales contracts for the recovered coal.

3

Figure 17.1 (continued)

The report is organized into three major sections: Background (introduction), The Fire Control Plan (body), and Cost Summary (ending). The sections are set off by headings. The longest section of the report—The Fire Control Plan—is further divided into two subsections, each explaining a stage of the plan. The subsections are identified by subheadings. The segments of the subsections are further marked off by subordinate headings.

Most of the well-known journalistic topics—*who, what, where, when, why, how*—are used throughout the report. However, *who* is not emphasized. Most of the action taken by the company's fire control team is written in the passive voice, probably because the writer assumed that the primary readers already knew who did what or that they and the secondary readers were primarily interested in what action was taken rather than in who performed the action. The report focuses on what was done, what was accomplished, and what it cost. The active voice is used, however, to explain additional information, for example, "Containment of the fire protected the important area . . . ," "The burning garbage probably ignited the coal . . . ," "Table I provides . . . ," "A gasoline-driven pump powered . . . ," "The second step under Stage 2 involved. . . ."

A review of the background section reveals the writer's use of the remaining journalistic topics:

- *What*—A fire in Bevo #3 mine.

- *When*—Discovered on July 11, 1998; initial action taken between October 1 and November 1, 1998.

- *Where*—The fire is close to a residential area and threatens an industrial park; the fire is in the Newcome bed and perhaps has invaded the Courtney bed just below it. Figure 1, which is not included in this sample, is a map showing the location of the mine, the fire, and the surrounding area. Figure 2, which also is not included, is a cross-sectional view of the mine showing the Newcome and Courtney beds.

- *Why*—Proximity of the fire to the residential area and the industrial park made it important to contain the fire.

The *why* topic is a version of the *so-what* principle that we discuss in Chapters 3, 16, and 18. This report contains many *so-whats* that explain the purpose or importance of the actions or the significance of the facts. For instance, the writer explains the purposes of containing the fire, drilling the boreholes, widening the original Newcome trench and deepening it to the Courtney bed, and constructing the wet-sand seal. In addition, the writer explains the significance of facts given: the elevated temperatures, the water freezing in the Newcome bed, and the recovery of coal during the operations. Where the writer does not provide *so-whats*, the action or the facts are self-defining or obvious: extinguishing the hot material, restoring the surface, drilling boreholes from the Newcome bed into the Courtney bed, the 1,000° Fahrenheit temperature in the Newcome bed, and the 500° Fahrenheit temperature in the Courtney bed.

Process description also explains how research or tests were conducted. Research reports often contain a methodology section describing the work done so that readers can evaluate, even replicate, the methods. Thus, the explanation should be complete and clear enough that readers could use it as a guide to repeat the original investigation or experience. Most methodology sections are relatively brief, although on occasions of important breakthroughs in science and technology, entire books are devoted to the description. One such book is James D. Watson's famous account of his and Francis Crick's research leading to the discovery of the structure of the DNA molecule: *The Double Helix* (New York: Atheneum, 1968).

Figure 17.2 shows a section from a research report that describes the results of an experimental process to improve the baking characteristics of frozen par-fried French fries. Each of the six steps in preparing the potatoes for evaluation is set off by a heading. The writers discuss the materials, equipment, and methods in enough detail so readers know exactly what was done and how. Readers can evaluate the methods and replicate the experiment if they choose. Notice the writers' use of passive verbs:

Russet Burbank potatoes . . . were cut. . . .

The cut strips were washed and held briefly. . . .

The potato chips were placed. . . .

The passive voice is used often in research reports to focus attention on the action, not the researcher. Readers assume the researcher performed the action.

EXPLAINING HOW SOMETHING WORKS

Process description also explains how mechanisms and systems work: how a laser measures inaccessible, and sometimes invisible, points; how an image is telecast; how a laser printer works; how an inclinometer works; how the enzyme streptokinase dissolves blood clots. When you explain mechanical processes, you emphasize the interaction of parts and the underlying principles of those interactions that take place during a cycle of the mechanism's operation. Figure 17.3 is the description of how the parts of a tire gauge work together. Notice how the explanation concentrates on the operation, not on the physical hardware. Pictorials, not words, carry visual features.

The description of how the pressure gauge works consists of an introductory paragraph and three paragraphs of descriptive details. The introduction explains the pressure gauge's importance, its appearance, and its overall operation. Each of the other paragraphs explains the movement of the gauge's parts as it operates.

The large cutaway drawing, placed diagonally across the illustration, helps familiarize readers with both the external and internal features of the gauge. The drawing of the person using the gauge is an effective use of "window dressing" to attract readers' attention. The cross-sectional drawings, showing what happens in each step of the gauge's operation, illustrate

PREPARING THE PRODUCT

To evaluate the baking characteristics of the surface-treated fries, the product was prepared as follows:

- PREPARATION: Russet Burbank potatoes (commercial processing quality, specific gravity 1.086–1.096) held at 45°F were cut into 3/8-in.-square and 1/4-in.-square × 3-1/2-to-4-in.-long strips with a hand-operated French fry cutter. Shorter strips 3/8-in.-square × 1-1/2-to-2-in.-long were also cut for use in pre-cooked frozen dinners. The cut strips were washed and held briefly in tap water until used.

- SURFACE FREEZING: The potato strips were placed on a dripping rack and then immersed and agitated in R-12 held in a Dewar flask (Nonaka et al., 1972). The immersion time in R-12 (−21.6°F) was standardized at 7 sec.

- LEACHING: The 3/8-in.-square surface-frozen strips were leached in 125°F water for 15 min. and the 1/4-in.-square strips for 10 min. The strips were immersed in heated water contained in a stream-jacketed kettle and agitated with a rotating propeller-type stirrer. The strips were not rotated.

- PAR-FRYING: A Wells fryer using 5 qts. vegetable oil heated at 365°F was used for par-frying. The duration of par-frying was varied depending upon whether the French fries were to be baked on a cookie sheet or in a frozen dinner such as a TV dinner. Duration was also varied to change the degree of final crispness.

  For the product to be baked alone, a par-fry time of 1 min. at 365°F was used to more or less duplicate the conventional practice of the industry. However, durations of 1-to-2-1/2 min. will increase the crispness of a 3/8-in.-square fry. For a 1/4-in.-square fry, a most desirable product was obtained with a 1 min. 15 sec. par-fry.

  For the product to be baked with a precooked frozen dinner, the par-frying time was lengthened to 2, 3, and 4 min. to produce varying degrees of crispness. Frozen dinners are cooked for a specified length of time under conditions of steam heating, and the French fry must withstand this environment and still maintain the quality of a desirable fry.

- FINAL FREEZING: The par-fried French fry was frozen in a tunnel blast freezer for 15 min. at −34°F and held at 210°F until used.

- BAKING: The surface-treated fries were baked in the usual manner—placing the fries in a single layer on a cookie sheet and baking them in an oven. The 3/8-in.-square par-fries were baked 7 min. at 450°F, then turned and baked an additional 8 min. The 1/4-in.-square par-fries were baked 4-1/2 min. at 450°F, then turned and baked an additional 4-1/2 min.

Figure 17.2 Process description is used to explain research and experimentation methods.
Source: Nonaka, M. and M. L. Weaver. "Texturizing Process Improves Quality of Baked French-Fried Potatoes." *Food Technology* 27 (Mar. 1973): 50. Reprinted by permission of The Institute of Food Technology.

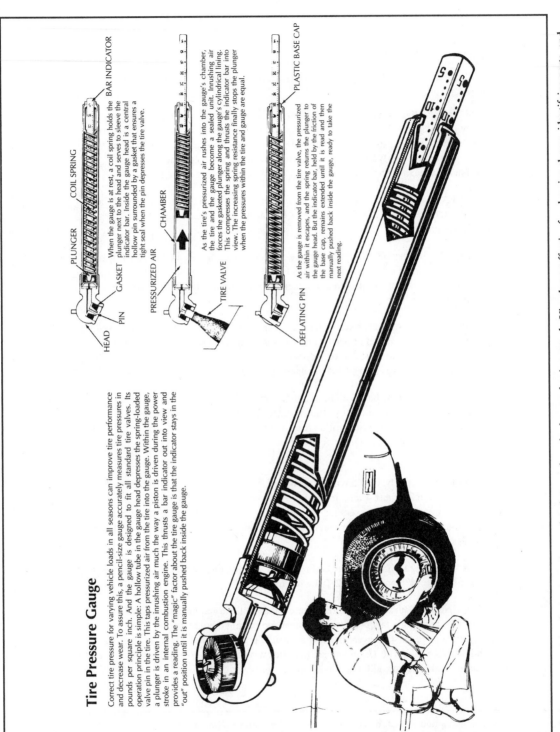

Tire Pressure Gauge

Correct tire pressure for varying vehicle loads in all seasons can improve tire performance and decrease wear. To assure this, a pencil-size gauge accurately measures tire pressures in pounds per square inch. And the gauge is designed to fit all standard tire valves. Its operation principle is simple: A hollow tube in the gauge head depresses the spring-loaded valve pin in the tire. This taps pressurized air from the tire into the gauge. Within the gauge, a plunger is driven by the inrushing air much the way a piston is driven during the power stroke in an internal combustion engine. This thrusts a bar indicator out into view and provides a reading. The "magic" factor about the tire gauge is that the indicator stays in the "out" position until it is manually pushed back inside the gauge.

BAR INDICATOR

When the gauge is at rest, a coil spring holds the plunger next to the head and serves to sleeve the indicator bar. Inside the gauge head is a central hollow pin surrounded by a gasket that ensures a tight seal when the pin depresses the tire valve.

As the tire's pressurized air rushes into the gauge's chamber, the tire and the gauge become a sealed unit. Inrushing air forces the gasketed plunger along the gauge's cylindrical lining. This compresses the spring and thrusts the indicator bar into view. The increasing spring resistance finally stops the plunger when the pressures within the tire and gauge are equal.

PLASTIC BASE CAP

As the gauge is removed from the tire valve, the pressurized air within it escapes, and the spring returns the plunger to the gauge head. But the indicator bar, held by the friction of the base cap, remains extended until it is read and then manually pushed back inside the gauge, ready to take the next reading.

COIL SPRING
PLUNGER
GASKET
HEAD
PIN
CHAMBER
PRESSURIZED AIR
TIRE VALVE
DEFLATING PIN

Figure 17.3 Process description is used to explain how tools and other mechanisms work. Visuals are effective for showing shapes, identifying parts, and explaining how parts move during operation.

Source: Excerpt from Rudolph Graf and George M. Whalen, *How It Works Illustrated: Everyday Devices and Mechanisms*, Popular Science Books (New York: Popular Science/Outdoor Life Book Division, Times Mirror Magazines, Inc., 1974), 20. Reprinted with permission from *Popular Science Magazine*, copyright 1974, Times Mirror Magazines, Inc.

the changing positions of the expanding chamber of air, the plunger, the spring, and the bar indicator.

ARRANGING THE DETAILS OF THE DESCRIPTION

As you have seen, process description is the method of the storyteller. You have to do more than merely explain a process. One of the biggest problems readers have in following the description of a complex process is being thrust into the first stage of the process without orientation. It is often best to precede your description of the initial stage with some information to help them get their bearings. If you move too quickly, you are likely to lose readers.

To help you describe complex processes that require more than just a "then-this-happens" story, let us study the arrangement and the kinds of information that will aid readers in following your explanation.

The three-part arrangement illustrated in Figure 17.4, which resembles the one used in mechanism description (see Figure 16.4), will usually be satisfactory for describing a process.

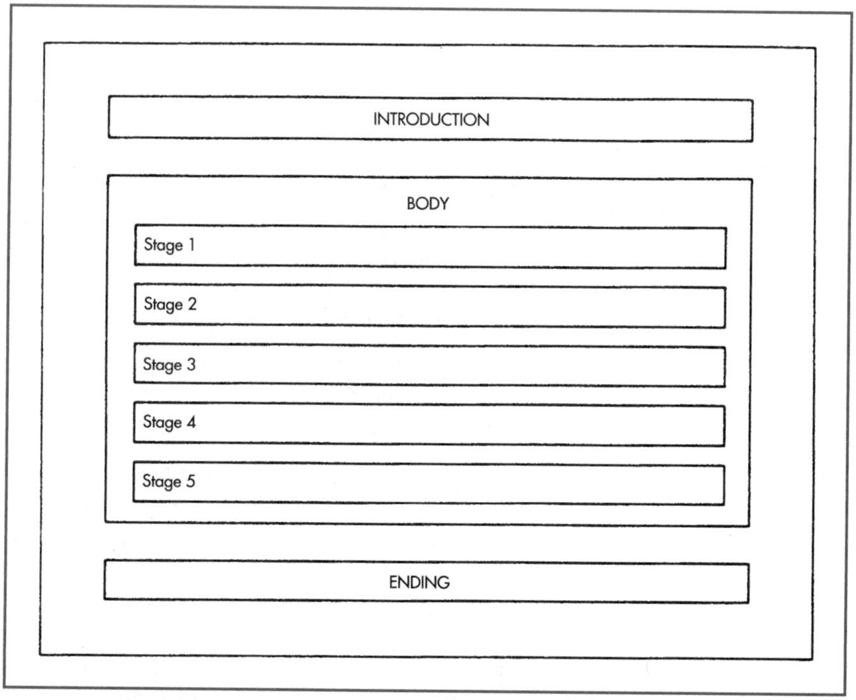

Figure 17.4 Basic organizational pattern of process description. The introduction provides an overview of the purpose, importance, duration, and major stages of the process. The body describes each major stage of the process. The ending, if necessary, summarizes important points about the process and describes the process through one complete cycle of activity.

THE TITLE

The title need not be terribly snappy, but it should be specific enough to identify the process. If submerged-welding techniques are your subject, include those words in the title. "Liquid Fuels from Coal by the SRC-Process" and "Using Helium to Trace Gases in Oilfields" are good descriptive titles of process reports.

THE INTRODUCTION

The introduction, which may require one paragraph or several, prepares readers for the details of the process. It identifies the process, states its purpose and significance, and traces briefly the main course of the process by naming its major stages. A well-written introduction may be the key to your readers' understanding of the process, so spend some time working on it.

Identifying the Process

Often just naming the process is adequate (taping an ankle, how sediments build up on the ocean floor, recruiting personnel). Sometimes, though, you must use a sentence or more to explain the nature of the process.

> Like a refrigerator, an air conditioner cools a pace by removing heat from the air and pumping it elsewhere.

> Dew is the result of the condensation of moisture from the air. As air cools, it is able to hold smaller and smaller amounts of water vapor. At a certain low temperature—the dew point—the air is saturated with water vapor, and dew begins to form as water droplets on cool surfaces, such as grass.

Sometimes it is important to explain why a particular process is used:

> The ultrasound scanner produces pulses of ultrasound (sound with a frequency range above the limit of human hearing). It is used, not to save the patient's hearing, but because it has a short wavelength and enables a computer to produce more detail in the image.

Remember to remind or inform your readers of the general principle behind what's familiar to you but little understood by them.

Going Through the Main Stages

Readers will always find it easier to follow the explanation of a process when they have first been given an overview of the process. The process is divided into its main stages, which are listed in the order in which they occur. Because the process may involve many separate actions, group closely related steps as a single main stage. In this way you can keep your readers from getting lost in the forest of individual steps and protect them against a monotonous "and-then" sequence. For instance, the transmission of electrical power from large generators in power plants to private homes involves a multitude of steps, but the main stages of the process are four: (1) power-plant generators produce high-voltage current, (2) transmission transformers increase the high voltage even higher to reduce energy losses, (3) powerlines carry the current over long distances, and (4) distribution transformers reduce the voltage for distribution to industry and private homes. Each main stage consists of several steps. For example, the fourth stage—reducing the voltage for distribution—consists of two substages: (a) reducing the current so that it can be distributed to factories with high-voltage machines and to high-speed electric trains and (b) further reducing the current to 220 and 110 volts before it reaches private homes.

You may present the overview two ways—by list or flowchart.

The following are examples of sentences that list the major stages of a process:

Executive recruitment consists of six steps: (1) making the position opening known to potential applicants, (2) screening the applicants, (3) interviewing qualified applicants, (4) selecting the best-qualified applicant, (5) offering employment, and (6) responding to the applicant's decision.

A fuse "blows" when the electrical current through the fuse becomes too great, creating heat that melts away the narrow center strip of the fuse, thereby interrupting the operation of the electrical circuit.

Making paper consists of four major stages:

1. Preparing the pulp

2. Removing impurities from the pulp

3. Turning the pulp into paper strips

4. Wrapping the paper around a roller or cutting the paper into separate sheets

The formation of salt deposits occurs in three stages: (1) deposit of alkaline earth metals in bodies of water, (2) concentration of salt in waters with limited inflow, and (3) sedimentation of carbonates into layers of salt.

Mitosis, the process by which the nucleus of a cell divides into two parts, consists of four separate stages, known as the prophase, metaphase, anaphase, and telephase.

The shield budding method of grafting involves five steps:

1. A bud is cut from a twig.

2. A T-shaped cut is made in the bark of the stock.

3. The bark is raised to admit the bud.

4. The bud is placed in the cut.

5. The stock and bud are wrapped.

The relationship of the RITE 1080's three main components is as follows:

1. Copy is typed onto the screen from the keyboard.

2. The copy is transferred from the screen to the disk for storage.

3. The disk is removed from the RITE 1080 and taken to the RITE 9200 where the copy is justified and typeset.

As you can easily see from some of these examples, listing the main stages in a column makes them easier to see, to remember, and to refer to. The surrounding blank space draws attention to the list. Notice also that the sample processes range from three to six main stages. That is about the right number. No simple rule governs how many stages to divide a process into, but too many stages (or too many steps within a stage) can give readers trouble. The human mind has a limited capacity for retaining pieces of information, and you don't want to overload it. We do not want to be too rigid in recommending that you restrict the number of major stages to no more than six in every instance, but when you find that you have more than eight or nine stages in a process or more than eight or nine steps in a major stage, consider repartitioning to reduce the number and to lessen the processing load on the reader's mind.

In making an overview list, make sure that the items in the list are grammatically parallel; that is, use groups of words of the same grammatical type. (See also, "Parallelism" in Unit V, The Writer's Guide.) Compare the following two lists of the steps for forming laminate wood bowls and plates. The first is ungrammatically parallel:

1. making a plastic form

2. the veneering is then cut to fit the form

3. build up the laminations

4. to cure the laminations

5. finishing the laminations

A grammatically parallel list would read like this:

1. *making* a plastic form

2. *cutting* the veneer to fit the form

3. *building* up the laminations

4. *curing* the laminations

5. *finishing* the laminations

Items in a list may either be single-spaced or doubled-spaced. However, if any item is more than a line long, double-space after each item in the list.

THE BODY

The body of the process description describes each main stage in the order given by the list or the flowchart in the introduction. The stage-by-stage description provides much the same information for each stage that the introduction did for the process as a whole. Again, as we suggested when we discussed mechanism description, simply think of each single stage of the process as a miniature process.

Here are some suggestions for describing specific stages.

• **If the stages of the process are complex or lengthy, introduce them with headings.** Give each stage proper emphasis by devoting at least a paragraph or section to it. Early in each paragraph or section explain what the stage is and what happens. If the stage is complex and the detail is necessary, provide an overview of its substages just as you did for the process as a whole.

• **Use topic sentences to explain the result of each stage or summarize the action that takes place in that stage.** The topic sentences of a series of paragraphs describing how an ultrasound scanner works to produce an image of an unborn child might read like this:

First, a probe emits an ultrasound pulse that scans the interior of the mother's body. . . .

Second, the returning echoes of the pulse from the womb and the baby are received as electrical signals by a computer. . . .

Third, the computer uses the returning echoes to build up a cross-section image of the mother and baby.

And so on to the end of the process. Each of these sentences starts a paragraph that may be expanded to the length and degree of detail the writer thinks the reader needs to understand what occurs in that stage.

• **As you describe each stage of the process, use flowcharts to partition each stage visually into substages or steps.** One way to do this is to provide a multilevel diagram that shows the main stages and their substages. Such a flowchart is illustrated in Figure 17.5, which provides an overview of the marketing chain for beef cattle. The first level of the flowchart identifies the three main stages—assembling, processing, and distributing. The second level of the flowchart identifies the substages of each main stage. The vertical broken lines arrange the substages under the appropriate main stage.

Block flowcharts that describe processes as complicated as the marketing chain for beef cattle leave much to be desired because they use a poor format or present too much information for the limited memory of most readers. However, the visual segments of the flowchart in Figure 17.5 make the process fairly easy to follow. Readers need not grasp more than five activities at a time: first the three main stages, then the substages of

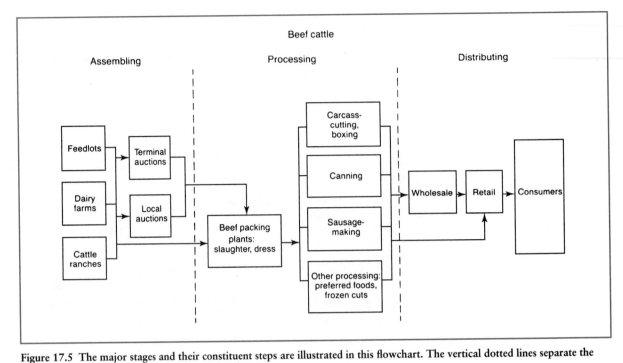

Figure 17.5 The major stages and their constituent steps are illustrated in this flowchart. The vertical dotted lines separate the major stages: assembling, processing, and distributing.
Source: Uhl, John N. "Who Does What in the Marketing Field." *1982 Yearbook of Agriculture.* Washington: GPO, 1982. 145.

each substage (five at the most in the assembling and the processing stages). Thus readers see the entire process and keep the big picture in mind while reading about the stages and substages.

Another way to illustrate multiple levels of a process is to use a series of flowcharts—one depicting the main stages and subsequent ones detailing the substages of each main stage, as in Figures 17.6 through 17.9. The simple one-level flowchart in Figure 17.6 identifies the three main stages of a community relations plan developed as part of an organization's management program. The three blocks provide an overview of the entire

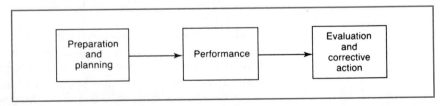

Figure 17.6 Flowchart showing the three main stages of a community relations plan.

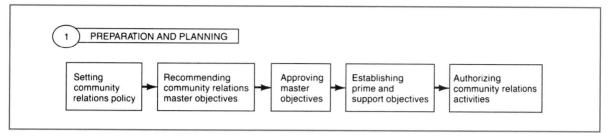

Figure 17.7 Flowchart showing the first stage and its substages of a community relations plan.

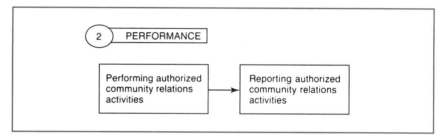

Figure 17.8 Flowchart showing the second stage and its substages of a community relations plan.

process at its most general level. As each of the three main stages is described in more detail in the body of the process description, a one-level flowchart shows that stage in greater detail, as shown in Figures 17.7, 17.8, and 17.9. The interrelated flowcharts work together to emphasize visually the key information in each stage and how it relates to the rest of the process.

The decision of whether to describe the process in a series of interrelated one-level flowcharts or to use one multilevel flowchart, such as the ones illustrated in Figures 17.5 and 17.10, depends on your analysis of your readers. Readers who are generally familiar with the process should have little difficulty following multilevel flowcharts. Readers who are not so familiar with the process or who are following an oral presentation will probably find the series of interrelated one-level flowcharts easier to read. For some readers you might want to provide both a full-page or full-screen multilevel flowchart that shows all levels of the process (see Figure 17.10) and a series of diagrams that detail the steps of each main stage.

The important thing is to use flowcharts. They take up space, but if they are easy to read, they minimize reading time and help readers keep track of how each activity fits into the overall process.

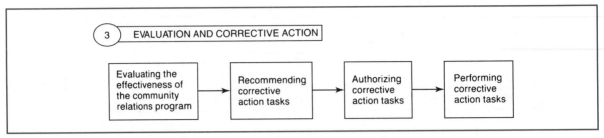

Figure 17.9 Flowchart showing the third stage and its substages of a community relations plan.

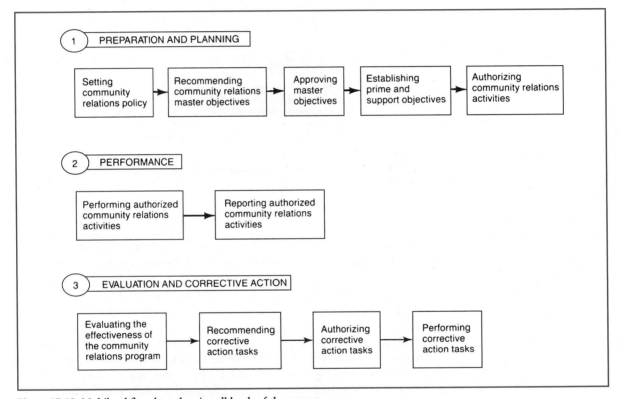

Figure 17.10 Multilevel flowchart showing all levels of the process.

THE ENDING

There is no set way to end the process description. It might simply end with an explanation of the last main stage, like this:

> The gases have lost almost half of their velocity and about one-third of their temperature before entering the turbine. As the gases pass through the turbine, they move through the converging exhaust nozzle (see Figure 5) and out of the engine. By going through the venturi-shaped tail pipe, the exhaust gases gain velocity to increase the propulsion of the craft.

The description might end with a brief summary of the main stages and a statement of the duration of the procedure:

The process—from the time the dough is placed in the hopper until the finished product is ready for shipment—takes only two minutes and fifteen seconds.

Or the description might end with additional comments on the process as a whole:

When a metal is cold worked—that is, shaped at normal temperatures— it nearly always ends up harder because the force that changed the shape of the piece also caused some changes inside the metal. Although the increased strength is useful for finished parts, it makes further cold working of unfinished pieces more difficult. Cold-worked metal can be made soft again by heating it, a process called "annealing."

PLANNING AND REVISING CHECKLIST: PROCESS DESCRIPTION

Think about the following while planning and revising process descriptions.

PLANNING

- How familiar is your intended audience with the process? Will any terms need to be defined? Will any *so-whats* need to be explained?

- What is the purpose of the description? Is it to help your audience understand what happens during the process? Evaluate the process? Compare it to a similar process?

- What visuals and analogies enable your audience to visualize and gain a conceptual understanding of the process?

REVISING

- Is the description of the process complete and accurate enough for you and your audience's purposes?

- Does your description provide a clear initial overview of the purpose, the duration, and the major stages of the process?

- Are the cause(s), effect(s), and the activity of each major stage of the process clearly explained?

- Are details, analogies, and references to time sequences clear to the intended audience?

- Are the visuals clear and easy to understand, considering the intended audience?

SUGGESTIONS FOR APPLYING YOUR KNOWLEDGE

1. Analyze the use of *so-whats* in the descriptions in Figure 17.2 and Figure 17.3. Divide a sheet of paper into two columns and list the actions or facts in the left column and the *so-whats* in the right column. If you believe that additional actions or facts require *so-whats,* add them to the list and provide the *so-whats.*

2. Analyze and discuss in class the description in Figure 17.11 of the filtration of domestic water supplies by use of a rapid sand filter.

3. Choose a process with which you are familiar, explain its purpose, partition it into its main stages and the main stages into steps. Submit for your instructor's and fellow students' evaluation: (1) a sentence or two that explains the purpose and importance of the process, (2) a list of the main stages, (3) a list of the steps in each stage, and (4) a flowchart depicting the main stages.

4. Team up with a classmate or group of classmates to give an oral explanation of a process with which you and your partner or group are familiar. Prepare the necessary visuals large enough to be seen by the rest of the class. One of you make the initial introduction of the process; the others describe the main stages and steps in the process. Time: 10 to 15 minutes.

5. Write an explanation of a process with which you are familiar.

   A. Explain how something is made, such as:

beer	nylon
bricks	paint
butter	paper
clay flowerpots	pencils
coins	printed circuits
glass	shingles
honey	soap
nails	wire

   B. Explain how something is done: how, for example,

   an auction is conducted

   a credit rating is checked

   a letter goes through the mail

   an organization hires an employee

   a student registers for courses at your school

continued

THE OPERATION OF A RAPID SAND FILTER

Domestic water supplies can be filtered simply and efficiently by a rapid sand filter. A rapid sand filter, as illustrated in Figure 1, consists of a rectangular concrete box, open at the top, with a depth of 8-1/2 feet. The depth must be adequate to accommodate a water depth of 3 to 4 feet, beds of sand and gravel, and the underdrain system. The sides of the filter are roughened to prevent water from streaming between the walls and the sand. The process comprises three main stage: (1) filtering the raw water, (2) draining the filtered water into storage tanks, and (3) washing the filter.

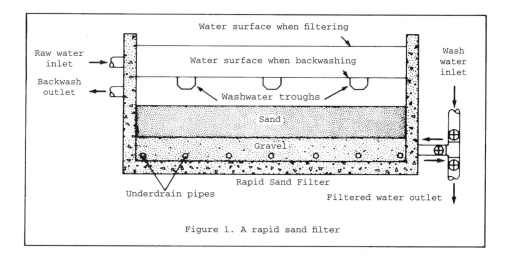

Figure 1. A rapid sand filter

Filtering the Raw Water

The filter consists of a bed of sand 24 inches deep, supported by gravel 12 inches deep. The raw water comes into the filter from primary sedimentation at the raw water inlet. As the water seeps through the pores of sand, the bacteria, finely divided clay, and other foreign particles in the water come into contact with the sand surfaces and are retained. The process is aided by the curved flow paths around the grains, throwing the particles against the sand grain surfaces. As the pores fill, the velocity of the water increases through the porous sand, and some of the

Figure 17.11 Description of a rapid sand filter.

deposited material is removed and washed farther down into the bed of sand. Most of the particles are collected on the first 3 to 4 inches of the sand bed.

Because much of the filtration is accomplished in the upper portion of the sand, the rest of the sand and the gravel bed catch any particles that fail to stick in the upper 3 to 4 inches. The depth of the additional sand and gravel also gives a more nearly uniform rate of filtration over the entire bed at all times. Without the uniform flow throughout the bed, some parts of the bed might dry and crack, causing the water to stream through without proper filtration.

Draining the Filtered Water

After the filtered water passes through the gravel, it collects in the underdrain system, which is a series of 16-inch diameter manifold pipes running lengthwise along the bottom of the rapid sand filter. Extending at right angles to the manifold pipes are 4-inch diameter pipes with 1/2-inch diameter holes spaced every 6 inches. The holes are located near the bottom of the lateral pipe to prevent clogging. Filtered water seeps through the holes and flows through the lateral pipes to the manifold pipes. The water then travels through the manifold pipes to the filtered water outlet, where it flows into storage tanks.

Washing the Filter

After 24 to 72 hours of continuous filtration, the filter beds become clogged with an accumulated mass of particles. To free the bed of these particles, the filter beds must be washed. Washing consists of passing filtered water in at the wash water outlet and through the underdrain system at such velocity that it causes the sand bed to expand to 50 percent greater than during the filtration process. The sand grains move through the turbulent water, rub against each other, and are cleaned of the accumulated particles. The rising washwater, after passing through the sand, flows into the washwater troughs and is wasted through the backwash outlet.

After the backwash, the filter is then ready for another filtration cycle.

Figure 17.11 (continued)

continued

C. Explain how something works, such as

a chainsaw	a remote controller
a circuit breaker	a rotary engine
a drill press	a sewage-treatment plant
an EKG machine	a solar heating system
a fireplace	a speedometer
the gall bladder	a telephone answering machine
the heart	a toaster
an odometer	a vacuum cleaner
an optical scanner	a water cannon
the pancreas	

D. Explain how a natural process occurs, such as

the digestion of proteins	pollination
an earthquake	sound
fog	a volcano
a hurricane	yawning
the growth of a particular plant or organism	

CHAPTER 18

INSTRUCTIONS

Learning how to do something new can be either enjoyable or frustrating. Often, the key is how clear and complete the instructions are. Some instructions, written by persons who do not know how to perform the procedure, are full of misinformation. Other instructions, written by persons who know the procedure thoroughly and who assume that everybody else does too, contain directions that are too general or incomplete. Good instructions are written by people who know the procedure inside out and who know how much detailed instruction their readers need—whether the readers are novice learners or experienced and highly skilled learners who want more conceptual understanding and more opportunities to explore and experiment on their own.

Whatever work you specialize in, you are certain to have to produce instructions. When you become good at producing instructions, you also become one of your organization's most valuable people, because good instructions can aid your organization in two ways:

1. Good instructions are effective customer-relations tools that help customers use the products and services they lease or purchase. If products and services are difficult to learn and use, customers will not lease or buy. On the other hand, good instructions enhance an organization's reputation by helping customers and clients get maximum value for their purchases and leases.

2. Good instructions are also useful in helping employees learn to do many jobs quickly and easily—from assembling, stocking, and shipping to operating, repairing, overhauling, and storing.

Your instructions should present straightforward help in solving problems for either customers or employees. Instructions can be oral, written, or, as shown in Figure 18.1, visual, but they should be put in writing and visuals when a mistake in the procedure is likely to be serious or when it is inconvenient, unfeasible, or impossible to communicate orally with your audience.

Written instructions come in all sizes and for different purposes and for different users. In this chapter we discuss the more common classifications of written instructions:

- Brief instructions presented in correspondence, on panels on packages, on sheets and leaflets

- Longer instructions presented in booklets and manuals

- Troubleshooting and error-management procedures

Our discussion covers collecting information, writing brief and lengthy sets of instructions, creating troubleshooting guides, and testing instructions for usability.

Figure 18.1 Sample instruction visuals. Some instructions, especially those designed for international audiences, rely heavily, if not solely, on visuals. *Source: Installation Guide for HP LaserJet Toner Cartridge C3903A,* reprinted with permission of Hewlett-Packard Company.

COLLECTING THE INFORMATION TO WRITE INSTRUCTIONS

Because readers of instructions expect you to write with *authority*, you must know the procedure inside out before you try to tell others how to do it. But knowing how to perform a procedure does not automatically mean you can write good instructions. Beginners who will use your instructions often lack the background or technical skills to perform what you may regard as commonly understood procedures. You must have the additional abilities to (1) put yourself in the shoes of the beginner so that you can predict their difficulties and (2) express to others what you know and do intuitively.

To conduct a comprehensive analysis of the procedure and your readers, you must consider eight topics—eight kinds of information that you need to collect:

- The reader's goal or goals, which identify what the user of your instructions should be able to do after reading the instructions

- The materials and equipment needed to perform the procedure

- The major stages of the procedure

- The duration of the procedure (how long it will take to perform the procedure)

- The step-by-step activities of each major stage

- The precautions to be observed when performing the procedure

- The visuals that illustrate situations, equipment, actions, and other aspects of the procedure

- The degree of difficulty that users of your instructions might experience in learning or performing the procedure

To gather this information, you must spend time learning the procedure and analyzing your readers and their goals and the environment in which they will use the instructions. To record the essential information you will need in working with these topics, we suggest that you use the Plan Sheet for Instructions (Figure 18.2), which is similar to those used by directors of training in preparing training manuals and other instructional material.

READER'S GOAL OR GOALS

(A) **The statement of the reader's goal or goals (see Figure 18.2) defines what the reader should be able to do when he or she finishes using the instructions.** A good goal statement should complete a "how-to" statement:

[How to] replace a fuel pump.

[How to] check the credit rating of a customer.

Plan Sheet for Instructions

(A) **Reader's Goal or Goals:**

(B) **Materials:**

   Equipment:

(C) **Major Stages:**

(D) **Duration of the Procedure:**

(E) Step No.	(F) Steps in Performing the Procedure	(G) Precautions	(H) Notes about Visuals	(I) Notes about Learning and Performance Difficulties

Figure 18.2 Plan Sheet for Instructions. This form is good for handwritten plans. You can modify the form for a computer-generated draft.

[How to] send an attachment by e-mail.

[How to] identify igneous rock.

[How to] conduct a pre-sentence investigation.

[How to] calibrate a centrifuge using a tachometer.

[How to] evaluate a long-term health-care insurance policy.

[How to] use a peripheral device on a computer, such as a modem, digitizer, or switcher.

[How to] inspect an oil cooler for cracks, damaged threads, and evidence of wear.

[How to] determine moisture content in textiles.

The reader's goal or goals should be stated quite specifically, such as "[How to] unjam a Bunscomb Bob Cat Chipper/Shredder, Model No. 1464." The goal or goals can also be developed into quantitative statements. For instance, a goal can be stated as "The reader will be able to replace the fuel pump in thirty minutes." Such a concrete, specific goal helps you clarify your objectives and write instructions that will aid the reader in achieving that goal. Identifying the reader's goals is a good starting point, because it focuses on yours and the reader's purposes and will be reflected in the title of the instructions. Focus early and continuously on what the reader hopes to achieve in using the instructions.

MATERIALS AND EQUIPMENT

(B) The materials and equipment lists (see Figure 18.2) specify the items needed to perform the procedure. Materials are those items consumed during the procedure. Equipment is the "hardware." In baking bread, the ingredients (flour, yeast, water, salt, etc.) are the materials; the measuring cup, mixing bowl, spoon, bread board, loaf pans, and oven (or bread machine) are the equipment. You must know your reader's needs as best you can so you can decide how much the reader knows and understands and whether the reader needs to be motivated to assemble the materials and equipment you list. To make the list as useful as possible, place it in the introduction, be as specific as the reader and the situation call for, and, if necessary, try to persuade the reader to use the equipment, tools, and materials you specify.

• *Put the list in the introduction.* Tell the reader exactly what to use so that he will know, before starting the procedure, the exact tools, parts, and test equipment required to complete the job. Don't wait until the middle of the procedure to tell him he needs an essential part to finish the job. It is conventional to list materials and tools in the order in which they are used in the procedure.

- *Be specific. Be complete.* In explaining to somebody how to ice-fish, do not tell her to use a fishing pole, line, and hook if she needs a 2-foot pole, 15 feet of 2-pound-test monofilament line, and a size 10 hook. If raw sunflower seeds are part of a recipe, be specific, or the chef may order salted, roasted, barbecue-flavored, or garlic-flavored sunflower seeds. If a high-intensity candling light of 80 to 100 ohms is needed, do not simply state that a light source is required. If a specific part is needed, include the manufacturer's part number or acceptable replacement stock number. Even persons who are familiar with a procedure can benefit from a friendly reminder of specificity, such as to use an insulated-handle screwdriver when working on electrical circuits.

- *Use consistent terminology.* Be consistent in choosing nomenclature and labeling equipment and material. It is difficult to produce a good set of instructions—and even more difficult for readers to follow instructions—for procedures in which procedures, units, functions, and features have been inconsistently labeled. One of your authors, for example, has used software in which a feature is labeled *tone presentation* on one screen and *present* on another. How many readers, do you suppose, would know that a feature labeled an *antenna* in one section of a report is the same as an item labeled *air terminal* in another section?

- *If necessary, try to persuade the reader to use the material and equipment you specify.* You must take into account the tendency of some readers to not believe it necessary to use the precise material or equipment you specify. Too many readers have an appalling lack of knowledge about the necessity for wearing protective eyeware when performing certain procedures. Others won't understand why the latest, more expensive version of a software program is needed instead of an older, less expensive version. To respond to the reader's belief that "it doesn't seem necessary to use that . . . ," consider adding parenthetical statements. For example, in Figure 18.5 on page 501, "one sheet of medium grit sandpaper *to smooth the wood frame*" explains to users of the instructions why that particular item is needed and might motivate them to use it.

Major Stages

Ⓒ The overview of the major stages of the procedure (see Figure 18.2) provides important conceptual information. For instance, let's assume that we are teaching readers how to change the points in the distributor of an automobile. Our overview of the major stages might look like this:

> The three major stages in changing the points in a distributor are (1) removing the old points, (2) installing the new points, and (3) adjusting the new points.

This highly condensed version of the procedure presents three ways to help readers grasp the big picture before they become immersed in the details of the procedure.

First, because the overview organizes the procedure into three major stages, it reduces the amount of information the reader needs to process at any given time. For example, the process might well involve 50 or more individual steps—which at first might appear intimidating to a beginner. However, organizing the work into three major stages makes the procedure appear more manageable. Thinking initially about accomplishing three major actions is less overwhelming than thinking about performing 50+ steps and will reduce the tendency of readers to worry in advance about whether they are going to fail.

Second, because each of the major stages in the overview identifies the task to be accomplished in each stage, the overview enables the reader to create a mental model of what is involved in each stage and to identify the major subgoals of that part of the procedure: at the end of the first stage, the old points will have been removed; at the end of the second stage, the new points will have been installed; at the end of the third stage, the new points will have been adjusted. These status descriptions help reassure the reader that the action can be accomplished, perhaps even easily and confidently, by following the instructions.

Third, because the major stages are listed in the order in which they are to be completed, the overview is a content map that helps the reader read selectively or predictably. Sometimes, of course, readers attempt to perform a procedure without even bothering to look at the instructions. Few readers will deliberately read a set of instructions from beginning to end. But for those who do, each major stage is the core of a heading, and the two (the overview list and the headings) help the reader keep the big picture in mind. Instead of reading a set of instructions from beginning to end, most readers are more likely to start trying to do the procedure, figuring things out as they go along, and to resort to the instructions only when they are stuck. Or they may want to review only the steps in a particular stage—for example, adjusting the points. Such a chronological overview provides nonlinear access to specific parts of the procedure, enabling some readers to read ahead if they wish. But all readers will share one thing in common—the desire to find quickly just the information they need.

When a major stage turns out to be long and complicated, consider providing an overview of it, just as you do for the entire procedure:

Estimating Storm Runoff

After determining the adequacy of drainage needed to maintain water in the pond during droughts, you need to estimate the potential storm runoff. To do this, you must identify (1) the kind of soil in the drainage area, (2) the types of vegetation in the drainage area, and (3) the steepness and shape of the watershed. Tables I through III show a range of runoff computations for different pond sizes.

A table of contents (see pages 356–360) might be appropriate for longer sets of instructions. Listing the major stages of a procedure or major steps of a stage responds to the diverse needs of different readers. Not to include these kinds of overviews is likely to be a major flaw in the design of your instructions.

DURATION OF THE PROCEDURE

Ⓓ The duration of the procedure (see Figure 18.2) is the amount of time necessary to perform the procedure. Stating the duration of the procedure might not seem important to you, but beginners need to know approximately how much time a procedure requires. For instance, if we rewrote our earlier overview statement about replacing points in a distributor as follows, the reader could estimate the amount of time he or she should set aside to perform the procedure:

> If you have never changed the points in a distributor, it will take you approximately one hour to (1) remove the old points, (2) install the new points, and (3) adjust the new points.

When a major stage in a procedure is long and complicated or you anticipate your reader not knowing how long it might take to complete, you can provide a similar overview for that stage:

> **Installing the Pool Liner**
>
> Before installing the liner, check the pool bottom to be sure there are no stones, twigs, or sharp objects that might damage the liner. After the liner is unboxed and placed at the deep end of the pool, it will take four to six people (see Figure 4) approximately 25 to 30 minutes to pull it into position and adjust it properly.

Remember that you should estimate the approximate amount of time it takes beginners to do the work, not you and other experts. In time, as they become more proficient in performing the process, they will be able to reduce the time needed.

STEP-BY-STEP PROCEDURE

Ⓔ Ⓕ The step-by-step part of the instructions explains the process in detail for novice readers. **State each step in terms of what the reader** *does* when performing the step (see Figure 18.2). This is where you must think through the process in detail—sequencing steps logically. What does the user do first? Second? Third? As you develop the steps, keep these three matters in mind: sequence the steps in the best order for the reader to complete the instructions, use imperative verbs, and avoid ambiguities.

Sequence the steps in logical order. Your instructions should state explicitly the sequence of steps (1, 2, 3, and so on) and should clearly distinguish instructional material from conceptual or background material. Numbering the steps is important because readers typically switch back and forth between instructions and work, reading a bit, then performing an action, then reading some more. The numbered steps make it easier for readers to find their place in the instructions. Numbering the steps makes clear the order in which steps are performed, which may or may not be a crucial consideration. Even in situations in which the reader can choose the order of action (for instance, it makes no difference in cleaning a double-barrel shotgun which barrel is cleaned first—assuming they are of the same gauge), you should set the sequence based on your experience of what is the best recommended practice. Show the reader one good way to perform the step.

Use imperative verbs. To present instructions in short, distinct steps, use a single imperative verb and as few words as possible to tell the reader exactly what to do. An imperative verb will usually be the first word of the instruction:

1. *Disengage* the clutch.

However, you will often begin an instruction with an adverbial phrase:

4. Before cutting the first strip, *check* to ensure that the pattern is straight.

or

2. Using the wire feeler gauge, *set* the gap between the electrodes to the correct clearance (see Figure 2A).

Use a specific imperative verb (one that states a command) to tell the reader the statement is *instructional*:

Instructional: 1. Disengage the clutch. (Use this style for instructions.)

Descriptive: The clutch is disengaged.

Subjunctive: The clutch should be disengaged.

The descriptive and subjunctive verbs are not instructional in that they don't tell the reader explicitly to *do* anything.

Avoid ambiguous statements. Be aware that statements can have multiple meanings that confuse and befuddle readers. For instance, it is essential that the user of instructions for mixing concentrated sulfuric acid and water know the precise way to do it. The statement: "Mix the concentrated sulfuric acid and water" sounds simple enough, right? However, the reader must decide how to mix the two. Is the acid added to the water? Is the water added to the acid? Are the acid and water poured simultaneously into a third container? The instruction is unclear, ambiguous, which can lead to poor or, as in this case, potentially dangerous results. Pouring the water into the acid or pouring the two simultaneously into a third container creates a volatile gas that can be messy and perhaps even cause an explosion. The safe procedure is to pour the acid into the water. Thus, to reduce ambiguity, the instruction should read: "Pour the concentrated sulfuric acid into the water." If necessary, explain why it is done that way.

Write instructions so that it will be difficult for someone to misunderstand them. To prevent costly errors in instructions and to check the clarity of the instructions, try them out yourself. Or better yet, find an inexperienced person (but one who is a reasonable representative of the intended audience) to try the instructions, while you watch and take notes for possible revisions. (See pages 523–526 for information about conducting usability tests.)

PRECAUTIONS

(G) Identify precautions (see Figure 18.2) that readers should observe while performing the step. According to the National Safety Council, approximately 4 million disability accidents occurred on the job in the United States in 1996.[1] Because learners make many mistakes, giving precautions to help reduce the risks of personal injury and property damage are among your most important responsibilities. Place precautions into one of three categories:

Caution: to prevent damage to tools, equipment, and materials.

Warning: to prevent injury to the person performing the procedure or to others nearby.

Danger: to warn of life-threatening situations to the person performing the procedure or to others nearby.

Use headings, bold print, color, and other typographical features to highlight precautions and make them visibly distinct from surrounding text. Any of the forms shown in Figure 18.3 may be used.

You must be on the lookout for points in the procedure where a precaution might be helpful. It is not easy to foresee when users of instructions will have a problem, a question, are likely to make a mistake, or might need to recover from an error. Relying on your own memories of the difficulties you had as a novice, the experience of others, and data derived from user testing will help you target places where probable problems and errors are most likely to occur.

Figure 18.3 provides examples of caution, warning, and danger statements. Use a consistent format for precautions throughout the set of instructions so that all warnings have the same look and are easy to spot. Place precautions where they seem most appropriate: general safety information needed to establish a safe and secure environment for performing the procedure or that applies throughout the procedure should go in the introductory section of the instructions. Specific safety information that

[1] *Accident Facts. Work, 1996.* 30 June 1998 ⟨http://www.nsc.org/irs/statinfo/AFP48.htm⟩.

CAUTION!

Tighten the nut to 25-30 pounds per inch. If you tighten the nut too hard, you will strip the threads.

CAUTION!
Oil rags are combustible. Wash or destroy them immediately.

CAUTION!

If the old gasket is not completely removed from the engine block, the new filter will not seal properly and will result in oil leaks and possible engine damage.

WARNING

Do not get under vehicle held up by a jack or by concrete blocks. The jack might slip and a concrete block will not hold the car's weight. Use jack stands or ramps.

 **DANGER!**

High frequency electromagnetic **radiation can cause fatal internal burns.** If you feel the slightest warming effect while near the equipment, **move away quickly.**

ELECTROMAGNETIC RADIATION

WARNING

Before making adjustments, shut off the engine, allow the cutting blades to come to a complete stop, and disconnect the spark plug.

Figure 18.3 These are sample cautions and warning statements. The words *caution, warning, danger,* or other suitable words are highlighted to make the statements visually prominent. Warnings and cautions are usually amplified with statements that explain the importance of observing the precaution, the consequences of not following the caution or warning, and the preventive or corrective action to be taken.

pertains to a specific step should be included within the instruction for performing that step.

Ideally, readers should follow instructions exactly. Unfortunately, many readers ignore them because they fail to understand their implications or they underestimate the potential problems in performing a task. Be aware of many readers' tendencies to think that precautions really don't seem necessary. To encourage readers to do exactly as the precaution says and to help them avoid making a mistake, explain the potential difficulty or danger:

> Extinguish all cigarettes and flames. A spark can ignite hydrogen gas from the battery.

"Extinguish all cigarettes and flames" is the precaution. "A spark can ignite hydrogen gas from the battery" describes the potential consequences of making a mistake and explains the importance of following the precaution. Adding this *so-what* provides the supplementary conceptual information that some readers need.

VISUALS

(H) **Identify the visuals that will help readers develop a mental picture of what they are to do in the step (see Figure 18.2).** Visuals are important enough in instructions to be regarded as equal partners with words. Decide early in your planning the visuals that will be helpful to your reader. Sometimes, as exemplified in Figure 18.1, visuals are the only medium of instructions. Keep the following questions in mind when you write instructions. Have I *told* the reader *what* to do? Have I *shown* the reader *how* to do it? Use column H in the Plan Sheet for Instructions to remind yourself of visuals you will want to use to illustrate the written instructions. Notice the use of visuals in instructions in Figures 18.1, 18.7, 18.8, and 18.12.

LEARNING AND PERFORMANCE DIFFICULTY

(I) **Estimate the degree of difficulty readers might experience in learning or performing the step (see Figure 18.2).** The degree of difficulty refers to the time and effort it takes to learn how to perform an action. Some tasks, of course, are more difficult to learn and perform than others. As you fill out this column in the Plan Sheet for Instructions, try to indicate how easy or difficult the task is to learn, remember, and perform by using words such as *difficult, moderate to difficult, moderate, moderate to easy, easy,* and so on. Just remember that you are considering the degree of difficulty for users of your instructions, not for you.

Don't fall into the trap of assuming that because you know how to do certain things that your reader also will know how to do them and will be bored by elementary instruction. A good way to learn the reader's needs is to recall your own experiences in learning the task. This might take some real memory work, because now that you are able to perform the procedure well, you have probably forgotten the difficulties you encountered as a learner. Another reliable way to learn the reader's needs is to conduct a user testing of the set of instructions (see pages 523–526).

Such analysis will help you decide how detailed your instruction for the task should be. You can also use column I to remind yourself of any prior knowledge or special skill that the reader may need to perform the task. For instance, if the reader is to check the electrolyte level in a battery, you must decide whether you can simply assume that the reader has the prior knowledge to do it or whether you must provide step-by-step instructions. If the reader at some point in a procedure has to transfer a file to another computer, you must decide whether the reader already knows how to do it or whether you must explain the process. Keep asking yourself: Now that I have told the reader *what* to do, should I tell the reader *how* to do it? Column I in Figure 18.2 is where you make notations about adding supplementary material for readers who may require more information about performing a troublesome step.

Sometimes the primary information in the instructions fails and the reader needs supplemental information to perform a task successfully. For instance, it may not be enough to state: "Disconnect the main electric cable from the generator outlet." This direction, as clear as it seems, omits a great deal of information that the reader must supply:

- the location of the main electric cable and generator outlet

- the identity of the main electric cable

- the tools needed to disconnect them

- the correct way to disconnect them

- the importance of disconnecting them correctly

A reader who lacks this necessary information risks making mistakes. A note, such as the one shown in Figure 18.4, is the best way to walk the reader through a task that is unfamiliar, difficult or dangerous to perform, or that results in an unexpected or undesired outcome. Learners need help both on what to do and why to do it.

Figure 18.5 is an example of a completed Plan Sheet for Instructions. Moving from the completed plan sheet to the first draft of your instructions should go fairly smoothly. The statement of the reader's goal or goals, the list of materials and tools or equipment, the duration of the procedure, and the list of the major steps give you the core of the introduction. The numbered steps, safety precautions, and notations give you the blueprint for the step-by-step procedure. In fact, your entries for Steps in Performing the Procedure (F) will use language much

Step 4.   Disconnect the main electric cable (the large cable with the shiny green protective cover) from the generator outlet (located just behind the large air vent). See Figure 2.

How?   Pull the cable boot straight out to disconnect the cable.

Why?   Do not pull on the cable itself. Doing so may damage the carbon conductor inside the cable and increase the chance of an electrical short or spark, which might result in an electrical shock or fire.

Or

Step 4.   Disconnect the main electric cable (the large cable with the shiny green protective cover) from the generator outlet (located just behind the large air vent). See Figure 2.

Note: Pull the cable boot straight out to disconnect the cable. Do not pull on the cable itself. Doing so may damage the carbon conductor inside the cable and increase the chance of an electrical short or spark, which might result in an electrical shock or fire.

Figure 18.4 Sample versions of a note that provides information that can help users of instructions perform an unfamiliar task. The first version is more effective because the reader sees the how and why sections labeled.

like that you will use in writing the instructions. As you examine the examples of different kinds of instructions in the rest of this chapter, you will notice that the completed plan sheet gives you the important information in the order in which you will most likely use it in writing the instructions.

Once you have completed the plan sheet, review it carefully to make sure it contains no misinformation, irrelevant information, vague instructions, or logical gaps. Leave nothing to chance.

Now, let us analyze the first of the three types of instructions listed earlier—brief instructions presented in correspondence, on packages and panels, and in sheets and leaflets.

WRITING BRIEF SETS OF INSTRUCTIONS

CORRESPONDENCE

You will often write letters, memos, and e-mail that provide brief but specific instructions to clients, potential clients, and co-workers. Such a letter is

Plan Sheet for Instructions

Reader's Goal or Goals: *Build a silkscreen frame (the first of six stages in printing your own t-shirts)*

Materials: *Two 20" lengths of 2" x 2" pine (to make the frame)*
Two 16" lengths of 2" x 2" pine (to make the frame)
One sheet of medium grit sandpaper to smooth the wood frame
Eight corrugated fasteners to secure the corners of the wood frame
Wood glue (such as Elmer's)

Equipment: *Carpenter's square and pencil to mark wood pieces*
Handsaw to saw wood
Miter box to cut 45° angles at the ends of the wood pieces
Table saw with dado blade to make grooves in the wood pieces
Hammer to drive corrugated fasteners into the wood frame

Major Stages: *1. Cutting and grooving the wood pieces*
2. Sanding the wood pieces
3. Gluing the wood pieces together
4. Fastening the corners together

Duration of the Procedure: *Approximately one hour (if the reader already knows how to use a miter box and saw with a dado blade)*

Step No.	Steps in Performing the Procedure	Precautions	Notes about Visuals	Notes about Learning and Performance Difficulties
Stage 1.	*Cutting and Grooving the Wood*			
1.	*Using the handsaw and miter box, cut the ends of the wood pieces to make miter joints.*	*Cut the wood at the correct angles so that….*	*drawing to show how each corner should be cut*	*must know how to use the miter box*
2.	*Using the carpenter's square and pencil, draw a line down each piece of wood 3/8" from the edge away from the print or long side of the wood.*	*none*	*drawing to show where the line is to be drawn*	*easy*
3.	*Using the table saw with a dado blade, carefully cut a 3/16" groove in each piece of wood as shown.*	*Wear safety goggles to protect eyes from flying wood particles. Make sure the….*	*drawing to show cross-sectional view of the board*	*must know how to use table saw with dado blade*

Figure 18.5 Sample of a completed Plan Sheet for Instructions.

Wunderbar Haus
Rhinelander Park, WI 54529-5204

Dear Guest:

Thank you for staying at the Wunderbar Haus. We hope that you enjoyed the fine facilities, programs, and services provided for your convenience.

Because we are expecting a large number of people to depart the guesthouse tomorrow, you are encouraged to use our express check-out service. If you have left a major credit card imprint upon registration, simply use our express video checkout (available from 6 a.m. to 12 noon). **The procedure takes only a minute or two.**

1. Using the remote control, tune the guest room television to the **Menu Screen** (channel 1).

2. Select **Account Review/Checkout**.

3. Select **Account Review** to view the current charges posted to your room account.

4. If you agree, and wish to check out, select **Check Out**. Or, if you disagree, please contact the Front Desk by dialing 7 on your guest room telephone.

When you select **Check Out**, the charges are applied to your credit card and a copy of your bill is available at the Concierge Desk in the main lobby.

The hotel check-out time is 12 noon. Departures after 12 noon may be subject to a half-day room charge. Should you require assistance with luggage carrying or storage, please press the Belldesk button on your guest room telephone.

We hope you have enjoyed your stay with us. We have certainly enjoyed serving you and look forward to accommodating you in the future whether you are traveling on business or pleasure.

Sincerely,

Hans Kroeber

Hans Kroeber, Assistant Manager
Guest Relations

Figure 18.6 Sample instructional letter.

shown in Figure 18.6. The letter instructs guests on how to use a hotel's express check-out service. Though brief, the letter contains a lot of information:

- The first two paragraphs introduce the instructions. The first paragraph contains statements designed to create goodwill.

- The second paragraph explains why the reader is receiving the instructions and introduces the instructions that are presented in the numbered, displayed list that follows.

- The list presents the instructions simply and directly, with sufficient detail so that the reader will know what to do.

- The third and fourth paragraphs provide additional useful information.

- The fifth and final paragraph "resells" the hotel's services and attempts to continue the goodwill established with the reader.

The instructions also illustrate the following five conventional strategies for explaining step-by-step actions:

1. **The reason for performing the procedure is explained.** The reader is motivated to perform the procedure by having the *so-what* explained (here is a way to avoid the wait at the front desk at check-out time). Once the reader realizes how the procedure is useful or important, he or she is likely to do it.

2. **The instructions are written in the imperative voice.** That is, the reader is told to perform some action, as in "*tune* the guest room television" and "*Select* Account Review/Checkout." Notice that the imperative is simply the "you" sentence form—"You turn the guest room television to the Menu Screen"—with the *you* missing. Imperative statements sound a bit brusque when taken out of context as we have done here, but they do not really trouble anyone. You have read imperative sentences many times in instructions, we suspect, and we are sure you have never been disturbed by them. Remember that instructions tell how to do something. Readers rely on you to tell them what to do and how to do it.

3. **The instructions are short and to the point.** They run from a low of 4 words to a high of 17, averaging about 11 words each. From 10 to 14 words is average in instructions.

4. **The instructions are presented in an uncluttered, simple format.** Each step is emphasized by being separated from the others and displayed in a numbered list, each in its own paragraph, surrounded by white space.

5. **Important words are emphasized.** Bold print highlights the menu items.

These strategies serve equally well in memo or e-mail instructions.

INSTRUCTIONAL SHEETS AND LEAFLETS

Instructions also appear on sheets and leaflets enclosed with goods, as shown in Figure 18.7, which explains how to mount decorative ceiling

HOW TO INSTALL CEILING HOOKS

CAUTION: Do not use hooks on radiant-heating ceiling. Do not drape electrical wire on the hook. Slide the chain link only over the hook. Weight of object should not exceed 15 pounds.

FOR PLASTER OR PLASTER BOARD CEILINGS (Fig. 1)

1. Drill hole in the ceiling to the same diameter as the closed flaps of the enclosed toggle bolt assembly (A).
2. Insert flaps and bolt into the ceiling with the toggle bolt protruding through the ceiling.
3. Lock the assembly by screwing on the hook as shown.

FOR WOOD OR ACOUSTICAL TILE CEILINGS (Fig. 2)

1. Screw steel screw (B) into hook (C).
2. Screw the assembly into the wood.

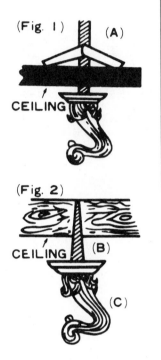

(Fig. 1) (A)

CEILING

(Fig. 2)

CEILING (B)

(C)

Figure 18.7 Step-by-step procedures. Note the contingent instructions depending on the type of ceiling into which the hooks are to be installed.

hooks for hanging flowerpots, chimes, or chains for swag lamps. Here are some guidelines for developing instructional sheets and leaflets:

- **Use a title that is specific enough to assure readers that they have the right instructions for the right job.** Usually the first thing readers look for on an instruction sheet is the title. The title should specifically link the right information to the right job. Words such as *directions, instructions, procedures,* and *how to* . . . confirm what type of document it is. Naming the procedure in the title also helps: "How to Install Ceiling Hooks."

- **Emphasize precautions.** Warnings and cautions should be placed where they cannot be overlooked easily.

- **If the instructions contain several steps or series of steps, use a numbered system instead of bullets, dashes, or other marks.** As readers look over the instructions, they should see down the left margin each instruction beginning with an arabic numeral and period (or some other mark).

- **Use visuals to help readers understand and follow an instruction.** The visual should be placed as close as possible to the instruction. Include captions and call-outs (references to visuals in the text) to identify visuals and relate them to the instructions. Otherwise, readers may not refer to them at all.

WRITING INSTRUCTION BOOKLETS AND MANUALS

As you can see from the samples in this chapter, the design of instructions is important. You must think carefully about the amount of space they will occupy. Some instructions must be squeezed into small panels on the side of a box, others fill a manual. Instruction booklets and manuals share many characteristics with briefer forms of instructions: directions are given in short imperative sentences; are separately paragraphed; are emphasized by surrounding white space, numbering, and different fonts; and are supported by visuals. In addition to these characteristics, longer instructional booklets and manuals include features that help readers quickly find a particular section that contains needed information for a specific action. Such guides include a table of contents; an overview statement and flowchart that maps the contents verbally, visually, or both; an index; tabs to mark the beginning of major sections; and sometimes even different colored paper for each section.

To see these characteristics in more detail, we include two types of instructional booklets and manuals. The first, which we call *workbench* instructions, instructs readers as they actually perform a procedure. The earlier examples in this chapter are examples of workbench instructions. The second type, which we call *armchair* instructions, teaches new techniques and procedures to readers in the calm of their offices or homes before they actually attempt to perform the procedure.

WORKBENCH INSTRUCTIONS

Read the instructions for building an accident-free tree stand (Figure 18.8) and then let us analyze its format, arrangement, and style.

Format

Layout and design of instructions are quite important. Notice the heavy reliance on visuals, bold type, and headings. Visuals *show* the reader how to do the work. The two-column format beginning on page 3 places the visuals next to the written instructions they illustrate. (One

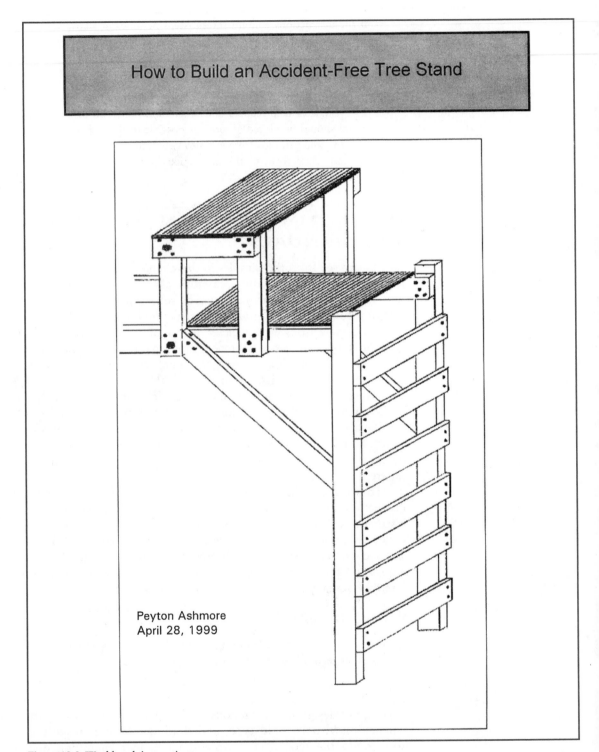

How to Build an Accident-Free Tree Stand

Peyton Ashmore
April 28, 1999

Figure 18.8 Workbench instructions.
Source: Unpublished student report, printed with permission of T. Peyton Ashmore, the author.

How to Build an Accident-Free Tree Stand

Many hunting accidents occur due to inadequate tree stands. These tree-stand accidents can be attributed to rotted wood, rusted nails, and stress failures. These instructions explain how to construct a tree stand that should prevent all types of accidents caused by faulty construction or inadequate materials. The assembly, which should take approximately two hours, consists of five major stages: 1) constructing the ladder, 2) constructing the foot platform, 3) constructing the seat platform, 4) attaching the chain to the foot and seat platforms, and 5) chaining the tree stand to a tree.

Materials Needed

The materials will cost approximately $50.

Quantity	Unit	Material
1	box	#8 galvanized penny nails
1	sheet	½" treated exterior plywood
2	each	twist tight fasteners
2	each	8' link chain (⅝" diameter)
2	each	2"x4"x14' treated wood
4	each	2"x4"x12' treated wood
2	each	1" hex head bolts

Tools Needed

- Hammer
- Adjustable wrench
- Pliers
- Hand saw or power saw
- 45° triangle
- Tape measure

1

Figure 18.8 (continued)

Stage I Constructing the Ladder

Step 1   Cut one of the 2"x4"x12' boards into 6 equal lengths of 2 feet. These pieces form the steps of the ladder portion of the tree stand.

Step 2   Place the two 2"x4"x14' boards parallel to one another on the ground. Be sure to position the boards so that the 2" side is facing up. Leave approximately 2 feet spacing between the two 2"x4"s.

Step 3   Beginning at the bottom of the ladder, nail the steps of the ladder to the 2'x4'x14' boards, spacing the steps 14 inches apart. The 4" side of the steps face up (Figure A). Two nails on each side should be sufficient.

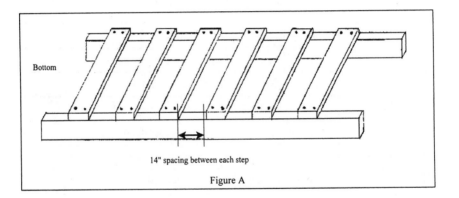

Bottom

14" spacing between each step

Figure A

Stage II Constructing the Foot Platform

This stage consists of making the supports (steps 1, 2, and 3) and braces (steps 4, 5, and 6) for the foot platform and making the foot platform itself (steps 7 and 8).

Making the Supports . . . . . .

Step 1   To make the supports for the foot platform, cut one of the 2"x4"x12' boards into three lengths: two pieces 4-½ feet long and one piece 4 feet long.

2

Figure 18.8 (continued)

Step 2   Place the ladder on its side and nail one of the 4 ½-foot-long sections above the last step on the inside part of the ladder (Figure B). The maximum distance between this brace and the last step should be 14". Use 5 nails to secure the foot support.

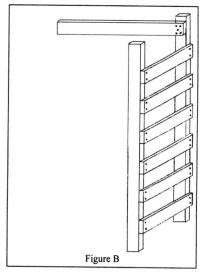

Figure B

Step 3   Repeat step 2 for the opposite side of the ladder at the same end (Figure C).

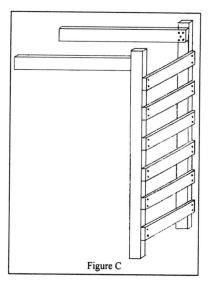

Figure C

3

Figure 18.8 (continued)

Making the Braces . . . .

Step 4   Take one of the 2"x4"x12" boards and cut two 3-½-feet sections.

Step 5   Trim the ends of the two 3-½-feet sections to a 45° angle (Figure D). Be sure to cut the ends so that they are both parallel.

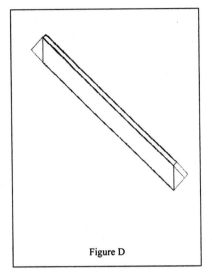

Figure D

Step 6   Nail the braces to the ladder as shown in Figure E. The portion of the braces that connect to the ladder should be toe-nailed.

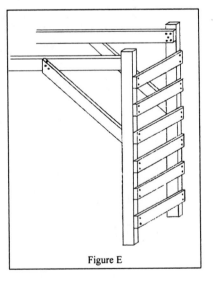

Figure E

4

Figure 18.8 (continued)

Making the Foot Platform . . . .

Step 7   Cut a 2-½'x2-½' section from the sheet of treated plywood. Be sure there is enough plywood left to cut a 1'x1-¹/₆' seat.

Step 8   Nail the plywood to the top of the 4-½-feet long support boards. Be sure that plywood is placed flush with the ladder (Figure F). Nail the plywood at each corner and at a couple of places along the support boards.

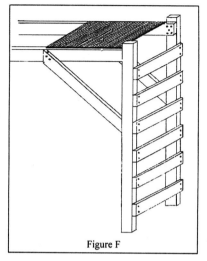

Figure F

Stage III Constructing the Seat Platform

This stage consists of making the seat braces (steps 1, 2, and 3) and the seat itself (steps 4 and 5).

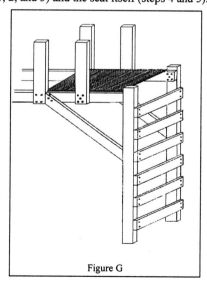

Making the Seat Braces . . . .

Step 1   Cut four 2-feet lengths from another 2"x4"x12" board. Place two of these 2-feet lengths flush with the 45° brace and the 4-½-feet sections.

Step 2   Place the other 2-feet lengths one foot from the rear of the plywood (Figure G). Use 5 nails to secure the front posts to the foot support. Use only four nails for the back posts arranged as shown in Figure G.

Figure G

5

Figure 18.8 (continued)

Step 3   Cut two more lengths from the 2"x4"x12" board and apply them horizontally to the tops of the previously placed braces. These are the supports for the seat of the tree stand (Figure H). Use 5 nails to secure the seat brace to the front vertical supports. Use only 4 nails, arranged as shown in Figure G, for the back supports.

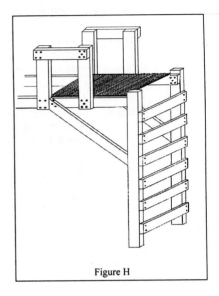

Figure H

Making the Seat . . . .

Step 4   Cut a 1'x2-½'-feet piece from the plywood.

Step 5   Place the piece of plywood on the two horizontal braces (Figure I). Place nails at each corner and at several places along the brace.

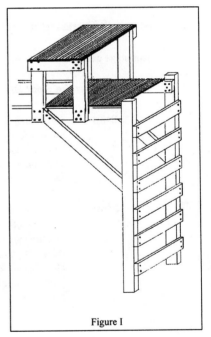

Figure I

6

Figure 18.8 (continued)

Stage IV Attaching the Chain to the Foot and Seat Platforms

If you are uncomfortable with the chain attachment, you can use the extended foot platform boards to nail the stand to the tree.

Step 1   Using a 1" hex head bolt, attach the link chain on the foot platform (Figure J).

Step 2   Using a 1" hex head bolt, attach the link chain on the seat platform (Figure J).

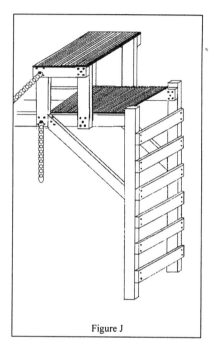

Figure J

Stage V Chaining the Tree Stand to a Tree

Step 1   Using a 1" hex head bolt, attach the twist tight fastener to the platforms on the opposite sides of the platforms from the chains.

Step 2   Place the tree stand parallel against the tree.

Step 3   Bring the chains around the tree and connect them to fasteners.

Step 4   Twist the fasteners to take up the slack in the link chain to secure the tree stand to the tree.

7

Figure 18.8 (continued)

common fault in preparing instructions is failing to place visuals where they are immediately useful.) Headings and subheadings help readers keep their place as they look back and forth between their work and the instructions.

Arrangement

Many instructions contain only the steps of the procedure, as illustrated in Figure 18.7. However, instructions for complicated procedures may contain an introduction, a body (the step-by-step instructions), and an ending section—essentially the same arrangement as for describing a mechanism or a process.

At the beginning of the instructions for assembling the accident-free tree stand are a title page that illustrates the finished product (the accident-free tree stand as it will look when fully assembled) and a one-page introduction. The one-page introduction explains the problem for which the stand is a solution, reassures that the procedure will be easy and fairly inexpensive, lists the major stages in the procedure, and lists the equipment and materials for the job.

The body of the instructions—the step-by-step procedure for making the tree stand—is on the next 6 pages. Here the writer and readers narrow their focus from an overall view of the procedure to the individual steps. Each step is emphasized by a numbered heading and by being stated in the imperative.

These instructions require no formal ending. They end after the instructions for completing the last step on page 7.

Style

Keep three stylistic considerations in mind when you write instructions.

• **Avoid writing in a telegraphic style.** As we mentioned earlier, keep your sentences short and to the point but write with natural, grammatical expression.

Natural Expression Used in Accident-Free Tree Stand Instructions	*Telegraphic Style*
Place the ladder on its side and nail one of the 4½ foot long sections above the last step on the inside of the ladder. . . .	Place ladder on side and nail one 4½ foot section above last step on inside of ladder . . .

• As you can see, telegraphic style omits most articles and conjunctions. But even when readers can understand the telegraphic style, many will avoid it because it looks different from natural prose. Telegraphic style is too choppy and does not save all that much space anyway.

- **Know when to use the imperative voice.** Use the imperative when you are writing an instruction. For example, you should write

> Nail the braces to the ladder.

not

> You should nail the braces to the ladder.

not

> The braces are to be nailed to the ladder.

not

> The braces must be nailed to the ladder.

Only the first sentence is imperative. The last three do not tell the reader what to do, and the reader may fail to recognize them as instructions.

ARMCHAIR INSTRUCTIONS

The four most noticeable differences between workbench instructions and armchair instructions are that armchair instructions have (1) a different purpose, (2) a more leisurely pace, and (3) a longer introduction, and (4) they often *look* more like essays. Armchair instructions explain a procedure before the reader attempts to perform it. Their essay-like format indicates that they are to be read beforehand, much like a "think" piece that provides some underlying principles, rather than as a guide to immediate action. They are not designed for reading while actually performing a procedure. As a "think" piece, armchair instructions tend to have a fairly lengthy introduction that identifies a problem or problems and discusses the benefits of the proposed solution or solutions before explaining the suggested procedure (similar to recommendation reports—see Chapter 14). Such a purpose, introduction, pace, and format is illustrated in Figure 18.9.

"Using Strategic Planning to Prepare for the Future" explains to operators and managers of agricultural businesses the process of thinking and researching necessary to develop a strategic business plan. The value of this kind of process description is that it explains the various factors that make up a strategic business plan. Because business owners cannot possibly know what will happen in the future, a detailed, carefully worked out set of workbench instructions is neither possible or appropriate. However, this article functions as a "think" piece in describing the process of strategic planning. It opens with a six-paragraph introduction that discusses the importance of strategic planning, distinguishes (with examples) the differences between strategic and tactical planning, explains the reasons for planning, and identifies who should do the planning.

Beginning with the heading "Steps in Strategic Planning," each of the eight steps is described in detail. Figure 1 is a block diagram that presents an overview of the entire process. Each major step is expressed in the

Using Strategic Planning To Prepare for the Future

What separates a successful agribusiness firm from an unsuccessful one? Numerous factors— quality of the land, managerial skill, and sufficient equity capital—are all important. And yet, some firms that seem to have these basics are less successful than other firms that are not so well endowed.

An important attribute of good management is to be able to step away from the trees and be able to see the forest. Strategic planning is analyzing the forest—the business and the environment in which it operates—in order to create a broad plan for the future. Strategic planning may bring to mind images of corporate executives meeting at luxurious retreats and staff members preparing multicolored visuals and reams of statistical and financial data. The result may be a 2-inch thick document on the chief executive's bookshelf.

For smaller agribusinesses and farms, the most effective planning may take place at the kitchen table. To establish an appropriate atmosphere for strategic planning, it is important to set aside time away from the day-to-day problems and interruptions so that the key participants—owners, managers, family members—can reach a common understanding about what they want to do in the next 3-5 years, and how they want to do it.

It is important that management takes a broad overview of the economy and the industry to determine the major opportunities and threats. Tactical planning is concerned with day-to-day and week-to-week decisions, such as what and how much pesticide to use, which cows to cull next, or whether to overhaul the old tractor or buy a new one. The results of strategic planning could lead to new enterprises, major capital investments, or perhaps even an exit from farming. This broader focus over a longer time distinguishes strategic planning from tactical planning.

Why Do Strategic Planning?

Strategic planning permits you to make more profits, in the long run, by:

Gerald B. White, Associate Professor of Agricultural Economics, Cornell University, Ithaca, NY

16

Farm Management

Figure 18.9 "Armchair" instructions.
Source: White, Gerald B. "Using Strategic Planning to Prepare for the Future." *1989 Yearbook of Agriculture.* Washington: GPO, 1989. 16–22.

• Establishing a clear direction for management and employees to follow,

• Defining in measurable terms what is most important for the firm,

• Anticipating problems and taking steps to eliminate them,

• Allocating resources (labor, machinery and equipment, buildings, and capital) more efficiently,

• Establishing a basis for evaluating the performance of management and key employees, and

• Providing a management framework which can be used to facilitate quick response to changed conditions, unplanned events, and deviations from plans.

Who Should Do Strategic Planning?

The planning should be initiated by the operator/manager of the agricultural business. In some cases, this process could involve a hired manager, but for most firms the operator/manager and other members of the family involved with management should be involved in the planning. In strategic planning, the process is as important as the final product. Getting the whole management team involved is critical. Strategic planning with typically close-knit farm families cannot be done in isolation from other family members, particularly when goals are set for the business. In such operations, business and family considerations are often so interwoven that it becomes artificial to try to separate the two.

Steps in Strategic Planning

Strategic planning involves the first seven steps shown in figure 1; an eighth step—implementation—is strategic management. This chapter focuses on the seven steps in the planning process.

Step 1. Define the Firm's Mission. The mission statement defines the purposes of the firm and answers the question, "What business or businesses are we in?" Defining the firm's mission forces the operator/manager to carefully identify the products, enterprises, and/or services toward which the firm's production is oriented. This statement answers the question, what is our current situation?

• What markets are likely to produce the best opportunities?

• What type of agricultural commodities or service can we produce to take advantage of these opportunities?

• What, if any, other activities are we involved in, and what are the priorities of these activities?

Establishing strategic goals, however, is the key element of the mission statement.

• Why are we in business?

• For profits?

• To provide employment/security for other family members?

• To increase wealth?

• To gain community status?

Answering these questions will suggest goals that will help to clarify objectives in the next step.

A mission statement is not necessarily a long document. In fact, it should contain fewer than 100 words, and two or three sentences may be sufficient.

Here is an example of a mission statement:

We operate a 70-cow dairy farm to support a modest level of living for two families. Our goals are to (1) build net worth, (2) stay in farming if at all possible, (3) gainfully employ two full-time family members (partners), (4) provide a good environment in which to raise our children, and (5) allow each partner suitable time off to enjoy family living, community activities, and hobbies. We would like to provide for the transfer of the farm to (partner) and to provide retirement income to (partner) within 5 years.

Part II / Strategic Management   17

Figure 18.9 (continued)

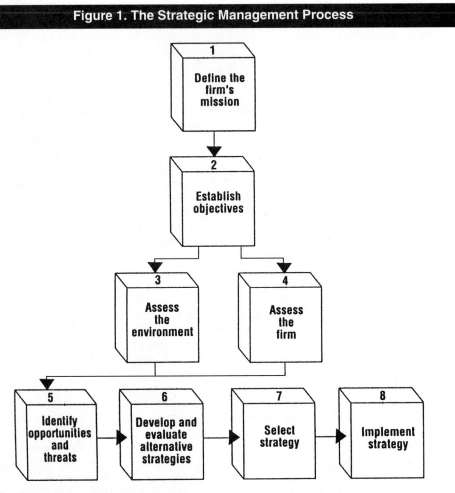

Figure 1. The Strategic Management Process

1 Define the firm's mission

2 Establish objectives

3 Assess the environment

4 Assess the firm

5 Identify opportunities and threats

6 Develop and evaluate alternative strategies

7 Select strategy

8 Implement strategy

Step 2. Establish Objectives. Goals, which are the more general, long-term desires of operator/managers, clarify the firm's purpose. Objectives should translate the mission into concrete terms. Objectives should be quantifiable and straightforward statements such as the following: increase sales by 100 percent over the next 5 years, reduce labor costs by 25 percent in the next 3 years, increase production per acre of grapes by 30 percent in the next 5 years, and provide health insurance coverage and Social Security coverage for two family employees next year. These objectives should be chosen in such a way that they contribute to attainment of the goals identified in Step 1. Each objective has two characteristics: (1) it can be measured, and (2)

18

Farm Management

Figure 18.9 (continued)

Strategic planning is as important to the family farmer who plans over the kitchen table as it is in the board rooms of large corporate farms. (USDA photo, 0986 X1092-10)

there is a given time in which to accomplish it. This allows management to evaluate progress in implementing the plan.

Step 3. Assess the External Environment. Every agricultural firm faces uncertainties, threats, and opportunities that are beyond its control. Market forces may cause prices to plunge, either in the long-run or short-run. Large crops, declining consumer demand, a strong dollar, high interest rates, changing Government policies, and regulation of labor and pesticides are external threats that can cut profits or make business more difficult. New market opportunities are created by demographic changes, changing consumer lifestyles, population growth in selected regions, and technological breakthroughs.

It is important in this step that the operator/manager understand the economic, social, and technological forces that will affect the firm. Then reasonable expectations may be formulated about what will happen to product prices, interest rates, the rate of inflation, labor markets, and input price over the next 3-5 years.

Step 4. Assess the Firm's Strengths and Weaknesses. The quality and quantity of resources within the control of the operator/man-

Part II / Strategic Management   19

Figure 18.9 (continued)

ager is the first part of this assessment. What are the abilities and limitations of the operator/manager? What skills and abilities do the employees have? How modern and efficient is the physical plant? How large is the resource base? What are the soils on the farm? What is the cash position of the firm? It is important that these resources be compared against those of competitors. Many farms have an unrealistic view of their own resources and operation because they do not compare themselves to others in the same business. The process of providing candid answers to these questions forces the operator/manager to recognize that every firm is constrained in some way by the internal environment—its physical resources as well as its human skills and abilities.

Step 5. Identify Opportunities and Threats. Combine the data gathered in Steps 3 and 4 to determine the threats and opportunities the firm might encounter in the planning period. Difficulties in the external environment can present opportunities in another segment of agriculture. For example, concern about cholesterol in meat products has created new markets for poultry and fish products. Concern about carcinogens in the environment, including some pesticides, has brought about new opportunities for cruciferous crops. Consumers are rediscovering oatmeal. Some firms have avoided problems by creatively turning an external threat into an opportunity. For example, Monfort of Colorado, a large feedlot operation, developed leaner and less costly cuts of meat packaged for microwave cooking. Promotional efforts were aimed at younger, more health-conscious consumers and two-career couples.

Step 6. Develop and Evaluate Alternative Strategies. Step 6, along with Step 7, is at the heart of the strategic planning process. This is the point at which the firm develops the alternative plans that describe the methods for attaining objectives and obtaining greater long-run profits.

In what ways can production agriculture firms gain a competitive advantage?

The answer to this question depends to a great extent on whether or not the farmer is a price-taker. Farmers are traditionally price-takers. An individual farmer has little, if any, power in the market to influence the price of commodities such as milk, grain, eggs, grapes, and potatoes because there is a very large number of producers and a homogeneous product is produced. Each quart of milk, bushel of grain, or dozen eggs is very similar to that produced by thousands of other farmers. These farmers have no "market power" because buyers can obtain the commodity at a price dictated by supply and demand considerations, after adjusting for transportation costs. High cost regions or firms are at a distinct disadvantage in these markets.

Some agricultural firms, such as landscape contractors or small wineries selling premium wines, are in less competitive markets where there are only a few smaller firms in the surrounding area and products or services can be differentiated. While these producers are also conscious of their competitors' prices, there is no clear "market price" for each product or service. In less competitive markets, the operator/manager is faced with the problem of pricing his or her product.

What types of strategies can operator/managers in price-taking firms employ to attain a competitive advantage?

1. *Become More Efficient.* Increase profits by:
   • Reducing input use, holding product and price (quality) constant,
   • Using more, or higher quality, inputs, increasing revenue more than costs.
2. *Seek Out Alternative Enterprises.*
3. *Exploit Quality Differences.* Obtain price premiums for quality that more than offset the additional costs involved in producing higher quality commodities.

20   **Farm Management**

Figure 18.9 (continued)

4. *Integrate Horizontally.* Farm more units, or add enterprises, enlarge enterprises to gain more complete use of existing unused resources; acquire additional resources. Spread fixed costs over more units of output.

5. *Integrate Vertically.* Obtain more profit by moving higher or lower into the marketing and distribution channels—add storage or packing facilities, trucks to haul products, and direct marketing; acquire resources to produce inputs that formerly were purchased.

6. *Reduce Risks Through Diversification and Hedging.*

7. *Identify New Markets.*

Firms that have some degree of control in the market, because there are fewer competitors or because there is the possibility for differentiation of products and services, have the potential for additional strategies to gain a competitive advantage, including these:

A *differentiation strategy* emphasizes high quality, excellent service, innovative design of products or services, or an unusually positive brand image. The key element in this strategy is that the attribute to be emphasized must be different from those offered by rival firms; in addition, the differences must be significant enough so that the price premium exceeds the additional cost of differentiating. The Monfort emphasis on leaner cuts of beef is one such successful strategy. Ben and Jerry's ice cream is another. (See the 1988 Yearbook of Agriculture, *Marketing U.S. Agriculture*, for more information on innovative marketing strategies.)

A *focus strategy* aims at a cost advantage or differentiation by focusing on a narrow segment of the market—a niche. In this strategy, the operator/manager selects a segment or group of segments (such as product variety, type of end buyer, distribution channel, or geographic location of buyer) for which to tailor a product or service and excludes other markets. The goal is to exploit a narrow segment of the market. Again, the feasibility of this strategy depends upon the size of the segment and whether or not it can support the additional cost of focusing.

Swedish Hill Vineyard and Winery of Romulus, NY, has successfully used a focus strategy. The owners, Dick and Cynthia Peterson, have established an image with the Scandinavian community in Upstate New York by holding an annual Scandinavian Festival that features food and entertainment that appeal to people of Swedish, Danish, Norwegian, and Finnish descent. To reinforce this image, the Petersons have developed two wine labels, Svenska Blush and Svenska White. Even though none of the Scandinavian countries has a significant wine industry, identification with the ethnic group has been an important part of Swedish Hill's recent growth in sales. Swedish Hill is presently negotiating a contract with the alcoholic beverage control agency in Sweden for exporting to that country.

Farmers who are price takers do not have the options for employing such strategies as differentiation and focusing. Of course, the option remains for price takers to move into new areas or businesses where they have more control over prices and more market power. Operator/managers who consider this option, however, should be forewarned that it is very easy to underestimate the difficulty or cost in attaining additional market power.

It is possible that no identified alternatives will permit a particular farm family to attain its objectives; therefore, nonfarming alternatives may need consideration. It may be possible, for example, to sell some farm assets, keeping part or all of the land and residence, and to seek off-farm employment. Non-farming alternatives should not be neglected in selecting alternatives.

Once alternatives are developed, Step 6 is only half completed. These alternative strategies must be evaluated. In [text continues]

Part II / Strategic Management   21

Figure 18.9 (continued)

imperative: Define the Firm's Mission, Establish Objectives, Assess the External Environment, and so on. The substeps of major steps—such as those in step 6 (Develop and Evaluate Alternative Strategies)—are also stated in the imperative: Become More Efficient, Seek Out Alternative Enterprises, and so on.

If you think that your readers need to understand why they must do something in a certain way, explain why. But keep the instructions and the explanation distinct. It is particularly important when giving instructions to analyze the job from the point of view of readers unfamiliar with, perhaps even totally ignorant of, the job or the importance of doing things a particular way. This advice also applies when you give a specific command. Ask yourself whether a general command such as "Remove the oil filter" is clear enough, or whether the action of removing the oil filter should be broken down into a subroutine—into the smallest possible steps. Remember, just as some people who own or operate agribusinesses do not know how to "grow" a company by using strategic planning, some people who have cars do not know how to remove an oil filter. Spell out instructions; do not be afraid of being too simple. For instance, the writer of "Using Strategic Planning to Prepare for the Future," in explaining how to define the firm's mission, explains how to write a mission statement and provides an example of one.

TROUBLESHOOTING AND UNDOING ERRORS

When something goes wrong during a procedure, the reader will likely look for troubleshooting procedures to aid in isolating and correcting the problem. Troubleshooting information contributes greatly to a set of instructions, because being able to recognize and correct errors successfully reduces the frustration and problems of learning how to perform new procedures. Readers want to be able to diagnose the problem, bring about the desired result, and get on with completing the task.

User testing your instructions will help you predict difficulties that readers might experience and help you identify the kinds of information readers need to identify problems and take corrective actions.

Troubleshooting guides must be context sensitive and brief and uncluttered, as illustrated in Figure 18.10, and placed where they are needed. They may accompany a specific step, come at the end of a major section of the procedure, or at the end of the instructions. A three-column table with headings such as *Problem, Probable Cause,* and *Solution* is apt to be the easiest way to lead readers quickly from the symptom of the problem to the solution with a minimum amount of information. List the most frequent or most likely problems first. Any one problem may have several possible causes. List the possible causes and solutions in order from the most frequent to the least frequent occurrence.

TROUBLESHOOTING TABLE

Note: Many video cassette problems are caused by defective cassettes. Check the cassette by substituting a known good cassette.

Problem	Probable Cause	Solution
Motor does not run when cassette is inserted	1. Power is not on.	Check to see if power is on. If not, turn on.
	2. Micro-actuating arm is bent or broken.	Bend the actuating arm (Fig. 2) far enough to actuate the micro-switch (Fig. 3) when the cassette is inserted, or replace.
	3. Micro-switch is defective.	Replace.
	4. Motor is defective.	Replace.
Poor visual or audio quality	1. Cassette is defective.	Check by inserting a known good cassette.
	2. Drive surfaces are dirty.	Using isopropyl (rubbing) alcohol, clean and wipe dry the outer edge of the flywheel, motor drive pulley, capstan shaft, and tape head (Fig. 4 A, B, C, and D).
	3. Drive belt is defective or incorrectly installed.	If the drive belt (Fig. 5) is stretched, replace. If the belt is not installed with the stripes on the outside (Fig. 5), reinstall. If the drive belt rides too high or too low on the motor pulley (Fig. 6), readjust.

Figure 18.10 A troubleshooting table is an effective way to present information on how to solve problems associated with performing a procedure.

TESTING INSTRUCTIONS FOR USABILITY

As with any document, your instructions are doomed to almost certain failure if you

- slap them together quickly in the haste of meeting a deadline (either to get a product or service out or to make the instructions available)

- rely on your own ability to follow the instructions to determine whether the instructions are clear and understandable for the eventual user

To avoid both mistakes, (1) schedule the project to allow time for testing the instructions and (2) test the instructions in an operational context (instead of sitting at your desk going over the procedure for the umpteenth time).

As you create a set of instructions, work through the procedure several times, attempting to put yourself in the user's shoes, walking through the steps and trying to anticipate problems. Look for statements that are too general, for inconsistencies between written and visual material, for insufficient clues on how to access specific information, or for places where information has been omitted. Remember, the more knowledgeable you are about the procedure, the more difficulty you will have predicting problems for users. Ultimately, to see if your careful and thorough consideration for the eventual user has been adequate and if your instructions will work, you must test them on persons who can represent the eventual user.

Testing for usability takes time, but doing it right will save time and money and prevent trouble later on. Here are some guidelines for testing your instructions for usability:

• **Maintain a positive attitude about testing your instructions.** Assume that you have lots of opportunities to improve them. Once you make the psychological commitment to conduct user testing, you will likely receive plenty of help. Here's what one of our students recently wrote about her experience with user testing:

> The user test helped me a lot. I admit that when I first learned that we were required to have another student test our sets of instructions, I was more than a bit skeptical—I assumed the testing was busywork to keep the project on our minds. Now, I know nothing could be further from the truth. The user test gave me the opportunity to see my own writing being used for something, which I thoroughly enjoyed. The tester's assessment memo to me gave me a solid basis for revisions that I needed to focus on. In my own testing of another student's set of instructions, I was put in the place of a learner, and I realized how much I looked for clarity. The difficulty I had in attempting to use another person's set of instructions helped me identify ways to improve my own.[2]

Listen carefully to what your tester says, and if the tester provides a written report, read it carefully. Don't argue with the tester or take issue with the tester's findings. Instead, pay careful, respectful attention to the opinions of the tester, who represents the opinions of the eventual users of your instructions. Be willing to make changes.

• **Estimate the time it takes to prepare, arrange, and administer a user test** and, if necessary, to repeat the test or to retest certain parts of the instructions after they have been revised. Sometimes testing results only in minor tweaking of the instructions. At other times, extensive revision is required and corrections can be time consuming.

---

[2]Used with permission of Anne L. Casey.

Name of the author(s) of the instructions _____

Your signature as tester_____

The title page (if there is one)

- Does the title page contain the title of the document, the author's name and affiliation, and date?
- Are these elements placed attractively on the page? The title should be in the upper third of the page; the author's name and affiliation should be in the middle third or lower third of the page; the date should be at the bottom of the page. Do you have suggestions for the design of the title page?
- Does the title of the document identify the task clearly? Do you have suggestions concerning the title?

The introduction

- Is it clear when the procedure is to be performed?
- Is it clear how long it will probably take to perform the procedure?
- Is there an attempt to motivate users to perform the procedure instead of paying somebody else or relying on somebody else to do it?
- Are the equipment and materials specified to inform the user of what is needed to perform the procedure?
- If any special precautions are needed to ensure that the procedure will be performed safely and successfully, are those precautions explained?
- Is there an overview of the major stages to help users anticipate what is to follow in the step-by-step instructions?
- What do you like best about the introduction?
- Do you have any suggestions concerning the introduction?

The step-by-step procedure

- Are headings used to indicate the sections that deal with each major stage? Does the wording of the headings repeat the wording in the overview statement? Do you have suggestions regarding headings?
- Are the instructions numbered and in the correct chronological order?
- Are the instructions written as instructions; that is, are imperative verbs used?
- Does each instruction explain to the user how to perform the step? In other words, it's often not sufficient to tell the user *what* to do; the user must be told *how* to do it and sometimes *why*.
- Are the visuals adequate and placed where the user can read the instruction and visualize the action together?
- Do you have suggestions regarding any of the instructions?

The format

- Are the pages numbered?
- Are approximately 1" margins maintained consistently?
- Is the type font and size appropriate?
- What do you like best about the format?
- Do you have suggestions regarding the format?

Mechanics, grammar, and style

- Identify grammar, punctuation, and spelling errors.
- List terms (abbreviations, words, symbols, phrases, etc.) that you believe should be defined.

Figure 18.11 Sample checklist for user testing.

- **Prepare the test carefully.** Decide whether you will test the entire set of instructions or just certain parts. You may decide to test only those steps that you are not sure you explain well. But it is usually better to test the entire set of instructions to see if users have difficulty even where you think there will be none. If the instructions are to be used by several groups of users—say systems analysts, applications programmers, and computer operators—design tests to see if the instructions are usable by them all.

   The quality of the test is extremely important. Have a specific plan for the test to help you and the tester of the instructions stay organized and focused. Developing a checklist will help. If you use a check sheet, introduce the tester or testers to it to see if they understand what they are to do. Figure 18.11 is an example of testing guidelines that are easily formatted into a checklist.

- **Prepare the tester or testers.** Testers are collaborators with you on the project, and if they are to assist you they need to know the objectives of the test. Some who agree to test your instructions may be a bit apprehensive about what they are to do and unsure about the objectives of the test. Explain to them that you are testing the instructions, not them, and that you want them to point out problems when they encounter them. Review the checklist with them, and remind them that the test is not to be performed perfunctorily.

- **Observe closely while the tester uses the instructions.** Watch the user go through each step, noticing where he or she works with ease and when he or she has difficulties. When problems arise with the instructions, ask the user what he or she believes is the source of the difficulty and solicit suggestions about how to correct it.

PLANNING AND REVISING CHECKLIST: INSTRUCTIONS

Think about the following while planning and revising instructions.

PLANNING

- Determine whether the instructions are essentially workbench or armchair instructions.

- Who is the intended audience? Are there special considerations to keep in mind? Do readers need to be motivated to perform the procedure the way you have explained? Should theory, terminology, and other background information be presented and explained? How detailed should information and instructions be, considering the audience?

- Are there places in the procedure where cautions, warnings, and notes should be provided?

- What equipment and materials are required to perform the procedure? What special materials or equipment might be needed under certain circumstances?

- What actions in the procedure should be illustrated? What visuals are most appropriate, and where should they be placed in the instructions?

- Will you need to include any routine maintenance, repair, or troubleshooting procedures that the intended audience could be expected to perform?

REVISING

- Is the introduction to the instructions adequate, considering the audience?

- Is it easy to follow the chronology of steps, and if necessary, the substeps? Is it clear why one section follows another?

- Are the instructions written in the imperative voice?

- Are steps adequately explained? Is enough information given that readers require? Has anything been left out that might help readers?

- Is nomenclature consistent throughout the instructions?

- Are the instructions free of jargon?

- Are the cautions, warnings, and notes presented clearly and formatted appropriately?

- Are appropriate visuals used and are they positioned effectively?

- Are maintenance, repair, and troubleshooting procedures within the area of expertise of the intended audience?

SUGGESTIONS FOR APPLYING YOUR KNOWLEDGE

1. Your textbooks, especially lab manuals, probably contain many examples of instructions. Bring one example to class to examine in the light of the information provided in this chapter.

2. Either as an individual or as a member of a group, discuss a hobby procedure that you recently learned. Who instructed you? Were the instructions written? Oral? Visual? A combination of the three? Did you have any initial problems in following the instructions? If so, what were they and how could they be corrected? What were other weaknesses or particular strengths in the instructions?

3. Elaborate on each of the following safety precautions in instructions on how to jump-start a car. Be sure that your *so-whats* would be clear to the intended readers.

   Make sure the vehicles do not touch.

   Do not jump-start unless both batteries are the same voltage.

   Do not jump-start if the battery is frozen.

   Wear goggles.

4. Either as an individual or as a member of a group, analyze the instructions in Figure 18.12.

There are three *general* situations where you will be meeting, crossing, or overtaking another boat. By learning these rules the rest should be easy. OK then, case number one....

1. Meeting head-on

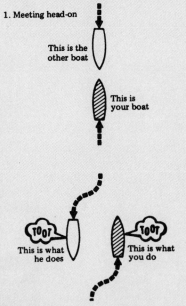

This is the other boat

This is your boat

This is what he does

This is what you do

You give him *one short* toot on the horn
and
He gives you *one short* toot back

Over half of the boats that got into an accident did so by smashing into another boat or some immovable object. If you think that's bad news — then how about the fact that most of these accidents happened because the operator of the boat *wasn't even looking ahead!* It would seem that these people, from the time they stepped into their boats were no better than an accident going somewhere to happen. In other cases the operator was looking ahead but he *didn't know what to do!*

It can be truly said that there are old boatmen.....and there are bold boatmen.....but there ain't no old, bold, boatmen. Not for long anyway.

To keep from running into things with your boat you must learn and use the "Rules of the Water Roads". In this little program we can only give you the smallest amount of all those things you need to know about the rules. For the rest, take an advanced boating course from the Coast Guard Auxiliary. OK, here we go.....

There are many different sets of rules of the road. Which set *you* use depends on *where* you are going to use your boat. You must understand that conditions are often very different on various water areas. The Coast Guard Auxiliary course, and other advanced courses will give you the straight scoop and we can promise you it *all* makes good horsesense.

Figure 18.12 Armchair instructions for following the "rules of the water road."
Source: (Almost) Everything You Ever Wanted to Know About Boating—But Were Ashamed to Ask. Washington: U.S. Coast Guard, February 1972.

5. Complete a Plan Sheet for Instructions for a procedure from your field of study, from your work, or from one of your hobbies.

6. Using the filled-out plan sheet from suggestion 5, write a set of instructions for either a do-it-yourselfer or a technician.

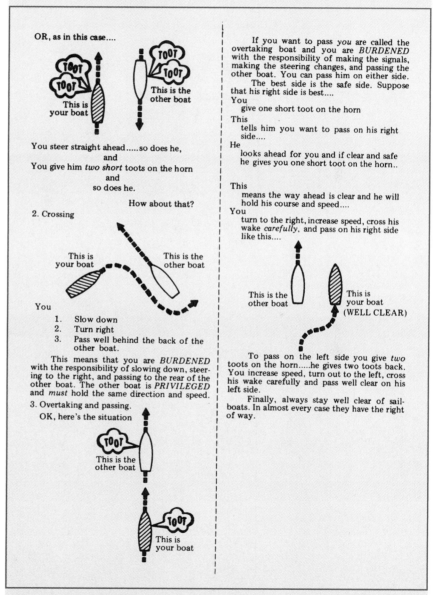

OR, as in this case....

This is your boat

TOOT TOOT

This is the other boat

TOOT TOOT

You steer straight ahead.....so does he,
and
You give him *two short* toots on the horn
and
so does he.

How about that?

2. Crossing

This is your boat

This is the other boat

You
1. Slow down
2. Turn right
3. Pass well behind the back of the other boat.

This means that you are *BURDENED* with the responsibility of slowing down, steering to the right, and passing to the rear of the other boat. The other boat is *PRIVILEGED* and *must* hold the same direction and speed.

3. Overtaking and passing.

OK, here's the situation

TOOT

This is the other boat

TOOT

This is your boat

If you want to pass *you* are called the overtaking boat and you are *BURDENED* with the responsibility of making the signals, making the steering changes, and passing the other boat. You can pass him on either side.

The best side is the safe side. Suppose that his right side is best....

You
give one short toot on the horn

This
tells him you want to pass on his right side....

He
looks ahead for you and if clear and safe he gives you one short toot on the horn..

This
means the way ahead is clear and he will hold his course and speed....

You
turn to the right, increase speed, cross his wake *carefully*, and pass on his right side like this....

This is the other boat

This is your boat (WELL CLEAR)

To pass on the left side you give *two* toots on the horn.....he gives two toots back. You increase speed, turn out to the left, cross his wake carefully and pass well clear on his left side.

Finally, always stay well clear of sailboats. In almost every case they have the right of way.

Figure 18.12 (continued)

UNIT IV

RESEARCH

CHAPTER 19

RESEARCH STRATEGIES

You conduct research in whatever workplace setting you find yourself. The research may be as easy as locating a vendor to supply a video splitter. You go to the company's Web site to get ordering information and the telephone number. The research may be as involved as conducting a 2- to 4-year on-site study of the migration patterns of gray wolves. The research may require you to use the library, interview subject matter experts, and visit sites. Or, you may search the Web from your office or send out a questionnaire to employees.

The chapters in this unit suggest effective research strategies (Chapter 19, Research Strategies) and identify several of the many research sites for gathering information (Chapter 20, Research Sites and Sources: Library and Internet Research, and Chapter 21, Research Sites and Sources: Field Research). Chapter 22, Documenting Sources, provides guidelines for showing the source of your research.

IDENTIFYING THE PROBLEM

In the workplace, you solve problems daily: situations that require a solution so that you can do your job more efficiently and the organization you work for can stay in business. You take some sort of *action* to change the current situation for the better. You are solving practical problems.[1]

In Chapter 14, Recommendation Reports, we describe several ways to report problems and solutions. For example, in Scott Pahl's study of the problem mowing grass along Minnesota highways, the cost had increased so significantly that the department of transportation began to look for an alternative to mowing. If you have not already read Chapter 14, review pages 378–392 now. We will refer to Pahl's study in the following pages.

DESCRIBE THE CURRENT SITUATION

For practical problems, you must study the current situation, identify the problem, and provide a timely solution. You don't know what might change in the future. Technology changes, our perceptions change, scientists develop a more effective solution, the seriousness of a problem grows. For example, the landfill can hold no more solid waste, or planes built in the 1970s and flown without major accidents for 30 years now begin to have serious and even fatal accidents. Ten years ago, in his original report, Scott Pahl recommended testing *Embark,* a plant-growth regulator; however, *Embark* is no longer available because of environmental concerns that showed up with its use over several years. When Scott did his research

---

[1]Carolyn D. Rude, in "The Report for Decision Making: Genre and Inquiry," classifies problems as theoretical ("problems of values, principles, and concepts"), empirical problems ("facts that can be observed or tested"), and practical problems ("require choice about action"). *Journal of Business and Technical Communication* 9 (1995): 177. We focus on practical problems in the workplace, although you will certainly encounter theoretical and empirical problems as well.

and wrote his report, *Embark* was the best product available. Ten years later, it is not. (We adjusted the report slightly so that we could continue to use it as an example.)

As you describe the current situation, you explore the problem in depth. You probably will discover that there's more to the problem than you thought. As you talk with different people familiar with the problem, you will get different perspectives on the problem and suggestions for possible solutions. Note the different perspectives and suggestions as you look for solutions. The need for a video splitter (mentioned in the first paragraph) evolved out of a need to solve a problem. Finding a video splitter was not the problem. The problem was that every time the projection system was hooked to the computer the monitor cable had to be unplugged and the LCD cable plugged into the computer. The computer was positioned such that it was difficult to reach the back of the computer. Setting up the LCD soon resulted in bent pins on the monitor cable and costly repairs. In addition, users complained of spending 10 minutes before and after the presentation to set up and take down the LCD. The technician saw the problem only as the bent pins; the end user saw the problem as set up time. The video splitter solved both the problem of bent pins and set up time. Users now run the projection system without unhooking the monitor from the computer.

IDENTIFY THE CRITERIA FOR STUDYING THE PROBLEM

Carolyn Rude identifies criteria to consider when solving problems:

> Criteria are those factors that predict whether a decision will yield desirable consequences. They are the reasons for making a decision. Criteria vary with problem and context. Establishing criteria is part of constructing the reality of the community—what is possible, true, and important in a particular context.[2]

She identifies three broad areas of criteria: technical, managerial, and social. **Technical criteria** provide a way to judge if it is *possible* to solve the problem. For example: Are the equipment, the laws, and the resources available? Is it possible to have one video input and two video output signals? Is there enough room to install the workstation? Can the fence be placed inside the property line without removing trees? **Managerial criteria** focus on such issues as cost, personnel, and schedules. Managers look at feasibility: The technical aspects of the problem can be solved, but is the solution cost effective? Are there enough work crews and support staff to take on the new client and meet the deadlines? **Social criteria** respond to issues such as *should* the solution be implemented? What will its effect be on the environment? How many deaths can be expected?

Only a few criteria for selecting a video splitter required attention: the cost (managerial criteria) and the availability of and sources for the feature to create two video outputs from one video input (technical criteria). There are no social considerations here. A simple problem; a simple solution.

[2]Rude 195.

Among the criteria Scott Pahl considered in the recommendation report on mowing Minnesota highways are

technical criteria	*SlowGrowth* plant-growth regulator works; available equipment can be adapted to spread the product
managerial criteria	cost of application; number of crew needed to apply the product
social criteria	low risk to workers; environmentally safe chemical; aesthetically pleasing

Spend time identifying the criteria. The criteria provide you with specific points to compare as you look for a solution to a problem. Figure 3.2 is an example of the criteria summarized in a table from *Consumer Reports* on printers. Not all problems and the criteria selected with it can be displayed in a table—but don't overlook how helpful a table might be in showing at least some of the comparisons.

GENERATE POSSIBLE SOLUTIONS AND FOLLOW THE LEADS

After you identify a problem, generate several possible solutions. Rarely will you look for solutions by yourself. You will meet with others affected by the problem; you will study the history of the problem. The list of possible solutions provides a starting point for your research. Some of the solutions you will eliminate immediately. For example, constructing a new building just so a more effective presentation room is available is not a solution (too costly). Renovating the current room is a possibility, but even that requires decisions that limit the extent of the renovation: for example, replace current furniture or work with the current furniture.

Your research will lead you to other possible solutions. Follow the leads. For example, in interviewing the manager of a computer classroom about security concerns, you learn that the use of fiber optic cables is not enough assurance that the computers will be secure. You must also padlock the computer case to prevent access to the chips, boards, and drives inside the computer. Or, say you need to improve the yield for your cotton crop. One of the works cited at the end of a government report looks like it might discuss the advantages and disadvantages of using a fertilizer developed from telephone books and chicken manure. You go to your library's Web site and locate the report.

LOCATING THE INFORMATION

You have identified solutions and have a list of leads to follow. Now you must locate the information that will help you make decisions and recommend a solution to the problem. The list of possible solutions will direct where you go for the information needed to solve the problem. The information will either exist because others have solved the problem or a similar problem or the information must be gathered because the problem is unique. If others have already done the research on a portion of the problem or if the solution exists, you need only locate the solution. If the problem is unique, you may have to gather information firsthand using interviews, questionnaires, or direct observations. These sources are frequently referred to as *primary sources. Secondary sources* are those you go to for help or information, rather than developing the information on your own. These might include sources inside your organization (for example, the accounting department), on the Web (such as a site that publishes government reports), or a publication located in your school, company, or local library.

More than likely, you will have to locate information from both primary and secondary sources. For example, assume that you have just been promoted to Web coordinator for your organization and that you have been given $40,000 to purchase the computer, software, and other peripherals you and your assistants will need to create the Web site. You have some experience with designing Web sites, so you can list fairly quickly what you need; however, you have also heard about some new technology and software. First, you decide to call a friend in a similar position at another company. She suggests you join the online discussion group for Web site developers. You also attend the monthly meeting of the local chapter of the Society for Technical Communication and meet others doing similar work. You ask several software and hardware vendors for demonstrations or you visit colleagues who are using some of the products you need. You locate the current prices and specifications online at vendors' Web sites. You are gathering information firsthand—interviews, networking, hands-on experience. You also go to your library and read the latest reviews on the products in publications such as *PC World* and *Internet World*. You gather this information from others and rely on their thorough research to help you evaluate the products.

In the Minnesota highway study, Scott Pahl used on-site visits, interviews with Minnesota Department of Transportation workers and vendors of products, and library research to find reports of experiments on controlling grass in medians. The research for a video splitter required less diverse sources. A visit to a classroom equipped with the splitter, the recommendation by a colleague of a source for the splitter, and a visit to the Web site of the company selling video splitters yielded a quick, inexpensive solution.

In the next two chapters, we describe some of the common locations for gathering information. Chapter 20, Research Sites and Sources: Library and Internet Research, focuses on library and Internet research—research we think of as text-based and in most cases research that someone else has done (secondary sources). You are borrowing from the work of others. For example, say you cannot possibly remember the hurricanes and their level of intensity that have moved through your region in the past 10 years, but you need this information because you manage the emergency supply inventory. You locate the information on the National Weather Service Web site. Or, you need to know what experiments have been conducted in the past 20 years on cigarette smoking. You search the library database for scientific journals that publish the results. Chapter 21, Research Sites and Sources: Field Research, describes research methods you most likely will use to gather information. For example, you will conduct the interviews with the campus police and the locksmith shop to explore the best security system for the computer classroom. Or, you will count the cars that move through a busy intersection and observe how many line up waiting to turn left before recommending a turn lane and turn light.

Consider locating the information a challenge—a challenge that involves detective work. When you are thorough, you will be successful in finding a solution to the problem.

TAKING NOTES

It is important to take notes on the information you are gathering. You cannot possibly remember all of the details you need to make the final report (even if it is a simple memo identifying the computer and software you need for a Web production workstation). You need to record the information from the articles and books you have found. Careful notetaking is essential. Our memories are simply too short to hold the information we have found, and we need to transform what we read into our own words. We need to adapt the information gathered to the problem we are researching.

Good notetaking also assures you that you have the necessary bibliographic information to attribute the information gathered to the original source (see Chapter 22, Documenting Sources). You must acknowledge the sources of the information in your reports—avoid plagiarism. Readers much prefer knowing the source of the information you gather rather than finding out later that what you produced as your own was originally someone else's idea. Taking careful notes on your sources helps when you write the report.

HOW TO TAKE NOTES

How you take notes will depend upon how you gathered the information and where you found the information. You will take notes whether you gather the information through firsthand observations or from secondary sources. And, you will need to note more than just the information you need to solve the problem. You need to note who or what was your source, where to go if you need to refer back to the information, when the information was gathered, and when you located the information. *Always* note the source and the date you collected information whether you are recording information from primary sources or secondary sources.

You have several options for taking notes:

- write notes on the source

- make electronic notes

- record notes using an audio or video recorder

- use notecards

In the following paragraphs we suggest ways to be an efficient note-taker for each of these options. You may use several of these methods depending upon the type of sources you will consult and how many sources you use. As you gather the information and take notes, refer back to the problem frequently. If you have worked through our suggestions in the earlier section, "Identifying the Problem," you have drafted a problem statement and brief history of the problem and listed the solutions you are researching. If you have written the problem and history in a computer file, you can add to it and modify the problem statement and solutions as you proceed through your research.

Notes on the Source

Frequently, when you find information in a periodical or on an organization's Web site, you make a copy of it or you print out a copy from the Web. You can read the source and make notations on the copy as you read—annotations. In working with a source, you might number and underline the major points, mark unfamiliar terms and provide synonyms, highlight statements that you agree or disagree with, cross-reference related ideas, and record ideas that occur to you as you read the material. Figure 19.1 illustrates one way to make such annotations.

Here are some suggestions for making useful notes on the copy and for keeping track of the information so you can use it to write up the solution to the problem.

- Immediately after you copy the information or print it from the Web, write on the source all the information you need to document it. You can lose a lot of time going back to sources for missing documentation information. Some magazines and journals include bibliographical information on each page, but many do not. Refer to Chapter 22, Documenting Sources, for a complete description of what you need to record and the format to use. You must identify the title of the work, the author(s), and the publication date. For material from the Web, be sure to get the address (if it does not show on the printed version) and note the date you collected the information.

- Skim the source to get an idea of how the information is organized. Be an active reader—that is, interact with the material by making notes or signaling with lines or other marks key areas of the text. If you find your mind wandering, stop reading. You probably won't have time to reread the material, so pay attention as you read and make notes and other marks that will direct you to the information when you refer back to it to write your report.

• Have 2 to 3 different color marking pens and paper or notecards with you as you begin to read. You will come up with your own system of

CONSUMER PRODUCT SAFETY REVIEW

SPRING 1998
VOL. 2, NO. 4

U.S. Consumer Product Safety Commission

Ann Brown, *Chairman*
Mary Sheila Gall, *Commissioner*
Thomas H. Moore, *Commissioner*

Includes recalls from the **National Highway Traffic Safety Administration**

Bike Helmets: A ⟨New⟩ Safety Standard

To help protect bikers, the U.S. Consumer Product Safety Commission (CPSC) recently issued a new federal safety standard for bicycle helmets. This standard will provide, for the first time, one uniform mandatory safety standard for all bike helmets, as well as special requirements for young children's helmets.

By March 1999, all bike helmets manufactured or imported for sale in the U.S. must comply with the CPSC standard. A bike helmet will carry a label or sticker stating that it meets CPSC's new safety standard. Bike helmets currently conform to several different voluntary standards.

CPSC's new bike helmet standard includes requirements for helmet performance during a crash, greater coverage for young children's heads, and chin strap requirements to help keep helmets on the head during a fall or collision.[1] This new standard was developed as a result of the Children's Bicycle Helmet Safety Act of 1994.

Injury Data

In recent years, about <u>900 people were killed</u> annually in bicycle-related incidents.[2] Most (90%) of these deaths were associated with <u>motor vehicle collisions.</u>   *bikes and cars*

Bike-related injuries took an especially high toll on children. More youngsters, ages 5 to 14, went to U.S. hospital emergency rooms for bicycle-related injuries than for injuries associated with any other sport. For children under age 5, bike-related injuries were number two for sports-related injuries, behind playground injuries.[3]

In 1996, among all age groups, an estimated 566,000 people were treated for bike-related injuries in U.S. hospital emergency rooms. About 356,000 of those injured were children under age 15. A CPSC study of bicycle hazards indicated that the injury risk for children under age 15 was more than five times that for older riders.[4]

children under 15 – most accidents

Head Injuries

Approximately 60% of all bike-related deaths involved head injuries. For children under age 5, about 64% of the deaths involved head injuries.   *most*

Of total injuries, approximately 30% involved the head and face. Young children incurred almost twice the proportion of head and facial injuries as older victims.   *were head injuries*

In the CPSC study, about one-half of the injuries to children under age 10 involved the head, compared with one-fifth of the injuries to older riders. This may have been partly due to the fact that only 5% of the victims younger than 15 in that study were wearing a helmet, compared with 30% of those 15 and older.

helmet not used by younger riders

Continued on page 2

Figure 19.1 Handwritten annotations on a photocopied article. You will create your own system of making notes on your sources. In this example, we make notes in the margins to call attention to important information. The notes at the end are ideas that occurred while reading the article.
Source: "Bike Helmets: A New Safety Standard." *Consumer Product Safety Review* (Spring 1998): 23 September 1998 ⟨http://www.cpsc.gov/cpscpub/pubs/cpsr_nws8:pdf⟩.

Consumer Product Safety Review Spring 1998

In several studies, bike helmet usage has been associated with dramatically reducing the risk of head and brain injury. One widely-cited study puts this reduction at 85% for head injury and 88% for brain injury.[5]

Major Provisions of the Standard

CPSC's new bike helmet safety standard mandates several important safety requirements. These include the following: *the new standard requires* ↓

✓ ■ *Impact protection in a crash:* The standard establishes a performance test to ensure that helmets will adequately protect the head in a collision or fall. This test involves dropping a helmet attached to a headform from specified heights onto a fixed steel anvil. Three shapes of anvils (flat, hemispherical, and curbstone) are used to represent different surfaces that may be encountered in actual riding conditions.

The impact tests are performed on different helmets of each model being evaluated. Each is subjected to one of four differing environmental conditions. These include high, low, and room temperatures, as well as immersion in water for several hours.

Test helmets are impacted at several different points to ensure that the helmet provides protection all around the head.

✓ ■ *Children's helmets and head coverage*: The new bike helmet standard specifies an increased area of head coverage for young children, ages 1 to 5. This additional coverage is to account for the different characteristics of young children's heads and will provide added head protection for this age group.

greater head coverage

✓ ■ *Chin strap strength and stability:* The performance tests for chin straps measure whether they are strong enough to prevent breakage or excessive elongation, and whether they work to resist a helmet's rolling off the head during a collision or fall.

stronger strap

In the strength test, the chin strap, when subjected to a weight falling a specified distance, must remain intact and not elongate more than a certain amount.

prevents roll off

In the roll-off test, a helmet is secured onto a test headform. A falling weight is attached to the edge of the helmet shell to attempt to pull the helmet off the headform. The helmet must remain on the test headform to pass the test.

Additional Requirements

In addition to the provisions above, the new bike helmet standard includes requirements for the following:

look for ↓ also

■ *Peripheral vision:* The standard requires that a helmet allow a field for vision of 105 degrees to both the left and right of straight ahead. ✓

■ *Labels and instructions:* Helmets must carry labels including information on, among other things, how to care for the helmet, what to do if the helmet is damaged, and how a helmet should be fitted and worn. ✓

■ *Certification labels, testing, and recordkeeping provisions:* To help ensure that bicycle helmets meet the CPSC requirements, manufacturers must have a certification test program and maintain test records. Bike helmets must have a label stating that they meet the CPSC standard. ✓

— *Scott Heh, Directorate for Engineering Sciences*

more info ↓ follow up

For More Information

To obtain a copy of the Safety Standard for Bicycle Helmets briefing package, contact: Office of the Secretary, U.S. Consumer Product Safety Commission, Washington, DC 20207/ 301-504-0800.

The *Federal Register* notice with the final CPSC bike helmet standard is posted on the CPSC web site a www.cpsc.gov. Click on "Business," then "Official Federal Information," and then "CPSC Federal Register Notices of Interest." The web site also lists numerous CPSC brochures on bikes and bike helmet safety. Click on "Consumer," then "CPSC Publications," then "Recreational Safety."

need to find out —
what state law is for Illinois?
helmet required??
might poll class members —
see who uses?
have children — do children use?

Figure 19.1 (continued)

notation as you read. You might highlight key information as you read through the article and then go back with a different color pen and place a star by the information you will need for your report. Or, you might write notes in the margin as you read and then go back and highlight the most important information. Because you most likely will find more than one bit of information in the article, you may want to note on the front of the copy, on a separate piece of paper or notecard, or in a computer file the information you want to refer back to. Be sure to cross-reference this additional sheet with the source in case it gets separated. For the example in Figure 19.1, the cross-reference might be *Bike Helmets, CPSR*, Spring '98. Note the page number with a brief description to help.

• Have the copy and your notes with you when you sit down to write your report.

You need to be careful with this method of notetaking. You can easily overlook or forget relevant information if you do not review the source as you write your report. As you outline your report, you may need to make notations where you plan to insert the information. When you write the section, the notation will point you to the source.

Electronic Notes

You will use a computer to send and receive information and to write your report. If you also use a computer to gather and record your research notes, your notes will already be in a form that you can move into your document file, and you won't need to retype or recopy them. Laptop computers make this easy, but even without a laptop you can most likely find a computer to record your notes as you gather information. Many libraries now have workstations available for you to write up your findings—particularly for sources that cannot leave the library. Everyone has different access to computers and different ways of writing electronically, but here are a few suggestions for making notes electronically:

• Establish a filenaming convention (for example, last name of author) and create a folder (a keyword from the problem, for example *Security-Locks*) to hold your notes.

• Once you create a file for each source, immediately identify the source. If you use the documentation format (Chapter 22) you plan to use in your report, you can copy and paste this information straight into your report and avoid rekeying it.

• Read the source and then type your notes. Be sure to identify page number(s) for each selection. You might want to double-space the notes to allow plenty of white space in your electronic word-processing file. By doing so, you can more easily review the information and cut and paste it quickly into the final document. You may find it helpful to print a copy of your notes and use scissors to cut the notes so you can order them with the other information you have gathered.

• Tag each block of information with a brief identifying keyword that links the note to the source. The tag identifies the source in some abbreviated format—either formally using one of the documentation styles described in Chapter 22 or informally with an abbreviated name for the source. For example: (Hey 2) identifies the author and the page number.

• More and more you will find yourself gathering information electronically. For example, you can copy a passage from the Web, or a colleague might send you an electronic file with information to incorporate in your report. The same general guidelines apply: establish a filenaming convention and a folder to store the information. Open the file and document the source—using the appropriate bibliographic entry.

If you are just developing your electronic notetaking strategies, a few suggestions: (1) be consistent in naming the files, (2) always save your electronic notes in at least two places, and (3) don't hesitate to print a hard copy if you need one.

Notes Recorded

Frequently the notes you take on primary sources will be recorded either using videotape, audiotape, or both. Or, you will develop survey forms or logsheets for an experiment and need to take notes. More than likely you will develop a form to record direct observations. We discuss field research in Chapter 21. Here we suggest some basic procedures for recording notes using equipment and forms:

Equipment

• If you use any type of equipment such as a laptop, video recorder, or audio recorder, check the equipment at least three separate times to make sure it works. Know how to use the equipment and be prepared to troubleshoot any problems that may occur. Have additional batteries, power cords, tapes, and other supplies.

• Get written permission to record an interview or visit a site. Identify the source of the information in your research notebook or an electronic file on your laptop and on each tape used (see Chapter 22, Documenting Sources).

• If possible, survey the site before you begin recording so you can adjust how you will record the information. Prepare for interviews and rehearse questions, if necessary.

• Label the tapes you use with the date and keywords (such as the location or the name of the person you interview).

Forms

• Develop a systematic collection process guided by a form you complete to record observations. The form will probably need to be revised several times before it is tested and revised again after it is tested. You want to develop a format that is easy to use but that provides enough options to gather all the relevant information.

• Know the form and rehearse the questions before you try to gather information. Practice on others in your organization before conducting the survey, for example, in a busy mall or as visitors leave a theme park.

Notecards

Notecards are the traditional method for keeping track of information—particularly, library research. Notecards are portable and easy to use and relatively inexpensive. Here are some suggestions for using notecards:

• Buy a couple of packs of 3″ x 5″ notecards for keeping track of your sources and 4″ x 6″ notecards for information in the sources. The size of the card identifies the purpose of the card immediately. Take notes as you read. Use a pen to make notes because the ink will hold up to the use you are going to give the information on the cards. Notecards are easy to handle and rearrange and they withstand multiple handling better than pieces of paper.

• When you compile a list of potential source material, make a bibliography card for each source. Use the 3″ x 5″ cards for this. The format should be similar for all of your resources: author's name, title, publisher, location, date. As Figure 19.2 shows, you can divide the bibliographical information for a periodical into four parts: (1) author's name, (2) title of the article, (3) title of the periodical, and (4) volume number, date, and page numbers. Figure 19.3 shows a bibliography card for a government

---

Richardson, Lorraine S.

"Creating Value with a Training Program"

Employee Benefits Journal
23.2 (Sept 1998): 6-7

Figure 19.2 A bibliography card for a periodical article should have the author's name on the first line, the title of the article on the second line, followed by the title of the periodical, the volume number (and issue number, if available), date, and page numbers. Limit yourself to one source per card so you can arrange the cards easily.

Office of Policy Development and Research

The State of the Cities 1998

Washington: US Department of Housing and Urban Development, 1998.

Figure 19.3 A bibliography card for a government document should have the name of the agency on the first line, the title of the publication on the second line, and the city, publishing organization, and date on final lines. The publication identifies Andrew Cuomo as secretary of HUD, but he is not the author. He represents HUD. (Use italics for the title instead of underline when you create the bibliography in your computer-generated report.)

document. Don't forget the Web address and date if you get something from the Web. If you interview someone, make a notecard so you won't forget to include the bibliographic information in your list of resources. Review Chapter 22, Documenting Sources.

• When you take notes during your reading, create a notecard for each note and write on one side of the card only. Use the 4″ x 6″ cards for this purpose because you can get more information on the card. As shown in Figure 19.4, you should put three kinds of information on each notecard: (1) a brief descriptive heading at the top to help you with sorting and arranging notecards as you organize your material, (2) the note itself, and (3) the author and page(s) used at the bottom to identify the source of the note. If you note more than one work by the author or more than one author with the same last name, indicate the title and author's initials as well as the author's last name and pages.

• Write down all the information you will need, so you will not have to go back to the source. The source may not be there. Keep informed about the topic you are researching. Be alert for changes in information and update if possible.

• Write legibly so you can read your own handwriting.

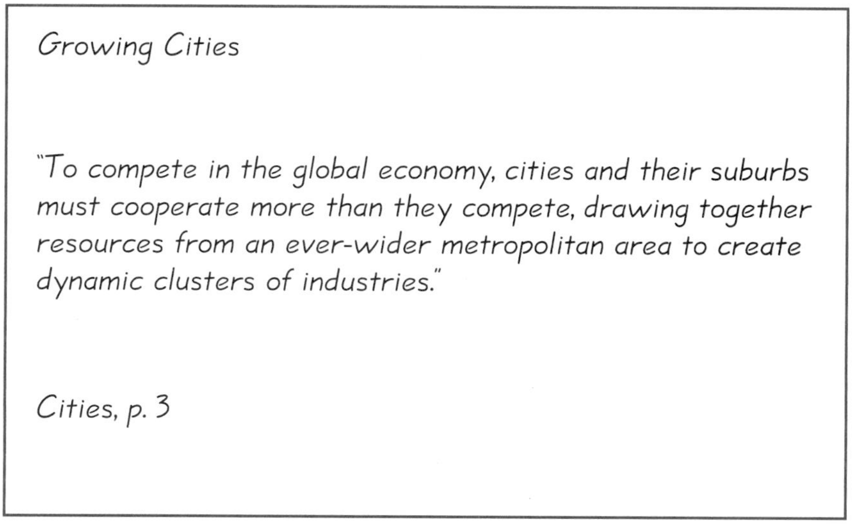

Growing Cities

"To compete in the global economy, cities and their suburbs must cooperate more than they compete, drawing together resources from an ever-wider metropolitan area to create dynamic clusters of industries."

Cities, p. 3

Figure 19.4 Limit yourself to one note per card so you can arrange them easily. A typical notecard has a topic heading at the top, the note itself, and enough bibliographical information to identify the specific source without having to write it all out.

TYPES OF NOTES

You will probably take three kinds of notes using any of the methods described above:

- quotations

- paraphrases

- summaries

The type of notes you make depend upon how you plan to use the information, who is going to read the information, and the source of the information.

Quoting

Quotations are appropriate when you need to record the exact words of the original source. Figure 19.4 is an example of a quotation note.

- Quotations are fairly easy to note. Copy the passage word for word exactly as it is printed, and put quotation marks around the passage to remind you that the passage is a direct quotation.

- Indicate the exact page(s) where the quotation appears. Or, if you have transcribed the quote from audiotapes, note the source and date.

• If you want to omit part of the source's words, indicate the omitted part with ellipsis points. (See "Ellipsis Points" in the Writer's Guide.)

• If you want to insert some explanatory word or phrase of your own inside the quotation, indicate the insertion by putting it inside brackets. (See "Brackets" in the Writer's Guide.)

Do not hesitate to include quotes in your report; however, review the report to make sure your own words provide a substantial amount of the report. Quotes from sources should support your ideas, not be the only ideas you present.

Paraphrasing

Paraphrases are appropriate when you want to state facts taken from another person's writing. They require you to put the author's ideas or statements in your own words.

• Rephrase the original passage to fit the context of your report. That is, use your own words and sentence structure to relay the information. However, that does not mean that you can distort or change the gist of the original passage. Let us illustrate the paraphrasing of a passage. An original passage and the paraphrased note are shown in Figure 19.5. You paraphrase the original passage to fit your needs.

• If you want to jot down a personal note that occurs to you while you are making a notecard, do so below the quotation or paraphrase (Figure 19.5). Making such personal notes is an excellent practice, for it helps you recall the ideas you had about the topic when you were working on it. Bracket the personal note to keep it separate from the quoted or paraphrased material.

You will paraphrase or summarize much of the research you gather in the workplace.

Summarizing

Summaries consist of a few sentences in your own words to condense the essence or major ideas of what you have read. Knowing how to paraphrase also equips you to write summaries of longer passages—a useful way to jog your memory about research materials or to provide readers with a usable condensed version of a longer document. An original two-paragraph passage and a summary of that passage are shown in Figure 19.6.

• Read the author's opening and closing statements and condense and reword them into your own words, making sure not to distort the author's intended meaning.

• Write the topic sentences of each paragraph or block of paragraphs. If the document is long, identify the main points of each major section. Condense and reword these, adding whatever transitions are necessary to make the relationship among the ideas clear.

Original passage

Increase the Federal Housing Administration (FHA) loan limit so that more middle-income city residents and minorities, who have traditionally tended to rely on FHA mortgage insurance, can enjoy the benefit of FHA single-family mortgage insurance, including down payments of less than 5 percent, and more flexible underwriting criteria. Raising the loan limit to a single nationwide threshold of $227,150 would also provide borrowers more room to finance housing rehabilitation costs under FHA's purchase rehab program—an important consideration in older urban housing markets.

Increase FHA Loan Limits

The FHA provides two incentives that encourage middle-income wage earners and minorities to purchase a home in the city. First, the FHA offers low down payment (less than 5%) and mortgage insurance. Second, the FHA increased the loan amount to $227,150 in part to encourage the refurbishing of older city homes.

[Will this help the River Edge area of the city?]
[Get an estimate of how many potential buyers.]
Cities, p. 31

Figure 19.5 Compare the original information (top) with a paraphrase of the information (bottom). The important information is captured in the paraphrase, but the sentence structure and the words are changed.

• Check to see that you have reconstructed the main ideas or the line of thought in the original.

Frequently in workplace reports you will use information gathered from a number of sources within the company. Whether you quote, paraphrase, or summarize the information, always acknowledge your source. The acknowledgment will frequently be phrases used within the report

Original passage

The Prebiotic Chemistry in the Outer Solar System Campaign seeks to identify and map the distribution of organic compounds, assay and understand details of organic chemical processes, and search for evidence of prebiological or protobiological activity on satellites of the gas giants. Europa and Titan, the two most likely sites for life, can be used as natural biological laboratories to understand how planetary environments can lead to life. Figure 3-2 illustrates activities related to the Campaign.

Europa, one of Jupiter's four major satellites, is a Moon-sized body. Its high albedo and spectral characteristics indicate the presence of surface water ice or frost. *Galileo* spacecraft observations indicate liquid water or even oceans under the surface. Water appears to be a critical precursor to life, and furthermore, internal heating of Europa by Jupiter's gravity may produce hydrothermal vents, similar to those on the terrestrial sea floor that support living communities by chemosynthesis rather than photosynthesis. Thus, detection and characterization of any Europa oceans is an integral part of our search for evidence of any life outside of Earth.

Titan, Saturn's largest satellite, has a thick nitrogen-methane atmosphere with a surface pressure 1.5 times that of the Earth. Laboratory simulations and *Voyager* data strongly suggest prodigious atmospheric organic chemistry powered by sunlight. The Cassini/Huygens mission will provide an initial survey of the nature of the surface and how the surface and atmosphere interact chemically. Then, advanced missions will provide detailed characterization of Titan's surface and atmosphere. These data may provide clues to the conditions on early Earth that led to the emergence of life.

Organic evidence in the gases of Europa and Titan

Scientists want to focus one part of space research on Europa and Titan, satellites of Jupiter and Saturn, respectively. Each has at least two significant features that provide a favorable environment for organic activity. Evidence of water and significant internal heat have been found on Europa. Saturn's nitrogen-methane atmosphere and surface pressure provide an environment suitable to initiate life.

Solar System, p. 3.4

Figure 19.6 Compare the original information (top) with a summary of the information (bottom). The important information is captured in the summary, but the sentence structure and words are changed.
Source: Mission to the Solar System: Exploration and Discovery: A Mission and Technology Roadmap (Pasadena, CA: Jet Propulsion Laboratory, National Aeronautics and Space Administration, 1997).

such as "Susan DuBois, Chief Information Officer, provided . . ." or "the Facilities Management Committee is the source. . . ." The acknowledgment in such phrases may appear less structured and somewhat informal. It is not. Your reader needs to know where you found your information and the authority behind the information. In the last section of this chapter, Evaluating Information, we discuss this further. In Chapter 22, Documenting Sources, we give several formats acknowledging sources.

EVALUATING THE INFORMATION

You have identified the problem and completed some of the research. Now you need to step back from the research and evaluate what you have found and what you still need to do to resolve the problem.

You can adjust the standard questions, who? what? when? where? and how? to evaluate the sources of your information. Figure 19.7 summarizes how these standard questions are applied to evaluating the information.

AUTHORITY AND SOURCE

Knowing who the source is lends authority to the information. That is, readers evaluate how much they trust the information as accurate and usable for their needs in part by knowing who is the source. You probably trust a medical doctor's recommendation about the best way to clean a wound more than you do that of the person you sit next to in the doctor's office. However, if the doctor recommends an ointment that he helped develop, and he is now paid by the pharmaceutical company for each sale, you might question the impartiality of his advice. If an organization

Who?	Who is the source of the information?	Authority	**Source**
Where?	Where can the reader locate and verify the information?	Source/Location	
What?	What is the information?	Content	**Information**
How?	How valid and reliable is the information? How is the information developed? Is it believable?	Worth of Info Valid/Reliable	
When?	When did the information originate?	Timeliness	**Place in your report**
Why?	Why are you including the information? Do you need the information?	Relevance	

Figure 19.7 Evaluate information before you include it in your report. You can use the six questions (left column) or remember the three areas: source, information, and place in report (right column). Include only information that applies to the problem you are solving.

promotes its product as the only (or best) solution, you should compare its claims with those of its competitors. You compare different makes and models of cars before you buy; as a researcher, you should do the same thing when comparing solutions to a problem.

Sources of information give readers of reports, memos, and other workplace documents one more way to evaluate the information. For example, professional journals earn credibility by having experts in the field review an author's work before printing the article. Publications such as *Consumer Reports* or *PC Magazine* describe the test procedures and criteria used when they make recommendations about products and services. Their reputation for fair evaluations gives you some assurance that you can rely on their recommendations. Just as there are reliable and unreliable sources in print, there are reliable and unreliable sources on the Web. Review pages 47–50 (Chapter 2) on Web sources and Chapter 20 for guidelines for evaluating the location of information. Regardless of the location, you should read critically and evaluate the information before incorporating it into your report, memo, or other workplace writing.

CONTENT—RELIABLE AND VALID

As you research your topic, you need to evaluate the information you find. Have the technical, managerial, and social criteria been researched thoroughly? What methods were used to develop the information? What sources did the producers of the information rely on?

You must evaluate the content of the information to make sure it is accurate and reliable. Statisticians use the terms *reliable* and *valid* to evaluate the research methods used. Simplified to suit our purposes here, *reliable* data means that the procedures used have been done correctly and another researcher can duplicate the process and expect similar results. Likewise, *valid* data means the procedure tests what it is intended to test.

As you collect information, you should make sure that the information was developed in some systematic way. For example, the cost accountant used standard accounting procedures to determine production costs for the tennis rackets, and you can rely on those costs to establish the wholesale and retail price. If the accountant provides production costs that are too low, most likely you will price the tennis rackets too low and lose money. However, you cannot rely just on the production costs figures. You must know what your competitors charge and what consumers will pay. If the accountant provides you with production costs for racquetball rackets, you cannot use these costs to establish pricing for tennis rackets. The comparison is neither valid nor relevant. And, production costs will be only one of several factors you must consider.

TIMELINESS AND RELEVANCE

The immediacy of problems you encounter in the workplace requires timely and relevant information. Production costs for tennis racquets produced 10 years ago has little relevance if you are establishing pricing now.

Computer prices hold for maybe a month. Technology changes rapidly and consumers' perceptions and needs change. For example, concern for the environment prompted a shift from pull-off tabs on soft drink cans to the pop-top tab that stays attached to the can. Drugs once thought safe have been pulled from the market when shown as unacceptably harmful.

Be aware of the development and publication dates of the information you gather. Note that the dates may not coincide. It may take awhile to get the information published. You have to evaluate if the time frame is appropriate and if the information is still reliable and valid.

You probably will not have much trouble collecting enough information. Actually the hard part is selecting relevant information from the vast amount of information available. For example, if the environmental impact studies on *SlowGrowth* do not report on conditions similar to those in Minnesota, Scott Pahl would not be able to make any argument for *SlowGrowth*'s impact there. Likewise, rather than include a visual showing the rainfall across the United States, which would have little relevance to the rainfall in Minnesota, Pahl would prefer a visual that targeted that state.

As you read Chapters 20 and 21, evaluate the information you are gathering for your report, memo, or other workplace document. Chapter 22 provides examples of widely accepted formats for identifying your sources. Identifying your sources in a standard way gives your readers a way to evaluate the information you provide for solving the problem. They readily can see who originated the information and where they can locate this source, and they see from the date when the information originated.

SUGGESTIONS FOR APPLYING YOUR KNOWLEDGE

Choose a problem to research. Write a one-paragraph description of the problem. After you have described the problem, do the following:

1. Find an article in a periodical and try two of the three notetaking types— write on the source, make electronic notes, and use notecards. Which process worked best for you? Do you need to modify how you made your notes? How? Why?

2. Select a passage from an article. Paraphrase the passage. Summarize the passage.

3. Locate a source on a U.S. government Web site that might have information to solve the problem you are researching. Describe your search process and the information found.

4. Use the search engines available on the World Wide Web to locate information related to the problem. What did you find? How easy or difficult was it to find timely and relevant information?

CHAPTER 20

RESEARCH SITES AND SOURCES—LIBRARY AND INTERNET RESEARCH

Take a tour of your school or community library, or, if you are working, check to see if your company has a library (many do). Tours are frequently part of your orientation to school or company resources. Listen carefully and note areas you most likely will use in your research. If you visited the library your freshman year, you probably should take a refresher tour if you are now a junior or senior. You will view the library from a different perspective because more than likely your interests are now more focused and specialized. You probably have a better idea of what you need to locate in the library.

You will also see how technology has changed the library and how you look for information. Most library catalogs are online, and many give you access to the library through the World Wide Web. Electronic databases provide access to abstracts and entire articles from periodicals. You must develop effective search strategies for the electronic environment to make the best possible use of the vast amount of information available.

In this chapter, we first describe library and Internet sources. We provide examples; you must explore the library sites. In the second section, we focus on search strategies. We suggest strategies for finding information to help you solve the problem you are researching. You must select and evaluate the sources to make sure they are worthwhile, reliable sources that provide relevant and timely information.

LIBRARY SITES

You can now visit a library without going there in person. You can find the complete texts for many articles from periodicals and government reports on the Web. Books are available in electronic form—no paper version. In this section we describe the traditional library (the building) and electronic libraries available to you. We encourage you to visit all of the sites.

TRADITIONAL LIBRARIES—THE BUILDINGS

The traditional library offers a good place to start for understanding the resources in a library and how to locate information in a library. Plan to visit the library and orient yourself to its organization so that your research trips are efficient searches for information.

On your first trip to the library, pick up a map of the library. You will soon learn which areas you will frequent most, but on your first trip look for the following areas:

- Card catalog (a rare sight now) and online catalog access (the computer terminals) to the library's holdings

- Newspapers and current periodicals

- The "stacks"—location of most of the books that can be checked out

- Reference section(s)—location of publications such as dictionaries and handbooks that must be used in the library

- Circulation desk—where you check out materials

- Microfilm section

- Specialized databases available on CD-ROM

As you look for these sections, you may see other parts of the library that interest you: music-listening rooms, computers to use for writing papers, children's book section, government documents, and so on. Explore.

You need to understand the classification system the library uses to organize the material. Most libraries have adopted the Library of Congress (LC) classification system. Figure 20.1 identifies the major divisions of the LC system. The series of numbers associated with the major division pinpoint the topic and location. As you work with your research problem, you will find yourself returning to the same sections of the library. However, you should also follow leads to other sections of the library. You might be

Library of Congress Call Numbers	
General Works	A
Philosophy and Religion	B
Auxiliary Sciences of History	C
History: General and Old World	D
History: America	E-F
Geography. Maps. Anthropology.	G
Economics and Business	H-HJ
Sociology	HM-HX
Political Science	J
Law (General)	K
Education	L
Music	M
Fine Arts	N
Language and Literature	P
Science	Q
Medicine	R
Agriculture	S
Technology	T
Military Science	U
Naval Science	V
Bibliography. Library Science.	Z

Figure 20.1 Library of Congress call numbers. Each general heading is broken into categories with letters and numbers assigned such that each work has a unique call number. For example, the call number for this textbook is HF5721.P39 signaling the general area is business communication. The *P* in *P39* is the initial letter of the first author's last name, **Pearsall**.

surprised at what you find. You will probably find a discussion of the problem that brings in information that you had not considered.

Understanding the physical layout of the library and the organization of the information in the library may make it easier for you to understand and locate information online. The physical layout places related sources together. For example, one library houses all reference sources (sources such as indexes, handbooks, and dictionaries) in one central location apart from the materials that can be checked out. Another library places related reference sources and circulating material on the same floor. The science and technology materials are on the fourth floor, the business, the social sciences, and education materials are on the third floor, the humanities on the second, and government documents are on the first floor. Learn the general organization and layout of the library you use.

ONLINE LIBRARIES

Few libraries remain that rely on the card (hard copy) catalog. At the very least, most have their holdings cataloged in a database that you access at terminals throughout the library. These libraries also have computers that give users access to a CD-ROM for reading databases available on a CD and probably several computers that provide access to the World Wide Web. However, most libraries now not only have the holdings online for users, but they also give users access to databases electronically. The access may be limited to the holdings of the library only, but again, libraries are changing. Libraries are sharing databases. When you access the holdings of the library, you may be connecting to the Internet and using databases shared by several libraries. The library is a part of a consortium of libraries (often organized by states) and the databases for the libraries are on the Web. Keep in mind that libraries have certain areas of the online catalog open for anyone to visit, but other areas require a user name and password.

User interfaces for the electronic "card catalog" look different for each library, but the information is the same. Figure 20.2 is an example of the information for the book *User and Task Analysis for Interface Design,* by JoAnn T. Hackos and Janice C. Redish, found in the Auburn University electronic catalog. Not only do you get the publication information (author, title, publisher, and publication date), but you also get the call number, the book's location in the library, and whether the book is on the shelf or checked out. The links (the underlined text) take you to other books by the author(s), related subjects (Figure 20.3), and publications with a call number (QA76.9.U83 in the example in Figure 20.4). The **previous** and **next** buttons (Figure 20.3) allow you to move to the next set of entries or back to the earlier set. Some electronic catalogs give you the option of saving the information to a disk, printing the information, or sending it to an e-mail address. You might save the information to disk when you want to gather a lot of information and need time to carefully review the sources.

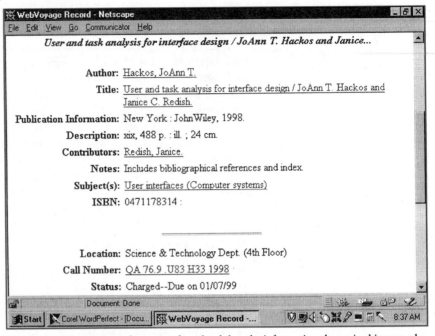

Figure 20.2 The catalog information for a book has the information shown in this example. The look of the user interface varies to meet the needs of the library's user and the institution's image.
Source: Computer screen reprinted with permission of Endeavor Information Systems, Inc. ⟨http://roo.lib.auburn.edu⟩ (14 October 1998)

Many libraries also provide services online so that you can gather information easily. If you find a source, but it is checked out, you can have it recalled. You also can view your account and see which books you have checked out and when they are due.

Electronic access to library holdings and electronic connections to databases give us access to such a vast amount of information that it becomes difficult to focus our search on the information we need. We suggest how to search online catalogs, databases, and the Web in the section Electronic Search Strategies.

COMMERCIAL AND ORGANIZATION SITES

The Web has revolutionized how companies and organizations transmit information about products, services, and activities to their customers and members. Some companies have created knowledge databases to store information about products, company procedures, employment opportunities, reports, instructions, membership forms, directories, shipping information, and so on. The information may be text, photographs, drawings, audio or video files, pictures of events as they happen, slide presentations, weather maps, and satellite feeds. The electronic environment is constantly changing.

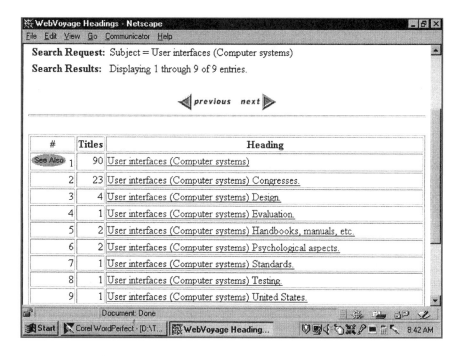

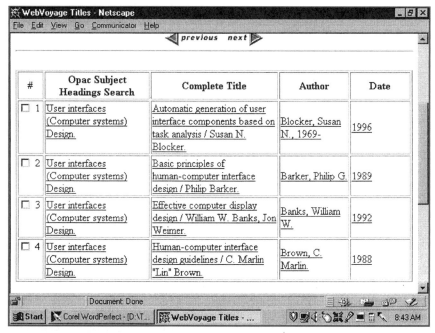

Figure 20.3 Selecting the Subjects link shown in Figure 20.2 leads to the top screen. Selecting #3 leads to the bottom screen. Following the Subject link yields four more possible sources on interface design.

Source: Computer screen reprinted with permission of Endeavor Information Systems, Inc. ⟨http://roo.lib.auburn.edu⟩ (14 October 1998).

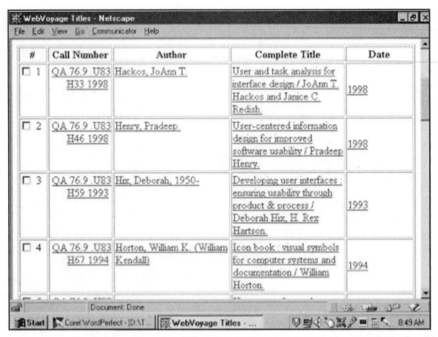

Figure 20.4 Selecting the call number link shown in Figure 20.2 results in a list of 20 related sources beginning with the call number QA76.9.U83. The last set of numbers signal the specific document: the initial letter of the first author's last name and the date of publication. *Source:* Computer screen reprinted with permission of Endeavor Information Systems, Inc. ⟨http://roo.lib.auburn.edu⟩ (14 October 1998).

The organization you work for may also have information available to only those in the organization. For example, financial records, customer order records, information on product prototypes, and other proprietary information may provide you with the information you need to solve the problem you are researching. You must be careful with proprietary information—information that belongs to the organization your work for. If your report will be read outside of the company, check with others (your supervisor or the legal department) before releasing the information.

Locating information on company and organization Web sites requires you to read carefully and follow the links (leads) to other information. Site maps help (see Figure 5.10, for example), but you must be alert, patient, and careful to keep track of your search paths.

While electronic access generally makes locating information easier and gives you access to more information, you should also check your organization's library. The library specializes in the interests of the organization and often stores the company archives. For example, you might review the report completed 10 years ago on providing an on-site day-care center to employees before you propose a day-care center now. Reviewing the older report may suggest issues you have not thought of. Similar to other libraries, corporate libraries are moving to electronic databases.

Don't overlook the small collections of information in companies and organizations that tend to build as they are used. The collections may start with one person's interest and research into a problem or a department may start a library of frequently used resources and reports published by the department. Search out these areas and the people who are building them.

GOVERNMENT SITES

City, state, and federal governments have Web sites. You find such information as the demographic, economic, and geographic features of the population the government represents. You can also find out information about the government, such as who to call if you have a question about the city recycling activities, how to contact your state legislator, or a report from NASA on the latest mission.

U.S. government Web sites are phenomenally rich sources of information.[1] Throughout this textbook we have used examples from government sites in part because of the variety and ease of locating information and in part because the information is public information, not copyrighted (although we still must acknowledge the source). You might start at the Library of Congress Web site, lcweb.loc.gov, but explore other sites. You can guess at the address for many of the U.S. government sites: www.nasa.gov (National Aeronautics and Space Administration), www.epa.gov (Environmental Protection Agency), www.hud.gov (Department of Housing and Urban Development).

Larger libraries around the country serve as federal depositories for U.S. government publications. That is, they receive many of the government publications and make them available for anyone to borrow. Figure 20.5 identifies the major subject headings for U.S. government documents. State governments have similar libraries that house state publications such as the laws of the state, brochures published by the agricultural extension agency, or reports from the state's board of education.

You have access to physical sites—library buildings, corporate libraries, and government agencies—and you have access to online libraries and companies, organizations, and government Web sites. The amount of information is overwhelming. To make the best possible use of these vast resources, you must define the problem you are researching as clearly and distinctly as possible. Focus on your immediate task: reporting a solution to a problem (specific information) to a specific audience for a specific purpose. In the next section, we describe search strategies that will help you locate information.

---

[1]See Judith Schick Robinson's *Tapping the Government Grapevine: The User-Friendly Guide to U.S. Government Information Sources,* 3d ed. (Phoenix: Oryx, 1998).

Government Documents Classification SuDoc Number		
Agricultural	A	
Commerce	C	
Census Bureau		C3
Defense	D	
Energy	E	
Education	ED	
General Accounting Office	GA	
General Services Administration	GS	
Health and Human Services	HE	
Interior	I	
U.S. Geological Survey		I19
Justice	J	
Judiciary	JU	
Labor	L	
Library of Congress	LC	
National Aeronautics and Space Administration	NAS	
State Department	S	
Smithsonian Institute	SI	
Treasury	T	
Internal Revenue Service		T22
Congress	X, Y	
Congressional Committees		Y4

Figure 20.5 Government publications are assigned SuDoc numbers (SuDoc for Superintendent of Documents). The SuDoc number points directly to the publication. For example,

HH	issuing agency	U.S. Department of Housing and Urban Development (HUD)
1.2	bureau within agency	Office of Policy Development and Research (general publication)
:C49/13	specific to title	The State of the Cities
998	year of publication	1998

ELECTRONIC SEARCH STRATEGIES

Search strategies require patience and methodical digging through information. The complete version of much of the information you find will be in a traditional format such as a book or magazine article or a videotape or photograph; however, you will probably do most of your searching for information using an electronic database. We provide search strategies that begin in an electronic environment. As you dig for information, refer back to your problem and the criteria you identified (see Chapter 19).

SEARCHING ELECTRONIC DATABASES

Your search for sources to complement your field research (Chapter 21) begins with a search using an electronic database. The database may be the holdings of a library, a database that focuses on a topic or field (for example, *National Trade Data Bank* and *Textile Technology Digest*) or on selected publications (for example, *InfoTrac* or *NewsBank NewsFile*), or a company's knowledge base (for example, Hewlett Packard's Web site for printer drivers www.hp.com). Each database has its own user interface (what you see on the screen) and each requires you to enter the search in a slightly different way. However, the behind-the-scenes search process is similar for all of the databases.

The search strategy and process relies on Boolean logic. Boolean logic is shown graphically using Venn diagrams in Figure 20.6. You will not see the process, but you will use *and, or,* and *not* in the corresponding phrases *all of these* or *as a phrase* for *and* and *any of these* for *or*. Using *as a phrase* looks for words in the same order used in the phrase. You may also use the symbols *?, *, or $* for truncating terms. The symbol used depends upon the database; look for instructions. You truncate a term in order to broaden the search, for example, *financ?* will locate finance, finances, financial, and so on. Figure 20.7 illustrates what the search screen might look like.

Your responsibility is to select keywords, words that signal the database what to look for. The keywords you select will depend upon the purpose of your search and the information you are trying to gather. You might begin with specific keywords. For example, if you are searching a company's knowledge base for information about printers, you can enter the model number of the printer you are interested in. Or, if you are searching a library's database, you enter the title of a book. If the printer and book are in the databases, you will have a successful search. However, if you lack specific information on the printer or instead of locating one book by an author you want all of the books by one author, you must modify your search. Entering the type of the printer will give you a list of models to select from. If you want to locate all of the books by an author in a library, you enter the author's name.

Searching using a subject keyword requires you to either expand or narrow your search depending on the results. For example, the keyword *golf* might produce 482 entries, but when the keyword *women* is added to the search only 29 entries appear. When you begin with a narrow topic, *graphite golf clubs* (as a phrase) you might find no entries. But changing the search strategy to treat *graphite* and *golf clubs* separately with *golf clubs* as a phrase, you might find only 1 entry. You might want to look through 482 entries if you are doing thorough research or 29 entries or 1 entry might be enough for your purpose. Review the database screen

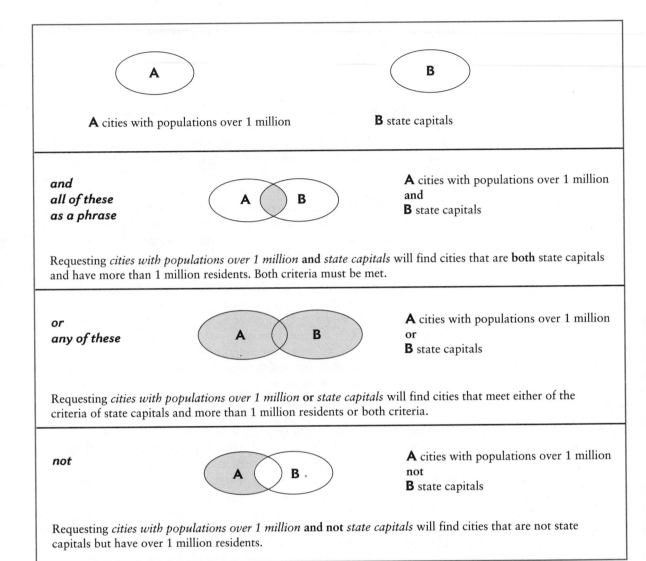

Figure 20.6 If you could *see* the Boolean logic behind the search process, you might see this. You identify the sets of data using keywords. The ovals represent a set of data, a keyword. When you provide more than one keyword or set, more than one oval, you must identify how you want to relate the sets. The *and* and *or* establish the relationship. *Not* is used to limit the search further.

before you begin your search. Most provide suggestions and options for conducting an efficient search. You can modify your search strategies in most databases without reentering the keywords. Before you give up on a search, double-check the keyword(s) you entered. A misspelled word or name will result in no matches or unintended matches. For instance, typing *gofl* instead of *golf* will yield no matches.

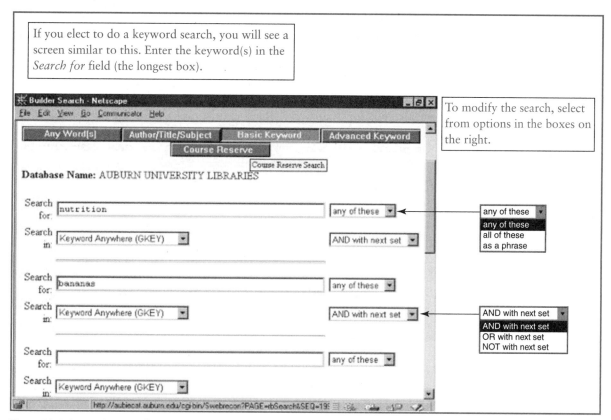

Figure 20.7 A sample screen for a keyword search. Review Figure 20.6 to determine the relationships you want to establish your search.
Source: Computer screen reprinted with permission of Endeavor Information Systems, Inc. ⟨http://aubiecat.auburn.edu⟩ (20 October 1998).

Many library databases first prompt you to select whether the keyword(s) are part of the title, journal title, author's name, subject, or call number. This selection narrows the area of the database, the field, for the search. The search for the keyword will be quicker because it assumes, for example, that the words you enter for the title must appear in that order with *and* or *as a phrase* assumed. When you go into a company's knowledge base through a series of links on the Web site, you are narrowing the search. Hewlett Packard, for example, sells more than printers. A series of choices will take you from the home page to printers and eventually to printer drivers.

USING SEARCH ENGINES

Yahoo!, Excite, and *AltaVista* are just three of the search engines currently available on the Web. Each has its own interface, organization, and areas it specializes in—Web sites on particular topics that it covers. Read the screen to begin your search. For most search engines, you will find the search most efficient if you first select one of the categories given on the opening screen. After you go to that category site, enter the keyword(s) you want to search for. The results identify Web sites that match the keyword(s) in some way and many list the possibilities in descending order of probable match (indicated by a percentage). Figure 20.8 shows the results of a search for *North Dakota* sites. (Search engines are developing into *portals,* the opening screen onto the Web. You can customize the portal for direct links to Web sites you visit frequently. You can also customize the search process so that you will be prompted when a new Web site appears that covers topics in which you are interested.)

Searching the Web and Web sites requires patience. You don't want to stop and write down every path you take. Navigation aids such as the Back key on the browser tool bar and Home key or links on Web sites help. Links change color if you activate them so you can retrace your steps to some extent. Using the bookmark feature in your Web browser helps once you find a site. However, searching sites until you find the information you need takes time. When you find the information, record the Web site address. You can print out the information, and in most cases the Web address will print in the top right corner of the page, or you can open a file in your word-processing software (perhaps the file with your notes on the problem you are researching) and record the address with notes from the site. It is easy to copy text and visuals from Web sites directly into word-processing or other software files—just be sure to acknowledge your source (see Chapter 22, Documenting Sources).

REFERENCE SOURCES

In this section, we provide an overview of commonly used and readily available reference sources: periodical and abstract indexes, directories, and online periodicals and news media. (Periodicals are magazines, newspapers, journals, and other publications published at regular intervals— daily, weekly, monthly, quarterly, for example). The reference sources we identify represent only a few of the many sources available. The sources you use will depend in part on what is available. Some of the reference sources will be in electronic form only and others are published in hard-copy and electronic form.

The hardest part of using reference sources is locating the information in them. Frequently the sources have more than one way to access the information. Because most sources are now electronic, you need not worry about how to access the information. However, you must construct an effective search strategy using meaningful keywords. In hard-copy versions, the information may be listed in alphabetical order, chronological order, or topical order—or all of the above. Review the overall organization of the reference source before you begin your search.

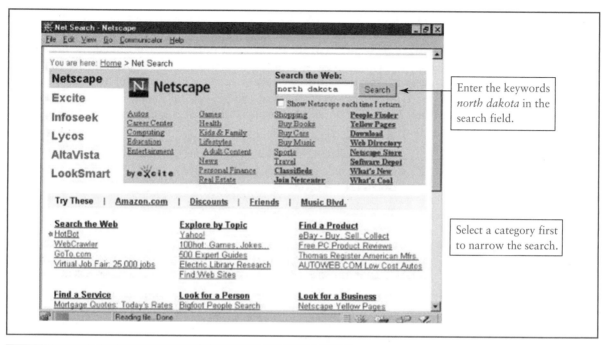

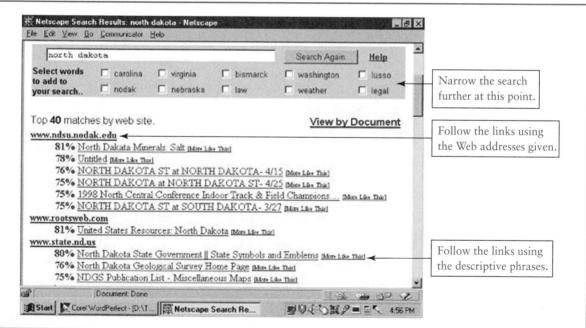

Figure 20.8 Example of the search engine feature for Netscape. You see the top screen first. Entering the keywords *north dakota* yielded 40 matches (only a few are shown here). The percentage indicates the probability of a match. The results change frequently as new sites develop.

Source: Portions of this figure copyright © Netscape Navigator, 1998. All Rights Reserved. Netscape, Netscape Navigator, and the Netscape "N" Logo are registered trademarks of Netscape in the United States and other countries. Reprinted with permission. 〈http://search.netscape.com v6〉 (12 October 1998).

Two Cautions　　We have two cautions before we give examples. First, **know the overall content and purpose of the reference source and be aware of what it covers and what it does not cover.** Read the description of the electronic database or the hard-copy source before you begin your search. The descriptions are not easy to find and not too informative—particularly for electronic databases. The following is the description for *InfoTrac's Expanded Academic ASAP:*

> Indexes over 1500 journal titles in a variety of subject areas including astronomy, religion, law, history, psychology, humanities, current events, sociology, communications, and the general sciences. Articles in over 500 journals are full text.[2]

Ask yourself if the topic you are researching falls into one of these subject areas. The topic areas are broad, so even if you can place your topic in one of these areas, you may not find anything in the database. Try another database. If you know the title of the magazine you want to search, enter the title. If you receive no results, try another database. If you do find material using the title or keywords, do not assume you have found all or even the most important information on the topic. The 1500 periodicals indexed by *InfoTrac,* for example, represent only a small number of the thousands of periodicals published.

The second caution: **recognize the gap between the time an article is published and the time it is picked up by a database.** The time span advertised by the publisher of the database does not mean that every article published in the periodicals has been indexed in the database. For example, a search in *ERIC* (the leading electronic database for periodicals related to education) in October 1998 found the latest issue of *College English* indexed to be October 1997. The *ERIC* database covered 1966 through July 1998. However, for issues after October 1997, you may have to go to another index with more recent issues cataloged, visit the Web site of the publisher of the periodical (in this case, www.ncte.org, National Council of Teachers of English), or go to the library's current periodicals section and look at the periodical. The delay in indexing *College English* may be a backlog of processing entries at *ERIC* or it may be a delay in receiving the journal from the publisher.

Reference sources vary in how much information they provide and in what form the information is presented. You will find the information in electronic form either on the Web, on the library's computer (a local server), or on a CD you load into a personal computer—many publishers have stopped issuing print versions. The following references are examples of the types of sources available.

---

[2]From the Auburn University Web site ⟨http://www.lib.auburn.edu/otherindexes.html#infotrac⟩ (10 October 1998).

PERIODICAL AND ABSTRACT INDEXES

Periodical and abstract indexes catalog together related publications and topics. These electronic indexes were once separated into indexes, bibliographies, and abstracts, but technology has provided publishers with the ability to combine the information into one form. The database entry has some or all of the following features: the bibliographic citation for the source, an abstract, the complete article (referred to as *fulltext*), and options for saving the information to a disk and ordering information if you want a hard copy of the article. You search using keywords, titles, authors, or other descriptors.

Visit your library online for a list of periodical and abstract indexes. Here are a few to look for:

ABI/Inform (American Business Information)

ERIC (education-related sources)

InfoTrac (see the description on page 566)

DIRECTORIES

Directories give brief, concise information on companies, organizations, and people. Search them to find such information as who owns Xerox, what is the largest advertising agency in the world, when Joe Camel was introduced, or which automobile was first in U.S. sales last year. If you need to locate companies in a certain industry or companies that manufacture a certain product, a good business directory will provide the names, addresses, and telephone numbers. Check your library for electronic versions of the directories or use a search engine on the Web to go directly to the company or organization's site. Here are a few of the most popular directories:

Directory of Foreign Manufacturers in the United States

Standard & Poor's Corporate Records

Thomas Register of American Manufacturers

US Government Periodicals Index

Other reference sources include almanacs, atlases, dictionaries, encyclopedias, handbooks, and yearbooks. Some focus on a particular topic or field of study; others provide a broader coverage of topics. Reference librarians know how to search the library's print material, Web sites, and other electronic sources. You can help them by clearly stating the problem you are researching and being familiar with the organization of the library.

ONLINE PERIODICALS AND NEWS MEDIA

Many news services and publications now have Web sites—some require you to subscribe, others limit what information you receive at no charge, and others provide the full text. For example, cnn.com or msnbc.com provide clips from the television broadcast and other information that complements the content of the television broadcast. The Web sites for magazines such as www.forbes.com or time.com present information from the print versions as well as additional information. Online periodicals and news media have developed rapidly over the past two years and continue to evolve as sources for immediate news.

EVALUATION OF INFORMATION

As you collect sources from the library and Internet, you will probably quickly evaluate the source to help narrow the search for information. In Chapter 19, we describe three factors to consider as you evaluate sources: (1) authority and source, (2) content reliability and validity, and (3) timeliness and relevance (see Figure 19.7). In Chapter 2, we provide guidelines for evaluating a Web site (see pages 47–50 and Figure 2.5). Review both chapters before you read the rest of this chapter. In this section, we provide several quick ways to evaluate information as you collect it. You will be using your critical thinking skills. You may incorporate these suggestions into your note-taking strategies.

Use the suggestions to help you narrow your search and evaluate the sources. Review the sources closely before incorporating information into your report.

AUTHORITY AND SOURCE

As you collect information from library and Internet resources, you must be aware of who or what organization has produced the information. If you cannot find the author or sponsoring organization on the information, don't use it. Ask yourself these questions:

- Who is the author and/or sponsoring organization?
- Does the author or organization specialize in this area?
- How do I contact the source to verify the information?
- Who or what led me to this source?

CONTENT—RELIABLE AND VALID

Collecting information and evaluating the information sometimes overlap. Although you'll spend most of your time synthesizing the information you collect, first you must collect enough information to evaluate the problem. In the collection process, you'll do a quick evaluation as you go. To confirm most information, you want at least two sources that say the same thing. Review your note-taking strategies (Chapter 19), but you might also find it helpful to develop mental notes. Say, for example, that you hear a brief news story about AIDS on CNN. You search out a confirmation and clarification of the story by going to the Centers for Disease Control and Prevention's Web site, and you make mental notes and notes in your report draft to find out why. The notes you collect look like the following:

Information	Mental Notes	Source
deaths from AIDS declining	deaths, not cases	CNN news 10/7/98
still same rate of infections, but living longer	declining or leveling off?	www.cdc.gov 10/10/98 Centers for Disease Control and Prevention
	find info on why— successful treatments?	call specialist at local hospital for an interview

Next, you'll spend time with the notes developing the report and applying critical thinking strategies as you evaluate all of the information. Taking notes and developing the notes into a report take time—allow enough time to think about your findings and to write the report.

TIMELINESS AND RELEVANCE

Each research problem will have an appropriate time frame from which to draw information. If the problem is computer-related, you might need to pull from sources no more than 3 months old for software development issues, no more than a week for pricing, and across 20 years for historical information. As you first make notes about the problem and establish the criteria to research (Chapter 19), you will develop an idea of the time frame for relevant information.

Date Final Report Due	March 12, 1999
Date of Publication of Information	June 1998
Difference in days/months/years	9 months
Will the reader consider this information up-to-date?	less than a year old—ok

SUGGESTIONS FOR APPLYING YOUR KNOWLEDGE

1. Tour your school, community, or company library and pick up a map. Locate the section(s) of the library the majority of the information for your area of specialization is found. Spend half an hour browsing through that area(s) of the library and make a list of 5 to 10 reference sources you think will help you in your course work or in finding solutions to a problem you are studying.

2. Visit the Web site of three U.S. government agencies. Compare the sites and describe the type of information you found.

3. Select a topic (if possible, related to a problem you are researching). Conduct a search of articles on the topic using 3 to 5 electronic databases. Write a brief report comparing the results of your search across the databases. Be prepared to report your findings in class.

CHAPTER 21

RESEARCH SITES AND SOURCES—FIELD RESEARCH

Research frequently requires firsthand knowledge. That is, you must collect the information instead of relying on the reports of others. When you leave your desk to collect information outside your office, that is field research. In this chapter, we describe three methods for collecting information from the field: interviews, surveys, and direct observations. As a researcher, you may interview *subject matter experts* (SMEs). The SMEs may be within your organization or outside the organization. You may interview face to face or by telephone. When you must collect information from a number people but lack the time to interview each one, you might develop a set of questions—a survey—to collect the information. You may distribute the survey electronically by e-mail or on the Web, or you may send the survey by mail. Alternatively, you may find that a visit to the site of the problem or setting up a comparison test may provide helpful information for solving the problem. More than likely you will use several methods for gathering information to solve a problem.

We begin by suggesting ways to prepare for collecting the information. We review suggestions first made in Chapter 19 for evaluating the information gathered. We provide guidelines for conducting interviews, developing surveys, and using direct observations to gather information to help solve workplace problems. Every discipline has its own methods for conducting field research (and library research). Seek help from others in your organization with experience in conducting field research.

PREPARING FOR FIELD RESEARCH

Before you begin to collect information, you must establish some collection procedures. More than likely you will have only one opportunity to interview the person or a limited amount of time to visit the site or conduct the experiment. Be prepared. Plan carefully. Here are five suggestions for preparing to do your research:

• **Review your notes on the problem you are researching.** State the problem in specific language and figure out what sort of information you need to solve the problem. In the example in Chapter 14, Scott Pahl studied the problem of increased costs of mowing highway medians. In reviewing his notes on the problem, Pahl determined that he needed to know more about the existing process and to research alternatives to mowing and their costs and impacts.

• **Establish objectives for collecting the information.** The objectives should identify specific tasks you must complete. For example, Scott Pahl knew he needed to interview the supervisors of the work crews mowing the grass to get a better understanding of how frequently the crews had to mow and what sort of problems they encountered. He knew he needed to find environmental experts and agronomists who specialized in grass. He also thought it would be helpful to visit at least some portions of the highways to identify the type of grass growing and to consider the aesthetic issues raised in letters of complaint from commuters. His initial objectives were to interview the work crew supervisors and locate and interview SMEs on grass control.

You will add to your objectives at each stage of collecting the information. For example, after visiting the site, Scott Pahl decided he needed to return to the site with an environmental engineer to evaluate the safest application procedure for SlowGrowth.

• **Set up a schedule for completing each task identified in your objectives.** You might find a large wall calendar or an electronic calendar that alerts you to due dates. Project-management software has features that allow you to schedule and coordinate multiple tasks. Many of your projects will have a fixed due date. The date you must complete the work should be the first date you put on your calendar. You then work back from the due date to schedule the tasks. If you don't have a specific due date, impose one on yourself. As you build the schedule, allow some extra days for tasks that require more time than expected.

• **Test your interview questions, survey, and direct observations procedures before you implement them.** Draft questions, surveys, and observation procedures and ask others to review them before going to the source. Some of the major trouble spots you might encounter while conducting field research include the following:

Selecting the Wrong Subjects to Interview   Will a 21-year-old want the same features in a car as a 35-year-old or 60-year-old? Probably not. Will surveying mall-goers about improving access to the planned sports complex give the same results as polling sports fans leaving the basketball arena that the proposed sports complex will replace? The mall-goer may not attend sporting events at the arena.

Before you select the target population, review the research problem and describe the characteristics of the subjects. Age difference is an obvious factor to consider when selecting subjects to research; however, you should look at other factors—many that cannot be observed. For example, you may need to consider level of education, income level, eye and hand coordination, desire to learn a new skill, and so on.

Selecting the Wrong Sites to Visit   A successful test of *SlowGrowth* in the Southeast will not ensure that it will retard the growth of weeds in Minnesota (Chapter 14). You might find different factors affecting the problem if you visit a site in the morning instead of in the afternoon. As you develop the problem statement and focus on the problem(s), you must take into account where the problem occurs most frequently and if you can get to that site for direct observations or if you must simulate the problem in another location.

Observing Factors That Do Not Apply to the Research Problem   Pinpointing criteria to analyze the problem will help establish what and what not to observe. For example, the make and model of a vehicle that enters a parking lot may be unimportant when analyzing traffic flow and congestion. A simple count of vehicles or axles may be enough. A simple count can be collected easily using a machine, but identifying vehicles requires a member of the research team to observe and record each car's make and model or to analyze the videotapes of the traffic and note the types of vehicles.

Asking Ambiguous and Irrelevant Questions   You have limited time to ask questions—make every one count. Ask the SME who developed a new bullet-proof vest about the material used in the vest, the construction of the vest, the types of bullets it will repel. Don't ask the SME the advantages of using a vest. The advantages have been established, and you can gather the statistics that support the use of bullet-proof vests before interviewing the SME. However, it would be appropriate to ask the SME's prediction for an improved rate of survival with vests made with the new material.

Using Inconsistent Collection Procedures   Work with other members of the team to develop the research procedures. Depending upon the problem, several members of the team may be doing the same tasks. Each member may have to administer the survey, interview SMEs or make a site visit. Team members should be using identical research procedures. For example, one team member cannot read the survey questions to a respondent while another member lets the respondent read the questions and still another e-mails the questions. The different environments may affect how the responses are given. You will need to discuss each team member's responsibilities and ensure consistent gathering of information.

• **Evaluate your progress throughout the project and make adjustments as needed.** Few projects go so smoothly that you complete the tasks and solve the problem without interruptions to the schedule. Often you must rely on and adjust to others whose schedule may not fit yours.

You may have to make progress reports to your supervisor or client. Progress reports may be informal memos to the project coordinator in your organization or more formal reports to the client. In progress reports, you will first review the problem. How much review you provide will depend upon your reader's familiarity with the problem. Simply identifying the problem in the subject line of a memo may be enough, or you may need to give a 1- to 2-page summary of the problem.

The major portion of the progress report (frequently divided into several sections) will report on current activities and the status of the research tasks. You might include a calendar that shows which tasks are on schedule and which have fallen behind. You might include a summary of the current expenses and project future expenditures. If the project research is running into problems, you must alert your supervisor and the client receiving the progress report, but you should also assure them that the problem is under control. Supervisors and clients expect a few problems. Keep them informed.

You might end the progress report with a short conclusion or summary, or you might end with a list of objectives to guide the work both in the short term (until the next progress report is due) and long term (until the project is completed).

EVALUATING THE INFORMATION

In Chapter 19, Research Strategies, we describe three areas you should review as you work through the problem and look for solutions. Field research requires the same type of scrutiny as library and Internet research even though you are collecting information firsthand rather than relying on the reporting of others.

You must evaluate your field research sources, the information, and the place it has in your report. Ask the questions given in Figure 19.7 and reviewed below:

Source	Who are the sources of the information? What is their area of expertise? Why are they the authority on the problem?
Information	How valid and reliable is the information gathered? Have I asked the right questions in interviews and on surveys? Does the information gathered on-site provide the information needed?
Place in Report	How is the information gathered contributing to solving the problem? Did I gather the information in a timely manner?

In the remaining pages, we provide guidelines for conducting interviews, administering surveys, and making direct observations.

INTERVIEWS

You know the problem. You have a good idea of some of the information you need. You have identified the subject matter experts (SMEs) you need to meet with to discuss the problem or a portion of the problem. The SMEs may be a part of your organization: for example, the customer service department that provides you a list of the most frequent troubleshooting questions or the bench technicians who explain how the new microprocessor will work. Or, you may have to locate an SME. Library and Internet resources can help you here, or ask others.

The key to conducting effective interviews is *preparation*. You must prepare for interviews whether the interview is an informal telephone call to a vendor to get a price quote or a more formal meeting with the lead scientist of a research project. Start with library and Internet resources. For example, in choosing how to configure the computer system you need, you can begin at the Web site of a computer vendor. Your call to the vendor may be unnecessary or you may need help deciding which combination ethernet and modem card to put in the laptop. To get a better understanding of a lead scientist's expertise before your visit, you might search the *Applied Science and Technology* electronic database order and read the complete text of her reports.

Before the interview make a list of questions. The questions will evolve out of your preliminary research in preparation for the interview. Design the questions to gather the information you need. *Ask direct questions:* What steps do you take to process the travel voucher? or How long does it take the work crew to mow a mile of highway median? Of course, at times you will want to elicit the opinion of the SME: What options do we have for managing the software environment in the computer classroom? or How do you think the traffic should be rerouted? (A question requiring only a yes or no response, such as Do you think the traffic should be rerouted? doesn't help you explore solutions to the problem.)

Effective questions will get you a long way toward conducting a productive and informative interview, but you also must *listen to the responses.* You may need to ask follow-up questions to clarify responses and to extend the responses further. Often factors you have not considered come out in the discussion. You must be adept at adjusting your questions. For example, in discussing with the locksmith the problem of security in the textile research lab, the supervisor learned about a fiber optic system that can be installed, which is comparable in cost to a combination lock system and yet secures the equipment as well as the room. The supervisor asked many follow-up questions to learn about the fiber optic system. One caution—stay focused on the topic and areas related to your original purpose for the interview. The person you interview will appreciate your efficient use of time and your understanding of the problem.

You also must *be considerate* of the SME. Be on time for the appointment and stay only as long as needed to gather the information. If you want to tape the interview, request permission and be prepared to take notes if the person does not want to be taped. You might follow the interview with a short thank-you note or return the favor and answer the SME's questions when she calls.

Finally, *review your notes* as soon as possible after the interview to fill in information that you did not write down as you discussed the problem with the SME. If you have to go back to the SME for more information, think through your questions carefully before you go back. If you taped the interview, review the tape and transcribe the conversation so you can review the information easily.

SURVEYS

In this section, we describe the type of survey you develop in response to an immediate, local problem. Surveys (also referred to as *questionnaires*) provide you with a tool for collecting information from individuals you cannot interview easily. Donald Zimmerman and Michel Lynn Muraski caution that the survey "should not be the sole source of information. In gathering information, social scientists suggest triangulation—gathering data in different ways to validate the information. . . ."[1] You will want to take courses in statistics and survey development before you conduct a large-scale survey. We suggest guidelines for surveys you might conduct for local problems.

For example, say you want to offer health benefits to your employees. You need to know how many of your 45 employees currently have health insurance. You send out an e-mail to everyone asking for a simple yes or no response. In this instance, you should probably offer a brief explanation of your plans and invite suggestions. The main purpose of your e-mail is to find out who has insurance. You can track who responds with the return address on the e-mail message.

For most surveys you will have several questions to ask. Your audience will probably give you only a few minutes to gather the information. We suggest you do the following before distributing your survey:

- **Review your notes on the problem you are researching**. If you have a clear understanding of the problem, you will develop a survey focused on getting the information from respondents.

- **Draft and test a set of questions that will gather the information you need**. Testing surveys goes beyond passing it around to others in your office. You must test it on a group similar to the population you plan to survey. Expect revisions and changes.

We discussed reliable and valid in Chapter 19. A reliable survey may be given to a similar population and similar results will be found. A valid survey gathers the information that it is designed to gather. You need to know two other terms used in survey research: sample and population. In most cases, you cannot possibly ask everyone, the population, affected by the problem to respond to your survey. Instead you select a representative sample from the population to ask the questions. The size of your sample will depend upon the size of your population.

Figure 21.1 summarizes the types of questions you can use. The type you select will depend upon the topic, the amount of information you need, the decisions you must make based on the questions, and factors such as the budget for the survey, how you will reach the target population, and the time respondents are willing to give you. At the end of this section we include an example of a survey (Figure 21.2).

- **Design a survey form that is quick and easy to respond to**. An e-mail message, a postcard, a sheet of 8.5-by-11-inch paper are some of the formats you might use. Start with an introductory paragraph that identifies the purpose of the survey or omit an introduction. If you include an introduction, be careful not to influence your reader's responses by giving away your position on the topic.

---

[1]Donald Zimmerman and Michel Lynn Muraski, *The Elements of Information Gathering: A Guide for Technical Communicators, Scientists, and Engineers* (Phoenix: Oryx, 1995) 123. You should review this source. The authors provide guidelines for conducting a survey.

yes/no	Quick and easy to respond to and to tally, but may not supply appropriate or complete information. *Will the voice recognition software help?* A yes or no answer will not give you an idea of how it will or will not help the employee. *Will the voice recognition software run on the laptops the sales staff use?* A yes or no response is all that is needed here.
multiple choice	Quick and easy to respond to and to tally. The options must be designed so the choices cover the possible options without conflict in meaning. *How many special classes have you attended at the City Zoo?* ___ *no classes*　___ *1–2 classes*　___ *3–4 classes*　___ *more than 4*
ranking	Ranking gives a list of items and the respondent identifies his or her preference. *Indicate your preference for health insurance (1 most preferred, 4 least preferred)* __ *$30 a month　hospital stays only* __ *$50 a month　routine medical bills and full hospital coverage* __ *$80 a month　full coverage ($20 deductible per visit)* __ *$99 a month　full coverage with dental plan ($20 deductible per visit)*
rating	Rating questions ask the respondent to select from a range of choices. *Strongly Agree*　*Agree*　*No Opinion*　*Disagree*　*Strongly Disagree* 　1　　　　2　　　　3　　　　4　　　　　　5 *My chair is comfortable.*　　　　　　　　　　　1　2　3　4　5 *My chair provides me with adequate back support.*　1　2　3　4　5 *My work area has adequate lighting.*　　　　　　1　2　3　4　5
open-ended	Asking questions that allow respondents to write freely or to fill in a blank gives you a lot of information. The information, however, may or may not be easy to analyze. The amount of space you provide will influence the answer you receive. *If you could design a software program to help you in your job, what features would you like?*
demographic	You need to find out about the person answering the survey. Ask only the personal questions that matter. For example, when surveying accountants about the method of accounting they use, you probably don't need to know their gender; however, their job title and age may help you determine their level of experience.

Figure 21.1 Invest time in constructing the questions for your surveys. Select questions that will give you a meaningful response that can easily be totaled and evaluated.

Responses to 1 or 2 questions may be all you can get from customers entering a store. If your sample population receive the survey in the mail, they may be willing to spend 20 to 30 minutes on responding. Testing your survey will give you an idea of how much time most people will need. Know your audience and how long you can expect them to spend answering the questions. You might want to state in the introduction how long the survey will take.

• **Include in your report the size of your sample and a copy of the survey.** As you analyze the responses, focus on the trends you see in the data rather than isolate individual questions. Use the responses as one part of the information you gathered to solve the problem. Report the margin of error for the survey results, if appropriate. The margin of error indicates the range of percentage points the final results may vary. For example, if 46 percent respond "yes" and the error is ±5, as few as 41 percent or as many as 51 percent could vote yes in the population.

Two examples of surveys illustrate the range of possibilities for collecting information from a large number of people. This method of field research has developed in recent years into an effective and efficient means of gathering information from a sample of the population in order to make decisions that will affect the population.

Figure 21.2 is an example of a survey distributed through the campus newspaper of a university in the Southwest. The target population is students of the university. Students have more than likely stopped to read the newspaper, so they may also take the time to respond to the survey. The survey is designed to fill the front of one sheet of paper that can easily be distributed through the newspaper. Each question is important, because of the limited time to get information from the students and the limited space available on the sheet of paper. The survey sheet can be folded with the return address showing and dropped in campus mail.

This survey was designed to gather information from a cross-section of the student population. The cost of developing, distributing, and collecting the survey were minimal, but some problems arose. Lack of control after distribution led to such problems as who responded (faculty and staff also read the newspaper) and how many times a person responded. How might the survey developers change the distribution to control for who responds without increasing the cost of collecting the information? What changes do you suggest in the questions? Do the questions' formats yield useful responses (review Figure 21.1)? What additional questions might be asked if the front *and* back of the paper were used?

In the second example of a survey, we have included selections from a survey conducted by the National Science Foundation and reported in *Science & Engineering Indicators–1998*. Figure 21.3 describes the survey instrument developed to poll the attitudes of a sampling of U.S. citizens on science and technology. Figures 21.4, 21.5, and 21.6 illustrate how the survey results are interpreted and presented.

Survey for Public Transportation on Campus

The West River County Council, the City of Levelland, and University of South Plains are studying the feasibility of public transportation for the area. Please take 5–10 minutes to complete the survey.

1. Are you a _____ full-time student or a _____ part-time student?

2. Are you a _____ Freshman _____ Sophomore _____ Junior _____ Senior _____ Graduate Student?

3. Do you have a driver's license? _____ Yes _____ No

4. Do you live in a   _____ single family home
    _____ apartment or condominium
    _____ trailer park
    _____ on-campus housing (including dorm, fraternity, or sorority)

5. Identify the closest intersection to where you live while attending USP:

    _____ and _____

6. How do you get to classes most of the time?   Please check only one.
    _____ drive alone   _____ carpool   _____ bicycle   _____ motorcycle
    _____ apartment shuttle bus _____ taxi   _____ bus   _____ walk
    _____ other_____ (please identify)

7. Which USP building do you spend most of your time in? _____

8. If you drive to campus, where do you usually park? Please check only one.
    _____ university parking lot   _____ public parking lot
    _____ private parking lot   _____ other

9. How much do you pay to park on campus? $_____ per _____ (day, month, semester, year)

10. If free public transportation were available from your residence to campus, would you use it?
    _____ every day _____ 1 day/week _____ 2–3 times/week _____ never

11. If a free campus shuttle were available, would you use it?
    _____ every day _____ 1 day/week _____ 2–3 times/week _____ never

12. If you had to pay for public transportation from your residence, how much would you be willing to pay?
    _____ up to 25¢ _____ 26¢–50¢ _____ 51¢–75¢ _____ no more than $1

13. **Optional** Age ____ under 18 ____ 18–22 ____ 23–35 ____ 36–50 ____ 51–64 ____ over 65

14. **Optional** If you have a disability, please check the term that best describes your disability.
    _____ mobility _____ visual _____ hearing _____ speech _____ health _____ other

Comments?

Please fold the survey so the address for the Campus Police shows. Drop the form in any campus mail box.

Figure 21.2 A survey such as this one allows you to get information from a large group of people without a lot of expense. However, it is not a "scientific" survey. Because the survey was inserted in a campus newspaper, the controls for who responds and how many respond limit the usefulness of the results. The results yield general trends and provide a starting point for a more focused study.

Survey Methodology

Survey of Public Attitudes [14]

- ▶ Overview
- ▶ Survey Design
- ▶ Trend Data
- ▶ Availability of data

▲ 1. Overview

a. Purpose

The Survey of Public Attitudes monitors public attitudes towards science and technology, including the public's level of scientific understanding and policy preferences on selected issues. The survey provides information of interest to those who design education programs and is used by academic researchers. The survey is closely coordinated with surveys in several other countries in order to facilitate international comparisons.

b. Respondents

The survey is completed by adults in the United States.

c. Key variables

- Acceptance of science and technology
- Admiration of science and technology
- Age
- Attitudes towards science and technology policy areas
- Educational level
- Geographic location (within U.S.)
- Interest in science and technology
- Occupation
- Perceived impacts of science and technology
- Personal activities regarding science and technology
- Public knowledge about science and technology
- Race/ethnicity
- Sex

▲ 2. Survey design

a. Target population and sample frame

The target population for the 1992 survey consisted of noninstitutionalized adults, aged 18 or over, in the United States. The sample frame consisted of those individuals over 18 who had working residential phones.

b. Sample design

This survey used random digit dialing (RDD) sampling methods. The sample was prepared by Survey Sampling, Inc., of Fairfield, Connecticut. A random sample of household telephone numbers was selected using the prefix data base from American Telephone and Telegraph and selected Donnelley files. The person aged 18 or over in the household with the most recent birth date was selected for inclusion in the sample. Approximately 2,000 adults were interviewed in the 1992 survey.

Figure 21.3 Every research project has a method or guidelines for conducting the research. Those projects with more rigid and formal guidelines (a methodology) can withstand the tests of reliability and validity. The results provide a level of assurance that the results will not change if a different target population is surveyed. The methodology described in this example establishes the guidelines for surveying 2,000 adults from the U.S. population to find public attitudes toward science and technology.

Source: National Science Foundation. *Survey Methodology.* 20 Oct. 1998. 21 June 1999 〈http://www.nsf.gov/sbe/srs/spa/spameth.htm〉.

c. Data collection techniques

The 1997 survey (*PDF 1.4 MB*) was conducted by the Public Opinion Laboratory at Northern Illinois University under the direction of the Chicago Academy of Sciences under contract to SRS. Primary data collection was done using computer-assisted telephone interviewing (CATI) techniques. Up to 6 calls were made to each number selected to determine whether the number was a working residential phone and up to 10 additional calls were made to select a respondent and complete the interview.

d. Estimation techniques

Since the Public Attitudes survey focuses on the percentage distribution of variables within the U.S. adult population rather than on estimates of the number of individuals in the United States with certain characteristics, the weight adjustments result in a total equal to the number of individuals in the sample rather than to the total population of interest. The weights for the NSF sample were adjusted to compensate for the fact that only one of the eligible adults in each household was selected. This adjustment is done by multiplying by the ratio of the number of eligible adults in the selected household to the mean number of eligible adults per household in the complete sample.

Since it is known that response rates within RDD samples are disproportionately high for college graduates and disproportionately low for high school dropouts, the sample results are benchmarked against the Current Population Survey, conducted by the Bureau of the Census. This weight adjustment is done within 90 cells formed by cross-classifying 5 age strata, 3 racial-ethnic strata, 2 gender strata, and 3 educational strata. No imputation for missing data was performed.

e. Possible sources of error

(1) Sampling - The coefficient of variation for a percentage estimate of 50 percent in the total population in 1992 was approximately 2 percent. For percentages substantially lower than 50 percent or for subgroups of the population, coefficients of variation were larger.

(2) Coverage - Households without phones are excluded from the sample frame and thus are not covered. There is also some undercoverage of individuals with recently installed phones due to the time lag between the selection of phone numbers and interviewing. Since adjustments are not made for multiple phone lines associated with a given household, there is overcoverage for individuals in homes with multiple phone lines. The benchmark to the Current Population Survey is designed to correct for some of the known biases introduced by coverage errors.

(3) Unit nonresponse - The cooperation rate for the 1992 survey was 72 percent.[15] While the weighting algorithm presumably at least partially corrects for nonresponse, any differences in personality or other characteristics not reflected in demographic variables would not be corrected by weighting.

(4) Item nonresponse - Item nonresponse was under 1 percent for all items on the 1992 survey.

(5) Measurement - Opinion and attitude questions are by their nature relatively prone to measurement error, since slight changes in question wording or changes in question ordering can have significant impacts on responses. A large number of the items in the Science and Engineering Indicators studies have been repeated over several studies, and analyses of these results indicate that these items are stable and tend to correlate with other related information points, suggesting that they are measuring the same underlying constructs.

Figure 21.3 (continued)

▲ 3. Trend data

Science and Engineering Indicators has contained information on public attitudes toward science and technology in every biennial edition since 1972. A significant restructuring of the survey was undertaken in 1979, which has provided the framework for subsequent surveys. Time trends for many of the variables can be constructed for the years 1979, 1981, 1985, 1988, 1990, and 1992.

▲ 4. Availability of data

a. Publications

Information from this survey is included in Science and Engineering Indicators. In addition, Jon Miller has published a number of articles based on this survey.

b. Electronic access

A public use file for this survey and several of the foreign data sets can be obtained by contacting:

ICASL Archive Data
Chicago Academy of Sciences
2001 North Clark Street
Chicago, IL 60614
Phone: (773) 549-0606

c. Contact for more information

Additional information about this survey can be obtained by contacting:

Melissa Pollak
Senior Analyst, Science and Engineering Indicators Program
Division of Science Resources Studies, Room 965
National Science Foundation
4201 Wilson Boulevard
Arlington, VA 22230
Phone: (703) 306-1777
E-mail: mpollak@nsf.gov

▲ 14. The public attitudes survey described here is the survey sponsored by SRS. A related survey on public attitudes sponsored by NIH and coordinated with the SRS survey is not described here. For information, contact David Chananie, NIH, 6006 Executive Boulevard, Suite 312, Bethesda, MD 20892-7052; (301) 496-4418.

▲ 15. The cooperation rate for this survey is defined as the number of respondents divided by the number of in-scope households for which there was a response to the phone within the allowed six tries. Note that, by definition, the response rate is lower than the coverage rate.

Last Modified: Tuesday, 20-Oct-98 10:02:59 Comments to srsweb@nsf.gov

Figure 21.3 (continued)

Appendix table 7-26.
Public's access to computers from work and home, by selected characteristics: 1983-97

Characteristic	1983	1985	1988	1990	1995	1997
			Percentages			
All adults						
No access	70	66	62	58	46	43
Access from work or home	27	28	29	30	33	34
Access from work and home	3	6	9	12	21	23
Male						
No access	68	62	59	55	41	42
Access from work or home	28	30	30	30	34	32
Access from work and home	4	8	11	15	25	26
Female						
No access	72	69	66	61	50	44
Access from work or home	26	26	28	31	33	36
Access from work and home	2	5	6	8	17	20
Less than high school graduate						
No access	94	87	92	85	80	79
Access from work or home	6	13	8	14	18	18
Access from work and home	0	0	0	1	2	3
High school graduate						
No access	66	65	58	55	42	40
Access from work or home	31	30	35	34	38	39
Access from work and home	3	5	7	11	20	21
Baccalaureate or higher degree						
No access	47	40	33	29	18	12
Access from work or home	45	43	41	41	36	38
Access from work and home	8	17	26	30	46	50
Attentive public for science and technology[a]						
No access	61	56	50	44	31	34
Access from work or home	29	33	35	31	31	36
Access from work and home	10	11	15	25	38	30
			Sample size			
All adults	631	2,005	2,041	2,033	2,006	2,000
Male	775	950	958	964	953	930
Female	856	1,054	1,084	1,070	1,053	1,070
Less than high school graduate	404	507	530	495	418	420
High school graduate	941	1,147	1,158	1,202	1,196	1188
Baccalaureate or higher degree	282	349	353	336	392	392
Attentive public for science and technology	208	235	233	229	195	288

NOTE: In 1985, 1988, 1990, 1995 and 1997, the question was worded, "Do you use a computer in your work? About how many hours do you personally use your work computer in a typical week? Do you presently have a home computer in your household? About how many hours do you personally use your home computer in a typical week?" In 1983, the question was worded, "Do you use computers or word processing equipment in your work?..."

[a]The attentive public for science and technology contains the attentive public for new scientific discoveries and the attentive public for new inventions and technologies.

SOURCES: J.D. Miller and L. Kimmel, *Public Attitudes Toward Science and Technology, 1979-1997, Integrated Codebook* (Chicago: Chicago Academy of Sciences, International Center for the Advancement of Scientific Literacy, 1997); and unpublished tabulations.

See figures 7-20 and 8-24.

Science & Engineering Indicators – 1998

Figure 21.4 The *Science & Engineering Indicators–1998* report is an 8-chapter report with an appendix for each chapter. Much of the data are displayed in tables such as this one found in the appendix for Chapter 7. The data support the discussion and recommendations found in the body of the report.

Source: National Science Foundation. Chapter 7: Science and Technology: Public Attitudes and Public Understanding. *Science and Engineering Indicators 1998*. 21 June 1999 〈http://www.nsf.gov/sbe/srs/seind98/pdf/append7.pdf〉.

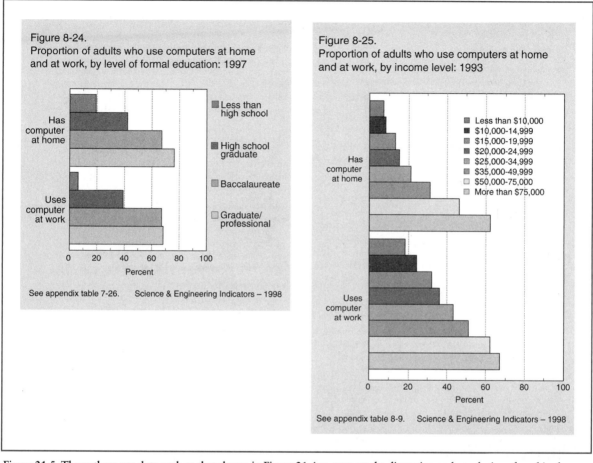

Figure 21.5 The authors use data such as that shown in Figure 21.4 to support the discussion and conclusions found in the report. They develop visuals that graphically display the data to help readers interpret the results. The horizontal bar graph shown on the left in this example uses data from the table shown in Figure 21.4.
Source: National Science Foundation. Chapter 8: Economic and Social Significance of Information Technologies. *Science and Engineering Indicators 1998.* 21 June 1999 〈http://www.nsf.gov/sbe/srs/seind98/pdf/c8.pdf〉.

Figure 21.3 describes the methodology, the design of the survey and the variables measured. Note the descriptors for the target population (noninstitutionalized adults, 18-years-old or over, residential telephone), the sample size (2,000), and the section describing errors that might occur in the sampling. Figure 21.4 illustrates a small portion of the data collected. The data is reported in a table found in the appendix of the report. Discussions and interpretation of data are found in the body of the report. In Figure 21.5, a portion of the data shown in Figure 21.4 is illustrated in the left bar graph (the report's Figure 8–24). The researchers use this and other data to interpret and report on the attitudes of U.S. citizens toward science and technology. The conclusions for a portion of the report are shown in Figure 21.6. Can you see how the survey developed from a

Highlights

IT AND THE ECONOMY

♦ **The use of information technologies (IT) is pervasive in the United States.** The real net computing capital stock in the private sector was $155.8 billion in 1995. And, in many industries, the number of employees who use a computer at work is more than 50 percent; in the banking industry, it is 85 percent.

♦ **IT is believed to have contributed to the country's structural shift to a service economy.** In the United States, growth in services as a proportion of gross domestic product has been led exclusively by IT and knowledge-intensive industries such as finance, insurance, real estate, and professional services.

♦ **The U.S. Bureau of Labor Statistics projects employment in IT-producing industries to nearly double from 1986 to 2006.** This expansion is due almost entirely to growth in computer and data processing services (including software manufacturing); employment declines are projected for the IT hardware industries. Since precise projections are always difficult, this should be taken as a general direction, not an exact level of employment.

♦ **Several comprehensive studies, using a variety of data and methods, indicate that there is an overall skill upgrading taking place in the labor force,** a trend attributed to the greater use of IT in many occupations.

♦ **The incidence of IT-related injury and employee surveillance in the workplace are on the rise,** but impacts on individuals are uncertain.

♦ **Recent research suggests—unlike past evidence of a "productivity paradox"—that there may be measurable productivity gains from IT.** Nonetheless, it is difficult to predict the precise organizational and firm-level conditions that foster the effective use of IT.

IT AND EDUCATION

♦ **By 1992, 80 percent of all K-12 schools had 15 or more microcomputers for instruction. In 1996, 85 percent of all schools had access to multimedia computers, 65 percent had Internet access, and 19 percent had a satellite dish.** Internet linkages are not necessarily widely accessible within schools—in 1996, only 14 percent of instructional classrooms had an Internet hook-up.

♦ **In fifth grade, more than half (58 percent) of the instructional use of computers is for teaching academic subject matter.** By 11th grade, less than half (43 percent) of computer-based instruction is for content; 51 percent is for computer skills training.

♦ **Meta-analyses of educational studies conducted between the late 1960s and the late 1980s consistently reveal positive impacts of computer-based instruction at the K-12 level.** Estimates of the order of magnitude vary, but one meta-analysis of 40 studies gave evidence of learning advantages that ranged from the equivalent of one-third to one-half of a school year for K-6 education.

♦ **The cost effectiveness of computer-based instruction relative to other forms of instruction has not been demonstrated.** As pressures to increase IT spending grow, it is likely that school districts will face greater opportunity costs between IT and other education-related expenses.

♦ **There is significant educational inequity in access to computers and the Internet.** Schools whose student body is represented primarily by minority or economically disadvantaged students have one-third to three times less access to these technologies than do schools attended primarily by white or nondisadvantaged students.

♦ **Poor and minority students cannot compensate for less computer access at school in their homes.** In 1993, blacks and Hispanics had half as much ownership of home computers as whites. The poorest and least educated groups had about one-tenth the access to home computers as the most affluent and educated groups. Research indicates that when the "informationally disadvantaged" are given access to computers and the Internet, they use these resources effectively for self-empowerment.

IT AND PRIVATE CITIZENS

♦ **Concerns about information privacy are growing larger and stronger.** In a 1996 Equifax/Harris privacy survey, two-thirds of the respondents said that protecting consumer information privacy was very important to them.

♦ **The vast majority of Americans believe that companies should be prohibited from selling information about consumers**—including their income, bill-paying history, and product purchases—and that stiff restrictions should be placed on access to medical records. Unfortunately, most Americans also believe that they have already lost control of personal information about themselves.

Figure 21.6 Each chapter in the *Science & Engineering Indicators—1998* report begins with the conclusions the researchers make from the survey of public attitudes on science and technology.
Source: National Science Foundation. Chapter 8: Economic and Social Significance of Information Technologies. *Science and Engineering Indicators 1998.* 21 June 1999 (http://www.nsf.gov/sbe/srs/seind98/pdf/c8.pdf).

methodology, to collected data, to interpretation of data, to conclusions? (We found these documents on National Science Foundation Web site, www.nsf.gov.)

DIRECT OBSERVATIONS

For many practical problems in the workplace, a firsthand look at the problem will give you a better understanding of contributing factors. Visiting the site, testing the product with those who will use the product, and running comparison tests provide opportunities to see the problem. Review the first two sections in this chapter on preparing and evaluating your research project.

SITE VISITS

A site visit might involve walking down several floors to see the room you have been given to convert to a Web development office for you and two assistants or it might involve a trip to your organization's production facilities in Brazil to witness firsthand the chicken-processing plant that is consistently 20 percent more productive than other plants. Regardless of the site, these three strategies will make your visit more productive:

• **Plan your visit.** Before you visit, understand your purpose for visiting the site. Review your notes and the problem statement. Define for yourself exactly what kind of information you need, and why. Make a list of what you must look for but also be prepared to see things you don't expect. Check to make sure that you have the equipment and material you need to gather data—maps, floor plans, measuring tapes, video and sound recorders, camera, specimen containers—whatever you need to collect and record data.

• **Take careful notes and videotape the site, if appropriate.** You may ask someone to give you an overview of the problem and the site. Or, you may walk around and observe before getting the opinions of those on the site. Regardless of how good an observer you are, you must record your observations—either in a notebook or by voice as you videotape. Memories cannot be trusted to recall what we observe.

• **Review your notes shortly after the visit.** You may need to clean up and add to your notes. Sometimes during a site visit you will take notes so fast that you will be unable to write complete sentences. Immediately after the visit, fill in the gaps while the details are still fresh in your mind. When you refer back to them several weeks or months later, you'll still clearly understand what you observed.

Firsthand knowledge of the problem provides you with the authority to make decisions about how to solve the problem. Readers of your report expect you to know all aspects of the problem and to answer their questions. Site visits contribute to your understanding of the problem.

USABILITY TESTS

Usability tests are a research tool that frequently save an organization from making a large investment in a product with no assurance that the product will be accepted by the consumer. Usability tests test the product with a group (a sample) of users of the product. For example, writers of software documentation have computer users with different ability levels work through the instructions for installing a printer or setting restrictions on the user access to network administration features. Or, you might be asked to write a set of instructions for new employees that will show them how to logon to the company's internal online knowledge base. Before you print 50 copies, test the instructions on several people with different levels of experience in using the online knowledge base.

Before you do large-scale usability testing, read more about how to set up the tests.[2] The suggestions we provide assume you are testing a fairly simple document or product for limited and almost immediate use. That is, you are responding to an immediate problem that requires a quick solution. For example, say the company you work for just loaded new customer-order-processing software that also gives the technician the specifications for making eyeglass lenses. No instructions are provided, so the first day the customer service representatives (CSRs) and technicians use the software is chaotic. In the evening, you write instructions so that the CSRs and technicians will have less trouble. You must test the instructions because you know the software too well. You might ask the first CSR and technician who arrive in the morning to work through the instructions. You can then make changes before the others arrive and test again. To develop your instructions, you followed these steps:

• **Identify the problem.** The problem was that customers were unhappy with the delay in processing their orders, and they would lose confidence that their order for new glasses is correct if the CSR struggled with entering the order. The CSRs and technicians needed to learn how to use the software quickly with little interruption of service to the customers.

• **Meet with the product developers and other SMEs to learn about the product.** If at all possible, work with the product developers. However, if you lack either time to do this or access to the developers, you may have to learn the product on your own so that you can help others. In the above case, you knew the software.

• **Select a representative sample of users.** Remember, you can only be certain of the effectiveness of the product with the users you tested the product on. You chose to have several CSRs and technicians review your instructions.

---

[2]For example, see JoAnn T. Hackos and Janice C. Redish, *User and Task Analysis for Interface Design* (New York: Wiley, 1998).

- **Conduct the test and record the results.** Most usability test sites have more than one means of collecting information about the product. In the case of testing software, the user's keystrokes may be recorded, a video camera may capture the eye movements of the user, another camera may record posture, audiotaping could capture any comments, and so on. In our example, you won't do all of this. You will either give the instructions to CSRs and technicians and ask them to write suggestions on the instructions as they work through them or you might sit beside them and note where they stop and ask you questions.

- **Evaluate the results and adjust the product's features.** In the example, all you probably need to do is go back to your office, fix the problem areas on the instructions, and retest, if necessary. You cannot change the software features. However, if you encounter numerous problems, you should write a memo describing the problems. Send the memo to the source of the software and your supervisor, if necessary.

Usability testing has become an important part of product development for software, hardware, and documentation. We commonly relate usability testing to products associated with the computer industry, but all businesses and industries test their products in some way before mass producing them.

COMPARISON TESTS

You may find that you must test a product or service before you recommend it as a solution to the problem you are researching. The test may be as simple as comparing price and durability features of a product (for example, snow plows for the company parking lots) or comparing vendor response time and length of service contracts for newly purchased oscilloscopes. Comparison tests help you focus on individual factors or criteria when considering more than one product or service.

The test may be a controlled experiment similar to what you would do for a chemistry or biology lab. You set up controlled experiments so that you narrow the causes of the problem. Scott Pahl's final recommendation called for testing *SlowGrowth*. He did not conduct the experiment, but if he were to construct the field test, he would probably test variables such as application season, amount of application, and rate of growth. He could not control the weather, but he could monitor the amount of rainfall as a variable that might influence the rate of growth.

As with surveys, you will need more specialized courses and experience before you can design and carry out a controlled experiment. However, for relatively simple, local problems, you can conduct comparison tests to study a relatively simple problem. Here are some suggestions for conducting comparison tests:

- **Review the problem and establish the purpose of the test.** To keep the comparison controllable, focus on reasonably small parts of the problem. You cannot test every laser toner cartridge available, but you can test the three brands of cartridges available from the local office supply store that fit your organization's laser printers.

- **Identify the variables or features to focus on.** As you select the variable to test, you are breaking the problem into small components. For the toner cartridges, you might measure features such as the ease of installation, the number of copies the cartridge makes, and the quality of the print judged by points per inch, darkness, and crispness of the letters.

- **Conduct the tests and record the results.** Using the toner cartridge example, you might ask 3 to 5 people to install the three ink cartridges you have selected for evaluation. For print quality, you first might print sample pages from several of the documents that your department produces (a memo, a letter, pages from a report with visuals) and ask 10 to 15 people to evaluate the results (possibly with a response as simple as acceptable/not acceptable).

- **Evaluate the results and make recommendations.** To compare the results for each feature side by side, you might construct a table similar to one *Consumer Reports* uses to show comparisons (see Figure 3.2). The comparisons won't always be easy and the *best* won't always be obvious. Some comparisons will require judgment calls. If you explain your decisions and back them up with test results, your audience will seriously consider your recommendations.

Acquiring firsthand knowledge takes time. Your reward will be your and your audience's greater confidence in the solutions you produce.

SUGGESTIONS FOR APPLYING YOUR KNOWLEDGE

Identify a problem that you can research by site visit, interview, survey, testing, or a combination of these methods. After you have identified a problem, do the following.

1. Visit the site of the problem and write a 1- to 2-page memo describing what you found. If others in your class also visit the same site, compare your description with theirs. Discuss any differences that may affect how you solve the problem.

2. Schedule an interview with an SME close to the problem. Before you conduct the interview, develop 5 to 10 questions you want to ask. Test your questions on a classmate before you interview.

3. Develop a set of questions for a survey. Bring the survey to class and ask your classmates to complete the survey. After you have had a chance to review the responses, ask the members of your class to suggest ways to improve the survey.

4. Create a form for collecting data from a usability test or comparison test you are conducting as part of your research of the problem.

CHAPTER 22

DOCUMENTING SOURCES

Readers rely on the information provided in workplace documents to make informed decisions about the problem at hand. As a writer, you need to know how to gather information from many sources—from primary sources such as personal experiences, surveys, interviews, direct observations (Chapter 21, Research Sites and Sources—Field Research) and from secondary sources found in the library and on the Internet (Chapter 20, Research Sites and Sources—Library and Internet Research). The more thorough and accurate you are in analyzing the problem and reporting your conclusions and recommendations, the more your audience will trust your solution to the problem.

In part, you project the thoroughness and accuracy of your report through the primary and secondary sources you use. However, you must identify these sources to your readers so that they can locate the sources and make independent judgments on the value of the information (see Figure 19.7). They will judge the authority of the source in part by the author's position and reputation and the quality of the periodical, Web site, or other form the information appears in. And, they will note the timeliness of the information. That is, are the information and sources current? Whether information is published in print format or electronically, whether it is an internal company document or a document found in a library, and whether it is a government source and considered public domain or is copyrighted or proprietary information—you must acknowledge your sources.

Some readers will rely solely on your evaluation of the information, but others will want to review the original source. In many cases, the readers do not go back to the original source to discredit your report. Instead, they want more background information on the problem, or they want to use your report and that of some of your sources to conduct their own research on another aspect of the problem. Show your readers where to find the information by providing the author(s), the title or other identifying description of the work, and the publication information, including the date and location of the source.

In the following pages, we describe several methods for citing sources and how to document the source. We begin by explaining how to handle quotations, paraphrases, summaries, and other material such as visuals that you use in the document. We briefly discuss the difference between proprietary, copyrighted, and public domain information—particularly information available electronically. Finally, we describe the documentation formats of the American Psychological Association (APA) and the Modern Language Association (MLA).

INCORPORATING INFORMATION

In Chapter 19, we describe how to take notes so that when you are ready to write the report you will have the information to support your ideas. Now we will discuss how to incorporate the notes into your document. An important tactic that helps readers follow *your* writing is the skillful handling of quoted and paraphrased material in your reports. If you make inept use of quotations, paraphrases, summaries, and other forms of information, you lose control of your report. It is important, therefore, to know when and how to quote, paraphrase, summarize, and incorporate nontext material. Here are some conventions that will help you stay on top of the information you have gathered and use it to support your views.

QUOTATIONS AND PARAPHRASES

Quotations and paraphrases are used to show support from authoritative sources. Be careful about how you incorporate them into your document. Here are some suggestions:

• **In general, avoid beginning and ending a report or paragraph with quotations or paraphrases.** There are two reasons for this: First, quotations and paraphrases in these positions produce a weak effect by drawing the focus away from *your* ideas. Because the beginning and end are the two most emphatic positions, you should place your ideas and conclusions in these positions. Second, quotations and paraphrases at the beginning of a report or a paragraph make you appear too indebted to the ideas of others, as if *your* writing serves only to comment on somebody else's thoughts. An important exception to these suggestions occurs when you want to use a quotation or a paraphrase as an attention-getting device. Just remember to use them for the added authority they can give to *your* ideas.

• **Introduce quotations and paraphrases by acknowledging them with a general comment,** such as "As one recent research study has found . . ." or with a specific reference, such as "Dr. Hiram Walton, head of the nuclear disposal site survey team, states that. . . ." Simply placing a quotation into the text without setting a context for it leaves readers trying to figure out the relevance of the quotation to what you are discussing.

• **Make sure that all quotations correspond exactly to the original wording, spelling, and interior punctuation.** Departures of any kind should be explained. If you choose to omit words from a quoted passage, you must indicate the omitted words by using ellipsis points (three or four spaced periods). See "Ellipsis Points" in the Writer's Guide. If you add a word or short phrase within a quotation, enclose the added words in brackets. Do not use parentheses, because readers will assume that the parenthetical statement exists in the original passage.

• **Except as noted in the next item, enclose all quotations inside quotation marks.** A quotation within a quotation is enclosed in single quotation marks (typed by using the apostrophe). See Writer's Guide, page 646.

• **Indent quotations longer than three lines and omit the quotation marks.** See Writer's Guide, page 645 and Figure 22.1.

SUMMARIES

The guidelines for summaries are not as specific as those for quotations and paraphrases because the information is usually gathered and synthesized from several sources. Just as the summaries from your notes have helped you review information and tie together key points, the summaries in your report should tie together key points for your readers. You may or may not be able to point to specific sources. Summaries are stronger if you use your own words rather than quoting or paraphrasing others (except, as we noted above, to grab readers' attention). Here are several suggestions:

• **Include summaries at key places in the document to help the reader review your main points.** Depending upon the length of the document, you may summarize the information at the end of sections of the document as well as at the end of the document. You may begin the document with a summary. If the summary is part of a report or research article, it may be identified as an Executive Summary or Abstract.

• **Do not introduce new information in the summary.** A summary reviews information that has already been presented. Because you have already cited the source of any new information in the body of the document, you need not cite it again in the summary—unless it is a quotation or paraphrase.

VISUALS, AUDIO- AND VIDEOTAPES, ELECTRONIC TEXT, AND OTHER SOURCES

Information gathered from a variety of media sources such as visuals, audio- and videotapes, unrecorded interviews, and text from electronic sources require special attention in incorporating and documenting the information. You need to acknowledge the source regardless of the form it takes. The following suggestions cover only a few possible forms. You will adapt how you acknowledge the source to the documentation style you choose and the special features of the material. Here are several suggestions:

• **For visuals, identify the source immediately after the caption or in an acknowledgment section at the end of the document.** Provide enough information for the reader to locate the source. We have done this throughout the textbook for visuals that we have received permission to use from other sources. Review Chapters 6 and 7 for information on types of visuals. In most cases, if you give the complete documentation information with the visual (in the caption), you need not list the source in the list of works cited or references.

• **Acknowledge audio- and videotaped material as you do text or visuals but note in the documentation the format (for example, videocassette, slides).** If you add taped material to a Web site, be sure to have permission to use the material.

- **Incorporate a phrase into the document that acknowledges particular contributions gathered in an interview.** For example, you might use the phrase "Dr. Karl Lawler, director of IMON's research and development, suggested...." If you follow MLA format, document the interview in the works cited section, particularly if you interviewed someone outside of your organization. APA format does not require you to document the interview, because it is considered "unrecoverable" information, but you should include the date and title of the person you interview at the first location you cite the person. If the interview is an informal discussion or with someone within your organization, you may not need to include it in your list of references or works cited.

- **Document information you have gathered electronically such as e-mail and listserv discussions and text from the Web or electronic databases.** Follow the guidelines for using quotes and paraphrases. Our caution here: It is easy to copy the material and easier still to lose track of the source. Take care with your notes as you gather information from electronic sources. We review the suggested APA and MLA format for this type of information on pages 603 and 609.

USING PROPRIETARY, COPYRIGHTED, AND PUBLIC DOMAIN INFORMATION

You will gather information from sources that may be proprietary, copyrighted, or within the public domain. Broadly speaking, these categories distinguish the extent to which you can use the information and the type of acknowledgment you must provide. Proprietary information belongs to a company or organization. The company or organization you work for more than likely has information (frequently recorded in internal documents such as memos or reports) that should not be released to clients or others outside of the company. Even if you developed the information, you developed it as an employee of the company. You must have permission before you release the information to someone outside the company. Obvious examples include software programs, financial statements, and marketing plans. However, memos and reports on issues such as security, travel reimbursements, or the description of a product development process also belong to the organization. You cannot include the information in a packet to a client or in your portfolio without permission.

Copyrighted work may be published or unpublished; it may be registered with the U.S. Copyright Office, but it does not have to be; it may carry the copyright symbol © or not. Works copyrighted in the United States do not automatically carry an international copyright—copyright laws vary among countries. The work belongs to the author(s) or organization that created the work. You must ask permission to use the work or information you gathered from the work, particularly if you will profit from using the material. For example, we have asked permission for some of the material used in this textbook because we did not create the material originally and because multiple copies of this textbook will be published, and we may benefit from the sale of the textbook. For more information about copyright laws, go to the Library of Congress Web site: lcweb.loc.gov/copyright.

U.S. government documents and works more than 75 years old belong to the public—they are part of the public domain. You do not need permission to use them; however, you must acknowledge any information you use. Remember, your reader may want to go to the original source to do further research. In the next section, we describe how you cite a document published by a government agency either in print form or electronic and provide the documentation for the source.

The World Wide Web provides easy access to a wide range of information. We use the term *information* broadly here to mean images and audio and video clips as well as text. Some of the information is part of the public domain. You can use it without permission, but you must provide the Web address and the date you located the information. Other information found on the Web is copyrighted material. The home page may have the copyright symbol ©, but the symbol is not required. You must obtain permission to use the information whether you use it in a printed document or in an electronic document such as your Web site. This includes obtaining permission to create a link to a Web site that is copyrighted or inserting an image from another site onto your page. You can create links and borrow images from the Web for your documents easily, but don't let the ease of use create a false sense of ownership. Information gathered from the Web requires the same care in obtaining permission to use and acknowledging the source as printed material found in the library.

To close this section, we have two points to make about information that is so readily available:

1. Acknowledge the source, whether it is copyrighted or not. You want your reader(s) to know where you found the information. The reader will know you have gone to experts on the problem and based your recommendations on research gathered from library, Internet, and field research.

2. Make every effort to obtain permission to use a copyrighted source. If you cannot secure permission, do not use the source. Find another source that has the same information and that will give you permission. You do not need permission from the holder of the copyright for class assignments, but for workplace assignments, you must have permission.

DOCUMENTING SOURCES

To acknowledge the sources you use, you must document the source. This acknowledgment is call *documentation* (literally meaning that you lead readers to other documents). Good documentation includes enough information about the source for readers to locate it. The following are two of the many style manuals giving guidelines for documenting sources.

APA   *Publication Manual of the American Psychological Association,* 4th ed. Washington, DC: American Psychological Association, 1994.

MLA   *MLA Handbook for Writers of Research Papers,* 5th ed. New York: Modern Language Association, 1999.

We describe APA and MLA in this chapter, but you should check with the technical communicators in your company or organization for guidelines on which style to use. Or, select the style commonly used in your field. Most provide essentially the same information so that the reader can locate the source: author information, title information, and publication information. The order the information is given and the format vary among the styles. We cannot possibly cover all of the types of sources you need to document—particularly the changing forms of electronic sources. You must make informed decisions about the format based on knowing the accepted format for commonly referred documents in your field of study or organization and the information needed for the documentation.

The reader needs to know the author(s), title (or other descriptive identifier), and publication information. The **author information** comes first in all documentation styles used. The author may be one or several individuals who developed the material or an editor who collects material from others and publishes a document. The editor's name appears first as the editor of the document if the entire work is cited. Sometimes a committee or defined group develops the document and does not single out individual authors, for example a government agency. The group's name appears in the author position.

The **title or other descriptive identifier** pinpoints the specific document. Accuracy is especially important when documenting the title. Many authors publish more than one document. The title identifies one document and, except in rare cases, a reference code is assigned to it. The Library of Congress classification system (see Figure 20.1), the SuDoc number for government documents (see Figure 20.5), or a classification system developed by an organization to track its documents identify the specific document. The classification is unique to the document and more than likely indicates where to locate the document in the library or resource room.

Publication information identifies where the document can be found— the original publisher, including the city or Web site where it is published and the date of publication. The date of publication is important because it allows the reader to judge the document's timeliness and relevancy to the information presented. If the document is part of a larger document, such as a journal, anthology, or Web site, information on the larger document is also included. Or, in the case of an interview, taped source, some electronic text, or other unpublished material, a brief descriptive phrase identifies the format of the document. Other information included in source documentation includes page numbers, editions, and any other information needed to help the reader locate the source and acknowledge the producers of the information.

Study the examples below for a better understanding of the type of information you must provide. We first give examples following the American Psychological Association's (APA) recommendations. We then use the same examples to illustrate the Modern Language Association's (MLA) recommendations. The most significant differences in documentation between the two are the location of the publication date, the use of initials for authors' first names by APA and written as published by MLA, and when words in titles are capitalized. APA does not use quotation marks to distinguish titles of articles. For in-text parenthetical citations, APA includes the date, MLA does not. And, APA does not require the page number unless you cite specific information (information that is paraphrased or quoted), whereas MLA includes the page number for all information.

APA—AMERICAN PSYCHOLOGICAL ASSOCIATION

The *Publication Manual of the American Psychological Association* (4th edition) recommends using in-text parenthetical citations and a list of ref-

---

Researchers seem to agree that the questionnaire should be as simple as possible. McKinney and Oglesby (1995) suggest testing the questionnaire for readability level "to insure that the content is pitched neither too high or too low for the respondents" (p. 322).

Recent studies (Griffey, 1999; Peavey & Abernathy, 1999) show that the questionnaire should be personalized, as well as simple. Every attempt should be made to get responses from all subjects. According to Griffey (1999), who returns the questionnaires can affect results:

> In a Wisconsin study with a 45.9% response, it was discovered that 78% of the former students in the top percentile of their class returned the questionnaire, while only 28% from the bottom percentile returned the questionnaire. (p. 83)

The tendency for successful students to return more questionnaires than their less successful counterparts can invalidate findings and conclusions.

Snelling (1997b) suggests that a high response rate is possible from all segments of the population if the questionnaire is highly personalized. To personalize the survey, she suggests...

Figure 22.1 The in-text parenthetical citations on this page follow the APA style. Note where the page numbers are placed and when the author(s)'s name is included inside the parentheses. In the center of the page is a direct quotation longer than three lines. Such quotations are indented. Quotation marks are unnecessary when long quotations are in this format.

erences at the end of the report to document sources. In this section, we explain and give examples of in-text parenthetical citations, which consists of two parts:

- An in-text parenthetical citation that identifies the author, the year of publication, and page or pages referenced so the reader can find it in the list of references at the end of the report (see Figure 22.1).

- A list of references at the end of the report, which is arranged alphabetically by author and which provides the publication information necessary to locate the source cited (see Figure 22.2).

Here's how the system works. The reader reads a passage like the following and sees the author or authors cited in parentheses:

Several nonmetallic materials have been considered for large wind turbine blades. Both fiberglass and wood composite appear to be alternatives to steel and aluminum, but because fiberglass and wood are both poor conductors, a direct lightning strike could cause severe damage. Fiberglass radomes have been shattered when no protection was provided

---

References

Griffey, R. L. (1999). The personalization of questionnaires. *Journal of Survey Techniques, 14,* 83–93.

Martin, G. M. (1998). Realizing a high response rate. *Journal of Survey Techniques, 13,* 312–325.

McKinney, J., & Ogelsby, F. (1995). *Designing surveys.* New York: Acme.

Peavey, J. M., & Abernathy, M. (1999). High-rate response: The standards set in a pilot study of HMO users and private health care users. *Studies in Research Techniques, 8,* 120–128.

Snelling, B. (1997a). Phrasing open-ended questions. *Journal of Survey Techniques, 14,* 106–107.

Snelling, B. (1997b). Designing questionnaires. *Studies in Research Techniques, 6,* 99–103.

Figure 22.2 Following APA style guidelines, the list of references for a report contains full publication information on each work cited in the report. Here are some guidelines for formatting the documentation on the reference page of workplace reports:

- Single-space entries for a workplace report.
- Indent the first line but all lines following should be against the left margin (about $\frac{1}{2}''$).
- Use author's initials and invert the names (for example, Smith, G. R.).
- Use capital letters only for the first word and proper nouns of titles and subtitles. Capitalize the titles of periodicals.
- Italicize the title of the work for workplace reports; do not use quotation marks around the article or essay found within the work.
- For periodicals, italicize the volume number as well as the title of the work.

(Fisher & Plumer, 1998, pp. 16–18). Other research has shown that epoxy-wood blades can be severely damaged if they are not protected (Bankaitis, 1999).

Notice that the author's or authors' last names, the year of publication, and the page or pages cited are enclosed in parentheses inside the normal sentence punctuation. The author's name, the year of publication, and the page numbers are separated by commas. The page number(s) are included when specific parts of the source are cited. Should readers wish to know more about the article by Fisher and Plumer or the report by Bankaitis, the list of references at the end of the report provides complete publication information.

The following examples demonstrate the various ways to present in-text parenthetical citations according to APA documentation style. Afterward, we illustrate format for entries in the list of references.

In-Text Parenthetical Citations

• One work by one author. Place the author's name, year of publication, and page number or numbers in parentheses:

> Land titling has caused some problems, most due to the bureaucracy involved with the titling process (Montgomery, 1996, p. 119).

Notice the use of commas between the author's name, the year of publication, and the page number. When you use the author's name as part of your sentence, cite the year after the author's name and the page number(s) in parentheses after the information you are citing:

> Montgomery's study (1996) revealed that while settlers paid only a nominal fee for land, the title process was cumbersome and caused several delays (p. 119).

• One work by two or three authors. When citing a work that has two authors, cite all names:

> Researchers have succeeded in fusing a myeloma tumor cell, capable of producing antibodies, with a spleen cell from an animal which previously had been primed with a known antigen (Kohler & Milstein, 1998).

• One work by three, four, or five authors. When citing a work that has three to five authors, cite all the authors the first time you refer to the work. After the first reference, include only the surname of the first author followed by *et al.* for the other authors:

> During the past decade several projects have used surge irrigation (Johnson, Martin, & Nordeen, 1999).

> Kleinmann, Morgan, Fenwick, and Dean (1994) discovered new evidence for changing the procedure. In recent tests, (Kleinmann et al., 1994, p. 86) show that although the grenade is effectively spin-stabilized in flight, it tends to drift to the right from its maximum ordinate.

- Work by a corporation or organizational author. Use the name of the corporation or organization as the author:

  > According to a recent study (Northeastern Commission on Higher Education [NCHE], 1999), more and more adults are returning to college.

Use the acronym for the source if you cite it more than once.

- Work with no identifiable author. Place the title of the article or book in the author position:

  > Soil resistivity can be decreased by adding moisture or chemicals to the soil ("Recommended Practice for Grounding of Industrial Power Systems," 1998).

  > There are three important sources of data-entry operators: (1) graduates from schools and colleges, (2) data-entry operators currently in the work force, and (3) secretarial and clerical personnel currently in the work force (*The Phosphorus on the Screen,* 1999, p. 29).

- Authors with the same surname. If you cite works by two or more authors who have the same surname, include the author's initials in all in-text citations:

  > C. D. Fulweiler (1996) reports that the average payload on the X-RD 70 is . . . (p. 117).

- Two or more works within the same parentheses. Use a semicolon to separate two or more references in the same parenthesis:

  > A slightly etched surface has better capillary action for the flow of the copper (Delong & Shinoda, 1994; Uhlig, 1999).

- Add a, b, c, and so on to the date when there are two or more works by the same author with the same date:

  > A recent study (Timmons, 1993b, p. 22) shows that . . .

The letters are assigned to work in the order they appear in the alphabetical listing of references.

- Personal communications:

  > Rose McClure of the University of Guelph, Ontario, Canada, believes that "contrary to popular opinion, electronic communication has generated more paperwork, not less" (personal communication, April 1, 1999).

  > In a recent research project on the social dynamics of Barnacle geese, investigators tested the relationship between "facial expressions" of the geese and dominance patterns (Jakob Probst, personal communication, July 16, 1999).

When you cite publications with in-text parenthetical entries, you must key them to the list of references listed at the end of the report. Personal communications are not listed in the list of references when APA documentation style is used.

References

At the end of the report all the sources cited are grouped in a list of references (see Figure 22.2). Every work cited must appear except personal communication, and each entry in the list must be cited in the report. In this section we explain the correct form and arrangement of entries in a list of references.

Forms for Print-Based Documents

- Book by one author:

  Moustakas, C. E. (1990). *Heuristic research: Design, methodology, and applications*. Newbury Park, CA: Sage.

- Book by two authors:

  Jasper, J. M., & Nelkin, D. (1992). *The animal rights crusade: The growth of a moral protest*. New York: Macmillan.

- Book by more than three authors:

  Hawisher, G. E., LeBlanc, P., Moran, C., & Selfe, C. L. (1996). *Computers and the teaching of writing in American higher education, 1979–1994: A history*. Norwood, NJ: Ablex.

- Book by corporate or organizational author (including government documents):

  Office of Policy Development and Research. (1998). *The state of the cities 1998*. Washington, DC: U.S. Department of Housing and Urban Development.

- Book with an editor:

  Fernstrom, J. D., & Miller, G. D. (Eds.). (1994). *Appetite and body weight regulation: Sugar, fat, and macronutrient substitutes*. Boca Raton: CRC Press.

- Parts of a book:

  Levine, A. S., & Billington, C. J. (1994). Dietary fiber: Does it affect food intake and body weight? In J. D. Fernstrom & G. D. Miller (Eds.), *Appetite and body weight regulation: Sugar, fat, and macronutrient substitutes*, (pp. 191–200). Boca Raton: CRC Press.

- Journal article:

  Vick, R. M. (1998). Perspectives on and problems with computer-mediated teamwork: Current groupware issues and assumptions. *Journal of Computer Documentation, 22*, 3–22.

- Popular magazine article. Give all the page numbers when the article appears on discontinuous pages:

  Gibbs, N. (1998, October 12). A week in the life of a hospital. *Time 152*, 54–63, 66, 68–77, 81–85, 89–91, 93–94, 97–100, 103.

- Newspaper article:

    Tam, P. (1998, October 23). From mutual-fund loser to tax-time winner. *The Wall Street Journal,* pp. C1, C13.

- Interviews and personal communications are not included in the list of references in APA style.

Forms for Electronic and Other Information

- Corporate or professional organization Web site:

    Hewlett Packard. HP 300 overview: The widescreen palmtop pc with enhanced Windows CE 2.0 operating system. Available: http://www.hp.com/jornada/palmtops/hp300lx/300_overview.html [25 October 1998].

- Online abstract or fulltext article from a periodical. The first date is the date of publication; the second date is the date the information was accessed:

    Markoff, J. (1998, September 23). Eyes for the mouse, wheels for the joystick: New company to create visual maps for navigating the Internet. [On-line]. *The New York Times,* p. C7. Abstract from: InfoTrac: Article A21151991 [1998, October 24].

- Online articles from an online periodical:

    Biren, A. N., Gregerman, S. R., Jonides, J., von Hippel, W., & Lerner, J. S. (1998). Undergraduate student-faculty research partnerships affect student retention. *The Review of Higher Education* [On-line serial], pp. 55–72. Available: http://muse.jhu.edu/journals/review_of_higher-education/v022/22.1nagda.html [1998, October 25].

- E-mail and listserv postings are cited in the text only (similar to personal communication):

    D. Nash, e-mail to D. Font, August 15, 1998.

- Television:

    Boyd, D. (Executive Producer). (1999, April 1). *Your local news in Vermont.* Burlington, VT: WVTT.

Arrangement of List of References

Entries in the list of references for APA documentation are arranged in alphabetical order by the surname of the first author or editor (see Figure 22.2). A work that has a corporate or organizational author is alphabetized by the first word of the corporation or organization (excluding *A, An, The*). A work that has no identifiable author is alphabetized by its title (excluding *A, An, The*).

When several works by the same author are listed, arrange them alphabetically by title. The author(s)' names are given for each entry in APA style.

Parrish, H. M. (1955). Early excision and suction of snakebite wounds in dogs. *North Carolina Medical Journal, 16,* 93–102.

Parrish, H. M. (1970). Hospital management in pit viper envenomations. *Clinical Toxicology, 3,* 501–502.

Parrish, H. M. (1963). Poisonous snakebite. *New English Journal of Medicine, 269,* 524–610.

Parrish, H. M. (1969). Seven pitfalls in treating pit viper bites. *Resident Physician, 67,* 108–120.

List one-author entries before multiauthor entries beginning with the same surname. Repeat the author's name.

Parrish, H. M. (1953). Early excision and suction of snakebite wounds in dogs. *North Carolina Medical Journal, 16,* 93–102.

Parrish, H. M. (1970). Hospital management in pit viper envenomations. *Clinical Toxicology, 3,* 501–502.

Parrish, H. M. (1969). Seven pitfalls in treating pit viper bites. *Resident Physician, 67,* 108–120.

Parrish, H. M., & C. Carr. (1967). Bites of copperheads in the United States. *Journal of the American Medical Association, 201,* 927–935.

MLA—MODERN LANGUAGE ASSOCIATION

The *MLA Handbook for Writers of Research Papers* (5th edition) recommends using either numbered notes (footnote or endnotes) or in-text parenthetical citations and list of works cited at the end of the document. We use the first method in our own documentation for this book. The numbered notes are placed at the bottom of the page the note appears on. Footnotes or endnotes frequently include the complete bibliographic information so that no list of works cited is needed. In this section, we explain and give examples of the second form, which consists of two parts:

1. An in-text parenthetical citation that identifies the author and page or pages referenced so the reader can find it in the list of works cited at the end of the report (see Figure 22.3).

2. A list of works cited at the end of the report, which is arranged alphabetically by author and which provides the publication information necessary to locate the source cited (see Figure 22.4).

Here's how the system works. The reader reads a passage like the following and sees the author or authors you have cited in parentheses:

Several nonmetallic materials have been considered for large wind turbine blades. Both fiberglass and wood composite appear to be alternatives to steel and aluminum, but because fiberglass and wood are both poor conductors, a direct lightning strike could cause severe damage. Fiberglass radomes have been shattered when no protection was provided (Fisher and Plumer 16–18). Other research has shown that epoxy-wood blades can be severely damaged if they are not protected (Bankaitis 82).

Notice that the author's or authors' last names and the page or pages cited are enclosed in parentheses inside the normal sentence punctuation and that there is no punctuation between the author's name and the page numbers. Should readers wish to know more about the article by Fisher and Plumer or the report by Bankaitis, the works cited list at the end of the report provides complete publication information.

The following examples demonstrate the various ways to present in-text parenthetical citations following MLA documentation style. Afterward, we illustrate formats for entries in the list of works cited.

In-Text Parenthetical Citations

• One work by a single author. Place the author's name and page number or numbers in parentheses:

> Land titling has caused some problems, most due to the bureaucracy involved with the titling process (Montgomery 119).

Researchers seem to agree that the questionnaire should be as simple as possible. McKinney and Oglesby suggest testing the questionnaire for readability level "to insure that the content is pitched neither too high or too low for the respondents" (322).

Recent studies (Griffey 83; Peavey and Abernathy 125) show that the questionnaire should be personalized, as well as simple. Every attempt should be made to get responses from all subjects. According to Griffey, who returns the questionnaires can affect results:

> In a Wisconsin study with a 45.9% response, it was discovered that 78% of the former students in the top percentile of their class returned the questionnaire, while only 28% from the bottom percentile returned the questionnaire. (83)

The tendency for successful students to return more questionnaires than their less successful counterparts can invalidate findings and conclusions.

Snelling (106) suggests that a high response rate is possible from all segments of the population if the questionnaire is highly personalized. To personalize the survey, she suggests...

Figure 22.3 The in-text parenthetical citations on this page follow the MLA style. Note where the page numbers are placed and when the author(s)'s name is included inside the parentheses. In the center of the page is a direct quotation longer than three lines. Such quotations are indented. Quotation marks are unnecessary when long quotations are in this format.

Works Cited

Griffey, R. L. "The Personalization of Questionnaires." *Journal of Survey Techniques* 14 (1999): 83–93.

Martin, Grace Morton. "Realizing a High Response Rate." *Journal of Survey Techniques* 13 (1998): 312–325.

McKinney, Joan, and Fred Ogelsby. *Designing Surveys.* New York: Acme, 1995. 16–17.

Peavey, John M., and M. Abernathy. "High-Rate Response: The Standards Set in a Pilot Study of HMO Users and Private Health Care Users." *Studies in Research Techniques* 8 (1999): 120–128.

Snelling, Britton. "Phrasing Open-Ended Questions." *Journal of Survey Techniques* 14 (1997): 106–107.

———. "Designing Questionnaires." *Studies in Research Techniques* 6 (1997): 99–103.

Figure 22.4 Following MLA style guidelines, the list of works cited section of a report contains full publication information on each work cited in the report. Here are some guidelines for formatting the documentation on the reference page of workplace reports:

- Single-space entries for a workplace report.
- Use a hanging indent so that the first line is against the left margin but lines following are indented (about $\frac{1}{2}''$).
- If an author has more than one work on the list, use 3 hyphens or the long dash in place of the author's name.
- Give authors' names as they appear on the work (for example, Smith, G. Robert) and invert only the first author's name when there is more than one author for the work.
- Use initial capitals for most of the words in the title and subtitle except for the articles (*a, an, the*), prepositions (for example, *of, with, for*), conjunctions (such as *and* and *but*), and the *to* in infinitives (to play).
- Italicize the title of the work for workplace reports; use quotation marks around the article or essay found within the work.

Notice that there is no comma between the author's name and the page number. When you use the author's name as part of your sentence, cite only the page number or numbers in parentheses:

> Montgomery's study revealed that while settlers paid only a nominal fee for land, the title process was cumbersome and caused several delays (119).

- One work by two or three authors. When citing a work that has two or three authors, cite all names:

> Researchers have succeeded in fusing a myeloma tumor cell, capable of producing antibodies, with a spleen cell from an animal which previously had been primed with a known antigen (Kohler and Milstein 44).

During the past decade several projects have used surge irrigation (Johnson, Martin, and Nordeen 72–73).

• **One work by more than three authors.** When citing a work that has more than three authors, include only the name of the first author followed by *et al.* for the other authors:

Recent tests (Kleinmann et al. 86) show that although the grenade is effectively spin-stabilized in flight, it tends to drift to the right from its maximum ordinate.

• **Work by a corporation or organizational author.** Use the name of the corporation or organization as the author:

According to a recent study (Northeastern Commission on Higher Education [NCHE] 9), more and more adults are returning to college.

Use the acronym for the source if you cite it more than once.

• **Work with no identifiable author.** Place the title of the article or book in the author position:

Soil resistivity can be decreased by adding moisture or chemicals to the soil ("Recommended Practice for Grounding of Industrial Power Systems" 428).

There are three important sources of data-entry operators: (1) graduates from schools and colleges, (2) data-entry operators currently in the work force, and (3) secretarial and clerical personnel currently in the work force (*The Phosphorus on the Screen* 29).

• **Authors with the same surname.** If you cite works by two or more authors who have the same surname, include the author's initials in all in-text citations:

C. D. Fulweiler reports that the average payload on the X-RD 70 is . . . (117).

• **Two or more works within the same parentheses.** Use a semicolon to separate two or more references in the same parenthesis:

A slightly etched surface has better capillary action for the flow of the copper (Delong and Shinoda 119; Uhlig 441–442).

• **Two or more works by the same author.** Add enough of the title to distinguish it from other works by the author and give the relevant page number or numbers:

A recent study (Timmons, *Bituminous* 22) shows that . . .

• **Personal communications:**

Rose McClure of the University of Guelph, Ontario, Canada, believes that "contrary to popular opinion, electronic communication has generated more paperwork, not less."

In a recent research project on the social dynamics of Barnacle geese, investigators tested the relationship between "facial expressions" of the geese and dominance patterns (Probst).

When you cite publications with in-text parenthetical entries, you must key them to a list of works cited at the end of the report.

List of Works Cited

At the end of the report all the sources cited are grouped in a list of works cited (see Figure 22.4). Every work cited must appear in the works cited list, and each entry in the works cited list must be cited in the report. In this section we explain the correct form and arrangement of entries in a list of works cited.

Forms for Print-Based Documents

- Book by one author:

  Moustakas, Clark E. *Heuristic Research: Design, Methodology, and Applications.* Newbury Park, CA: Sage, 1990.

- Book by two authors:

  Jasper, James M., and Dorothy Nelkin. *The Animal Rights Crusade: The Growth of a Moral Protest.* New York: Macmillan, 1992.

- Book by more than three authors:

  Hawisher, Gail E., Paul LeBlanc, Charles Moran, and Cynthia L. Selfe. *Computers and the Teaching of Writing in American Higher Education, 1979–1994: A History.* Norwood, NJ: Ablex, 1996.

- Book by corporate or organizational author (including government documents):

  Office of Policy Development and Research. *The State of the Cities 1998.* Washington: US Dept. of Housing and Urban Development, 1998.

- Book with an editor:

  Fernstrom, John D., and Gregory D. Miller, eds. *Appetite and Body Weight Regulation: Sugar, Fat, and Macronutrient Substitutes.* Boca Raton: CRC Press, 1994.

- Parts of a book:

  Levine, Allan S., and Charles J. Billington. "Dietary Fiber: Does it Affect Food Intake and Body Weight?" *Appetite and Body Weight Regulation: Sugar, Fat, and Macronutrient.* Boca Raton: CRC Press, 1994. 191–200.

- Journal article:

    Vick, Rita M. "Perspectives on and Problems with Computer-Mediated Teamwork: Current Groupware Issues and Assumptions." *Journal of Computer Documentation* 22 (1998): 3–22.

- Popular magazine article. The + indicates the article ran over several pages but was interrupted by advertisements. Give the page numbers for consecutive pages, for example, 54–56, when possible:

    Gibbs, Nancy. "A Day in the Life of a Hospital." *Time* 12 Oct. 1998: 54+.

- Newspaper article:

    Tam, Pui-Wing. "From Mutual-Fund Loser to Tax-Time Winner." *The Wall Street Journal* 23 Oct. 1998: C1+.

- Interviews and personal communications:

    Powell, Mary. Personal interview. Orlando, FL. 6 Sept. 1999.

    Martinez, Henri. Telephone interview. 10 Jan. 1999.

Forms for Electronic and Other Information

- Corporate or professional organization Web site:

    Hewlett Packard. *HP 300 Overview: The Widescreen Palmtop PC with Enhanced Windows CE 2.0 Operating System.* 25 October 1998 ⟨http://www.hp.com/jornada/palmtops/hp300lx/300_overview.html⟩.

- Online abstract or fulltext article from periodical that originated in print form. The first date is the date of publication; the second date is the date the information was accessed:

    Markoff, J. "Eyes for the Mouse, Wheels for the Joystick: New Company to Create Visual Maps for Navigating the Internet." *New York Times* 23 Sept. 1998: C7. InfoTrac, 24 Oct. 1998 ⟨http://web2.searchbank.com/infotrac/session/445/626/26770280w3/6!xrn_3⟩.

- Online articles from an online periodical:

    Biren, A. Nagda, Gregerman, Sandra R., Jonides, John, von Hippel, William, and Jennifer S. Lerner. "Undergraduate student-faculty research partnerships affect student retention." *Review of Higher Education* 22 (1998): 55–72. 25 Oct. 1998 ⟨http://muse.jhu.edu/journals/review_ of_higher-education/v022/22.1nagda.html⟩.

- E-mail and listserv postings are cited similar to personal communication:

    Nash, Debra. E-mail to Dean Font. 15 Aug. 1998.

- Television:

    Boyd, Dan, Executive Producer. *Your Local News in Vermont.* Burlington, VT: WVTT. 1 Apr. 1999.

Arrangement of List of Works Cited

Entries in the list of works cited (MLA) are arranged in alphabetical order by the surname of the first author or editor (see Figure 22.4). A work that has a corporate or organizational author is alphabetized by the first word of the corporation or organization (excluding *A, An, The*). A work that has no identifiable author is alphabetized by its title (excluding *A, An, The*).

When several works by the same author are listed, arrange them alphabetically by title. Using MLA style, give the author's name only in the first entry. For subsequent entries, type three hyphens (or one long dash) and a period, and cite the title.

Parrish, H. M. "Early Excision and Suction of Snakebite Wounds in Dogs." *North Carolina Medical Journal* 16 (1955): 93.

—. "Hospital Management in Pit Viper Envenomations." *Clinical Toxicology* 3 (1970): 501–2.

—. "Poisonous Snakebite." *New English Journal of Medicine* 269 (1963): 524–610.

—. "Seven Pitfalls in Treating Pit Viper Bites." *Resident Physician* 67 (1969): 108–20.

List one-author entries before multiauthor entries beginning with the same surname. Do not use the three hyphens (long dash) with coauthors. Repeat the author's name.

Parrish, H. M. "Early Excision and Suction of Snakebite Wounds in Dogs." *North Carolina Medical Journal* 16 (1955): 93–102.

—. "Hospital Management in Pit Viper Envenomations." *Clinical Toxicology* 3 (1970): 501–2.

—. "Seven Pitfalls in Treating Pit Viper Bites." *Resident Physician* 67 (1969): 108–20.

Parrish, H. M., and C. Carr. "Bites of Copperheads in the United States." *Journal of the American Medical Association* 201 (1967): 927–35.

Documenting sources pinpoints the location of the information for the reader. The examples we provide cover several widely accepted formats for identifying your sources. Identifying your sources in a standard way allows your readers to evaluate the information you provide for solving the problem. They readily can see who originated the information and where they can locate this source, and they see from the date when the information originated.

PLANNING AND REVISING CHECKLIST: DOCUMENTATION IN REPORTS

Think about the following while planning and revising documentation:

PLANNING

- Should the information source be acknowledged?
- Is a particular format for documentation required?
- If not, what would be the most appropriate format for documentation, considering the purpose and audience of the report?

REVISING

- Have you been consistent in your use of format for documentation?
- Does every reference cited in the text of the report have an entry on the list of works cited (MLA) or list of references (APA)?
- Is there an in-text citation for each entry in the list of works cited or reference section?
- Is permission needed to use any of the information in the report?

SUGGESTIONS FOR APPLYING YOUR KNOWLEDGE

1. The following sources are given in the order in which they are cited in a report. Arrange them in format and in proper order as they would appear in a list of works cited (MLA) or list of references (APA).

   - A book published by Van Nostrand Reinhold of New York, titled Painting of Steel Bridges and Other Structures, written by C. H. Hare, and published in 1996.

   - Bridge Pier Scour with Debris Accumulation is the title of an article appearing in the September 1992 issue of the Journal of Hydrological Engineering on pages 1306 through 1310 (volume 118). The authors are B. W. Melville and Donna M. Dongol.

   - J. Beth Kennedy and Marshall Z. Soliman are authors of an article titled Dynamic Response of Multigirder Bridges, which appeared on pages 2222–2238 of volume 118 in the August 1992 issue of Journal of Structural Engineering.

- A book titled Removing Concrete from Bridges published by the Transportation Research Board of the National Research Council located in Washington, DC in 1991. The author is David George Manning.

- Civil Engineering published an article titled Fifth Time Around, as California Pier Disappears, which identified no author. It appeared in the July 1997 issue on page 12 of volume 62.

- The Journal of Hydrological Engineering published an article titled Temporal Variation of Scour Around Circular Bridge Piers, written by U. C. Kothyari and others. It appeared on pages 1091–1106, August 1999, in volume 118.

- In 1998 the Government Printing Office in Washington, D.C., published a report written by the U.S. Congressional House of Representatives Committee on Public Works and Transportation's Subcommittee on Investigations and Oversight. The report is titled Bridge Safety: Hearings before the Subcommittee on Investigations and Oversight of the Committee on Public Work and Transportation, House of Representatives, 102nd Congress, First Session, 7–8 May 1997.

2. If you are planning to use a documentation system other than the one recommended in this chapter, prepare a brief explanation of it for your instructor. Explain at least these three basic features: (a) the method of citation used to lead the reader from the text to the documentation (footnote numbers, parenthetical identification of author and year, or whatever); (b) the arrangement of the documentation (footnotes arranged in the order of the appearance of the materials they document, bibliography citations arranged alphabetically, or another method); and (c) the form of the documentation entry in the bibliography or list of references.

UNIT V

WRITER'S GUIDE

WRITER'S GUIDE

This writer's guide contains a series of short descriptions of various writing techniques, conventions, and problems. We have arranged the guide alphabetically to make it easier for you to find your way around.

Whether you are a student or a company employee, you should check to see if you are required to use a specific style manual or guide. If you are in a writing class, your instructor may use the symbols on the inside back cover in marking your papers, correspondence, and reports. In this way your instructor will refer you to entries that should show you how to correct a problem in your writing. In some classes, you may be required to follow the guidelines presented in such style manuals as *The Council of Biological Editors Style Manual* or the *Publication Manual of the American Psychological Association.*

Once you are a professional in the workplace, you should also find out if the company or organization you work for has a style manual. Corporate style guides are common. They are developed to help ensure that the documents a company or organization produces present information in a professional and consistent manner. For example, *The Microsoft Manual of Style for Technical Publications* provides writers within Microsoft information on such topics as spacing after periods and use of quotation marks and hyphens.

If you are not required to follow a particular style guide or manual, you can use this writer's guide, for its guidelines are based on the most recent and best practice in workplace writing.

ABBREVIATIONS

Abbreviations are often used in workplace writing. However, they must be used with some care. Remember that abbreviations are primarily for the convenience of the writer. If they are likely to inconvenience the reader, they should not be used. Use without explanation only those abbreviations you are absolutely certain your reader will understand correctly. If you have any doubts at all, the first time you use a term, spell out the full expression and follow it with the abbreviation in parentheses—*Trunk Highway (TH)*—or use the abbreviation and follow it with the full expression—*TH (Trunk Highway).*

Any college-level dictionary will list the abbreviations you are likely to need. In most dictionaries the abbreviation will be listed twice—once as an abbreviation in normal alphabetical order and once behind the word for which it is an abbreviation. Another excellent source for standard abbreviations is *The Chicago Manual of Style.*

Guidelines concerning the acceptability of abbreviations vary from place to place, but the following rules are usable unless you have instructions to the contrary.

ACCEPTED ABBREVIATIONS

Some abbreviations are generally known and accepted, even preferred in all writing. The following is a representative list of such abbreviations:

Titles

Dr. Mr. Mrs. Ms.

These abbreviated titles are used only before the name, as in *Dr. Smith* or *Dr. Lois Smith*. By themselves, of course, titles are spelled out: The *doctor* drove a black car.

Time

A.M. P.M. B.C. A.D. C.S.T. (Central Standard Time)

Academic Degrees

A.A. B.A. M.A. M.D. M.B.A. Ph.D.

Organizations and Countries

In most of your writing you may also abbreviate the names of organizations and countries when names are long and unwieldy. Be careful to use a standard abbreviation and to spell out the first time if it is unfamiliar to the reader.

CBS	Columbia Broadcasting System
FBI	Federal Bureau of Investigation
NASA	National Aeronautics and Space Administration
USAF	United States Air Force
U.S.A.	United States of America
U.K.	United Kingdom

Although the practice is divided on using periods with abbreviations, it is quite common for abbreviations of countries to include periods. The abbreviations of organizations generally do not.

Common Measurements

Some commonly known measurements expressed in two or more words are usually abbreviated either in capitals or lowercase without periods:

MPG mpg MPH mph RPM rpm

Certain Latin Terms

Certain Latin terms, if used instead of their English equivalents, are always abbreviated:

etc. (and so forth) e.g. (for example) i.e. (that is)

ABBREVIATIONS ACCEPTED IN SPECIALIZED WRITING

Abbreviations are widely used in workplace writing. Terms of measurement of two or more words, such as *Brinnel hardness number* (Bhn), *British thermal unit* (Btu), and *cubic foot* or *feet* (cu ft), will be abbreviated both in lists and tables and in the textual prose. Workplace writers will use such abbreviations as *C.O.D.* (collect on delivery) and *f.o.b.* (free on board, meaning the receiver pays the transportation charges).

But even in workplace writing some restraint is called for. A document with a lot of abbreviations intimidates the reader and slows understanding. Therefore, many writers in the workplace do not abbreviate one-word measurements, such as *ounce* or *pound,* in their text. However, they may abbreviate them in lists and tables. (See "Metric Conversion Table," pages 631–632, which includes the abbreviations for many metric measurements.)

Internal consistency is important. Once you abbreviate a term, continue to do so throughout your text. A typical piece of workplace writing might look like this:

> The horizontal and vertical alignment of the highway is consistent with a freeway designed for 70 mph. The maximum mainline curve is 3 percent. Maximum speed on the frontage roads will be 30 mph.

ABBREVIATIONS TO AVOID

In any text, general or specialized, there are many abbreviations that you should avoid. We specify text because some of these abbreviations are suitable in lists, tables, illustrations, and addresses, where space may be limited. In your text, you should spell out

Titles
Professor, *not* Prof.

First Names
Charles, *not* Chas.

Geographical Locations
France, *not* Fr.   New York, *not* N.Y.
(Long names such as U.S.A. are an exception.)

Geographical Terms
street, *not* st.   road, *not* rd.   mountain, *not* mt.

Seasons, Months, Days
winter, *not* wtr.   January, *not* Jan.   Monday, *not* Mon.

Common Words
government, *not* gov't.   Protestant, *not* Prot.

APOSTROPHE

The apostrophe has three major uses: (1) to form the possessive case of nouns and indefinite pronouns, (2) to replace omitted letters and numerals, and (3) to form the plurals of numerals, letters, and symbols.

FORMING THE POSSESSIVE

Observe the following rules in forming the possessive case.

Singular Nouns

To form the possessive of singular nouns, including proper nouns, add an apostrophe and *s*. This is true even for nouns that already end in *s* or another sibilant sound such as *x* or *z*.

woman's   horse's   table's   lynx's   Jones's

There are a few exceptions to this rule. When adding an apostrophe and *s* results in an *s* or *z* sound that is hard to pronounce, add only the apostrophe:

Moses'   conscience'

Try these pronunciations for yourself. Notice that *lynx's* is easy to pronounce, where as *conscience's* is awkward to say.

Plural Nouns

Form the possessive of plural nouns by adding an apostrophe plus *s* to words that do not end with *s* or another sibilant. Add only the apostrophe to plural words that do end in *s* or a sibilant:

women's   alumni's   advisers'   actresses'

Pronouns

For indefinite pronouns add an apostrophe and *s* to form the possessive:

anyone's   everyone's   everybody's   nobody's
no one's   other's   neither's

Form the possessive of all other pronouns without the apostrophe:

my (mine)   your (yours)   his, her (hers)   its
our (ours)   their (theirs)   whose

Joint Possession

When there is joint possession, add the apostrophe or apostrophe and *s* only to the last name of the group:

Sigrid and Alfred's house

When there is separate possession, add the apostrophe and *s* to each member of the group:

Sigrid's and Alfred's houses

REPLACING LETTERS AND NUMERALS

In contractions we omit letters, and in numerical expressions we sometimes omit numerals. In both these uses the apostrophe replaces the missing element:

He doesn't work here now.
It's Mary at the door.
He graduated in '98.

FORMING PLURALS

Use the apostrophe and *s* to form the plural of letters and symbols:

Omitted is spelled with one *m* and two *t*'s.

This use of the apostrophe is for clarity—to prevent, for example, someone from confusing *a's* with *as*.

You may also use the apostrophe plus *s* to form the plural of numbers, but frequently the *s* is used alone:

The 1930's (*or* 1930s) were Depression years.

BRACKETS

The major use you are likely to have for brackets is to insert material of your own into a quoted passage. Such insertion is sometimes necessary for various reasons: (1) to add a date or fact not obvious from the passage, (2) to indicate by use of *sic* (Latin for *thus* or *so*) an error of fact or usage in the original and therefore not your error, or (3) to straighten out the syntax of a sentence you may have disturbed through the use of ellipses (see entry on "Ellipsis Points"). Brackets are the accepted signal to the reader that the inserted material is not part of the original. Therefore, do not use parentheses for this purpose.

In that month [January], the GNP fell.
He fell to erth [sic] from a plane.
I was encouraged to engage in others [partnerships] . . . on the same terms with those that I have in North Carolina.

BULLETS

Bullets are those little marks used in a displayed list instead of numbers to emphasize key points or topics. They are used when sequence is not an important concern (either because all items are equally important or because the items do not constitute a complete list).

For example, use bullets if items in the displayed list are of equal importance.

Additional projects funded by the society are these:
- Feasibility study for landfills in Lincoln County, New Mexico
- Comparative analysis of wood and steel in the construction of domestic houses
- Improved procedures for collecting data for analyzing food preferences of mourning doves in northwest Arkansas

Number items in a displayed list if the sequence is important.

The three major styles of supervision, and the order in which we discuss them, are as follows:
1. The autocratic supervisor
2. The democratic supervisor
3. The free-rein supervisor

Various marks can serve as bullets—circles, squares, triangles, arrows, and so forth—although the standard bullet is a small square or circular dot [•]. Be sure to use the same size and type of bullet for comparable items in a displayed list, either all 12-point [•] or 10-point [•] or 8-point [•].

CAPITALIZATION

Rules for capitalization vary from organization to organization, and the tendency is toward capitalizing fewer and fewer words. One of the most widely recognized style manuals, *The Chicago Manual of Style,* 14th edition (1994), is less prescriptive than its previous editions on the issue of capitalization. It identifies an "*up* style" (a tendency to use uppercase, that is, capital letters) and a "*down* style" (a tendency to use lowercase). The choice might be dictated by the organization you work for or it may be your own, but be consistent. The following general practices are fairly standard.

PROPER NOUNS

Capitalize proper nouns and the words that derive from them.

People
Charles Darwin, Darwinism

Geographic Entities

England, English	Texas, Texans	East 40th Street
the Ohio River	Mount Everest	

Languages

French	Russian	Swahili

Religious Terms

God	the Bible	the Old Testament	Judaism	
Jews	Jewish	Protestant	Catholic	Muslim

Days of the Week
Monday   Tuesday

Months
January   February

Holidays
Easter   Independence Day

Specific Buildings and Structures
Empire State Building   Hoover Dam   the Golden Gate Bridge

Organizations

United States Senate	United Nations
United States Navy	American Legion

Certain Historical Terms
Magna Carta   Constitution   Revolutionary War   Renaissance

Scientific Terms

Capitalize and italicize the phylum, class, order, family, and genus of plants and animals; italicize but do not capitalize the species:

> *Homo sapiens*   *Saxifrage stolonifera*

Brand Names

> Chevrolet   Nike   Ivory Snow   Xerox

Companies

> International Business Machines (IBM)   Southern Companies, Inc.

Course Titles

> Scientific and Technical Writing   Advanced Wood Chemistry

Ships

> *USS San Pablo*   *SS Titanic*

TITLES OF BOOKS, ARTICLES, PLAYS, MOVIES

Unless you are following a documentation style that requires another practice, capitalize the first word of every title. Capitalize all other words except prepositions of fewer than five letters, articles, and conjunctions:

> *Font and Function: Making the Right Choices*
> *Logical Construction: The Structure of Design*
> *Maxims and Instructions from the Boiler Room*
> "Getting Inside Your Camera"
> "What's a Camera for?"

OFFICIAL TITLES

Capitalize an official title when you place it before a person's name or use it to refer to a specific person:

> Congresswoman Smith
> Colonel Peter R. Moody
> The President is in his office.

Do not capitalize a title used in a general way:

> Most professors enjoy teaching.

COLON

The colon is a mark of introduction. You can use it to introduce quotations (particularly long quotations) and lists.

QUOTATIONS

The Environmental Impact Statement for I-35E clarifies the impact on wetlands as follows: "The most significant impact to water resources would be the direct displacement of wetlands. Of approximately 2,300 acres of wetlands in the study area, 28 acres would fall within the corridor of the proposed action and would be filled or altered."

LISTS

There will be three final steps: a location-design hearing, a final EIS, and a Design Study Report.

The Metropolitan Council's long-range planning indicates that expansion of the urban service limit should involve the following areas:

- Existing urban service area
- Addition to the urban service area
- Freestanding growth centers

Do *not* place a colon between a verb or a preposition and the objects that follow. Both the colons in the following examples are *incorrect* and should be removed:

Incorrect	The three steps are: a location report, a final EIS, and a design study report.
Incorrect	Public hearings have been scheduled for: Apple Valley, Eagan, and Mendota.

Place no punctuation at all after a verb or preposition:

Correct	The three steps are a location report, a final EIS, and a design study report.
Correct	Public hearings have been scheduled for Apple Valley, Eagan, and Mendota.

You may use a capital or a lowercase letter following colons. Generally, a complete sentence would start with a capital letter; a subordinate clause or a phrase with a lowercase letter.

CONVENTIONAL USES

Dear Mr. Rose: (formal salutation in a letter)
6:22 P.M.
8:4:1 (expression of proportion)

COMMA

Commas have so many uses that it is little wonder people despair of using them correctly. In this elementary guide we will keep things as simple as we can and still cover the major rules.

COMPOUND SENTENCES

When two independent clauses are joined by a coordinating conjunction *(and, but, for, nor, or, and yet)*, use a comma before the conjunction:

> Building the highway on the present alignment would have little impact on the north bluffs, but building it on the new alignment would create a severe impact.

See also the entries for "Run-on Sentences" and "Semicolon."

INTRODUCTORY ELEMENTS

We begin about 25 percent of our sentences with an introductory word, phrase, or subordinate clause. After such an introductory element, a comma is never wrong:

> Unfortunately, the bridge will be seen as an artificial object.
> Of the 36 Indian mounds, only 12 were well preserved.
> As speed increases, foreground details fade rapidly.

Sometimes, when the introductory element is short, you are not incorrect if you omit this comma. Do so with care, however. Make sure you don't cause your reader to overread. Look at the following sentence:

> Because foreground objects do not block viewing, bridge structures can provide an opportunity for outstanding vistas.

Remove the comma after *viewing* and readers will mistakenly read that the bridge structures are being viewed. When they realize their error, they must back up and begin again.

Unless you are quite sure of what you are doing, you may always want to use the comma after introductory elements. Be careful, however, not to confuse a long, complete subject with an introductory element. This error could cause you to put a comma incorrectly between subject and verb. You would want no punctuation at all at the spot we have marked with brackets in this example:

> Planned recreational development of the area[ ] includes a river valley trail system.

You may, however, have a parenthetical element between the subject and the verb that would call for two commas, one on each side of the element:

> This game refuge, as proposed, would cross the entire area.

FINAL ELEMENTS

Subordinate clauses or phrases that follow a main clause present more of a problem than do introductory elements. Generally, if they are not closely tied to the thought of the main clause, they are preceded by a comma. Definitely use a comma when the final element presents a turn of thought:

> Railroads and highways have contributed to the area's urbanization, although much of the area is still undeveloped.

However, when the final element is closely tied into the preceding main clause, you are better off without a comma:

> The highway will cross Indian mounds that have already been disturbed.

In this sentence the clause beginning with *that* is essential to the thought; therefore, a comma is not wanted. Reading aloud will usually help in this situation. If you pause before the final element while reading aloud, it is a good sign that a comma is needed.

PARENTHETICAL AND INTERRUPTING ELEMENTS

When a word, phrase, or clause is parenthetical to the main thought of the sentence or interrupts the flow of the sentence, set commas around it:

> The cultural features, mainly Indian mounds, are to the west of the highway.

The inserted phrase, *mainly Indian mounds*, adds information to the sentence, of course, but it is an aside. It interrupts the flow of the main clause. See also the entries for "Dash" and "Parentheses."

The phrase *of course* is usually set off by commas. So are conjunctive adverbs such as *consequently*, *however*, *nevertheless*, and *therefore*:

> The bridge is so high, of course, to allow river traffic to pass underneath.
> However, the most expansive vistas are to the east.

NONRESTRICTIVE MODIFIERS

Nonrestrictive modifiers are set apart from the rest of the sentence by commas. Restrictive modifiers are not. Sometimes, determining which is which is a puzzle. A restrictive modifier is essential to the meaning of the sentence. For instance:

> The design choices *for the Cedar Avenue Bridge* are all costly.

The italicized modifier defines and identifies which design choices, among all the possible design choices the writer could be talking about, are meant. The writer is not talking about the design choices for the Brooklyn Bridge or the Golden Gate Bridge. The writer is talking specifically and exclusively about the design choices for the Cedar Avenue Bridge. The modifier is therefore restrictive—it is essential to the meaning of the sentence. Look now at a nonrestrictive modifier:

> Old Shakopee Road, which is a two-lane asphalt highway with narrow shoulders, in 1999 became inadequate for handling commuter traffic.

In this case the italicized modifier adds important and useful information, but it is not essential to the sentence. The road's name provides the limits or restrictions needed: It is not any road; it is Old Shakopee Road. Therefore, the modifier is *nonrestrictive*.

If in doubt, try reading your sentence aloud. You will probably pause quite naturally at the breaks around nonrestrictive modifiers. These pauses are your clues to insert commas. See also the entries for "Dash" and "Parentheses."

SERIES

Commas are the normal punctuation used when you are constructing a series:

> This seepage emerges as natural springs that feed *tributary streams, lakes, and marshes.*
>
> The components of the recreation system range from *miniparks, neighborhood playgrounds, and community playfields to multipurpose parks, park reserves, and historic parks.*

For lists with internal punctuation see the entry for "Semicolon."

CONVENTIONAL USES

The comma is the conventional mark of punctuation in several situations:

Informal Salutation
> Dear Felicia,

Dates
> May 21, 1955, is my birthday.

(But *21 May 1955* and *May 1955* are both written without commas.)

Addresses
> 1269 River Valley Drive, Eagan, Indiana, is . . .

Titles and Degrees
> Margaret E. Norad, Dean, is . . .
> Margaret E. Norad, M.D., is . . .

DASH

The dash is essentially a mark of separation. It is a rather peculiar but also a rather useful mark of punctuation—as long as it is not overused. It is peculiar because it can be substituted for many other marks of punctuation, particularly the comma and parentheses. And, of course, it is this peculiarity that makes the dash useful.

When substituted for a comma, the dash indicates that the writer meant to be emphatic about the separation:

> The table lists the total acres of wetlands within the project—all of which would be eliminated.

Placing dashes around parenthetical material indicates a degree of formal separation greater than the comma would indicate and less than parentheses:

Several protective measures—wood fiber mats, mulches, and special seed mixtures—will prevent erosion.

You may also use the dash to emphasize items in a list or occasionally, instead of a colon, to introduce a list:

Several antierosion measures are available:
—wood fiber mats
—mulches
—special seed mixtures
—berms and dikes

Several antierosion devices are available—wood fiber mats, mulches, special seed mixtures, and berms and dikes.

The popularity of the dash may tempt you to overuse it, but it would quickly lose its emphatic value if you substituted the dash too freely for other marks. Used discreetly, the dash is a useful—even productive—mark of punctuation.

DICTION

You have good diction when you choose words and expressions suitable to the occasion and express your thoughts as simply and clearly as possible.

Most people recognize that words suitable for some occasions are not suitable for others. The happy slang of locker rooms and poker games would be inappropriate in an annual business report. A passage from an annual report on student housing, for instance, reads this way:

Dormitories were full and dorm waiting lists long as students began fall classes this year. More than 250 students were waiting to be assigned rooms. In some instances, students were temporarily housed in local hotels and motels.

The language is simple and serious and quite adequate to the occasion of the report. It is neither slangy nor heavy and pompous. Do not let the desire to be more formal lead you into windy pomposities such as *viable interface* and *at this point in time* or tired clichés such as *grim reality* or *Mother Nature*. Your cleaned-up everyday language, supported by whatever professional vocabulary both you and your readers need and understand, will probably serve you well. You don't have to *ascertain reality* to write formally. *Finding out the facts* will serve just as well.

Your ear, once again, is a good guide. Read your work aloud. If it *sounds* foolish or pompous, it probably is. If you are sure you would not say something the way you have written it, do not write it that way either.

Faulty diction can also be caused by a lack of precision in choosing the words needed to express your thoughts. You may say *communicating* when *talking* is the more precise word. You may have confused *enormity* with *enormousness*. Perhaps you wrote the nonstandard *irregardless* for *regardless*. Perhaps you used *good* as in "Johnny played good" instead of "Johnny played *well*." You may have windily talked about *factors* when you should have found some specific words to express what the factors really are.

You will not learn about good diction by reading about it. Rather you learn it by reading and listening to people who have it and by practicing what you have learned. And don't forget your *dictio*nary. (See also Chapter 4.)

ELLIPSIS POINTS

Ellipsis points consist of three spaced periods. They have several uses in workplace writing. Use ellipsis points to indicate that you have omitted something from a quoted passage. Use four periods rather than three when the omission comes at the end of the sentence, the first period of the four being the period of the sentence. For example, the preceding sentence could be quoted as follows:

> Use four periods . . . when the omission comes at the end of the sentence. . . .

Notice that we have removed supplemental material from the sentence but have been careful not to change its meaning.

On occasion you might use ellipsis points as an emphatic mark of separation between statements:

> Be sure to get your copy . . . ORDER NOW . . . Mail the coupon below with your check or money order for the full amount.

EXCLAMATION POINT

The exclamation point is placed after a statement to emphasize the statement. Its presence indicates that the information in the statement is particularly impressive, unusual, or emotional:

> The project engineer recommended the building despite knowing it was unsafe!

The exclamation point has limited use in workplace writing. Use it sparingly, and certainly never use more than one after a statement.

FRAGMENTARY SENTENCES

If you inadvertently punctuate a piece of a sentence as a complete sentence, you have written a fragmentary sentence. Fragmentary sentences most often lack a complete verb or are introduced by a relative pronoun or a subordinating conjunction.

INCOMPLETE VERB

Incorrect   The glaciers forming three striking and different natural features.

Correct this sentence by correcting the verb:

Correct   The glaciers formed three striking and different natural features.

RELATIVE PRONOUNS

The relative pronouns are *who, that, what, which, whoever,* and *whatever.* They signal that the clause they introduce needs to be connected to a complete sentence. When you make this connection, you have corrected the error.

Incorrect   The Minnesota River is an underfit river. That is too small for its valley.

Correct   The Minnesota River is an underfit river that is too small for its valley.

SUBORDINATING CONJUNCTIONS

Subordinating conjunctions, as the name implies, connect a subordinate clause with a main clause. Therefore, their presence at the beginning of a clause marks the clause as subordinate and unable to stand alone. Common subordinating conjunctions are *after, although, because, since, though, unless,* and *when.*

As with the relative clause, the answer here is to join the subordinate clause to the main clause.

Incorrect   Although the area is largely undeveloped. It does have some light industry.

Correct   Although the area is largely undeveloped, it does have some light industry.

Sometimes writers will deliberately write fragmentary sentences to gain some special effect. In the following example the writer attempts to catch the feeling of conversation:

Unbelievable? Not really. In *Highway to Life* you'll find out how modern, safe, multilane divided highways are reducing traffic fatalities by as much as 90 percent.

The source of the example is an advertising letter, where such use is appropriate. But use such devices with care, and be sure your deliberate use is so obvious it cannot be mistaken for an error.

HYPHEN

Hyphens are used in word division and in numbers. For these two uses see the entries for "Word Division" and "Numbers."

Here we are concerned with the use of the hyphen to combine two or more words to make them function as one word. Some publishers' or newspapers' style manuals devote dozens of pages to the use of the hyphen. We suspect that madness lies in that direction. We attempt to simplify matters by considering hyphens used in compound words and in compound modifiers.

COMPOUND WORDS

In English we form many new words by compounding two existing words, as in *wristband, wrist-drop,* and *wrist shot.* We have no trouble speaking such compounds, but we do have problems as soon as we attempt to write them. As our three examples rather maddeningly demonstrate, sometimes they are written as one word, sometimes hyphenated, sometimes as two words. No rules are observed uniformly enough to be much help to us here. Few of us will keep such fine distinctions in our heads.

What's the answer? When your piece of writing is important—perhaps a report or a letter of application—use your dictionary if you're not absolutely sure of the spelling. There is no better way. When the dictionary offers a choice of spellings, choose the first and use it consistently throughout the document.

COMPOUND MODIFIERS

Compound modifiers are compound words also, but here our problems are somewhat eased. Most compound modifiers, whether in the dictionary or of our own invention, are hyphenated when used before the words they modify. For example:

> a coarse-grained texture
> a close-mouthed man
> a light-blue coat
> the ready-to-go-to-college woman

In informal writing we might see all these examples and similar modifiers written without the hyphen. But in workplace writing it is a good idea to use the hyphen to avoid confusion. Take the example of *light-blue coat*. A *light, blue coat* is light in weight. If the hyphens were omitted, consider the possibilities for confusion in *heavy-machinery operator, used-car buyer,* and *pink-skinned pig.*

Note that we have specified that a compound modifier is hyphenated when it is placed *before* the word it modifies. In constructions where the modifier appears as a predicate adjective—that is, after a linking verb—it is usually not hyphenated.

> For the ready-to-go-to-college woman . . .
> For the woman who is ready to go to college . . .

In the second example the adjective phrase *ready to go to college* is joined to its pronoun by the linking verb *is*. (A linking verb is used to connect a subject to another noun or modifier. *To be* is the most usual linking verb, but many verbs, such as *seem, feel,* and *appear* can function as linking verbs.)

If in doubt about the hyphenation of compound words, whether they are used as modifiers or not, consult your dictionary. If you don't find an entry for the compound, use your own judgment and the principles given here. Remember, your goal is to avoid confusing the reader.

ITALICS

In print, italics are a special typeface or font, like this: *Modern Photography*. When writing in longhand, you italicize by underlining:

In preparing manuscripts to be submitted for publication, most editors will want you to underline words that will be italicized in print. Editors find it difficult to proofread words and expressions in italics. Check to see which form is preferred—<u>underlining</u> or *italics*. To help editors distinguish between words you want underlined and words you want italicized, insert a circled handwritten symbol— (und) or (Ital) —to clarify:

> (und)
> <u>Evaluating Company Web Sites.</u> Company Web sites have become a popular source for information about jobs. Such Web sites contain helpful background information about the company. However, there are some potential drawbacks to relying exclusively on the company's Web site for information about the company. For instance, companies put only positive features on their sites, giving a potential applicant only their view. A company that is ranked dead last in its industry by <u>Fortune</u> (Ital) magazine will not mention that ranking.

EMPHASIS

You can emphasize a word or several words by italicizing them:

> (Ital)
> <u>Do not</u> place a colon between a verb or a preposition and the objects that follow.
> *Do not* place a colon between a verb or a preposition and the objects that follow.

Like all emphatic devices, italics quickly lose their value if you overuse them.

FOREIGN WORDS

We sometimes incorporate foreign words into English. When they have been completely accepted—like *rendezvous,* for instance—we do nothing to make them stand out. If they are still considered exotic, we italicize them:

> The officer in charge of a firing squad has the unpleasant task of giving the *coup de grace.*

> The officer in charge of a firing squad has the unpleasant task of giving the <u>coup de grace.</u> (*Ital*)

If in doubt about how to handle a word, use your dictionary. Its entry for the word will indicate whether or not you should italicize it.

Italicize scientific names:

> American chars belong to the genus *Salvelinus.*

> American chars belong to the genus (*Ital*) <u>Salvelinus.</u>

WORDS AS WORDS

When you use words as words and letters as letters, italicize them to prevent misunderstanding. There are frequent examples of such uses in this book, for instance:

> *Omitted* is spelled with one *m* and two *t*'s.

> (*Ital*) (*Ital*) (*Ital*)
> <u>Omitted</u> is spelled with one <u>m</u> and two <u>t</u>'s.

TITLES

Italicize the titles of books, journals, magazines, newspapers, films, and television programs:

> *The Compact Edition of the Oxford English Dictionary*
> (*Ital*)
> <u>The Compact Edition of the Oxford English Dictionary</u>

> *Newsweek*
> (*Ital*)
> <u>Newsweek</u>

> *Wide World of Sports*
> (*Ital*)
> <u>Wide World of Sports</u>

If you refer to an article, chapter, or section of a work, use quotation marks. See the entry for "Quotation Marks."

METRIC CONVERSION TABLE

The metric system of measurement is used in virtually every country outside the United States and is increasingly used, especially in workplace contexts, in the United States. In research and writing it is often necessary, therefore, to be able to convert readily from the metric system to the U.S.

system and vice versa. The accompanying table provides multipliers for converting both ways; the multipliers have been rounded to the third decimal place and thus yield an approximate equivalent.

METRIC TO U.S.			U.S. TO METRIC		
to convert from	to	multiply the metric unit by	to convert from	to	multiply the U.S. unit by
Length					
kilometers (km)	miles	.621	miles	kilometers	1.609
meters (m)	yards	1.093	yards	meters	.914
meters	feet	3.280	feet	meters	.305
meters	inches	39.370	inches	meters	.025
centimeters (cm)	inches	.394	inches	centimeters	2.540
millimeters (mm)	inches	.039	inches	millimeters	25.400
Area and Volume					
square meters (m²)	square yards	1.196	square yards	square meters	.836
square meters	square feet	10.764	square feet	square meters	.093
square centimeters (cm²)	square inches	.155	square inches	square centimeters	6.451
cubic centimeters (cm³)	cubic inches	.061	cubic inches	cubic centimeters	16.387
Liquid Measure					
liters (L)	cubic inches	61.020	cubic inches	liters	.016
liters	cubic feet	.035	cubic feet	liters	28.339
liters	U.S. gallons*	.264	U.S. gallons*	liters	3.785
liters	U.S. quarts*	1.057	U.S. quarts*	liters	.946
milliliters (mL)	fluid ounces	.034	fluid ounces	milliliters	29.573
Weight and Mass					
kilograms (kg)	pounds	2.205	pounds	kilograms	.453
grams (g)	ounces	.035	ounces	grams	28.349
grams	grains	15.430	grains	grams	.065

*The British imperial gallon equals approximately 1.2 U.S. gallons or 4.54 liters. Similarly, the British imperial quart equals 1.2 U.S. quarts, and so on.

MISPLACED AND DANGLING MODIFIERS

Modifiers are words, phrases, or clauses that limit or restrict other words, phrases, or clauses. *Green* modifying *coat* limits the coat to that color. "The bridge *that fell down*" cannot be a bridge that remained standing. "A boy *moving downhill*" cannot at the same time also be a boy moving uphill. For the most part we use modifiers with little difficulty, seldom thinking about them. But if we become careless in their placement, we can create sentences that are vague or misunderstood or, on occasion, accidentally funny.

Modifiers that are in the wrong position to modify the words that the writer intended to modify are called *misplaced*. Modifiers that have nothing in the sentence to modify are called *dangling*.

MISPLACED MODIFIERS

To correct a misplaced modifier, place it as close as possible to the words it modifies. Let's look at some examples:

> *Incorrect*   The report about the resident students of *July 6, 1999,* reached me today.

Here the italicized modifier is located properly to modify *students* but incorrectly to modify *report*. If *report* is to be modified, move the phrase:

> *Correct*   The report of *July 6, 1999,* about the resident students reached me today.

Another example:

> *Incorrect*   Many researchers are attempting to identify factors that contribute to student development *in residential college life.*

If we move the italicized modifier, we have quite a different statement:

> *Correct*   Many researchers are attempting to identify factors *in residential college life* that contribute to student development.

You are the writer in charge of the sentence. Put the modifier next to the words modified and say exactly what you mean.

DANGLING MODIFIERS

Unlike misplaced modifiers, which modify the wrong word, dangling modifiers have nothing to modify.

> *Incorrect*   *Analyzing change during the first year of college,* students who lived at home participated in fewer extracurricular activities.

At first impression this sentence leads us to believe that the students were analyzing change. But the sentence doesn't make sense that way. Looking at the sentence again, we realize that the word meant to be modified by the italicized modifier is not in the sentence. Let's say the missing word is *she*. We can now correct the sentence:

> *Correct*   Analyzing change during the first year of college, she found that students who lived at home participated in fewer extracurricular activities.

Any time you begin a sentence with a phrase of the type represented by "Analyzing change" or "To analyze change," be alert. Be sure you include the words you intend to modify.

NUMBERS

The point at issue in writing numbers is whether they are written as a figure (26) or a word (twenty-six). The rules we give you are generally, though not universally, accepted. If the company or organization you work for has a style guide, check to see what it recommends. Whether you use these rules or others, be consistent throughout any piece of work.

FIGURES

Most style and usage books call for a number to be written as a figure in the following instances:

Addresses

1262 Pater Road, Dayton, OH 45419

Dates

July 25, 2001 or 25 July 2001

Time (with A.M. or P.M.)

6:20 P.M.

Exact Sums of Money with $ or ¢

$106.20   26¢

References to Pages, Figures, and Such

Page 6   See Figure 10.

Units of Measure

10 meters   20 amperes   42 feet   9 tons

Identifying Numbers

Her telephone number is (212) 626-6934.
His Social Security number is 010-18-7806.

Decimals

6.42 kilometers   3.5 liters

Percentages

61 percent   61%

Fractions Connected to Whole Numbers

42 ¼   6 ½

Tables and Illustrations

For reasons of space and clarity, all numbers in tables and illustrations are normally written as figures.

WORDS OR FIGURES

The general trend in workplace writing is to use figures more than words. However, in some instances a word is still preferred or optional.

Numbers over 10

In most workplace writing all numbers under 10 are written in words, and numbers 10 and over are written as figures:

We have three choices in how to cross the valley.
Only 36 Indian mounds are well preserved.

If numbers under and over 10 are linked together in a series, write them all as figures:

> Historical sites in the area include 36 Indian mounds, 2 Indian villages, and 3 pioneer cemeteries.

Some organizations and publications write textual numbers up to one hundred as words and over one hundred as figures. Under this system, hyphenate the two-word numbers between twenty-one and ninety-nine.

Numbers over 100

Numbers over 100 are spelled out only if they begin a sentence.

Large numbers are written with commas every three numerals, counting from the right:

> 3,125,400,000

If numbers under and over 100 are linked in a series, all are written as figures.

> In 129 historical sites, only 36 Indian mounds are well preserved.

Approximate Numbers

Often, numbers used in an approximate way are written as words, regardless of their size. The notion is that written as a figure the number might imply an exactness that is not meant:

> The bookstore sold more than three thousand hand calculators during the fall term alone.

Numbers at Beginnings of Sentences

Do not write any number that begins a sentence as a figure. This is a sensible rule. In certain circumstances a hurried reader might connect the number to the period of the preceding sentence and so read the number as a decimal. If writing the number as a word will be cumbersome, revise the sentence:

> Five hundred ten insurance policies were sold in September.
> In September, 510 insurance policies were sold.

Fractions

Fractions connected to whole numbers are always written as figures:

> 42 ½   6 ¼

Small fractions are often written as words; if the fraction stands alone, write it as an unhyphenated compound:

> one fourth   two thirds

Hyphenate a fraction written as an adjective:

one-third speed two-fifths full

If the numerator and denominator of a fraction already is hyphenated, omit the hyphen between the parts:

forty-two thousandths

This last circumstance will seldom occur because large fractions are usually expressed as decimals.

Time (with o'clock)

We normally use the term *o'clock* with the hour. And we generally write the hour as a word:

eleven o'clock

Compound-Number Adjectives

In workplace writing, two numbers frequently function together as a compound adjective. When such is the case, to avoid confusion write one as a number, one as a word:

3 two-lane highways two 12-foot driving lanes

Be careful about hyphenating number adjectives. There's considerable difference between 100 gallon drums and 100-gallon drums. In fact, it would be far safer to write the first as 100 one-gallon drums.

OUTLINES

To help you construct a formal outline, we present here an outline of a report you can see in final form in Figure 15.6, pages 412–416. To emphasize the rules of outlining, we have annotated the outline and followed it with a few comments. Remember that most word-processing software has a feature that helps you create an outline.

SAMPLE OUTLINE

Peer Advising Proposal

The purpose of this report is to request funding for a peer advising program to be established for Criminal Justice Studies students. The report will be sent to Janice H. Grumbacher, Director of The Center for Educational Development. **Purpose and audience statement**

I. Description of the program **1st-level heading, capital roman numerals**

  A. Creation of peer advising unit **2nd-level heading, capital letters**

  B. Duties of unit **No punctuation needed after any heading**

  C. Evaluation of unit

II. Work and management plan	**Capitalize only first letter of all headings and proper nouns**
A. Facilities	
B. Task breakdown	
1. Training	**3rd-level headings, arabic numerals**
2. Office hours	
3. Evaluation	
C. Management	
D. Detailed Budget	
1. Training time	
2. Office hours	
3. Evaluation time	
E. Personnel	
1. Martin A. Doyle	
2. William Morrell	

COMMENTS

Normally, you do not include headings in the outline for your introduction or conclusion. The organization of the body of your report is what concerns you. Some version of your purpose and audience statement is likely to end up in your introduction, however.

- **Make your headings statements of substance.** That is, use words that will give the reader of your outline a true idea of your material. Headings such as "Cause 1," and "Cause 2" are of far less use than "Residential waste," and "Commercial waste."

- **Put parallel headings into parallel form.** (See also the entry for "Parallelism.") All parallel headings must have the same phrase structure. They must all be noun phrases, for example, and not a mixture of noun phrases and infinitive phrases. Use whatever phrase structure best suits your needs, but stick to it. Our simple outline uses parallel structure. An example of *improper* form would be
  A. Creation of unit
  B. To accomplish duties of unit
  C. How to evaluate the unit

- **Logically, you cannot divide anything without ending up with at least two pieces.** This rule of logic holds true in outlining. Do not put just one subheading under any other heading; you must have at least two. An outline entry like the following would be *incorrect*:
  A. Management
     1. Supervision

If you have I, you have II; if an A, you must have a B; and so forth.

PARAGRAPHS

A typical paragraph is a central statement followed by opinions and facts that relate to or support the central statement—as in this example:

> Saint Anthony Falls, the only major cataract on the Mississippi River and the original reason for the existence of Minneapolis, is the focal point of this historic district. Father Louis Hennepin, the first European to see the falls, viewed it and named it in 1680. In 1823, soldiers from the recently established Fort Snelling harnessed its powers for grist and lumber mills. The first dam was built in 1847, and the first big sawmill in 1848. Within another ten years, four flour mills were in operation, and Minneapolis was on its way to national leadership in both lumber and flour milling.

Generally, the central statement comes first in the paragraph, as it does in this example. In this position it fulfills two jobs: It introduces the paragraph and it provides the necessary transition from the preceding paragraph. Sometimes, however, the central statement may be placed last:

> A check of deer-auto collisions recorded by the Department of Natural Resources within the study area showed 60 auto-killed deer in 1998 and 64 in 1999. Several locations had a high incident of deer-auto collisions. These locations are within linear bands of vegetation extending from the river valley to various woodlots and agricultural fields within the study area. Deer follow these vegetational bands in their movements between the valley and the higher ground. The proposed highway bisects several of these bands. Therefore, it seems likely that deer-auto accidents will continue and perhaps increase.

Placing the central statement last is useful in persuasion. You allow the facts to convince the reader before you draw the conclusion. It is a device to be used sparingly, however. Used too often, it can leave readers wondering why they have to plow through so many facts without proper guidance.

Paragraphs come in many lengths. A paragraph used as a transition between longer units might be only a sentence or two long. On the other hand, a paragraph in a scholarly book might be 250 to 300 words long.

Paragraphs also vary in length depending upon where they appear. Paragraphs in newspapers run only about 50 words long, in magazines about 100 words. These lengths relate to the narrowness of the columns being used. Newspapers and magazine editors avoid long columns of print without a break. They break the paragraphs at fairly slight shifts of thought. In nonfiction books of a general nature, paragraphs run 100 to 150 words long. Probably for most workplace writing an average of about 100 words per paragraph would be appropriate. In word-processed work, double-spaced, this would be about 2½ paragraphs to a page.

Paragraphs run shorter in letters, memos, and e-mail than in printed work. A one-page letter that is all one paragraph appears hard to read. Therefore, paragraphs in letters, memos, and e-mail may run only two or three sentences long—sometimes only one sentence.

Think of paragraphing as a way of guiding your reader through your material. Well-constructed paragraphs help the reader to spot your generalizations, usually the key to your organization. And, normally, your generalizations are your major statements—the ideas and opinions you want your reader to retain. Do not forget the visual impact of paragraphing. Large blocks of unbroken print may frighten off the reader. But too-short paragraphs may suggest a lack of organization. A document with paragraphs of varying lengths will probably present most material best.

PARALLELISM

When you start a series of sentence elements that serve the same function, put them into the same grammatical form. For instance, you will use many lists in workplace writing. Place all elements of the list in the same form, as in this example:

> Always consider the following factors in designing an exhibit:
> * distance of viewers from exhibit
> * average viewing time
> * material to be used
> * lighting conditions
> * visual acuity of viewers

In this example, each item on the list is based on a noun—*distance, time, material,* and so on. The writer would have had faulty parallelism if she had switched grammatical forms, as in this faulty list:

> * distance of viewers from exhibit
> * to consider viewing time
> * what material should be used?

In this faulty list the writer went from a noun phrase to an infinitive phrase to a complete clause. Use any grammatical form in your list that is convenient for you, but stick to the same form throughout.

We have many paired constructions in English, such as *both . . . and; either . . . or; neither . . . nor; not . . . but;* and *not only . . . but also,* that call for parallel forms after each part of the pair. Look at this example:

> *Correct*   Design your exhibit *either for a* technically skilled audience *or for* the general public.

Both elements are based upon prepositional phrases and are correctly parallel. You would have faulty parallelism with this next structure.

> *Incorrect*   Design your exhibit *either for a* technically skilled audience *or to* please the general public.

Here the parallelism breaks down with the introduction of the infinitive phrase *to please* in the second element.

In most compound sentences you will be wise to keep both clauses in the same voice—active or passive (see the entry for "Sentences"). In this example both sides of the compound sentence are in the active voice:

Correct   People want to excel, construct, and imitate; and they seek pleasure, recognition, friends, and security.

The reader would be disturbed if we switched to the passive voice in the second clause:

Incorrect   People want to excel, construct, and imitate; and pleasure, recognition, friends, and security are sought by them.

The following two main clauses read easily despite their length (36 words) because all the elements in both clauses are carefully balanced:

Speeding drivers passing a billboard off the highway will be able to read nine words at most, but slow-moving students passing a sign in a cafeteria line will be able to read several hundred words.

Any time you have elements in any kind of series, take a hard look at them. Be sure you have them in a parallel grammatical form.

PARENTHESES

Of the three marks of punctuation used to enclose parenthetical material (commas, dashes, and parentheses), parentheses are the "heaviest." They separate the inserted material more definitely and can enclose longer elements—up to several sentences, if necessary—than other marks. Look at the following examples. Pay particular attention to the punctuation inside and around the parentheses:

Norway spruce *(Picea abies),* a native of Europe, is similar to white spruce in most characteristics. The model tree would have a straight central stem, normal taper (forming a cone the base of which is 70 to 80 percent of its height), and foliage that would be progressively less dense going from the bottom of the tree to the topmost whorl.

The primary purpose of shaping is to control height and width and to develop uniform taper. (Other purposes are to correct deformities, to remove multiple leaders, and to prune lower branches to form a handle and a complete base whorl.) A variety of tools may be used in the shaping process.

Keep these matters of punctuation in mind when using parentheses:

- Place no punctuation before the first parenthesis.
- Delay any punctuation needed after the last word before the first parenthesis until after the second parenthesis.
- Use any capitalization and punctuation required by the sentence structure inside the parentheses.
- Use no special punctuation around parentheses placed between sentences.

A special conventional use of parentheses is to enclose figures or letters in lists. The numbering may use both parentheses or only the closing parenthesis, although use of both parentheses is more common:

> The two main steps in shearing any species with a regular whorled branching habit are (1) regulations of the terminal whorl and (2) clipping or shearing of the side branches.
> The two main steps in shearing any species with a regular whorled branching habit are 1) regulations of the terminal whorl and 2) clipping or shearing of the side branches.

Be consistent in the form you choose. See also the entries for "Comma," "Brackets," and "Dash."

PERIOD

Periods have the following conventional uses:

Abbreviations
Ms.   Mr.   etc.   Jr.

Decimal Point
.00236 $13.45

End Stop
He bought the farm.

Practices vary concerning the number of spaces following a period or other concluding mark of punctuation. Traditionally, in the United States the practice has been to use two spaces after concluding punctuation. However, the trend today is to leave only one space. Either practice may be acceptable. Check to see whether your instructor or editor has a preference. Whether you leave one space or two after concluding punctuation, be consistent.

Initials
Isabelle K. Thompson   J. P. Morgan

Leaders
A series of periods to lead the eye are sometimes used in tables and tables of contents:

TABLE OF CONTENTS

List of illustrations..ii
Abstract iv
Introduction...1

Word-processing software will create the dot leaders for you if you set the lead tab. See also the entry for "Ellipsis Points."

PRONOUNS

Take care with pronouns in regard to agreement, reference, and case.

AGREEMENT

Make a pronoun agree in number and gender with its antecedent—singular with singular, plural with plural, male with male, female with female, gender neutral with gender neutral:

> *John* monopolized the meeting, but *he* . . .
> The *woman* walked through the lobby; then *she* . . .
> Set the *table* down and put the lamp on *it*.
> The *group members*, when *they* meet . . .

Traditionally, when we could be referring to either a man or a woman, we have used the male pronoun:

> The *student* first gets a class card, then *he* . . .

Concern for equity in gender has made many people feel that this construction is unfair or at least insensitive. English still lacks a natural pronoun for such situations, but one way around this problem is to use a plural construction when you can:

> The *students* first get a class card, then *they* . . .

Be particularly careful with collective nouns (see the entry for "Verb Agreement"). They can be considered either singular or plural, depending on meaning. Make your pronoun agree with whatever number and verb you choose for the collective noun:

> The *committee* is having *its* last meeting tonight.
> The *committee* are arguing intensely among *themselves*; they . . .

See also material on collective nouns, page 654.

REFERENCE

Make sure your reader can tell without the slightest hesitation which word or word group your pronoun refers to. If you suspect any confusion, rewrite your sentence.

Despite the distance between the nouns and pronouns in the following sentence, the references are quite clear:

> The *speaker* should place the *notes* on the lectern provided. *He* should not wave *them* about.

In the following sentence, the reference is unclear. It could go back to either *leader* or *secretary*:

> Both the group leader and the secretary are responsible for the proper recording of motions. He should keep an accurate record.

In cases like this, repeat the needed noun: "The *secretary* should keep an accurate record."

In the following sentence, *this* clearly refers to the broad concept of considering all contributions worthwhile:

> Group members should believe that all contributions are worth considering. *This* in itself will prevent many arguments and unhappy members.

However, in the following sentence, *this* is an unclear reference.

> A faulty fact can usually be identified when placed next to an accurate statement. However, *this* may not occur.

We do not know what will not occur. We have three choices: (1) a faulty fact being identified, (2) a faulty fact being placed next to an accurate statement; (3) an accurate statement being made. A clear rewrite might be "However, *this identification* may not occur."

As the last example demonstrates, you should examine every reference for the possibility of misunderstanding. Remember that references clear to you may not be clear to your reader. Be particularly careful whenever you are using *this, that, which,* or *it.*

Case

A brief lesson from the history of English is appropriate here. At one time—about fourteen hundred years ago—all nouns in English had case. A noun used as the object of a sentence was in the nominative case, an indirect object in the dative case, and so forth. Thus, a hound eating a bone was a *hund,* but a hound given a bone was a *hunde.* Except for the possessive case—*a hound's bone*—these cases did not survive in nouns. Today, word order and prepositions tell us whether a noun is subject (S), object (O), or indirect object (IO):

> John gave the bone to the hound.
>   S   O   IO

But case did survive in pronouns. Correct case is seldom necessary for understanding. If someone incorrectly says, "Annette and me went fishing," we understand that person as well as if he or she had correctly said "Annette and I went fishing." If not necessary for understanding, however, case is still important. Quite frankly, status is involved. People who keep their pronouns sorted out correctly are considered by many other people to be more educated and cultured than those who do not.

A pronoun used as the subject of a sentence is in the nominative case—*I, he, she, we, they, who.* Pronouns used as objects of verbs and prepositions are in the objective case—*me, him, her, us, them, whom.* The pronouns *you* and *it* are the same in both cases.

Let's look at some examples:

He hit *me.*
We are going to *him* at once.
He gave *her* the hat.
She bought the car for *us* boys.
We women want equality.
Who is going to the exhibit?
He gave the car to *whom?*

Many people have no trouble sorting out pronouns until they have to use a double object. Then they go to pieces and use the nominative case rather than the objective, perhaps because it sounds more elegant to them. The following forms are *correct*:

He gave the book to *my brother and me.*
It's a matter between *him and me.*
She sent *them and us* an invitation.
Between *you and me,* I think I understand it.

If in doubt about a double object, try it in the singular. Few people would say, "He gave the car to *I.*" Therefore, "He gave the car to *my brother and I*" would be equally incorrect. "He gave the car to *my brother and me*" is correct.

There is only one tricky place in the whole sorting out of pronouns—the seldom-used predicate nominative. After any form of the verb *to be* (*is, are, was,* and so on), we use the nominative case rather than the objective:

It is *she.*
Is it *she?*

Despite this rule almost everyone says, "It's me," not, "It's I." As we say, this construction is seldom used, particularly in writing. And if you get it wrong, most people will not notice. But do pay attention to your other pronouns. They may be more important than you think.

QUESTION MARK

If you write a direct question, place a question mark at its end:

How far must you drill to reach stable bedrock?

Polite requests may be punctuated with a question mark or a period:

Will you please send me the noise analysis report before Tuesday?

Or

Will you please send me the noise analysis report before Tuesday.

Use a period, not a question mark after an indirect question:

Representatives of the Sierra Club asked what the impact of the larger dam would be.

QUOTATION MARKS

Use quotation marks to set off quotations and certain titles. You may also use them to set off words used as words. (For additional information on making and documenting quotations, see pages 592–596.)

QUOTATIONS

Use quotation marks to enclose a passage repeated from an earlier statement, whether written or spoken. The quotation marks signal that you have reproduced the passage word for word:

> Zoo director Sheryl Sikes stated, "The Zoo Board believes that most of the traffic will originate from the metropolitan area and will use the major freeways to reach the zoo."

You may make small, properly marked additions and omissions in quoted material, as explained in the entries for "Brackets" and "Ellipsis Points."

If your quotation runs longer than three lines, do not put it inside quotation marks. Instead, indent it on the page in the following manner:

> In a letter to the Highway Department, the Chairman of the Rockport Environmental Council expressed the Council's major concern about the new route:
>
>> The proposed route would cut a path across the marsh, destroying valuable habitat. Even though the new bridge would be supported by piers, the piers themselves and the associated construction activities would leave permanent scars and damaging effects on the landscape.

Note that in this example the quoted passage is not only indented but also single-spaced, in order to contrast it with double-spaced text. Use a colon to introduce indented quotations.

TITLES

Titles of works shorter than book length, such as magazine articles, short stories, and poems, are set inside quotation marks:

> Enclosed is the brochure "Comparing Your Options in Home Insurance," which we believe will help you decide which home insurance plan is best for you.
>
> Wallerstein and Kelly's "California's Children of Divorce" presents data gathered from both individual case studies and from group questionnaires.

WORDS AS WORDS

Words used as words may be italicized (see the entry on "Italics") or set inside quotation marks:

> What is meant by the term "annealing"?
> What is meant by the term *annealing*?

Whichever method you choose, be consistent within a piece of work.

QUOTATION MARKS WITH OTHER MARKS OF PUNCTUATION

Fairly definite rules govern the use of other punctuation marks with quotation marks.

Introductory Marks

Quotations that need an introduction are preceded by commas or, in more formal circumstances, by colons:

> The Rockport mayor said, "No major conflicts with the plans for existing development are anticipated."
>
> The Rockport mayor supported alternative C with this statement: "All Rockport land-use planning has anticipated the construction of alternative C. Therefore, we strongly recommend this alternative."

See also the entry for "Colon."

When a quotation is closely integrated into a sentence, use no introductory mark of punctuation:

> The zoo director supports the building of the freeway because she believes that "most of the major traffic will originate from the metropolitan area. . . ."

The use of the lowercase letter at the beginning of the quotation tells the reader that the preceding part of the sentence has been omitted. Therefore, no ellipsis is needed. However, an ellipsis is needed to signal the omission of the material at the end of the sentence. See also the entry for "Ellipsis Points."

Quotation Marks within Other Quotation Marks

When you use quotation marks within other quotation marks, use single quotes for the inside marks:

> In objection, the councilwoman said, "We question your use of the terms 'prudent and feasible' in this regard."

Commas and Periods

Two basic styles apply to using quotation marks with commas and periods: the American style and the British style. In the American style, a comma or a period at the end of any words set inside quotation marks is always set inside the marks, even when logic indicates it should go outside:

> The councilwoman questioned our use of the terms "prudent and feasible."

In the British style, a comma or period at the end of any words set inside quotation marks is always set outside the marks:

> The councilwoman questioned our used of the terms "prudent and feasible".

Generally, American readers expect the American style and British readers expect the British style. However, the distinction is disappearing as globalization grows. Regardless of which style you use, be consistent.

Colons and Semicolons

When a colon or semicolon is needed at the end of a quotation, always set it outside the marks:

> The councilwoman questioned our use of the terms "prudent and feasible"; we agreed that the issue is open to interpretation.

Dashes, Exclamation Points, and Question Marks

Dashes, exclamation points, and question marks follow the logic of the sentence. When they belong to the quotation, they go inside the marks. When they belong to the sentence, they go outside:

> Many new tree growers ask, "Why should trees be shaped?"
> What is meant by the term "shaping"?

Note that in the first example the question mark also serves as end punctuation for the sentence.

RUN-ON SENTENCES

The rule for avoiding run-on sentences is simple enough: Don't join two independent clauses with only a comma or with no punctuation at all. Normal punctuation between two independent clauses is one of the following:

- a period
- a semicolon
- a comma and a coordinating conjunction (*and, but, for, nor, or, yet*)

The trick is to recognize an independent clause when you see one. The following are all independent clauses, which means they have a subject and verb and can stand by themselves as a complete sentence. If you have difficulty with run-on sentences, memorize these patterns:

> Overhead projection is a dramatic method of presenting facts and ideas clearly, concisely, and effectively.
> The instructor controls the equipment with a switch of her fingertips.
> Put your overhead visuals on a transparent base.
> Most inks can be washed off easily.
> They are safe to use.

Placing a conjunctive adverb before an independent clause does not make the clause subordinate. Nor does the conjunctive adverb serve as a strong connective. Therefore, you must use normal punctuation as defined in this section before an independent clause beginning with a conjunctive adverb. The major conjunctive adverbs are *accordingly, also, anyhow, besides, consequently, furthermore, however, indeed, likewise, moreover, nevertheless, then, therefore.*

Observe carefully these examples of correct punctuation:

Most inks can be washed off easily. Therefore, they are safe to use.
Most inks can be washed off easily; therefore, they are safe to use.
Most inks can be washed off easily, and, therefore, they are safe to use.

See also the entries for "Colon," "Comma," "Fragmentary Sentence," "Period," and "Semicolon."

SEMICOLON

The semicolon is used in certain situations between independent clauses and when internal commas make it necessary in a series. It really has quite limited uses. Do not confuse a semicolon (;) with a colon (:). Do not use it to introduce lists or quotations, and do not use it after the salutation in a letter. See the entries for "Colon" and "Run-on Sentences."

INDEPENDENT CLAUSES

You can use the semicolon between two independent clauses at any time instead of the more normal period; however, the semicolon is most widely used when the link between the two clauses is one of the conjunctive adverbs: *consequently, however, nevertheless, therefore,* and so on. In this situation the comma is not considered strong enough punctuation, and the period is perhaps too strong:

The outlet will be below water level; therefore, it will be entirely submerged and not visible from the bank.

Sometimes, independent clauses between which you would normally use a comma and a coordinating conjunction already have strong internal commas. In this case substitute a semicolon for the comma:

The buildings, mainly flour- and sawmills, are gone; but foundations, penstocks, tailraces, and some machinery remain.

SERIES

When the elements of a series have internal commas, substitute a semicolon at the breaks where you would normally use commas:

The schools examined were Normandale, a two-year public community college; Hamline, a four-year private school; and the University of Illinois, a four-year public school.

SENTENCES

Elsewhere in this guide we tell you about various sentence faults (see the entries for "Fragmentary Sentences," "Misplaced and Dangling Modifiers," "Run-on Sentences," "Parallelism," and "Verb Agreement"). In this section we give some positive advice about writing better sentences. Specifically, we discuss choice of the proper voice, sentence length, sentence order, and directness.

VOICE

English sentences are in either of two voices—active or passive:

Active   The glaciers formed three striking and different natural features.

Passive   Three striking and different natural features were formed by the glaciers.

In the active-voice sentence the subject acts; in the passive-voice sentence the subject is acted upon. Active-voice sentences use fewer words and state more directly what you have to say. With the passive voice you run the risk of forgetting the final prepositional phrase—*by the glaciers*—and leaving the actor unknown.

For simple instructions the imperative mood of the active voice is clearly superior to the passive. A passage in a safety brochure reads this way:

Keep your distance. Never operate a crane beneath the power lines without adequate clearance. Play it safe. Leave more than the minimum six feet required. Remember, too, a boom may rebound when a load is released.

The passage is clear and direct, and clearly says: "This means you!" Compare the active version with the passive:

Distance should be kept. A crane should not be operated beneath power lines without adequate clearance. More than the minimum six feet should be allowed for safety reasons. It should be remembered that a boom may rebound when a load is released.

The second version is indefinite and needlessly long.

Compare   It is requested that you send me a copy of your speech.
With   I would appreciate a copy of your speech.

The second, active-voice version is far closer to normal speech, and far more polite than the impersonal passive-voice version.

However, the passive voice has many uses. Use it when the person or thing acted upon is more important than the actor or when you wish to de-emphasize the actor. Do not use the passive voice by accident. Know it when you see it, and use it only when it is clearly better than the active-voice version of the same idea. (See also pages 86–88.)

SENTENCE LENGTH

Professional writers average about 21 words a sentence whether they are writing for high school graduates or PhDs. For an audience with less than a high school education they might scale down their sentences to 14 to 18 words. Take a lesson from the professional writer and work for similar averages. Remember that we are talking about averages. Do not cookie-cut a series of 21-word sentences. Rather, let your sentences range over a spread of about 5 to 35 words. Being conscious of your sentence length will prevent the two extremes of poor writing—too short sentences and too long sentences. The former results in disconnected, primer-like sentences:

> The glaciers formed the topography of the study area. They left an accumulation of glacial drift. This drift is from 100 to 500 feet thick. [25 words in 3 sentences.]

Smoothly connecting the ideas, we get this result:

> The glaciers, leaving an accumulation of glacial drift from 100 to 500 feet thick, formed the topography of the study area. [21 words in 1 sentence.]

At the other extreme, too long sentences are too complex for the reader to follow. And sometimes, as in this example from a government document, the writer loses control over the material:

> As of the effective date of this memorandum, projects which have received design approval (as defined by PPM 90–1) may receive PS & E approval, if otherwise satisfactory, on the basis of past state highway submissions which identify and document the economic, social and environmental effects previously considered with respect to these advanced projects, together with a supplemental report, if necessary, covering the consideration and disposition of the items and not previously covered and now listed herein in paragraph 4.b. [78 words in 1 sentence—too many.]

SENTENCE ORDER

Normal English sentence order is subject first, verb second. Following the verb, a wide range of objects, modifiers, subordinate clauses, and additional main clauses is possible:

> Actual shearing *techniques differ* among growers.
>   S   V
> *Some prefer* to begin trimming at the base of the tree and work upward to
>   S   V
> the terminal leader.

Professional writers begin about 75 percent of their sentences with the subject. Another 23 percent of their sentences they begin with a simple adverbial opener, followed by the subject:

> *In the terminal whorl,* the grower will encounter some common situations that require corrective action.
> *However,* these are dangerous tools, and you should take extra precautions.

Professional writers begin less than two percent of their sentences with a subordinate clause or verbal phrase:

When the operation is repeated annually, it has the effect of developing a shorter, well-shaped, and compact tree.
To use any herbicide safely, follow the exact instructions on the label.

Sentence openers before the subject usually serve as transitional devices, linking the sentences to a previous idea.

We appreciate professional writing because it puts no roadblocks between us and the thought. Follow the professional pattern, and you will avoid the difficulties of sentences like the following:

It appears logical to use the same shoulder width and surface type as that in place on adjacent projects, or if aspects of traffic growth or traffic assignment splits would justify a different selection, or if stage construction is a consideration, it may be desirable to deviate from standards.

This sentence, poor on several counts, puts its main idea—permissible deviation from standards—last. Readers wander through the conditions, wondering why they are reading them. Reverse the order and use a list, and the result will be a far better statement:

You may deviate from standards under these conditions:
- If it appears logical to use the same width and surface type as that in place on adjacent projects.
- If aspects of traffic growth or traffic assignment splits would justify a different selection.
- If stage construction is a consideration.

DIRECTNESS

Write directly to your thought. Write to express ideas, not to line up words in a row. Do not follow old formulas that are word wasters. Do not *make application to;* simply *apply.* Do not *make contact* with people; instead, simply *see* them or *meet* them. Do you begin thank-you notes by saying, "I want to thank you for . . ."? Why not simply say "Thank you for . . ."? It sounds fairly pompous to say or write *at this point in time* rather than *now.* If something happens *due to the fact that,* simply say *because.* If something is *in accordance with the regulation,* it is really *under* or *by the regulation.* The list of such tired, indirect ways of saying things is unfortunately all too long. You will avoid most of them if you think about what you want to say and say it in the most direct way you can.

We also waste a good many words by not recognizing the value of the verb in English:

| *Compare* | What is the conclusion to be drawn from this research? |
| *With* | What can we conclude from this research? |

The second sentence saves three words. How was this achieved? By taking the action idea in *conclusion* and putting it in the verb *conclude,* where it belongs.

Besides using fewer words when you put your action into verbs, you will make your writing more vivid. This first version of a sentence is pallid and indirect.

A blockage of debris in the conduit could cause a flood in the upper pool.

By putting action into verbs, we have this far better sentence:

Debris blocking the conduit could flood the upper pool.

Look at the use of verbs and verb forms in the opening paragraph of an advertising letter (the italics are ours):

To *help prevent* highway deaths, engineers *may* someday *control* traffic with computers. For long distances, the computer *may steer, accelerate, and brake* the car *as needed.* The driver will *lounge, read, play cards, even sleep* while *being whisked* down the highway.

The professional writer of this paragraph knew that verbs snap people to attention. He used verbs to express ideas vividly and directly. He did not hide his ideas behind a smoke screen of needless words. (See also pages 84-86.)

SPELLING

Spelling correctly is important. Many people are quick to judge your competence and intelligence by how well you spell. A misspelled word or two in a letter of application may block you from a job as quickly as would lack of experience or education. This may be unfortunate or even unwise, but it is one of the facts of life.

For many historical reasons, such as changes in pronunciation and the introduction of foreign words, English is a difficult language to spell. Nevertheless, it has certain rules, explained in numerous books. Look for them in your library—under either *spelling* or *orthography*—or in your bookstore. The rules really do help and are worth mastering.

If you keep a dictionary handy and use it, you probably spell the difficult words correctly. If you are like most people, it's the everyday words that you misspell the most. Most of us are reluctant to lift the heavy dictionary off the shelf when we need it only to check the spelling of a common word. All too often our confidence is misplaced. Here is another approach:

- Use the spell checker on your computer.
- Proofread. Stop at words that cause you problems. Read carefully for correctly spelled words that are the wrong words. That is, if you use *too* for *to* or *accept* for *except,* the spelling checker will not catch your error.

- Consult one of the small books that list without definition 20,000 to 30,000 of the most commonly used words. These books also divide words into syllables, so they are useful for breaking a word at the end of a line.

TRANSITION

Transitions move the reader from one idea to the next. More importantly they show the relationships among ideas as shown in the relationship of one sentence to the next or of one paragraph to a previous paragraph. You may need a transition to tie a sentence or paragraph into the overall purpose of a report.

Transitions take many forms. You can make a transition with words such as *however, therefore,* and *consequently,* as in this sentence:

Generally, the system adapts best to large operations; *however*, it is a flexible system and may, in some instances, fill the needs of small operations.

You can provide transition by repeating key words from one paragraph or sentence to the next. Read the first sentence in this paragraph and in the previous two paragraphs, and you will see that we have done exactly that with the key word *transition*. Sometimes you will need a more obvious transition to move from one part of a report to the next, as in this example:

Before making specific recommendations for design and management of natural-air drying systems, we will describe the principles involved.

The use of headings, particularly when combined with a good lead-in, can provide excellent transition:

FILLING SCHEDULES
Three types of filling schedules can be used when operating a natural-air drying bin: fast-fill, layer-fill, and weekly-fill.
Fast-fill Schedule
　With the fast-fill schedule . . . .
Layer-fill Schedule
　If filled in layers . . . .
Weekly-fill Schedule
　The weekly-fill schedule . . . .

Notice in these last examples the repetition of the key words in the sentences that follow the headings. Including the key words in the opening sentence reinforces for readers that they are in the right section. Also, avoid sentences that begin with vague openings such as "This is. . . ."

However you provide them, transitions are a key to the coherent and logical presentation of your material. Do not leave your readers without them.

UNDERLINING

See "Italics."

VERB AGREEMENT

Make the verb agree with its subject. Normally, this will not be a problem, but some trouble spots exist.

INTERVENING PREPOSITIONAL PHRASES

When a prepositional phrase with a plural object—for example, *of the women*—comes between a singular noun or pronoun and its verb, writers often go astray and use a plural verb:

Incorrect   The *stack* of letters are . . .
Correct   The *stack* of letters is . . .

The pronouns most likely to cause difficulty in this construction are *each, either, neither,* and *none,* all of which take singular verbs. Grammar often is at war with meaning here, but grammar decides the verb:

Incorrect   If *each* of the group members have . . .
Correct   If *each* of the group members has . . .

COMPOUND SUBJECTS

Compound subjects connected by *and* take a plural verb:

Hydrogen and oxygen are . . .

When you have a compound subject in an *either . . . or* construction, the noun closest to the verb decides the form of the verb. Note the reversal in these two examples:

Either the group members or the *leader is* . . .
Either the leader or the group *members are* . . .

COLLECTIVE NOUNS

We have a good many collective nouns in English, nouns such as *audience, band, committee, group, company,* and *class.* Collective nouns can take either singular or plural verbs, depending on the meaning of the sentence:

The *committee is* having *its* last meeting tonight.
The *committee are* arguing intensely among *themselves.*

However, most Americans feel uncomfortable using a plural verb after a collective noun. (The British do it naturally.) We are more likely to say, "The *committee members are* arguing among *themselves.*" (See also the entry on "Pronouns.")

PLURAL-SOUNDING NOUNS

Some nouns sound plural but are not—for instance, *electronics, econom-ics, mathematics, physics,* and *measles.* Despite their sound, such nouns take singular verbs:

> *Mathematics is* necessary in . . .

NOUNS OF MEASUREMENT, TIME, AND MONEY

Plural nouns that express measurement, time, or money take singular verbs:

> *One hundred yards is* the distance from goal line to goal line.
> *Ten years was* the sentence.
> *Five thousand dollars is* a lot of money.

WORD DIVISION

Word-processing software and laser printing technology have eliminated many word division problems. The word either fits on a line or moves to the next line. Occasionally, you may need to hyphenate a word. If so, re-view the following guidelines and consult a dictionary.

When you have to carry part of a word over to another line, break it between syllables and hyphenate it:

> Even more important than the dormitory pro-
> gram is the . . .

Your dictionary will show the syllabic division of words:

> croc • o • dile   gum • my   gra • cious

A few standard rules cover the proper way of dividing words:

- When a vowel ends a syllable or stands by itself, break after the vowel:
  paro-chial
  esti-mate (not est-imate)
- Break between double consonants, unless the double consonant ap-pears in the root of the word:
  occur-ring
  bril-liant
- but
  spell-ing
  toll-ing
- Do not carry over single letters or *-ed* when the *e* is silent. For instance, you would not carry over the *-y* of *busy* or the *-ed* of *bucked.* You could break *darted* before the *-ed* because the *-ed* is pronounced. (However, usually it is better not to carry over only two letters. Leave them on the line above or carry the whole word over.)

INDEX